McDougal Littell
CLASSZONE

MW00906697

Visit **classzone.com** and get connected.

ClassZone resources provide instruction, practice and learning support for students and parents.

 **History & Geography**

- Brings history to life with interactive activities and visuals
- Provides interactive maps, charts, and graphs

Current Events

- Takes you beyond the text and keeps you up-to-date on world events
- Reflects the most recent political, economic, and social issues
- Provides weekly current events quizzes to help check comprehension

Interactive ←→ Review

- Provides a unique way to review key concepts and events
- Includes geography games, crossword puzzles, and matching games
- Helps ensure lesson comprehension through graphic organizers, animated flipcards, and review/study notes

Research and Writing

- Includes links to primary sources, chapter resources, biographies, and state-specific resources
- Provides support for your writing assignments through complete writing models, rubrics, and research guides

Access the online version of your textbook at **classzone.com**

Your complete text, along with animated maps, charts and infographics, is available for immediate use!

McDougal Littell
Where Great Lessons Begin

MICHIGAN EDITION

McDougal Littell

American HISTORY

BEGINNINGS to 1914

Robert Dallek

Jesus Garcia

Donna M. Ogle

C. Frederick Risinger

Senior Consultants

Dr. Robert Dallek is an acclaimed historian of the American presidency and an authority on leadership and crises. His biography of President John F. Kennedy, *An Unfinished Life*, spent eight weeks on *The New York Times* bestseller list. A former professor of History at Boston University, Dr. Dallek also spent three decades as a professor at UCLA, and a year as a visiting professor at Oxford. In recent years he has also been a visiting professor at Dartmouth College. In addition to his books, he is the author of more than 100 publications and the recipient of numerous honors and awards. He is a frequent commentator on radio and television networks, including NPR, CNN, and NBC, on subjects concerning the presidency, current events, and foreign policy.

Dr. Jesus Garcia is professor of Curriculum and Instruction at the University of Nevada, Las Vegas, and past president of the National Council for the Social Studies. A former social studies teacher, Dr. Garcia has co-authored many books and articles on subjects that range from teaching social studies in elementary and middle schools to seeking diversity in education. Dr. Garcia has also worked for both the Chicago and Washington, D.C., public schools and the Arkansas Department of Education as a consultant on social studies standards.

Dr. Donna Ogle is professor of Reading and Language at National-Louis University in Chicago, Illinois, and is a specialist in reading in the content areas, with an interest in social studies. She is past president of the International Reading Association and a former social studies teacher. Dr. Ogle is currently directing two content literacy projects in Chicago schools and is Senior Consultant to the Striving Readers Research Project. She continues to explore applications of the K-W-L strategy she developed and is adding a Partner Reading component—PRC2 (Partner Reading and Content 2).

C. Frederick Risinger is the former Director of Professional Development and coordinator for Social Studies Education at Indiana University. He is past president of the National Council for the Social Studies as well as past president of the National Social Studies Supervisors Association. Mr. Risinger also served on the coordinating committee for the National History Standards Project. He writes a monthly column on technology in the social studies classroom for *Social Education* and is the current president of the Social Science Education Consortium.

Copyright © 2008 McDougal Littell, a division of Houghton Mifflin Company. All rights reserved.

Maps on pages A20-A39 © Rand McNally & Company. All rights reserved.

Acknowledgments for copyrighted material begin on page R79 and constitute an extension of this page.

Warning: No part of this work may be reproduced or transmitted in any form or by any means, electronic or mechanical, including photocopying and recording, or by any information storage or retrieval system without the prior written permission of McDougal Littell unless such copying is expressly permitted by federal copyright law. With the exception of not-for-profit transcription in Braille, McDougal Littell is not authorized to grant permission for further uses of copyrighted selections reprinted in this text without the permission of their owners. Permission must be obtained from the individual copyright owners as identified herein. Address inquiries to Supervisor, Rights and Permissions, McDougal Littell, P.O. Box 1667, Evanston, IL 60204.

ISBN-13: 978-0-547-12710-1
ISBN-10: 0-547-12710-3

03 04 05 06 07 08 09 0868 12 11 10 09

Internet Web Site: http://www.mcdougallittell.com

Consultants and Reviewers

MICHIGAN REVIEWERS

Jeannie M. Brousseau
Pierce Middle School
Grosse Pointe, MI

Sharon Goralewski
Oakland Schools
Waterford, MI

Theresa L. Groves
Grand Blanc Schools
Grand Blanc, MI

David Hales
Wayne County Regional Educational
Service Agency
Wayne, MI

Susan Laninga
Kent Intermediate School District
Grand Rapids, MI

Brenda L. Rice
Athens High School
Troy, MI

Renee Tull
Birmingham Public Schools
Birmingham, MI

Student Panel

The following Middle School Student Panel reviewed textbook
materials and technology products for this program.

Jessica Baker
Nelly Benitez
Ameer Cannon
Katie Conley
Murad Dajani
Will DiFrancesca
Tom Foydel
Philippa Gillette
Jenny Gorelick
Michael Grassle
Danielle Jackson
DeJauna Jackson
Mark Johnson
David Lenz
Andrew Mack

Madelaine Martin
Jabari McIntyre
Victoria Meliska
Sarah Peters
Brianna Ransom
Andrés Rivera-Thompson
Simone Samuels
Ben Shoaf
Gabriel Siegal
Kyle Siegal
Brock Snider
Hank Strickler
Jasmine Wright
Hannah Wyler

Teacher Consultants

The following educators provided ongoing review of key components or contributed teaching ideas and activities for this program.

Venise N. Battle
Shady Hill School
Cambridge, Massachusetts

Paul C. Beavers
J.T. Moore Middle School
Nashville, Tennessee

Cristy Berger
Wilkinson Middle School
Madison, Michigan

Holly West Brewer
Buena Vista Paideia Magnet
Nashville, Tennessee

David Brothman
North Chicago School District
North Chicago, Illinois

Ron Campana
United Federation of Teachers
New York, New York

Patricia B. Carlson
Swanson Middle School
Arlington, Virginia

Meg DeWeese
Thoreau Academy-Tulsa Public
School System
Tulsa, Oklahoma

Kelly Ellis
Hamilton Middle School
Cypress, Texas

James Grimes
Middlesex County Vocational-
Technical High School
Woodbridge, New Jersey

Julie Guild
Carl Albert Junior High
Oklahoma City, Oklahoma

Brent Heath
De Anza Middle School
Ontario, California

Suzanne Hidalgo
Serrano Middle School
Highland, California

Cathryn Mahan Hinesley
Seneca Ridge Middle School
Sterling, Virginia

Alan Hornbecker
Walt Whitman Middle School
Alexandria, Virginia

Barbara Kennedy
Sylvan Middle School
Citrus Heights, California

Pamela Knifflin
Navasota Junior High
Navasota, Texas

Tammy Leiber
Navasota Junior High
Navasota, Texas

Lori Lesslie
Cedar Bluff Middle School
Knoxville, Tennessee

Christine Loop
Glasgow Middle School
Alexandria, Virginia

Brian McKenzie
Buffalo Public School #81
Buffalo, New York

Kayne Miller
Longfellow Middle School
Falls Church, Virginia

Ronnie Moppin
Sunny Vale Middle School
Blue Springs, Missouri

Caroline Ona
Washington Irving Middle School
Springfield, Virginia

Jean Price
St. John's School
Houston, Texas

Meg Robbins
Wilbraham Middle School
Northampton, Massachusetts

Philip Rodriguez
McNair Middle School
San Antonio, Texas

Leslie Schubert
Parkland School
McHenry, Illinois

Robert Sisko
Carteret Middle School
Carteret, New Jersey

Jim Sorenson
Chippewa Middle School
Des Plaines, Illinois

Amy Smith
Lanier Middle School
Fairfax, Virginia

Marci Smith
Hurst-Euless-Bedford ISD
Bedford, Texas

Nicholas Sysock
Carteret Middle School
Carteret, New Jersey

Susan Weber
Maple Point Middle School
Langhorne, Pennsylvania

Becky Wedeking
Eisenhower Middle School
Topeka, Kansas

Lisa Williams
Lamberton Middle School
Carlisle, Pennsylvania

OVERVIEW
Michigan Student Edition

- Additional in-depth review for Eras 1 and 2 can be found on the eEdition

USHG Content Expectations	American History: Beginnings to 1914
Foundational Issues in USHG	Prologue and Chapters 6 & 7
Introduction to Era 6	Chapters 19-22

- Guide to Understanding Michigan's Grade Level Content Expectations
- Guide to the MEAP (Michigan Educational Assessment Program)

Lessons with Embedded GLCE Annotations

 Look for the Michigan symbol throughout this book. It highlights targeted grade level content expectations to help you succeed on your test.

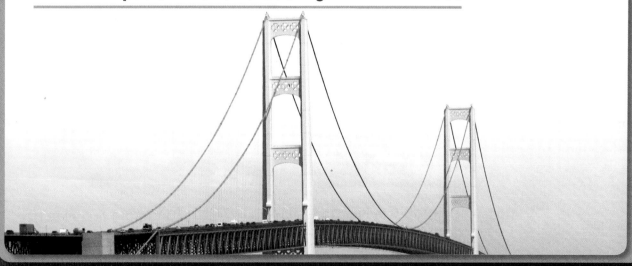

Mackinac Bridge, Michigan © Ilene MacDonald/Alamy

MICHIGAN CONTENTS

UNIT 1
MICHIGAN

Three Worlds Meet

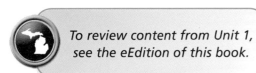

To review content from Unit 1, see the eEdition of this book.

Online Activities
at CLASSZONE.COM

Animated HISTORY
Early Native American Life

Experience the activity and commerce of a Native American market, p. 10.

Interactive Review

Play the GeoGame to test your knowledge of the European explorations of North America, p. 21.

✓ Online Test Practice
Review test-taking strategies and practice for your test, pages 23, 55.

2 MICHIGAN

The English Colonies

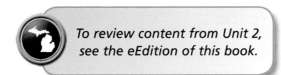

To review content from Unit 2, see the eEdition of this book.

Animated HISTORY
A New England Seaport

Visit a busy New England seaport in the 1700s, p. 108.

Interactive Review

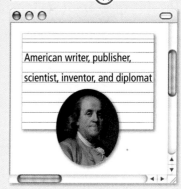

American writer, publisher, scientist, inventor, and diplomat

Use Interactive Flipcards to review key people, places, and events in the American colonies, p. 149.

Online Test Practice
Review test-taking strategies and practice for your test, pages 91, 123, 151.

UNIT 3 MICHIGAN

Creating A New Nation

Online Activities at CLASSZONE.COM

Animated HISTORY
Battle Tactics

See a Revolutionary War battle come alive, p. 202.

Interactive Review

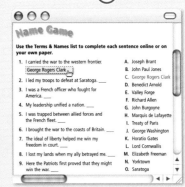

Play the Name Game to test your knowledge of the Revolutionary War, p. 229.

Online Test Practice

Review test-taking strategies and practice for your test, pages 191, 231, 259, 299.

UNIT 4 MICHIGAN

The Early Republic

Online Activities
at CLASSZONE.COM

Animated HISTORY
An American Textile Mill

Experience what life was like in an 1800s mill town, p. 370.

Interactive Review

Play the GeoGame to test your knowledge of the new republic, p. 333.

Online Test Practice

Review test-taking strategies and practice for your test, pages 335, 361, 389.

MI9

UNIT 5 MICHIGAN

A Changing Nation

Online Activities
at CLASSZONE.COM

Animated HISTORY
The Journey West

Endure the hardships and dangers of the westward journey across America's wilderness, p. 424.

Interactive Review

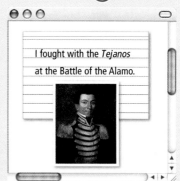

I fought with the *Tejanos* at the Battle of the Alamo.

Use Interactive Flipcards to review key people, places, and events of the mid-1800s, p. 445.

Online Test Practice

Review test-taking strategies and practice for your test, pages 415, 447, 475.

UNIT 6 MICHIGAN

A Nation Divided and Rebuilt

Online Activities
at CLASSZONE.COM

Animated HISTORY
Naval Action at Vicksburg

See Union naval power in action at Vicksburg, p. 556.

Interactive Review

Slave States

Play the GeoGame to test your knowledge of the history and geography of the Civil War, p. 505.

Online Test Practice
Review test-taking strategies and practice for your test, pages 507, 533, 567, 591.

UNIT 7 MICHIGAN

America Transformed

Online Activities
at CLASSZONE.COM

Animated HISTORY
Ellis Island

Visit historic Ellis Island to experience the immigration process in turn-of-the-century America, p. 648.

Interactive Review

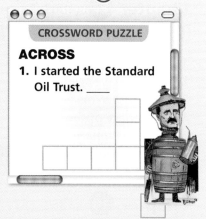

CROSSWORD PUZZLE

ACROSS
1. I started the Standard Oil Trust. _____

Solve a crossword of key terms and names for the era of Industrialization and Immigration, p. 667.

Online Test Practice
Review test-taking strategies and practice for your test, pages 627, 669, 691, 715.

Epilogue

FEATURES

PRIMARY SOURCES

HISTORICAL MAPS

Election 1876

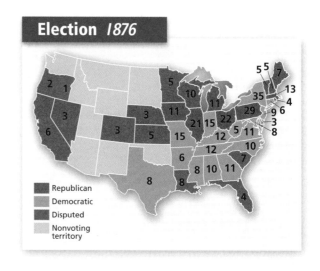

Republican
Democratic
Disputed
Nonvoting territory

Graphs

Tables and Charts

Essential Question Charts

Timelines

Infographics

Four Steps to Being a Strategic Reader

These pages explain how the *American History* chapters are organized. By using the four key strategies below, you will become a more successful reader of history, and more knowledgeable about your state's standards.

1 Set a Purpose for Reading

2 Build Your Social Studies Vocabulary

3 Use Active Reading Strategies

4 Check Your Understanding

Can you find it?

Find the following items on this and the next three pages.

- **one** chapter Essential Question and **one** chart that helps answer it
- **two** places where important words are defined
- **three** online games
- **four** key strategies for reading

---

1 Set a Purpose for Reading

Key features at the beginning of each chapter and section help you set a purpose for reading.

(A) **Essential Question** This key question sets the main purpose for reading.

(B) **Connect Geography & History** This feature helps you to consider geography's impact on history.

(C) **Animated Geography & History** sets the stage for where the history you'll study takes place.

(D) **Before, You Learned** and **Now You Will Learn** This information helps you to connect what you've studied before to what you'll study next.

(E) **Key Question** Each topic covered in the chapter is followed by a Key Question that sets your purpose for reading about that topic.

2 Build Your Social Studies Vocabulary

The Reading for Understanding pages provide three important ways to build your vocabulary.

(A) **Terms & Names** cover the most important events, people, places, and social studies concepts in the section.

(B) **Background Vocabulary** lists words you need to know in order to understand the basic concepts and ideas discussed in the section.

(C) **Visual Vocabulary** features provide visual support for some definitions.

(D) **Terms & Names** and **Background Vocabulary** are highlighted and defined in the main text so that you'll understand them as you read and study.

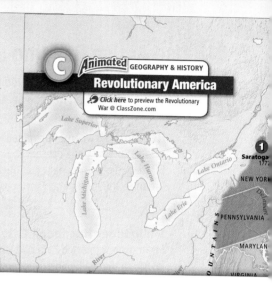

CHAPTER
7

The American Revolution

1775–1783

1. The Early Years of the War
2. The War Expands
3. The Path to Victory
4. The Legacy of the War

A ESSENTIAL QUESTION

How was it possible that American Patriots gained their independence from the powerful British Empire?

C Animated GEOGRAPHY & HISTORY
Revolutionary America
Click here to preview the Revolutionary War @ ClassZone.com

B CONNECT Geography & History

How might the geography of the United States have affected the course of the war?

Think about:

1 how **Saratoga** lies in the Hudson River valley, a major ... the Appalachian Mountains

---

Connecting History

Expansion
Europeans would continue to settle and claim lands in the West until they reached the Pacific Ocean. You will see this theme emerge when you study westward expansion in later chapters.

Americans Seize the Frontier Determined to retake Fort ... and his men set out for Vincennes from Kaskaskia in Februar... ilton wasn't expecting an attack because the rivers were flood... But Clark's men slogged through miles of icy swamps and ... chest-deep water. They caught the British at Vincennes by su...

When Hamilton and his troops tried to remain in ... pretended to have a larger force than he really had. Clark also ... Native American allies of the British in plain view of the fort. ... to do the same to the British unless they surrendered. Frighte... gave up.

Clark's victory gave the Americans a hold on the vast re... the Great Lakes and the Ohio River (even though Fort Detro... remained in the hands of the British). This area was more tha... size of the original 13 states. The expansion of the war into th... had another consequence: it forced the British again to sprea... over a larger area and further weakened the British war effort...

▲ **CAUSES AND EFFECTS** Explain why the war spread to the fronti...

War on the Waves

E ▶ **KEY QUESTION** How did Americans expand the naval war?

The war expanded not only west into the frontier but also e... high seas. By 1777, Britain had over 200 warships off the Ameri... allowed Britain to control the Atlantic trade routes to Europea...

British Trade Disrupted Because the American navy was sm... Congress encouraged American **privateers** to attack British m...

A privateer is a privately owned ship that has ... permission by a wartime government to atta... merchant ships. After capturing a ship ... a privateer sold its cargo and share... America commissioned more than 1,... to prey on the British. They capture... ships, causing British merchants to ... government to end the war.

Though outnumbered, the Con... scored several victories. A daring ... **John Paul Jones** inspired America... across the Atlantic to attack Britis... the coast of Britain itself.

"I Have Not Yet Begun to Figh... Jones became the commander of a... *Bonhomme Richard*. With four oth... patrolled the English coast. In Septe... vessels approached a convoy in which... warships were guarding a number of supp...

James Forten, who later became famous for his efforts to end slavery, joined a privateer at the age of 14.

---

2 Reading for Understanding

Key Ideas

D

BEFORE, YOU LEARNED
Despite the Continental Army's difficulties, the Patriots triumphed at Saratoga.

NOW YOU WILL LEARN
The expansion of the war weakened the British by forcing them to spread their military resources around the world.

Vocabulary

A **TERMS & NAMES**

Marquis de Lafayette (mahr•KEE•deh laf•eye•EHT) French aristocrat who volunteered to serve in Washington's army

Valley Forge site in southeast Pennsylvania where Washington and his army camped in the winter of 1777–1778

George Rogers Clark frontiersman who helped defend the Western frontier

John Paul Jones sea commander who attacked British ships near the British coast

Wilderness Road a trail into Kentucky

B **BACKGROUND VOCABULARY**

ally (AL•eye) a country that agrees to help another country achieve a common goal

desert (duh•ZERT) to leave military duty without permission

privateer (pry•vuh•TEER) a privately owned ship that has been granted permission by a wartime government to attack an enemy's merchant ships

C Visual Vocabulary
privateer

photograph courtesy of Peabody Essex Museum

Reading Strategy

Recreate the diagram shown at right. As you read and respond to the **KEY QUESTIONS**, use the center box to record the main idea; use the outer ovals to note important details. Add ovals or start a new diagram as needed.

📖 See Skillbuilder Handbook, page R2.

MAIN IDEAS AND DETAILS

Other nations join the war.

The War Expands

🖱 **GRAPHIC ORGANIZERS**
Go to Interactive Review @ ClassZone.com

READING FOR UNDERSTANDING

③ Use Active Reading Strategies

Active reading strategies help you note the most important information in each section.

Ⓐ Reading Strategy Each Reading for Understanding page contains a Reading Strategy diagram to help you track and organize the information you read.

Ⓑ Skillbuilder Handbook Every Reading Strategy is supported by a corresponding lesson in the Skillbuilder Handbook section at the back of this book.

Ⓒ Active Reading Strategies in the Skillbuilder Handbook will help you to read and study *American History*.

Battle of Charles Town British siege of Charles Town (Charleston), South Carolina, in May 1780, in which the Americans suffered their worst defeat of the war

Lord Cornwallis (korn•WAHL•ihs) British general whose campaigns in the South led to his defeat at Yorktown

Battle of Yorktown final battle of the war, in which French and American forces led by George Washington defeated British General Cornwallis

BACKGROUND VOCABULARY
redoubt (re•DOWT) a small fort

Visual Vocabulary
redoubt at Yorktown

▶ **Reading Strategy** Ⓐ

Re-create the diagram shown at right. As you read and respond to the **KEY QUESTIONS**, use the diagram to record important events in the order in which they occurred.

📖 See Skillbuilder Handbook, page R5.

SEQUENCE EVENTS

British capture Savannah, 1778.	British capture Charles Town, 1780.
	British capture Georgia.

212 Chapter 7

🖱 **GRAPHIC ORGANIZERS**
Go to **Interactive Review @ ClassZone.com**

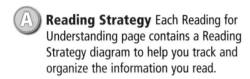

Skillbuilder Handbook

Ⓑ Table of Contents

Ⓒ

1.3 Finding Main Ideas

Defining the Skill

The **main idea** is a statement that summarizes the main point of a speech, an article, a section of a book, or a paragraph. Main ideas can be stated or unstated. The main idea of a paragraph is often stated in the first or last sentence. If it is the first sentence, it is followed by sentences that support that main idea. If it is the last sentence, the details build up to the main idea. To find an unstated idea, you must use the details of the paragraph as clues.

Applying the Skill

The following paragraph describes the role of women in the American Revolution. Use the strategies listed below to help you identify the main idea.

How to Find the Main Idea

Strategy ❶ Identify what you think may be the stated main idea. Check the first and last sentences of the paragraph to see if either could be the stated main idea.

Strategy ❷ Identify details that support that idea. Some details explain the main idea. Others give examples of what is stated in the main idea.

> **WOMEN IN THE REVOLUTION**
>
> ❶ Many women tried to help the army. Martha Washington and other wives followed their husbands to army camps. ❷ The wives cooked, did laundry, and nursed sick or wounded soldiers. ❷ A few women even helped to fight. ❷ Mary Hays earned the nickname "Molly Pitcher" by carrying water to tired soldiers during a battle. ❷ Deborah Sampson dressed as a man, enlisted, and fought in several engagements.

Make a Chart

Making a chart can help you identify the main idea and details in a passage or paragraph. The chart below identifies the main idea and details in the paragraph you just read.

> *Main Idea: Women helped the army during the Revolution.*
>
> *Detail: They cooked and did laundry.*
> *Detail: They nursed the wounded and sick soldiers*
> *Detail: They helped to fight.*
> *Detail: One woman, Molly Pitcher, carried water to soldiers during battles.*

Practicing the Skill

Turn to Chapter 5, Section 2, "Roots of American Democracy." Read "Parliament and Colonial Government" on page 137, and create a chart that identifies the main idea and the supporting details.

④ Check Your Understanding

One of the most important things you'll do as you study *American History* is to check your understanding of events, people, places, and issues as you read.

Ⓐ Connect to the Essential Question
This chart summarizes the information that will help you understand the most important ideas in the chapter.

Ⓑ Interactive Review includes a Name Game and provides two online activities to test your knowledge of the history you just studied.

Ⓒ Section Assessment reviews the section Terms & Names, revisits your Reading Strategy notes, and provides key questions about the section.

---

large segments of the population were actively involved in a poli Even if the British had succeeded in defeating an American army, would never have been able to conquer the American people.

Ⓐ CONNECT to the Essential Question

How was it possible that American Patriots gained their independence from the powerful British Empire?

AMERICAN STRENGTHS		BRITISH WEAKNESSES
Patriots fought for their lives, their property, and their political ideals.	Motivation	The British and their Hessian mercenaries fought merely for pa
Many civilians actively supported the Revolution technique Rebellion	Popular support	The British were unprepared for a popular uprising. There was no wi
Ameri mistakes patriotism		
France su and Spain expandin French m		
America		

Ⓑ CHAPTER 7 Interactive Review

Chapter Summary

① Key Idea
Although the Continental Army had difficulty fighting in a divided America, the Patriots triumphed at Saratoga.

② Key Idea
The expansion of the war weakened the British by forcing them to spread their military resources around the world.

③ Key Idea
The Continental Army, their allies, and the American people brought about an American victory.

④ Key Idea
Americans emerged from the Revolution as citizens of a unified nation that valued the ideal of liberty.

To create **Review and Study Notes** go to **Interactive Review** @ ClassZone.com

Name Game

Use the Terms & Names list to comple your own paper.

1. I carried the war to the western frontier. _George Rogers Clark_
2. I led my troops to defeat at Saratoga. ___
3. I was a French officer who fought for America. ___
4. My leadership unified a nation. ___
5. I was trapped between allied forces and the French fleet. ___
6. I brought the war to the coasts of Britain. ___
7. The ideal of liberty helped me win my freedom in court. ___
8. I lost my lands when my ally betrayed me. ___
9. Here the Patriots first proved that they migh win the war. ___
10. Here the Continental Army endured a difficu winter. ___

Activities

CROSSWORD PUZZLE
Complete the online crossword puzzle to show what you know about the American Revolution.

ACROSS
1. _____ captured the British warship *Serapis*.

GEOGAME
Use this online map to reinforce your understanding including the locations of important battles and geog drop each place name in the list at its location on the you keep track of your progress online.

Trenton
Saratoga
Lake Ontario
Valley Forge
Hudson River

Lake Ontario

More place names online

Defining Religious Freedom For many Americans, central to the liberty was the idea that religion is a private matter and that people have the right to choose and practice their personal religious belief such as James Madison and Thomas Jefferson called for a "separ church and state," meaning that the state should not be involved in affairs.

In 1777 Thomas Jefferson proposed his **Virginia Statute for Religiou** In it, he claimed that people have a "natural right" to freedom of including religious opinion. Jefferson opposed state laws that p Jews or Catholics from holding public office. He also opposed the using tax money to support churches, because, he wrote, "to com to furnish contributions of money for the propagation of opini he disbelieves, is sinful and tyrannical."

Jefferson's statute was eventually adopted as law in Virgin became the basis of the religious rights guaranteed by the Bill the U.S. Constitution.

Uniting the States For almost two centuries each colony ha erned independently of its neighbors. The colonies had been and often uncooperative. However, as the war turned colonie Americans saw how important it was for these states to work nation. The great challenge that lay ahead was how to remai nation of independent states, despite regional and religious d

▲ **SUMMARIZE** Describe the ideals that emerged from the Revolutio

Ⓒ Section Assessment

ONLINE Q For test practi Interactive

TERMS & NAMES
1. Explain the importance of
   • Treaty of Paris
   • Elizabeth Freeman
   • Richard Allen
   • Virginia Statute for Religious Freedom

USING YOUR READING NOTES
2. **Categorize** List and categorize the major results of the Revolutionary War.

KEY IDEAS
3. What groups gained least from
4. How did the goals of the Revol toward a more just society afte

CRITICAL THINKING
5. **Connect Economics & History** Treaty of Paris protect America's economic interests?
6. **Causes and Effects** How did the Patriot victory affect Native Americans?
7. **Historical Perspective** What might have happened if, during the peace negotiations, each state had tried to negotiate independently?
8. **Writing** **Citizenship Report** Use the Internet to research Elizabeth Freeman and Richard Allen.

Themes of American History

Themes are ideas and issues that arise and reappear through American history. Understanding these themes will help you to connect the past and the present and to make sense of U.S. history. *American History* focuses on nine of these themes.

Democratic Ideals

Americans have built their society around the principles of democracy. In a democracy, power lies with the people, and every individual enjoys basic rights that cannot be taken away. Throughout the nation's history, however, some Americans— mainly women and minorities—have had to struggle to gain their full rights. Still, the ideals of democracy remain the guiding principles of this land.

Citizenship

The citizens of the United States enjoy rights and freedoms found in very few other places in the world. Yet Americans know that with such freedoms come responsibilities and duties. Whether they stand in line to vote or spend a weekend to clean up a local river, Americans recognize that citizen participation is what keeps a democracy strong.

Diversity and Unity

The United States has been a land of many peoples, cultures, and faiths. Throughout the nation's history, this blend of ethnic, racial, and religious groups has helped to create a rich and uniquely American culture. The nation's many different peoples are united in their belief in American values and ideals.

Impact of the Individual

The history of the United States is the story not only of governments and laws but of individuals. Indeed, individuals have made the United States what it is today through their extraordinary and ordinary achievements. American history provides a variety of examples of the impact of the individual on society in both the United States and the world.

Immigration and Migration

This country was settled by and has remained a magnet for immigrants. Also, within the United States, large numbers of people have migrated to different regions of the country. However, movements to and within the United States have not always been voluntary. Africans were brought against their will to this country. Native Americans were forced from their homelands in order to make room for European settlers.

Martin Luther King, Jr.

Economics in History

Economics has had a powerful impact on the course of U.S. history. For example, the desire for wealth led thousands to join the California Gold Rush in 1849. The nation as a whole has grown wealthy, thanks to its abundant resources and the hard work of its citizens. An important economic issue, however, has been how to make sure that all people have opportunities to share fully in the nation's wealth. This issue will continue to be important in the 21st century.

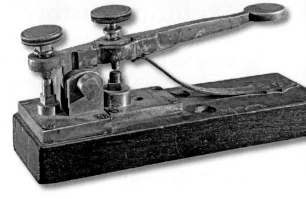

Mid-1800s telegraph

Science and Technology

Americans have always been quick to embrace inventions and new ways of doing things. After all, this country was settled by people who turned away from old ways and tried new ones. In the past two centuries, new inventions, new technologies, and scientific breakthroughs have transformed the United States—and will continue to do so in our lifetimes and beyond.

America and the World

As the power and influence of the United States have grown, the nation has played a much more active role in world affairs. Indeed, throughout the 20th century, the United States focused much of its energy on events beyond its borders. The nation fought in two world wars and tried to promote democracy, peace, and economic growth around the globe. As one of the world's political and economic leaders, the United States continues to be a key player in world affairs.

Expansion

When the United States declared its independence from Great Britain, it was only a collection of states along the Atlantic Ocean. But the new country would not remain that way for long. Many Americans shared a sense of curiosity, adventure, and a strong belief that their destiny was to expand all the way to the Pacific Ocean. Driven by this belief, they pushed westward. Americans' efforts to increase the size of their nation is a recurring theme in early U.S. history.

Exploring History Online

American History provides a variety of tools to help you explore history online. See history come to life in the Animation Center. Find help for your research projects in the Research and Writing Center. Review for tests with the Interactive Review, or create your own activities in the Activity Center. Go to ClassZone.com to make *American History* interactive!

ClassZone.com

is your gateway to exploring history. Explore the different **ClassZone** Centers to help you study and have fun with history.

A **Interactive Review**
provides you with flip cards, a crossword puzzle, section quizzes, drag-and-drop map activities, and more.

B **Activity Center**
You'll find a variety of interactive tools that will help you engage with history *your* way.

C **Activity Maker**
lets you create your own activities so that you can focus on what *you* need to review.

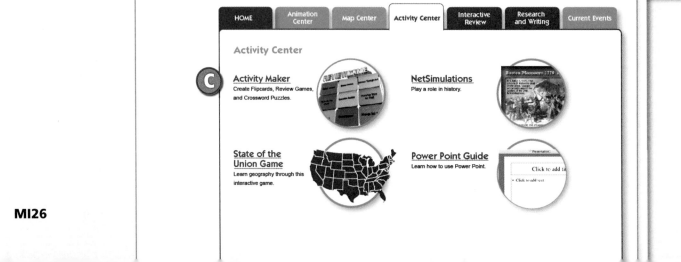

Animation Center

A rich collection of interactive features and maps on a wide variety of historical eras and topics

 Roll-overs
Explore the illustration by clicking on areas you'd like to know more about. This Battle Tactics animation links to features about tactics, cannon loading, a soldier's gear, and more.

 3D models
Study this soldier's gear by rotating the 3D model.

 In-depth Views and Information
Click each box to find out what a soldier carried during the war.

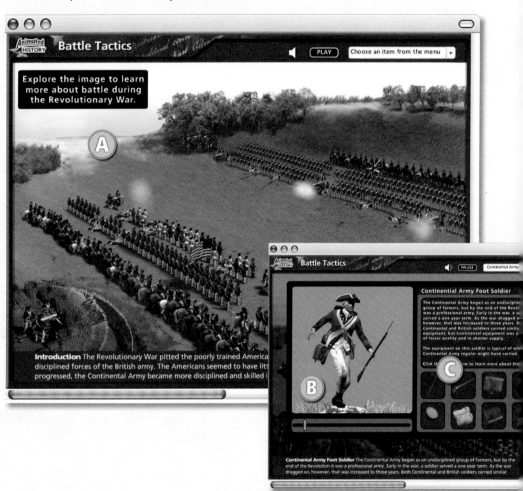

Review Game

- Create your own review game to study history *your* way.

- Select your own topics from any chapter to help you focus on specific people, places, or events to review.

- Help your friends to explore history online. Challenge them to play a review game that you create and modify!

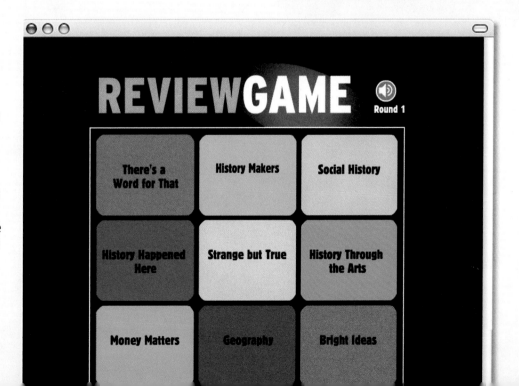

MICHIGAN

STEPS TO SUCCESS

Guide to Understanding
Michigan's Grade Level Content Expectations   MI31

- The Michigan Integrated United States History Content Expectations are organized into a short set of foundational expectations, four eras, and a section on public discourse, decision making, and citizen involvement. Each section lists the content you will learn and may be assessed on the MEAP.

Guide to
The MEAP (Michigan Educational Assessment Program)   S1

- The MEAP (Michigan Educational Assessment Program) is designed to measure your understanding of the grade level content expectations.

 For a complete list of the Michigan Grade Level Content Expectations for Grade Eight, see page R85.

Mackinac Bridge, Michigan © Ilene MacDonald/Alamy

Why Study History?

When you study U.S. history, you will see how the past informs your everyday life. Many things, such as the clothes you wear and the music you listen to, have been influenced by America's past.

Learn how to think like a historian! Dive into the dramatic events of America's past and uncover the lives of the people who shaped our nation's history.

▶ *Be An Informed Citizen* Your textbook will show you how the United States were founded, and how our current government came into existence.

Your textbook will also encourage you to be a more active participant in your community and to make a difference in our nation's future.

▶ *Become a Better Critical Thinker* Many questions throughout this book will encourage you to form your own opinion.

For example, what would *you* have done during the Civil War if fighting for what you believed in meant fighting against your own family?

▶ *Know Your Heritage* By learning about the diverse cultures that make up the United States, you will gain a better understanding of your own heritage.

What Will I Learn?

Guide to Understanding

Michigan's Grade Level Content Expectations

Michigan's Grade Level Content Expectations for Integrated United States History explore the American experience by integrating geography, civics/government, and economics into the study of history. The grade level content expectations are organized into the following groups:

Foundations in United States History and Geography—Review of Eras 1–3
Era 3—Revolution and the New Nation (1754–1800s)
Era 4—Expansion and Reform (1792–1861)
Era 5—Civil War and Reconstruction (1850–1877)
Era 6—The Development of an Industrial, Urban, and Global United States (1870–1898)
Public Discourse, Decision Making, and Citizen Involvement

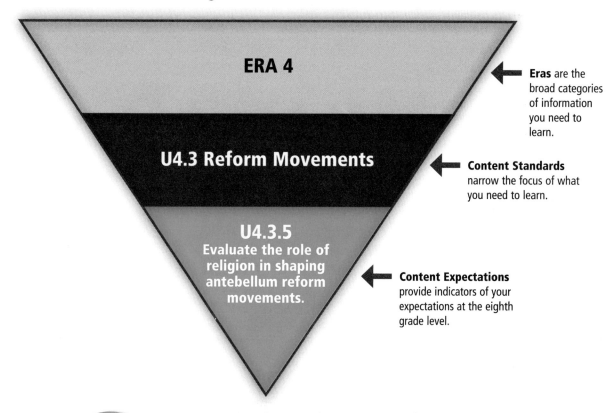

ERA 4

U4.3 Reform Movements

U4.3.5
Evaluate the role of religion in shaping antebellum reform movements.

Eras are the broad categories of information you need to learn.

Content Standards narrow the focus of what you need to learn.

Content Expectations provide indicators of your expectations at the eighth grade level.

CONNECT *To Your Michigan Test*

In the ninth grade, you will take the social studies portion of the **MEAP (MICHIGAN EDUCATIONAL ASSESSMENT PROGRAM).** This test is designed to measure your understanding and mastery of the grade level content expectations.

Overview

Michigan Grade Level Content Expectations

The charts that follow provide a brief overview of the grade level content expectations. The grade level content expectations are the skills and knowledge you need to succeed on the **MEAP**. Look for them at the beginning of each section.

For a complete list of the Michigan Grade Level Content Expectations for Grade Eight, see page R85.

FOUNDATIONS IN UNITED STATES HISTORY AND GEOGRAPHY		Review of Eras 1–3
Content Expectations		**What It Means to *You***
F1	Political and Intellectual Transformations	The foundational issues are a review of your previous study of American history and geography. These content expectations will help you apply what you learned in fifth grade to your Integrated United States History course.

ERA 3 — Revolution and the New Nation (1754–1800s)	What It Means to *You*
Era 3 focuses on why and how our nation's founders created the U.S. Constitution. The founders knew that they needed a national government to unite the states, but many people feared a strong central government. They wanted to maintain the independence of the states and protect the rights of individuals. Thus, the Articles of Confederation—the nation's first plan—gave limited power to the national government. This plan proved to be too weak. It could not deal with the many challenges the new nation faced. Attempts to create a strong national government that protected the rights of individuals and the states led to the U.S. Constitution.	Studying this era will help you understand the issues involved in creating a democratic government. This will help you appreciate the challenges faced by modern nations that are on the road to democracy.

ERA 4 — Expansion and Reform (1792–1861)

Era 4 focuses on the early decades of the United States. This period was a time of great change and challenge. Events in Europe created problems for the U.S. government. Political parties and economic differences divided the nation along regional lines. New industries and inventions changed the way people lived and worked. The cotton gin and the addition of new western lands caused slavery to spread. As the nation grew and changed, tensions increased between the North and South, and people called for social reforms.

What It Means to *You*

Understanding this era will help you appreciate elements of continuity and change in American society. The United States still faces many challenges. People still debate the role of the United States in world affairs. Political and economic differences often divide regions, and people still work for social reform.

ERA 5 — Civil War and Reconstruction (1850–1877)

Era 5 focuses on slavery, the Civil War, and Reconstruction. The issue of slavery divided the nation. The government attempted several political compromises, but tensions grew. When Abraham Lincoln won the presidency in 1860, seven Southern states left the Union. Soon, more Southern states followed. The country plunged into a bloody Civil War that ended in the South's defeat. After the war, the nation set out to reconstruct, or rebuild, the South. During Reconstruction, millions of freed African Americans worked to improve their lives, aided by the Thirteenth, Fourteenth, and Fifteenth Amendments to the U.S. Constitution.

What It Means to *You*

The Civil War was the greatest threat to the survival of the republic that our nation has ever faced. We still debate why the war was fought, how the Union won, and how we rebuilt the nation.

ERA 6 — The Development of an Industrial, Urban, and Global United States (1870–1898)

What It Means to *You*

Era 6 focuses on the growth of industry and cities and changes in the West. The period was a time of major changes in communication, transportation, and population. These changes had both good and bad effects. The railroad helped open the West to settlers, but this threatened the way of life of Native Americans. New inventions spurred industrialization and created great wealth for some people. Cities grew as millions of immigrants came to the United States in search of work. Life improved for many city dwellers, but others faced urban slums, dangerous factories, and discrimination.

Studying this era will help you understand how change affects people and society. Understanding the past will help you make sense of the effects of change today.

Era 6 also focuses on investigating topics in U.S. history that continue to be important today. These topics include the balance of power and the movement of people.

Public Policy Issues — Public Discourse, Decision Making, and Citizen Involvement

What It Means to *You*

This section focuses on public policy issues. You will research an issue and write an essay for or against that issue. This activity will help you prepare for the persuasive essay on the **MEAP (Michigan Educational Assessment Program)**. The essay will take the form of a letter to a government official concerning a public policy issue.

Guide to

the MEAP (Michigan Educational Assessment Program)

This section of your book helps you develop and practice the skills you need to study history and to prepare for the **MEAP (Michigan Educational Assessment Program)**.

The **MEAP Strategies and Practice** offer specific strategies for tackling many of the items you'll find on the **MEAP**. It gives tips for answering multiple-choice questions and persuasive essays. In addition, it offers guidelines for analyzing primary and secondary sources, maps, political cartoons, charts, graphs, and timelines. Each strategy is followed by a set of questions you can use for practice.

CONTENTS for MEAP Strategies and Practice

The chart below provides a guide to the test-taking strategies that will help prepare you for the MEAP.

**Find online test practice
@ ClassZone.com**

- **Learn** each strategy by reviewing the numbered steps on the page listed in the column.

- **Practice** the strategy on the following page.

- **Apply** the strategies you learned in the **MEAP Practice** at the end of each chapter.

Strategy	Learn	Practice	Apply
Multiple Choice	p. S2	p. S3	p. 191, Chapter 6
Primary and Secondary Sources	pp. S4, S6	pp. S5, S7	p. 55, Chapter 2 p. 231, Chapter 7 p. 335, Chapter 9
Political Cartoons	p. S8	p. S9	p. 361, Chapter 10 p. 415, Chapter 12 p. 669, Chapter 20
Charts	p. S10	p. S11	p. 22, Chapter 1 p. 334, Chapter 9
Line and Bar Graphs	p. S12	p. S13	p. 335, Chapter 9 p. 361, Chapter 10
Pie Graphs	p. S14	p. S15	p. 123, Chapter 4
Thematic Maps	p. S16	p. S17	p. 447, Chapter 13 p. 507, Chapter 15 p. 533, Chapter 16 p. 591, Chapter 18
Timelines	p. S18	p. S19	p. 360, Chapter 10
Constructed Response	pp. S20–21	pp. S22–23	p. 23, Chapter 1 p. 55, Chapter 2 p. 91, Chapter 3
Persuasive Essays	pp. S24–S25	pp. S26–S27	p. 81, Chapter 3 p. 431, Chapter 13

Multiple Choice

A multiple-choice question consists of a stem and a set of choices. The stem is usually in the form of a question or an incomplete sentence. One of the choices correctly answers the question or completes the sentence.

1 Read the stem carefully and try to answer the question or complete the sentence without looking at the choices.

2 Pay close attention to key words in the stem. They may direct you toward the correct answer.

3 Read each choice with the stem. Don't jump to conclusions about the correct answer until you've read all of the choices.

4 Take great care with statements that are stated negatively.

5 After reading all of the choices, eliminate any that you know are incorrect.

6 Use modifiers to help narrow your choice.

7 Look for the best answer among the remaining choices.

stem

1 At the beginning of the Revolution, *most* Americans were

2 *Most* is a key word here. Replacing it with *all* or *some* changes the sentence and calls for a different answer.

3 choices

A united in support of the war.

B Patriots who wanted independence from Great Britain.

C against a war with Great Britain.

D Loyalists who supported the British point of view.

2 Which of the following present-day states was **NOT** ceded to the United States in the Treaty of Guadalupe Hidalgo?

4 *Not* is the keyword here. Eliminate any states that you know were ceded as part of the treaty.

A Arizona

B California

C New Mexico

D Washington

3 At the outset of the Civil War, both the Union and the Confederacy wanted the support of the border states

A Delaware, Marlyand, Kentucky, and Oklahoma.

5 You can eliminate **A** if you remember that Oklahoma was not a state at the time of the Civil War.

B Delaware, Maryland, Kentucky and Missouri.

C Delaware, Maryland, West Virginia, Kentucky, and Missouri

D *all* the states bordering the Missouri Compromise line.

6 Absolute words, such as *all, never, always, every,* and *only,* often signal an incorrect choice.

7 In **C**, West Virginia did lie on the border between the Union and the Confederacy. However, it broke away from Virginia early in the war and became a state in 1863. Therefore, **B** is the correct answer.

answers: 1 (C), 2 (D), 3 (B)

MEAP PRACTICE

Directions: Read the following questions and choose the *best* answer from the four choices.

1 Which of the following inventions did **NOT** help open the Great Plains to farming?

   A the steel windmill

   B barbed wire

   C the spring-tooth harrow

   D cotton gin

2 Which of the following statements *best* explains why, by the year 1500, there were hundreds of Native American groups with diverse religious beliefs, economies, and languages?

   A The local environment influenced each group in different ways.

   B Spiritual beliefs dictated many groups' distinct cultural growth.

   C Contagious disease caused the people to form smaller groups.

   D Trading practices led to the establishment of specialized cultures.

3 During the presidency of Thomas Jefferson, the United States was able to foster westward expansion when it acquired territory in what is known as

   A Seward's Folly.

   B the Missouri Compromise.

   C the Kansas-Nebraska Act.

   D the Louisiana Purchase.

4 The movement of Puritans from England to North America in the 1620s and 1630s is known as the Great

   A Awakening.

   B Compromise.

   C Debate.

   D Migration.

MEAP STRATEGIES AND PRACTICE

Primary Sources

Primary sources are materials written or made by people who took part in or witnessed historical events. Letters, diaries, speeches, newspaper articles, and autobiographies are all primary sources. So, too, are legal documents, such as wills, deeds, and financial records.

1 Look at the source line and identify the author. Consider what qualifies the author to write about the events discussed in the passage.

2 Skim the document to form an idea of what it is about.

3 Note special punctuation. Ellipses indicate that words or sentences have been removed from the original passage. Brackets indicate words that were not in the original. Bracketed words often are replacements for difficult or unfamiliar terms.

4 Carefully read the passage and distinguish between facts and the author's opinions.

5 Consider for whom the author was writing. The intended audience may influence what and how an author writes.

6 Before rereading the passage, skim the questions to identify the information you need to find.

The Flight from the White House

Wednesday Morning, twelve o'clock. Since sunrise I have been turning my spy-glass in every direction, (. .)but alas! I can (see) **3** only groups of military, wandering in all directions, as if there **4** was a lack of arms, or of spirit to fight for their own fireside.

2 *Three o'clock.* Will you believe it, my sister? We have had a battle, or skirmish, near Bladensburg, and here I am still, within sound of the cannon!. . . Two messengers covered with dust come to bid me fly. . . . At this late hour a wagon has been [found], and I have had it filled with plate and the most valuable portable articles belonging to the house. Whether it will reach its destination . . . or fall into the hands of British soldiery, events must determine. Our kind friend, Mr. Carroll, has come to hasten my departure, and is in a very bad humor with me, because I insist on waiting until the large picture of General Washington is secured. . . . It is done! and the precious portrait placed in the hands of two gentlemen of New York, for safe keeping. And now, dear sister, I must leave this house. . . . When I shall again write to you, or where I shall be tomorrow, I cannot tell!

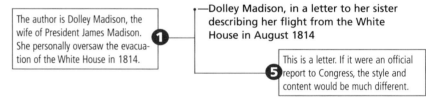

The author is Dolley Madison, the wife of President James Madison. She personally oversaw the evacuation of the White House in 1814.

1

—Dolley Madison, in a letter to her sister describing her flight from the White House in August 1814

This is a letter. If it were an official **5** report to Congress, the style and content would be much different.

6 1 Dolley Madison's letter describes her preparations to flee the White House in advance of a British attack. In which war did this attack take place?

   A War of Jenkins' Ear

   B French and Indian War

   C Revolutionary War

   D War of 1812

2 Why might Dolley Madison be considered a good source of information on the British attack on Washington, D.C.?

   A She was the wife of President James Madison.

   B She was an eyewitness to the attack.

   C She helped her husband develop military policy.

   D She had intercepted British war plans.

answers: 1 (D), 2 (B)

Directions: Use this passage and your knowledge of U.S. history to answer questions 1 through 4.

Life in Texas, Mid-1800s

I wish that I could emphasize this feature of our early Texan life. *The spirit of helpfulness and friendly fellowship always prevailed. It was one of the best of the good things of the new country.* We were all strangers together, always willing to lend or borrow. . . . Once Mr. Van Zandt was called away from home . . . [and] another man came and took our gun and killed a deer, for he knew we needed meat. . . . When our need for things was pressing, we usually found a way for making them. One time Mr. Van Zandt needed a saddle—he made it, having only a drawing knife from which to fashion the saddle-tree from a dead sassafras tree which he cut down for the purpose. His shoes were gone and he could get no others. He bought some red leather, made a last [a foot-shaped, wooden block] and manufactured some very respectable shoes.

—Frances Cook Lipscomb Van Zandt,
Texas settler, 1839–1846

1 What was a good thing about the new Texas country that the author writes was important to her?

A Being hungry

B Being a stranger

C The spirit of helpfulness and friendliness

D Getting deer meat whenever she wanted it

2 Mr. Van Zandt used leather, wood, and simple tools to

A build a wagon.

B make goods to trade for meat.

C build a spinning wheel.

D make a saddle and shoes.

3 According to the passage, which of the following is **NOT** one of the ways the Van Zandts and their Texas neighbors got their supplies?

A lending or borrowing things

B making them by hand with simple tools

C buying them from mail-order catalogs

D volunteering to help each other

4 Frances Van Zandt wrote, "We were all strangers together," to explain that hardships on the Texas frontier

A left people isolated and alone.

B drew people together to help each other.

C were shared only by close friends and relatives.

D made people suspicious of one another.

Passage from "Frances Cook Lipscomb Van Zandt Reminisces About the Early Years in Texas, 1839–1846," from the Van Zandt Folder, Mary Daggett Lake Papers, series IV, box 3, Fort Worth Public Library, Fort Worth, Texas. Courtesy of the Fort Worth Public Library, Fort Worth, Texas.

Secondary Sources

Secondary sources are descriptions or interpretations of historical events made by people who were not at those events. The most common types of written secondary sources are history books, encyclopedias, and biographies. A secondary source often combines information from several primary sources.

1 Read titles to preview what the passage is about.

2 Look for topic sentences. These, too, will help you preview the content of the passage.

3 As you read, use context clues to help you understand difficult or unfamiliar words. (You can tell from the description of the battle in the previous sentences that the word *fiasco* must mean something like "disaster," "failure," or "blunder.")

4 As you read, ask and answer questions that come to mind. You might ask: Why did Dolley Madison take a bed with her? Why would the British burn public buildings?

5 Before rereading the passage, skim the questions to identify the information you need to find.

1 **The British Offensive**

2 Ironically, Britain achieved a far more spectacular success in an operation originally designed as a diversion from their main thrust down Lake Champlain. In 1814 a British army sailed from Bermuda for Chesapeake Bay, landed near Washington, and met a larger American force . . . at Bladensburg, Maryland, on August 24. The Battle of Bladensburg quickly became the "Bladensburg races" as the American militia fled, almost without firing a shot. The British then descended on Washington. Madison, who had **3** witnessed the Bladensburg fiasco, escaped into the Virginia hills. His wife, Dolley, pausing only long enough to load her silver, a bed, and a portrait of George Washington onto her carriage, hastened to join her husband, while British troops ate the supper prepared for the Madisons at the presidential **4** mansion. Then they burned the mansion and other public buildings in Washington. A few weeks later, the British attacked Baltimore, but after failing to crack its defenses, they broke off the operation.

—Paul S. Boyer, et al., *The Enduring Vision*

5 **1** Why do you think the authors refer to the Battle of Bladensburg as a "fiasco"?

  A because the American forces fled almost without a fight

  B because President Madison had to flee the White House

  C because it allowed the British to attack Washington, D.C.

  D because it was a famous victory for the British forces

2 What, according to the authors, did the British raid on Washington, D.C., accomplish?

  A It paved the way for the British capture of Baltimore.

  B It drove all the American militia out of the city.

  > Remember to be wary of choices that contain absolutes, such as *all*, *every*, or *only*.

  C It helped the British offensive on Lake Champlain.

  D It burned down the presidential mansion and other public buildings.

answers: 1 (A), 2 (D)

Directions: Use this passage and your knowledge of U.S. history to answer questions 1 through 3.

African-American Sailors

African Americans contributed greatly to the growth of maritime commerce in the United States. Beginning in colonial times, slaves, with their masters' permission, hired themselves out as sailors. Some served as translators on slave ships. Merchant ships also offered a means of escape for runaway slaves. A few escapees even took to the sea as pirates.

Seafaring was one of the few occupations open to free African Americans. They served on clippers, naval vessels, and whaling ships from the 1700s into the late 1800s. Federal crew lists from Atlantic seaports show that during this time, African Americans made up 10 percent or more of sailors on American ships. Seafaring was an especially dangerous line of work for free blacks. They risked capture in southern ports, where they were often thrown in jail or sold into slavery.

1 What records show that African Americans made up 10 percent or more of sailors on American ships?

A shipyard records

B family bibles

C federal crew lists

D ships' logs

2 Based on the passage, which of the following is **NOT** one of the reasons free and enslaved African Americans went to sea?

A to escape slavery

B to live as pirates

C to earn wages as sailors

D to discover new lands

3 The author states that life was especially dangerous for free African-American sailors because

A American prosperity depended on their work alone.

B the worst jobs on board ship were always assigned to them.

C they ran the risk of capture and enslavement in southern ports.

D they were more likely than white sailors to contract scurvy.

MEAP STRATEGIES AND PRACTICE

Political Cartoons

Political cartoons are drawings that express views on political issues of the day. Cartoonists use symbols and such artistic styles as caricature—exaggerating a person's physical features—to get their message across.

1 Identify the subject of the cartoon. Titles and captions often indicate the subject matter.

2 Identify the main characters in the cartoon. Here, the main character is Horace Greeley, a candidate in the 1872 presidential election.

3 Note the symbols—ideas or images that stand for something else—used in the cartoon.

4 Study labels and other written information in the cartoon.

5 Analyze the point of view. How cartoonists use caricature often indicates how they feel. The exaggeration of Greeley's physical appearance—short and overweight—makes him appear comical.

6 Interpret the cartoonist's message.

The cartoonist shows Tammany Hall, New York's Democratic political machine, as a tiger. Uncle Sam, a symbol for the United States, is shown looking on.

The writing on the wall suggests that Tammany Hall wants reform. The "Whitewash" label on the bucket suggests that the tiger's true, corrupt, stripes are just being covered up.

Thomas Nast, *Harper's Weekly*, August 31, 1872

1 "What are you going to do about it, if 'Old Honesty' lets him loose again?"

1 Based on the cartoon, what do you think was Horace Greeley's major issue in the 1872 presidential campaign?

A political reform

B states' rights

C abolition

D temperance

2 Which one of the following statements do you think *best* represents the cartoonist's point of view?

A Horace Greeley is an honest man.

B Tammany Hall supports political reform.

C Tammany Hall, regardless of Greeley's view, is still corrupt.

D Horace Greeley, like most Tammany politicians, is corrupt.

answers: 1 (A), 2 (C)

Directions: Use the cartoon and your knowledge of U.S. history to answer questions 1 through 3.

THE LITTLE GIANT IN THE CHARACTER OF THE GLADIATOR.

Anonymous, 1858

1 Stephen A. Douglas is portrayed as a gladiator armed with the sword and shield of

   A Congress and the rule of law.

   B freedom of speech and of the press.

   C constitutional and property rights of slaveholders.

   D voting rights and self-government for the territories.

2 Popular sovereignty was used in the 1850s to address the issue of

   A states' rights.

   B federalism.

   C slavery.

   D voting rights.

3 The cartoon illustrates the fight over whether to

   A admit Kansas into the Union as a free state or a proslavery state.

   B grant freedom of the press to newspapers in the territories.

   C allow sword fighting and dueling as legal activities in the 1850s.

   D replace a system of majority rule with a monarchy.

MEAP STRATEGIES AND PRACTICE

Cartoon: Copyright © Bettman/Corbis

Charts

Charts present information in a visual form. History textbooks use several types of charts, including tables, flow charts, Venn diagrams, and concept webs. The type of chart most commonly found in standardized tests is the table. It organizes information in columns and rows for easy viewing.

1 Read the title and identify the broad subject of the chart.

2 Read the column and row headings and any other labels. This will provide more details about the subject of the chart.

3 Compare and contrast the information from column to column and row to row.

4 Try to draw conclusions from the information in the chart. Ask yourself: What trends does the chart show?

5 Read the questions, and then study the chart again.

Review difficult or unfamiliar words. Here, the term *nativity* means "place of birth."

1 **United States Population by Region and Nativity** *1890–1920*

2	1890	1900	1910	1920
Northeast				
Total Population	17,407,000	21,047,000	25,869,000	29,662,000
% Native Born	78	77	74	77
% Foreign Born	22	23	26	23
North Central				
Total Population	22,410,000	26,333,000	29,889,000	34,020,000
% Native Born	82	84	84	86
% Foreign Born	18	16	16	14
South				
Total Population	20,028,000	24,524,000	29,389,000	33,126,000
% Native Born	97	98	97	97
% Foreign Born	3	2	3	3
West				
Total Population	3,134,000	4,309,000	7,082,000	9,214,000
% Native Born	78	75	76	79
% Foreign Born	22	25	24	21

4

Source: *Historical Statistics of the United States*

Compare changes in population over time and contrast statistics among regions. **3**

5 **1** The two regions with the *highest* percentage of foreign-born inhabitants are the

  A Northeast and the West.

  B West and the South.

  C South and the North Central.

  D North Central and the Northeast.

2 When did immigration to the Northeast peak?

  A between 1910 and 1920

  B before 1900

  C between 1900 and 1910

  D after 1920

answers: 1 (A), 2 (C)

Directions: Use the chart and your knowledge of U.S. history to answer questions 1 through 4.

Percentage of Population Free and Enslaved, by States and Territories *1790*					
North			**South**		
States/Territories	**Free**	**Enslaved**	**States/Territories**	**Free**	**Enslaved**
Connecticut	98.9	1.1	Georgia	64.5	35.5
Delaware	85.0	15.0	Kentucky	83.1	16.9
Maine	100.0	0.0	Maryland	67.8	32.2
Massachusetts	100.0	0.0	North Carolina	74.5	25.5
New Hampshire	99.9	0.1	South Carolina	57.0	43.0
New Jersey	93.8	6.2	Virginia	60.9	39.1
New York	93.8	6.2			
Pennsylvania	99.1	0.9			
Rhode Island	98.6	1.4			
Vermont	100.0	0.0			

Source: Inter-University Consortium for Political and Social Research

1 The state with the *highest* percentage of enslaved people was

 A New Hampshire.

 B North Carolina.

 C Rhode Island.

 D South Carolina.

2 Which of the following *best* describes *most* states in the North?

 A The population was more than 98 percent free.

 B More than 10 percent of the population was enslaved.

 C Less than 60 percent of the population was free.

 D The population was more than 20 percent enslaved.

3 Which statement about the percentage of enslaved people is *true*?

 A It is much lower in the South.

 B It is much higher in the South.

 C There is no difference between the regions.

 D There is a slight difference between the regions.

4 What economic factor *best* explains the population differences between the regions?

 A The North focused on manufacturing.

 B The North was wealthy enough to free enslaved people.

 C The South focused on plantation agriculture.

 D The South needed enslaved people for factory work.

Line and Bar Graphs

Graphs show statistics in a visual form. Line graphs are particularly useful for showing changes over time. Bar graphs make it easy to compare numbers or sets of numbers.

① Read the title and identify the broad subject of the graph.

② Study the labels on the vertical and horizontal axes to see the kinds of information presented in the graph. Note the intervals between amounts and between dates. This will help you read the graph more efficiently.

③ Look at the source line and evaluate the reliability of the information in the graph. Government statistics on education tend to be reliable.

④ Study the information in the graph and note any trends.

⑤ Draw conclusions and make generalizations based on these trends.

⑥ Read the questions carefully, and then study the graph again.

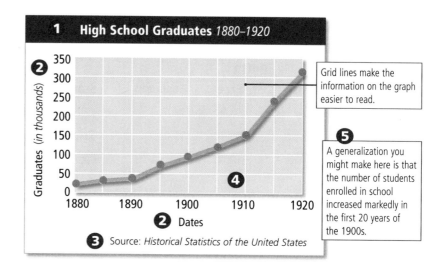

1 High School Graduates *1880–1920*

② Graduates (in thousands)

Grid lines make the information on the graph easier to read.

⑤ A generalization you might make here is that the number of students enrolled in school increased markedly in the first 20 years of the 1900s.

② Dates

③ Source: *Historical Statistics of the United States*

⑥ 1 How many students graduated from high school in 1905?

A exactly 100,000   C about 150,000

B about 125,000   D exactly 175,000

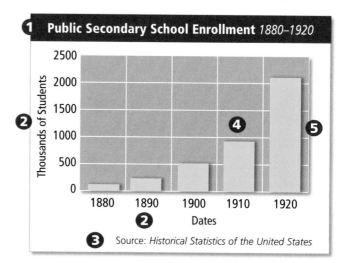

1 Public Secondary School Enrollment *1880–1920*

② Thousands of Students

② Dates

③ Source: *Historical Statistics of the United States*

⑥ 2 Which one of the following sentences do you think *best* describes the trend shown in the bar graph?

A The number of students enrolled steadily increased.

B The number of students enrolled showed little change.

C The number of students enrolled rose and fell.

D The number of students enrolled steadily decreased.

answers: 1 (B), 2 (A)

Directions: Use the graphs and your knowledge of U.S. history to answer questions 1 through 4.

Growth of the African-American Population, 1820–1860

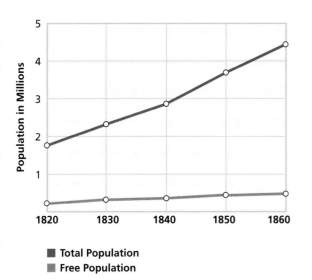

■ Total Population
■ Free Population

Source: Gilder Lehrman Institute of American History

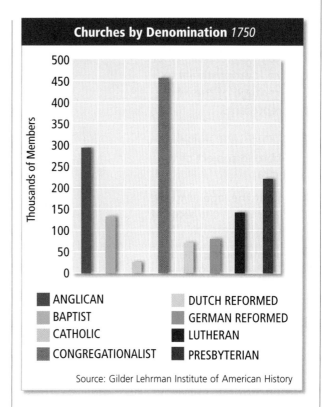

Churches by Denomination *1750*

■ ANGLICAN   ◻ DUTCH REFORMED
■ BAPTIST   ■ GERMAN REFORMED
▦ CATHOLIC   ■ LUTHERAN
▨ CONGREGATIONALIST ▦ PRESBYTERIAN

Source: Gilder Lehrman Institute of American History

1 In which decade did the total African-American population *first* exceed 3.5 million?

   A 1820–1830

   B 1830–1840

   C 1840–1850

   D 1850–1860

2 About how many times larger than the free African-American population was the total population in 1860?

   A four

   B five

   C six

   D nine

3 Which one of the following statements accurately reflects information in the graph?

   A There were more Congregationalist churches than all other denominations combined.

   B There were more Presbyterian churches than Anglican churches.

   C The Baptists had the fewest churches.

   D The Congregationalists had the most churches.

4 Which denomination had the *fewest* members?

   A Anglican   C German Reformed

   B Catholic   D Lutheran

Pie Graphs

A pie, or circle, graph shows relationships among the parts of a whole. These parts look like slices of a pie. The size of each slice is proportional to the percentage of the whole that it represents.

❶ Read the title and identify the broad subject of the pie graph.

❷ Look at the legend to see what each of the slices of the pie represents.

❸ Read the source line and note the origin of the data shown in the pie graph.

❹ Compare the slices of the pie and try to make generalizations and draw conclusions from your comparisons.

❺ Read the questions carefully and review difficult or unfamiliar terms.

❻ Eliminate choices that you know are wrong.

❶ **The Popular Vote in the 1860 Presidential Election**

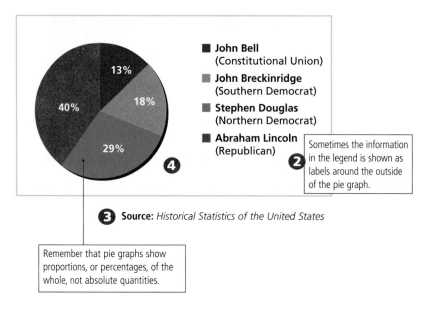

- ■ **John Bell** (Constitutional Union)
- ■ **John Breckinridge** (Southern Democrat)
- ■ **Stephen Douglas** (Northern Democrat)
- ■ **Abraham Lincoln** (Republican)

❷ Sometimes the information in the legend is shown as labels around the outside of the pie graph.

❸ **Source:** *Historical Statistics of the United States*

Remember that pie graphs show proportions, or percentages, of the whole, not absolute quantities.

1 In the 1860 presidential election, Abraham Lincoln won

A by a landslide.

B a majority of the votes cast.

C a plurality of the votes cast.

D by a narrow margin.

❺ In electoral terms, the word *landslide* refers to an overwhelming victory, *majority* means "more than 50 percent," and *plurality* means "the most but less than 50 percent."

2 What political situation in 1860 does the pie graph show?

A The Democratic Party was split into northern and southern wings before the 1860 election.

B The Republican Party was not yet an important force in national politics.

C Douglas won fewer popular votes than Lincoln but won more electoral votes.

D Because no candidate won a majority of the popular votes, the House of Representatives decided the election.

❻ You can eliminate **B** when you notice that the Republican Party received more votes than any other.

answers: 1 (C), 2 (A)

Directions: Use the pie graphs and your knowledge of U.S. history to answer questions 1 through 4.

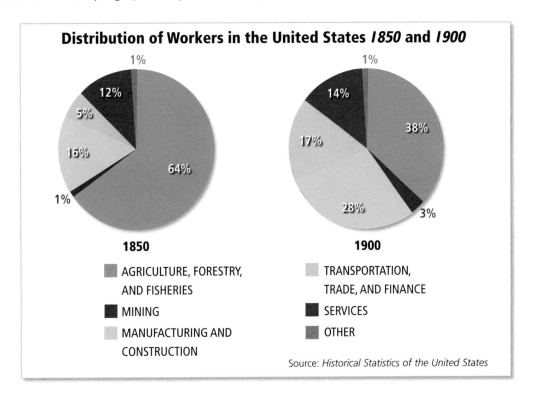

Distribution of Workers in the United States *1850* and *1900*

1850

1%
12%
5%
16%
64%
1%

1900

1%
14%
38%
17%
28%
3%

■ AGRICULTURE, FORESTRY, AND FISHERIES
■ MINING
■ MANUFACTURING AND CONSTRUCTION

■ TRANSPORTATION, TRADE, AND FINANCE
■ SERVICES
■ OTHER

Source: *Historical Statistics of the United States*

1 In 1850, *most* people worked in

A agriculture, forestry, and fisheries.

B mining.

C services.

D transportation, trade, and finance.

2 In 1900, more people worked in manufacturing and construction than in

A agriculture, forestry, and fisheries.

B mining and agriculture, forestry, and fisheries combined.

C services and transportation, trade, and finance combined.

D transportation, trade, and finance.

3 Which occupation category showed an increase between 1850 and 1900?

A manufacturing and construction

B services

C transportation, trade, and finance

D agriculture, foresty, and fisheries

4 What helped to bring about the changes reflected in the two pie graphs?

A the passage of new immigration laws

B the growth of industry

C the decline of world agricultural markets

D decrease in factory wages

Thematic Maps

A thematic map, or special-purpose map, focuses on a particular topic. The location of baseball parks, a country's natural resources, election results, and major battles in a war are all topics you might see illustrated on a thematic map.

1 Read the title to determine the subject and purpose of the map.

2 Examine the labels on the map to find more information about the map's subject and purpose.

3 Study the legend to find the meaning of the symbols and colors used on the map.

4 Look at the colors and symbols on the map and try to identify patterns.

5 Use the compass rose or North arrow to determine directions on the map.

6 Use the scale to estimate distances between places shown on the map.

7 Read the questions and then carefully study the map to determine the answers.

1 Southern Military Districts, 1867

3 While a thematic map focuses on one topic, it often offers several kinds of information on that topic. Therefore, the legend for a thematic map is usually very detailed.

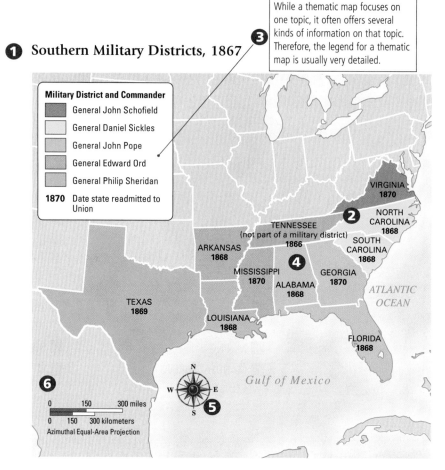

Military District and Commander
- General John Schofield
- General Daniel Sickles
- General John Pope
- General Edward Ord
- General Philip Sheridan
- **1870** Date state readmitted to Union

7 **1** Which former Confederate state was the *first* to be readmitted to the Union?

A Tennessee

B South Carolina

C Florida

D Alabama

2 The military district in which Texas was located was commanded by

A General Edward Ord.

B General John Pope.

C General Philip Sheridan.

D General Daniel Sickles.

answers: 1 (A), 2 (C)

MEAP PRACTICE

Directions: Use the map and your knowledge of U.S. history to answer questions 1 through 4.

The Battle of San Jacinto, 1836

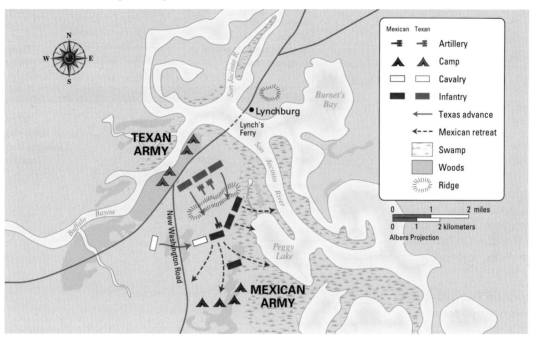

1 The Texan camp was located in what type of area?

A swamp

B ridge

C woods

D open plains

2 In which direction did the Texan forces move to attack the Mexican army?

A directly south

B northeast

C directly east

D southeast

3 An attack was launched on the Mexican forces from the west by

A Texan artillery.

B Texan cavalry.

C Texan infantry.

D Texan artillery, cavalry, and infantry.

4 What was the importance of the Battle of San Jacinto?

A Texas won its independence from Mexico.

B It avenged the defeats at Goliad and the Alamo.

C Texas gained U.S. support in the struggle for freedom.

D It proved that the Texans were better fighters than the Mexicans.

Timelines

A timeline is a type of chart that lists events in the order in which they occurred. In other words, timelines are a visual method of showing what happened when.

1 Read the title to discover the subject of the timeline.

2 Identify the time period covered by the timeline by noting the earliest and latest dates shown. On vertical timelines, the earliest date is shown at the top. On horizontal timelines, it is on the far left.

3 Read the events and their dates in sequence. Notice the intervals between events.

4 Use your knowledge of history to develop a fuller picture of the events listed in the timeline. For example, place the events in a broader context by considering what was happening elsewhere in the world.

5 Note how events are related to one another. Look particularly for cause-effect relationships.

6 Use the information you have gathered from the above strategies to answer the questions.

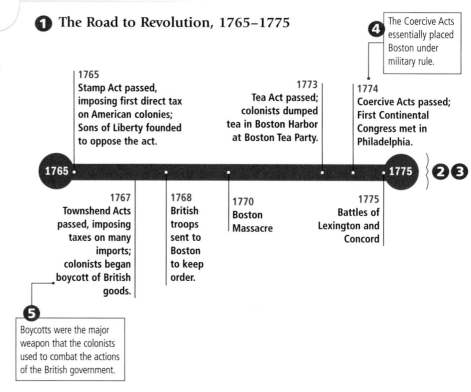

1 The Road to Revolution, 1765–1775

4 The Coercive Acts essentially placed Boston under military rule.

1765 Stamp Act passed, imposing first direct tax on American colonies; Sons of Liberty founded to oppose the act.

1773 Tea Act passed; colonists dumped tea in Boston Harbor at Boston Tea Party.

1774 Coercive Acts passed; First Continental Congress met in Philadelphia.

1767 Townshend Acts passed, imposing taxes on many imports; colonists began boycott of British goods.

1768 British troops sent to Boston to keep order.

1770 Boston Massacre

1775 Battles of Lexington and Concord

5 Boycotts were the major weapon that the colonists used to combat the actions of the British government.

6 1 How did the colonists respond to the passage of the Townshend Acts?

A They founded the Sons of Liberty.

B They dumped British tea in Boston Harbor.

C They began a boycott of British goods.

D They called the First Continental Congress

2 About how much time passed between the Coercive Acts and the first battles of the Revolutionary War?

A one year

B three years

C seven years

D nine years

answers: 1 (C), 2 (B)

Directions: Use the timeline and your knowledge of U.S. history to answer questions 1 through 3.

The Erie Canal, 1816–1840s

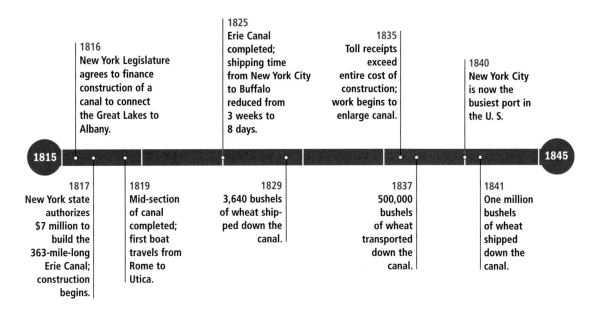

1816
New York Legislature agrees to finance construction of a canal to connect the Great Lakes to Albany.

1825
Erie Canal completed; shipping time from New York City to Buffalo reduced from 3 weeks to 8 days.

1835
Toll receipts exceed entire cost of construction; work begins to enlarge canal.

1840
New York City is now the busiest port in the U. S.

1815

1845

1817
New York state authorizes $7 million to build the 363-mile-long Erie Canal; construction begins.

1819
Mid-section of canal completed; first boat travels from Rome to Utica.

1829
3,640 bushels of wheat shipped down the canal.

1837
500,000 bushels of wheat transported down the canal.

1841
One million bushels of wheat shipped down the canal.

1 The Erie Canal was completed and ready for water traffic between Buffalo and Albany in

A 1817.

B 1819.

C 1825.

D 1840.

2 About how many years after the canal was finished did work begin to enlarge it?

A 4 years

B 6 years

C 11 years

D 21 years

3 Which of the following statements about the Erie Canal is **NOT** *true*?

A The canal greatly reduced the time it took to ship goods between the Great Lakes and New York.

B From 1837 to 1841, the volume of wheat shipped through the canal doubled.

C The cost of building the canal was greater than the amount of tolls collected.

D The mid-section of the canal was completed in 1819.

Constructed Response

Constructed-response questions focus on various kinds of documents. Each document is usually accompanied by a series of questions. These questions call for short answers that, for the most part, can be found directly in the document. Some answers, however, require knowledge of the subject or time period addressed in the document.

1 Read the title of the document to discover the subject addressed in the questions.

2 Study and analyze the document. Take notes on what you see.

3 Read the prompt and then study the document again to locate the answers.

4 Carefully write your answers.

1 Joseph Glidden's Patent

2 Constructed-response questions use a wide range of documents, including short passages, cartoons, charts, graphs, maps, timelines, posters, and other visual materials. This is a copy of a legal document called a patent.

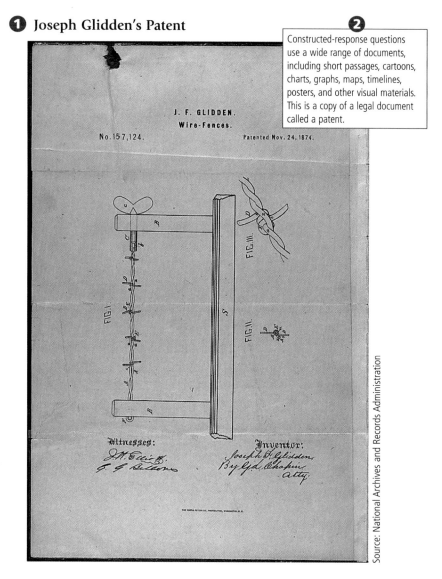

J. F. GLIDDEN.
Wire-Fences.
No. 157,124.   Patented Nov. 24, 1874.

Witnesses: Inventor:

Source: National Archives and Records Administration

3 Joseph Glidden received the patent shown above.

- Identify the invention that is illustrated on this patent.
- Identify what evidence indicates this is a legal document.
- Identify what other developments had a major impact on farming in the 1800s.

4 *The patent is for the invention of barbed wire. The fact that a witness and an attorney signed the patent suggests that it is a legal document. In addition to barbed wire, steel plows, reapers, threshers, and dry farming had a major impact on farming.*

First Amendment Rights: the Five Basic Freedoms

Freedom of Religion	People have the right to practice the religion of their choice.
Freedom of Speech	People have the right to state their ideas.
Freedom of the Press	People have the right to publish their ideas.
Freedom of Assembly	People have the right to meet peacefully in groups.
Freedom to Petition	People have the right to make requests and complain to the government.

The First Amendment to the U.S. Constitution protects five basic freedoms.

- Identify what religious right the First Amendment protects.

- Identify which of the five basic freedoms you would be exercising if you wrote a letter to the mayor asking for a stop sign at an intersection near your school.

- Explain how freedom of speech and freedom of the press are related.

Freedom of religion gives you the right to belong to any religious group you choose. Freedom of speech and freedom to petition give you the right to state your ideas and to make a request of or to complain to the government. You exercise these two rights when you write a letter to the mayor. Freedom of speech and freedom of the press guarantee that the government cannot prevent people or the press from expressing views on such things as politics, religion, social conditions, art, and daily life. Both freedoms protect the free exchange of ideas and opinions.

Use the chart and your knowledge of U.S. history to answer the constructed-response item.

Ratifying the Constitution

State	Date Ratified
Connecticut	January 9, 1788
Delaware	December 7, 1787
Georgia	January 2, 1788
Maryland	April 28, 1788
Massachusetts	February 6, 1788
New Hampshire	June 21, 1788
New Jersey	December 18, 1787
New York	July 26, 1788
North Carolina	November 21, 1789
Pennsylvania	December 12, 1787
Rhode Island	May 29, 1790
South Carolina	May 23, 1788
Virginia	June 25, 1788

The U.S. Constitution took several years to ratify.

- Identify which state was the first to ratify the U.S. Constitution and in what year.

- Identify which state was the last to ratify the U.S. Constitution and in what year.

- Explain why the Bill of Rights was important to the ratification of the U.S. Constitution.

Use the chart and your knowledge of U.S. history to answer the constructed-response item.

A Country Dividing

Act	Provisions
Missouri Compromise, 1820–1821	**1.** Slavery was to be prohibited in the Louisiana territory north of the 36° 30′ parallel. **2.** Maine was admitted as a free state. **3.** Missouri was admitted as a slave state.
Compromise of 1850	**1.** The territories of New Mexico and Utah were created without restrictions on slavery. **2.** California was admitted as a free state. **3.** The slave trade was abolished in Washington, D.C. **4.** Congress passed a strong fugitive slave law for the return of escaped slaves.
Kansas-Nebraska Act, 1854	**1.** Two new territories, Kansas and Nebraska, were created. **2.** Popular sovereignty would be used to decide whether a territory became a slave or a free state. **3.** The provision overturned the Missouri Compromise.

As the United States grew during the 1800s, Congress and American citizens argued about what form of government each new territory and state would have. Congress passed three acts in hopes of settling the issue.

- Identify the common issue addressed by the three acts.
- Explain how the Kansas-Nebraska Act overturned the Missouri Compromise.
- Discuss why the Kansas-Nebraska Act created conflict in Kansas.

Persuasive Essays

The ability to communicate your views about political issues is an important citizenship skill. On the Grade 9 Social Studies MEAP, you will be asked to write a persuasive essay in the form of a letter to a government official. In the letter, you will take a stand for or against a public policy issue. Like all persuasive essays, the letter will need to make a clear and forceful claim and support that claim with reasons and evidence.

❶ Read the information in the Introduction to learn about the issue you are to address in your letter.

❷ On the MEAP, you will use information from the Data Section to support the claim you make in your letter. Carefully study and analyze the information.

Introduction

❶ During President George Washington's first term, political parties started to develop around the beliefs of two members of Washington's cabinet, Secretary of the Treasury Alexander Hamilton and Secretary of State Thomas Jefferson. Despite Washington's opposition to political parties, they had a great influence in American domestic and foreign policy.

❷ Data Section

Read the following information. Use it along with your knowledge of U.S. history to complete the tasks that follow.

Part A: A Warning on Political Parties

Let me . . . warn you in the most solemn manner against the baneful [harmful] effects of the spirit of party generally. This spirit, unfortunately, is inseparable from our nature, having its root in the strongest passions of the human mind. . . .

It serves always to distract the public councils and enfeeble [weaken] the public administration. It agitates the community with illfounded jealousies and false alarms; kindles the animosity [hatred] of one part against another; foments occasionally riot and insurrection. It opens the door to foreign influence and corruption, which find a facilitated access [easy entry] to the government itself through the channels of party passions.

—George Washington, Farewell Address

Part B: Positions of the First United States Political Parties

Federalist Party	Democratic-Republican Party
Strong central government	Weak central government
Loose interpretation of the Constitution	Strict interpretation of the Constitution
Government should pay states' Revolutionary War debts	Each state should pay its own debts
Favored a national bank	Opposed a national bank
Favored business interests	Favored agricultural interests
Pro-British foreign policy	Pro-French foreign policy

❸ In Task I, you will be asked to answer a multiple-choice question to help you see relationships in the data.

❹ Persuasive essays involve issues that have two sides. Think about the two sides of the issue in the Task II prompt. Choose which side you want to support.

❺ Write your essay using persuasive language. Include at least one core democratic value of American constitutional democracy. Core democratic values include such beliefs and principles as public or common good, popular sovereignty, patriotism, rule of law, representative government, checks and balances, and individual rights.

Part C: Policy Dispute in Congress Hall, Philadelphia

Prints Division, The New York Public Library, Astor, Lenox, and Tilden Foundations.

❸ Task I: Interpreting Information

Read the information in Part A of the Data Section.

1 Which of the following statements *best* describes George Washington's views on the *relationship between* **political parties** and **how the government operates?**

  A Political parties help the government address important problems.

  B Political parties make the government less effective.

  C Political parties help voters make good decisions.

  D Political parties block foreign influences and corruption.

❹ Task II: Taking a Stand

Write a letter to a government official supporting or opposing the following public policy issue.

2 **Should the creation of multiple political parties be encouraged?**

Support your position by using a core democratic value of American constitutional democracy, prior knowledge, and information from the Data Section. ❺

Essay Rubric The best essays will clearly state and support the position; include support based on a core democratic value; draw on prior knowledge from history, geography, civics, or economics; and use information from the Data Section. It is not enough to simply state an opinion.

Introduction

In 1775, Great Britain had an army of 48,647 men located throughout the world, more than 8,500 of them in the Americas. A rebellion by the small group of 13 colonies in America did not scare the keepers of such a large colonial empire. Nevertheless, the Americans won the Revolution, thanks in part to the colonists' belief and alliances with European Nations.

Data Section

Read the following information. Use it with your knowledge of U.S. history to complete the tasks that follow.

Part A: Philadelphia, September 12, 1777

I close this paper with a short address to General Howe. . . . We know the cause which we are engaged in, and though a passionate fondness for it may make us grieve at every injury. . . . We are not moved by the gloomy smile of a worthless king, but by the ardent glow of generous patriotism. We fight not to enslave, but to set a country free, and to make room upon the earth for honest men to live in. In such a case we are sure that we are right; and we leave to you the despairing reflection of being the tool of a miserable tyrant.

—Thomas Paine, *The American Crisis No. IV*

Part B: The Battle of Yorktown, 1781: Winning the American Revolution

Estimated American, French, and British Forces and Casualties		
Generals and Their Divisions	**Forces**	**Casualties**
General Washington (American colonies)	11,100	76
General Rochambeau (France)	7,800	186
General Cornwallis (Britain)	8,000	482

Source: U.S. Army Center of Military History

Estimated French and British Naval Strength*		
French and British Fleets	**Ships**	**Guns on Board Ship**
Admiral Graves (Britain)	19	1,450
Admiral DeGrasse (France)	24	2,610

*D++small craft or transport ships

Task I: Interpreting Information

Read the information in Part B of the Data Section.

1 Which of the following statements *best* describes the *relationship between* **France's assistance during the American Revolution** and **the outcome of the war**?

A France had little to do with the American victory.

B France defeated the British navy.

C France provided soldiers and ships that helped offset British strength.

D The Americans won even though the French suffered heavy casualties.

Task II: Taking a Stand

Write a letter to a government official supporting or opposing the following public policy issue.

2 Just as France and other European nations supported the Americans during the American Revolution, should the United States support other nations in their quest for freedom today?

Support your position by using a core democratic value of American constitutional democracy, prior knowledge, and information from the Data Section. Core democratic values include life, liberty, justice, equality, rule of law, representative government, and individual rights.

MEAP STRATEGIES AND PRACTICE

The Landscape of America

The best place to begin your study of American history is with the geography of America. Geography is more than the study of the land and people. It also involves the relationship between people and their environment.

The United States is part of the North American continent. The United States ranks third in both total area and population in the world. It is filled with an incredible variety of physical features, natural resources, climactic conditions, and people. This handbook will help you to learn about these factors and to understand how they affected the development of the United States.

Chicago's waterways—its river system, canals, and location on Lake Michigan—have made it the commercial hub of the Midwest.

Turbines in a California "wind farm" use coastal winds to generate electricity. California is the birthplace of both windsurfing and America's first wind farms.

ROCKY MOUNTAINS

WEST

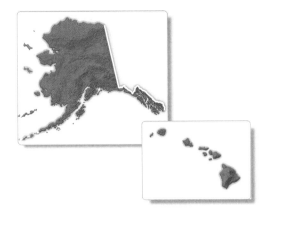

Rhode Island is world-renowned for its commercial fishing.

NORTHEAST

MIDWEST

APPALACHIAN MOUNTAINS

SOUTH

The climate and soil of Alabama are well-suited for growing cotton. The United States grows over 4 million tons of cotton annually.

The Landscape of America **A1**

Themes of Geography

One useful way to think about geography is in terms of major themes or ideas. These pages examine the five major themes of geography and show how they apply to Boston, Massachusetts.

Location

"Where am I?" Your answer is your location. One way to answer is to use absolute location. That means using the coordinates of longitude and latitude (see page A6). For example, if you're in Boston, your absolute location is approximately 42° north latitude and 71° west longitude.

More likely, however, you'll use relative location to answer the question. Relative location describes where an area is in relation to another area. For example, Boston lies in the northeast corner of the United States, next to the Atlantic Ocean.

THINKING ABOUT GEOGRAPHY What is the relative location of your school?

One of the world's best natural ports, Boston has been a center of international shipping for more than 300 years.

Region

Geographers can't easily study the whole world at one time. So they break the world into regions. A region can be as large as a continent or as small as a neighborhood. A region has certain shared characteristics that set it apart. These characteristics might include political division, climate, language, or religion. Boston is part of the northeast region. It shares a climate—humid continental—with the cities of New York and Philadelphia.

THINKING ABOUT GEOGRAPHY What characteristics does your city or town share with nearby cities or towns?

Place

"What is Boston like?" Place can help you answer this question. Place refers to the physical and human factors that make one area different from another. Physical characteristics are natural features, such as physical setting, plants, animals, and weather.

Human characteristics include cultural diversity and the things people have made—including language, the arts, and architecture. For instance, Boston includes African Americans, as well as people of Irish, Italian, Chinese, and Hispanic ancestry.

THINKING ABOUT GEOGRAPHY What physical and human characteristics make where you live unique?

The dragon dance is a holiday tradition in Boston's vibrant Chinatown neighborhood.

Movement

Movement refers to the shifting of people, goods, and ideas from one place to another. People constantly move in search of better places to live, and they trade goods with one another over great distances. Movement also causes ideas to travel from place to place. In recent years, technology has quickened the movement of ideas and goods.

Boston became known as the Cradle of Liberty because of the movement of ideas. The concepts of freedom and self-government that developed in Boston spread to the other colonies and helped to start the American Revolution.

THINKING ABOUT GEOGRAPHY What are some of the different ways you spread information and ideas?

Boston's subway system, which runs both above and below ground, is the oldest in the nation.

Human-Environment Interaction

Human-environment interaction refers to ways people interact with their environment, such as building a dam, cutting down a tree, or even sitting in the sun.

In Boston, human-environment interaction occurred when officials filled in swampy areas to make the city larger. In other ways, the environment has forced people to act. For example, people have had to invent ways to protect themselves from extreme weather and natural disasters.

THINKING ABOUT GEOGRAPHY What are ways that people in your city or town have changed their environment?

Themes of Geography **Assessment**

MAIN IDEAS

1. What is the relative location of your home?
2. What are three characteristics of the region in which you live?
3. What are at least three ways in which you have recently interacted with the environment?

CRITICAL THINKING

4. **Forming and Supporting Opinions** Which aspect of geography described in these themes do you think has most affected your life? Explain.

Think about
- ways that you interact with your environment
- how you travel from place to place

Map Basics

Geographers use many different types of maps, and these maps all have a variety of features. The map on the next page gives you information on a historical event—the final two years of the Civil War. But you can use it to learn about different parts of a map, too.

Types of Maps

Physical maps Physical maps show mountains, hills, plains, rivers, lakes, oceans, and other physical features of an area. (See Atlas p. A29.)

Political maps Political maps show political units, such as countries, states, provinces, counties, districts, and towns. Each unit is normally shaded a different color, represented by a symbol, or shown with a different typeface. (See Atlas p. A28.)

Historical maps Historical maps illustrate such things as economic activity, migrations, battles, and changing national boundaries.

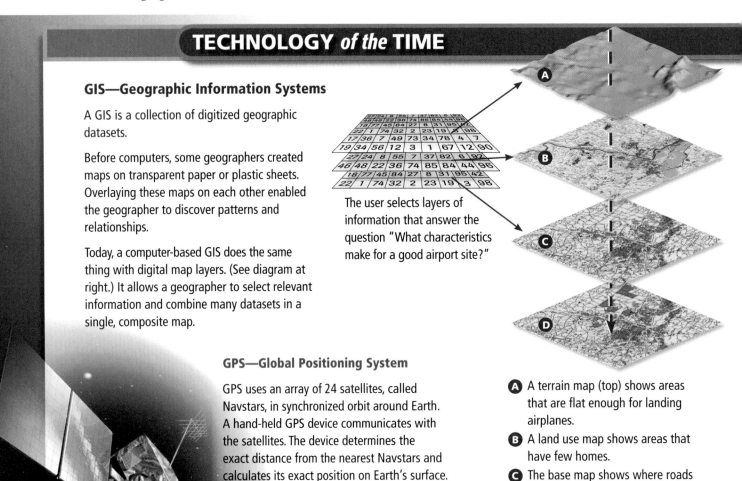

TECHNOLOGY *of the* TIME

GIS—Geographic Information Systems

A GIS is a collection of digitized geographic datasets.

Before computers, some geographers created maps on transparent paper or plastic sheets. Overlaying these maps on each other enabled the geographer to discover patterns and relationships.

Today, a computer-based GIS does the same thing with digital map layers. (See diagram at right.) It allows a geographer to select relevant information and combine many datasets in a single, composite map.

The user selects layers of information that answer the question "What characteristics make for a good airport site?"

GPS—Global Positioning System

GPS uses an array of 24 satellites, called Navstars, in synchronized orbit around Earth. A hand-held GPS device communicates with the satellites. The device determines the exact distance from the nearest Navstars and calculates its exact position on Earth's surface.

A A terrain map (top) shows areas that are flat enough for landing airplanes.

B A land use map shows areas that have few homes.

C The base map shows where roads are located.

D The layers are combined to create a composite map showing possible sites for the airport.

Reading a Map

A Lines Lines indicate political boundaries, roads and highways, human movement, and rivers and other waterways.

B Symbols Symbols represent such items as capital cities, battle sites, or economic activities.

C Labels Labels are words or phrases that explain various items or activities on a map.

D Compass Rose A compass rose shows which way the directions north (N), south (S), east (E), and west (W) point on the map.

E Scale A scale shows the ratio between a unit of length on the map and a unit of distance on the earth. A typical one-inch scale indicates the number of miles and kilometers that length represents on the map.

F Colors Colors show a variety of information on a map, such as population density or the physical growth of a country.

G Legend or Key A legend or key lists and explains the symbols, lines, and colors on a map.

H Lines of Longitude These are imaginary, north-south lines that run around the globe.

I Lines of Latitude These are imaginary, east-west lines that run around the globe. Together, latitude and longitude lines form a grid on a map or globe to indicate an area's absolute location.

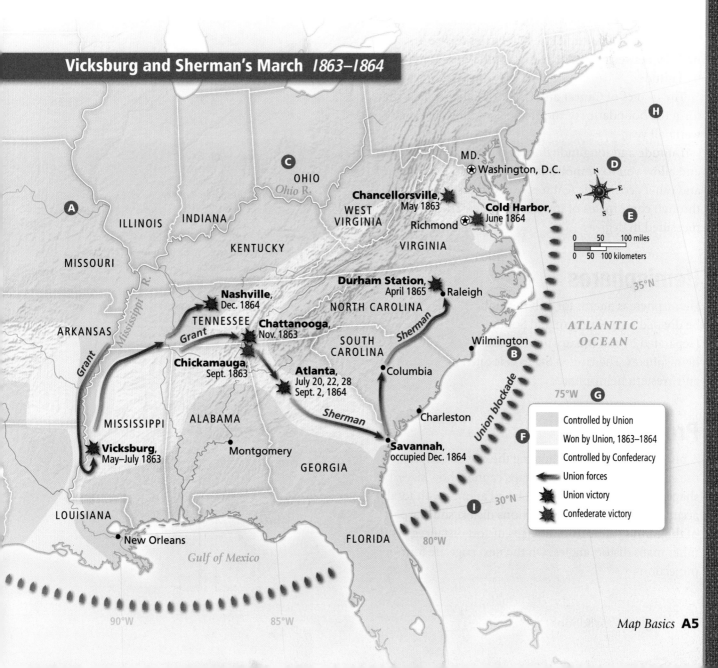

Vicksburg and Sherman's March *1863–1864*

Longitude lines

- are imaginary lines that run north to south around the globe and are known as meridians
- show the distance in degrees east or west of the prime meridian

The prime meridian is a longitude line that runs from the North Pole to the South Pole. It passes through Greenwich, England, and measures 0° longitude.

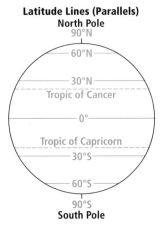

Longitude Lines (Meridians)
North Pole
150°W 180° 150°E
120°W   120°E
90°W   90°E
Prime Meridian
60°W   60°E
30°W   30°E
West Longitude   0°   East Longitude

Latitude lines

- are imaginary lines that run east to west around the globe and are known as parallels
- show distance in degrees north or south of the equator

The equator is a latitude line that circles the earth halfway between the North and South poles. It measures 0° latitude.

The tropics of Cancer and Capricorn are parallels that form the boundaries of the Tropics, a region that stays warm all year.

Latitude and longitude lines appear together on a map and allow you to pinpoint the absolute location of cities and other geographic features. You express this location through coordinates of intersecting lines. These are measured in degrees.

Latitude Lines (Parallels)
North Pole
90°N
60°N
30°N
Tropic of Cancer
0°
Tropic of Capricorn
30°S
60°S
90°S
South Pole

Hemispheres

Hemisphere is a term for half the globe. The globe can be divided into Northern and Southern hemispheres (separated by the equator) or into Eastern and Western hemispheres. The United States is located in the Northern and Western hemispheres.

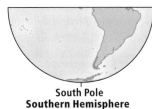

Northern Hemisphere
North Pole

Equator

South Pole
Southern Hemisphere

Projections

A projection is a way of showing the curved surface of the earth on a flat map. Flat maps cannot show sizes, shapes, and directions on a globe all at once with total accuracy. As a result, all projections distort some aspect of the earth's surface. Some maps distort distances, while other maps distort angles. On the next page are four projections.

Western Hemisphere   Eastern Hemisphere

Mercator Projection

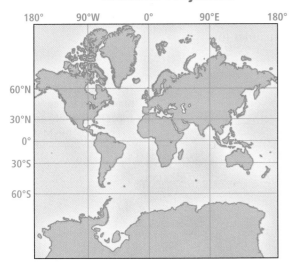

The Mercator projection shows most of the continents as they look on a globe. However, the projection stretches out the lands near the North and South poles. The Mercator is used for all kinds of navigation.

Azimuthal Projection

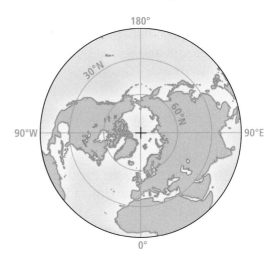

An azimuthal projection shows the earth so that a straight line from the central point to any other point on the map gives the shortest distance between the two points. Size and shape of the continents are also distorted.

Homolosine Projection

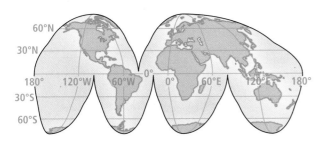

This projection shows the accurate shapes and sizes of the landmasses, but distances on the map are not correct.

Robinson Projection

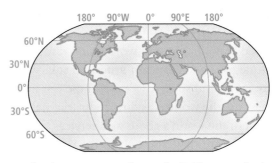

Textbook maps commonly use the Robinson projection. It shows the entire earth with nearly the true sizes and shapes of the continents and oceans. However, the shapes of the landforms near the poles appear flat.

Map Basics Assessment

MAIN IDEAS

1. What is the longitude and latitude of your city or town?

2. What information is provided by the legend on the map on page A5?

3. What is a projection? Compare and contrast Antarctica on the Mercator and the Robinson projections.

CRITICAL THINKING

4. **Making Inferences** Why do you think latitude and longitude are so important to sailors?

Think about

• the landmarks you use to find your way around

• the landmarks available to sailors on the ocean

Physical Geography of the United States

Physical geography involves all the natural features on the earth. This includes the land, resources, climate, and vegetation.

Land

Separated from much of the world by two oceans, the United States covers 3,717,796 square miles and spans the entire width of North America. To the west, Hawaii stretches the United States into the Pacific Ocean. To the north, Alaska extends the United States to the Arctic Circle. On the U.S. mainland, a huge central plain separates large mountains in the West and low mountains in the East. Plains make up almost half of the country, while mountains and plateaus make up a quarter each.

An abundance of lakes—Alaska alone has three million—and rivers also dot the landscape. Twenty percent of the United States is farmed. Urban areas cover only about two percent of the nation.

These sandstone buttes in Monument Valley Navajo Tribal Park (Utah) are nicknamed "the Mittens."

THINKING ABOUT GEOGRAPHY What is the land like around your city or state?

Resources

The United States has a variety of natural resources. Vast amounts of coal, oil, and natural gas lie underneath American soil. Valuable deposits of lead, zinc, uranium, gold, and silver also exist. These resources have helped the United States become the world's leading industrial nation—producing more than 20 percent of the world's goods and services.

These resources have also helped the United States become both the world's largest producer of energy (natural gas, oil, coal, nuclear power, and electricity) and the world's largest consumer of it. Other natural resources include the Great Lakes, which are shared with Canada. They contain about 20 percent of the world's total supply of fresh surface water. Refer to the map on the next page to examine the nation's natural resources.

THINKING ABOUT GEOGRAPHY What are the different natural resources that you and your family use in your daily lives?

Coal mining is an important industry in parts of the Northwest, the Southwest, and the East.

Melting glaciers thousands of years ago left deposits of sand and gravel in ridges, called eskers, like this one in North Dakota.

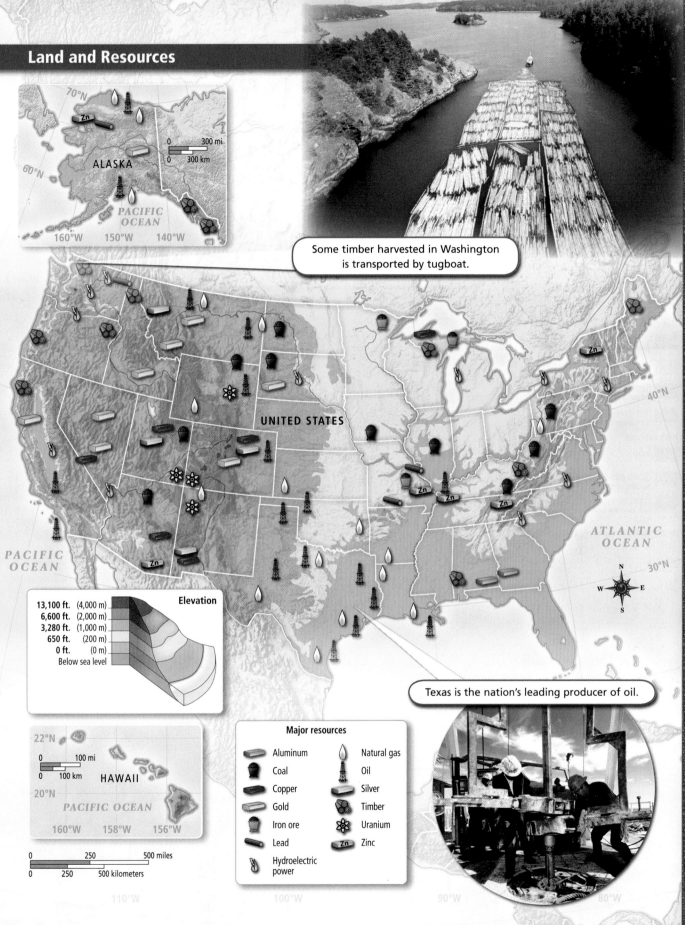

Land and Resources

ALASKA

PACIFIC
OCEAN

70°N

60°N

160°W   150°W   140°W

0   300 mi
0   300 km

Some timber harvested in Washington
is transported by tugboat.

UNITED STATES

PACIFIC
OCEAN

ATLANTIC
OCEAN

40°N

30°N

Elevation

13,100 ft.   (4,000 m)
6,600 ft.   (2,000 m)
3,280 ft.   (1,000 m)
650 ft.   (200 m)
0 ft.   (0 m)
Below sea level

N
W   E
S

Texas is the nation's leading producer of oil.

22°N

HAWAII

PACIFIC OCEAN

20°N

0   100 mi
0   100 km

160°W   158°W   156°W

Major resources

Aluminum		Natural gas	
Coal		Oil	
Copper		Silver	
Gold		Timber	
Iron ore		Uranium	
Lead		Zn Zinc	
Hydroelectric power			

0   250   500 miles
0   250   500 kilometers

110°W   100°W   90°W   80°W

Climate Zones

ALASKA
(U.S.)

Tropical
- Tropical wet (always hot and wet)
- Tropical wet and dry (hot with wet and dry seasons)

Dry
- Desert (very hot summers, with cold nights, very dry)
- Semiarid (hot summers, cold winters, dry)

Mid-Latitude
- Mediterranean (mild wet winters, hot dry summers)
- Marine west coast (mild year round)
- Humid subtropical (hot summers, mild winters, rainy)
- Humid continental (mild-to-hot summers, cold winters)

High Latitude
- Subarctic (very cold winters, cold summers)
- Tundra (bitterly cold winters, freezing summers)
- Highland (temperature varies with elevation from tropical to glaciers)

ARCTIC OCEAN

Baffin Bay

Arctic Circle

60°N

40°W

Hudson

A single Northeast blizzard can dump two feet or more of snow.

40°N

60°N

ATLANTIC OCEAN

UNITED STATES

PACIFIC OCEAN

Tropic of Cancer

N
W   E
S

0   250   500 miles
0   250   500 kilometers

Gulf of Mexico

20°N

Southern Florida is warm enough for beach activities almost year-round.

PACIFIC OCEAN

22°N

HAWAI
(U.S.)

0   75   150 miles
0   75   150 kilometers

20°N

160°W   158°W   156°W

120°W   100

Climate

The United States contains a variety of climates. For example, the mean temperature in January in Miami, Florida, is 67°F, while it is 11°F in Minneapolis, Minnesota. Most of the United States experiences a continental climate, or distinct change of seasons. Some regional climatic differences include hot and humid summers in the Southeast versus hot and dry summers in the Southwest. Harsh winters and heavy snow can blanket parts of the Midwest, the Northeast, and the higher elevations of the West and Northwest. Refer to the map on the previous page to see the nation's climatic regions.

Human activities have affected the climate, too. For example, pollution from cars and factories can affect local weather conditions and are contributing to a dangerous rise in the earth's temperature.

THINKING ABOUT GEOGRAPHY How would you describe the climate where you live?

Vegetation

Between 20,000 and 25,000 species and subspecies of plants and vegetation grow in the United States—including over 1,000 different kinds of trees. Climate often dictates the type of vegetation found in a region. For instance, cold autumns in the Northeast contribute to the brilliantly colored autumn leaves. Rain nourishes the forests in the Northwest and Southeast. The central plains, where rainfall is less heavy, are covered by grass. Cactus plants thrive in the dry southwestern deserts.

Along with natural vegetation, climate dictates the nation's variety of planted crops. For example, temperate weather in the Midwest helps wheat to grow, while warm weather nourishes citrus fruit in Florida and California.

THINKING ABOUT GEOGRAPHY What kinds of trees or plants grow in your region?

Spanish moss grows in coastal areas from Virginia south to Venezuela. This scene is of Cumberland Island, Georgia.

Physical Geography Assessment

MAIN IDEAS

1. What are the different aspects of physical geography?
2. Which state contains the largest variety of climates?
3. What two states contain most of the country's oil resources?

CRITICAL THINKING

5. **Drawing Conclusions** What do you think are the advantages of living in a country with diverse physical geography?

Think about
- the different resources available in your region
- the variety of recreational activities in your region

Geography Dictionary

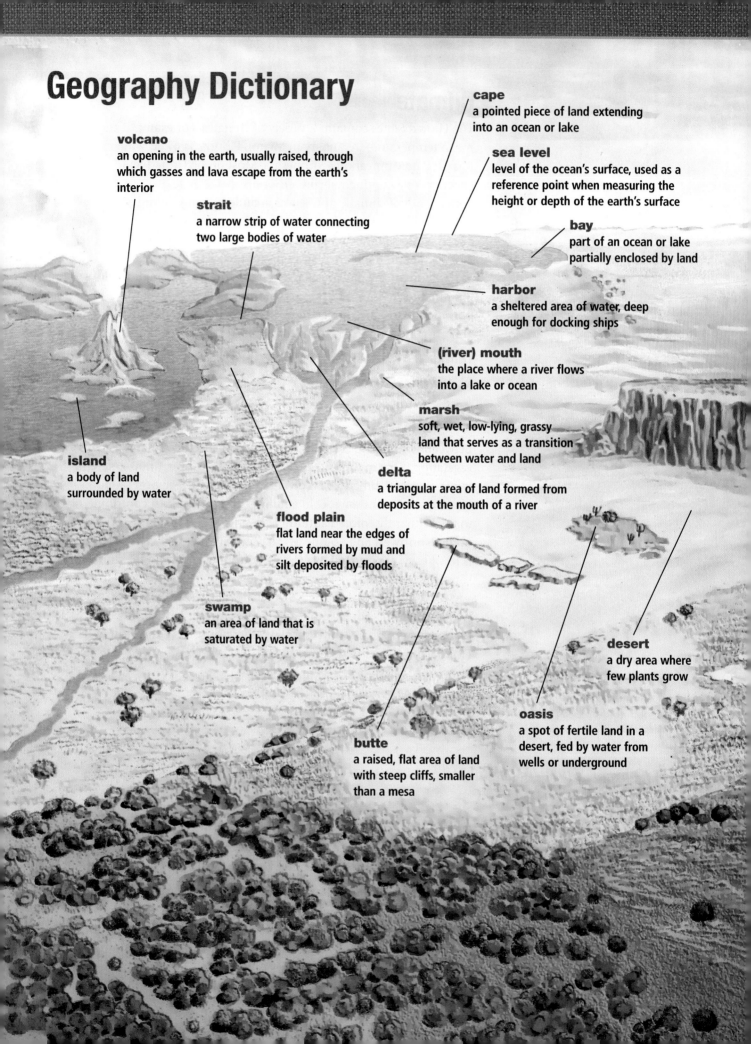

cape
a pointed piece of land extending into an ocean or lake

sea level
level of the ocean's surface, used as a reference point when measuring the height or depth of the earth's surface

volcano
an opening in the earth, usually raised, through which gasses and lava escape from the earth's interior

strait
a narrow strip of water connecting two large bodies of water

bay
part of an ocean or lake partially enclosed by land

harbor
a sheltered area of water, deep enough for docking ships

(river) mouth
the place where a river flows into a lake or ocean

marsh
soft, wet, low-lying, grassy land that serves as a transition between water and land

island
a body of land surrounded by water

delta
a triangular area of land formed from deposits at the mouth of a river

flood plain
flat land near the edges of rivers formed by mud and silt deposited by floods

desert
a dry area where few plants grow

swamp
an area of land that is saturated by water

oasis
a spot of fertile land in a desert, fed by water from wells or underground

butte
a raised, flat area of land with steep cliffs, smaller than a mesa

prairie
a large, level area of grassland with few or no trees

steppe
a wide, treeless plain

mountain
natural elevation of the earth's surface with steep sides and greater height than a hill

valley
low land between hills or mountains

glacier
a large ice mass that moves slowly down a mountain or over land

mesa
a wide, flat-topped mountain with steep sides, larger than a butte

cataract
a large, powerful waterfall

canyon
a narrow, deep valley with steep sides

cliff
the steep, almost vertical edge of a hill, mountain, or plain

plateau
a broad, flat area of land higher than the surrounding land

Human Geography of the United States

Human geography focuses on people's relationships with each other and the surrounding environment. It includes two main themes of geography: human-environment interaction and movement. The following pages will help you to better understand the link between people and geography.

Humans Adapt to Their Surroundings

Humans have always adapted to their environment. For example, in North America, many Native American tribes burned forest patches to create grazing area to attract animals and to clear area for farmland. In addition, Americans have adapted to their environment by building numerous dams, bridges, and tunnels. More recently, scientists and engineers have been developing building materials that will better withstand the earthquakes that occasionally strike California.

THINKING ABOUT GEOGRAPHY What are some of the ways in which you interact with your environment on a daily basis?

The Fred Hartman Bridge, completed in 1995, crosses the Houston Ship Channel, connecting two suburbs of Houston, Texas.

The multi-level cliff dwellings of Mesa Verde, Colorado, were built by Ancestral Pueblo people between 700 and 900 years ago.

Humans Affect the Environment

When humans interact with the environment, sometimes nature suffers. In the United States, for example, major oil leaks or spills occur each year—fouling shorelines and harming wildlife. Building suburbs and strip malls has also destroyed forests, farmland, and valuable wetlands.

THINKING ABOUT GEOGRAPHY What are some of the environmental problems in your city or town?

Workers use heavy equipment to attack a Gulf of Mexico oil spill.

Preserving and Restoring

In 2003, Americans recycled more than 30% of their garbage—about 72 million tons. In 2005, the Kyoto Protocol began to take effect, requiring the signing countries to limit or reduce greenhouse gas emissions. As of 2006, 165 nations had ratified Kyoto.

THINKING ABOUT GEOGRAPHY
What are some of the ways in which you help the environment?

Destruction of Original Forests

1620

1850

1926

This maps show that, over the years, human beings have nearly cut down all the original forests in the United States. Each dot represents 25,000 acres.

More than 3,000 volunteers each year participate in Hands on Miami Day by planting trees and cleaning up neighborhoods.

Human Geography of the United States **A15**

Human Movement

In prehistoric times, people roamed the earth in search of food. Today, people move from place to place for many different reasons. Among them are cost of living, job availability, and climate. Since the 1950s, many Americans—as well as many new immigrants—moved to the Sunbelt. This region runs through the southern United States from Virginia to California. Since 1990 the nation has seen a population shift from the North and East to the South and West.

- The fastest growing county in the United States—Riverside—and three of the country's ten fastest growing cities are in Southern California. Yet the state has seen a steady outmigration.

- Cities such as Dallas-Forth Worth, Atlanta, and Minneapolis-St. Paul show net outmigration while their surrounding suburbs have net immigration.

THINKING ABOUT GEOGRAPHY

Has your family ever moved? If so, what were some of the reasons?

Clark County, home to Las Vegas, is one of the nation's fastest growing metropolitan areas. In just six years (1999 to 2005), school enrollments grew from about 217,000 to 291,000—more than one third.

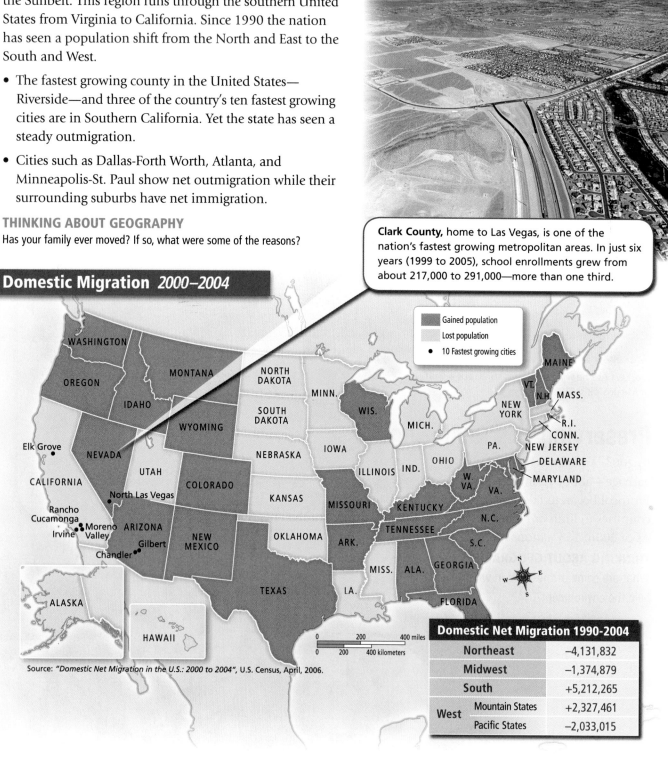

Domestic Migration *2000–2004*

Legend:
- Gained population
- Lost population
- • 10 Fastest growing cities

Source: "Domestic Net Migration in the U.S.: 2000 to 2004", U.S. Census, April, 2006.

Domestic Net Migration 1990-2004		
Northeast		−4,131,832
Midwest		−1,374,879
South		+5,212,265
West	Mountain States	+2,327,461
	Pacific States	−2,033,015

Humans Spread Ideas and Information

Throughout U.S. history, people from all over the world have come to the United States. They have brought with them food, music, language, technology, and other aspects of their culture. As a result, the United States is one of the most culturally rich and diverse nations in the world. Look around your town or city. You'll probably notice different people, languages, and foods.

Today, the spreading of ideas and customs does not rely solely on human movement. Technology—from the Internet to television to satellites—spreads ideas and information throughout the world faster than ever. This has created an ever-growing, interconnected world. As the 21st century continues, human geography will continue to play a key role in shaping the United States and the world.

THINKING ABOUT GEOGRAPHY How have computers and the Internet affected your life?

American consumer products are for sale around the globe.

Puertorriqueños celebrate the National Puerto Rican Day Parade in New York City.

Human Geography **Assessment**

MAIN IDEAS

1. What are some of the ways that people have helped to restore the environment?

2. What are some of the ways that residents of your region have successfully modified their landscape?

3. What are some of the reasons that people move from place to place?

CRITICAL THINKING

4. **Recognizing Effects** In what ways has technology helped bring people in the world together?

   Think about

   • the different ways in which people communicate today

   • the speed in which people today can communicate over long distances

Geography Handbook Assessment

TERMS

Briefly explain the significance of each of the following.

1. physical map
2. political map
3. longitude
4. latitude
5. hemisphere
6. projection
7. flood plain
8. sea level
9. human geography
10. human movement

Compare and contrast each pair of terms.

11. place; location
12. parallel; meridian
13. climate; temperature

REVIEW

Themes of Geography (pages A2–A3)

14. What is the difference between absolute location and relative location?

15. What is meant by the theme of place?

16. What are the themes of movement and human-environment interaction?

Map Basics (pages A4–A7)

17. What do you think are some of the benefits of using technology to study geography?

18. What are the three major kinds of maps?

19. What are latitude and longitude lines?

Physical Geography (pages A8–A11)

20. How have the natural resources in the United States helped its economic development?

21. What are the different climates within the United States?

Human Geography (pages A14–A16)

22. How is human geography different from physical geography?

23. What aspects of human geography might cause people to move?

CRITICAL THINKING

24. **Forming and Supporting Opinions** Which of the five themes of geography do you think has had the most impact on history? Why?

25. **Causes and Effects** How do the climate and natural resources of an area affect its economy?

26. **Categorizing** Create a diagram to organize information from this Handbook about the regions of the United States.

	West	South	Midwest	Northeast
Landforms	Rocky Mountains	Mississippi Delta		
Resources				

27. **Drawing Conclusions** How have computers helped geographers make more accurate maps?

28. **Making Inferences** Why do you think the Mercator projection is used for all types of navigation?

Use the photograph below to answer 29–31.

29. What region of the United States is pictured here?

30. What are some of the physical features of this area?

31. What is the climate of the area pictured?

Standards–Based Assessment

✓ **TEST PRACTICE**

- **Online Test Practice @ ClassZone.com**
- **Test-Taking Strategies & Practice** at the front of this book

MULTIPLE CHOICE

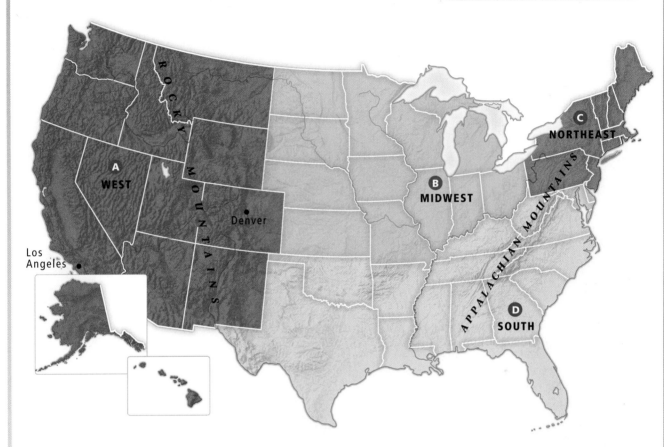

Use the map and your knowledge of geography to answer questions 1–3.

1. **Which describes the absolute location of Denver?**

   A. approximately 39°N 105°W, elev. 5,280 feet

   B. 844 miles ENE of Los Angeles

   C. mountainous; highland climate

   D. state capital of Colorado

2. **Which region is a source for uranium ore?**

   A. A **B.** B **C.** C **D.** D

3. **Which region has a primarily humid subtropical climate?**

   A. A **B.** B **C.** C **D.** D

Read each question and choose the best answer.

4. **The United States is located in which hemispheres?**

   A. Northern and Western

   B. Southern and Western

   C. Northern and Eastern

   D. Southern and Eastern

5. **Constructing a breakwater in Boston harbor is an example of how humans—**

   A. adapt to their environment.

   B. affect their environment.

   C. spread ideas and information.

   D. restore their environment.

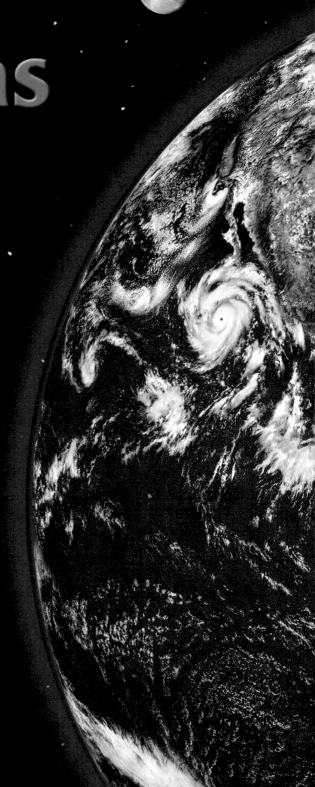

RAND McNALLY
World Atlas

CONTENTS

Legend for Physical and Political Maps

Water Features

ATLANTIC OCEAN   Ocean or sea

   Lake (physical map)

   Lake (political map)

   Salt lake (physical map)

   Salt lake (political map)

   Seasonal lake

   River

   Waterfall

Land Features

Mt. Mitchell 6,684 ft. 2,037 m. △   Mountain peak

Mt. McKinley 20,320 ft. 6,194 m. ▲   Highest mountain peak

Great Basin   Physical feature (mountain range, desert, plateau, etc.)

Nantucket Island   Island

Cultural Features

———   International boundary

———   State boundary

CANADA   Country

KANSAS   State

Population Centers

National capital	State capital	Town	Population
✪	✪	■	Over 1,000,000
✪	✪	▣	250,000 – 1,000,000
✪	✪	•	Under 250,000

Land Elevations and Ocean Depths

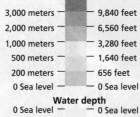

Land elevation

3,000 meters	9,840 feet
2,000 meters	6,560 feet
1,000 meters	3,280 feet
500 meters	1,640 feet
200 meters	656 feet
0 Sea level	0 Sea level

Water depth

0 Sea level	0 Sea level
200 meters	656 feet
2,000 meters	6,560 feet

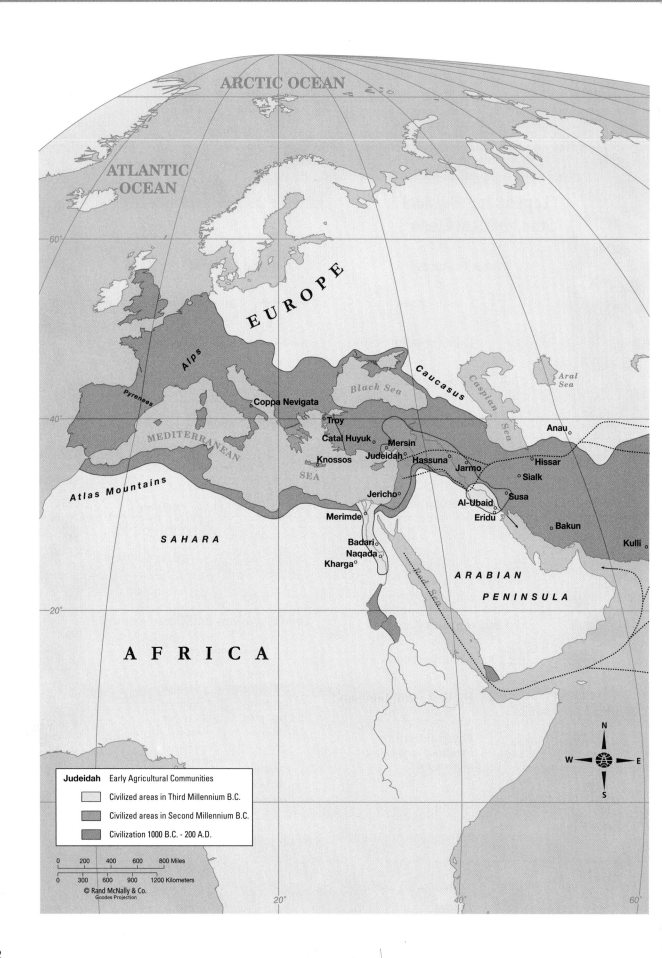

ARCTIC OCEAN

ATLANTIC OCEAN

EUROPE

Alps

Pyrenees

Black Sea

Caucasus

Caspian Sea

Aral Sea

Anau

Coppa Nevigata

Troy

Catal Huyuk

Mersin

Judeidah

Hassuna

Jarmo

Hissar

Sialk

Knossos

MEDITERRANEAN

SEA

Jericho

Al-Ubaid

Susa

Atlas Mountains

Eridu

Bakun

Merimde

Kulli

SAHARA

Badari

Naqada

Kharga

ARABIAN

PENINSULA

AFRICA

N
W   E
S

Judeidah   Early Agricultural Communities

    Civilized areas in Third Millennium B.C.

    Civilized areas in Second Millennium B.C.

    Civilization 1000 B.C. - 200 A.D.

| 0 | 200 | 400 | 600 | 800 Miles |

| 0 | 300 | 600 | 900 | 1200 Kilometers |

© Rand McNally & Co.
Goodes Projection

RAND MCNALLY

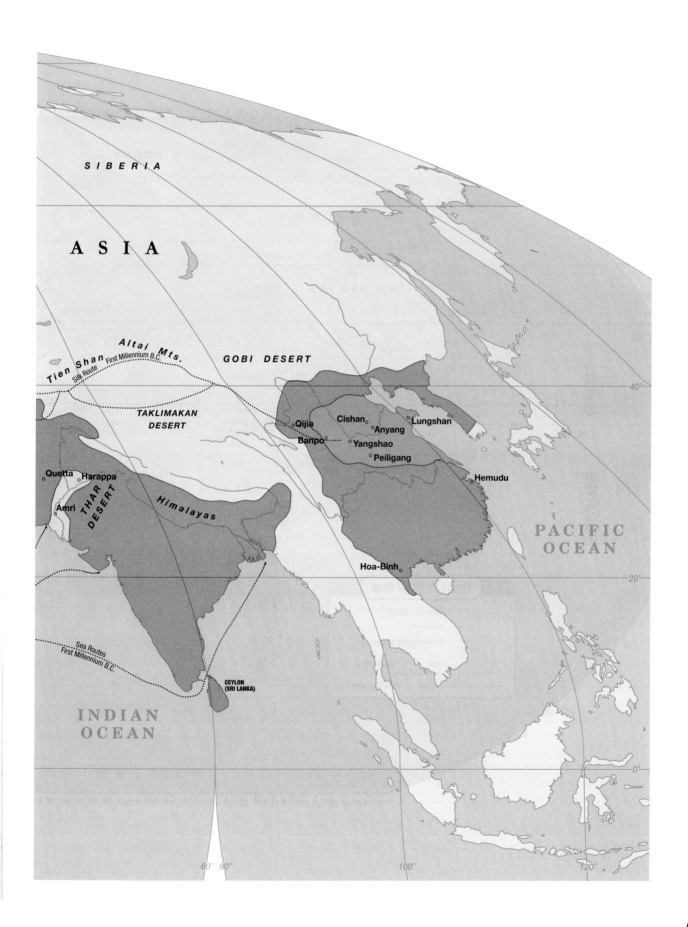

SIBERIA

ASIA

Altai Mts.

Tien Shan

Silk Route

First Millennium B.C.

GOBI DESERT

TAKLIMAKAN
DESERT

Qijia

Cishan

Anyang

Lungshan

Banpo

Yangshao

Peiligang

Hemudu

Quetta

Harappa

THAR
DESERT

Himalayas

Amri

Hoa-Binh

PACIFIC
OCEAN

Sea Routes
First Millennium B.C.

CEYLON
(SRI LANKA)

INDIAN
OCEAN

40°

20°

0°

80° 80°

100°

120°

RAND M?NALLY

The English Colonies
1585–1763

Because Puritans wanted everyone to be able to read the Bible, most New England children went to school. Students learned by copying from hornbooks like this one.

The New England Colonies

Key Idea: English colonists settled New England, where they established many political and religious traditions.

The Pilgrims and Puritans sought religious and political freedom in New England. They established freedom of speech, democracy, and a Protestant work ethic, but did not tolerate religious dissent. A short growing season, rocky soil, and hills supported small, diversified farms. Merchants and shipbuilders exported fish and timber to the world through the region's seaports.

An 18th-century school

The Middle Colonies

Key Idea: Religious tolerance and ethnic diversity characterized the Middle Colonies

The tolerance of the Quaker and Dutch colonists attracted a diverse population. Skilled immigrant farmers profited from the fertile soil and mild climate. Rivers encouraged shipping and commerce, and harbors became large cities. Although the region did not depend on slave labor, the slave trade was important to the economy.

1585

1603 Elizabeth I dies; England and Scotland united under James I

1619 Virginia Company forms House of Burgesses

1632 Lord Baltimore establishes Maryland colony for Catholics

1648 English Revolution

English found Roanoke colony

1607 English found Jamestown colony

1620 Pilgrims land at Plymouth

1630 Puritans found Massachusetts Bay

1651 First Navigation Act

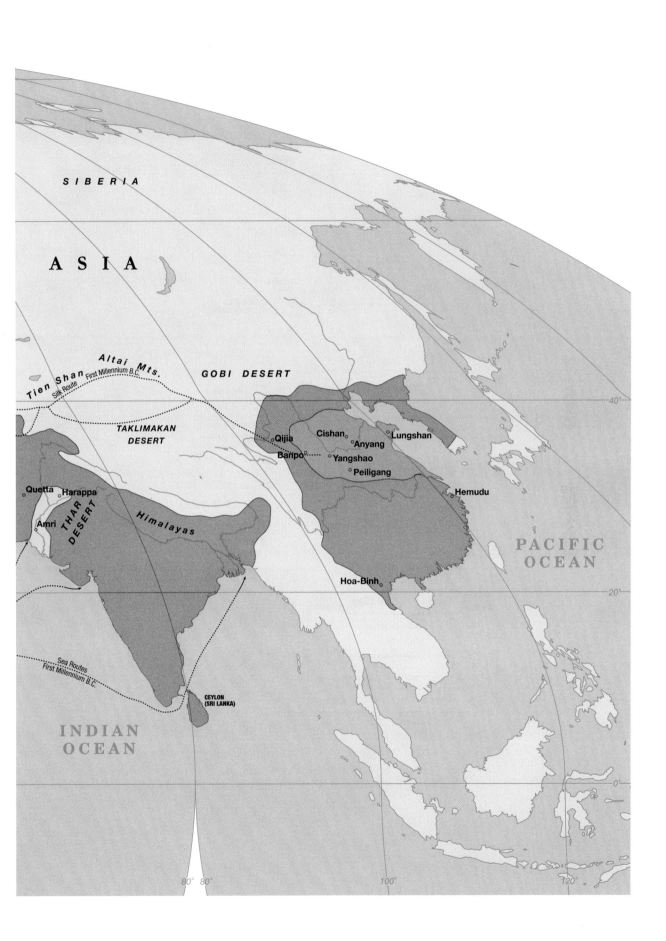

SIBERIA

ASIA

Tien Shan
Altai Mts.
Silk Route
First Millennium B.C.

GOBI DESERT

TAKLIMAKAN
DESERT

Qijia
Cishan
Anyang
Lungshan
Banpo
Yangshao
Peiligang

Hemudu

Quetta
Harappa
THAR
DESERT
Himalayas

Amri

Hoa-Binh

PACIFIC
OCEAN

Sea Routes
First Millennium B.C.

CEYLON
(SRI LANKA)

INDIAN
OCEAN

40°

20°

0°

80°   80°

100°

120°

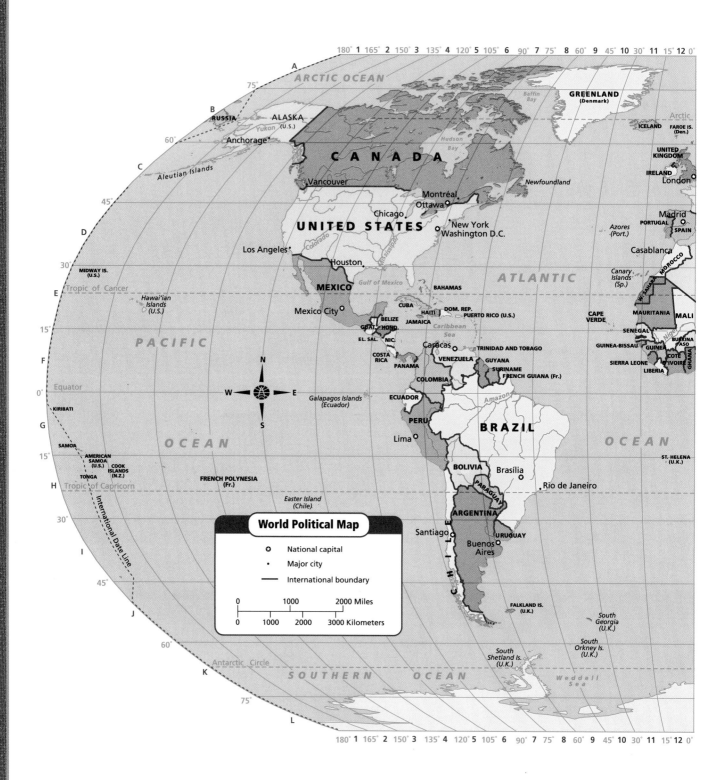

World Political Map

- ⊙ National capital
- • Major city
- — International boundary

0   1000   2000 Miles
0   1000   2000   3000 Kilometers

RAND M^CNALLY

13 15° 14 30° 15 45° 16 60° 17 75° 18 90° 19 105° 20 120° 21 135° 22 150° 23 165° 24 180°

ARCTIC OCEAN A

Franz Josef Land

Spitsbergen
(Nor.)

Novaya
Zemlya

75°

Circle B

NORWAY FINLAND

*North
Sea* SWEDEN DEN.

R U S S I A

60°

*Bering
Sea* C

EST.
LAT.
LITH.

Volga

Moscow

Novosíbirsk

Sea of Okhotsk

NETH. POLAND
GERMANY BELARUS

Ob

KAZAKHSTAN

MONGOLIA

45°

FRANCE UKRAINE
HUNG.
ROM.
MOLD.

UZBEKISTAN
KYRG.

Beijing

NORTH
KOREA

Sea of Japan

JAPAN D

ITALY
BUL.
Rome
ALB.
GREECE

Black Sea
GEO.
ARM. AZER.

TURKMENISTAN TAJIK.

C H I N A

Seoul

SOUTH
KOREA

Tōkyō

30°

Yenisey

Lena

TURKEY

CYPRUS
SYRIA
LEB.
ISRAEL
JORDAN

IRAQ

IRAN

AFGHANISTAN

Yangtze

Shanghai

PACIFIC

Crete

TUNISIA

Mediterranean Sea

Cairo

KUWAIT

PAKISTAN

NEPAL
BHU.

Kolkata
(Calcutta)

TAIWAN

Hong Kong

Tropic of Cancer E

ALGERIA LIBYA EGYPT

SAUDI
ARABIA

QATAR
U.A.E.

Karáchi

BNG.

INDIA

MYANMAR
LAOS

*South China
Sea*

NORTHERN
MARIANA ISLANDS
(U.S.)

WAKE ISLAND
(U.S.)

15°

NIGER CHAD

OMAN

Mumbai
(Bombay)

*Arabian
Sea*

*Bay of
Bengal*

THAILAND

Bangkok

VIETNAM
CAMBODIA

Manila

PHILIPPINES

GUAM
(U.S.)

O C E A N F

NIGERIA
Lagos

Nile

SUDAN

YEMEN

ERITREA
DJIBOUTI

Addis
Ababa

SRI LANKA

PALAU

FED. STATES OF
MICRONESIA

BENIN

CENTRAL
AFRICAN
REPUBLIC

ETHIOPIA

SOMALIA

MALDIVES

BRUNEI

MARSHALL
ISLANDS

CAMEROON

SINGAPORE

Equator 0°

EQUATORIAL
GUINEA

GABON

Congo

UGANDA

KENYA

MALAYSIA

Borneo

New Guinea

DEM. REP.
OF THE CONGO

RWANDA

BURUNDI

SEYCHELLES

Sumatra

Jakarta

INDONESIA

PAPUA
NEW GUINEA

SOLOMON
ISLANDS

G

TANZANIA

I N D I A N

Java

EAST TIMOR

15°

ANGOLA

ZAMBIA

MALAWI

COMOROS

Coral Sea

VANUATU

MOZAMBIQUE

MADAGASCAR

MAURITIUS

NEW CALEDONIA
(Fr.)

FIJI

NAMIBIA
ZIMBABWE

BOTSWANA

REUNION
(Fr.)

O C E A N

Tropic of Capricorn H

Johannesburg

SWAZILAND

AUSTRALIA

Brisbane

SOUTH
AFRICA
LESOTHO

Darling

Sydney

30°

Perth

Auckland

Melbourne

NEW ZEALAND I

*Îles Kerguélen
(Fr.)*

Tasmania

45°

J

60°

S O U T H E R N O C E A N

Antarctic Circle K

75°

A N T A R C T I C A

© Rand McNally & Co.
Made in U.S.A.
N-CLA10000-P1- -9-11-11

L

13 15° 14 30° 15 45° 16 60° 17 75° 18 90° 19 105° 20 120° 21 135° 22 150° 23 165° 24 180°

60°

45°

30°

International Date Line

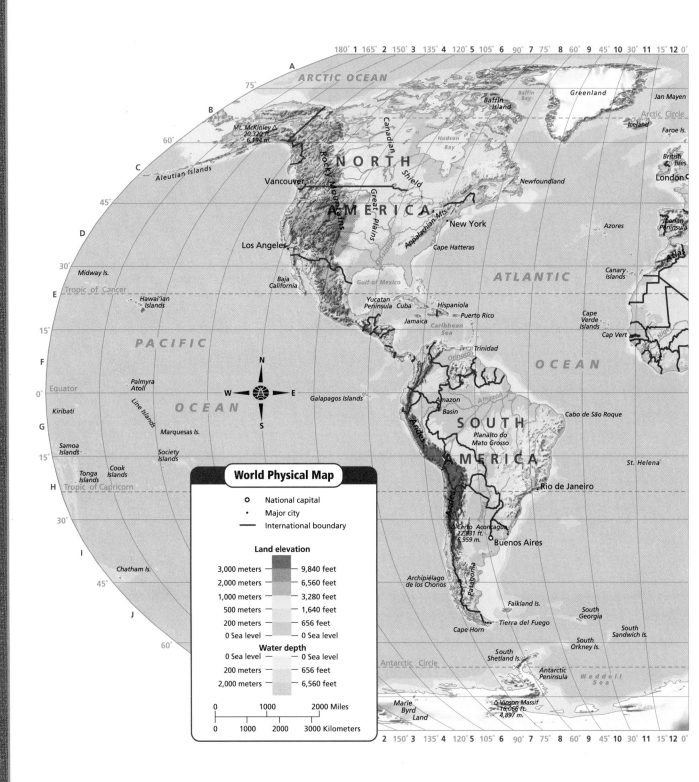

RAND McNALLY

13 15° 14 30° 15 45° 16 60° 17 75° 18 90° 19 105° 20 120° 21 135° 22 150° 23 165° 24 180°

ARCTIC OCEAN
A
75°
Spitsbergen
Franz
Josef Land
Nordkapp
Novaya
Zemlya
B
Scandinavia
Siberia
60°
Bering
Sea
North
Sea
C
Moscow
Volga
Kamchatka
Peninsula
Sea of Okhotsk
Sakhalin
45°
Caucasus
Don
Aral
Black Sea
Gora Elbrus
18,510 ft.
5,642 m.
Pamir
Gobi Desert
Hokkaidō
Honshū
Sea of Japan
D
Alps
Balkan
Peninsula
Sardinia
Sicily
Creté Cyprus
Zagros Mts.
Beijing
Plateau
of
Tibet
Himalayas
Mt. Everest
29,028 ft.
8,848 m.
East
China
Sea
Kyūshū
30°
Mts.
Cairo
Nile
Taiwan
PACIFIC
Tropic of Cancer
E
S a h a r a
AFRICA
Arabian
Peninsula
Mumbai
(Bombay)
Decan
Mariana
Islands
Wake
Island
15°
Sahel
Arabian
Sea
Bay of
Bengal
Hainan Dao
South China
Sea
Luzon
Guam
Socotra
Lakshadweep
OCEAN
F
Gulf of
Guinea
Ethiopian
Plateau
Sri Lanka
Malay
Peninsula
Mindanao
Palau
Islands
Caroline
Islands
Marshall
Islands
Congo
Congo
Basin
Maldive
Islands
Borneo
Celebes
Equator
0°
Kilimanjaro
19,340 ft.
5,895 m.
Sumatra
New Guinea
Solomon
Islands
G
Seychelles
Java
INDIAN
Cocos
Islands
15°
Madagascar
New
Hebrides
Coral Sea
Mauritius
New Caledonia
Fiji
Is.
Reunion
Kalahari
Desert
Great
Sandy
Desert
AUSTRALIA
Tropic of Capricorn
H
Johannesburg
OCEAN
Darling
Great Dividing Range
30°
Cape of Good Hope
Cape Leeuwin
Sydney
North Island
Aoraki
(Mt. Cook)
12,316 ft.
3,754 m.
I
Tasmania
South Island
45°
Îles Kerguélen
J
60°
SOUTHERN
OCEAN
Antarctic Circle
K
Queen Maud
Land
Enderby
Land
Wilkes Land
Victoria Land
75°
© Rand McNally & Co.
Made in U.S.A.
N-CLA10000-A1- -5- -7
ANTARCTICA
L

13 15° 14 30° 15 45° 16 60° 17 75° 18 90° 19 105° 20 120° 21 135° 22 150° 23 165° 24 180°

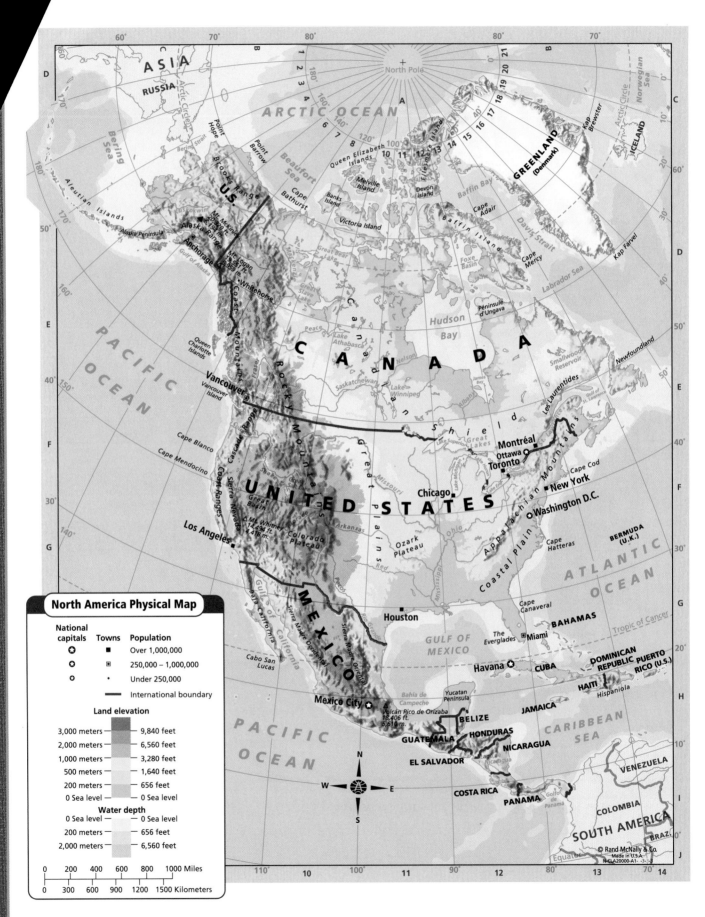

North America Physical Map

National capitals

⊛ Over 1,000,000 (population)

⊕ 250,000 – 1,000,000

⊚ Under 250,000

Towns   **Population**

■ Over 1,000,000

▣ 250,000 – 1,000,000

• Under 250,000

— International boundary

Land elevation

3,000 meters	9,840 feet
2,000 meters	6,560 feet
1,000 meters	3,280 feet
500 meters	1,640 feet
200 meters	656 feet
0 Sea level	0 Sea level

Water depth

0 Sea level	0 Sea level
200 meters	656 feet
2,000 meters	6,560 feet

0 200 400 600 800 1000 Miles

0 300 600 900 1200 1500 Kilometers

RAND M℃NALLY

© Rand McNally & Co.
Made in U.S.A.
N-CLA20000-A1- -3- -

A28

South America Physical Map

National capitals

⊕ Over 1,000,000
⊕ 250,000 – 1,000,000
⊙ Under 250,000

Towns **Population**

■ Over 1,000,000
▣ 250,000 – 1,000,000
• Under 250,000

━━━ International boundary

Land elevation

3,000 meters	9,840 feet
2,000 meters	6,560 feet
1,000 meters	3,280 feet
500 meters	1,640 feet
200 meters	656 feet
0 Sea level	0 Sea level

Water depth

0 Sea level	0 Sea level
200 meters	656 feet
2,000 meters	6,560 feet

0 200 400 600 800 1000 Miles
0 300 600 900 1200 1500 Kilometers

GULF OF MEXICO

NORTH AMERICA

MEXICO
BELIZE
GUATEMALA
HONDURAS
EL SALVADOR
NICARAGUA
COSTA RICA
PANAMA

CUBA
Yucatan Channel
Greater Antilles
JAMAICA
HAITI
DOMINICAN REPUBLIC
PUERTO RICO (U.S.)
Lesser Antilles

CARIBBEAN SEA

Punta Gallinas
Pico Cristóbal Colón 18,947 ft. 5,775 m.
Caracas
TRINIDAD AND TOBAGO
Boca Grande

Golfo de Panamá
Maracaibo
Llanos
Orinoco
VENEZUELA
GUYANA
SURINAME
FRENCH GUIANA (FR.)
Cabo Orange

Bogotá
COLOMBIA
Nev. del Huila 18,865 ft. 5,750 m.
Pakaraima

Punta Galera
ECUADOR
Chimborazo 20,702 ft. 6,310 m.
Galapagos Islands (Ec.)
Equator

Putumayo
Napo
Amazon
Amazon Basin
Manaus
Ilha de Marajó
Equator

Punta Pariñas
Juruá
Purus
Madeira
Tapajós
Xingu
Tocantins
BRAZIL
Cabo de São Roque

Selvas
PERU
Nev. Huascarán 22,133 ft. 6,746 m.

Lima
Andes
Planalto do Mato Grosso
Represa de Sobradinho
Recife

Punta Carreta
Lago Titicaca
Nev. Illampu 21,066 ft. 6,421 m.
La Paz
BOLIVIA
Brasília
Serra do Espinhaço
São Francisco

Nev. Sajama 21,463 ft. 6,542 m.
Cordillera Real

Atacama Desert
Gran Chaco
PARAGUAY
São Paulo
Cabo de São Tomé
Rio de Janeiro

PACIFIC OCEAN

Isla San Ambrosio (Chile)
Isla San Felix (Chile)
Nev. Ojos del Salado 22,615 ft. 6,893 m.
Andes
Paraná
Iguaçu Falls
Paraná
Uruguay
Lagoa dos Patos
Tropic of Capricorn

Archipiélago Juan Fernández (Chile)
Cerro Aconcagua 22,831 ft. 6,959 m.
Santiago
CHILE
ARGENTINA
Buenos Aires
URUGUAY
Lagoa Mirim

Punta Lavapié
Pampas
Río de la Plata

Patagonia
Golfo San Matías
Península Valdés
N
W   E
S

Isla Grande de Chiloé
Archipiélago de los Chonos
Cabo Dos Bahías
Golfo San Jorge
Cabo Tres Puntas

ATLANTIC OCEAN

Isla Wellington
Bahía Grande
FALKLAND ISLANDS (U.K.)
West Falkland
East Falkland

Isla Santa Inés
Tierra del Fuego
Strait of Magellan

Cape Horn
South Georgia (U.K.)

Drake Passage
South Shetland Islands (U.K.)
South Orkney Islands (U.K.)
South Sandwich Islands (U.K.)

ATLANTIC OCEAN

© Rand McNally & Co.
Made in U.S.A.
N-CLA40000-A1- -4- -4

RAND McNALLY

A29

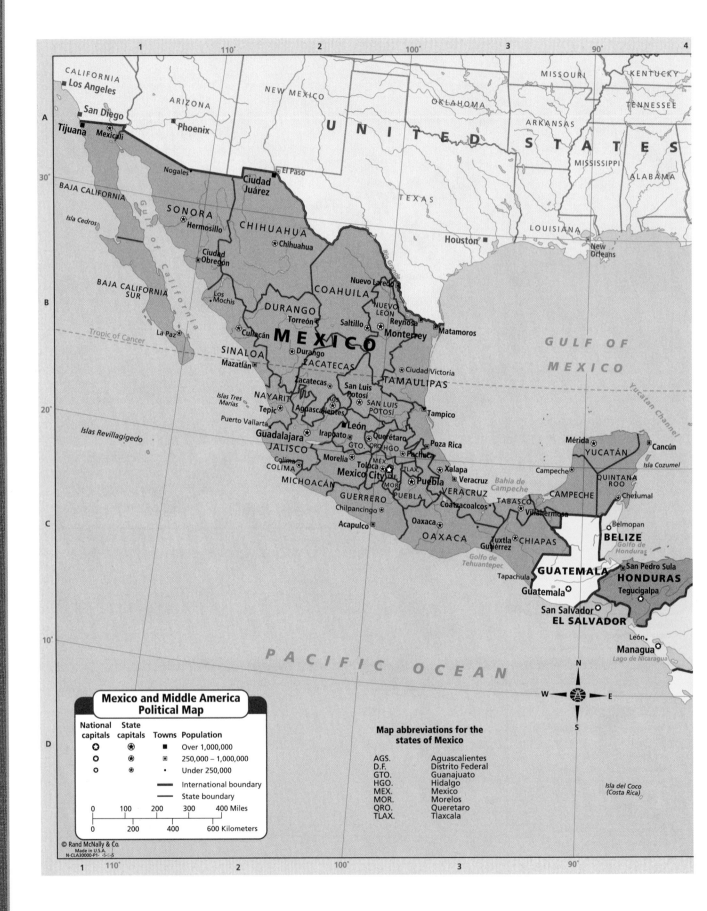

CALIFORNIA
Los Angeles
San Diego
Tijuana Mexicali
ARIZONA
Phoenix
NEW MEXICO
OKLAHOMA
MISSOURI
KENTUCKY
TENNESSEE
ARKANSAS
U N I T E D   S T A T E S
MISSISSIPPI
ALABAMA
Nogales
El Paso
Ciudad Juárez
BAJA CALIFORNIA
Isla Cedros
SONORA
Hermosillo
Ciudad Obregón
CHIHUAHUA
Chihuahua
TEXAS
Houston
LOUISIANA
New Orleans
BAJA CALIFORNIA SUR
Los Mochis
DURANGO
Torreón
COAHUILA
Nuevo Laredo
NUEVO LEÓN
Saltillo Reynosa
Monterrey Matamoros
GULF OF MEXICO
Gulf of California
La Paz
Tropic of Cancer
Culiacán
M E X I C O
SINALOA
ZACATECAS
Durango
Mazatlán
Ciudad Victoria
TAMAULIPAS
Zacatecas
San Luis Potosí
Islas Tres Marías
NAYARIT
Tepic
Aguascalientes
AGS.
SAN LUIS POTOSÍ
Tampico
Yucatán Channel
Islas Revillagigedo
Puerto Vallarta
León
Irapuato
Guadalajara
JALISCO
GTO.
Querétaro
QRO.HGO.
Pachuca
Poza Rica
Mérida
YUCATÁN
Cancún
Isla Cozumel
Colima
COLIMA
Morelia
Toluca
MEX.
Mexico City
D.F.
TLAX.
Puebla
PUEBLA
Xalapa
Veracruz
Campeche
QUINTANA ROO
Chetumal
MICHOACÁN
MOR.
VERACRUZ
Bahía de Campeche
CAMPECHE
Chilpancingo
GUERRERO
Coatzacoalcos
TABASCO
Villahermosa
Belmopan
BELIZE
Golfo de Honduras
Acapulco
Oaxaca
OAXACA
Tuxtla Gutiérrez
CHIAPAS
Golfo de Tehuantepec
San Pedro Sula
Tapachula
GUATEMALA
HONDURAS
Tegucigalpa
Guatemala
San Salvador
EL SALVADOR
León
Managua
Lago de Nicaragua
P A C I F I C   O C E A N
N W E S

Mexico and Middle America Political Map

National capitals	State capitals	Towns	Population
⊕	✸	■	Over 1,000,000
✪	✹	▣	250,000 – 1,000,000
⊙	✺	•	Under 250,000

——— International boundary

——— State boundary

0 100 200 300 400 Miles

0 200 400 600 Kilometers

© Rand McNally & Co.
Made in U.S.A.
N-CLA30000-P1- -5- -5

Map abbreviations for the states of Mexico

AGS.	Aguascalientes
D.F.	Distrito Federal
GTO.	Guanajuato
HGO.	Hidalgo
MEX.	Mexico
MOR.	Morelos
QRO.	Queretaro
TLAX.	Tlaxcala

Isla del Coco (Costa Rica)

RAND McNALLY

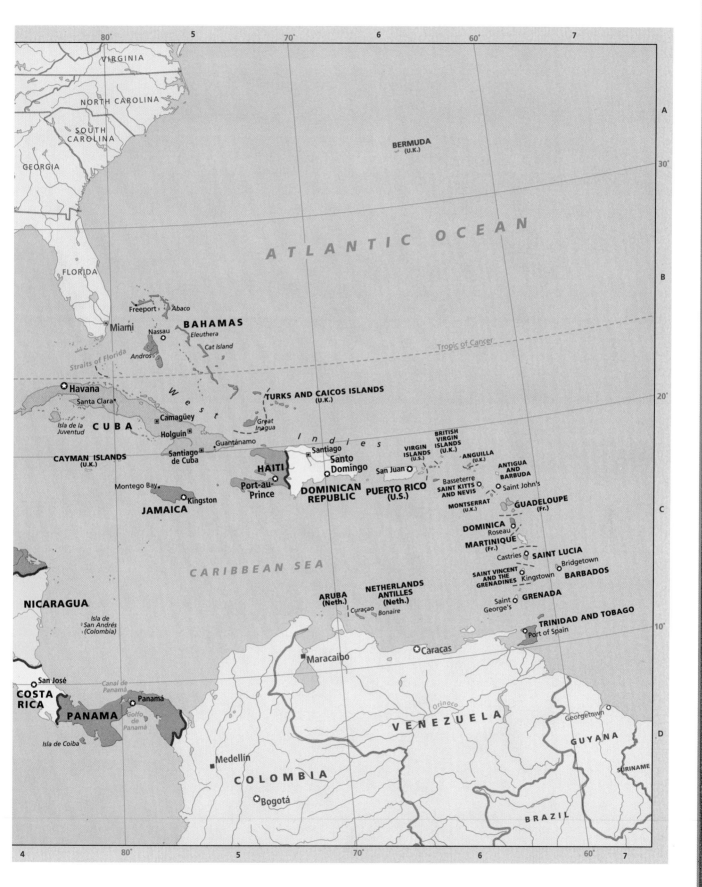

VIRGINIA

NORTH CAROLINA

SOUTH
CAROLINA

GEORGIA

FLORIDA

BERMUDA
(U.K.)

ATLANTIC OCEAN

Straits of Florida

Miami

Freeport ○ Abaco

BAHAMAS

Nassau
Eleuthera

Cat Island

Andros

Tropic of Cancer

Havana ✪

Santa Clara

CUBA

Isla de la
Juventud

Camagüey ▣

Holguín ▣

Guantánamo

Great
Inagua

TURKS AND CAICOS ISLANDS
(U.K.)

W
e
s
t

I
n
d
i
e
s

CAYMAN ISLANDS
(U.K.)

Santiago
de Cuba ▣

Montego Bay

Kingston ✪

JAMAICA

Santiago ○

HAITI

Port-au-
Prince ✪

Santo
Domingo

DOMINICAN
REPUBLIC

San Juan ○

PUERTO RICO
(U.S.)

VIRGIN
ISLANDS
(U.S.)

BRITISH
VIRGIN
ISLANDS
(U.K.)

ANGUILLA
(U.K.)

Basseterre
SAINT KITTS
AND NEVIS ○

MONTSERRAT
(U.K.)

ANTIGUA
AND
BARBUDA

Saint John's ○

GUADELOUPE
(Fr.)

DOMINICA
Roseau ○

MARTINIQUE
(Fr.)

Castries ○ ✪ SAINT LUCIA

Bridgetown ○

CARIBBEAN SEA

NICARAGUA

Isla de
San Andrés
(Colombia)

ARUBA
(Neth.)
○ Curaçao

NETHERLANDS
ANTILLES
(Neth.)
○ Bonaire

SAINT VINCENT
AND THE
GRENADINES

Kingstown ○

BARBADOS

Saint
George's ○ ✪ GRENADA

TRINIDAD AND TOBAGO

Port of Spain ✪

San José ○

COSTA
RICA

Panamá ✪

PANAMA

Canal de
Panamá

Golfo
de
Panamá

Isla de Coiba

Maracaibo ■

Caracas ✪

VENEZUELA

Georgetown ○

GUYANA

SURINAME

Medellín ○

COLOMBIA

Bogotá ✪

BRAZIL

Orinoco

✪ RAND McNALLY

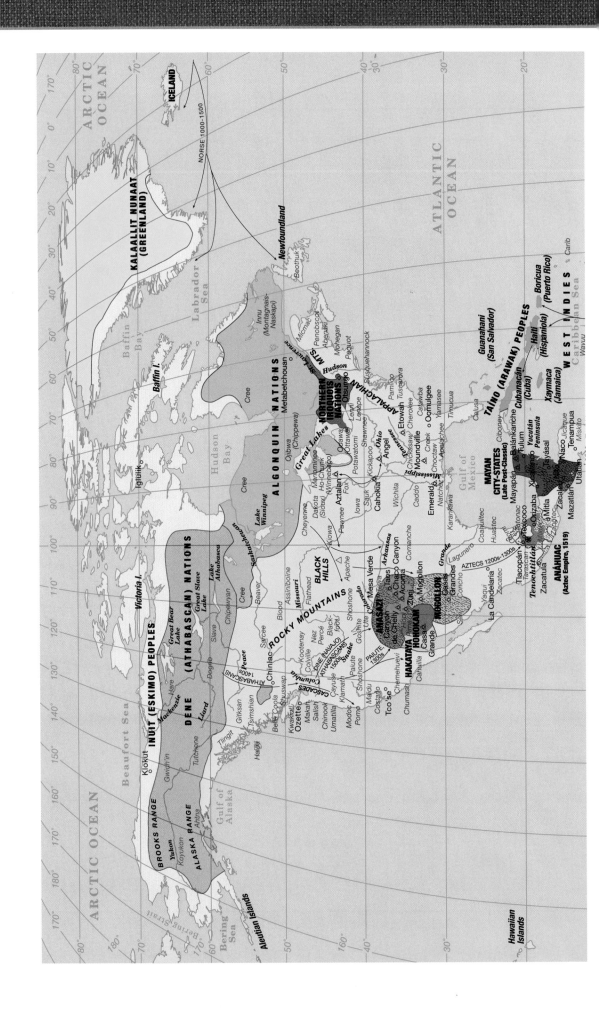

RAND MCNALLY

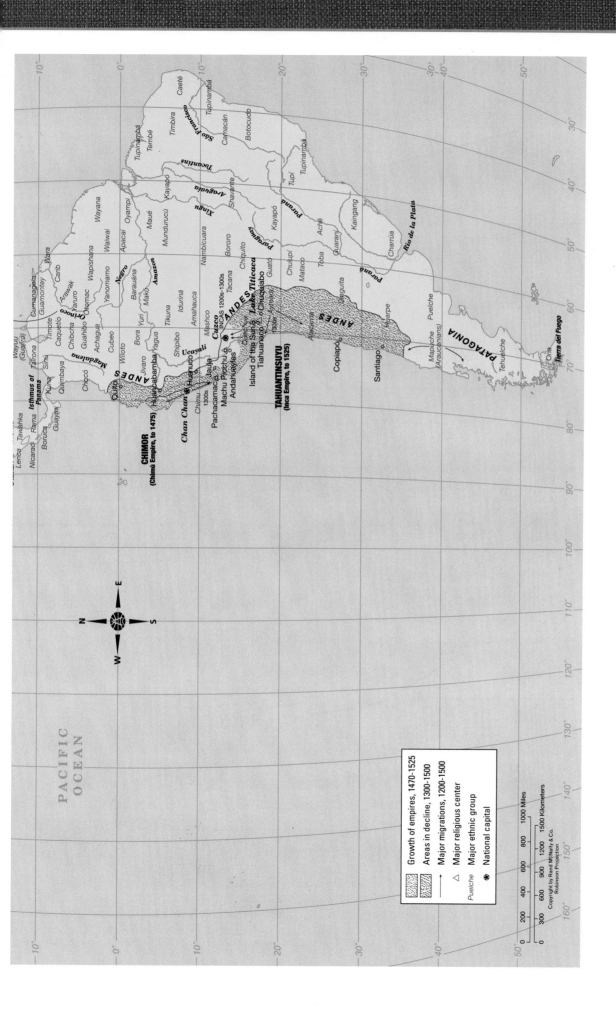

PACIFIC
OCEAN

N
W — E
S

Lenca
Tawahka
Nicarao
Rama
Boruca
Guaymí
Kuna
Sihu
Timbté
Quimbaya
Guahíbo
Chocó
Wiloto
Jívaro
Huánuco
Jauja
Chimu
Machu Picchu
Andahuaylas
Island of the Sun
Tiahuanaco
Atacama
Copiapó
Santiago
Wayuu
(Guajiro)
Guamagneia
Tairona
Guamontey
Wara
Carib
Yaruro
Otomac
Arawak
Yanomamo
Orinoco
Chibcha
Achagua
Cubeo
Bora
Yuri
Makú
Tikuna
Idurina
Amahauca
Mashco
Negro
Amazon
Nambicuara
Tacana
Aymará
Uru
Ayaviri
Chuquiabo
Diaguita
Huarpe
Mapuche
(Araucanians)
Puelche
Tehuelche
Ona
Tierra del Fuego
PATAGONIA

Caetê
Tupinambá
Tembé
Timbira
Camacán
Botocudo
Kayapó
Mundurucú
Maué
Apacaí
Oyampi
Wayana
Waiwai
Wapishana
Baraúna
Shipibo
Ucayali
Xingu
Araguaia
Tocantins
São Francisco
Shavante
Bororo
Chiquito
Guató
Kayapó
Paraguay
Acré
Paraná
Tupi
Kaingang
Chamua
Rio de la Plata
Guaraní
Toba
Mataco
Chulupí
Pilcomayo
Porung
Porú

Magdalena
Quito
ANDES
Huancabamba
CHIMOR
(Chimú Empire, to 1475)
Chan Chan
Pachacamac
Cuzco
INCAS 1200s–1300s
ANDES
Lake Titicaca
TAHUANTINSUYU
(Inca Empire, to 1525)
ANDES
1300s

Isthmus of
Panama

Growth of empires, 1470–1525

Areas in decline, 1300–1500

Major migrations, 1200–1500

△ Major religious center

Puelche Major ethnic group

⊛ National capital

Copyright by Rand McNally & Co.
Robinson Projection

0   200   400   600   800   1000 Miles
0 300 600 900 1200 1500 Kilometers

⊛ RAND McNALLY

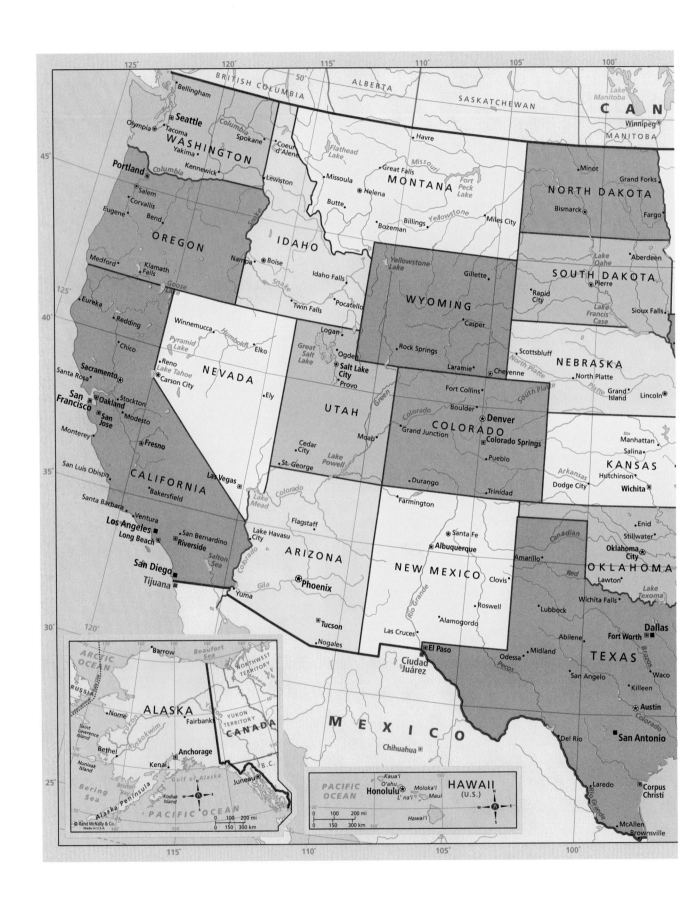

BRITISH COLUMBIA ALBERTA SASKATCHEWAN C A N
50°
Bellingham
Seattle
Olympia ⊕ Tacoma Spokane Coeur
Yakima d'Alene Havre
WASHINGTON Flathead Winnipeg ⊕
45° Lake MANITOBA
Columbia Great Falls Missouri
Portland ⊡ Kennewick Lewiston Missoula Fort Minot Grand Forks
Salem Helena MONTANA Peck NORTH DAKOTA
Corvallis Butte Lake
Eugene Bend Bozeman Billings Yellowstone Miles City Bismarck ⊕ Fargo
OREGON Yellowstone Aberdeen
Medford Klamath IDAHO Lake Gillette Lake
Falls Nampa • Boise Oahe SOUTH DAKOTA
Goose Snake Rapid Pierre
Lake Idaho Falls WYOMING City
125° Eureka Twin Falls Pocatello Rock Springs Casper Lake Sioux Falls
40° Redding Francis
Chico Logan Scottsbluff Case
Winnemucca Humboldt Ogden North Platte NEBRASKA
Santa Rosa Reno Great Salt Lake Laramie ⊕ Cheyenne North Platte
Sacramento ⊕ Lake Tahoe Salt City Fort Collins Grand Lincoln
San Oakland Carson City Lake Provo Boulder Island
Francisco Stockton NEVADA Denver South Platte
San Modesto UTAH Grand Junction COLORADO Colorado Springs Manhattan Salina
Jose Ely Moab Pueblo KANSAS
Monterey Fresno Cedar Durango Dodge City Hutchinson
City Lake Arkansas Wichita ⊕
San Luis Obispo Las Vegas ⊡ Powell Trinidad
35° St. George Colorado Farmington
CALIFORNIA Lake Flagstaff Santa Fe ⊕ Enid
Santa Barbara Bakersfield Mead Stillwater
Ventura Lake Havasu Albuquerque ⊡ Oklahoma OKLAHOMA
Los Angeles ⊡ San Bernardino City ARIZONA NEW MEXICO Amarillo • City ⊕
Long Beach Riverside ⊡ Clovis Lawton Lake
San Diego ⊡ Salton Colorado Texoma
Tijuana Sea Phoenix ⊕ Roswell Wichita Falls
Yuma Gila Lubbock Dallas ⊡
30° Tucson ⊡ Alamogordo Fort Worth ⊡
120° Nogales Las Cruces Abilene Midland TEXAS Waco
El Paso ⊡ Odessa Pecos Killeen
Ciudad San Angelo Austin ⊕
Juárez Colorado
MEXICO Del Rio San Antonio ⊡

⊕ RAND McNALLY

ARCTIC Beaufort NORTHWEST Laredo Corpus
OCEAN Barrow Sea TERRITORY Christi
RUSSIA ALASKA Mackenzie
Nome Fairbanks YUKON
Saint Lawrence Kuskokwim TERRITORY CANADA McAllen
Island Bethel Anchorage Brownsville
Nunivak Kenai B.C.
Island Bristol Yukon
Bay Gulf of Alaska Juneau PACIFIC Kaua'i 155° HAWAII
Bering Kodiak OCEAN O'ahu ⊕ Moloka'i (U.S.)
Sea Island Honolulu Maui
Alaska Peninsula L'na'i
⊕ Rand McNally & Co. PACIFIC OCEAN 0 100 200 mi 0 100 200 mi
Made in U.S.A. 0 150 300 km Hawai'i 0 150 300 km

A34

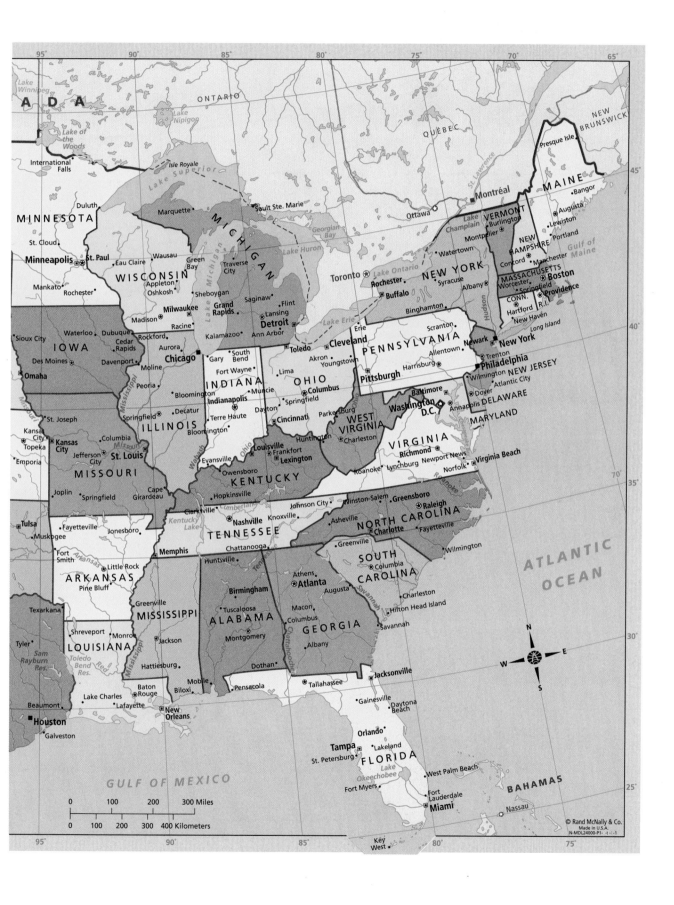

95°   90°   85°   80°   75°   70°   65°

CANADA

ONTARIO

Lake Winnipeg

Lake of the Woods

Lake Nipigon

QUÉBEC

NEW BRUNSWICK

International Falls

Lake Superior

Isle Royale

Sault Ste. Marie

Marquette

MINNESOTA

Duluth

Ottawa

St. Lawrence

Montréal

MAINE

Presque Isle

45°

St. Cloud

Lake Huron

Georgian Bay

Lake Champlain

VERMONT

Bangor

Augusta

Lewiston

Minneapolis   St. Paul

Wausau

Eau Claire

MICHIGAN

Toronto   Lake Ontario

Watertown

Montpelier   Burlington

NEW HAMPSHIRE

Concord   Manchester

Portland

Gulf of Maine

Mankato

Rochester

WISCONSIN

Green Bay

Appleton

Oshkosh

Traverse City

Saginaw

Flint

Rochester

Buffalo

NEW YORK

Syracuse

Albany

MASSACHUSETTS

Worcester   Springfield   Boston

CONN.   Providence

Hartford   R.I.

New Haven

Sioux City

IOWA

Waterloo

Dubuque

Cedar Rapids

Rockford

Milwaukee

Madison   Racine

Sheboygan

Grand Rapids

Lansing

Kalamazoo   Ann Arbor

Detroit

Lake Erie

Erie

Binghamton

Scranton

PENNSYLVANIA

Allentown   Newark   New York

Long Island

40°

Des Moines

Davenport

Moline

Aurora

Chicago

Gary   South Bend

Fort Wayne

Toledo

Akron

Cleveland

Youngstown

Harrisburg

Trenton

Philadelphia   NEW JERSEY

Atlantic City

Omaha

Peoria

Bloomington

INDIANA

Muncie

Lima

OHIO

Columbus

Springfield

Pittsburgh

Wilmington   Dover   DELAWARE

St. Joseph

Springfield

Decatur

Indianapolis

Terre Haute

Dayton

Cincinnati

Parkersburg

Baltimore

Washington D.C.

Annapolis

MARYLAND

Kansas City

Topeka

Columbia

ILLINOIS

Bloomington

Evansville

Louisville   Frankfort

Lexington

Huntington

WEST VIRGINIA

Charleston

VIRGINIA

Richmond

Newport News

70°

Emporia

Kansas City

Jefferson City

St. Louis

MISSOURI

Cape Girardeau

Owensboro

Ohio

KENTUCKY

Hopkinsville

Roanoke

Lynchburg

Norfolk   Virginia Beach

35°

Joplin

Springfield

Cumberland

Kentucky Lake

Clarksville

Johnson City

Winston-Salem   Greensboro

Raleigh

Roanoke

Tulsa

Fayetteville

Jonesboro

Nashville

Knoxville

Asheville

NORTH CAROLINA

Charlotte   Fayetteville

Muskogee

Memphis

TENNESSEE

Chattanooga

Greenville

Wilmington

Fort Smith

Arkansas

Little Rock

ARKANSAS

Pine Bluff

Huntsville

Greenville

Birmingham

Athens   Atlanta

Augusta

SOUTH CAROLINA

Columbia

Charleston

Hilton Head Island

ATLANTIC OCEAN

Texarkana

Tyler

Sam Rayburn Res.

LOUISIANA

Shreveport   Monroe

MISSISSIPPI

Jackson

Tuscaloosa

ALABAMA

Montgomery

Macon

Columbus

GEORGIA

Albany

Savannah

Chattahoochee

30°

Toledo Bend Res.

Red

Hattiesburg

Mobile

Pensacola

Dothan

Tallahassee

Jacksonville

Gainesville

Daytona Beach

Beaumont

Lake Charles

Baton Rouge

Biloxi

Lafayette

New Orleans

Houston

Galveston

GULF OF MEXICO

Mississippi

Orlando

Tampa   Lakeland

St. Petersburg

FLORIDA

Lake Okeechobee

West Palm Beach

BAHAMAS

25°

Fort Myers

Fort Lauderdale

Miami

Key West

Nassau

N
W   E
S

0   100   200   300 Miles

0   100   200   300   400 Kilometers

© Rand McNally & Co.
Made in U.S.A.
N-MDL24000-P1- -1 -1 -1

95°   90°   85°   80°   75°

RAND MCNALLY

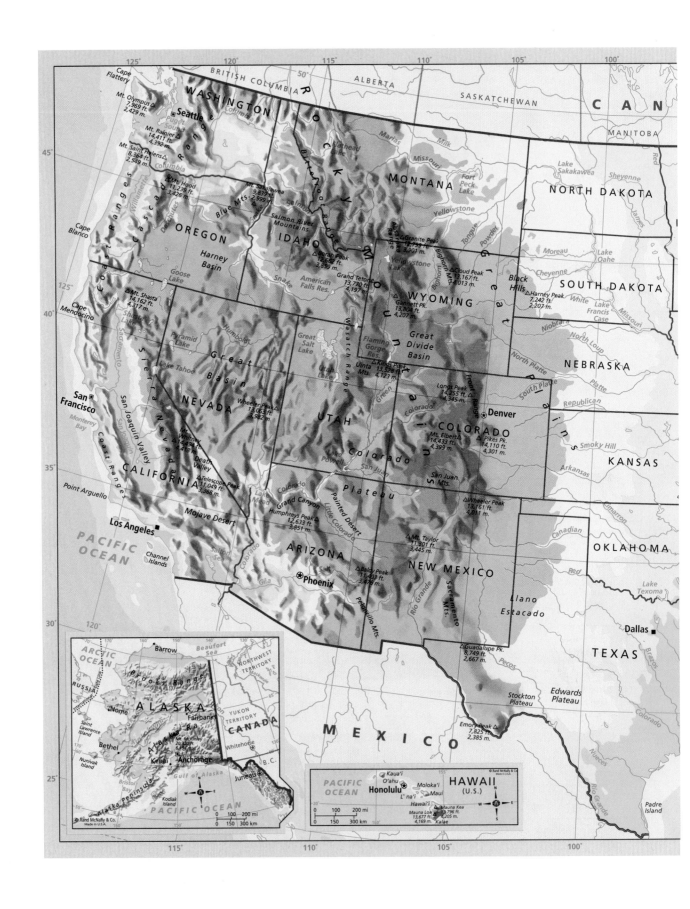

RAND M^{c}NALLY

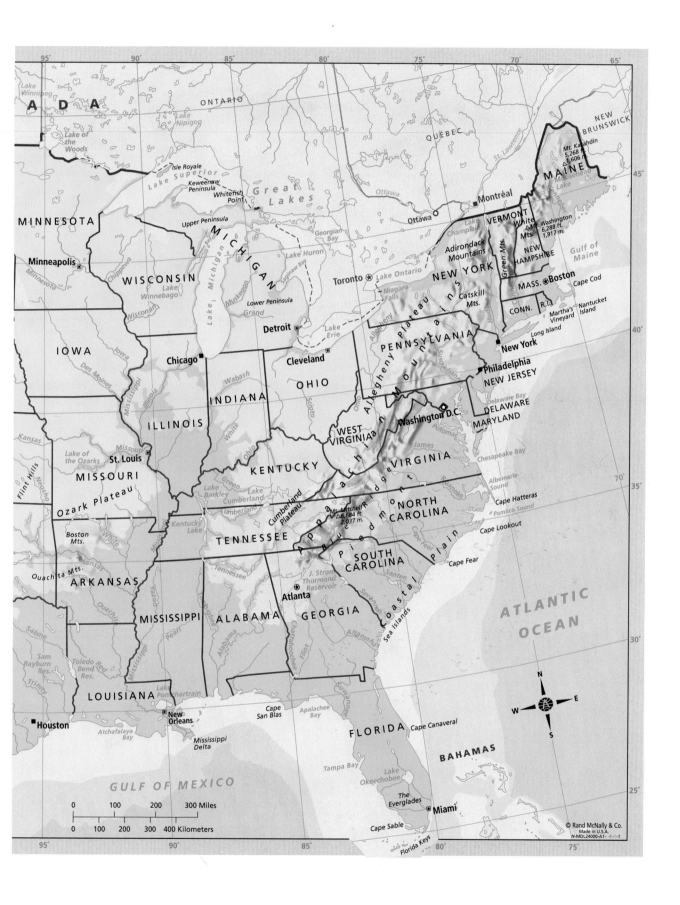

A D A

ONTARIO

Lake
Winnipeg

Lake of
the
Woods

Lake
Nipigon

QUÉBEC

MINNESOTA

Isle Royale

Keweenaw
Peninsula

Whitefish
Point

Lake Superior

Great
Lakes

Ottawa

St. Lawrence

Montréal

MAINE

Mt. Katahdin
5,268 ft.
1,606 m.

Moosehead
Lake

Minneapolis

Chippewa

WISCONSIN

Upper Peninsula

Lake
Winnebago

MICHIGAN

Georgian
Bay

Lake Huron

Saginaw Bay

Lake Michigan

Toronto

Lake Ontario

Niagara
Falls

VERMONT

Adirondack
Mountains

White
Mts.

Mt. Washington
6,288 ft.
1,917 m.

NEW
HAMPSHIRE

Green Mts.

Gulf of
Maine

Wisconsin

Minnesota

IOWA

Des Moines

Wabash

Muskegon

Grand

Lower Peninsula

Detroit

Lake
Erie

Cleveland

NEW YORK

Plateau

Allegheny

Catskill
Mts.

MASS.

Boston

Cape Cod

CONN.

R.I.

Martha's
Vineyard

Nantucket
Island

Chicago

Illinois

OHIO

White

Scioto

PENNSYLVANIA

Mountains

Long Island

New York

ILLINOIS

INDIANA

Philadelphia

NEW JERSEY

Kansas

Lake of
the Ozarks

St. Louis

Missouri

WEST
VIRGINIA

Washington D.C.

Delaware Bay

DELAWARE

MARYLAND

MISSOURI

Ohio

KENTUCKY

Appalachian

VIRGINIA

James

Potomac

Chesapeake Bay

Flint Hills

Ozark Plateau

Neosho

Green

Lake
Barkley

Lake
Cumberland

Cumberland

Cumberland
Plateau

Roanoke

Albemarle
Sound

Cape Hatteras

70°

Boston
Mts.

White

Kentucky
Lake

Mt. Mitchell
6,684 ft.
2,037 m.

Blue Ridge

NORTH
CAROLINA

Pamlico Sound

Ouachita Mts.

Arkansas

Tennessee

TENNESSEE

Appalachian

Piedmont

Cape Fear

Cape Lookout

ARKANSAS

Ouachita

SOUTH
CAROLINA

Cape Fear

Santee

Coastal

Sabine

Mississippi

Yazoo

MISSISSIPPI

ALABAMA

Atlanta

GEORGIA

Savannah

Plain

Sea Islands

ATLANTIC
OCEAN

Sam
Rayburn
Res.

Toledo
Bend
Res.

Pearl

Alabama

Chattahoochee

Flint

Altamaha

30°

Trinity

LOUISIANA

Lake
Pontchartrain

New
Orleans

Cape
San Blas

Apalachee
Bay

Suwannee

Houston

Atchafalaya
Bay

Mississippi
Delta

FLORIDA

Cape Canaveral

BAHAMAS

N

W   E

S

GULF OF MEXICO

Tampa Bay

Lake
Okeechobee

The Everglades

Miami

25°

Cape Sable

Florida Keys

0   100   200   300 Miles

0   100   200   300   400 Kilometers

© Rand McNally & Co.
Made in U.S.A.
N-MDL24000-A1- -1-1-1

95°   90°   85°   80°   75°

RAND McNALLY

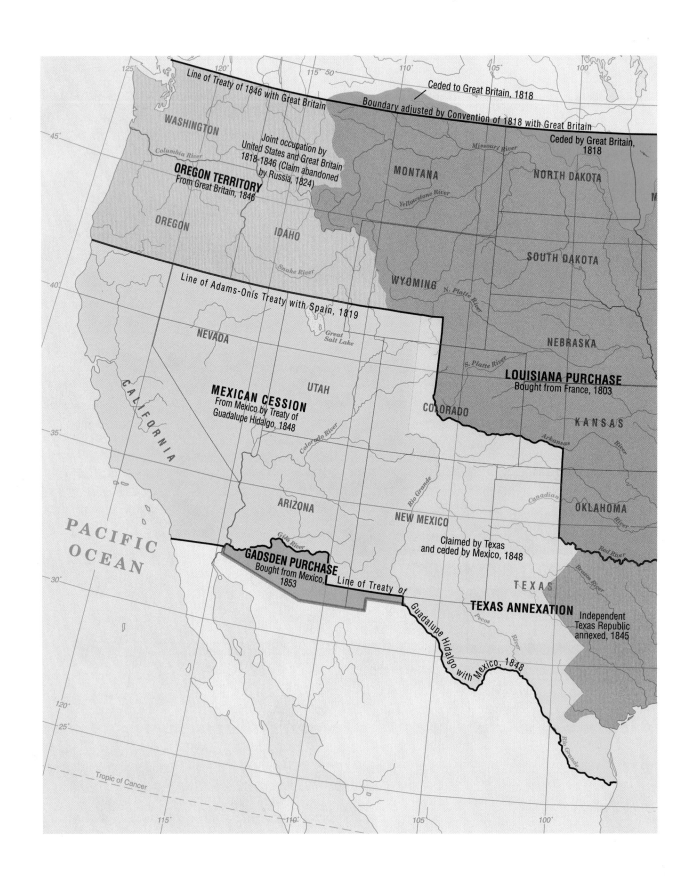

Line of Treaty of 1846 with Great Britain

Ceded to Great Britain, 1818

Boundary adjusted by Convention of 1818 with Great Britain

Ceded by Great Britain, 1818

WASHINGTON

Columbia River

Missouri River

MONTANA

NORTH DAKOTA

Joint occupation by
United States and Great Britain
1818-1846 (Claim abandoned
by Russia, 1824)

OREGON TERRITORY
From Great Britain, 1846

OREGON

IDAHO

Yellowstone River

Snake River

SOUTH DAKOTA

WYOMING

N. Platte River

Line of Adams-Onís Treaty with Spain, 1819

NEVADA

*Great
Salt Lake*

NEBRASKA

S. Platte River

LOUISIANA PURCHASE
Bought from France, 1803

UTAH

MEXICAN CESSION
From Mexico by Treaty of
Guadalupe Hidalgo, 1848

COLORADO

KANSAS

Arkansas
River

CALIFORNIA

Colorado River

ARIZONA

Rio Grande

NEW MEXICO

Canadian

OKLAHOMA

Red River

Claimed by Texas
and ceded by Mexico, 1848

PACIFIC
OCEAN

Gila River

GADSDEN PURCHASE
Bought from Mexico,
1853

Line of Treaty of

Pecos

T E X A S

Brazos River

TEXAS ANNEXATION

Independent
Texas Republic
annexed, 1845

Guadalupe Hidalgo with Mexico, 1848

River

Rio Grande

Tropic of Cancer

RAND MᶜNALLY

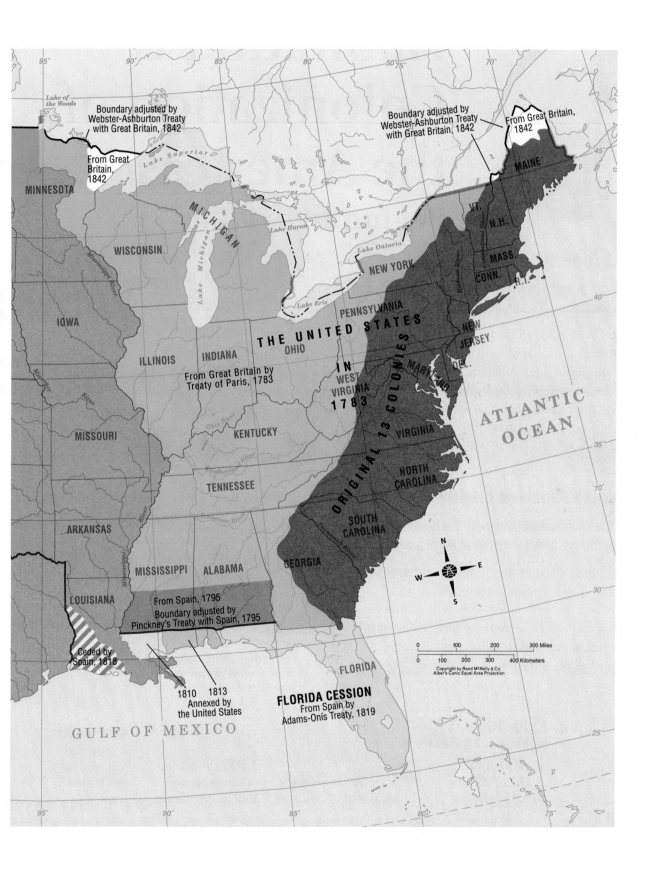

Boundary adjusted by Webster-Ashburton Treaty with Great Britain, 1842

From Great Britain, 1842

Boundary adjusted by Webster-Ashburton Treaty with Great Britain, 1842

From Great Britain, 1842

MAINE

VT.

N.H.

MASS.

CONN.

R.I.

Lake of the Woods

MINNESOTA

Lake Superior

MICHIGAN

WISCONSIN

Lake Michigan

Lake Huron

Lake Ontario

NEW YORK

Lake Erie

PENNSYLVANIA

Hudson River

Connecticut River

IOWA

ILLINOIS

INDIANA

OHIO

THE UNITED STATES

IN

NEW JERSEY

DEL.

Mississippi River

Missouri River

From Great Britain by Treaty of Paris, 1783

WEST VIRGINIA

1783

MARYLAND

ATLANTIC OCEAN

MISSOURI

KENTUCKY

Ohio River

ORIGINAL 13 COLONIES

VIRGINIA

Cumberland River

TENNESSEE

Tennessee River

NORTH CAROLINA

ARKANSAS

SOUTH CAROLINA

Savannah River

MISSISSIPPI

ALABAMA

GEORGIA

LOUISIANA

From Spain, 1795
Boundary adjusted by Pinckney's Treaty with Spain, 1795

N

W   E

S

Ceded by Spain, 1818

1810   1813
Annexed by the United States

FLORIDA

0   100   200   300 Miles
0   100   200   300   400 Kilometers

Copyright by Rand McNally & Co.
Alber's Conic Equal Area Projection

GULF OF MEXICO

FLORIDA CESSION
From Spain by Adams-Onís Treaty, 1819

Habitation & Colonization of the Americas
Beginnings–1700

Inca earrings,
A.D. 200

The First American Civilizations

Key Idea: After humans populated the Americas, advanced
civilizations and cultures developed.

Thousands of years ago, humans migrated from Asia
to North America in search of food and shelter. As
they spread throughout the Americas, they developed
complex societies, including the Olmec and the Maya in
Mesoamerica. After these great civilizations declined, the
vast Inca and Aztec empires developed in their place.

Native North America c.1492

Key Idea: The environment influenced the development
of diverse native societies in North America.

By 1492, millions of Native Americans lived throughout
North America. The continent's many unique
environments encouraged the development of a range
of advanced societies. Although these societies interacted
with each other, sometimes traveling great distances,
they were isolated from the rest of the world.

European colonization of the
Americas led to blendings of
several distinct cultures.

c. 1200–400 B.C.
Olmec thrive in Mesoamerica

late 1400s
Kongo and
Ndongo run
world slave
trade

**c. 400 B.C.–
A.D. 1700**
Mound Builders

1300s Feudalism
in Europe wanes;
Renaissance begins

A.D. 700s–1000s
Empire of Ghana

35,000 B.C.
▼
Humans begin to
populate North America

c. A.D. 600
Muhammed founds Islam

1100s–1200s
Growth and rule of
empire of Mali

c. 1440 Gutenberg's
printing press

Replicas of the *Niña*, *Pinta*, and *Santa María*, the three ships with which Columbus first crossed the Atlantic.

European Exploration & Colonization

Key Idea: European exploration and colonization created permanent changes in the Americas and in Europe.

Starting in the 1300s, Europeans were driven to explore the world. After Columbus's voyages, the trans-Atlantic trade brought new people, plants, animals, and diseases to both the Americas and to Europe. As European nations competed with each other for North America's riches, they conquered Native Americans, claimed their lands, and often enslaved them. Although conflict prevailed, there was much cultural interchange.

The Slave Trade

Key Idea: European colonists brought enslaved Africans to the Americas.

African kingdoms often went to war to enslave enemy populations, and their slave trade was well-established by the time Europeans arrived in Central Africa in the 1480s. In the Americas, European colonists enslaved Native Americans and came to depend on enslaved Africans as a permanent source of cheap labor. Millions of enslaved people suffered cruelly as a result.

The hold of a slave ship, as depicted by a crew member. Roughly 20 percent of Africans did not survive the trans-Atlantic journey to the Americas.

1488 Dias reaches Cape of Good Hope

1492 Columbus crosses Atlantic Ocean, lands in the Americas

1494 Treaty of Tordesillas

c. 1500 Iroquois Confederacy formed

1519 Luther begins Protestant Reformation

1521 Cortés conquers Aztecs

1534 Anglican Church splits from Roman Catholicism

1565 Spanish found St. Augustine

1585 English found Roanoke colony

1588 Defeat of Spanish Armada

1651 First Navigation Act

1680 Popé's Rebellion

1700

The English Colonies
1585–1763

Because Puritans wanted everyone to be able to read the Bible, most New England children went to school. Students learned by copying from hornbooks like this one.

The New England Colonies

Key Idea: English colonists settled New England, where they established many political and religious traditions.

The Pilgrims and Puritans sought religious and political freedom in New England. They established freedom of speech, democracy, and a Protestant work ethic, but did not tolerate religious dissent. A short growing season, rocky soil, and hills supported small, diversified farms. Merchants and shipbuilders exported fish and timber to the world through the region's seaports.

An 18th-century school

The Middle Colonies

Key Idea: Religious tolerance and ethnic diversity characterized the Middle Colonies

The tolerance of the Quaker and Dutch colonists attracted a diverse population. Skilled immigrant farmers profited from the fertile soil and mild climate. Rivers encouraged shipping and commerce, and harbors became large cities. Although the region did not depend on slave labor, the slave trade was important to the economy.

1585

English found Roanoke colony

1603 Elizabeth I dies; England and Scotland united under James I

1607 English found Jamestown colony

1619 Virginia Company forms House of Burgesses

1620 Pilgrims land at Plymouth

1630 Puritans found Massachusetts Bay

1632 Lord Baltimore establishes Maryland colony for Catholics

1648 English Revolution

1651 First Navigation Act

The Southern Colonies

Key Idea: New Southern colonies were settled by fortune-seekers, religious refugees, enslaved Africans, and the poor.

The Southern soil and climate was ideal for cash crops such as tobacco, rice, and indigo. Southern planters grew rich using the unpaid labor of slaves imported from Africa. Each colony was governed by an elected representative assembly modeled on Virginia's House of Burgesses, yet slaves had no rights.

Plantation owners became wealthy, but Bacon's Rebellion in 1676 (*right*) demanded rights for poor frontier settlers: Backcountry Virginians wanted lower taxes and protection from Native American attacks.

The Backcountry and Frontier

Key Idea: Increased contact between English settlers, Native American groups, and other European colonists led to conflicts over frontier lands and resources.

As poorer settlers pushed west into the Backcountry, they competed for land, furs, and other resources with Native American peoples, as well as with French and Spanish colonists. These conflicts led to the French and Indian War, which united the English colonies against a common enemy.

(*above*) Philadelphia, late 1700s. The Middle Colonies provided a haven for ethnic and religious minorities who were often persecuted in England, such as Catholics and (*left*) Quakers.

1660 Restoration of English monarchy

1664 England takes New Amsterdam from Dutch

1675 King Philip's War

1676 Bacon's Rebellion

1681 Penn granted charter for Pennsylvania

1688 Glorious Revolution of William and Mary

1689 English Bill of Rights

1732 Georgia founded

1739 Stono Rebellion

1751 George III crowned

1754–1763 French and Indian War

UNIT 3

Creating a New Nation

1763–1791

Why It Matters Now

America at the beginning of its history was an experiment
—a trial to see if democratic and representative government
could work. Patriot colonists imperiled "their lives, their
fortunes, their sacred honor" for the sake of principle. The
values they fought for, and the decisions they wrote into
the Constitution, echo through our history and shape our
government and our lives to this day.

Is life so dear, or peace so sweet, as to be purchased at the price of chains and slavery? Forbid it, Almighty God! I know not what course others may take; but as for me, give me liberty or give me death!
—Patrick Henry, 1775

The Road to Revolution

1763–1776

 ESSENTIAL QUESTION

What drove the colonists to declare independence from Great Britain?

② To Lexington and Concord

CONNECT 🔄 **Geography & History**

What role did the geography of 18th-century Boston play in the early days of the Revolution?

Think about:

1 why it was so difficult to invade the town

2 the routes from Boston to Lexington and Concord

3 the strategic importance of the surrounding hills

① The only road connecting Boston to the mainland

King George III

No Stamp Act

Teapot decorated to protest Stamp Act, 1766

1763

Proclamation of 1763 restricts westward expansion.

1765 Parliament passes Stamp Act.

Effect Colonists organize boycott of British goods.

1767 Parliament passes Townshend Acts.

Effect Boycott is resumed; political activism spreads.

Animated GEOGRAPHY & HISTORY

Battle of Bunker Hill *1775*

Click here to preview the events that
led to the American Revolution
@ClassZone.com

Charlestown burns
during the battle.

3

Bunker Hill and Breed's Hill
overlook the town.

BOSTON

harbor

British patrols

Massachusetts
Minuteman

1774 Intolerable Acts
are passed.

▼

Effect Colonists organize
First Continental Congress.

1775 Fighting
begins at Lexington
and Concord.

1776

1773 Parliament passes
Tea Act.

▼

Effect Colonists destroy
tea in Boston Tea Party.

Bedford, MA
militia flag,
1775

Declaration of
Independence
announces
American
separation from
Britain.

The Road to Revolution **155**

▶ Key Ideas

BEFORE, YOU LEARNED

The British tried to stop colonists from settling on the western frontier.

NOW YOU WILL LEARN

Colonists saw British efforts to increase control over the colonies as violations of their rights.

▶ Vocabulary

TERMS & NAMES

King George III British monarch who reigned during the American Revolution

Quartering Act act requiring the colonists to quarter, or house, British soldiers and provide them with supplies

Sugar Act law placing a tax on sugar, molasses, and other products shipped to the colonies

Stamp Act law requiring all legal and commercial documents to carry an official stamp showing that a tax had been paid

Patrick Henry member of Virginia's House of Burgesses

Sons of Liberty secret society formed to oppose British policies

BACKGROUND VOCABULARY

speculate to buy as an investment

boycott refusal to buy

REVIEW

Proclamation of 1763 British proclamation that forbade the colonists from settling west of the Appalachian Mountains

Visual Vocabulary
King George III

▶ Reading Strategy

Re-create the diagram shown at right. As you read and respond to the **KEY QUESTIONS**, use the boxes to record the opposing points of view of Parliament and the American colonists.

 See Skillbuilder Handbook, page R8.

COMPARE AND CONTRAST

Parliament	Colonists
Colonies should help pay for their own defense.	

🖱 **GRAPHIC ORGANIZERS**
Go to **Interactive Review** @ ClassZone.com

SECTION 1

Tighter British Control

F1.1.1 Political and Intellectual Transformations – colonial ideas about government (e.g., limited government, republicanism, protecting individual rights and promoting the common good, representative government, natural rights)
F1.1.3 Political and Intellectual Transformations – changing interactions with the royal government of Great Britain after the French and Indian War

One American's Story

In 1765 Sally Franklin's father—the famous American diplomat Benjamin Franklin—was in London to protest the Stamp Act. During his stay, Sally Franklin wrote her father long and detailed letters that were filled with news from the colonies. Often she wrote about family and friends, but Sally also had a keen interest in political affairs. In one letter, she vividly described the colonial reaction to the repeal of the Stamp Act:

PRIMARY SOURCE

❝ We have heard by a round-about way that the Stamp Act is repealed. . . . The bells rung, we had bonfires and one house was illuminated. Indeed I never heard so much noise in my life; the very children seem distracted. ❞

—Sally Franklin, quoted in *Founding Mothers*

Sally Franklin (Bache)

Similar celebrations occurred throughout the colonies. Many thought the difficulties between Britain and America had finally come to an end.

The Colonies and Britain Grow Apart

🔻 **KEY QUESTION** Why were the colonists threatened by Parliament's new laws?

During the French and Indian War, American colonists helped the British defeat the French. The colonists took pride in the British victory, but soon found that their relationship with Britain had soured. In earlier days, the colonies had been allowed, for the most part, to manage their own affairs. In the 1760s, however, Parliament's new laws and restrictions threatened the colonists' freedom.

Westward Expansion Restricted After the French and Indian War, **King George III**, the British monarch, issued many reforms to tighten his control of the American colonies. First, he issued the **Proclamation of 1763**, which forbade the colonists from settling beyond the Appalachian Mountains. Although designed to maintain peace between the colonists and Native Americans, this law angered settlers who hoped to **speculate**, or buy as an investment, in western lands. In addition, King George decided to keep 10,000 soldiers in the colonies to enforce the proclamation. But housing the troops proved very expensive. Therefore, Parliament passed the **Quartering Act**, a law that required colonists to house all British soldiers.

These new laws created great anxiety in the colonies. The colonists feared that Parliament intended to use the troops to control their movements and restrict their freedom.

Parliament Taxes the Colonists In addition to the cost of keeping troops in the colonies, Britain owed massive debts from the French and Indian War. To pay off these debts, Britain needed more revenue, or income. As a result, Parliament looked to the colonies to pay part of the costs for frontier defense and colonial government.

In 1765, Parliament passed the **Sugar Act**. This law placed a tax on sugar, molasses, and other products shipped to the colonies. Making matters worse, in the following year Parliament passed the **Stamp Act**, a law that required all legal and commercial documents to carry an official stamp showing that a tax had been paid. In addition to wills and contracts, all newspapers and diplomas also had to carry a stamp.

From Parliament's perspective, the Sugar and Stamp Acts were reasonable ways to raise money in the colonies to pay off Britain's debt. From the colonist's perspective, however, these acts were seen as serious threats to their political rights. Their anger focused on two complaints: First, that Parliament had no right to tax the colonies—that was a job for the colonial assembly. And second, that no tax should be created without their consent.

▲ **COMPARE AND CONTRAST** Explain why the colonists disagreed with Parliament.

Colonists Defy Parliament

▼ **KEY QUESTION** How did the colonists react when Parliament took over the assemblies' power to tax?

The Stamp Act enraged the colonists. Everywhere people took up the cry "No taxation without representation!" to protest the attack on their rights. **Patrick Henry**, a member of Virginia's House of Burgesses, demanded resistance. When another member shouted that resistance was treason, Henry is said to have replied, "If *this* be treason, make the most of it!"

The Colonists Organize In 1765, delegates from nine colonies formed the Stamp Act Congress in New York. During this meeting, delegates drafted a petition to the king protesting the Stamp Act and declared that the right to tax the colonists belonged to the colonial assemblies, not to Parliament. This was the first time the colonies had united in opposition to British policy.

Meanwhile, some colonists formed secret societies, such as the **Sons of Liberty**, to oppose British policies. Occasionally they encouraged

Under the Stamp Act of 1765, royal stamps such as these were required on legal documents.

people to attack customs officials and burn the stamps. As a result, many customs officials quit their jobs and returned to England.

Colonists Threaten British Profits The colonists' complaints against Parliament were bitter, loud, and sometimes violent. But the most effective protest took the form of a **boycott**, a widespread refusal to buy British goods. By refusing to buy goods from England, the colonists targeted British merchants. The colonists hoped that these merchants, faced with declining sales, would influence Parliament to repeal the Stamp Act. Some British politicians sided with the colonists. Parliamentary leader William Pitt spoke out against the Stamp Act:

PRIMARY SOURCE

❝ The Americans have not acted in all things with prudence and [good] temper. They have been driven to madness by injustice. Will you punish them for the madness you have [caused]? . . . . My opinion . . . . is that the Stamp Act be repealed absolutely, totally, and immediately. ❞

—William Pitt, quoted in *Patriots*

The colonists' tactic worked, and Parliament finally repealed the Stamp Act in 1766. But at the same time, Parliament passed the Declaratory Act, which stated that Parliament had supreme authority to govern the colonies. Although the colonists celebrated the repeal of the Stamp Act, the great argument between Parliament and the colonies had just begun.

 CAUSES AND EFFECTS Explain how the colonists reacted when Parliament took over the assemblies' power to tax.

(*above*) During the crisis with Great Britian, colonists often met under the Liberty Tree, a symbol of liberty, individuality, and freedom.

Michigan Grade Level Content Expectations *Review*

ONLINE QUIZ
For test practice, go to
Interactive Review @ ClassZone.com

TERMS & NAMES

1. Explain the importance of

- King George III
- Quartering Act
- Sugar Act
- Stamp Act
- Patrick Henry
- Sons of Liberty

USING YOUR READING NOTES

2. Compare and Contrast Complete the diagram that you started at the beginning of this section.

Parliament	Colonists
Colonies should help pay for their own defense.	

KEY IDEAS

3. Why did Parliament pass new laws governing the colonies?

4. How did the colonists oppose the new acts?

CRITICAL THINKING

5. Analyze Point of View Why would Britain's new laws have convinced Americans that their freedom was under threat?

6. Connect Economics & History Why was boycotting British goods an effective way to protest the Stamp Act?

7. Writing Protest Song Imagine that you are one of the Sons of Liberty. Write a song protesting Parliament's new laws.

Reading for Understanding

▶ Key Ideas

BEFORE, YOU LEARNED

Colonists saw British efforts to increase control over the colonies as violations of their rights.

NOW YOU WILL LEARN

Many colonists organized to oppose British policies.

▶ Vocabulary

TERMS & NAMES

Crispus Attucks sailor of African-American and Native American ancestry who died at the Boston Massacre

Boston Massacre incident in 1770 in which British troops fired on and killed American colonists

Townshend Acts acts passed by Parliament in 1767 to tax imports in the colonies

writs of assistance search warrants used to enter homes or businesses to search for smuggled goods

Daughters of Liberty organization of colonial women formed to protest British policies

Samuel Adams leader of the Boston Sons of Liberty

committee of correspondence organization formed to exchange information about British policies and American resistance

Boston Tea Party incident in 1773, when colonists protested British policies by boarding British ships and throwing their cargoes of tea overboard

BACKGROUND VOCABULARY

duties taxes placed on imported goods

REVIEW

John Adams lawyer who defended British soldiers accused of murder in the Boston Massacre

▶ Reading Strategy

Re-create the diagram shown at right. As you read and respond to the **KEY QUESTIONS**, use the boxes to record how each aspect of the Townshend Acts angered the colonists.

 See Skillbuilder Handbook, page R7.

CAUSES AND EFFECTS

Townshend Acts...	anger colonists because...
writs of assistance	*customs officials invaded their homes and businesses*
duties on imports	

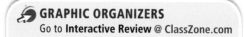

GRAPHIC ORGANIZERS
Go to **Interactive Review** @ ClassZone.com

Colonial Resistance Grows

 F1.1.1 Political and Intellectual Transformations – colonial ideas about government (e.g., limited government, republicanism, protecting individual rights and promoting the common good, representative government, natural rights)
F1.1.3 Political and Intellectual Transformations – changing interactions with the royal government of Great Britain after the French and Indian War

One American's Story

Crispus Attucks was born into slavery in Framingham, Massachusetts, around 1723. It is believed that Attucks was the son of an African-American father and a Native American mother. As a young man, Attucks escaped slavery by running away to sea.

In March 1770, Attucks was in Boston, where feelings against British rule were reaching a fever pitch. He joined a crowd who were protesting British troops. A witness described what happened next.

PRIMARY SOURCE

❝ [The British officer] is said to have ordered [the troops] to fire, and to have repeated that order. One gun was fired first; then others in succession and with deliberation, till ten or a dozen guns were fired. **❞**

—anonymous account of the Boston Massacre

Crispus Attucks

When the smoke cleared Attucks was dead, one of the victims of the **Boston Massacre**. Throughout America, tension between Britain and its colonies was exploding into violence.

Tightening British Control

🔻 **KEY QUESTION** Why did the Townshend Acts anger the colonists?

After the uproar over the Sugar and Stamp Acts, Britain hoped to avoid further conflict with the colonies. Yet Parliament faced a serious dilemma: how to control the unruly colonists without angering the people with a new set of taxes. The answer, Parliament decided, was the Declaratory Act.

Passed in 1766, the Declaratory Act affirmed Parliament's right to legislate for the colonies "in all cases whatsoever." Importantly, however, no new tax accompanied the act. The purpose of the Declaratory Act was simply to reassert Parliament's control over all colonial affairs.

Most colonists did not feel threatened by the Declaratory Act. Although some politicans did protest the new law in colonial assemblies, most people were not bothered by Parliament's bold political statement. Instead, colonists simply ignored the act and went on with their lives as best they could.

The Townshend Acts Are Passed Parliament's new strategy, however, had one major flaw: with the Stamp Act repealed, Britain still needed to raise money in the colonies to pay for troops and other expenses. So Britain's finance minister, Charles Townshend, proposed a new series of **duties**, or taxes on imports, to raise revenue in America.

Approved by Parliament in 1767, the **Townshend Acts** placed duties on numerous imports to the colonies such as glass, paper, paint, lead, and tea. In addition, the acts allowed British officers to issue **writs of assistance**, or search warrants, to enter homes and businesses to search for smuggled or illegal goods.

Daily Life *The Colonial Marketplace*

By the 1760s, English merchants were sending hundreds of ships to America with goods for sale to the colonists. Beyond the daily necessities of life—tools, knives, nails, and axes—colonists were eager to buy the latest luxuries and fashions from England, including (**A**) clothing, (**B**) glass and building materials, (**C**) glassware, (**D**) scientific and medical instruments, (**E**) books and periodicals, (**F**) furniture, and (**G**) fine silks.

BOYCOTT PRESSURES MERCHANTS

When the colonists boycotted British goods, many English merchants, shippers, and manufacturers lost business as their products went unsold. As a result, in 1765 many merchants pressured Parliament to repeal the acts so their businesses could recover.

CRITICAL THINKING Make Generalizations
How did the colonial boycotts affect British merchants?

Anger Over the Townshend Acts News of the Townshend Acts sparked immediate protest throughout the colonies. People were furious that Parliament had once again passed a tax without their consent. Colonists felt that only locally elected officials—rather than Parliament—should have the right to create laws and taxes in the colonies. Many people, such as Pennsylvania lawyer John Dickinson, thought the acts were illegal. Dickinson explained his beliefs in a famous pamphlet:

PRIMARY SOURCE

❝ We cannot be happy without being free . . . we cannot be free without being secure in our property . . . we cannot be secure in our property, if [taxed] without our consent. ❞

—John Dickinson, *Letters from a Farmer in Pennsylvania*

The colonists were also angry about the writs of assistance. Many believed that the writs went against their natural rights, as defined by English philosopher John Locke. The law of nature, wrote Locke, teaches that "no one ought to harm another in his life, health, liberty, or possessions."

🔺 **CAUSES AND EFFECTS** Explain why the Townshend Acts angered the colonists.

Colonists Protest

🔻 **KEY QUESTION** In what ways did colonists protest British laws?

In response to the Townshend Acts, merchants in Boston organized another boycott of British goods. By October 1767, other colonies had joined the Massachusetts protests. The colonists were uniting for a common cause.

Political Activism Spreads As the boycott spread throughout the colonies, more people became politically active. Many colonists who had not previously participated in politics now had a way of making their voices heard. For example, some women formed their own protest organization called the **Daughters of Liberty**. They urged colonists to weave their own cloth and to use American products instead of British goods.

Meanwhile, colonial leaders urged the people to remain calm and not to protest violently. "No mobs," the *Boston Gazette* suggested, "Constitutional methods are best." Regardless, some colonists continued to protest with anger and threatened to form a mob.

Fearing disorder in the colonies, British officials called for more troops. This angered the colonists—even those who wanted peace. **Samuel Adams**, a leader of the Boston Sons of Liberty, stated, "We will destroy every soldier that dare put his foot on shore. . . . I look upon them as foreign enemies!"

The Boston Massacre In the fall of 1768, more than 1,000 additional British soldiers (known as redcoats for their bright red jackets) arrived in Boston under the command of General Thomas Gage. With their arrival, tensions erupted into violence.

Connecting History

Representative Government
Ever since the House of Burgesses was established in Jamestown in 1619, colonists had the right to raise their own taxes. See *Chapter 3, page 64.*

Paul Revere's etching of the Boston Massacre fueled anger in the colonies.

Are the soldiers represented fairly in Revere's etching?

On March 5, 1770, a group of colonists—mostly youths and dockworkers—surrounded some soldiers in front of the State House. Soon, the two groups began trading insults, shouting at each other and even throwing snowballs. As the crowd grew larger, the soldiers began to fear for their safety. Thinking they were about to be attacked, the soldiers fired into the crowd. Five people, including Crispus Attucks, were killed.

The people of Boston were outraged at what came to be known as the Boston Massacre. In the weeks that followed, the colonies were flooded with anti-British propaganda in newspapers, pamphlets, and political posters. Attucks and the four victims were depicted as heroes who had given their lives for the cause of freedom. The British soldiers, on the other hand, were portrayed as evil and menacing villains.

At the same time, the soldiers who had fired the shots were arrested and charged with murder. **John Adams**, a lawyer and cousin of Samuel Adams, agreed to defend the soldiers in court. Many people criticized Adams and some even threatened to harm the lawyer. But Adams believed that everyone—including the British soldiers—was entitled to a fair trial. Although Adams supported the colonists' cause, he wanted to demonstrate that everyone was subject to the rule of law.

Adams argued that the soldiers had acted in self-defense. The jury agreed and acquitted the soldiers. To many colonists, however, the Boston Massacre would stand as a symbol of British tyranny in the colonies.

▲ **SUMMARIZE** Describe how colonists protested British laws.

Economic Interference

🔻 **KEY QUESTION** How did colonists in the port cities react to the Tea Act?

In April 1770, Parliament repealed the Townshend Acts. Once again, the colonial boycott had worked—British trade had been hurt and Parliament had backed down. But Parliament kept the tea tax to show that it still had the right to tax the colonists.

The Tea Act Increases Anger To demonstrate their displeasure with the remaining tax on tea, many colonists chose not to purchase luxuries from British merchants. Instead, they drank tea that was smuggled from Holland. As a result, many British tea companies lost money in America as their tea went unsold and rotted in ports.

Attempting to save British tea merchants, Parliament passed the Tea Act in 1773. This law gave one company, the East India Company, the exclusive right to sell tea in the colonies. Although the act lowered the price of tea for colonists, it also restricted colonists from acting as shippers and merchants of the valuable product.

Many colonists—particularly those who had traded in smuggled tea—were enraged by the new tax. Colonists saw the tea act as another attempt by Parliament to interfere in the economic life of the colonies.

Colonial Unity Expands By this time, colonial leaders understood the importance of unity among the colonies. Therefore, Samuel Adams urged many towns in Massachusetts to establish **committees of correspondence** to communicate with their neighboring towns and colonial leaders.

In the months that followed, these groups exchanged numerous secret letters on colonial affairs and resistance to British policy. Before long, many other colonies—such as New York, South Carolina, and Rhode Island—had created similar committees of correspondence.

History Makers *Revolutionary Leaders*

Samuel Adams   1722–1803

When Parliament levied taxes upon the colonies, no one responded with greater passion and fury than Boston merchant Samuel Adams. A skillful writer, orator, and popular leader of the Sons of Liberty and the Boston Committee of Correspondence, Samuel Adams persuaded many colonists to unite against British policy and taxation. "It does not require a majority to prevail," Samuel Adams wrote, "but rather an irate, tireless minority keen to set brush fires in people's minds."

John Adams   1735–1826

While his cousin Samuel planned fiery public protests, John Adams used a quieter tactic—the law—to counter British policy. "Facts are stubborn things," Adams wrote, "and whatever may be our wishes, our inclinations, or the dictates of our passions, they cannot alter the state of facts and evidence." Putting this theory into practice, Adams helped draft a legal petition to the king suggesting that Parliament had no right to tax the colonies.

COMPARING *Leaders*

How did Samuel and John Adams differ in the way they protested British actions?

ONLINE BIOGRAPHY For more information about Samuel and John Adams, go to the **Research & Writing Center** @ ClassZone.com

The Boston Tea Party Protests against the Tea Act took place throughout the colonies. In Charlestown, South Carolina, colonists unloaded tea and let it rot on the docks. In New York City and Philadelphia, colonists blocked tea ships from landing. In Boston, the Sons of Liberty organized what came to be known as the **Boston Tea Party**.

On the evening of December 16, 1773, a group of men disguised as Native Americans boarded three tea ships docked in Boston harbor. One of the men, George Hewes, a Boston shoemaker, later recalled the events.

PRIMARY SOURCE

❝ We then were ordered by our commander to open the hatches and take out all the chests of tea and throw them overboard. . . . In about three hours from the time we went on board, we had thus broken and thrown overboard every tea chest to be found in the ship; while those in the other ships were disposing of the tea in the same way, at the same time. ❞

—George Hewes, quoted in *A Retrospect of the Boston Tea-Party*

That night, Hewes and the others destroyed 342 chests of tea to protest the Tea Act. Many colonists rejoiced at the news. British officials, however, were angered by the destructive protest and wanted to punish the culprits.

In the days that followed, some colonial leaders offered to pay for the tea if Parliament agreed to repeal the hated Tea Act. But Britain ruled out any compromise. This decision pushed many Americans into open rebellion.

 CAUSES AND EFFECTS Describe how colonists reacted to the Tea Act.

Michigan Grade Level Content Expectations *Review*

🖱 **ONLINE QUIZ**
For test practice, go to
Interactive Review @ ClassZone.com

TERMS & NAMES

1. Explain the importance of

- Crispus Attucks
- Daughters of Liberty
- Boston Massacre
- Samuel Adams
- Townshend Acts
- John Adams
- writs of assistance
- Boston Tea Party

USING YOUR READING NOTES

2. Causes and Effects Complete the diagram that you started at the beginning of this section.

Townshend Acts...	anger colonists because...
writs of assistance	*customs officials invaded their homes and businesses*
duties on imports	

KEY IDEAS

3. Why did colonists oppose the Townshend Acts?

4. How did the colonists express their discontent?

5. What prompted the Boston Tea Party?

CRITICAL THINKING

6. Draw Conclusions Why did Parliament keep trying different ways of raising revenue?

7. Problems and Solutions Why did the colonists react so violently to the Tea Act?

8. Summarize Explain the impact of Paul Revere's etching of the Boston Massacre.

9. **Writing** Letter Write a letter to Parliament, urging the British government not to interfere in colonial trade.

American Spirit

POPULAR RESISTANCE

The colonists found many ways to resist the new laws passed by Parliament. Americans from all walks of life joined in the popular protests.

PROTESTS IN THE STREETS

Popular protests echoed through the streets of colonial towns. In this illustration, an angry crowd of colonists burns the hated stamps.

WOMEN BECOME ACTIVISTS

For the first time in American history, large numbers of women became involved in a political cause. Women played a leading role in the boycotts of British goods. They also organized and signed petitions. This British cartoon shows the women of Edenton, North Carolina signing a promise not to buy British products.

POLITICS IN DAILY LIFE

Protests against the Stamp Act appeared everywhere, from newspapers and periodicals to ordinary household items.

A mock stamp printed by a Pennsylvania journal to protest the Stamp Act

Join the Boycott

Imagine you have joined the boycott of imported goods. Create a political pamphlet that expresses your opinion about British products.

▶ Key Ideas

BEFORE, YOU LEARNED

Many Americans organized to oppose British policies.

NOW YOU WILL LEARN

The tensions between Britain and the colonies led to the outbreak of the Revolutionary War.

▶ Vocabulary

TERMS & NAMES

Minutemen group of armed civilians, trained to be ready to fight "at a minute's warning"

Intolerable Acts series of laws, known in Britain as the Coercive Acts, meant to punish Massachusetts and clamp down on resistance in other colonies

First Continental Congress meeting of delegates from most of the colonies, called in reaction to the Intolerable Acts

Paul Revere Boston silversmith who rode into the countryside to spread news of British troop movement

Lexington and Concord first battles of the Revolutionary War

Loyalists Americans who supported the British

Patriots Americans who sided with the rebels

BACKGROUND VOCABULARY

militia a force of armed civilians pledged to defend their community

Visual Vocabulary Paul Revere

▶ Reading Strategy

Re-create the diagram shown at right. As you read and respond to the **KEY QUESTIONS**, record information to support the generalization.

 See Skillbuilder Handbook, page R11.

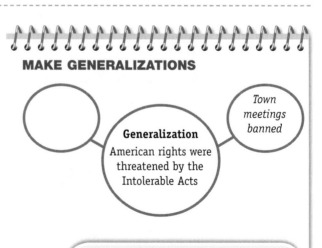

MAKE GENERALIZATIONS

Generalization
American rights were threatened by the Intolerable Acts

Town meetings banned

 GRAPHIC ORGANIZERS
Go to **Interactive Review** @ ClassZone.com

The Road to Lexington and Concord

F1.1.1 Political and Intellectual Transformations – colonial ideas about government (e.g., limited government, republicanism, protecting individual rights and promoting the common good, representative government, natural rights)
F1.1.3 Political and Intellectual Transformations – changing interactions with the royal government of Great Britain after the French and Indian War

One American's Story

At dawn on April 19, 1775, Captain John Parker and 70 of his men stood on the grassy common at the center of Lexington, a village near Boston. The men under Parker's command belonged to the local **militia**—a force of armed civilians pledged to defend their community. About one-third of the Lexington militia were **Minutemen**, colonists trained to be "ready to act at a minute's warning." A soldier described what happened next:

PRIMARY SOURCE

❝ There suddenly appeared a Number of King's troops . . . They were . . . on a quick pace Towards us with Three officers in there front on horse back and on full gallop Towards us the foremost of which cryed through down your arms you villains you Rebels." ❞

—**John Robbins, quoted in** *Redcoats and Rebels*

Colonists battle Redcoats at Lexington, 1775.

Captain Parker was wounded and eight of his men were killed in the first fighting of the War of Independence. Colonial protests had turned into violent revolution.

The Intolerable Acts

🔻 **KEY QUESTION** What rights were threatened by the Intolerable Acts?

The Boston Tea Party infuriated Parliament. One British official said the people of Boston "ought to be knocked about their ears." King George III declared, "We must master them or totally leave them to themselves and treat them as aliens." Britain chose to "master" the colonies.

Attacks on Rights and Liberties In 1774, Parliament passed a series of laws to punish the Massachusetts colony and to clamp down on resistance in other colonies. The British called these laws the Coercive Acts, but they were so harsh that the colonists called them the **Intolerable Acts**. These acts were a direct attack on colonists' traditional rights and liberties, because they

- closed the port of Boston until colonists paid for the destroyed tea
- altered the Massachusetts charter to ban town meetings
- replaced the elected council with an appointed one
- increased the governor's power over the colonists
- protected British officials accused of crimes in the colonies from being tried by colonists
- allowed British officers to house troops in private dwellings

To enforce the acts, Parliament appointed General Thomas Gage governor of Massachusetts.

ANALYZING *Political Cartoons*

HISTORICAL CARTOONS

Historical cartoons show how people viewed the important events of their time. Each cartoon on these pages expresses the point of view of the cartoonist. Notice how the cartoonists use symbols, exaggeration, and humor to get their points across.

The Bostonians in Distress

This cartoon uses symbols to show the situation in Boston after the Intolerable Acts stopped all ships from entering the town's harbors.

Bostonians are trapped in a cage symbolizing the restrictions of the Intolerable Acts.

Other colonists are shown helping the Bostonians by feeding them fish.

The First Continental Congress Meets In 1772, Sam Adams had written, "I wish we could arouse the continent." The Intolerable Acts answered his wish. Other colonies immediately offered Massachusetts their support. They sent food and money to Boston. The committees of correspondence also called for a meeting of colonial delegates to discuss what to do next.

In September 1774, delegates from all the colonies except Georgia met in Philadelphia. At this meeting, called the **First Continental Congress**, delegates voted to ban all trade with Britain until the Intolerable Acts were repealed. They also called on each colony to begin training troops. Georgia agreed to be a part of the actions of the Congress even though it had voted not to send delegates.

The First Continental Congress marked a key step in American history. Although most delegates were not ready to call for independence, they were determined to uphold colonial rights. This meeting planted the seeds of a future independent government. John Adams called it "a nursery of American statesmen." The delegates agreed to meet again in seven months.

The Bostonians Paying the Excise-Man

This cartoon was published in London in 1774. It shows how Tories (those supporting the King) viewed colonial protests.

A customs informer, who has been tarred and feathered, is being tormented.

The protesters are shown as violent thugs.

CRITICAL THINKING

1. **Make Inferences** Which cartoon is sympathetic to the colonists?

2. **Synthesize** How would these images have helped unite the colonists against British policies?

 See Skillbuilder Handbook, page R24.

History Makers

Abigail Adams 1744–1818

Abigail Smith was born on November 11, 1744, in Weymouth, Massachusetts. She married John Adams in 1764, the same year that Britain enacted the Sugar Act. She was often left alone to manage the family farm and raise their children.

During their long separations, Abigail wrote her husband many letters about government and politics. Often she expressed her opinions to her husband and even gave him advice when creating new laws. In one letter, Abigail asked John to give women more rights. "Remember the ladies," she wrote him, "and be more generous and favorable to them than your ancestors." Abigail's views were well ahead of her time, although it was years before women achieved equal rights.

CRITICAL THINKING Draw Conclusions What might Abigail Adams think about women's rights today?

 **ONLINE BIOGRAPHY** For more on on Abigail Adams, go to the **Research & Writing Center** @ ClassZone.com

British Control Begins to Slip The colonists hoped that another trade boycott would force a repeal of the Intolerable Acts. After all, past boycotts had led to the repeal of the Stamp Act and the Townshend Acts. This time, however, Parliament stood firm. It even increased restrictions on colonial trade and sent more troops in the colonies. However, in the countryside, British authorities were already losing control of government. Throughout the colonies, Americans acted forcefully to reestablish the rights that Parliament was taking away. In the summer of 1774 in towns throughout Massachusetts, large crowds gathered to prevent British-appointed judges from holding court. They also forced many unelected officials to resign. In defiance of the royal governor, the people of Massachusetts elected a provincial congress with the power to collect its own taxes and raise its own army.

By the end of 1774, some colonists were preparing to fight. In Massachusetts, John Hancock headed the Committee of Safety, which had the power to call out the militia. In Virginia, House of Burgess member Patrick Henry delivered his most famous speech, calling for war:

PRIMARY SOURCE

❝ Gentlemen may cry peace, peace—but there is no peace. The war is actually begun! The next gale that sweeps from the north will bring to our ears the clash of resounding arms! Our brethren are already in the field! Why stand we here idle? . . . I know not what course others may take; but as for me, give me liberty or give me death. ❞

—**Patrick Henry, quoted in** *Patriots*

But most colonial leaders believed that any fight with Britain would be short. They thought that a public show of force would make the British Parliament change its policies.

▲ **SUMMARIZE** Explain what rights were threatened by the Intolerable Acts.

The Revolution Begins

🔻 **KEY QUESTION** Why did the fighting begin at Lexington?

Since 1770, Sam Adams had been building a network of informants to keep watch over British activities. The British had their spies too. It was from these spies that General Gage learned that the Massachusetts militia was storing arms and ammunition in Concord, about 20 miles northwest of Boston. He also heard that Sam Adams and John Hancock were nearby in Lexington. On the night of April 18, 1775, Gage ordered his troops to arrest Adams and Hancock in Lexington and to destroy the supplies in Concord.

The Midnight Ride The Sons of Liberty had prepared for this moment. **Paul Revere**, a Boston silversmith, and a second messenger, William Dawes, were sent to spread the news about British troop movements. Revere would cross the harbor from Boston to Charlestown. From there he would ride to Lexington and Concord. Dawes would take the land route.

Revere had arranged a system of signals to alert colonists across the harbor in Charlestown. One lantern burning in the Old North Church steeple signaled that the British troops were taking the land route out of Boston; two lamps meant that the troops were leaving Boston by water.

CONNECTING 🔄 *History*

NEW ENGLANDERS OPPOSE THE KING

New Englanders had a long history of fierce opposition to royal authority. During the English Civil War of the 1640s, many New England Puritans returned to England to fight the king. They rejoiced when a republic was set up in England following the king's execution.

Over a century later, in the 1760s and 1770s, descendants of the Puritans were still angered by the same issues that had upset their ancestors:

- the levying of taxes without the people's consent
- the extent of the king's power
- the creation of a standing army that might threaten their freedom

Puritans execute King Charles I in London in 1649.

CRITICAL THINKING **Make Generalizations** Why was New England a hotbed of political protest?

When the British moved, so did Revere and Dawes. They galloped over the countryside on their "midnight ride," spreading the news. In Lexington, they were joined by Dr. Samuel Prescott. When Revere and Dawes were stopped by a British patrol, Prescott broke away and carried the message to Concord.

Lexington and Concord At dawn on April 19, 1775, more than 700 British troops reached Lexington. There they found Captain John Parker and about 70 colonial militiamen waiting. The British commander ordered the Americans to drop their muskets. The colonists refused. No one knows who fired first, but within a few minutes eight militiamen lay dead. The British then marched to Concord, where they destroyed military supplies. A battle broke out at a bridge north of town, forcing the British to retreat.

Nearly 4,000 Minutemen and militiamen arrived in the area. They lined the road from Concord to Lexington and peppered the retreating redcoats with musket fire. "It seemed as if men came down from the clouds," one British soldier later recalled. Only the arrival of 1,000 more troops saved the British from total destruction as they scrambled back to Boston.

Lexington and Concord were the first battles of the Revolutionary War. As Ralph Waldo Emerson later wrote, colonial troops had fired the "shot heard 'round the world." Americans would now have to choose sides and back up their political beliefs by force of arms. Those who supported the British were called **Loyalists**. Those who sided with the rebels were known as **Patriots**. The Revolution had begun.

 CAUSES AND EFFECTS Explain why fighting began at Lexington.

Michigan Grade Level Content Expectations *Review*

ONLINE QUIZ
For test practice, go to
Interactive Review @ ClassZone.com

TERMS & NAMES

1. Explain the importance of

- Minutemen
- Paul Revere
- Intolerable Acts
- Lexington and Concord
- First Continental Congress
- Loyalists
- Patriots

USING YOUR READING NOTES

2. Make Generalizations Complete the diagram that you started at the beginning of this section.

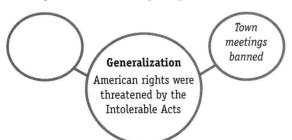

KEY IDEAS

3. Why did Britain pass the Intolerable Acts?

4. Why were British troops sent to Concord?

CRITICAL THINKING

5. Draw Conclusions Why did the colonists fear the Intolerable Acts?

6. Analyze Causes What democratic traditions were threatened by Parliament's policies?

7. Make Inferences Why were the British worried about the weapons being stored in Lexington?

8. Geography In the 18th century the landscape of Boston was very different than it is today. Research and write a short paper on how much the landscape around Boston has changed, or build a model of Boston in the 18th century.

Connect to Literature

Johnny Tremain by Esther Forbes

In 1775, 16-year-old Johnny Tremain lives in Boston and works as a delivery boy for a newspaper. Because he travels so much around the city, he is able to help the Patriots gather information about what the British are doing.

On the night of April 18, Johnny learns that British troops will be leaving on an expedition to seize the gunpowder at Lexington and Concord. He rushes to tell this news to Dr. Joseph Warren, who is a Patriot. Then Johnny goes to bed, wondering if the war has begun.

So Johnny slept. It was daylight when he woke with Warren's hand upon his shoulder. Outside on Tremont Street he could hear the clumping of army boots. A sergeant was swearing at his men. The soldiers were paraded so close to the house, which stood **flush**[1] with the sidewalkless street, that Johnny at first thought they must be in the room.

Doctor Warren dared speak no louder than a whisper.

"I'm going now."

"Something's happened?"

"Yes." He motioned Johnny to follow him into the kitchen. This room was on the back of the house. They could talk without danger of being overheard by the troops in the street.

Doctor Warren had on the same clothes as the day before. He had not been to bed. But now his hat was on his head. His black bag of instruments and medicines was packed and on the table. Silently he put milk, bread, herrings beside it, and gestured to Johnny to join him.

"Where did it begin?" asked Johnny.

"Lexington."

"Who won?"

"They did. Seven hundred against seventy. It wasn't a battle. It was . . . just target practice . . . for them. Some of our men were killed and the British **huzzaed**[2] and took the road to Concord."

"And did they get our supplies there?"

"I don't know. Paul Revere sent for me just after the firing on Lexington Green."

The young man's usually fresh-colored face was **haggard**.[3] He knew the seriousness of this day for himself and for his country.

"But everywhere the alarm is spreading. Men are grabbing their guns—marching for Concord. Paul Revere did get through in time last night. Billy Dawes a little later. Hundreds—maybe thousands— of Minute Men are on the march. Before the day's over, there'll be real fighting—not target practice. But Gage doesn't know that it's begun. You see, long before Colonel Smith got to Lexington—just as soon as he heard that Revere had warned the country—he sent back for reinforcements. For Earl Percy. You and I, Johnny, are just about the only people in Boston who know that blood has already been shed."

ADDITIONAL READING

Give Me Liberty! by Russell Freedman An exciting and well illustrated account of the events leading up to the Declaration of Independence.

Concise History of the American Revolution, by David C. G. Dutcher This publication from the National Park Service provides a good narrative of the American Revolution.

1. **flush:** in a line with
2. **huzzaed:** cheered
3. **haggard:** tired

▶ Key Ideas

BEFORE, YOU LEARNED

Rising tensions between Britain and the colonies led to the outbreak of the Revolutionary War.

NOW YOU WILL LEARN

As fighting continued, Americans decided to declare their independence from Britain.

▶ Vocabulary

TERMS & NAMES

Ethan Allen leader of a Patriot group of fighters known as the Green Mountain Boys

Second Continental Congress America's government during the Revolutionary War

Continental Army America's Patriot army during the Revolutionary War

Thomas Paine political radical and the author of *Common Sense*

Declaration of Independence document that declared American independence from Britain

Thomas Jefferson delegate from Virginia who wrote the Declaration of Independence

BACKGROUND VOCABULARY

siege when enemy forces surround a town or city in order to force it to surrender

artillery cannon and large guns

Visual Vocabulary Thomas Jefferson

▶ Reading Strategy

Re-create the diagram shown at right. As you read and respond to the **KEY QUESTIONS**, use the boxes to sequence events.

 See Skillbuilder Handbook, page R5.

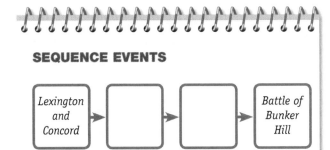

SEQUENCE EVENTS

Lexington and Concord → ☐ → ☐ → *Battle of Bunker Hill*

GRAPHIC ORGANIZERS
Go to **Interactive Review** @ ClassZone.com

Declaring Independence

F1.2.1 Political and Intellectual Transformations – colonists' views of government
F1.2.2 Political and Intellectual Transformations – their reasons for separating from Great Britain

One American's Story

No one knows who warned the colonists about the British plan to march on Concord. But suspicion has always fallen on Margaret Kemble Gage, the American-born wife of British General Thomas Gage. Despite her husband's lofty position as commander-in-chief of the British army in America, Margaret's loyalty remained torn between England and America. Explaining her mixed feelings about the war, Margaret Gage quoted Blanche from Shakespeare's play *King John*:

PRIMARY SOURCE

❝ The Sun's o'ercast with blood: fair day, adieu!
Which is the side that I must go withal?
I am with both: each army hath a hand;
And in their rage, I having hold of both,
They whirl asunder and dismember me . . .
Whoever wins, on that side shall I lose.
Assured loss, before the match be played. **❞**

— Margaret Kemble Gage, quoted in *Paul Revere's Ride*

Margaret Kemble Gage
by John Singleton Copley

After the British retreat at Lexington and Concord, even Margaret's husband suspected his wife had revealed the secret plans. Fearing she might do the same again, Gage sent his wife back to England. Like many others, Margaret Gage was forced to make difficult choices as the conflict began to spread.

The Siege of Boston

🔻 **KEY QUESTION** What events led to the Battle of Bunker Hill?

After the fighting at Lexington and Concord, British troops retreated to safety in Boston. As General Gage considered his next move, over 15,000 militiamen from all over New England surrounded the town. Boston was now

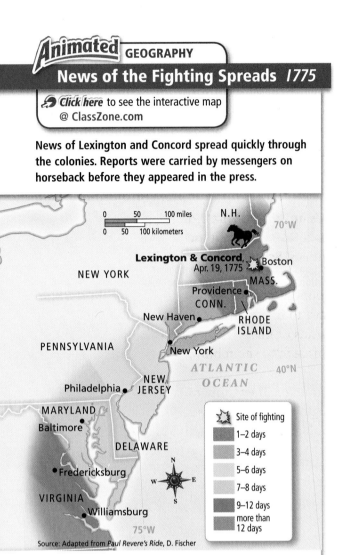

Animated GEOGRAPHY

News of the Fighting Spreads 1775

Click here to see the interactive map
@ ClassZone.com

News of Lexington and Concord spread quickly through the colonies. Reports were carried by messengers on horseback before they appeared in the press.

0   50   100 miles
0   50   100 kilometers

N.H.
70°W

Lexington & Concord, Boston
Apr. 19, 1775

NEW YORK

MASS.

Providence

CONN.

New Haven

RHODE
ISLAND

New York

PENNSYLVANIA

ATLANTIC
OCEAN
40°N

NEW
JERSEY

Philadelphia

MARYLAND

Baltimore

DELAWARE

N
W   E
S

Fredericksburg

75°W

VIRGINIA

Williamsburg

Site of fighting
1–2 days
3–4 days
5–6 days
7–8 days
9–12 days
more than
12 days

Source: Adapted from *Paul Revere's Ride*, D. Fischer

Connect Geography & History

Draw Conclusions How many miles could news spread in a two-day period?

under **siege**—encircled by military forces determined to force the British to surrender.

The Continental Army Is Formed In 1775, Boston stood at the tip of a long peninsula that connected the town to the mainland. Because the town was almost completely surrounded by water, it could not be attacked easily by land. However, if the Americans succeeded in placing cannon on the hills overlooking the bays that surrounded the town, the British would be forced to surrender.

The Americans came up with a daring plan. They would capture a British fort, far to the north, and drag the fort's cannon back to Boston. On May 10, 1775, Americans attacked Britain's Fort Ticonderoga on Lake Champlain. **Ethan Allen** led this band of backwoods fighters known as the Green Mountain Boys. They captured the fort and its large supply of **artillery**, or cannon and large guns.

On the same day as the attack on Fort Ticonderoga, the **Second Continental Congress** began meeting in Philadelphia. This would be America's government during the war. Delegates included John and Samuel Adams, John Hancock, Benjamin Franklin, George Washington, and Patrick Henry. They agreed to create a **Continental Army**. George Washington, who was from Virginia, was chosen as its commanding general.

Battle of Bunker Hill Meanwhile, tensions were building in Boston in June 1775. Across the harbor from Boston stood the town of Charlestown. Militiamen were positioned on Bunker Hill and Breeds Hill, which rose above the town. They built fortifications on Breeds Hill. Alarmed, the British decided to attack.

General William Howe crossed the bay with 2,200 British soldiers. Bostonians watched in horror as the British set fire to Charlestown. Then, marching in ranks, the British climbed Breeds Hill toward the American militia. On the hilltop, the militia waited. According to legend, Colonel William Prescott ordered, "Don't fire until you see the whites of their eyes!" When the British got close, the militia unleashed a barrage of fire. The British fell back and then charged again. Eventually, they forced the militia off the hill.

The redcoats had won the Battle of Bunker Hill, but at tremendous cost. More than 1,000 were killed or wounded, compared with some 400 militia casualties. "The loss we have sustained is greater than we can bear," wrote General Gage. The inexperienced colonial militia had held its own against the world's most powerful army.

▲ **SEQUENCE EVENTS** Describe the events that led to the Battle of Bunker Hill.

The Conflict Spreads

▼ **KEY QUESTION** Why were the British forced to leave Boston?

In their coffee houses, inns, and taverns, colonists discussed the deepening crisis. Most colonists still hoped for peace. Even some Patriot leaders still considered themselves loyal subjects of the king. They blamed Parliament for the terrible events taking place.

The Olive Branch Petition In July 1775, moderates in Congress drafted the Olive Branch Petition and sent it to London. This document asked the king to restore harmony between Britain and the colonies. Some members opposed the petition but signed it anyway as a last hope.

The king rejected the petition, however, and announced new measures to punish the colonies. He would use the British navy to block American ships from leaving their ports. He would send thousands of hired German soldiers to fight in America. "When once these rebels have felt a smart blow, they will submit," he declared.

The colonial forces were not going to back down, though. They thought they were equal to the British troops. George Washington knew otherwise. The British soldiers were professionals, while the colonial troops had little training and were poorly equipped. The Massachusetts militia barely had enough gunpowder to fight one battle.

Washington Arrives During the summer of 1775, Washington arrived at the militia camp near Boston. He immediately began to gather supplies and train the army. In the fall, Washington approved a bold plan. Continental Army troops would invade Quebec, in eastern Canada. They hoped to defeat British forces there and draw Canadians into the Patriot cause. One of the leaders of this expedition was Benedict Arnold. He was an officer who had played a role in the victory at Fort Ticonderoga.

After a grueling march across Maine, Arnold arrived at Quebec in November 1775. Under harsh winter conditions, the Americans launched their attack but failed. After several months, they limped home in defeat.

The British Retreat from Boston In Massachusetts, the Continental Army continued its siege of Boston. The British lay trapped in the town, which stood like an island protected by the surrounding waters of the bays. They gazed nervously across the bays to the opposite shores, where thousands of American forces waited on the hills.

Neither side was able or willing to break the standoff. However, help for Washington was on the way. Cannon were being hauled from Fort Ticonderoga. This was a difficult job, since there were no roads across the snow-covered mountains. It took soldiers, under the leadership of American General Henry Knox, two months to drag the 59 heavy weapons to Boston, where they arrived in January 1776.

Washington positioned these cannon on Dorchester Heights, overlooking Boston. The Americans, now in a position of power, threatened to bombard the city. General Howe, who was in charge of

(*below*) This statue, which stands in the Boston Public Garden, commemorates the day General Washington drove the British from the city.

the British forces, decided to withdraw his troops. On March 17, over 7,000 British soldiers departed Boston in more than 100 ships. Boston Patriots joyfully reclaimed their city. Although the British had damaged homes and destroyed possessions, Boston was still standing. The British would never return.

▲ **CAUSES AND EFFECTS** Explain how the British were forced to leave Boston.

Rebellion Becomes Revolution

▼ **KEY QUESTION** What ideas can be found in the Declaration of Independence?

As the British evacuated Boston, Americans debated the crisis. Most Americans hoped to avoid a final break with Britain. However, the publication of a pamphlet titled *Common Sense* helped convince many Americans that it was time to fight for independence.

***Common Sense* Changes Minds** *Common Sense* had been written by **Thomas Paine**, a recent immigrant from England. Paine was considered a political radical. He believed that all men, not just landowners, should have the right to vote. He also ridiculed the idea that kings ruled by the will of God. Calling George III "the Royal Brute," Paine argued that all monarchies were corrupt. He also disagreed with the economic arguments for remaining with Britain. "Our corn," he said, "will fetch its price in any market in Europe." He believed that America should follow its own destiny.

PRIMARY SOURCE

❝ Everything that is right or natural pleads for separation. The blood of the slain, the weeping voice of nature cries, " 'Tis time to part." Even the distance at which the Almighty had placed England and America is a strong and natural proof that the authority of the one over the other was never the design of heaven. ❞

—Thomas Paine, *Common Sense*

(*above*) political writer Thomas Paine (*below*) the pamphlet, *Common Sense*, that moved many colonists toward revolution

Common Sense was an instant success. Published in January, it sold more than 100,000 copies in three months. Americans were beginning to understand that it was time to fight for independence.

A Time for Decision The Continental Congress remained undecided. A majority of the delegates did not support independence. Even so, in May 1776, Congress adopted a resolution authorizing each of the 13 colonies to establish its own government.

On June 7, Richard Henry Lee of Virginia introduced a key resolution. It called the colonies "free and independent states" and declared that "all political connection between them and the state of Great Britain is . . . totally dissolved." Congress debated the resolution, but not all the delegates were ready to vote on it.

In the meantime, however, Congress appointed a committee to draft a

Declaration of Independence. The committee included Benjamin Franklin, John Adams, Roger Sherman, Robert Livingston, and **Thomas Jefferson**.

The group chose Jefferson to compose the Declaration. Two reasons for selecting Jefferson were that he was an excellent writer and that he came from Virginia. The members knew that no independence movement could succeed without Virginia's support.

Jefferson immediately went to work. In two weeks, he had prepared most of the Declaration. (See pages 184–188.) On July 2, 1776, Congress considered Lee's resolution again. Despite some opposition, the measure passed. The colonies now considered themselves independent from Great Britain.

COMPARING *Symbols of Freedom*

REVOLUTIONARY FLAGS

During the Revolution, Patriot militiamen created elaborate flags to represent their colony and military traditions. Often these flags were carried into battle.

This flag was carried to the Battle of Bunker Hill by Massachusetts militiamen in 1775. The Liberty Tree represented freedom in the colonies.

Regiments from South Carolina adorned their flag with a crescent. Another version had the word "Liberty" stitched in the crescent.

This flag was carried to Boston by Rhode Island militiamen in 1775.

This flag, created in 1775, was adorned with the British Union, as well as 13 red and white stripes.

The North Hampton County Militia adorned its flag with 13 white stars, a blue field, and 13 red and white stripes.

This was the flag of Gadsden, South Carolina's Continental Navy. The snake was a warning to those who would tread on liberty.

DONT TREAD ON ME

Activity

Create a Revolutionary Flag

Create a flag that might have been carried in the Revolution. Use symbols to represent your state or hometown.

CRITICAL THINKING Make Inferences Why did some Patriot flags include British symbols? What does that tell you about some colonists' desire for independence?

The Declaration is Adopted Two days later, on July 4, 1776, Congress adopted the document that proclaimed independence—the Declaration of Independence. John Hancock, the president of the Congress, was the first to sign the Declaration. According to tradition, he wrote in large letters and commented, "There, I guess King George will be able to read that." The core idea of the Declaration is based on the philosophy of John Locke. This idea is that people have natural and unalienable rights, or rights that government cannot take away. Jefferson stated this belief in what was to become the Declaration's best-known passage.

 CONNECT *to the Essential Question*

What drove the colonists to declare independence from Great Britain?

All regions and groups	Southern Colonies	New England and Middle Colonies	Backcountry
• feared that British troops might be used against colonists • suffered from tax increases (Stamp Act 1765) • were angered that the right to tax had been taken away from colonial assemblies (Stamp Act 1765) • suffered from duty on imports (Sugar Act 1764; Townshend Acts 1767)	• Planters were angry that the Proclamation of 1763 restricted them from speculating in land beyond the Appalachian Mountains.	• Merchants suffered from interference in colonial trade (Tea Act 1773). • New England merchants suffered from the Sugar Act of 1764, which raised duty on sugar • New Yorkers were angry they had to pay to house troops in New York (Quartering Act 1765)	• angered by Proclamation of 1763, which restricted movement west • Some Scots-Irish had never felt loyalty to Britain.

CRITICAL THINKING **Draw Conclusions** What issues united the colonists against Great Britian?

PRIMARY SOURCE

❝ We hold these truths to be self-evident, that all men are created equal, that they are endowed by their Creator with certain unalienable Rights, that among these are Life, Liberty, and the pursuit of Happiness. ❞

—Thomas Jefferson, The Declaration of Independence

If a government disregards these rights, Jefferson explained, it loses its right to govern. The people then have the right to abolish that government, by force if necessary. They can form a new government that will protect their rights. When Jefferson spoke of "the people," however, he meant only free, white, landowning men. Women, the enslaved, and those without property were left out of the Declaration.

The Declaration also explained the reasons for breaking with Britain. It declared the colonies to be free and independent states. This was a very serious action—treason from the British point of view—and the delegates knew it. John Hancock urged the delegates to stand together in mutual defense. He realized that if the war were lost, they might all be hanged.

The Declaration closed with this pledge: "And for the support of this Declaration, with a firm reliance on the protection of divine Providence, we mutually pledge to each other our Lives, our Fortunes, and our sacred Honor."

Americans had declared independence. Now they had to win their freedom on the battlefield.

 MAIN IDEAS & DETAILS Explain what ideas can be found in the Declaration of Independence.

Michigan Grade Level Content Expectations _Review_

🖱 **ONLINE QUIZ**
For test practice, go to
Interactive Review @ ClassZone.com

TERMS & NAMES

1. Explain the importance of
- Ethan Allen
- Thomas Jefferson
- Continental Army
- Thomas Paine
- Second Continental Congress
- Declaration of Independence

USING YOUR READING NOTES

2. Sequence Events Complete the diagram that you started at the beginning of this section.

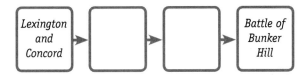

KEY IDEAS

3. Make Inferences What forced the British to leave Boston?

4. Analyze Primary Sources What does the Declaration of Independence say about government and the rights of the people?

CRITICAL THINKING

5. Draw Conclusions Why did it take the colonists so long to declare independence?

6. Make Inferences Why do you think _Common Sense_ was so popular?

7. Sequence Events Why do you think militiamen surrounded the British in Boston?

8. **Math** **Graph** Research the population statistics of colonial Boston. Make a graph to show how the population of Boston changed during the Revolution.

The Road to Revolution **183**

The Declaration of Independence

Setting the Stage On July 4, 1776, the Second Continental Congress adopted what became one of America's most cherished documents. Written by Thomas Jefferson, the Declaration of Independence voiced the reasons for separating from Britain and provided the principles of government upon which the United States would be built.

Preamble

When in the Course of human events, it becomes necessary for one people to dissolve the political bands which have connected them with another, and to assume among the powers of the earth, the separate and equal station to which the Laws of Nature and of Nature's God entitle them, a decent respect to the opinions of mankind requires that they should declare the causes which impel them to the separation.

The Right of the People to Control Their Government

We hold these truths to be self-evident, that all men are created equal, that they are **endowed**[1] by their Creator with certain **unalienable**[2] Rights, that among these are Life, Liberty and the pursuit of Happiness; that, to secure these rights, Governments are instituted among Men, deriving their just powers from the consent of the governed; that whenever any Form of Government becomes destructive of these ends, it is the Right of the People to alter or to abolish it, and to institute new Government, laying its foundation on such principles and organizing its powers in such form, as to them shall seem most likely to effect their Safety and Happiness. Prudence, indeed, will dictate that Governments long established should not

Rights of the People

The ideas in this passage reflect the views of John Locke. Locke was an English philosopher who believed that the natural rights of individuals came from God, but that a government's power comes from the consent of the governed. This belief is the foundation of modern democracy.

1. In what way can American voters bring about changes in their government?

---

1. endowed: provided.   **2. unalienable:** unable to be taken away.

be changed for light and transient causes; and accordingly all experience hath shewn that mankind are more disposed to suffer, while evils are sufferable, than to right themselves by abolishing the forms to which they are accustomed. But when a long train of abuses and **usurpations**,[3] pursuing invariably the same Object, evinces a design to reduce them under absolute **Despotism**,[4] it is their right, it is their duty, to throw off such Government, and to provide new Guards for their future security.

Such has been the patient sufferance of these Colonies; and such is now the necessity which constrains them to alter their former Systems of Government. The history of the present King of Great Britain is a history of repeated injuries and usurpations, all having in direct object the establishment of an absolute Tyranny over these States. To prove this, let facts be submitted to a **candid**[5] world.

Tyrannical Acts of the British King

He has refused his Assent to Laws, the most wholesome and necessary for the public good.

He has forbidden his Governors to pass Laws of immediate and pressing importance, unless suspended in their operation till his assent should be obtained; and, when so suspended, he has utterly neglected to attend to them.

He has refused to pass other Laws for the accommodation of large districts of people, unless those people would **relinquish**[6] the right of Representation in the Legislature, a right inestimable to them, and formidable to tyrants only.

He has called together legislative bodies at places unusual, uncomfortable, and distant from the depository of their public Records, for the sole purpose of fatiguing them into compliance with his measures.

He has dissolved Representative Houses repeatedly, for opposing with manly firmness his invasions on the rights of the people.

He has refused for a long time, after such dissolutions, to cause others to be elected; whereby the Legislative powers, incapable of Annihilation, have returned to the people at large for their exercise; the State remaining in the mean time exposed to all the dangers of invasions from without, and **convulsions**[7] within.

He has endeavoured to prevent the population of these States; for that purpose obstructing the Laws for **Naturalization**[8] of Foreigners;

Grievances Against Britain

The list contains 27 offenses by the British king and others against the colonies. It helps explain why it became necessary to seek independence.

2. Which offense do you think was the worst? Why?

Loss of Representative Government

One of the Intolerable Acts of 1774 stripped the Massachusetts Legislature of many powers and gave them to the colony's British governor.

3. Why was this action so "intolerable"?

---

3. usurpations: unjust seizures of power.

4. Despotism: rule by a tyrant with absolute power.

5. candid: fair, impartial.

6. relinquish: give up.

7. convulsions: violent disturbances.

8. Naturalization: process of becoming a citizen.

refusing to pass others to encourage their migration hither, and raising the conditions of new Appropriations of Lands.

He has obstructed the Administration of Justice, by refusing his Assent to Laws for establishing Judiciary powers.

He has made Judges dependent on his Will alone, for the **tenure**[9] of their offices, and the amount and payment of their salaries.

He has erected a multitude of New Offices, and sent hither swarms of Officers to harass our people and eat out their **substance**.[10]

He has kept among us, in times of peace, Standing Armies, without the Consent of our legislatures.

He has affected to render the Military independent of and superior to the Civil power. He has combined with others to subject us to a jurisdiction foreign to our constitution and unacknowledged by our laws; giving his Assent to their Acts of pretended Legislation:

For **quartering**[11] large bodies of armed troops among us;

For protecting them, by a mock Trial, from punishment for any Murders which they should commit on the Inhabitants of these States;

For cutting off our Trade with all parts of the world;

For imposing Taxes on us without our Consent;

For depriving us, in many cases, of the benefits of Trial by Jury;

For transporting us beyond Seas to be tried for pretended offenses;

For abolishing the free System of English Laws in a neighboring Province, establishing therein an **Arbitrary**[12] government, and enlarging its Boundaries so as to render it at once an example and fit instrument for introducing the same absolute rule into these Colonies;

For taking away our Charters, abolishing our most valuable laws, and altering fundamentally the Forms of our Governments;

For suspending our own Legislatures, and declaring themselves invested with power to legislate for us in all cases whatsoever.

He has **abdicated**[13] Government here, by declaring us out of his Protection and waging War against us.

He has plundered our seas, ravaged our Coasts, burnt our towns, and destroyed the lives of our people.

He is at this time transporting large Armies of **foreign Mercenaries**[14] to compleat the works of death, desolation, and tyranny, already begun

Quartering Troops without Consent

The Quartering Act of 1765 required colonists to provide housing and supplies for British troops in America.

4. Why did colonists object to this act?

Taxation without Representation

The colonists believed in the long-standing British tradition that Parliament could tax only those citizens it represented—and the colonists claimed to have no representation in Parliament.

5. How do persons today give consent to taxation?

---

9. **tenure:** term.
10. **eat out their substance:** drain their resources.
11. **quartering:** housing or giving lodging to.
12. **Arbitrary:** not limited by law.
13. **abdicated:** given up.
14. **foreign Mercenaries:** professional soldiers hired to serve in a foreign army.

with circumstances of Cruelty & **perfidy**[15] scarcely paralleled in the most barbarous ages, and totally unworthy the Head of a civilized nation.

He has constrained our fellow Citizens, taken Captive on the high Seas, to bear Arms against their Country, to become the executioners of their friends and Brethren, or to fall themselves by their Hands.

He has excited domestic **insurrections**[16] amongst us, and has endeavoured to bring on the inhabitants of our frontiers the merciless Indian Savages, whose known rule of warfare is an undistinguished destruction of all ages, sexes and conditions.

Efforts of the Colonies to Avoid Separation

In every stage of these Oppressions We have **Petitioned for Redress**[17] in the most humble terms; Our repeated Petitions have been answered only by repeated injury. A Prince, whose character is thus marked by every act which may define a Tyrant, is unfit to be the ruler of a free people.

Nor have We been wanting in attentions to our British brethren. We have warned them from time to time of attempts by their legislature to extend an unwarrantable jurisdiction over us. We have reminded them of the circumstances of our emigration and settlement here. We have appealed to their native justice and **magnanimity,**[18] and we have conjured them by the ties of our common kindred, to disavow these usurpations, which would inevitably interrupt our connections and correspondence. They too have been deaf to the voice of justice and of **consanguinity.**[19] We must, therefore, **acquiesce**[20] in the necessity, which denounces our Separation, and hold them, as we hold the rest of mankind, Enemies in War, in Peace Friends.

The Colonies Are Declared Free and Independent

We, therefore, the Representatives of the United States of America, in General Congress, Assembled, appealing to the Supreme Judge of the world for the **rectitude**[21] of our intentions, do, in the name, and by the Authority of the good People of these Colonies solemnly publish and declare, That these United Colonies are, and of Right ought to be, Free and Independent States; that they are Absolved from all Allegiance to the British Crown, and that all political connection between them and

Petitioning the King

The colonists sent many petitions to King George III. In the Olive Branch Petition of 1775, the colonists expressed their desire to achieve "a happy and permanent reconciliation." The king rejected the petition.

6. Why did the colonists at first attempt to solve the dispute and remain loyal?

Powers of an Independent Government

The colonists identified the ability to wage war and agree to peace; to make alliances with other nations; and to set up an economic system as powers of a free and independent government.

7. What other powers are held by an independent government?

---

15. **perfidy:** dishonesty, disloyalty.

16. **domestic insurrections:** rebellions at home.

17. **Petitioned for Redress:** asked for the correction of wrongs.

18. **magnanimity:** generosity, forgiveness.

19. **consanguinity:** relationship by a common ancestor; close connection.

20. **acquiesce:** accept without protest.

21. **rectitude:** moral uprightness.

the State of Great Britain is, and ought to be, totally dissolved; and that as Free and Independent States, they have full Power to levy War, conclude Peace, contract Alliances, establish Commerce, and do all other Acts and Things which Independent States may of right do.

And for the support of this Declaration, with a firm reliance on the protection of divine Providence, we mutually pledge to each other our Lives, our Fortunes, and our sacred Honor. [Signed by]

John Hancock *President, from Massachusetts*

[**Georgia**] Button Gwinnett; Lyman Hall; George Walton

[**Rhode Island**] Stephen Hopkins; William Ellery

[**Connecticut**] Roger Sherman; Samuel Huntington; William Williams; Oliver Wolcott

[**North Carolina**] William Hooper; Joseph Hewes; John Penn

[**South Carolina**] Edward Rutledge; Thomas Heyward, Jr.; Thomas Lynch, Jr.; Arthur Middleton

[**Maryland**] Samuel Chase; William Paca; Thomas Stone; Charles Carroll

[**Virginia**] George Wythe; Richard Henry Lee; Thomas Jefferson; Benjamin Harrison; Thomas Nelson, Jr.; Francis Lightfoot Lee; Carter Braxton

[**Pennsylvania**] Robert Morris; Benjamin Rush; Benjamin Franklin; John Morton; George Clymer; James Smith; George Taylor; James Wilson; George Ross

[**Delaware**] Caesar Rodney; George Read; Thomas McKean

[**New York**] William Floyd; Philip Livingston;Francis Lewis; Lewis Morris

[**New Jersey**] Richard Stockton; John Witherspoon; Francis Hopkinson; John Hart; Abraham Clark

[**New Hampshire**] Josiah Bartlett; William Whipple; Matthew Thornton

[**Massachusetts**] Samuel Adams; John Adams; Robert Treat Paine; Elbridge Gerry

---

Declaration Signers

The Declaration was signed by 56 representatives from the 13 original states.

8. Which signers do you recognize? Write one line about each of those signers.

DOCUMENT–BASED QUESTIONS

Short Answer

1. What is the purpose of the Declaration of Independence as stated in the Preamble?

2. What are the five main parts of the Declaration?

3. What are three rights that all people have?

Extended Answer

4. Why did the colonies feel that they had to declare their independence?

Chapter Summary

1 Key Idea
Colonists saw British efforts to increase control over the colonies as violations of their rights.

2 Key Idea
Many colonists organized to oppose British policies.

3 Key Idea
The tensions between Britain and the colonies led to the outbreak of the Revolutionary War.

4 Key Idea
As fighting continued, Americans decided to declare their independence from Britain.

For detailed Review and Study Notes go to **Interactive Review** @ ClassZone.com

Name Game

Use the Terms & Names list to complete each sentence online or on your own paper.

1. _____ wrote the Declaration of Independence.
   Thomas Jefferson

2. The _____ was a secret society established to oppose British policy.

3. _____ rode into the countryside to warn of British troop movement.

4. The British used _____ to enter and search the colonists' homes.

5. The African-American sailor who died at the Boston Massacre was _____.

6. During the Revolutionary War, George Washington commanded the _____.

7. The _____ placed a tax on molasses.

8. Parliament passed the _____ in 1767 to tighten control on the colonies.

9. At the _____ in Philadelphia, delegates voted to ban all trade with Britain.

10. The _____ required colonists to house and feed British soldiers.

A. Quartering Act
B. Continental Army
C. First Continental Congress
D. Sons of Liberty
E. Townshend Acts
F. Paul Revere
G. Sugar Act
H. Thomas Jefferson
I. Crispus Attucks
J. Philadelphia
K. Boston Tea Party
L. Writs of Assistance

Activities

FLIPCARD

Use the online flipcards to quiz yourself on the terms and names introduced in this chapter.

He was a political radical and author of *Common Sense*

ANSWER:
Thomas Paine

CROSSWORD PUZZLE

Complete the online crossword puzzle to show what you know about the American Revolution.

ACROSS
1. _____ could fight at a minute's warning.

VOCABULARY

Explain the significance of each of the following

1. King George III
2. Sugar Act
3. Boston Tea Party
4. Townshend Acts
5. Boston Massacre
6. First Continental Congress
7. Minutemen
8. Intolerable Acts
9. Stamp Act
10. Lexington and Concord
11. Thomas Jefferson
12. Declaration of Independence

Explain how the terms and names in each group are related.

13. Sons of Liberty, King George III, Daughters of Liberty
14. First Continental Congress, committees of correspondence, Boston Massacre
15. Sugar Act, Boston Tea Party, Stamp Act
16. Thomas Paine, Patrick Henry, Samuel Adams

KEY IDEAS

1 Tighter British Control (pages 156–159)

17. How did Parliament's new laws reflect a change in British treatment of the colonies?
18. How did the colonists get the Stamp Act repealed?

2 Colonial Resistance Grows (pages 160–166)

19. In what ways did the Townshend Acts attack colonists' rights and freedoms?
20. How did Americans protest the Townshend Acts?
21. Why did protests against the Tea Act take place in the port cities?

3 The Road to Lexington and Concord (pages 168–174)

22. In what ways were the Intolerable Acts harsher than Parliament's previous laws?
23. What did the British troops hope to achieve in Lexington and Concord?

4 Declaring Independence (pages 176–183)

24. How did the Americans force the British to leave Boston?

25. What does the Declaration of Independence say about the relationship between government and the people?

CRITICAL THINKING

26. **Make Inferences** Why were the boycotts of British products so effective?

27. **Summarize** How did protests against British policies encourage women to become politically active?

28. **Make Generalizations** How did the committees of correspondence help unite the colonies?

29. **Make Inferences** Why were the colonists storing weapons in Concord?

30. **Categorize** Fill in the chart below to show how Parliament's new laws threatened the colonists economically and politically.

Economic Threat	Threat to Political Traditions

31. **Causes and Effects** How did ordinary people help change British government policies?

32. **Connect Geography and History** Study this map of Boston during the Battle of Bunker Hill. Why were the British so alarmed when the Americans occupied the hills above Charlestown?

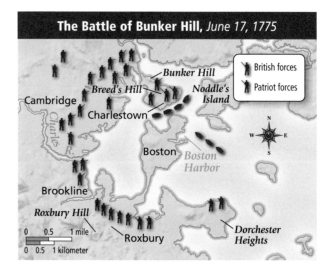

The Battle of Bunker Hill, *June 17, 1775*

Bunker Hill
Breed's Hill
Noddle's Island
Cambridge
Charlestown
Boston
Boston Harbor
Brookline
Roxbury Hill
Roxbury
Dorchester Heights

British forces
Patriot forces

Charles R.

0 0.5 1 mile
0 0.5 1 kilometer

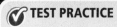 **TEST PRACTICE**

• **Online Test Practice @ ClassZone.com**
• Use the **MEAP Strategies & Practice,** pages S1-S27, at the front of this book

MULTIPLE CHOICE

Use the artifact below and your knowledge of U.S. history to answer question 1.

ARTIFACT

1 Examine this teapot that was created to protest the Stamp Act. Why did colonists use this ordinary household item to carry a political message?

   A to openly demonstrate their support of the cause

   B to remind themselves which items were taxed

   C to offend British soldiers and government officials

   D to declare independence

Use the quotation and your knowledge of U.S. history to answer question 2.

PRIMARY SOURCE

❝ It is inseparably essential to the freedom of a people, and the undoubted rights of Englishmen, that no taxes should be imposed on them, but with their own consent, given personally, or by their representatives. ❞

—from The Declaration of Rights of the Stamp Act Congress

2 According to this declaration, what is essential to freedom?

   A No taxes should be imposed.

   B Taxes need the consent of the governed.

   C America should be independent.

   D Englishmen should have rights.

YOU BE THE HISTORIAN

33. **Causes and Effects** What were the unexpected consequences of Britain's victory in the French and Indian War?

34. **Problems and Solutions** Was the American Revolution a conflict that could have been avoided? Explain your answer.

35. **Make Inferences** What was so unusual about women becoming politically involved in the 1760s and 1770s?

36. **Make Generalizations** How did British policies plant the seeds of a future American national government?

37. **Draw Conclusions** How did the political protests of the 1760s and 1770s help prepare the American people for the Revolution?

38. **Analyze Point of View** Do you think that any of Parliament's new laws were justified? Explain your answer.

 Answer the

ESSENTIAL QUESTION

What drove the colonists to declare independence from Great Britain?

Written Response Write a four-paragraph response to the Essential Question. Be sure to consider the key ideas of each section as well as the most significant facts that helped determine your answer. Use the Response Rubric below to guide your thinking and writing.

Response Rubric
A strong response will

• discuss why Parliament increased its control and taxation of the colonists

• explain how Parliament's actions threatened the economy and democratic political traditions of the colonies

• describe how the colonists reacted to Parliament's increased control.

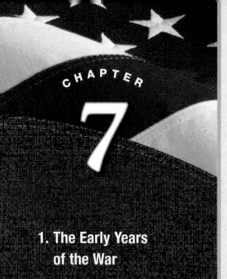

1. The Early Years
   of the War

2. The War Expands

3. The Path to Victory

4. The Legacy
   of the War

The American Revolution

1775–1783

 ESSENTIAL QUESTION

How was it possible that American Patriots gained their independence from the powerful British Empire?

CONNECT ↻ **Geography & History**

How might the geography of the United States have affected the course of the war?

Think about:

1. how **Saratoga** lies in the Hudson River valley, a major gap through the Appalachian Mountains

2. how **Yorktown** stands on the Chesapeake Bay, a wide body of water that allowed ships access to ports and plantations

3. the distance between Britain and America, roughly 3,400 miles

Travel time:
4 weeks to 4 months

Battle of Lexington

1775

Revolution begins at **Lexington** and **Concord.**

1776 Declaration of Independence

After their victory at the **Battle of Long Island**, the British make New York their base of operations.

1777 The American victory at **Saratoga** convinces foreign powers that America can win.

Effect France enters the war on the American side.

1778 The British capture **Savannah**, Georgia—their first major victory in their new Southern campaign.

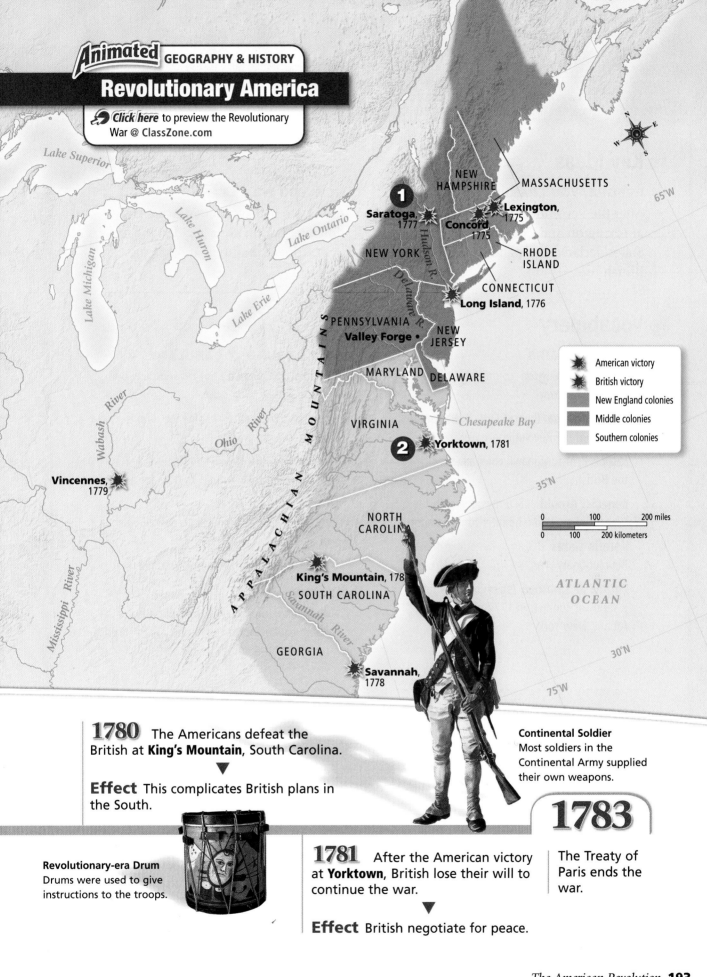

Animated GEOGRAPHY & HISTORY

Revolutionary America

Click here to preview the Revolutionary
War @ ClassZone.com

NEW HAMPSHIRE
MASSACHUSETTS

1

Saratoga, 1777
Lexington, 1775
Concord 1775

NEW YORK
RHODE ISLAND
CONNECTICUT

Hudson R.
Delaware R.

Long Island, 1776

PENNSYLVANIA
Valley Forge •
NEW JERSEY

MARYLAND
DELAWARE

VIRGINIA
Chesapeake Bay

2 **Yorktown**, 1781

Vincennes, 1779

Wabash River
Ohio River

NORTH CAROLINA

Mississippi River

A P P A L A C H I A N   M O U N T A I N S

King's Mountain, 178

SOUTH CAROLINA
Savannah River

GEORGIA
Savannah, 1778

Lake Superior
Lake Michigan
Lake Huron
Lake Erie
Lake Ontario

ATLANTIC OCEAN

65°W
35°N
30°N
75°W

Legend:
- ✸ American victory
- ✸ British victory
- New England colonies
- Middle colonies
- Southern colonies

0   100   200 miles
0   100   200 kilometers

1780 The Americans defeat the
British at **King's Mountain**, South Carolina.

▼

Effect This complicates British plans in
the South.

Revolutionary-era Drum
Drums were used to give
instructions to the troops.

1781 After the American victory
at **Yorktown**, British lose their will to
continue the war.

▼

Effect British negotiate for peace.

Continental Soldier
Most soldiers in the
Continental Army supplied
their own weapons.

1783

The Treaty of
Paris ends the
war.

▶ Key Ideas

BEFORE, YOU LEARNED

After the Revolutionary War broke out at Lexington and Concord, the United States declared independence from British rule.

NOW YOU WILL LEARN

Although the Continental Army had difficulty fighting in a divided America, the Patriots triumphed at Saratoga.

▶ Vocabulary

TERMS & NAMES

George Washington commander of the Continental Army

John Burgoyne (buhr•GOIN) British army general in the Revolutionary War

Joseph Brant Mohawk chief allied with the British

Benedict Arnold U.S. army general in the Revolutionary War who later turned traitor

Horatio Gates U.S. army general in the Revolutionary War

Battles of Saratoga (sair•uh•TOH•guh) a series of conflicts in 1777 near Albany, New York

BACKGROUND VOCABULARY

neutral (NEW•truhl) not favoring any one side

pacifist (PAS•uh•fist) someone who is opposed to all war

mercenary (MUR•suh•NAIR•ee) a professional soldier hired to fight for a foreign country

strategy (STRA•tuh•jee) an overall plan of action

rendezvous (RAHN•day•voo) a meeting

REVIEW

guerrillas (guh•RIL•uhz) small bands of fighters who weaken the enemy with surprise raids and hit-and-run attacks

▶ Reading Strategy

Re-create the diagram shown at right. As you read and respond to the **KEY QUESTIONS**, use the diagram to note important events and their effects. Add boxes or start a new diagram as needed.

 See Skillbuilder Handbook, page R7.

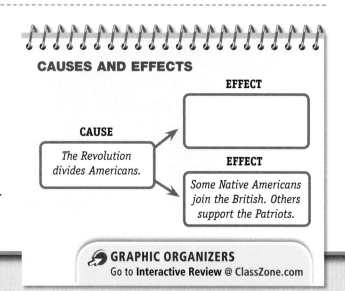

CAUSES AND EFFECTS

CAUSE

The Revolution divides Americans.

EFFECT

EFFECT

Some Native Americans join the British. Others support the Patriots.

GRAPHIC ORGANIZERS
Go to **Interactive Review** @ ClassZone.com

SECTION 1

The Early Years of the War

8 – U6.2.1 United States History Investigation Topic and Issue Analysis, Past and Present – Use historical perspectives to analyze issues in the United States from the past and the present; conduct research on a historical issue or topic, identify a connection to a contemporary issue, and present findings (e.g., oral, visual, video, or electronic presentation, persuasive essay, or research paper); include causes and consequences of the historical action and predict possible consequences of the contemporary action.

One American's Story

When John Singleton Copley painted this portrait of his own Loyalist family, the Copleys had only recently escaped the violence of the Revolution. Copley's father-in-law (shown seated) lost his investments during the Boston Tea Party. Copley's wife (in the blue dress) lost her infant son during the siege of Boston. In the background stands Copley himself—an American who became one of the greatest painters in the British Empire.

Copley was born and raised in Boston. Before the war, he left Boston to study overseas. When he received news of the fighting in America, he wrote to his half-brother.

The Copley Family, by John Singleton Copley

PRIMARY SOURCE

❝ Could anything be more fortunate than the time of my leaving Boston? Poor America. I hope for the best, but I fear the worst. Yet certain I am she will finally emerge from her present calamity and become a mighty empire. ❞

—John Singleton Copley, letter to Henry Pelham

Copley worried about his family as he traveled through Europe. Eventually, he found them safe in London. They had arrived with the first wave of Loyalist refugees. Copley painted this portrait after their reunion.

Americans Divided

🔻 **KEY QUESTION** In what ways was the Revolution like a civil war?

The issue of separating from Britain divided American society. Historians estimate that 20 to 30 percent of Americans were Loyalists, 40 to 45 percent were Patriots, and the rest were **neutral**, or not favoring any one side.

Americans Choose Sides The conflict divided Americans along social, religious, and ethnic lines. New England and Virginia had many Patriots. Loyalists were numerous in cities, New York State, and the South. Judges, councilors, and governors tended to be Loyalists. Many Loyalists were clergy or members of the Church of England. Some Quakers were active Loyalists, although many were **pacifists**—people opposed to all war. The Patriots drew support from Congregationalists, Presbyterians, and Baptists.

Most Southern states did not allow African Americans to enlist. They feared that armed African Americans might lead slave revolts. In contrast, the British offered enslaved persons their freedom if they joined British forces. Many slaves ran away to fight for the British. In the North, however, about 5,000 African Americans served in the Continental Army.

The American Revolution was the largest Indian war in American history. All Native American nations east of the Mississippi were caught up in the fighting. Some Native Americans, like the Mohawks, joined the British because they feared Americans would take Native American land. Others, who lived within areas settled by the colonists, sided with the Americans.

▲ **CAUSES AND EFFECTS** Explain how the Revolution caused divisions among the population.

Connecting History

Dissent and Rebellion
The oldest English settlements were in New England and Virginia. They both had a tradition of dissent and rebellion. *See Chapter 3, p. 72, Chapter 4, p. 104.*

🔊 ONLINE PRIMARY SOURCE

Hear the debate at the **Research & Writing Center** @ ClassZone.com

---

COMPARING Perspectives

Patriots and Loyalists (or "Tories") viewed the political situation from radically different perspectives. These were some of the arguments heard as debate gave way to bloodshed.

🔊 Patriots Speak

❝ [Shall] a body of men in Great Britain, who . . . know nothing of us . . . invest themselves with a power to command our lives and properties . . . ?
—*a lady from Philadelphia*

If our Trade be taxed, why not our Lands, or Produce . . . in short, everything we possess? They tax us without having legal representation. ❞
—*Samuel Adams*

🔊 Loyalists Speak

❝ They call me a brainless Tory; but tell me, which is better—to be ruled by one tyrant three thousand miles away, or by three thousand tyrants not one mile away?
—*Mather Byles*

Whenever a . . . people . . . prevent the execution of laws, or destroy the property of individuals . . . there is an end of all order and government. . . ❞
—*Massachusetts Gazette, and Boston News-Letter*

CRITICAL THINKING

1. **Analyze Primary Sources** What were the Loyalists' greatest fears? What angered the Patriots most?

2. **Analyze Point of View** What would you have said to oppose each argument listed above?

Preparing for War

▼ **KEY QUESTION** Why did both America and Britain have trouble raising an army?

In June 1775, Congress named **George Washington** commander of the Continental Army. This army faced many problems.

Problems of the Army At first, this new national army was formed from state militias, made up of untrained and undisciplined volunteers. The militia were part-time, emergency fighters who were not prepared for the hardship of a long war.

Washington's main goal was to keep the Revolution alive. To do so, he needed to keep an army in the field, win some battles—no matter how small—and avoid a crushing defeat. He knew he could not win a major battle until he had a large, well-trained army.

At the start of the war, Congress asked men to enlist only for one year. When the soldiers' time was up, they went home. As a result, Washington's army never numbered more than 17,000 men. In the early years of the war, Washington always worried about losing men whose enlistments had expired.

Congress's inability to supply the army also frustrated Washington. The soldiers lacked blankets, shoes, food, and even guns and ammunition.

Fortunately, many women helped the army. George Washington's wife Martha and other wives followed their husbands to camp. The women cooked, did laundry, and nursed sick or wounded soldiers. Some women even disguised themselves to help fight. Twenty-two-year-old Deborah Sampson dressed as a man, enlisted, and fought in several battles. But many women who never ventured near a battlefield also helped the nation by managing farms and businesses while their husbands were away fighting. In the days when women had few civil rights and freedoms, the war brought them greater responsibilities.

History Makers

George Washington   1732–1799

When Washington saw the army he was asked to lead, he was shocked by its disunity. Soldiers shared a common enemy but had no sense of national unity. Officers from different regions refused to co-operate with each other. Troops would only obey officers from their own province. Angrily, Washington wrote, "Could I have foreseen what I have experienced, and am likely to experience, no consideration upon earth would have induced me to accept this command." But Washington was determined to hold the army together. His efforts helped create a model of unity for the nation.

COMPARING *Leaders*

As you read through the chapter, look for other examples of Washington's leadership. Compare his leadership qualities to those of British generals described in this chapter.

🔊 **ONLINE BIOGRAPHY** For more on the life of George Washington, go to the **Research & Writing Center** @ ClassZone.com

Britain Prepares Many British viewed the Americans as disorganized, inexperienced rebels who would be easily defeated. In contrast to Washington's troops, the British army was experienced and professional. But the British military faced problems of its own. For personal and political reasons, many British officers refused to fight the Americans. Many British people were not enthusiastic about the war, so the king had trouble recruiting soldiers in

Britain. In addition, British soldiers signed up for life—which discouraged enlistment. Because of these problems, Britain had to hire mercenaries. A **mercenary** is a professional soldier hired to fight for a foreign country. The British mercenaries were called "Hessians" (HEH•shunz) because many came from the German region of Hesse.

▲ **CAUSES AND EFFECTS** Describe why each side had trouble raising an army.

War in the Middle States

▼ **KEY QUESTION** How did Washington reverse a series of American defeats?

As Chapter 6 explains, Washington had forced the British to retreat from Boston in March 1776. He then hurried his army to New York City, where he expected the British to go next. One British goal was to occupy coastal cities so that their navy could land troops and supplies. From these bases on the coast, they could then launch their military campaigns.

Patriot Retreat Washington's hunch was correct. In July 1776, Britain's General William Howe arrived in New York with a large army. Then in August, more soldiers arrived, including about 9,000 Hessian mercenaries. At the Battle of Long Island the Americans were defeated.

For several months, the British and American armies fought to control New York. Finally, the British forced Washington to retreat through New Jersey. (See map below.) By December, when the American army crossed the Delaware River into Pennsylvania, it was in terrible condition.

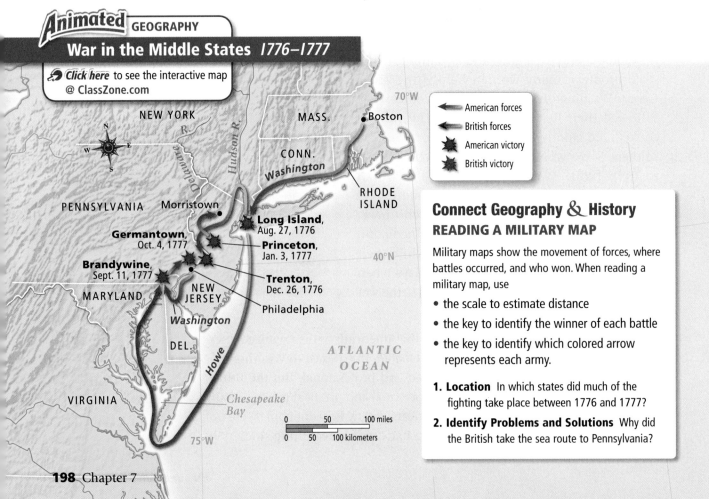

Animated GEOGRAPHY

War in the Middle States 1776–1777

↪ *Click here* to see the interactive map @ ClassZone.com

Legend:
- ← American forces
- ← British forces
- ★ American victory
- ★ British victory

Long Island, Aug. 27, 1776
Germantown, Oct. 4, 1777
Princeton, Jan. 3, 1777
Brandywine, Sept. 11, 1777
Trenton, Dec. 26, 1776
Philadelphia
Morristown
Boston

NEW YORK
MASS.
CONN.
RHODE ISLAND
PENNSYLVANIA
MARYLAND
NEW JERSEY
DEL.
VIRGINIA
Chesapeake Bay
ATLANTIC OCEAN
Hudson R.
Delaware R.
Washington
Howe

0 50 100 miles
0 50 100 kilometers

Connect Geography & History
READING A MILITARY MAP

Military maps show the movement of forces, where battles occurred, and who won. When reading a military map, use

- the scale to estimate distance
- the key to identify the winner of each battle
- the key to identify which colored arrow represents each army.

1. **Location** In which states did much of the fighting take place between 1776 and 1777?

2. **Identify Problems and Solutions** Why did the British take the sea route to Pennsylvania?

Political writer Thomas Paine witnessed the low spirits of the soldiers during the retreat. To urge Americans to keep fighting, Paine published the first in a series of pamphlets he called *The American Crisis.*

PRIMARY SOURCE

" These are the times that try men's souls. The summer soldier and the sunshine patriot will, in this crisis, shrink from the service of their country; but he that stands it now, deserves the love and thanks of man and woman. "

—Thomas Paine, *The American Crisis*

Washington needed something to encourage his weary men. He also knew that he must attack the British quickly because most of his soldiers would leave once their enlistments ended on December 31.

Victory at Trenton Late on December 25, 1776, Washington's troops rowed across the icy Delaware River to New Jersey. From there, they marched in bitter, early-morning cold to Trenton (see map on page 198) to surprise the Hessians, some of whom were sleeping after their Christmas celebration. The Americans captured or killed more than 900 Hessians and gained needed supplies. Washington's army won another victory at Princeton eight days later before setting up winter camp at Morristown, New Jersey. These victories proved that the American general was better than many had thought. The American army began to attract new recruits.

A Hessian mercenary

🔺 **SUMMARIZE** Explain how Washington reversed a series of defeats.

Britain's Northern Strategy

🔻 **KEY QUESTION** What was Britain's northern strategy?

Meanwhile, the British were pursuing a **strategy**—an overall plan of action— to seize the Hudson River valley. They believed that New England was the source of the rebellion. If they controlled the Hudson River valley, they could cut off New England from the other states. The strategy called for three armies to meet at Albany, New York.

- General **John Burgoyne** would lead a force south from Canada.
- Lt Colonel Barry St. Leger would come down the Mohawk valley.
- General Howe would follow the Hudson north from New York City.

Burgoyne left Canada in June 1777 with an army of British, Hessians, and Iroquois. In July, they captured Fort Ticonderoga and continued south. (See map on page 200.)

Burgoyne's Slow March Called "Gentleman Johnny" by his soldiers, Burgoyne threw elaborate parties to celebrate victories. But his mood changed as he marched deeper into hostile territory. Not only was the countryside filled with rebel sympathizers, but the forests were swarming with militia from New York and New England. The militia cut down trees to slow Burgoyne's progress. They burned crops and drove off cattle, leaving no food

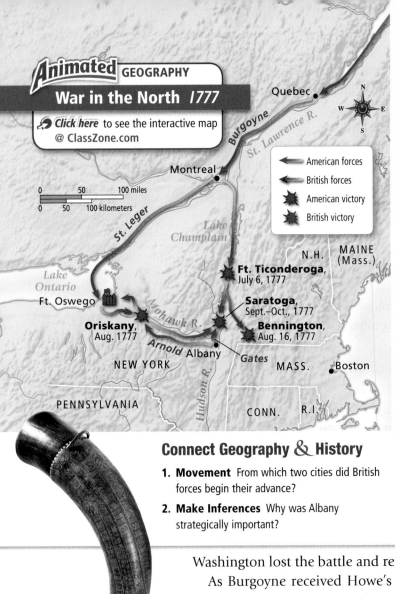

Animated GEOGRAPHY

War in the North 1777

Click here to see the interactive map @ ClassZone.com

Quebec

Montreal

Burgoyne

St. Lawrence R.

St. Leger

0   50   100 miles
0   50   100 kilometers

Lake Champlain

Lake Ontario

Ft. Oswego

Oriskany,
Aug. 1777

Ft. Ticonderoga,
July 6, 1777

Saratoga,
Sept.–Oct., 1777

Bennington,
Aug. 16, 1777

Mohawk R.

Arnold   Albany

Gates

Hudson R.

N.H.   MAINE
(Mass.)

NEW YORK

MASS.

Boston

PENNSYLVANIA

CONN.   R.I.

American forces
British forces
American victory
British victory

Connect Geography & History

1. **Movement** From which two cities did British forces begin their advance?

2. **Make Inferences** Why was Albany strategically important?

Powder Horn
Revolutionary-era soldiers used horns like this to carry gunpowder.
Why was horn a good material in which to store gunpowder?

for the British. Burgoyne realized that the countryside was rising up against him. It was a lesson that other British generals would soon learn: they were not simply fighting an enemy army, they were fighting an entire people.

Britain's Strategy Unravels Burgoyne still looked forward to the **rendezvous**, or meeting, with St. Leger and Howe in Albany. But on August 4, Burgoyne received a message that Howe would not be coming north; instead, he had decided to try to capture Philadelphia—where the Continental Congress met. "Success be ever with you," wrote Howe. Yet Burgoyne needed Howe's soldiers, not his good wishes.

When Washington heard that Howe was heading south, he rushed to protect Philadelphia. However, in September 1777, Howe defeated Washington at Brandywine. (See map on page 198.) Howe then occupied Philadelphia. In October, Washington attacked Howe at Germantown. Again, Washington lost the battle and retreated to winter camp.

As Burgoyne received Howe's message, St. Leger faced his own obstacle in reaching Albany. In the summer of 1777, he was trying to defeat a small American force at Fort Stanwix, near Oriskany in the Mohawk River valley of New York. St. Leger's forces included Iroquois led by Mohawk chief **Joseph Brant**, also called Thayendanegea (thi•ehn•DAH•nah•gee•ah). Brant had been promised that the British would protect Iroquois land.

During August 1777, American general **Benedict Arnold** led an army up the Mohawk River. He wanted to chase the British away from Fort Stanwix. Arnold sent a captured Loyalist and some Iroquois to spread the rumor that he had a large army. The trick worked, and the British retreated to Fort Oswego. Now no one was left to rendezvous with Burgoyne.

🔺 **MAIN IDEAS & DETAILS** Explain Britain's northern strategy—and why it failed.

Saratoga: A Turning Point

🔻 **KEY QUESTION** Why has Saratoga been called a "turning point"?

Burgoyne's army was running out of supplies. A raiding party was sent into Vermont where it was defeated by New England militia at the Battle of Bennington on August 16, 1777.

British Advance on Albany Despite these setbacks, Burgoyne's army continued south. But an American force led by General **Horatio Gates** blocked their way on a ridge called Bemis Heights, near Saratoga, New York. There the Polish engineer Tadeusz Kosciuszko (TAH•deh•oosh KAWSH•choosh•kaw) had helped the Americans create fortifications, or built-up earthen walls.

Starting on September 19, Burgoyne attacked the fortifications. While Gates commanded the Americans on the ridge, Benedict Arnold led an attack on nearby Freeman's Farm. His men repeatedly charged the British, with Arnold galloping through the battlefield "like a madman." Despite heavy casualties, the British held their position, but on October 7, Burgoyne was forced to retreat.

Burgoyne Surrenders Burgoyne's army moved slowly through heavy rain to a former army camp at Saratoga. By the time they arrived, the men were exhausted. The Continental Army then surrounded Burgoyne's army and fired on it day and night until Burgoyne surrendered. The series of conflicts that led to this surrender is known as the **Battles of Saratoga**.

The victory at Saratoga was a turning point. It prevented the British from dividing the States and isolating New England. It also showed Europeans that the Americans might win their war for independence. Because of this, some European nations hostile to Great Britain decided to help.

▲ **CAUSES AND EFFECTS** Explain why Saratoga has been called "a turning point."

Connect *to the* **World**

In London, after hearing the news of Burgoyne's surrender, William Pitt (Lord Chatham) warns Parliament: "You cannot conquer America."

Michigan Grade Level Content Expectations *Review*

 ONLINE QUIZ
For test practice, go to
Interactive Review @ ClassZone.com

TERMS & NAMES

1. Explain the importance of
- George Washington
- John Burgoyne
- Joseph Brant
- Benedict Arnold
- Horatio Gates
- Battles of Saratoga

USING YOUR READING NOTES

2. Analyze Causes and Effects Complete the diagram you started at the beginning of this section. Then create a diagram for each of the other main events in this section.

CAUSE

The Revolution divides Americans.

EFFECT

EFFECT

Some Native Americans join the British. Others support the Patriots.

KEY IDEAS

3. Why did the British want to control the Hudson River valley?

4. Why were the Battles of Saratoga important?

CRITICAL THINKING

5. Analyze Graphs
The graph shows how colonists were divided in 1776. Why is it surprising that the Patriots won?

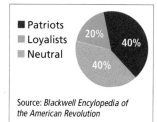

■ Patriots
■ Loyalists
■ Neutral

20%
40%
40%

Source: *Blackwell Encyclopedia of the American Revolution*

6. Connect *to* **Today** Use of mercenaries was banned by a United Nations agreement in 1989. Why do you think this was?

7. Writing Letter Write a one-page letter from Burgoyne to General Howe. Respond to Howe's letter in which he says he will head to Pennsylvania. Describe how this news affects your strategy.

The American Revolution **201**

Animated HISTORY
BATTLE TACTICS

🔊 *Click here* to enter a Revolutionary War battlefield @ ClassZone.com

Formal Battle

The majority of Revolutionary War battles followed a standard sequence. A battle would begin after the armies formed rows, or lines, facing each other. Americans used lines of both "regulars" (members of the Continental Army) and militia.

🔊 *Click here* **First,** field artillery (cannon) blast the enemy's lines.

🔊 *Click here* **Next,** front line soldiers advance to 50–100 yards of the enemy and fire muskets.

🔊 *Click here* **Finally,** soldiers attack with bayonets (knives attached to the end of a gun), while cavalry (soldiers on horseback) charge.

COMPARING *Tactics*

Formal Battle and Guerrilla War

The militia's expert marksmanship played an important role in formal battles. However, the militia often practiced more informal guerrilla fighting. As part-time soldiers, they operated locally to disrupt supplies and communication and ambush enemy units. The militia ensured that the British could not depend on the countryside for supplies or support.

Activity

Take to the Battlefield!

1. Divide into two armies, one on each side of the room.
2. Each group then selects a "general," who divides them into these groups:
   - artillery
   - infantry (front & second lines)
   - cavalry
3. The two "generals" command their "troops" to move forward as they would in a formal battle.

Reading for Understanding

▶ Key Ideas

BEFORE, YOU LEARNED

Despite the Continental Army's difficulties, the Patriots triumphed at Saratoga.

NOW YOU WILL LEARN

The expansion of the war weakened the British by forcing them to spread their military resources around the world.

▶ Vocabulary

TERMS & NAMES

Marquis de Lafayette (mahr•KEE•deh laf•eye•EHT) French aristocrat who volunteered to serve in Washington's army

Valley Forge site in southeast Pennsylvania where Washington and his army camped in the winter of 1777–1778

George Rogers Clark frontiersman who helped defend the Western frontier

John Paul Jones sea commander who attacked British ships near the British coast

Wilderness Road a trail into Kentucky

BACKGROUND VOCABULARY

ally (AL•eye) a country that agrees to help another country achieve a common goal

desert (duh•ZERT) to leave military duty without permission

privateer (pry•vuh•TEER) a privately owned ship that has been granted permission by a wartime government to attack an enemy's merchant ships

Visual Vocabulary
privateer

photograph courtesy of Peabody Essex Museum

▶ Reading Strategy

Recreate the diagram shown at right. As you read and respond to the **KEY QUESTIONS**, use the center box to record the main idea; use the outer ovals to note important details. Add ovals or start a new diagram as needed.

 See Skillbuilder Handbook, page R2.

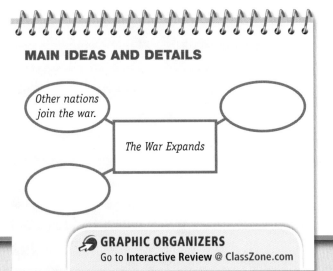

MAIN IDEAS AND DETAILS

Other nations join the war.

The War Expands

⚡ GRAPHIC ORGANIZERS
Go to **Interactive Review** @ ClassZone.com

The War Expands

8 – U6.2.1 United States History Investigation Topic and Issue Analysis, Past and Present – Use historical perspectives to analyze issues in the United States from the past and the present; conduct research on a historical issue or topic, identify a connection to a contemporary issue, and present findings (e.g., oral, visual, video, or electronic presentation, persuasive essay, or research paper); include causes and consequences of the historical action and predict possible consequences of the contemporary action.

One American's Story

In 1778, General Washington hoped to take Newport, Rhode Island, from the British. The French had just entered the war, and their fleet had arrived to help the Americans. But a storm damaged the ships, and the Americans retreated, pursued by the British. A regiment of African Americans saved the day by holding the enemy at bay. An eyewitness described the bravery of the all-black First Rhode Island Regiment.

The First Rhode Island Regiment, by David R. Wagner

© David Wagner
http://davidrwagner.com

PRIMARY SOURCE

❝ There was a black regiment in the same situation. Yes, a regiment of negroes, fighting for our liberty and independence,—not a white man among them but the officers. . . . Had they been unfaithful, or given way before the enemy, all would have been lost. Three times in succession were they attacked . . . and three times did they successfully repel the assault, and thus preserve our army from capture. ❞

—Dr. Harris, a veteran of the Battle of Rhode Island

In 1778 the war was expanding on many fronts. Not only were some states allowing African Americans to enlist, but foreign soldiers began arriving to help the American cause.

Help from Abroad

▼ **KEY QUESTION** Why did France and Spain enter the war?

The French were still bitter over their defeat by Britain in the French and Indian War, in which France lost its North American colonies. The French hoped to weaken the British by helping Britain's American colonies break free. In 1776, France began to give secret aid to the Americans. However, the French didn't become an overt American **ally** until the Americans had proved they could win a conventional battle against British forces. An ally is a country that helps another country achieve a common goal.

France and Spain Enter the War After hearing of the American victory at Saratoga, King Louis XVI of France publicly recognized U.S. independence. In 1778, France signed two treaties of alliance with the United States. By doing so, France went to war with Britain. As part of its new alliance, France promised to send badly needed funds, supplies, and troops to America.

In 1779, France persuaded its ally Spain to help the Americans, too. Spain was also Britain's rival. The Spanish governor of Louisiana, General Bernardo de Gálvez, acted quickly. He captured the British strongholds of Natchez and Baton Rouge in the lower Mississippi Valley. From there, his small army went on to take Mobile and, in 1781, Pensacola, in West Florida. These victories prevented the British from attacking the United States from the southwest. However, like France, Spain wanted more than just to help the United States. Gálvez's victories helped extend Spain's empire.

By entering the war against Britain, France and Spain forced the British to fight a number of enemies on land and sea. For instance, the British expected to have to fight the French in the West Indies, so they sent troops there. And thousands of British troops were busy fighting Gálvez in the west. The British now had to spread their military resources over many fronts.

ANALYZE *Political Cartoons*

This cartoon was published in London in 1779, a year after France had formed an alliance with the United States. In political cartoons, sometimes a nation is represented by a figure wearing clothes associated with that nation. For example, in 18th-century cartoons, a Native American symbolized America. Here, figures representing different nations surround a sleeping figure representing Great Britain.

France is on the attack.

Scotland defends Britain.

Britain sleeps through the war.

THE PRESENT STATE OF GREAT BRITAIN.

America steals the cap of liberty.

Holland (whose merchants were trading with the Americans) picks Britain's pocket.

Skillbuilder Handbook, page R18.

CRITICAL THINKING

1. **Analyze Point of View** Why would the cartoonist have shown Britain as sleeping?

2. **Make Inferences** Why is Holland shown picking Britain's pocket?

3. **Synthesize** What is the basic meaning of the cartoon?

Foreign Officers Arrive European military officers from France, Poland, and the German states came to Washington's aid. One of these was the **Marquis de Lafayette** (laf•eye•EHT), a 19-year-old French aristocrat who volunteered to serve in Washington's army. He wanted a military career, and he believed in the American cause. Soon after Lafayette arrived in June 1777, he was given the command of an army division and quickly gained Washington's confidence. Lafayette won his men's respect and love by sharing their hardships. Called "the soldier's friend," he used his own money to buy warm clothing for his ragged troops. Washington regarded him as a son.

Lafayette fought in many battles and also persuaded the French king to send a 6,000-man army to America. He became a hero in both France and the United States. Later he took part in France's own revolution.

Along with Lafayette came the Baron de Kalb, a German officer who had served in the French army. He became one of Washington's generals with a reputation for bravery.

Marquis de Lafayette

▲ **MAIN IDEAS & DETAILS** Tell why France and Spain entered the war.

Winter at Valley Forge

▼ **KEY QUESTION** How did Valley Forge transform the American army?

Help from France and Spain came when the Americans desperately needed it. As you have read, in late 1777 Britain's General Howe had forced Washington to retreat from Philadelphia. In the winter of 1777–1778, Washington and his army camped at **Valley Forge** in southeast Pennsylvania.

Hardship at Valley Forge On the march to Valley Forge, Washington's army lacked supplies. Many soldiers had only blankets to cover themselves. They also lacked shoes. The barefoot men left tracks of blood on the frozen ground as they marched.

The soldiers' condition did not improve at camp. Over the winter, the soldiers at Valley Forge grew weak from not having enough food or warm clothing. Roughly a quarter of them died from malnutrition, exposure, or diseases such as smallpox and typhoid fever. Because of this suffering, the name Valley Forge came to stand for the great hardships that Americans endured in the Revolutionary War.

Washington appealed to Congress for supplies, but it was slow in responding. Luckily, private citizens sometimes helped the soldiers. On New Year's Day 1778, a group of Philadelphia women drove ten teams of oxen into camp. The oxen were pulling wagons full of supplies and 2,000 shirts. The women had the oxen killed to provide food for the troops.

Patriotism Unites the Army Despite the hardships, American soldiers showed amazing endurance. Under such circumstances, soldiers often **desert**, or leave military duty without permission. Soldiers did desert, but Lieutenant

A Deadly Winter

Due to poor planning, thievery, and muddy roads, supplies were lacking during the army's winter camp at Valley Forge. An estimated 2,500 to 3,000 men died from exposure, disease, or malnutrition. According to the Marquis de Lafayette,

> The unfortunate soldiers were in want of everything; they had neither coats nor hats, nor shirts, nor shoes. Their feet and their legs froze until they were black, and it was often necessary to amputate them. **"**

◄ The **amputation saw** was an important piece of the surgeon's kit.

STRANGE BUT TRUE

A soldier in pain hated to see a surgeon approaching with this tool.

What is it?

ANSWER: A tooth extractor

Data File

WHO approx. 12,000 regulars, officers, and advisers

WHAT 14' x 16' log huts housed 12 privates each; officers had more space, depending on rank

WHERE 25 miles NW of Philadelphia

WHEN Dec. 19, 1777, to June 19, 1778

WHY near major crossroads, with plenty of wood and water

HARDSHIPS AT VALLEY FORGE

- In February, almost 5,000 soldiers were too sick to fight; another 3,700 lacked either shoes or clothes.

- Shipments intended for troops were often stolen by government employees.

- Many local farmers were Loyalist and refused to sell food to the army. Others would not sell food because American currency was worthless.

- Common ailments included typhus and dysentery.

- Desertions exceeded 2,000. By February, 8–10 men were deserting each day.

- When frostbitten flesh dies, it turns black. The condition, called gangrene, can spread through the body and can be fatal. Amputations were performed without anesthetics or antiseptics, so amputees often died from infections anyway.

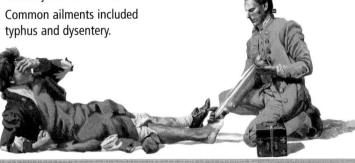

Colonel John Brooks wrote that the army stayed together because of the "Love of our Country." Once again, Washington's determination and patriotic vision inspired the troops to keep fighting.

The Army Grows Stronger Thanks to a German officer, the Baron von Steuben, the inexperienced American army was transformed into a skilled fighting force. Von Steuben began by forming a model company of 100 men. He taught them how to handle weapons properly. He also showed them how to fight the kind of formal battles favored by the British. (See Battle Tactics on page 202.) Within a month, the troops were executing drills with speed and precision. Because of this, the American army emerged from Valley Forge as a more efficient and stronger fighting machine.

▲ **SUMMARIZE** Describe how Valley Forge transformed the American army.

Frontier Fighting

▼ **KEY QUESTION** Why did the war spread to the frontier?

In the late 18th century, the region between the Appalachian Mountains and the Mississippi River was known as the frontier; colonists had only just begun to settle there. In 1763, the British had tried to restrict settlement in this area and had built forts in the region. But some believed that the frontier should be open to settlement. In 1775 Daniel Boone helped build the **Wilderness Road**, a trail into Kentucky. Because Kentucky was claimed by Virginia in 1777, 24-year-old Kentuckian **George Rogers Clark** persuaded Virginia's governor, Patrick Henry, to allow him to raise an army to capture British outposts on the Western frontier. Clark wanted to expand the war into the frontier by attacking the British and their Native American allies in what is now Indiana and Illinois.

Clark's Army In May 1778, Clark led a group of frontiersmen to Kaskaskia, a British fort guarding the Mississippi River. They captured Kaskaskia without a fight.

Then they moved east to take Fort Sackville at Vincennes, in present-day Indiana. Earlier, a small force sent by Clark had taken Vincennes, but British forces under Henry Hamilton had recaptured it. Settlers called Hamilton the "Hair Buyer" because he supposedly paid rewards for American scalps.

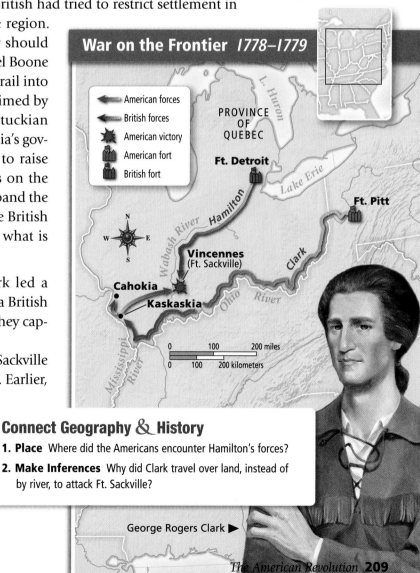

War on the Frontier 1778–1779

American forces
British forces
American victory
American fort
British fort

PROVINCE OF QUEBEC

L. Huron
Lake Erie
Ft. Detroit
Ft. Pitt
Hamilton
Wabash River
Vincennes (Ft. Sackville)
Clark
Cahokia
Kaskaskia
Ohio River
Mississippi River

0   100   200 miles
0   100   200 kilometers

Connect Geography & History

1. **Place** Where did the Americans encounter Hamilton's forces?
2. **Make Inferences** Why did Clark travel over land, instead of by river, to attack Ft. Sackville?

George Rogers Clark ▶

Connecting History

Expansion
Europeans would continue to settle and claim lands in the West until they reached the Pacific Ocean. You will see this theme emerge when you study westward expansion in later chapters.

Americans Seize the Frontier Determined to retake Fort Sackville, Clark and his men set out for Vincennes from Kaskaskia in February 1779. Hamilton wasn't expecting an attack because the rivers were flooding the woods. But Clark's men slogged through miles of icy swamps and waded through chest-deep water. They caught the British at Vincennes by surprise.

When Hamilton and his troops tried to remain in the fort, Clark pretended to have a larger force than he really had. Clark also executed some Native American allies of the British in plain view of the fort. He threatened to do the same to the British unless they surrendered. Frightened, the British gave up.

Clark's victory gave the Americans a hold on the vast region between the Great Lakes and the Ohio River (even though Fort Detroit on Lake Erie remained in the hands of the British). This area was more than half the total size of the original 13 states. The expansion of the war into the frontier also had another consequence: it forced the British again to spread their troops over a larger area and further weakened the British war effort.

🔺 **CAUSES AND EFFECTS** Explain why the war spread to the frontier.

War on the Waves

🔻 **KEY QUESTION** How did Americans expand the naval war?

The war expanded not only west into the frontier but also eastward to the high seas. By 1777, Britain had over 200 warships off the American coast. This allowed Britain to control the Atlantic trade routes to European markets.

James Forten, who later became famous for his efforts to end slavery, joined a privateer at the age of 14.

British Trade Disrupted Because the American navy was small and weak, Congress encouraged American **privateers** to attack British merchant ships. A privateer is a privately owned ship that has been granted permission by a wartime government to attack an enemy's merchant ships. After capturing a ship, the crew of a privateer sold its cargo and shared the money. America commissioned more than 1,000 privateers to prey on the British. They captured hundreds of ships, causing British merchants to call on their government to end the war.

Though outnumbered, the Continental Navy scored several victories. A daring officer named **John Paul Jones** inspired Americans by sailing across the Atlantic to attack British ships along the coast of Britain itself.

"I Have Not Yet Begun to Fight" In 1779, Jones became the commander of a ship named *Bonhomme Richard*. With four other ships, he patrolled the English coast. In September, Jones's vessels approached a convoy in which two British warships were guarding a number of supply ships.

Jones closed in on the *Serapis*, the larger of the two warships. At one point, the *Bonhomme Richard* rammed the better-armed British vessel. As the two ships locked together, the confident British captain demanded that Jones surrender. In words that have become a famous U.S. Navy slogan, Jones is said to have replied, "I have not yet begun to fight!"

The two warships were virtually locked together; the muzzles of their guns almost touched. They blasted away, each seriously damaging the other. On the shore, crowds of Britons gathered under a full moon to watch the fighting. After a fierce three-and-a-half-hour battle, the main mast of the *Serapis* cracked and fell. The ship's captain then surrendered. The *Bonhomme Richard* was so full of holes that it eventually sank, so Jones and his crew had to sail away in the *Serapis*!

Jones's success angered the British and inspired the Americans. Even so, the Americans knew that the war had to be won on land. The next section discusses the major land battles in the closing years of the war.

 SUMMARIZE Explain how Americans expanded the naval war.

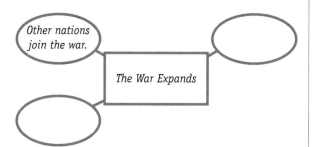
John Paul Jones,
by N. C. Wyeth

Michigan Grade Level Content Expectations *Review*

🌀 **ONLINE QUIZ**
For test practice, go to
Interactive Review @ ClassZone.com

TERMS & NAMES

1. Explain the importance of
- Marquis de Lafayette
- John Paul Jones
- Valley Forge
- Wilderness Road
- George Rogers Clark

USING YOUR READING NOTES

2. Main Ideas & Details List the ways in which the war expanded from 1776–1779. For each, identify one key event and explain its importance.

Other nations join the war.

The War Expands

KEY IDEAS

3. List reasons why France decided to help America. Were Spain's reasons the same or different? Explain.

4. How did foreign officers help General Washington?

CRITICAL THINKING

5. Connect Economics & History How did the alliance with France alter America's financial situation?

6. Analyze Point of View Why do you think so many Native Americans on the frontier supported the British?

7. **Connect** *to* **Today** Why has Valley Forge remained an important symbol of America's heritage?

8. **Math** Research to find out how many soldiers fought in Washington's army during each year of the Revolution. Then calculate the average size of the army throughout the war.

Reading for Understanding

▶ Key Ideas

BEFORE, YOU LEARNED

The expansion of the war forced the British to spread their military resources over a wide area.

NOW YOU WILL LEARN

The Continental Army, their allies, and the American people brought about an American victory.

▶ Vocabulary

TERMS & NAMES

Battle of Charles Town British siege of Charles Town (Charleston), South Carolina, in May 1780, in which the Americans suffered their worst defeat of the war

Lord Cornwallis (korn•WAHL•ihs) British general whose campaigns in the South led to his defeat at Yorktown

Battle of Yorktown final battle of the war, in which French and American forces led by George Washington defeated British General Cornwallis

BACKGROUND VOCABULARY

redoubt (re•DOWT) a small fort

Visual Vocabulary
redoubt at Yorktown

▶ Reading Strategy

Re-create the diagram shown at right. As you read and respond to the **KEY QUESTIONS**, use the diagram to record important events in the order in which they occurred.

 See Skillbuilder Handbook, page R5.

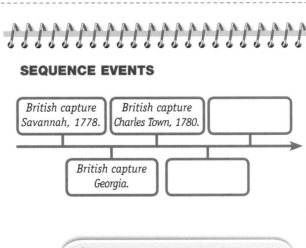

SEQUENCE EVENTS

| *British capture Savannah, 1778.* | *British capture Charles Town, 1780.* | |

| | *British capture Georgia.* | |

GRAPHIC ORGANIZERS
Go to **Interactive Review** @ ClassZone.com

The Path to Victory

8 – U6.2.1 United States History Investigation Topic and Issue Analysis, Past and Present – Use historical perspectives to analyze issues in the United States from the past and the present; conduct research on a historical issue or topic, identify a connection to a contemporary issue, and present findings (e.g., oral, visual, video, or electronic presentation, persuasive essay, or research paper); include causes and consequences of the historical action and predict possible consequences of the contemporary action.

One American's Story

James P. Collins, a 16-year-old American, found himself in the midst of a civil war as the Revolution raged in the South. He watched as both sides committed war crimes. At the Battle of King's Mountain, fought on the border of North and South Carolina in October 1780, he saw American Patriots surround and slaughter about 1,000 American Loyalist militia, led by Major General Patrick Ferguson. Collins described the scene.

The Battle of King's Mountain

PRIMARY SOURCE

❝ The dead lay in heaps on all sides, while the groans of the wounded were heard in every direction. I could not help turning away from the scene before me with horror and, though exulting in victory, could not refrain from shedding tears. ❞

—James P. Collins, quoted in *The Spirit of Seventy-Six*

As James Collins's story demonstrates, fighting in the South was vicious.

The War Moves South

🔻 **KEY QUESTION** What happened when the British shifted the war to the South?

After three years of fighting in the North, the British were no closer to victory. Although they had captured many important Northern coastal cities, they didn't have enough troops to control the countryside.

The British Change Their Strategy In 1778 the British decided to move the war to the South. They believed that most Southerners were Loyalists, who would support an invading British army.

The British also expected Southern slaves to escape and join them because they had promised to grant the slaves freedom. Although thousands of African Americans did join the British, not all were set free.

Savannah and Charles Town Fall In December 1778, the British captured the port of Savannah, Georgia. (See Map Ⓐ on p. 215.) They then conquered most of Georgia. In 1780, a British army led by General Henry Clinton landed in South Carolina. They trapped American forces in Charles Town (now Charleston), the largest Southern city. **The Battle of Charles Town** ended when the city surrendered. The Americans lost almost their entire Southern army. It was the worst American defeat of the war.

After that loss, Congress assigned General Horatio Gates—the victor at Saratoga—to form a new Southern army. Continental soldiers led by Baron de Kalb formed the army's core. Gates added about 2,000 new and untrained militia. He then headed for Camden, South Carolina, to challenge the army led by the British general **Lord Cornwallis**. (Cornwallis had assumed control of British forces after Clinton returned to New York.)

In August 1780, Gates's army ran into British troops outside Camden. (See Map Ⓐ on p. 215.) The Americans were in no condition to fight. They were out of supplies and half-starved. Even worse, Gates put the inexperienced militia along part of the frontline instead of behind the veterans. When the British attacked, the militia panicked and ran. Gates also fled,

CONNECT To Today

MILITARY COMMUNICATION

In the 18th century, military communications were painfully slow. Ships from London might take up to four months to bring orders to British generals.

Mail did not travel much faster within America itself. British General Cornwallis was frustrated by the "delay and difficulty of conveying letters" and "the impossibility of waiting for answers." Not only were journeys long, but bands of Patriots made sure that British lines of communication were constantly disrupted.

Today, wars are fought with the help of technology that provides instant communication. Computers and satellites relay information quickly between sea, air, and ground forces. For example, a video of an attack on enemy forces in Afghanistan can be sent via satellite to the Florida command center and then relayed live to the White House.

A woman gives a message to an officer of the Continental Army.

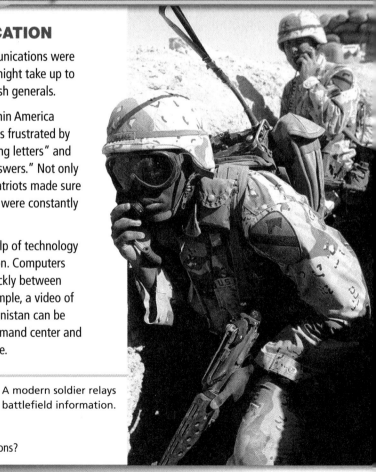

A modern soldier relays battlefield information.

CRITICAL THINKING

1. **Draw Conclusions** Which side in the Revolutionary War would have suffered most from slow communications? Why?

2. **Evaluate** What are the advantages of today's faster communications?

War in the South 1778–1781

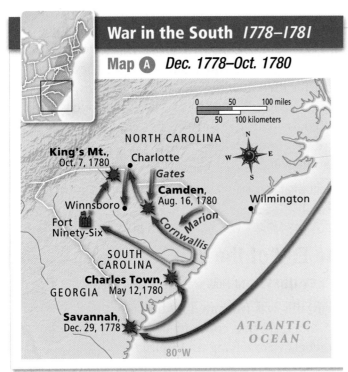

Map A *Dec. 1778–Oct. 1780*

NORTH CAROLINA

King's Mt., Oct. 7, 1780
Charlotte
Gates
Camden, Aug. 16, 1780
Winnsboro
Wilmington
Fort Ninety-Six
Cornwallis *Marion*
SOUTH CAROLINA
Charles Town, May 12,1780
GEORGIA
Savannah, Dec. 29, 1778

ATLANTIC OCEAN

0 50 100 miles
0 50 100 kilometers

80°W

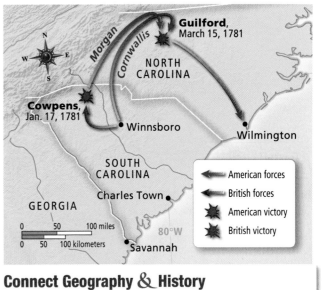

Map B *Jan. 1781–April 1781*

Guilford, March 15, 1781
Morgan *Cornwallis*
NORTH CAROLINA
Cowpens, Jan. 17, 1781
Winnsboro
Wilmington
SOUTH CAROLINA
Charles Town
GEORGIA
Savannah

American forces
British forces
American victory
British victory

0 50 100 miles
0 50 100 kilometers

80°W

Connect Geography & History

1. **Place** Where did the British begin their attacks in the South?
2. **Identify Problems and Solutions** Why do you think Cornwallis headed for the coast after the Battle of Guilford?

but de Kalb remained with his soldiers and received fatal wounds. This second defeat in the South ended Gates's term as head of an army. American spirits fell to a new low.

Guerrilla War Although the Americans had been defeated at Camden, the British were having difficulty controlling the South. The countryside was hostile and filled with more rebel sympathizers than Loyalists. Rebel guerrillas repeatedly attacked British messengers. This made it difficult for British forces moving inland to keep in touch with their bases on the coast. British commanders in the South were discovering what General Burgoyne had realized in the North: the countryside was a dangerous place for the British army.

One of the most famous rebel guerrilla leaders was Francis Marion, called the "Swamp Fox" because he led cunning attacks from his base in the swamps. An American officer described Marion's guerrilla band: "Their number did not exceed 20 men and boys, some white, some black, and all mounted, but most of them miserably equipped." Despite their poor equipment, Marion's men were able to cut the British supply line that led inland from Charles Town.

General Greene Takes Charge After Gates's defeat at Camden, Washington put Nathanael Greene in charge of the Southern army. Greene was one of Washington's best generals. In January 1781, he sent part of his army south to confront Cornwallis. In a formal, linear battle, the Americans won a spectacular victory at Cowpens. (See Map **B** above.) The victory proved that Americans had mastered the formal battle tactics of the British.

Cornwallis's main army now pursued Greene up into North Carolina. The British still had the advantage in a full-scale battle due to their greater firepower. However, the Americans used their knowledge of the landscape to keep one step ahead of the advancing British. Greene's strategy was to let the British wear themselves out. When the Americans did fight, they did their best to make sure the British suffered heavy losses. In fact, Cornwallis lost so many men at the Battle of Guilford Court House that he decided to retreat to Wilmington, on the coast. With his army exhausted, Cornwallis had to face a bitter truth: there were more active Patriots than Loyalists in the South. Britain's southern strategy had failed.

🔺 **CAUSES AND EFFECTS** Explain what happened when the British shifted the war to the South.

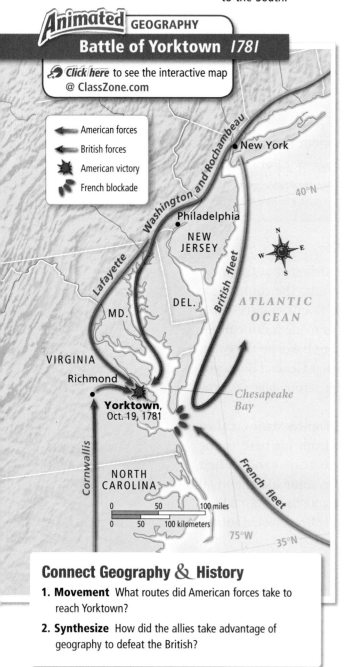

Animated GEOGRAPHY

Battle of Yorktown *1781*

🔎 *Click here* to see the interactive map @ ClassZone.com

← American forces
← British forces
✦ American victory
⬤ French blockade

Connect Geography & History

1. **Movement** What routes did American forces take to reach Yorktown?

2. **Synthesize** How did the allies take advantage of geography to defeat the British?

The End of the War

🔻 **KEY QUESTION** How was Cornwallis trapped?

Cornwallis was frustrated by his setbacks in the Carolinas. He had come to believe that Southern rebels were relying on Virginia for their supplies. So, in 1781, without waiting for orders, he marched north into Virginia. In August Cornwallis set up his base at Yorktown, located on a peninsula in Chesapeake Bay. From there, his army could receive supplies by ship from New York. It was a fatal mistake.

Setting the Trap Cornwallis's decision gave Washington a golden opportunity to trap the British on the peninsula. Washington first joined forces with General Jean Rochambeau's French army in New York and headed south. In August 1781, as these armies came south, a large French fleet arrived from the West Indies and blocked Chesapeake Bay. (See map at left.) The French fleet prevented the British ships from reaching Yorktown and delivering supplies—and prevented the British in Yorktown from escaping.

Meanwhile, the **Battle of Yorktown** had begun. The British tried to protect themselves by encircling the town with numerous **redoubts**, or small forts. These forts were meant to keep the allies' artillery at a distance from the town. But as the allies captured British redoubts, they brought their artillery closer to the town's defenses. The American and French cannon bombarded Yorktown, turning its buildings to rubble. Cornwallis had no way out. On October 19, 1781, he surrendered his force of about 8,000.

Although fighting continued in the South and on the frontier, Yorktown was the last major battle of the war. When the British prime minister, Lord North, heard the news, he gasped, "It is all over!" Indeed, he and other British leaders were soon forced to resign. Britain's new leaders began to negotiate a peace treaty, which is discussed in the next section.

▲ **SUMMARIZE** Describe how Cornwallis was trapped.

Why the Americans Won

▼ **KEY QUESTION** How were the Americans able to defeat the British?

By their persistence, the Americans won independence even though they faced many obstacles. As you have read, the American army lacked training and experience. American soldiers served only for short periods of time. They often lacked proper supplies and weapons. In contrast, the British forces ranked among the best trained in the world. Yet the Americans had advantages that had not been obvious at first; only as the war progressed did American strengths become apparent. The chart on the next page sets these American strengths against the weaknesses of the British.

The British were defeated not only by the American army, but by civilians who kept the resistance alive. The British were not prepared for a popular uprising. In Europe, only armies fought the wars, and civilians either fled or hid before advancing forces. In America, however, the British discovered that

History through Art

The Surrender of Lord Cornwallis by John Trumbull shows a British officer surrendering to a mounted American officer, with French troops on the left and Americans on the right. Unwilling to face public humiliation, Cornwallis pretended to be ill, sending General Charles O'Hara to offer his sword to the French. The French sent O'Hara to General Washington, who allowed General Benjamin Lincoln to accept the sword of surrender.

CRITICAL VIEWING How does the positioning of the troops symbolize the British defeat?

large segments of the population were actively involved in a political cause. Even if the British had succeeded in defeating an American army, they likely would never have been able to conquer the American people.

CONNECT to the Essential Question

How was it possible that American Patriots gained their independence from the powerful British Empire?

AMERICAN STRENGTHS		BRITISH WEAKNESSES
Patriots fought for their lives, their property, and their political ideals.	**Motivation**	The British and their Hessian mercenaries fought merely for pay.
Many civilians actively supported the Revolution. Patriots used many techniques to rally popular support. Rebellion broke out across the continent.	**Popular support** 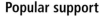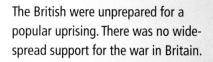	The British were unprepared for a popular uprising. There was no wide-spread support for the war in Britain.
American generals learned from their mistakes. Washington inspired loyalty and patriotism in his troops.	**Leadership**	British generals were overconfident and disunited, their efforts often uncoordinated.
France supplied money and troops. France and Spain weakened British forces by expanding the war. The Dutch helped carry French military supplies to the Americans.	**Foreign allies**	No allies. As more European countries turned against Britain, the British were forced to fight many enemies.
Americans fought close to home; the militia made sure that the British could not live off the land.	**Communication and supplies**	Orders from London might take months to reach America. The British were also forced to transport food and supplies over 3,000 miles of ocean.
Although Americans had fewer troops, local militia helped swell American forces. Altogether, 250,000 may have fought for the Patriot cause.	**Troop strength**	By 1781 the British army had around 54,000 troops fighting rebel forces.

CRITICAL THINKING **Compare and Contrast** Which strength do you think was most important to the American victory?

Fond Farewells In late 1783, the last British ships and troops left New York City. As the American army disbanded, soldiers such as Joseph Plumb Martin of Connecticut had mixed emotions. Martin had enlisted in 1776, at the age of 15. He experienced the terrible winter at Valley Forge and the winning battle at Yorktown. Many years later, he wrote about his last day as a regular.

PRIMARY SOURCE

❝ There was as much sorrow as joy. . . . We had lived together as a family of brothers for several years, . . . had shared with each other the hardships, dangers, and sufferings incident to a soldier's life; had sympathized with each other in trouble and sickness; . . . And now we were to be . . . parted forever. **❞**

—Joseph Plumb Martin, quoted in *The Revolutionaries*

In his farewell letter to his armies, George Washington wrote that the army's endurance "through almost every possible suffering and discouragement for the space of eight long years, was little short of a standing miracle." Like Washington—and the British—American Patriots were astonished at their achievement.

 SUMMARIZE Explain how the Americans were able to defeat the British.

Michigan Grade Level Content Expectations *Review*

🔊 **ONLINE QUIZ**
For test practice, go to
Interactive Review @ ClassZone.com

TERMS & NAMES

1. Explain the importance of
   • Battle of Charles Town
   • Lord Cornwallis
   • Battle of Yorktown

USING YOUR READING NOTES

2. **Sequence** Complete the diagram to show the most importance events of this section.

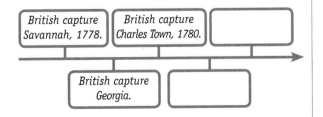

British capture Savannah, 1778. → *British capture Charles Town, 1780.* → ☐

British capture Georgia. ☐

KEY IDEAS

3. Why didn't the British control of coastal cities bring them victory in the South?

4. When and why did Congress form a new Southern army?

5. How did the allies force the British to surrender?

CRITICAL THINKING

6. **Make Generalizations** Does military superiority always guarantee victory? Why or why not?

7. **WHAT IF?** What might have happened at Yorktown without the aid of the French fleet?

8. **Connect *to* Today** What can the history of the Revolution teach us about modern conflicts?

9. **Writing** Letter Use books or the Internet to find out about the actions of Lord North after the British defeat at Yorktown. As North, write a letter to your king explaining the defeat.

RALLYING TO THE CAUSE

During the Revolution, American Patriots supported the war effort in a variety of ways. Why was popular support so important for the American victory?

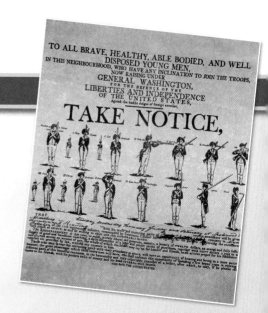

Teens in History

RAISING THE LIBERTY POLE

Americans imagined liberty as a tree grown from a seed planted by the early colonists. Many American communities had a liberty tree (or pole) in the center of town that served as a meeting spot where Patriots rallied supporters and exchanged news.

THE YOUNG ENLIST

Although the Continental Army was not supposed to enlist boys younger than sixteen, recruiters did not usually ask for proof of age. In fact, teenage boys made up a large proportion of the army. Posters like this one were designed to persuade young men to enlist.

" To the enemies of our country! May they have cobweb breeches, a *porcupine saddle*, a hard-trotting horse, and an eternal journey!"

"May the enemies of America be destitute of (lacking in) beef and claret (wine) "

PATRIOTIC CURSES

Patriots raised their spirits by laughing at the enemy.

PATRIOT POET

Phillis Wheatley, the first African-American writer to achieve fame, was a poet who supported the Patriot cause. During the war, Washington invited her to his headquarters after she sent him a poem that ended with this verse:

"Proceed, great chief,
with virtue on thy side,
Thy ev'ry action
let the goddess guide.
A crown, a mansion,
and a throne that shine,
With gold unfading,
Washington be thine."

SPYING FOR THE CAUSE

Many women spied for the Patriots. The American-born Patience Wright worked in London as a sculptor. Some historians believe that she coaxed military information out of her subjects as she sculpted their likenesses. Then she apparently passed on the information to Patriot agents in London.

SECRET CODES

Information was often coded, in case letters fell into enemy hands. One kind of secret message did not look like a code at all, but lay hidden in an innocent-looking letter like the one shown here. By cutting the right shape out of another piece of paper and laying it on top of the letter, the secret message would be revealed.

Activity

Decode a secret message!

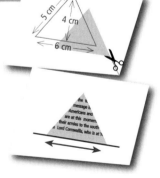

1 In the middle of a sheet of paper, cut out a triangle with these dimensions:
Base: 6 cm; Height: 4 cm; Sides: 5 cm.

2 Place the sheet over the message below. Align the base of the triangle with the blue line below the message. Then slide the sheet slowly from left to right until you find the secret message.

M. may have told you the secret news by this time. But, if you have not heard, the message is that the city of New York will be attacked by some Americans and French, who are growing bolder day by day and are at this moment moving their armies there. They will not take their armies to the south to attack British forces there because my Lord Cornwallis, who is at Yorktown, is not a threat.

▶ Key Ideas

BEFORE, YOU LEARNED
A combination of factors brought about an American victory.

NOW YOU WILL LEARN
Americans emerged from the Revolution as citizens of a unified nation that valued the ideal of liberty.

▶ Vocabulary

TERMS & NAMES

Treaty of Paris the 1783 treaty that ended the Revolutionary War

Elizabeth Freeman enslaved African American who won her freedom in court

Richard Allen African-American preacher who helped start the Free African Society

Virginia Statute for Religious Freedom statement of religious liberty, written by Thomas Jefferson

BACKGROUND VOCABULARY

disputes (dis•PYOOTS) disagreements

outposts (OWT•posts) military bases, usually located on the frontier

nondenominational not favoring any particular religion

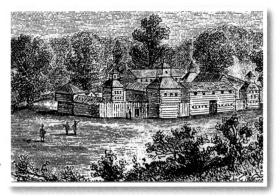

Visual Vocabulary
outpost

▶ Reading Strategy

Re-create the spider diagram shown at right. As you read and respond to the **KEY QUESTIONS**, use the main branches to note categories of facts about results of the war. Add stems to record important details in each category.

 See Skillbuilder Handbook, page R6.

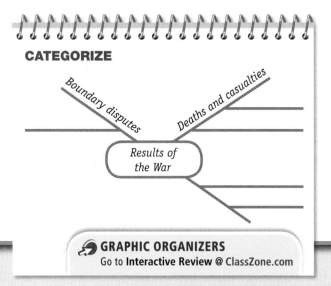

CATEGORIZE

Boundary disputes

Deaths and casualties

Results of the War

GRAPHIC ORGANIZERS
Go to **Interactive Review** @ ClassZone.com

The Legacy of the War

F1.3.1 Describe the consequences of the American Revolution by analyzing the – birth of an independent republican government

F1.3.4 Describe the consequences of the American Revolution by analyzing the – concerns over distribution of power within governments, between government and the governed, and among people

One American's Story

Haym Salomon, a Jew living in Poland, moved to New York before the Revolution in search of liberty. He soon became a successful merchant and banker. During the war, Salomon supported the Patriot cause.

When the British captured New York in 1776, Salomon was arrested. Because he spoke many languages, the British thought he could help them deal with foreign merchants, so they let him out of prison. Unfortunately, prison had permanently damaged his health.

In 1778, Salomon fled to Philadelphia. He loaned the new government more than $600,000, which was never repaid. Like many other Americans, Salomon had sacrificed his health and fortune to help his country survive.

A 1975 U.S. postage stamp honors Haym Salomon.

Costs of the War

▼ **KEY QUESTION** What were the costs of the war?

No one knows exactly how many people died in the war, but eight years of fighting took a terrible toll. An estimated 25,700 Americans died in the war, and 1,400 remained missing. Over 8,200 Americans were wounded. Some were left with permanent disabilities, such as amputated limbs. The British military suffered about 10,000 deaths.

Debts and Losses Many soldiers who survived the war left the army with no money. They had received little or no pay. Instead of back pay, the government gave some soldiers certificates for land in the West. Many men sold that land to get money for food and other basic needs.

Both the Congress and the states had borrowed money to finance the conflict. The war left the nation with a debt of about $27 million—a debt that would prove difficult to pay off.

Those who supported the losing side in the war also suffered. Thousands of Loyalists lost their property. Between 60,000 and 100,000 Loyalists

PAYING FOR THE WAR

The Continental Congress—our first national government—did not have the power to tax; it asked for funds and then hoped that the states would pay. It did have the power to borrow, however. Fighting the Revolutionary War cost America around $100 million, and by 1782, the new U.S. government was approximately $30 million in debt. To fund the Continental Army, the United States borrowed money in several ways.

TREASURY NOTES	CERTIFICATES	PERSONAL NOTES
A treasury note states the government's promise to repay a specified amount at a specified date. Notes were sold to **patriotic investors** and to **foreign countries** such as France.	Printed money, known as "certificates," could be exchanged for an amount of silver—*if* the government had enough. This is how many **"regulars"** (soldiers), **farmers**, and **tradespeople** were paid.	**Wealthy individuals**, such as Haym Salomon and Robert Morris—the country's first superintendent of finance—issued personal notes (or loans) to pay government expenses.

Connect *to* **Today** Do you think it's a good idea for a modern government to borrow money? Why or why not?

left the United States during and after the war. Among them were several thousand African Americans and Native Americans, including Mohawk chief Joseph Brant. Most of the Loyalists went to Canada. There they settled new towns and provinces. They also brought English traditions to areas that the French had settled. To this day, Canada has both French and English as official languages.

The Revolution had been a civil war that left both Patriots and Loyalists with bitter memories. Patriots found it especially difficult to forgive the former American general Benedict Arnold. In 1780 Arnold had betrayed his country by trying to turn over an American fort to the British. Throughout American history, the name Benedict Arnold is used to mean traitor.

▲ **SUMMARIZE** List some of the costs of the war.

The Treaty of Paris

🔻 **KEY QUESTION** What did America gain most from the Treaty of Paris?

Benjamin Franklin, John Adams, and John Jay began formal peace negotiations with the British on September 27, 1782. The final **Treaty of Paris**, which ended the Revolutionary War, was signed on September 3, 1783.

Favorable Terms The Americans won favorable terms in the peace treaty:

- The United States was independent.
- Its boundaries would be the Mississippi River on the west, Canada on the north, and Spanish Florida on the south.
- The United States would receive the right to fish off Canada's Atlantic Coast, near Newfoundland and Nova Scotia.
- Each side would repay debts it owed the other.
- The British would return any enslaved persons they had captured.
- Congress would recommend that the states return any property they had seized from Loyalists.

Neither Britain nor the United States fully lived up to the treaty's terms. Americans did not repay the prewar debts they owed British merchants or return Loyalist property. The British did not return runaway slaves.

Boundary Disputes The Treaty of Paris led to boundary **disputes**, or disagreements, with Spain, who could now claim control of both banks of the Mississippi river for over 100 miles north of the Gulf of Mexico. This Spanish control threatened American shipping. In the northwest, the British refused to give up military **outposts**, or bases, in the Great Lakes area, such as Fort Detroit.

COMPARING *Prewar and Postwar Boundaries*

Prewar Boundaries *1775*

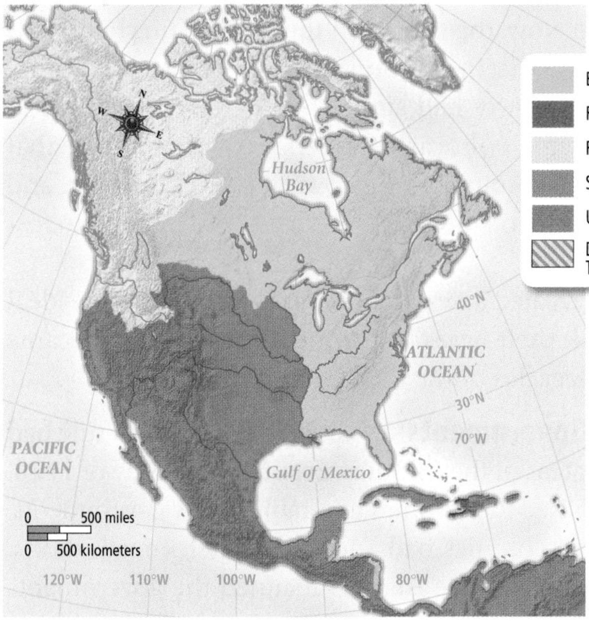

Postwar Boundaries *1783*

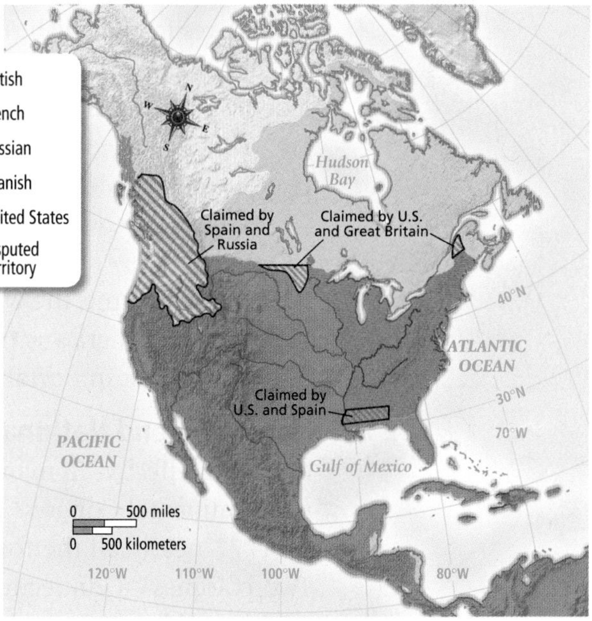

British
French
Russian
Spanish
United States
Disputed Territory

Connect Geography & History

1. Place What was the southern limit of British territory in 1775?

2. Evaluate Which foreign nation benefited most from the Treaty of Paris?

The Threat to Native American Lands The Treaty of Paris redrew the national boundaries with little concern for Native American interests. In Chapter 5, you learned that the British had attempted to keep white settlers away from Native American territory by establishing the Proclamation Line of 1763. Because of this, many tribes had supported the British in the war. But in the treaty, the British handed over Native American lands without even consulting their former allies. When Mohawk chief Joseph Brant heard the news, he was horrified by the betrayal.

PRIMARY SOURCE

❝ When I joined the English in the beginning of the War, it was purely on account of my forefathers' engagements with the King. I always looked upon these engagements, or covenants between the King and the Indian nation, as a sacred thing. ❞

—Joseph Brant, 1783

Joseph Brant, or Thayendanegea, was not born to be a chief but earned the esteem of his people by his leadership. The giant shell he wears is a symbol of wealth and status.

Native Americans who lived east of the Mississippi found themselves living within the boundaries of a new nation that was intent on westward expansion. Their lands were now at risk.

▲ **MAIN IDEAS & DETAILS** Identify what America gained from the Treaty of Paris.

Creating a New Nation

▼ **KEY QUESTION** What ideals emerged from the Revolution?

"Liberty" had been the rallying cry of the Revolution as Americans freed themselves from British rule. Now, the success of the Revolution challenged the existing world order. For the first time in the Americas, a colonial rebellion against an imperial power had succeeded. By destroying British authority, the Revolution offered political reformers a chance to prove that republicanism, the idea that a country can be governed by the people, and without a king, could work. Imperial powers around the world began to fear this new threat.

At the same time, the war created a new nation—one that valued the ideal of liberty. As Americans built their new society, the ideal of liberty became one of the most important legacies of the Revolution.

New State and National Governments As early as 1775 British rule had become ineffective in many areas of the colonies. Eventually, in May of 1776, the Continental Congress advised the colonies to establish new governments. By 1777 nearly all the former colonies had adopted written constitutions. Two colonies—Connecticut and Rhode Island—retained the governments established by their royal charters.

All the new state constitutions contained some enumeration of individual rights and liberties. For instance, Virginia's new Constitution of 1776 was based on the Virginia Declaration of Rights. It protected many rights and guaranteed freedom of the press and freedom of religion. Some states, including Delaware, prohibited slavery and a state-supported religion. Georgia's constitution established public schools.

The states also realized early on that they needed a national government, if only to conduct the war. By 1777, the Continental Congress had drafted a plan: the Articles of Confederation. (The new government finally took charge in 1781.) The Articles gave very limited powers to the central government—little more than waging war and signing treaties. (See Chapter 8.)

Freedom and Slavery During the Revolution, some people began to see a conflict between slavery and the ideal of liberty. In response, Vermont outlawed slavery, and Pennsylvania passed a law to free slaves gradually. Individual African Americans also fought to end slavery, sometimes suing for freedom in the courts. For example, **Elizabeth Freeman** sued for her freedom in a Massachusetts court and won. Her victory in 1781 and other similar cases ended slavery in that state.

Freed African Americans formed their own institutions. For example, in Philadelphia **Richard Allen** helped start the Free African Society, a **nondenominational** group that encouraged people to help each other. (*Nondenominational* means not favoring any particular religion.) Richard Allen had earned the money to buy his freedom by working for the Revolutionary forces. As a preacher, Allen's leadership was shaped by his belief that he had a special duty to teach and help people, of all backgrounds, who had suffered from discrimination. Allen also founded the African Methodist Episcopal Church, the first African-American church in the United States.

Despite the efforts to end slavery in the North, in the South slavery continued. However, many people, including Southern plantation owners, were troubled by the new nation's dependence on slavery. In 1784, Thomas Jefferson, a slave owner himself, wrote of his fears for America if slavery were allowed to continue: "I tremble for my country when I reflect that God is just; that his justice cannot sleep forever."

Connecting History

Regionalism
The South's dependence on slavery would lead to a terrible civil war that threatened to tear apart the United States itself. You will see this theme emerge as you study events leading to the Civil War.

Richard Allen

Defining Religious Freedom For many Americans, central to the ideal of liberty was the idea that religion is a private matter and that people should have the right to choose and practice their personal religious beliefs. People such as James Madison and Thomas Jefferson called for a "separation of church and state," meaning that the state should not be involved in religious affairs.

In 1777 Thomas Jefferson proposed his **Virginia Statute for Religious Freedom**. In it, he claimed that people have a "natural right" to freedom of opinion, including religious opinion. Jefferson opposed state laws that prohibited Jews or Catholics from holding public office. He also opposed the practice of using tax money to support churches, because, he wrote, "to compel a man to furnish contributions of money for the propagation of opinions which he disbelieves, is sinful and tyrannical."

Jefferson's statute was eventually adopted as law in Virginia. Later, it became the basis of the religious rights guaranteed by the Bill of Rights in the U.S. Constitution.

Uniting the States For almost two centuries each colony had been governed independently of its neighbors. The colonies had been quarrelsome and often uncooperative. However, as the war turned colonies into states, Americans saw how important it was for these states to work together as a nation. The great challenge that lay ahead was how to remain united as a nation of independent states, despite regional and religious differences.

SUMMARIZE Describe the ideals that emerged from the Revolution.

Michigan Grade Level Content Expectations *Review*

 ONLINE QUIZ
For test practice, go to
Interactive Review @ ClassZone.com

TERMS & NAMES

1. Explain the importance of

- Treaty of Paris
- Richard Allen
- Elizabeth Freeman
- Virginia Statute for Religious Freedom

USING YOUR READING NOTES

2. Categorize List and categorize the major results of the Revolutionary War.

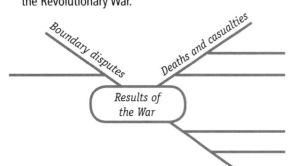

KEY IDEAS

3. What groups gained least from the Treaty of Paris?

4. How did the goals of the Revolution guide Americans toward a more just society after the war?

CRITICAL THINKING

5. Connect Economics & History How did the Treaty of Paris protect America's economic interests?

6. Causes and Effects How did the Patriot victory affect Native Americans?

7. Historical Perspective What might have happened if, during the peace negotiations, each state had tried to negotiate independently?

8. **Writing** **Citizenship Report** Use the Internet to research Elizabeth Freeman and Richard Allen. Write a brief report explaining how their efforts helped improve their communities.

Chapter Summary

① Key Idea
Although the Continental
Army had difficulty fighting in
a divided America, the Patriots
triumphed at Saratoga.

② Key Idea
The expansion of the war
weakened the British by forcing
them to spread their military
resources around the world.

③ Key Idea
The Continental Army, their allies,
and the American people brought
about an American victory.

④ Key Idea
Americans emerged from the
Revolution as citizens of a
unified nation that valued the
ideal of liberty.

To create **Review and Study Notes**
go to **Interactive Review**
@ ClassZone.com

Name Game

**Use the Terms & Names list to complete each sentence online or on
your own paper.**

1. I carried the war to the western frontier.
   George Rogers Clark 🖱

2. I led my troops to defeat at Saratoga. ____

3. I was a French officer who fought for
   America. ____

4. My leadership unified a nation. ____

5. I was trapped between allied forces and
   the French fleet. ____

6. I brought the war to the coasts of Britain. ____

7. The ideal of liberty helped me win my
   freedom in court. ____

8. I lost my lands when my ally betrayed me. ____

9. Here the Patriots first proved that they might
   win the war. ____

10. Here the Continental Army endured a difficult
    winter. ____

A. Joseph Brant
B. John Paul Jones
C. George Rogers Clark
D. Benedict Arnold
E. Valley Forge
F. Richard Allen
G. John Burgoyne
H. Marquis de Lafayette
I. Treaty of Paris
J. George Washington
K. Horatio Gates
L. Lord Cornwallis
M. Elizabeth Freeman
N. Yorktown
O. Saratoga

Activities

CROSSWORD PUZZLE

Complete the online crossword
puzzle to show what you know about
the American Revolution.

ACROSS
1. _____ captured
   the British
   warship *Serapis*.

GEOGAME

Use this online map to reinforce your understanding of the Revolutionary War,
including the locations of important battles and geographic features. Drag and
drop each place name in the list at its location on the map. A scorecard helps
you keep track of your progress online.

Trenton

Saratoga

Lake Ontario

Valley Forge

Hudson River

More place names online

Lake Ontario

VOCABULARY

Explain the significance of each of the following:

1. Joseph Brant
2. Treaty of Paris
3. Battles of Saratoga
4. privateer
5. Battle of Yorktown
6. neutral
7. Richard Allen
8. Valley Forge
9. guerrilla
10. George Washington

Explain how the terms and names in each group are related.

11. George Washington, Marquis de Lafayette, Valley Forge, mercenary

12. John Burgoyne, Horatio Gates, Benedict Arnold

13. Lord Cornwallis, Battle of Yorktown, redoubt

Marquis de Lafayette

KEY IDEAS

① The Early Years of the War (pages 194–201)

14. What difficulties did the Americans have in readying a military force to fight the Revolutionary War?

15. What events led to British defeat at Saratoga?

② The War Expands (pages 204–211)

16. Explain the importance of George Rogers Clark and John Paul Jones in expanding the war.

17. Explain three effects of America's alliances with France and Spain.

③ The Path to Victory (pages 212–219)

18. Why did the British decide to attack the South?

19. Describe the tactics and technologies used during the fighting in the Southern colonies.

④ The Legacy of the War (pages 222–228)

20. In what ways did the Treaty of Paris of 1783 favor America?

21. Describe three challenges America faced after defeating Britain.

CRITICAL THINKING

22. **Causes and Effects** How did shortages of soldiers and supplies affect Washington's plans at the start of the war?

23. **Summarize** Summarize the role of Britain's navy in the war.

24. **Compare** Create a table to compare and contrast the battles of Saratoga and Yorktown. After you complete your table, explain the significance of each battle.

Battles of Saratoga	Battle of Yorktown
mountainous	*town*
wooded terrain	*flat land*

25. **Synthesize** Why did the war last such a long time?

26. **Evaluate** Refer to the "American Strengths/British Weaknesses" chart on page 218. Which British weakness do you think proved most important in the Patriot victory? Explain your choice.

27. **Draw Conclusions** How was America able to overcome its lack of resources and soldiers?

28. **Interpret Graphs** Study the graph below. How do you explain the change in data from 1779 to 1780?

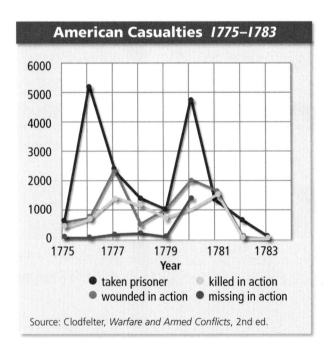

American Casualties 1775–1783

● taken prisoner ● killed in action
● wounded in action ● missing in action

Source: Clodfelter, *Warfare and Armed Conflicts*, 2nd ed.

MEAP PRACTICE

DOCUMENT-BASED QUESTIONS

Analyze each document, and answer the questions that follow.

DOCUMENT 1

1 This artwork shows Catherine Van Rensselaer Schuyler, the wife of American general Phillip Schuyler, setting fire to her own family's fields near Saratoga, New York, in 1777. Why is Mrs. Schuyler burning her fields?

A to distract the British from taking over her home

B she is mentally ill

C to keep the British from taking her crops

D to clear the field for replanting

DOCUMENT 2

PRIMARY SOURCE

" When . . . it [became] impossible for any but the wealthiest to import anything to eat or wear, and all had to be raised and manufactured at home, from bread stuffs, sugar, and rum to the linen and woollen for our clothes and bedding, you may well imagine that my duties were not light. "

—Temperance Smith

2 Temperance Smith wrote this while her husband was serving at Fort Ticonderoga during the American Revolution. How did Temperance Smith's life change during the war?

A She had to grow her own food and make her own clothing.

B She was able to buy food and clothing from the British.

C She became more independent.

D She was able to do less housework.

YOU BE THE HISTORIAN

29. Make Judgments Do you think America was stronger before or after the war? Explain and justify your opinion.

30. Causes and Effects How did the war change the daily life of an average merchant or farm family?

31. WHAT IF? Suppose France had not come to America's aid. In what ways would this have affected Washington's ability to defeat the British?

32. Analyze Motives Why do you think most Patriots who fought the Revolutionary War to protect liberty did not try to banish slavery?

33. Citizenship How did independence change Americans' responsibilities as citizens?

Connect *to* **Today** Give some examples of how people in your community fulfill these responsibilities today.

 Answer the

ESSENTIAL QUESTION

How was it possible that American Patriots gained their independence from the powerful British Empire?

Written Response Write a four-paragraph response to the Essential Question. Be sure to consider the key ideas of each section as well as the most significant factors that led to the American victory. Use the Response Rubric below to guide your thinking and writing.

Response Rubric

A strong response will

• discuss major events that led to the American victory

• analyze American strengths and British weaknesses

• explain the importance of strong leadership

• describe the role of allies in the war.

1. The Confederation Era

2. Creating the Constitution

3. Ratifying the Constitution

Confederation to Constitution

1776–1791

 ESSENTIAL QUESTION

How did Americans create a national government that respected both the independence of states and the rights of individuals?

CONNECT ⟲ **Geography & History**

How might the geography of the United States have affected the policies of the new national government?

Think about:

❶ the newly acquired territory between the Appalachian Mountains and the Mississippi River

❷ the regions with the densest population concentration

❸ the distance between Maine and Georgia, about 1,300 miles

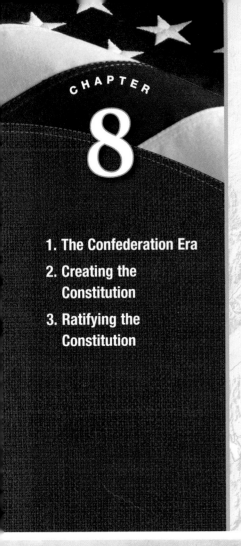

Independence Hall as it appeared in 1776.

1781 Articles of Confederation passed.
▼
Effect The United States has its first national government.

1776

American independence

1777 Continental Congress passes the Articles of Confederation.

This early flag has 13 stars representing the original 13 colonies.

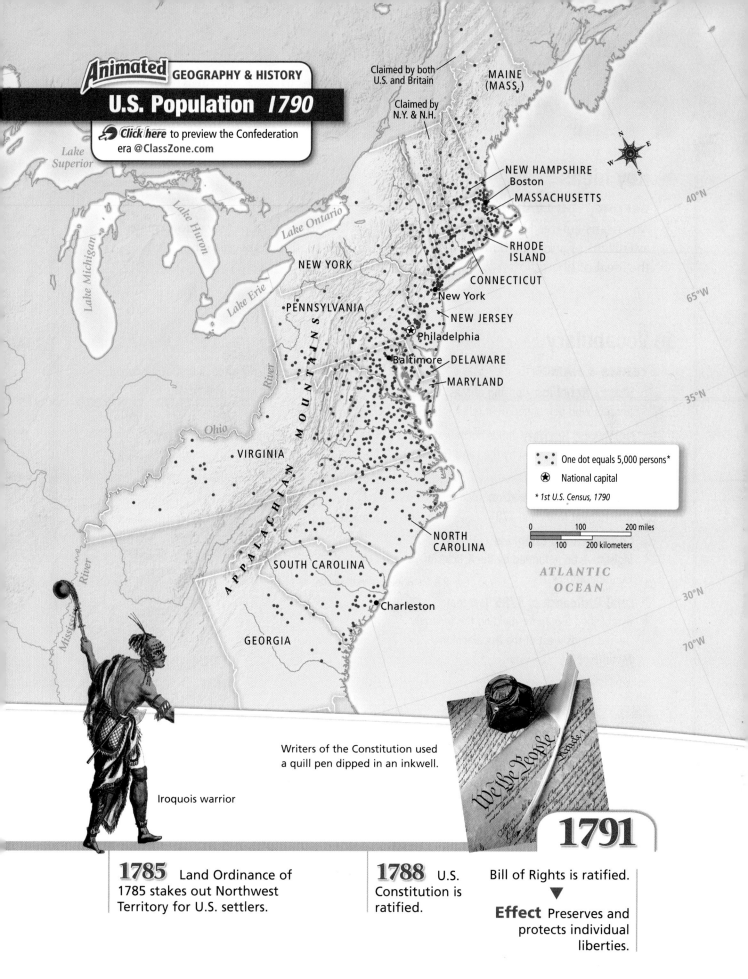

U.S. Population *1790*

Click here to preview the Confederation era @ClassZone.com

Lake Superior

Lake Michigan

Lake Huron

Lake Ontario

Lake Erie

Claimed by both U.S. and Britain

MAINE (MASS.)

Claimed by N.Y. & N.H.

NEW HAMPSHIRE
Boston
MASSACHUSETTS

RHODE ISLAND

CONNECTICUT

NEW YORK

New York

NEW JERSEY

PENNSYLVANIA

Philadelphia

Baltimore   DELAWARE

MARYLAND

River

Ohio

VIRGINIA

APPALACHIAN MOUNTAINS

Mississippi River

NORTH CAROLINA

SOUTH CAROLINA

Charleston

GEORGIA

ATLANTIC OCEAN

40°N

65°W

35°N

30°N

70°W

- One dot equals 5,000 persons*
- ⊛ National capital
- * 1st U.S. Census, 1790

0   100   200 miles
0   100   200 kilometers

N E W S

Iroquois warrior

Writers of the Constitution used a quill pen dipped in an inkwell.

We the People

1785 Land Ordinance of 1785 stakes out Northwest Territory for U.S. settlers.

1788 U.S. Constitution is ratified.

1791

Bill of Rights is ratified.
▼
Effect Preserves and protects individual liberties.

Reading for Understanding

▶ Key Ideas

BEFORE, YOU LEARNED
Americans emerged from the Revolution as citizens of a unified nation that valued the ideal of liberty.

NOW YOU WILL LEARN
The Articles of Confederation created a weak national government.

▶ Vocabulary

TERMS & NAMES

Shays's Rebellion uprising of Massachusetts farmers who demanded debt relief

Northwest Territory lands northwest of the Appalachians, covered by the Land Ordinance of 1785

Articles of Confederation plan for national government ratified in 1781

Confederation Congress national legislative body formed by the Articles of Confederation

Land Ordinance of 1785 law that established a plan for dividing the federally owned lands west of the Appalachian Mountains

Northwest Ordinance law that described how the Northwest Territory was to be governed

BACKGROUND VOCABULARY

republic state, country or nation in which people elect representatives to govern.

ratification act of official confirmation

levy impose or raise a tax

arsenal place where weapons are stored

REVIEW

neutral not siding with one country or another

▶ Reading Strategy

Create an outline like the one shown at right. As you read and respond to the **KEY QUESTIONS**, note the main ideas and supporting details about the Articles of Confederation.

 See Skillbuilder Handbook, page R9.

MAIN IDEAS & DETAILS

> The Articles of Confederation
>
> I. Features of the A. of C.
>   —
>   —
> II. Needs addressed by the A. of C.
>   —
>   —

 GRAPHIC ORGANIZERS
Go to **Interactive Review** @ ClassZone.com

The Confederation Era

F1.3.2 Describe the consequences of the American Revolution by analyzing the – creation of Articles of Confederation
8 – U3.3.1 Explain the reasons for the adoption and subsequent failure of the Articles of Confederation (e.g., why its drafters created a weak central government, challenges the nation faced under the Articles, Shays' Rebellion, disputes over western lands).

One American's Story

After the Revolutionary War, the nation faced hard economic times. People had little money, but the states continued to levy high taxes. In Massachusetts, many farmers fell deeply into debt.

PRIMARY SOURCE

❝ I have been obliged to pay and nobody will pay me. I have lost a great deal by this man and that man . . . and the great men are going to get all we have, and I think it is time for us to rise and put a stop to it. . . . ❞

—Plough Jogger, quoted in *The People Speak: American Voices, Some Famous, Some Little Known*

Shays's rebels take over a Massachusetts courthouse. Today a stone marker rests on the spot of the rebellion.

From August 1786 to February 1787, Daniel Shays, a Revolutionary War veteran, led Jogger and other farmers in an armed uprising. To protest what the farmers viewed as unfair taxation, they attacked county courts in Massachusetts. At first, using force, they succeeded in stopping the courts from selling farmers' possessions and jailing people who couldn't pay their debts.

The state militia put down **Shays's Rebellion**, as the uprising came to be known. But many people sided with the farmers. America's leaders realized that a popular armed uprising spelled danger to the new nation. It was clearly time to talk about a stronger national government.

Forming a New Government

🔽 **KEY QUESTION** What did the states want from a national government?

Ten years before Shays's Rebellion, the colonists had resisted the harsh rule of a distant government. As Americans planned their first national government, in 1776-1777, their main goal was to prevent governmental tyranny from reappearing in the new nation.

Republicanism and Citizenship American leaders felt strongly that the people needed to exercise control over their government. It was decided that the new nation would be a **republic**, a country in which the people choose representatives to govern them. But not everyone in the United States would be allowed to help select these representatives. Most states had fairly high property qualifications, and only property owners, who were considered citizens, would be allowed to vote. African Americans were generally not allowed to vote. Some states granted voting rights to all white males. All states, except Pennsylvania and Georgia, made property ownership a requirement for voting. Women were also denied the right to vote in most states.

State Constitutions Lead the Way Once the American colonies declared independence in 1776, each of the states set out to create its own government. The framers, or creators, of the state constitutions did not want to destroy the political systems that they had had as colonies. They simply wanted to make those systems more representative.

Some states experimented with giving different powers to different parts of government. By creating separate branches of government, Americans hoped to prevent any one part of the government from becoming too powerful. All state governments limited the powers of their governors because of the colonists' unpleasant experience with the British king.

Some states included a Bill of Rights in their constitutions. Based on the English Bill of Rights of 1689, these bills were lists of freedoms that Americans were most eager to protect. The first constitutional document in the United States was Virginia's constitution of 1776. It protected freedom of the press and freedom of religion.

As citizens set up their state governments, they discussed how to form a national government. During the Revolutionary War, Americans realized that they had to unite to win the war against Britain. Forming a national government was key to national unity. And diplomat John Dickinson's words, "By uniting we stand, by dividing we fall," became a popular slogan.

The Articles of Confederation In 1776, the Continental Congress began to plan for a national government. Congress agreed that the government should be a republic. But the delegates disagreed about whether each state should have one vote or voting should be based on population.

They also disagreed about who should control the **Northwest Territory**, or the lands west of the Appalachians. The Continental Congress eventually arrived at a plan called the **Articles of Confederation**. In the Articles, the national government would be run by a legislative body to be called the **Confederation Congress**. Congress had the power to wage war, make peace, sign treaties, run Indian affairs, and issue money. Each state had only one vote in the Congress.

Connecting History

Growth of Government
The English Bill of Rights limited the power of the English monarch. Among other things, it prevented the monarch from levying taxes, and maintaining an army in peacetime without the consent of Parliament.

Powers Granted and Denied Congress

GRANTED CONGRESS	DENIED CONGRESS
• Conduct foreign affairs	• Establish executive branch
• Declare war and make peace	• Enforce national laws
• Issue or borrow money	• Enact and collect taxes
• Control Western territories	• Regulate interstate or foreign trade
• Control Indian affairs	• Establish federal courts
• Run postal service	• Amend the Articles

CRITICAL THINKING Evaluate Why did the powers denied Congress lead to a weak government?

But the Articles left most important powers to the states. These powers included the authority to set taxes and enforce national laws. The proposed Articles left the individual states in control of the lands west of the Appalachian Mountains.

The Articles Are Ratified The Continental Congress passed the Articles of Confederation in November 1777. It then sent the Articles to the states for **ratification,** or approval. By July 1778, eight states had ratified the Articles. But some of the small states that did not have Western land claims refused to sign. These states worried that they would be at a disadvantage unless the Western lands were placed under the control of the national government. The states with Western lands could sell them to pay off debts left from the Revolution and possibly become overwhelmingly powerful. But states without lands would have difficulty paying off the high war debts.

Gradually, all the states gave up their claims to Western lands. This led the small states to ratify the Articles. In 1781, Maryland became the 13th state to accept the Articles. As a result, the United States finally had an official government.

🔺 **SUMMARIZE** Discuss the powers of the states under the Articles of Confederation.

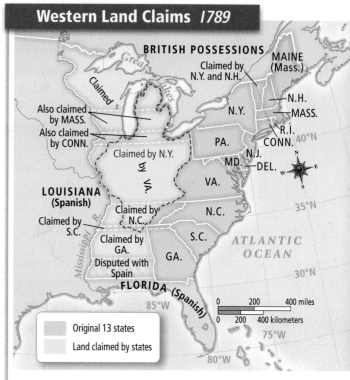

Western Land Claims 1789

Connect Geography & History

1. **Location** How far west did the Western land claims extend?

2. **Draw Conclusions** The western lands were vast. What might be some of the challenges of governing such a large territory?

Strengths and Weaknesses of the Articles

🔻 **KEY QUESTION** What were the weaknesses of the national government?

The Confederation Congress had run the country during the Revolutionary War and had some success in handling land issues. But Americans began to realize the Confederation Congress was too weak to deal with most other national issues.

The Land Ordinance of 1785 One issue the Confederation Congress successfully handled was what to do with the Western lands that it now controlled. Starting in 1785, the Congress passed important laws on how to divide and govern these lands.

The **Land Ordinance of 1785** called for surveyors to stake out six-mile-square plots, called townships, in the Western lands. These lands later became known as the Northwest Territory. The Northwest Territory included land that formed the states of Ohio, Indiana, Michigan, Illinois, Wisconsin, and part of Minnesota.

Governing the Northwest Territory The **Northwest Ordinance** of 1787 outlined how the Northwest Territory was to be governed. The bill had many democratic features. As the territory grew in population, it would gain rights to self-government. When there were 5,000 free adult males in an area, men who owned at least 50 acres of land could elect an assembly. When there were 60,000 people, they could apply to become a new state. Slavery was outlawed. Rivers were to be open to navigation for all. Freedom of religion and trial by jury were guaranteed.

The Northwest Ordinance was a big success for the Confederation Congress. The bill created a model for the orderly growth of the United States well into the 19th century. But the Northwest Ordinance was bad for the lands' original inhabitants. The Ordinance promised Native Americans fair treatment, and Native American lands were not to be taken from them. However, the increased contact between settlers and natives led to territorial conflicts that were not easily resolved.

Problems with Britain and Spain To fight the Revolutionary War, Congress had borrowed large sums of money. With the war over, it was now time to pay back the loans. Yet the Confederation Congress did not have the money to do so. Congress also found that it did not have the power to deal on an equal basis with other nations. Some of the challenges Congress faced with other nations were:

- Britain competed against the American fur trade by refusing to evacuate its military forts south of the Great Lakes.
- Britain barred American-owned ships from British waters in the Caribbean.
- Spain also put up barriers to American shipping in the Caribbean.
- Spain refused to allow Americans to use the Mississippi River or to deposit goods in New Orleans.
- Spain and Congress argued over the boundary of Florida.

In the late 1700s, Spain held the crucial port of New Orleans. **Why did this have an impact on American traders?**

The problems the Confederation faced in foreign relations revealed the basic weaknesses of the national government. The United States did not have the strength to face up to the superior forces of the British or the Spanish.

Economic Problems and Shays's Rebellion With American trade weakened, the nation was facing a serious economic crisis. Much of the Confederation's debt was owed to soldiers of the Revolutionary army. Upset at not being paid, approximately 300 soldiers demonstrated before the Pennsylvania State House where Congress was meeting in June 1783. The delegates were forced to flee the city. The event was another clear sign of Congress's weakness.

One reason Congress was unable to raise money to pay the soldiers was that it did not have the power to **levy**, or collect, taxes. The national government depended on the states to send money. The states, who also owed money because of the war, tried to raise money through taxes. However, few ordinary Americans could afford to pay them. Taxes on imported goods raised the cost of everyday necessities, further hurting average Americans.

Taxes in Massachusetts were some of the highest in the nation. The government's refusal to grant debt relief led to an uprising known as Shays's Rebellion. In January 1787, Shays led a march on a federal **arsenal**, a place where weapons are stored. Around one thousand soldiers from the state militia quickly defeated Shays's men.

America's leaders realized that an armed uprising of common farmers spelled danger for the nation. Some leaders hoped that the nation's ills could be solved by giving more power to the national government.

▲ **PROBLEMS AND SOLUTIONS** Identify the reasons why the national government was not strong enough.

Michigan Grade Level Content Expectations *Review*

 ONLINE QUIZ
For test practice, go to
Interactive Review @ ClassZone.com

TERMS & NAMES
1. Explain the importance of
   - Shays's Rebellion
   - Northwest Territory
   - Articles of Confederation
   - Confederation Congress
   - Land Ordinance of 1785
   - Northwest Ordinance

USING YOUR READING NOTES
2. **Problems and Solutions** Complete the outline you started at the beginning of this section.

   > **The Articles of Confederation**
   >
   > I. *Features of the A. of C.*
   >   —
   >   —
   > II. *Needs addressed by the A. of C.*
   >   —
   >   —

KEY IDEAS
3. How did the Articles of Confederation prevent the national government from becoming too powerful?
4. Why was the Confederation Congress unable to resolve problems with Britain and Spain?

CRITICAL THINKING
5. **Connect Economics and History** Which side would you have supported in Shays's Rebellion—the farmers or the officials who called out the militia? Why?
6. **Analyze** Why were the states afraid of centralized authority and a strong national government?
7. **Writing** **Letter** Write a one-page letter from Daniel Shays to the governor of Massachusetts. In your letter, ask the governor to pardon, or forgive, your rebellion against the government.

The Northwest Territory

In the mid-1780s, Congress decided to sell the land known as "the Territory Northwest of the river Ohio" to settlers—although this policy was often fiercely resisted by the Native Americans living in the region. The sale of land solved two problems. First, it provided cash for the government. Second, it increased American control over the land. The first organized American settlement in the Northwest Territory was Marietta, Ohio, founded in 1788.

The Land Ordinance of 1785 outlined how the land in the Northwest Territory would be divided. Congress created townships that could be divided into sections, as shown on the map below. Each township was six miles by six miles. This was an improvement over earlier methods of setting boundaries. Previously people had used rocks, trees, or other landmarks to set boundaries.

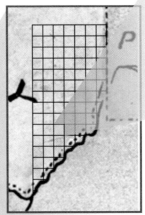

Township 1785

36	30	24	18	12	6
35	29	23	17	11	5
34	28	22	16	10	4
33	27	21	15	9	3
32	26	20	14	8	2
31	25	19	13	7	1

Each township contained 36 sections. Each section was one square mile.

NATIVE AMERICANS

This area that became the Northwest Territory was the homeland of many Native American tribes — such as the Miami and Shawnee. The tribes grew crops and supplemented their diet with hunting and fishing. Some built bark houses. Besides trading with European fur traders, Native Americans traded with other tribes. Miami corn, for example, was valued for its high quality and the ease with which it could be turned into fine flour.

Shawnee fishing

one square mile

GOVERNMENT SURVEYORS

Congress provided for official surveys of the Territory. Basic surveying tools included a compass, chain and stakes, a jacob staff (a long, straight wooden rod used as a base for instruments), and a theodolite. (See photo.) A theodolite consists of a telescope that can be moved from side to side and up and down. It measures angles and determines alignment.

Connect Geography & History

1. **Summarize** What was the land in the Northwest Territory like before American settlers moved there?

2. **Problems and Solutions** How did American settlers affect the landscape in the territory?

3. **Make Inferences** Why would geography have helped create an independent spirit in the territory?

See Geography Handbook, page A2.

Reading for Understanding

▶ Key Ideas

BEFORE, YOU LEARNED
The Articles of Confederation created a weak national government.

NOW YOU WILL LEARN
The Constitution created a new, stronger government that replaced the Confederation.

▶ Vocabulary

TERMS & NAMES

Constitutional Convention 1787 meeting at which the U.S. Constitution was created

Founders people who helped create the U.S. Constitution

James Madison prominent adviser to the Constitutional Convention

Virginia Plan proposal for a two-house legislature with representation according to each state's population or wealth

New Jersey Plan proposal for a legislature in which each state would have one vote

Great Compromise agreement to establish a two-house national legislature, with all states having equal representation in one house and each state having representation based on its population in the other house.

Three-Fifths Compromise agreement that three-fifths of a state's slave population would be counted for representation and taxation

executive branch government department that enforces laws

judicial branch government department that interprets laws

legislative branch government department that makes laws

checks and balances the ability of each branch of government to exercise checks, or controls, over the other branches

▶ Reading Strategy

Re-create the diagram shown at right. As you read and respond to the **KEY QUESTIONS**, use the ovals to show why there was a need for a Constitutional Convention.

 See Skillbuilder Handbook, page R3.

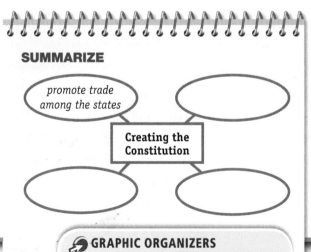

SUMMARIZE

promote trade among the states

Creating the Constitution

GRAPHIC ORGANIZERS
Go to **Interactive Review** @ ClassZone.com

Creating the Constitution

8 – U3.3.3 Describe the major issues debated at the Constitutional Convention including the distribution of political power, conduct of foreign affairs, rights of individuals, rights of states, election of the executive, and slavery as a regional and federal issue.

8 – U3.3.4 Explain how the new constitution resolved (or compromised) the major issues including sharing, separating, and checking of power among federal government institutions, dual sovereignty (state-federal power), rights of individuals, the Electoral College, the Three-Fifths Compromise, and the Great Compromise.

One American's Story

On May 15, 1787, Virginia Governor Edmund Randolph arrived in Philadelphia. The young nation faced conflict, as Shays's Rebellion had shown. Now delegates from throughout the states were coming to Philadelphia to discuss reforming the government.

Early in the convention Randolph spoke.

PRIMARY SOURCE

❝ Let us not be afraid to view with a steady eye the [dangers] with which we are surrounded. . . . Are we not on the eve of [a civil] war, which is only to be prevented by the hopes from this convention? ❞

—Edmund Randolph, quoted in *Edmund Randolph: A Biography*

The Pennsylvania State House is where (*inset*) Edmund Randolph attended the Constitutional Convention.

At first, many Americans doubted that the national government needed strengthening. But fear of rebellion and lawlessness had changed people's minds. For over four months, Congress debated how best to keep the United States from falling apart.

The Call for a Constitutional Convention

🔻 **KEY QUESTION** Why was there a call for a Constitutional Convention?

In September 1786, delegates from five states met in Annapolis, Maryland, to discuss ways to promote trade among the states. At the time, most states charged high taxes on goods imported from other states. The Annapolis delegates believed that creating national trade laws would help the economies of all the states. However, making such changes required amending the Articles of Confederation, because the national government had been granted no

History Makers

James Madison 1751–1836

James Madison was a soft-spoken, scholarly man. In the months before the convention, Madison studied the history of other confederacies that had failed. He saw that without a strong central government, states tended to concentrate too much on their individual interests and not enough on the common good. He came to believe that simply revising the Articles of Confederation would not be enough. Out of this research emerged the Virginia Plan, which provided the basic structure of the new government.

Madison may have made the greatest contribution of any of the Founders at the Constitutional Convention. His contributions were so important that he earned the title "Father of the Constitution."

COMPARING Leaders

As you read through the chapter, look for other examples of Madison's leadership. Compare his leadership qualities to those of American statesmen described in previous chapters.

 **ONLINE BIOGRAPHY** For more on James Madison, go to the **Research & Writing Center** @ ClassZone.com

power to regulate trade among the states. Some delegates, led by Alexander Hamilton, called for a convention in Philadelphia the following May. Twelve states sent delegates to the Convention. Only Rhode Island declined.

Constitutional Convention The convention opened on May 25, 1787. The first order of business was to nominate a president for the convention. Every delegate voted for the hero of the Revolution, George Washington. Washington's quiet and dignified leadership set the tone for the convention.

The delegates did not want to be pressured by the politics of the day. For this reason, they decided their discussions would remain secret. Much of what we know today about the debates and drama of the Constitutional Convention is thanks to Virginia delegate **James Madison**. In addition to contributing many ideas that shaped the Constitution, Madison took detailed notes on the proceedings.

Who Was There? The 55 delegates to the **Constitutional Convention**, as the Philadelphia meeting became known, were a very impressive group. Many had been members of their state legislatures and had helped write their state constitutions. Along with other leaders of the time, these delegates are called the **Founders**, or Founding Fathers, of the United States. Many of the delegates who helped draft the proposals presented at the Convention were already well known. Roger Sherman, a Connecticut delegate, was a signer of The Declaration of Independence and the Articles of Confederation. Pennsylvania's Gouverneur Morris had also signed the Articles of Confederation. Morris and Washington were friends.

Another prominent Pennsylvania delegate, Scots-born James Wilson, was known for his brilliant legal mind. Wilson worked with James Madison in pushing for a system of **popular sovereignty**, which is a government system in which the people rule. He backed the election of a national legislature by the people to be "not only the cornerstone, but the foundation of the fabric."

Who Was Missing? A number of key people were unable to attend. Thomas Jefferson and John Adams were overseas at their diplomatic posts. But they wrote home to encourage the delegates. Others had a less positive outlook. For example, Patrick Henry, who had been elected as a delegate from Virginia, refused to go. He said he "smelled a rat . . . tending toward monarchy."

Also, the convention did not reflect the diverse U.S. population of the 1780s. There were no Native Americans, African Americans, or women among the delegates. These groups of people were not recognized as citizens and were not invited to attend. However, the framework of government the Founders established at the Constitutional Convention is the very one that would eventually provide full rights and responsibilities to all Americans.

▲ **SUMMARIZE** Explain why the United States needed a constitutional convention.

Some Challenges of the Convention

▼ **KEY QUESTION** What were some of the major challenges facing the Convention?

By 1787, many Americans realized that people and states often came into conflict and needed a government that could keep order. They wanted a government that was strong enough to protect people's rights but not so strong that it would oppress them.

Disagreements over Representation As the Convention began, the delegates disagreed about what form the new government would take. Two plans emerged. James Madison and the other Virginia delegates had drawn up their plan while they waited for the convention to open. Edmund Randolph presented the plan. The **Virginia Plan** proposed a government with three branches. The **executive branch** would enforce the laws. The **judicial branch** would interpret the laws. The third branch, the **legislative branch,** would create the laws.

The Virginia Plan wanted the legislature to have two sections: an Upper House and a Lower House. In both houses, the number of representatives

COMPARING *Plans for Government*

	VIRGINIA PLAN	**NEW JERSEY PLAN**
Legislative branch	Two (branches) houses: representation determined by state population or wealth	One house: one vote for each state, regardless of size
	Lower House: elected by the people Upper House: elected by lower house	Elected by state legislatures
Executive branch	Appointed by Legislature	Appointed by Legislature
Judicial branch	Appointed by Legislature	Appointed by Executive

CRITICAL THINKING Analyze Which plan appealed more to the smaller states?

from each state would be based on the state's population or its wealth. The legislature would have the power to make laws "in all cases to which the separate states are incompetent [unable]."

As well as having its own distinct powers, each branch could check the powers of the other branches in certain circumstances. This system of **"checks and balances"** is a way of controlling the power of government. As James Madison said, "All power in human hands is liable to be abused." The Founders designed the new government to limit that abuse.

Delegates from the small states strongly objected to the Virginia Plan because it gave more power to states with larger populations. In response to the Virginia Plan, New Jersey delegate William Paterson presented an alternative. Like the Articles, the **New Jersey Plan** called for a single-house congress in which each state had an equal vote. Small states supported the New Jersey Plan.

The Great Compromise Emotions ran high as the delegates struggled to solve the problem of representation in the legislature. In early July, a committee led by Roger Sherman and other delegates from Connecticut offered a deal known as the **Great Compromise**. Sherman proposed:

PRIMARY SOURCE

❝ That the proportion of suffrage in the first branch should be according to the respective numbers of free inhabitants, and that in the second branch or Senate, each State should have one vote and no more. ❞

—Roger Sherman, June 11, 1787

In other words, to satisfy the smaller states, each state would have an equal number of votes in the Senate. To satisfy the larger states, representation in the House of Representatives was set according to state populations. On July 16, 1787, the convention passed the plan.

🔺 **PROBLEMS AND SOLUTIONS** Describe the major challenges of the Convention in creating a stronger national government.

Challenges Over Slavery

🔻 **KEY QUESTION** How did the Constitutional Convention compromise over slavery?

Because representation in the House of Representatives would be based on the population of each state, the delegates had to decide who would be counted in that population. For example, were slaves to be counted as part of the population?

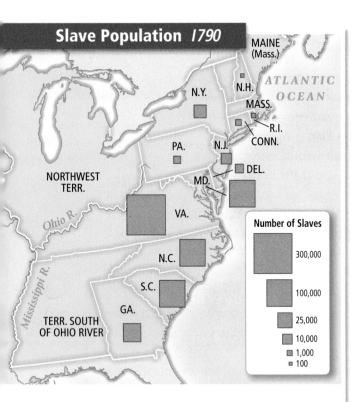

Slave Population 1790

Number of Slaves: 300,000 / 100,000 / 25,000 / 10,000 / 1,000 / 100

Connect Geography & History

1. **Place** Which state would have the greatest interest in having slaves counted as part of their population for purposes of representation?
2. **Clarify** Why did the North and the South have differing opinions on whether or not slaves should be counted as part of a state's population?

The Three-Fifths Compromise Representation based on population raised the question of whether slaves should be counted as people. The Southern states had many more slaves than the Northern states. Southerners wanted the slaves to be counted as part of the population for representation but not for taxation. Northerners, whose states had few slaves, argued that slaves were not citizens and should not be counted for representation but should be counted for taxation.

The delegates reached an agreement, known as the **Three-Fifths Compromise**. Three-fifths of the slave population would be counted for both purposes: representation in the legislature and taxation.

The delegates had another point of disagreement. Slavery had already been outlawed in several Northern states. Many Northerners wanted to see this ban extended to the rest of the nation. But Southern slaveholders disagreed. The delegates from South Carolina and Georgia stated that they would never accept any plan "unless their right to import slaves be untouched." Again, the delegates settled on a compromise. On August 29, they agreed that Congress could not ban the slave trade until 1808.

On September 17, 1787, the delegates passed the Constitution. All but three of the 42 delegates present signed the Constitution. It was then sent to each state for approval.

 ANALYZE POINT OF VIEW Explain how the Constitutional Convention compromised on the issue of slavery.

Connecting History

Individual Rights vs. Majority Rule
Congress decided to end the importation of Africans after 1808. However, the slave trade continued in the slave states.

Michigan Grade Level Content Expectations *Review*

 ONLINE QUIZ
For test practice, go to
Interactive Review @ ClassZone.com

TERMS & NAMES

1. Explain the importance of

- Constitutional Convention
- Founders
- James Madison
- legislative branch
- Virginia Plan
- checks and balances
- New Jersey Plan
- Great Compromise
- executive branch
- judicial branch
- Three-Fifths Compromise

USING YOUR READING NOTES

2. Summarize Summarize the important achievements of the Constitution.

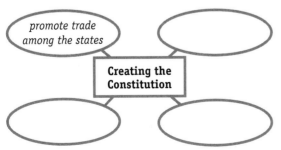

promote trade among the states

Creating the Constitution

KEY IDEAS

3. What was the relationship between the Annapolis Convention and the Constitutional Convention?

4. Why did the Virginia delegates insist that the new government have three branches?

5. Under the Three-Fifths Compromise, how would each state's population be decided?

CRITICAL THINKING

6. Analyze Point of View Why did supporters of the Virginia Plan believe their plan was the best way to create a new government?

7. **Connect** *to* **Today** What American political traditions can be traced back to the Constitutional Convention?

8. **Art** Think about the Three-Fifths Compromise. Draw a political cartoon that expresses your views on the issue.

▶ Key Ideas

BEFORE, YOU LEARNED
The Constitution created a new, stronger government that replaced the Confederation.

NOW YOU WILL LEARN
American liberties are protected by the U.S. Constitution and a Bill of Rights.

▶ Vocabulary

TERMS & NAMES

Antifederalists people who opposed ratification of the Constitution

federalism system of government in which power is shared between the national (or federal) government and the states

Federalists people who supported ratification of the Constitution

The Federalist papers ratification essays published in New York newspapers

Bill of Rights first ten amendments to the U.S. Constitution

BACKGROUND VOCABULARY

majority rule a system in which more than one half of a group holds the power to make decisions binding the entire group

amendment addition to a document

REVIEW

Parliament Britain's chief lawmaking body

Enlightenment 18th-century movement that emphasized the use of reason and the scientific method to obtain knowledge

▶ Reading Strategy

Re-create the diagram shown at right. As you read and respond to the **KEY QUESTIONS,** use the circles to compare the positions of Federalists and Antifederalists.

 See Skillbuilder Handbook, page R8.

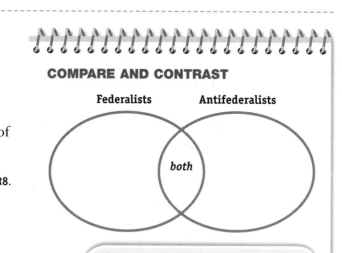

COMPARE AND CONTRAST

Federalists   Antifederalists

both

GRAPHIC ORGANIZERS
Go to **Interactive Review** @ ClassZone.com

Ratification and the Bill of Rights

8 – U3.3.5 Analyze the debates over the ratification of the Constitution from the perspectives of Federalists and Anti-Federalists and describe how the states ratified the Constitution.
8 – U3.3.6 Explain how the Bill of Rights reflected the concept of limited government, protections of basic freedoms, and the fear of many Americans of a strong central government.

One American's Story

In February of 1788, **Antifederalists**, people who opposed the Constitution, sent out a pamphlet voicing their concerns over the form of the new government. The title of the essay was "Observations on the New Constitution, and on the Federal and State Conventions." To the surprise of many people, a woman, Mercy Otis Warren, was responsible for the pamphlet. The pamphlet stressed the importance of a democratic nation ruled by the people.

PRIMARY SOURCE

❝ Government is instituted for the protection, safety and happiness of the people. . . . That the origin of all power is in the people, and that they have an [incontestable] right to check the creatures of their own creation, vested with certain powers to guard the life, liberty and property of the community. ❞

—Mercy Otis Warren, quoted in *Mercy Otis Warren*

Mercy Otis Warren was an Antifederalist and a respected historian of the American Revolution.

Warren's essay became an important part of the debate between supporters and opposers of the Constitution.

Federalists and Antifederalists

🔽 **KEY QUESTION** What key issues divided Federalists and Antifederalists?

By the time Warren's essay was published, Americans had already been debating the new Constitution for months. The document had been widely distributed in newspapers and pamphlets across the country. The framers of the Constitution knew that the document would cause controversy. At once they began to campaign for ratification, or approval, of the Constitution.

Concerns of the Federalists The framers suspected that people might be afraid the Constitution would take too much power away from the states. To address this fear, the framers explained that the Constitution was based on federalism. **Federalism** is a system of government in which power is shared between the central (or federal) government and the states. Linking themselves to the idea of federalism, the people who supported the Constitution took the name **Federalists**.

The Federalists promoted their views and answered their critics in a series of essays, known as *The Federalist* **papers**. Three well-known politicians wrote *The Federalist* papers—James Madison, Alexander Hamilton, and John Jay. These essays first appeared as letters in New York newspapers. Calling for ratification of the Constitution, *The Federalist* papers appealed both to reason and emotion. In *The Federalist* papers, Hamilton described why people should support ratification.

PRIMARY SOURCE

❝ Yes, my countrymen, . . . I am clearly of opinion it is your interest to adopt it [the Constitution]. I am convinced that this is the safest course for your liberty, your dignity, and your happiness. ❞

—Alexander Hamilton, *The Federalist* "Number 1"

ONLINE PRIMARY SOURCE

Hear the debate at the **Research & Writing Center** @ ClassZone.com

COMPARING *Perspectives*

Federalists and Antifederalists had very different ideas about how the United States should be governed. These were some of the arguments made as Americans passionately debated ratification of the Constitution.

Patrick Henry

◀)) Antifederalists

❝ Your president may easily become king: Your Senate is so imperfectly constructed that your dearest rights may be sacrificed by what may be a small minority; and a very small minority may continue for ever unchangeably this government, although horridly defective. Where are your checks in this government?

—*Patrick Henry*

The mode of levying taxes is of the utmost consequence; and yet here it is to be determined by those who have neither knowledge of our situation, nor a common interest with us. ❞

—*George Mason*

◀)) Federalists

❝ I am persuaded that a firm union is as necessary to perpetuate our liberties as it is to make us respectable; and experience will probably prove that the national government will be as natural a guardian of our freedom as the state legislature[s] themselves.

—*Alexander Hamilton*

As all the States are equally represented in the Senate, and by men the most able and the most willing to promote the interests of their constituents, they will all have an equal degree of influence in that body. ❞

—*John Jay*

John Jay

CRITICAL THINKING **Analyze** What was it about a strong federal government that frightened the Antifederalists?

Concerns of the Antifederalists The Antifederalists thought the Constitution took too much power away from the states and did not guarantee rights for the people. Some feared that a strong president might be declared king. Others feared the Senate might become a powerful ruling class. In either case, they thought, the liberties fiercely won during the Revolution might be lost.

Antifederalists received support from rural areas, where people feared a strong government that might add to their tax burden. Large states and those with strong economies, such as New York, which had greater freedom under the Articles of Confederation, also were unsupportive of the Constitution at first.

New Yorkers cheer a "Ship of State" float in honor of the new Constitution of 1798. **Why did Alexander Hamilton deserve a float in his honor?**

▲ **COMPARE AND CONTRAST** Describe the disagreements between Federalists and Antifederalists.

The Battle for Ratification

▼ **KEY QUESTION** How did the lack of a bill of rights endanger the Constitution?

The proposed U.S. Constitution contained no guarantee that the government would protect the rights of the people, or of the states. Some supporters of the Constitution, including Thomas Jefferson, wanted to add a bill of rights—a formal summary of citizens' rights and freedoms, as a set of amendments to the Constitution.

The Call for a Bill of Rights Virginia's convention opened in June of 1788. Antifederalist Patrick Henry fought against ratification, or approval, of the Constitution. George Mason, who had been a delegate to the Constitutional Convention in Philadelphia, also was opposed to it.

Antifederalists wanted written guarantees that the people would have freedom of speech, of the press, and of religion. They demanded assurance of the right to trial by jury and the right to bear arms.

Federalists insisted that the Constitution granted only limited powers to the national government so that it could not violate the rights of the states or of the people. They also pointed out that the Constitution gave the people the power to protect their rights through the election of trustworthy leaders. In the end, Federalists yielded to the people's demands and promised to add a bill of rights if the states ratified the Constitution.

Final Ratification In December 1787, Delaware, New Jersey, and Pennsylvania voted for ratification. In January 1788, Georgia and Connecticut ratified the Constitution, followed by Massachusetts in early February. By late June, nine states had ratified. The Constitution was officially ratified with nine votes. It was vital, however, to get the support of Virginia, the largest state, and New York. Without New York, the nation would be split geographically into two parts. James Madison recommended that Virginia ratify the Constitution, with the addition of a bill of rights.

As other states ratified, however, the Virginia Antifederalists played on Southern fear of Northern domination. Under the Articles of Confederation, each state had one vote, and major decisions required the approval of nine of the 13 states. The Constitution, however, provided for **majority rule**, which means that more than one half of a group holds the power to make decisions binding on the entire group. The North, Virginia Antifederalists warned, would then dictate policy in trade, slavery, and other important issues bearing on the southern economy.

After bitter debate, at the end of June, Virginia narrowly ratified the Constitution with 89 in favor and 79 opposed. The news of Virginia's vote arrived while the New York convention was in debate. Until then, the Antifederalists had outnumbered the Federalists. But with Virginia's ratification, New Yorkers decided to join the Union. New York also called for a bill of rights.

It would be another year before North Carolina ratified the Constitution, followed by Rhode Island in 1790. By then, the new Congress had already written a bill of rights and submitted it to the states for approval.

▲ **EVALUATE** Explain how the lack of a bill of rights made ratification of the Constitution more difficult.

CONNECT ⟲ *Citizenship and History*

DEBATE AND FREE SPEECH

To debate is to engage in argument by discussing opposing points of view. Debate has long been an important method of exploring public issues. The Founding Fathers engaged in intense debate before the ratification of the U.S. Constitution.

Today, many students learn about the ideas of democracy through programs like the YMCA Youth in Government program. Most of these programs consist of a model legislature composed of high school students writing legislation. Participants then meet to debate their proposed laws in their actual state capitol building.

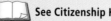

Organize a Debate!

1 Choose a debate opponent and an issue to debate. Research the topic you chose.

2 Agree on a format for your debate—presentation, rebuttal, and closing.

3 Debate your opponent in front of the class. Ask the audience to cast their votes; then report the result to the class.

📖 **See Citizenship Handbook, page 300.**

How did Americans create a national government that respected both the independence of states and the rights of individuals?

	CONFEDERATION WEAKNESSES	NEW GOVERNMENT STRENGTHS
Taxes	Congress could not levy or collect taxes.	Congress empowered to levy and collect taxes
Trade	Congress could not regulate trade carried on between states or with foreign nations.	Congress empowered to regulate interstate and foreign commerce
Courts	No regular Confederation courts; Congress depended on state courts to settle legal disputes arising from its laws.	A national system of courts set up with district and circuit courts and a supreme court
Executive	No national executive branch; enforcement of acts of Congress left to the states.	National government had the power to enforce federal laws.
States' Rights	Equality of states in voting, regardless of size or population	Proportional representation in the House; equality of states in the Senate.
Amendments	Unanimous vote required to amend Articles	Two-thirds vote in each House of Congress
Laws	Nine states had to approve an ordinary bill.	A majority required to pass a bill

CRITICAL THINKING Evaluate How were states' rights protected under the new government?

The Bill of Rights and the Constitution

▼ **KEY QUESTION** How does the Bill of Rights protect people's rights?

Madison, who took office in the first Congress in the winter of 1789, took up the cause of the bill of rights. Madison submitted ten **amendments**, or additions to a document, to the Constitution. Congress proposed that they be placed at the end of the Constitution in a separate section. These ten amendments to the U.S. Constitution became known as the **Bill of Rights.**

The Bill of Rights Of these amendments to the Constitution, the first nine guarantee basic individual freedoms. Jefferson and Madison believed that government enforcement of religious laws was the source of much social conflict. They supported freedom of religion as a way to prevent such conflict. Even before Madison wrote the Bill of Rights, he worked to ensure religious liberty in Virginia. (In 1786, Madison had helped pass the Virginia Statute for Religious Freedom, originally written by Jefferson in 1779.)

Connecting History

Religion in Public Life
Issues of religious freedom were widely debated as soon as the Puritans settled in the Massachusetts Bay Colony. Some colonists argued for and others argued against religious tolerance.

Freedom of religion is an important part of the First Amendment, which states: "Congress shall make no law respecting an establishment of religion, or prohibiting the free exercise thereof . . ." This means that the government may never support one particular religion, favor one faith above another, or interfere with anyone's religious freedom.

In this way, the Constitution put an end to the kind of religious conflict that had divided the early colonies. In the words of Thomas Jefferson, the first amendment built "a wall of separation between Church and State." Taken as a whole, the Bill of Rights creates an invisible but powerful shield that protects people from government abuse.

Amending the Constitution But the Bill of Rights was more than that. It was the first step in making the Constitution a living document, one that can be amended to reflect the changes in society. The Constitutional Convention provided for such changes. Two-thirds of each house of Congress or two-thirds of the state legislatures can propose an amendment. To become law, an amendment then needs the approval of three-fourths of the states. By this process, the Bill of Rights became the first ten amendments. Since then seventeen more amendments have been added to the Constitution.

 SUMMARIZE Explain how the Bill of Rights ensures American freedoms.

Michigan Grade Level Content Expectations *Review*

ONLINE QUIZ
For test practice, go to
Interactive Review @ ClassZone.com

TERMS & NAMES

1. Explain the importance of
- Antifederalists
- *The Federalist* papers
- federalism
- Bill of Rights
- Federalists

USING YOUR READING NOTES

2. Compare & Contrast Complete the diagram you started at the beginning of this section.

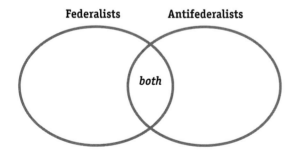

Federalists   Antifederalists

both

KEY IDEAS

3. What arguments did the Federalists use to convince people to support the Constitution? What arguments did the Antifederalists use against them?

4. Why was ratification of the Constitution in Virginia and New York especially important?

5. What did the framers of the Constitution do to prevent religious conflict?

CRITICAL THINKING

6. Compare & Contrast How was the battle over ratification similar to the conflicts among the states over the writing of the Constitution?

7. Analyze Point of View Why did the Antifederalists demand the Bill of Rights?

8. Language Arts Review the major arguments for and against ratification of the Constitution. Hold a press conference or write a news report on the ratification debate.

Reading Primary Sources

The Federalist "Number 51"

SETTING THE STAGE James Madison wrote 29 essays in *The Federalist* papers to argue in favor of ratifying the Constitution. In *The Federalist* "Number 51," Madison explains how the government set up by the Constitution will protect the rights of the people by weakening the power of any interest, or group, to dominate the government.

It is of great importance in a republic not only to guard the society against the oppression of its rulers, but to guard one part of the society against the injustice of the other part. Different interests necessarily exist in different classes of citizens. If a majority be united by a common interest, the rights of the minority will be insecure. There are but two methods of providing against this evil: the one by creating a will in the community independent of the majority—that is, of the society itself; the other, by **comprehending**[1] in the society so many separate descriptions of citizens as will render an unjust combination of a majority of the whole very improbable, if not **impracticable.**[2] . . .

Whilst[3] all authority in it will be derived from and dependent on the society, the society itself will be broken into so many parts, interests and classes of citizens, that the rights of individuals, or of the minority, will be in little danger from interested combinations of the majority. In a free government the security for civil rights must be the same as that for religious rights. It consists in the one case in the multiplicity of interests, and in the other in the multiplicity of **sects.**[4] . . .

In the extended republic of the United States, and among the great variety of interests, parties, and sects which it embraces, a **coalition**[5] of a majority of the whole society could seldom take place on any other principles than those of justice and the general good. . . .

It is no less certain than it is important . . . that the larger the society, provided it lie within a practicable sphere, the more duly capable it will be of self-government. And happily for the republican cause, the practicable sphere may be carried to a very great extent by a judicious **modification**[6] and mixture of the *federal principle*.

---

1. **comprehending:** understanding.
2. **impracticable:** not practical or realistic.
3. **whilst:** while.
4. **multiplicity of sects:** large number of groups.
5. **coalition:** alliance of groups.
6. **judicious modification:** careful change.

Minority Rights

In the 1700s, people feared that democratic majorities could turn into mobs that would violate other people's rights. Madison had to explain how the Constitution would prevent this.

1. What two methods does Madison suggest a society can use to protect minority rights?

Large Republics

For centuries, people believed that only small societies could be republics. But Madison argues that large societies are more likely to remain republics.

2. Why does Madison believe that a large republic is likely to protect justice?

Objections to the Constitution

SETTING THE STAGE George Mason was one of the leading Antifederalists. In "Objections to the Constitution of Government Formed by the Convention," he listed his reasons for opposing ratification. Above all, he feared that the Constitution created a government that would destroy democracy in the young nation.

Declaration Of Rights

At the time of the ratification debate, Americans across the nation complained that the Constitution did not include a bill of rights.

3. What arguments does Mason make about the lack of a Declaration of Rights?

Abuse Of Power

Mason believed that presidents might abuse the power to grant pardons for treason in order to protect the guilty.

4. What reasons might favor a presidential power to pardon?

There is no Declaration of Rights; and the Laws of the general Government being **paramount**[1] to the Laws and Constitutions of the several States, the Declaration of Rights in the separate states are no Security. Nor are the people secured even in the Enjoyment of the Benefits of the common-Law. . . .

In the House of Representatives, there is not the Substance, but the Shadow only of Representation; which can never produce proper Information in the Legislature, or inspire Confidence in the People; the Laws will therefore be generally made by Men little concern'd in, and **unacquainted**[2] with their Effects and Consequences.

The Senate have the Power of altering all Money-Bills and of originating Appropriations of Money and the **Sallerys**'[3] of the Officers of their own Appointment in **Conjunction**[4] with the President of the United States; altho' they are not the Representatives of the People, or **amenable**[5] to them. . . .

The President of the United States has the unrestrained Power of granting Pardon for Treason; which may be sometimes exercised to screen from Punishment those whom he had secretly **instigated**[6] to commit the Crime, and thereby prevent a Discovery of his own Guilt.

This government will **commence**[7] in a moderate **Aristocracy**;[8] it is at present impossible to foresee whether it will, in (its) Operation, produce a **Monarchy**[9] or a corrupt oppressive Aristocracy; it will most probably vibrate some Years between the two, and then terminate in the one or the other.

—George Mason

---

1. **paramount:** most important.
2. **unacquainted:** unfamiliar.
3. **sallerys:** salaries.
4. **conjunction:** joining.
5. **amenable:** agreeable.
6. **instigated:** caused.
7. **commence:** begin.
8. **aristocracy:** rule by a few, usually nobles.
9. **monarchy:** rule by one, usually a king.

DOCUMENT-BASED QUESTIONS

Short Answer

1. Why does Madison believe that a fragmented society will not endanger minority rights?

2. What does Mason argue might happen if the president had the power to pardon people?

Extended Answer

3. Compare how each writer supports his opinions with facts.

Chapter Summary

1 **Key Idea**
The Articles of Confederation created a weak national government.

2 **Key Idea**
The Constitution created a new, stronger government that replaced the Confederation.

3 **Key Idea**
American liberties are protected by the U.S. Constitution and a Bill of Rights.

For detailed Review and Study Notes go to **Interactive Review** @ ClassZone.com

Name Game

Use the Terms & Names list to complete each sentence online or on your own paper.

1. The first government of the United States was established by the Articles of Confederation

2. A group known as _____ opposed ratification of the Constitution.

3. Angered by new taxes, farmers attacked the courts in Massachusetts during _____

4. In a _____, the people elect representatives to govern them.

5. State representation in the House and Congress was determined by the _____

6. The _____ established law in the Northwest Territory.

7. _____ was the primary author of the Virginia Plan.

8. The Constitution was created at the _____ in 1787.

9. The _____ interprets the law.

10. The first ten amendments of the Constitution are known as the _____

A. New Jersey Plan
B. Constitutional Convention
C. Republic
D. Articles of Confederation
E. Legislative Branch
F. Shays's Rebellion
G. Antifederalists
H. James Madison
I. Northwest Ordinance
J. Judicial Branch
L. Land Ordinance of 1785
M. Founders
N. Bill of Rights
O. Great Compromise
P. Federalist Papers

Activities

CROSSWORD PUZZLE

Complete the online crossword puzzle to show what you know about the Constitution.

ACROSS
1. _____ is known as "Father of the Constitution."

GEOGAME

Use this online map to reinforce your knowledge of the Confederation Era, including the locations of important cities and events. Drag and drop each name in the list at its location on the map. A scorecard helps you keep track online.

Constitutional Convention

Shays's Rebellion

Northwest Territory

Confederation Congress

The Federalist papers published here

More items online

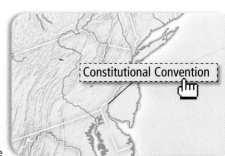

Constitutional Convention

VOCABULARY

Explain the significance of each of the following.

1. Shays's Rebellion
2. Great Compromise
3. Constitutional Convention
4. Bill of Rights
5. James Madison
6. Northwest Ordinance
7. Founders
8. Three-Fifths Compromise
9. Articles of Confederation
10. Confederation Congress

Explain how the terms and names in each group are related.

11. ratification, amendment
12. Virginia Plan, New Jersey Plan
13. Confederation Congress, Land Ordinance of 1785
14. Federalists, Antifederalists

KEY IDEAS

1 The Confederation Era (pages 234–239)

15. What problems did the Continental Congress successfully address?

16. How did Shays's Rebellion affect people's views on the Articles of Confederation?

2 Creating the Constitution (pages 242–247)

17. What groups of people were not represented at the Constitutional Convention?

18. What compromises did the delegates make during the convention?

3 Ratifying the Constitution (pages 248–254)

19. Why were Virginia and New York important in the battle for ratification of the Constitution?

20. Why did some states think that it was necessary to add a bill of rights to the Constitution?

CRITICAL THINKING

21. **Causes and Effects** How did America's history as a British colony cause the Confederation to fail?

22. **Evaluate** Why is the Northwest Ordinance sometimes called the Confederation Congress's only success?

23. **Problems & Solutions** Create a chart to identify the specific problems faced by the new nation, and the solutions it tried.

Problem	Solution
Western lands	Northwest Ordinance, 1787
Postwar depression	
Representation in the new government	

24. **Compare and Contrast** How do the Articles of Confederation and the Constitution each carry out democratic ideals?

25. **Evaluate** How did the Antifederalists have an impact on the Constitution?

26. **Interpret Maps** In which states did the Federalists have statewide majorities?

Ratification in Middle States 1790

Federalist majority
Anti-federalist majority
Evenly divided
Sparsely populated

NEW YORK

PENNSYLVANIA

NEW JERSEY

DELAWARE

✓ **TEST PRACTICE**

• **Online Test Practice** @ ClassZone.com
• Use the **MEAP Strategies & Practice,** pages S1-S27, at the front of this book

DOCUMENT-BASED QUESTIONS

Study each document carefully and answer the questions that follow.

DOCUMENT 1

THE CONSTITUTIONAL CONVENTION · 1787

1 This mural shows (left to right) Hamilton, Wilson, Madison, and Franklin. What does it tell you about the Constitutional Convention's delegates?

A They reflected the diversity of American society.

B Most were laborers and farmers.

C They were all very young.

D They were leaders of the time.

DOCUMENT 2

PRIMARY SOURCE

❝ I like much the general idea of framing a government which should go on of itself . . . [but] I do not like. . . . First, the omission of a bill of rights. . . . Let me add that a bill of rights is what the people are entitled to against every government on earth, general or particular; and what no just government should refuse. . . ❞

—Thomas Jefferson, December 20, 1787

2 Which of these would be *most likely* to support Jefferson's point of view?

A Federalists

B James Madison

C Antifederalists

D Alexander Hamilton

YOU BE THE HISTORIAN

27. Make Decisions How might the United States have developed if the Articles of Confederation had continued to provide the basis for government?

28. Draw Conclusions In what ways was the land of the Northwest Territory distributed democratically?

29. Connect Economics & History How did the Three-Fifths Compromise satisfy both North and South?

30. Compare & Contrast Consider the two groups that rebelled against the government: farmers and Revolutionary War veterans. Compare what life was probably like for these people as opposed to what life might have been like for the Founders.

31. **Connect** *to* **Today** How does the Constitution give Americans a voice in their national government?

Answer the

ESSENTIAL QUESTION

How did Americans create a strong national government that respected both the rights of states and the rights of individuals?

Written Response Write a two-to-three-paragraph response to the Essential Question. Be sure to consider the key ideas of each section as well as the ideals that Americans value today. Use the Response rubric to guide your thinking and writing.

Response Rubric

A strong response will

• discuss the values and ideals of modern America

• analyze the post-revolutionary events and conflicts out of which these ideals emerged

• explain the unique nature of the American constitution

Constitution Handbook

The Living Constitution

The Framers of the Constitution created a flexible plan for governing the United States far into the future. They also described ways to allow changes in the Constitution. For over 200 years, the Constitution has guided the American people. It remains a "living document." The Constitution still thrives, in part, because it echoes the principles the delegates valued. Each generation of Americans renews the meaning of the Constitution's timeless ideas. These two pages show you some ways in which the Constitution has shaped events in American history.

> **"** In framing a system which we wish to last for ages, we should not lose sight of the changes which ages will produce. **"**
>
> —James Madison, Constitutional Convention

1963
Reverend Dr. Martin Luther King, Jr. addresses demonstrators at the civil rights march on Washington in August 1963.

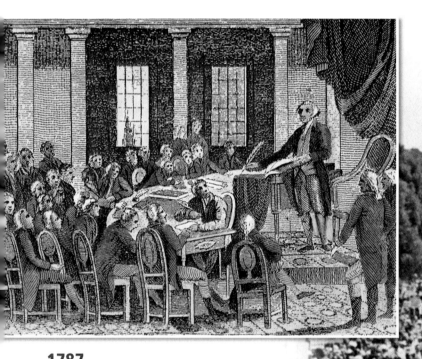

1787
Delegates in Philadelphia sign the Constitution.

1971

The 26th Amendment to the Constitution gives young people "18 years of age or older" the right to vote. Here, the Voters Project encourages young people to register and vote.

1981

A Supreme Court decision rules that Congress can exclude women from the draft. In the early 2000s, there were 215,243 women in the U.S. military.

2002

Attorney General John Ashcroft's positions on privacy and civil liberties issues made him a controversial figure in the George W. Bush cabinet. Ashcroft was a key supporter of the passage of the USA Patriot act. The act, which was dubbed the "anti-terrorism" act, drew fire from both liberals and conservatives. Critics of the act said it endangered the basic freedoms guaranteed under the U.S. Constitution.

Seven Principles of the Constitution

The Framers of the Constitution constructed a new system of government. Seven principles supported their efforts. To picture how these principles work, imagine seven building blocks. Together they form the foundation of the United States Constitution. In the pages that follow, you will find the definitions and main ideas of the principles shown in the graphic below.

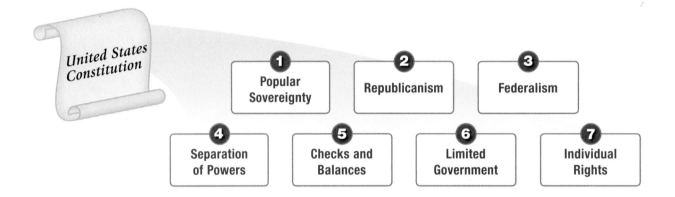

United States Constitution

1 **Popular Sovereignty**

2 **Republicanism**

3 **Federalism**

4 **Separation of Powers**

5 **Checks and Balances**

6 **Limited Government**

7 **Individual Rights**

1 Popular Sovereignty
Who Gives the Government Its Power?

"We the people of the United States . . . establish this Constitution for the United States of America." These words from the Preamble, or introduction, to the Constitution clearly spell out the source of the government's power. The Constitution rests on the idea of **popular sovereignty**—a government in which the people rule. As the nation changed and grew, popular sovereignty took on new meaning. A broader range of Americans shared in the power to govern themselves.

In 1987, Americans gathered in Washington, D.C. to celebrate the 200th anniversary of the Constitution.

② Republicanism
How Are People's Views Represented in Government?

The Framers of the Constitution wanted the people to have a voice in govern-ment. Yet the Framers also feared that public opinion might stand in the way of sound decision making. To solve this problem, they looked to **republicanism** as a model of government.

Republicanism is based on this belief: The people exercise their power by voting for their political representatives. According to the Framers, these lawmakers played the key role in making a repub-lican government work. Article 4, Section 4, of the Constitution also calls for every state to have a "republican form of government."

Senator Barack Obama, Democrat of Illinois, addresses a 2005 town meeting in Carrollton, IL.

③ Federalism
How Is Power Shared?

The Framers wanted the states and the nation to become partners in govern-ing. To build cooperation, the Framers turned to federalism. **Federalism** is a system of government in which power is divided between a central government and smaller political units, such as states. Before the Civil War, federalism in the United States was closely related to dual sovereignty, the idea that the federal government and the states each had exclusive power over their own spheres.

The Framers used federalism to structure the Con-stitution. The Constitution assigns certain powers to the national government. These are delegated powers. Powers kept by the states are reserved powers. Powers shared or exercised by national and state governments are known as concurrent powers.

Federalism

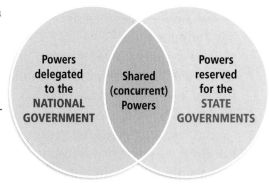

The overlapping spheres of power bind the American people together.

4 Separation of Powers
How Is Power Divided?

The Framers were concerned that too much power might fall into the hands of a single group. To avoid this problem, they built the idea of **separation of powers** into the Constitution. This principle means the division of basic government roles into branches. No one branch is given all the power. Articles 1, 2, and 3 of the Constitution detail how powers are split among the three branches.

Separation of Powers

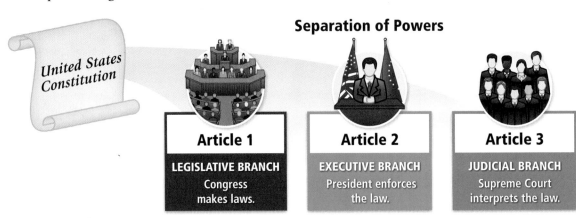

United States Constitution

Article 1	Article 2	Article 3
LEGISLATIVE BRANCH Congress makes laws.	**EXECUTIVE BRANCH** President enforces the law.	**JUDICIAL BRANCH** Supreme Court interprets the law.

5 Checks and Balances
How Is Power Evenly Distributed?

Baron de Montesquieu, an 18th-century French thinker, wrote, "power should be a check to power." His comment refers to the principle of **checks and balances**. Each branch of government can exercise checks, or controls, over the other branches. Though the branches of government are separate, they rely on one another to perform the work of government.

The Framers included a system of checks and balances in the Constitution to help make sure that the branches work together fairly. For example, only Congress can pass laws. Yet the president can check this power by refusing to sign a law into action. In turn, the Supreme Court can declare that a law, passed by Congress and signed by the president, violates the Constitution.

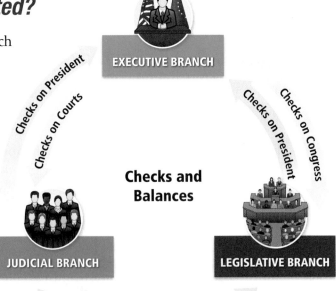

EXECUTIVE BRANCH

Checks on President
Checks on Courts
Checks on President
Checks on Congress

Checks and Balances

JUDICIAL BRANCH

LEGISLATIVE BRANCH

Checks on Congress
Checks on Courts

6 Limited Government
How Is Abuse of Power Prevented?

The Framers restricted the power of government. Article 1, Section 9, of the Constitution lists the powers denied to the Congress. Article 1, Section 10, forbids the states to take certain actions.

The principle of **limited government** is also closely related to the "rule of law": In the American government everyone, citizens and powerful leaders alike, must obey the law. Individuals or groups cannot twist or bypass the law to serve their own interests.

In mid-1987, Congress conducted a dramatic inquiry into the Iran-Contra affair. (*above*) Lieutenant Colonel Oliver North testifies before the hearings. North was found guilty of taking part in a cover-up.

7 Individual Rights
How Are Personal Freedoms Protected?

The first ten amendments to the Constitution shield people from an overly powerful government. These amendments are called the Bill of Rights. The Bill of Rights guarantees certain **individual rights**, or personal liberties and privileges. For example, government cannot control what people write or say. People also have the right to meet peacefully and to ask the government to correct a problem. Later amendments to the Constitution also advanced the cause of individual rights.

Students and teachers in Oakland, California, protest measures proposed in the 2005 election.

Seven Principles of the Constitution Assessment

MAIN IDEAS
1. What are the seven principles of government?
2. How does the Constitution reflect the principle of separation of powers?
3. Why did the Framers include a system of checks and balances in the Constitution?

CRITICAL THINKING
4. **Form Opinions** How do the rights and responsibilities of U.S. citizenship reflect American national identity?

   Think about
   • what it means to be an American
   • the rights and responsibilities of U.S. citizens

The Constitution of the United States

ESSENTIAL QUESTION
How has our 220-year-old Constitution remained a living document?

How to Read the Constitution
- The main column has the actual text.
- Notes in the side column point out or explain important aspects of the document.
- Some of the spellings and punctuation have been updated for easier reading.
- Headings and subheadings have been added to help you find specific topics.
- Those parts of the Constitution that are no longer in use have been crossed out.

PREAMBLE. Purpose of the Constitution

We the people of the United States, in order to form a more perfect Union, establish justice, insure domestic tranquility, provide for the common defense, promote the general welfare, and secure the blessings of liberty to ourselves and our posterity, do ordain and establish this Constitution for the United States of America.

Goals of the Preamble

Preamble	Explanation	Examples
"Form a more perfect Union"	Create a nation in which states work together	• Interstate road network • U.S. coins, paper money
"Establish justice"	Make laws and set up courts that are fair	• Court system • Jury system
"Insure domestic tranquility"	Keep peace within the country	• National Guard • Federal marshals
"Provide for the common defense"	Safeguard the country against attack	• Army • Navy
"Promote the general welfare"	Contribute to the happiness and well-being of all the people	• Safety in the workplace • Aid to the poor
"Secure the blessings of liberty to ourselves and our posterity"	Make sure future citizens remain free	• Commission on Civil Rights • Federal Election Commission

CRITICAL THINKING
1. Which goal of the preamble do you think is most important? Why?
2. How does the preamble reflect the principle of popular sovereignty?

Visitors hear a lecture on the Constitution at the National Archives Building, which also houses the Declaration of Independence and the Bill of Rights.

ARTICLE 1. **The Legislature**

▼ **KEY QUESTION** What is the main role of the legislative branch?

SECTION 1. **Congress**

All legislative powers herein granted shall be vested in a Congress of the United States, which shall consist of a Senate and House of Representatives.

SECTION 2. **The House of Representatives**

1. Elections The House of Representatives shall be composed of members chosen every second year by the people of the several states, and the **electors** in each state shall have the qualifications requisite for electors of the most numerous branch of the state legislature.

2. Qualifications No person shall be a Representative who shall not have attained to the age of twenty-five years, and been seven years a citizen of the United States, and who shall not, when elected, be an inhabitant of that state in which he shall be chosen.

3. Number of Representatives Representatives and direct taxes shall be apportioned among the several states which may be included within this Union, according to their respective numbers, which shall be determined by adding to the whole number of free persons, including those bound to service for a term of years, and excluding Indians not taxed, three-fifths of all other Persons. The actual **enumeration** shall be made within three years after the first meeting of the Congress of the United States, and within every subsequent term of ten years, in such manner as they shall by law direct. The number of Representatives shall not exceed one for every thirty thousand, but each state shall have at least one Representative; and until such enumeration shall be made, the state of New Hampshire shall be entitled to choose three, Massachusetts eight, Rhode Island and Providence Plantations one, Connecticut five, New York six, New Jersey four, Pennsylvania eight, Delaware one, Maryland six, Virginia ten, North Carolina five, South Carolina five, and Georgia three.

4. Vacancies When vacancies happen in the representation from any state, the executive authority thereof shall issue writs of election to fill such vacancies.

5. Officers and Impeachment The House of Representatives shall choose their Speaker and other officers; and shall have the sole power of **impeachment**.

SECTION 3. **Congress**

1. Numbers The Senate of the United States shall be composed of two Senators from each state, chosen by the legislature thereof, for six years; and each Senator shall have one vote.

BACKGROUND VOCABULARY

electors voters

enumeration an official count, such as a census

impeachment the process of accusing a public official of wrongdoing

Elections

Representatives are elected every two years. There are no limits on the number of terms a person can serve.

1. What do you think are the advantages of holding frequent elections of representatives?

Representation

Some delegates, such as Gouverneur Morris (*above*), thought that representation should be based on wealth as well as population. Others, such as James Wilson, thought representation should be based on population only. Ultimately, the delegates voted against including wealth as a basis for apportioning representatives.

2. How do you think the United States would be different today if representation were based on wealth?

2. Classifying Terms Immediately after they shall be assembled in consequence of the first election, they shall be divided as equally as may be into three classes. The seats of the Senators of the first class shall be vacated at the expiration of the second year, of the second class at the expiration of the fourth year, and of the third class at the expiration of the sixth year, so that one-third may be chosen every second year; ~~and if vacancies happen by resignation, or otherwise, during the recess of the legislature of any state, the executive thereof may make temporary appointments until the next meeting of the legislature, which shall then fill such vacancies.~~

3. Qualifications No person shall be a Senator who shall not have attained to the age of thirty years, and been nine years a citizen of the United States, and who shall not, when elected, be an inhabitant of that state for which he shall be chosen.

COMPARING *Federal Office Terms and Requirements*

Position	Term	Minimum Age	Residency	Citizenship
Representative	2 years	25	state in which elected	7 years
Senator	6 years	30	state in which elected	9 years
President	4 years	35	14 years in the U.S.	natural-born
Supreme Court Justice	unlimited	none	none	none

CRITICAL THINKING Why do you think the term and qualifications for a senator are more demanding than for a representative?

Impeachment

The House brings charges against the president. The Senate acts as the jury. The Chief Justice of the Supreme Court presides over the hearings.

3. How many presidents have been impeached?

4. Role of Vice President The Vice President of the United States shall be President of the Senate, but shall have no vote, unless they be equally divided.

5. Officers The Senate shall choose their other officers, and also a President **pro tempore**, in the absence of the Vice President, or when he shall exercise the office of President of the United States.

6. Impeachment Trials The Senate shall have the sole power to try all impeachments. When sitting for that purpose, they shall be on oath or affirmation. When the President of the United States is tried, the Chief Justice shall preside: and no person shall be convicted without the concurrence of two-thirds of the members present.

7. Punishment for Impeachment Judgment in cases of impeachment shall not extend further than to removal from office, and disqualification to hold and enjoy any office of honor, trust or profit under the United States; but the party convicted shall nevertheless be liable and subject to **indictment**, trial, judgment and punishment, according to law.

SECTION 4. **Congressional Elections**

1. Regulations The times, places and manner of holding elections for Senators and Representatives shall be prescribed in each state by the legislature thereof; but the Congress may at any time by law make or alter such regulations, except as to the places of choosing Senators.

2. Sessions The Congress shall assemble at least once in every year, ~~and such meeting shall be on the first Monday in December, unless they shall by law appoint a different day.~~

SECTION 5. **Rules and Procedures**

1. Quorum Each house shall be the judge of the elections, returns and qualifications of its own members, and a majority of each shall constitute a **quorum** to do business; but a smaller number may adjourn from day to day, and may be authorized to compel the attendance of absent members, in such manner, and under such penalties as each house may provide.

2. Rules and Conduct Each house may determine the rules of its proceedings, punish its members for disorderly behavior, and, with the concurrence of two-thirds, expel a member.

3. Congressional Records Each house shall keep a journal of its proceedings, and from time to time publish the same, excepting such parts as may in their judgment require secrecy; and the yeas and nays of the members of either house on any question shall, at the desire of one-fifth of those present, be entered on the journal.

4. Adjournment Neither house, during the session of Congress, shall, without the consent of the other, adjourn for more than three days, nor to any other place than that in which the two houses shall be sitting

SECTION 6. **Payment and Privileges**

1. Salary The Senators and Representatives shall receive a compensation for their services, to be ascertained by law, and paid out of the treasury of the United States. They shall in all cases, except treason, felony and breach of the peace, be privileged from arrest during their attendance at the session of their respective houses, and in going to and returning from the same; and for any speech or debate in either house, they shall not be questioned in any other place.

2. Restrictions No Senator or Representative shall, during the time for which he was elected, be appointed to any civil office under the authority of the United States, which shall have been created, or the emoluments whereof shall have been increased during such time; and no person holding any office under the United States, shall be a member of either house during his continuance in office.

Senate Rules

Senate rules allow for debate on the floor. Using a tactic called filibustering, senators give long speeches to block the passage of a bill. (*above*) Senator Strom Thurmond holds the filibustering record—24 hours, 18 minutes.

4. Why might a senator choose filibustering as a tactic to block a bill?

Connect to Today

Salaries Senators and representatives are paid $165,200 a year. The Speaker of the House is paid $212,100—the same as the vice president.

5. How do the salaries of members of Congress compare to those of adults—like teachers or famous sports figures?

SECTION 7. How a Bill Becomes a Law

1. Tax Bills All bills for raising **revenue** shall originate in the House of Representatives; but the Senate may propose or concur with amendments as on other Bills.

2. Lawmaking Process Every bill which shall have passed the House of Representatives and the Senate, shall, before it become a law, be presented to the President of the United States; if he approves he shall sign it, but if not he shall return it, with his objections to that house in which it shall have originated, who shall enter the objections at large on their journal, and proceed to reconsider it. If after such reconsideration two-thirds of that house shall agree to pass the bill, it shall be sent, together with the objections, to the other house, by which it shall likewise be reconsidered, and if approved by two-thirds of that house, it shall become a law. But in all such cases the votes of both houses shall be determined by yeas and nays, and the names of the persons voting for and against the bill shall be entered on the journal of each house respectively. If any bill shall not be returned by the President within ten days (Sundays excepted) after it shall have been presented to him, the same shall be a law, in like manner as if he had signed it, unless the Congress by their adjournment prevent its return, in which case it shall not be a law.

CONNECT TO GOVERNMENT → *How a Bill Becomes a Law*

| INTRODUCTION | COMMITTEE ACTION | FLOOR ACTION | |

1

The House introduces a bill and refers it to a committee.

The Senate introduces a bill and refers it to a committee.

2

The House committee may approve, rewrite, or kill the bill.

The Senate committee may approve, rewrite, or kill the bill.

3

The House debates and votes on its version of the bill.

The Senate debates and votes on its version of the bill.

4

The House and Senate committee members work out the differences between the two versions.

3. Role of the President Every order, resolution, or vote to which the concurrence of the Senate and House of Representatives may be necessary (except on a question of adjournment) shall be presented to the President of the United States; and before the same shall take effect, shall be approved by him, or being disapproved by him, shall be repassed by two-thirds of the Senate and House of Representatives, according to the rules and limitations prescribed in the case of a bill.

★ How a Bill Becomes a Law ★

Creating a Play

1 Study the diagram below.

2 Work with a small group to create a presentation to teach an audience of younger students how a bill becomes a law.

- Assign the tasks of actor, illustrator, narrator, and scriptwriter.
- Develop a script.
- Gather props and rehearse your presentations.

3 Present the drama to a class of younger students.

FINAL APPROVAL

ENACTMENT

5
Both houses of Congress pass the revised bill.

6
President vetoes the bill.
OR
President signs the bill.

7
Two-thirds majority vote of Congress is needed to approve a vetoed bill.

8
Bill becomes law.

BACKGROUND VOCABULARY

naturalization a way to give full citizenship to a person of foreign birth

tribunals courts

felonies serious crimes

appropriation public funds set aside for a specific purpose

militia an emergency military force, such as the National Guard, that is not part of the regular army

SECTION 8. Powers Granted to Congress

1. Taxation The Congress shall have power to lay and collect taxes, duties, imposts and excises, to pay the debts and provide for the common defense and general welfare of the United States; but all duties, imposts and excises shall be uniform throughout the United States;

2. Credit To borrow money on the credit of the United States;

3. Commerce To regulate commerce with foreign nations, and among the several states, and with the Indian tribes;

4. Naturalization, Bankruptcy To establish a uniform rule of **naturalization**, and uniform laws on the subject of bankruptcies throughout the United States;

5. Money To coin money, regulate the value thereof, and of foreign coin, and fix the standard of weights and measures;

6. Counterfeiting To provide for the punishment of counterfeiting the securities and current coin of the United States;

7. Post Office To establish post offices and post roads;

8. Patents, Copyrights To promote the progress of science and useful arts, by securing for limited times to authors and inventors the exclusive right to their respective writings and discoveries;

COMPARING Military Responsibilities

The president is the Commander-in-Chief of the U.S. Armed Forces. There are five military branches—the Army, Marine Corps (USMC), Navy (USN), and Air Force (USAF), and the Coast Guard (USCG). The National Guard is the home based militia.

U.S. Navy (USN) The branch of the U.S. armed forces responsible for naval operations. Unofficial motto: *"Non sibi sed patriae"* meaning "Not self but country."

United States Army The largest branch of the U.S. armed forces, the U.S. Army has its roots in the Continental Army which was formed in June 1775. The army is responsible for land-based military operations. Motto: "Call to Duty."

U.S. Air Force (USAF) The largest and most technologically advanced air force in the world, USAF is trained for "offensive and defensive air operations." Unofficial motto: "No One Comes Close."

9. Federal Courts To constitute **tribunals** inferior to the Supreme Court;

10. International Law To define and punish piracies and **felonies** committed on the high seas, and offenses against the law of nations;

11. War To declare war, grant letters of marque and reprisal, and make rules concerning captures on land and water;

12. Army To raise and support armies, but no **appropriation** of money to that use shall be for a longer term than two years;

13. Navy To provide and maintain a navy;

14. Regulation of Armed Forces To make rules for the government and regulation of the land and naval forces;

15. Militia To provide for calling forth the **militia** to execute the laws of the Union, suppress insurrections and repel invasions;

16. Regulations for Militia To provide for organizing, arming, and disciplining the militia, and for governing such part of them as may be employed in the service of the United States, reserving to the states respectively the appointment of the officers, and the authority of training the militia according to the discipline prescribed by Congress;

Connect *to* Today

Declaring War Only Congress can declare war. Yet in the following "undeclared" wars, Congress bowed to the president's power to take military action and send troops overseas: Korean War (1950–1953), Vietnam War (1957–1975), Persian Gulf War (1991), and Kosovo crisis (1999).

6. Why do you think the Constitution sets limits on the president's power to make war?

U.S. Marine Corps (USMC) The marines have a multi-purpose role, including providing presidential protection and helicopter service. Marines also provide security for American embassies and consulates overseas. Motto: "*Semper Fidelis*" meaning "Always Faithful."

U.S. National Guard

The National Guard is a component of the U.S. Army and USAF. National Guard units can be mobilized at any time to supplement regular armed forces.

CRITICAL THINKING

1. **Form and Support Opinions** Women now serve in combat roles in the U.S. Armed Forces? Do you agree or disagree with this policy?

2. **Connect *to* Today** Under what circumstances do you think the president should call out the National Guard?

BACKGROUND VOCABULARY

bill of attainder a law that condemns a person without a trial in court

ex post facto law a law that would make an act a criminal offense after it was committed

tender money

Residents of the District of Columbia elect a mayor and city council. However, Congress retains ultimate authority in the district and has veto power over the budget and legislative matters.

Habeas Corpus

A writ of habeas corpus is a legal order. It protects people from being held in prison or jail without formal charges of a crime. In 1992, the Supreme Court recognized that habeas corpus "is the [basic] instrument for safeguarding individual freedom."

7. How does habeas corpus help ensure fairness and justice?

Direct Tax

In 1913, the 16th Amendment allowed Congress to collect an income tax—a direct tax on the amount of money a person earns. Americans today pay much more in taxes than their ancestors would have imagined.

8. Why do you think the issue of taxes is so important to people?

17. District of Columbia To exercise exclusive legislation in all cases whatsoever, over such district (not exceeding ten miles square) as may, by cession of particular states, and the acceptance of Congress, become the seat of the government of the United States, and to exercise like authority over all places purchased by the consent of the legislature of the state in which the same shall be, for the erection of forts, magazines, arsenals, dockyards, and other needful buildings; and

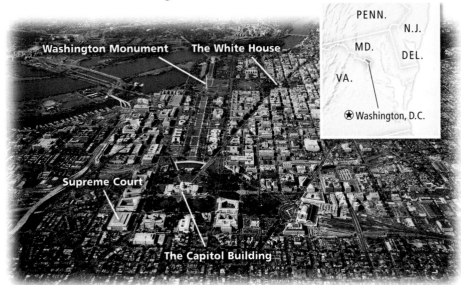

Washington Monument   The White House

Supreme Court

The Capitol Building

PENN.
N.J.
MD.
DEL.
VA.
★ Washington, D.C.

18. Elastic Clause To make all laws which shall be necessary and proper for carrying into execution the foregoing powers, and all other powers vested by this Constitution in the government of the United States, or in any department or officer thereof.

SECTION 9. Powers Denied Congress

1. ~~Slave Trade The migration or importation of such persons as any of the states now existing shall think proper to admit, shall not be prohibited by the Congress prior to the year one thousand eight hundred and eight, but a tax or duty may be imposed on such importation, not exceeding ten dollars for each person.~~

2. Habeas Corpus The privilege of the writ of habeas corpus shall not be suspended, unless when in cases of rebellion or invasion the public safety may require it.

3. Illegal Punishment No **bill of attainder** or **ex post facto** law shall be passed.

4. Direct Taxes No capitation, ~~or other direct,~~ tax shall be laid, ~~unless in proportion to the census or enumeration herein before directed to be taken.~~

5. Export Taxes No tax or duty shall be laid on articles exported from any state.

6. No Favorites No preference shall be given by any regulation of commerce or revenue to the ports of one state over those of another: nor shall vessels bound to, or from, one state be obliged to enter, clear, or pay duties in another.

7. Public Money No money shall be drawn from the treasury, but in consequence of appropriations made by law; and a regular statement and account of the receipts and expenditures of all public money shall be published from time to time.

8. Titles of Nobility No title of nobility shall be granted by the United States: and no person holding any office of profit or trust under them shall, without the consent of the Congress, accept of any present, emolument, office, or title, of any kind whatever, from any king, prince, or foreign state.

SECTION 10. Powers Denied the States

1. Restrictions No state shall enter into any treaty, alliance, or confederation; grant letters of marque and reprisal; coin money; emit bills of credit; make anything but gold and silver coin a **tender** in payment of debts; pass any bill of attainder, ex post facto law, or law impairing the obligation of contracts, or grant any title of nobility.

2. Import and Export Taxes No state shall, without the consent of the Congress, lay any imposts or duties on imports or exports, except what may be absolutely necessary for executing its inspection laws; and the net produce of all duties and imposts, laid by any state on imports or exports, shall be for the use of the treasury of the United States; and all such laws shall be subject to the revision and control of the Congress.

3. Peacetime and War Restraints No state shall, without the consent of Congress, lay any duty of tonnage, keep troops or ships of war in time of peace, enter into any agreement or compact with another state, or with a foreign power, or engage in war, unless actually invaded, or in such imminent danger as will not admit of delay.

Titles of Nobility

The Framers disapproved of titles of nobility. The list of grievances in the Declaration of Independence included numerous examples of King George III's abuses of power. Symbols of these abuses included English titles of nobility, such as "king," "queen," and "duke." The Framers said clearly that there would be no such titles in the new republic.

9. How do TV news reporters address members of Congress and the president?

Article 1 Assessment

MAIN IDEAS
1. What is the main role of the legislative branch?
2. What role does the vice president of the United States play in the Senate?
3. Why are there more members in the House of Representatives than the Senate?
4. What is one of the powers denied to Congress?

CRITICAL THINKING
5. **Draw Conclusions** How does Article 1 show that the Constitution is a clearly defined yet flexible document?

Think about
• the powers of Congress
• the "elastic clause"

natural-born citizen a citizen born in the United States or a U.S. commonwealth, or to parents who are U.S. citizens living outside the country

affirmation a statement declaring that something is true

ARTICLE 2. The Executive

🔻 **KEY QUESTION** What is the chief purpose of the executive branch?

SECTION 1. The Presidency

1. Terms of Office The executive power shall be vested in a President of the United States of America. He shall hold his office during the term of four years, and, together with the Vice President, chosen for the same term, be elected, as follows:

2. Electoral College Each state shall appoint, in such manner as the Legislature thereof may direct, a number of electors, equal to the whole number of Senators and Representatives to which the State may be entitled in the Congress; but no Senator or Representative, or person holding an office of trust or profit under the United States, shall be appointed an elector.

CONNECT TO GOVERNMENT ⟶ *Electoral College*

American voters do not choose their president directly. Members of a group called the Electoral College actually elect the president. Each state has electors. Together they form the Electoral College. In most states, the winner takes all. Except for Maine and Nebraska, all the electoral votes of a state go to one set of candidates.

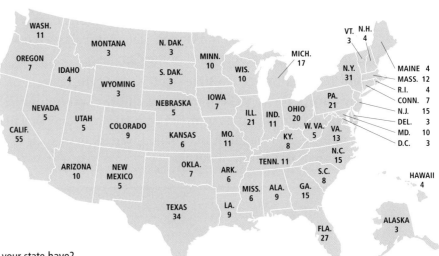

CRITICAL THINKING

1. **Place** How many electoral votes does your state have?

2. **Draw Conclusions** In which states would a presidential candidate campaign most heavily? Why?

Number of electors for each state = total number of its senators and representatives

---

~~3. Former Method of Electing President~~ ~~The electors shall meet in their respective states, and vote by ballot for two persons, of whom one at least shall not be an inhabitant of the same state with themselves. And they shall make a list of all the persons voted for, and of the number of votes for each; which list they shall sign and certify, and transmit sealed to the seat of the government of the United States, directed to the President of the Senate. The President of the Senate shall, in the presence of the Senate and House of Representatives, open all the certificates, and the votes shall then be counted. The person having the greatest number of votes shall be the President, if such number be a majority of the whole number of electors appointed; and if there be more than one who have such major-~~

ity, and have an equal number of votes, then the House of Representatives shall immediately choose by ballot one of them for President; and if no person have a majority, then from the five highest on the list the said House shall in like manner choose the President. But in choosing the President, the votes shall be taken by States, the representation from each state having one vote; a quorum for this purpose shall consist of a member or members from two-thirds of the states, and a majority of all the states shall be necessary to a choice. In every case, after the choice of the President, the person having the greatest number of votes of the electors shall be the Vice President. But if there should remain two or more who have equal votes, the Senate shall choose from them by ballot the Vice President.

4. Election Day The Congress may determine the time of choosing the electors, and the day on which they shall give their votes, which day shall be the same throughout the United States.

5. Qualifications No person except a **natural-born citizen**, or a citizen of the United States at the time of the adoption of this Constitution, shall be eligible to the office of President; neither shall any person be eligible to that office who shall not have attained to the age of thirty-five years, and been fourteen years a resident within the United States.

6. Succession In case of the removal of the President from office, or of his death, resignation, or inability to discharge the powers and duties of the said office, the same shall devolve on the Vice President, and the Congress may by law provide for the case of removal, death, resignation or inability, both of the President and Vice President, declaring what officer shall then act as President, and such officer shall act accordingly, until the disability be removed, or a President shall be elected.

7. Salary The President shall, at stated times, receive for his services, a compensation, which shall neither be increased nor diminished during the period for which he shall have been elected, and he shall not receive within that period any other emolument from the United States, or any of them.

8. Oath of Office Before he enter on the execution of his office, he shall take the following oath or **affirmation**: I do solemnly swear (or affirm) that I will faithfully execute the office of President of the United States, and will to the best of my ability, preserve, protect and defend the Constitution of the United States.

SECTION 2. Powers of the President

1. Military Powers The President shall be commander in chief of the Army and Navy of the United States, and of the militia of the several states, when called into the actual service of the United States; he may require the

Succession

Vice President Gerald Ford (*left*), next in the line of succession, takes the oath of office after the resignation of President Richard Nixon on August 9, 1974. Ford, like every U.S. president, promises to uphold the Constitution. The 25th Amendment sets up clearer procedures for presidential succession.

President's Salary

The president's yearly salary is $400,000. The president also gets special allowances, such as funds for travel expenses. Benefits include:

- living in a mansion, the White House
- vacationing at Camp David, an estate in Maryland
- using *Air Force One*, a personal jet plane

10. Why do you think the president needs to have a plane and a vacation spot?

Chief Executive

Like a business executive, the president solves problems and makes key decisions. President George W. Bush is shown in the oval office in 2006.

Commander in Chief

As a military leader, President Abraham Lincoln meets with General McClellan during the Civil War.

Head of a Political Party

President Andrew Jackson on his way to Washington, D.C. for his inauguration in 1829. Jackson was a leader of the Democratic-Republican Party—the forerunner of today's Democratic Party.

Chief Diplomat and Chief of State

As a foreign policy maker, President Ronald Reagan visits British Prime Minister Margaret Thatcher in 1984.

Legislative Leader

President Franklin D. Roosevelt signs the Social Security Act of 1935. All modern presidents have legislative programs they want Congress to pass.

CRITICAL THINKING

1. **Make Inferences** Why is it important that the commander in chief of the armed forces of the United States be a civilian (the president) rather than a military commander?

2. **Connect** *to* **Today** Why do you think the United States enjoys close relations with Britain?

opinion, in writing, of the principal officer in each of the executive departments, upon any subject relating to the duties of their respective offices, and he shall have power to grant **reprieves** and pardons for offenses against the United States, except in cases of impeachment.

2. Treaties, Appointments He shall have power, by and with the advice and consent of the Senate, to make treaties, provided two-thirds of the Senators present concur; and he shall nominate, and by and with the advice and consent of the Senate, shall appoint ambassadors, other public ministers and consuls, judges of the Supreme Court, and all other officers of the United States, whose appointments are not herein otherwise provided for, and which shall be established by law; but the Congress may by law vest the appointment of such inferior officers, as they think proper, in the President alone, in the courts of law, or in the heads of departments.

3. Vacancies The President shall have power to fill up all vacancies that may happen during the recess of the Senate, by granting commissions which shall expire at the end of their next session.

SECTION 3. Presidential Duties

He shall from time to time give to the Congress information of the State of the Union, and recommend to their consideration such measures as he shall judge necessary and expedient; he may, on extraordinary occasions, **convene** both houses, or either of them, and in case of disagreement between them, with respect to the time of adjournment, he may adjourn them to such time as he shall think proper; he shall receive ambassadors and other public ministers; he shall take care that the laws be faithfully executed, and shall commission all the officers of the United States.

SECTION 4. Impeachment

The President, Vice President and all civil officers of the United States shall be removed from office on impeachment for, and conviction of, treason, bribery, or other high crimes and **misdemeanors**.

BACKGROUND VOCABULARY

reprieves delays or cancellations of punishment

convene call together

misdemeanors violations of the law

Appointments

Recent presidents have used their power of appointment to add minorities and women to the Supreme Court. In 1967, President Lyndon Johnson appointed the first African-American justice, Thurgood Marshall. In 1981, President Ronald Reagan appointed the first woman, Sandra Day O'Connor.

11. What do you think influences a president's choice for a Supreme Court justice?

Connect *to* Today

State of the Union Major TV networks broadcast the State of the Union address to the whole nation. In this yearly message, the president urges Congress to achieve certain lawmaking goals. The president's speech also must gain the attention of TV viewers.

12. Why is the president's power to persuade an important political skill?

Article 2 Assessment

MAIN IDEAS

1. What is the chief purpose of the executive branch?

2. What are the requirements for becoming president?

3. How does the Constitution limit the president's power to make appointments and treaties?

CRITICAL THINKING

4. Analyze Issues Why do you think the Constitution states that the president must seek approval from the Senate for most political appointments and treaties?

Think about

• the abuse of power • the will of the voters

inferior courts courts with less authority than the Supreme Court

appellate having power to review court decisions

Federal Courts

The Judiciary Act of 1789, passed by the first Congress, included establishing a Supreme Court with a chief justice and five associate justices and other lower federal courts.

13. How many Supreme Court justices are there today?

Judicial Power

Judicial power gives the Supreme Court and other federal courts the authority to hear certain kinds of cases. These courts have the power to rule in cases involving the Constitution, national laws, treaties, and states' conflicts.

14. What federal cases have you seen reported on TV?

The Constitution actually creates only one court— the U.S. Supreme Court. (*right*) The members of the Supreme Court in 2006.

ARTICLE 3. **The Judiciary**

🔻 **KEY QUESTION** What is the main purpose of the judicial branch?

SECTION 1. **Federal Courts and Judges**

The judicial power of the United States shall be vested in one Supreme Court, and in such **inferior courts** as the Congress may from time to time ordain and establish. The judges, both of the Supreme and inferior courts, shall hold their offices during good behavior, and shall, at stated times, receive for their services a compensation, which shall not be diminished during their continuance in office.

SECTION 2. **The Courts Authority**

1. General Authority The judicial power shall extend to all cases, in law and equity, arising under this Constitution, the laws of the United States, and treaties made, or which shall be made, under their authority;—to all cases affecting ambassadors, other public ministers and consuls;—to all cases of admiralty and maritime jurisdiction;—to controversies to which the United States shall be a party;—to controversies between two or more states;—between a state and citizens of another state;—between citizens of different states;—between citizens of the same state claiming lands under grants of different states, and between a state, or the citizens thereof, and foreign states, citizens or subjects.

2. Supreme Court In all cases affecting ambassadors, other public ministers and consuls, and those in which a state shall be party, the Supreme Court shall have original jurisdiction. In all the other cases before mentioned, the Supreme Court shall have **appellate** jurisdiction, both as to law and fact, with such exceptions, and under such regulations, as the Congress shall make.

3. Trial by Jury The trial of all crimes, except in cases of impeachment, shall be by jury; and such trial shall be held in the state where the said crimes shall have been committed; but when not committed within any state, the trial shall be at such place or places as the Congress may by law have directed.

COMPARING Checks and Balances

EXECUTIVE BRANCH (President)

CHECKS ON COURTS	CHECKS ON CONGRESS
• Appoints federal judges • Can grant reprieves and pardons for federal crimes	• Can veto acts of Congress • Can call special sessions of Congress • Can suggest laws and send messages to Congress

JUDICIAL BRANCH (Supreme Court)

CHECKS ON PRESIDENT	CHECKS ON CONGRESS
• Can declare executive acts unconstitutional • Judges, appointed for life, are free from executive control	• Judicial review—Can declare acts of Congress unconstitutional

LEGISLATIVE BRANCH (Congress)

CHECKS ON COURT	CHECKS ON PRESIDENT
• Can impeach and remove federal judges • Establishes lower federal courts • Can refuse to confirm judicial appointments	• Can impeach and remove the president • Can override veto • Controls spending of money • Senate can refuse to confirm presidential appointments and to ratify treaties

CRITICAL THINKING

1. Why is judicial review an important action of the Supreme Court?

2. Which check do you think is the most powerful? Why?

SECTION 3. Treason

1. Definition Treason against the United States shall consist only in levying war against them, or in adhering to their enemies, giving them aid and comfort. No person shall be convicted of treason unless on the testimony of two witnesses to the same overt act, or on confession in open court.

2. Punishment The Congress shall have power to declare the punishment of treason, but no attainder of treason shall work corruption of blood, or forfeiture except during the life of the person attained.

Article 3 Assessment

MAIN IDEAS

1. What is the main purpose of the judicial branch?

2. What is judicial review?

3. What are two kinds of cases that can begin in the Supreme Court?

CRITICAL THINKING

4. Draw Conclusions Why might the Supreme Court feel less political pressure than Congress in making judgments about the Constitution?

Think about

• the appointment of Supreme Court justices

• Congress members' obligation to voters

immunities legal protections
suffrage right to vote

ARTICLE 4. Relations Among States

SECTION 1. State Acts and Records

Full faith and credit shall be given in each state to the public acts, records, and judicial proceedings of every other state. And the Congress may by general laws prescribe the manner in which such acts, records and proceedings shall be proved, and the effect thereof.

SECTION 2. Rights of Citizens

1. Citizenship The citizens of each state shall be entitled to all privileges and **immunities** of citizens in the several states.

2. Extradition A person charged in any state with treason, felony, or other crime, who shall flee from justice, and be found in another state, shall on demand of the executive authority of the state from which he fled, be delivered up, to be removed to the state having jurisdiction of the crime.

3. Fugitive Slaves No person held to service or labor in one state, under the laws thereof, escaping into another, shall, in consequence of any law or regulation therein, be discharged from such service or labor, but shall be delivered up on claim of the party to whom such service or labor may be due.

Extradition

Persons charged with serious crimes cannot escape punishment by fleeing to another state. They must be returned to the first state and stand trial there.

15. Why do you think the Framers included the power of extradition?

Activity

1 Form small groups to illustrate a chart showing the national, shared, and state powers.

2 Display the chart in your classroom.

COMPARING Federal and State Powers

Americans live under both national and state governments.

NATIONAL POWERS
- Maintain military
- Declare war
- Establish postal system
- Set standards for weights and measures
- Protect copyrights and patents

SHARED POWERS
- Collect taxes
- Establish courts
- Regulate interstate commerce
- Regulate banks
- Borrow money
- Provide for the general welfare
- Punish criminals

STATE POWERS
- Establish local governments
- Set up schools
- Regulate state commerce
- Make regulations for marriage
- Establish and regulate corporations

CRITICAL THINKING Evaluate What do you think is the purpose of dividing the powers between national and state governments?

SECTION 3. **New States**

1. Admission New states may be admitted by the Congress into this Union; but no new state shall be formed or erected within the jurisdiction of any other state; nor any state be formed by the junction of two or more states, or parts of states, without the consent of the legislatures of the states concerned as well as of the Congress.

2. Congressional Authority The Congress shall have power to dispose of and make all needful rules and regulations respecting the territory or other property belonging to the United States; and nothing in this Constitution shall be so construed as to prejudice any claims of the United States, or of any particular state.

SECTION 4. **Guarantees to the States**

The United States shall guarantee to every state in this Union a republican form of government, and shall protect each of them against invasion; and on application of the legislature, or of the executive (when the legislature cannot be convened) against domestic violence.

ARTICLE 5. **Amending the Constitution**

The Congress, whenever two-thirds of both houses shall deem it necessary, shall propose amendments to this Constitution, or, on the application of the legislatures of two-thirds of the several states, shall call a convention for proposing amendments, which, in either case, shall be valid to all intents and purposes, as part of this Constitution, when ratified by the legislatures of three-fourths of the several states, or by conventions in three- fourths thereof, as the one or the other mode of ratification may be proposed by the Congress; provided that no amendment which may be made prior to the year one thousand eight hundred and eight shall in any manner affect the first and fourth clauses in the ninth section of the first article; and that no state, without its consent, shall be deprived of its equal **suffrage** in the Senate.

Admission to Statehood

In 1998, Puerto Ricans voted against their island becoming the 51st state. A lawyer in Puerto Rico summed up a main reason: "Puerto Ricans want to have ties to the U.S., but they want to protect their culture and language." Also, as a U.S. commonwealth, Puerto Rico makes its own laws and handles its own finances

16. Do you think Puerto Rico should become a state? Why or why not?

Amending the Constitution

There are two ways to propose an amendment:

2/3 of each house of **Congress** vote to amend the Constitution*	**2/3** of **state legislatures** call for a national convention to amend the Constitution

*All 27 amendments have been proposed by this method.

There are also two ways to ratify an amendment:

3/4 of state legislatures approve the amendment	**3/4** of states approve the amendment at state conventions

CRITICAL THINKING Why do you think more votes are needed to ratify an amendment than to propose one?

BACKGROUND
VOCABULARY

ratification official approval

unanimous consent
complete agreement

Federal Supremacy

In 1957, the "supreme law of the land" was put to a test. The governor of Arkansas defied a Supreme Court order. The Court ruled that African-American students could go to all-white public schools. President Dwight D. Eisenhower then sent federal troops to protect the first African-American students to enroll in Central High School in Little Rock, Arkansas.

ARTICLE 6. Supremacy of the National Government

SECTION 1. Valid Debts

All debts contracted and engagements entered into, before the adoption of this Constitution, shall be as valid against the United States under this Constitution, as under the Confederation.

SECTION 2. Supreme Law

This Constitution, and the laws of the United States which shall be made in pursuance thereof; and all treaties made, or which shall be made, under the authority of the United States, shall be the supreme law of the land; and the judges in every state shall be bound thereby, anything in the constitution or laws of any state to the contrary notwithstanding.

SECTION 3. Loyalty to Constitution

The Senators and Representatives before mentioned, and the members of the several state legislatures, and all executive and judicial officers, both of the United States and of the several states, shall be bound by oath or affirmation to support this Constitution; but no religious test shall ever be required as a qualification to any office or public trust under the United States.

Members of the House of Representatives swear to support and defend the U.S. Constitution at the opening of the 109th Congress in 2005.

ARTICLE 7. Ratification

The **ratification** of the conventions of nine states shall be sufficient for the establishment of this Constitution between the states so ratifying the same. Done in convention by the **unanimous consent** of the states present, the seventeenth day of September in the year of our Lord one thousand seven hundred and eighty-seven and of the independence of the United States of America the twelfth. In witness whereof we have hereunto subscribed our names.

George Washington
President and deputy from Virginia

New Hampshire: *John Langdon, Nicholas Gilman*

Massachusetts: *Nathaniel Gorham, Rufus King*

Connecticut: *William Samuel Johnson, Roger Sherman*

New York: *Alexander Hamilton*

New Jersey: *William Livingston, David Brearley, William Paterson, Jonathan Dayton*

Pennsylvania: *Benjamin Franklin, Thomas Mifflin, Robert Morris, George Clymer, Thomas FitzSimons, Jared Ingersoll, James Wilson, Gouverneur Morris*

Delaware: *George Read, Gunning Bedford, Jr., John Dickinson, Richard Bassett, Jacob Broom*

Maryland: *James McHenry, Dan of St. Thomas Jenifer, Daniel Carroll*

Virginia: *John Blair, James Madison, Jr.*

North Carolina: *William Blount, Richard Dobbs Spaight, Hugh Williamson*

South Carolina: *John Rutledge, Charles Cotesworth Pinckney, Charles Pinckney, Pierce Butler*

Georgia: *William Few, Abraham Baldwin*

The Signers

The 39 men who signed the Constitution were wealthy and well educated. About half of them were trained in law. Others were doctors, merchants, bankers, and slaveholding planters. Missing from the list of signatures are the names of African Americans, Native Americans, and women. These groups reflected the varied population of the United States in the 1780s.

17. How do you think the absence of these groups affected the decisions made in creating the Constitution?

Articles 4–7 Assessment

MAIN IDEAS

1. What rights does Article 4 guarantee to citizens if they go to other states in the nation?

2. What are two ways of proposing an amendment to the Constitution?

3. What makes up "the supreme law of the land"?

CRITICAL THINKING

4. Form and Support Opinions Should the Framers of the Constitution have allowed the people to vote directly for ratification of the Constitution? Why or why not?

Think about

- the idea that the government belongs to the people
- the general public's ability to make sound political decisions

The Bill of Rights and Amendments 11–27

James Madison played a leading role in the creation of the U.S. Constitution.

In 1787, Thomas Jefferson sent James Madison a letter about the Constitution. Jefferson wrote, "I will now add what I do not like . . . [there is no] bill of rights." He explained his reasons: "A bill of rights is what the people are entitled to against every government on earth . . . and what no just government should refuse." Jefferson's disapproval is not surprising. In writing the Declaration of Independence, he spelled out basic individual rights that cannot be taken way. These are "life, liberty, and the pursuit of happiness." The Declaration states that governments are formed to protect these rights.

Several states approved the Constitution only if a list of guaranteed freedoms was added. While serving in the nation's first Congress, James Madison helped draft the Bill of Rights. In 1791, these first ten amendments became part of the Constitution.

AMENDMENTS 1–10. The Bill of Rights

▼ **KEY QUESTION** Why do some individual rights need special protection in the Constitution?

AMENDMENT 1. Religious and Political Freedom 1791

Congress shall make no law respecting an establishment of religion, or prohibiting the free exercise thereof; or **abridging** the freedom of speech, or of the press; or the right of the people peaceably to assemble, and to petition the Government for a redress of grievances.

The Five Freedoms

1. Freedom of Religion
2. Freedom of Speech
3. Freedom of the Press
4. Freedom of Assembly
5. Freedom to Petition

AMENDMENT 2. Right to Bear Arms 1791 A well-regulated militia, being necessary to the security of a free state, the right of the people to keep and bear arms, shall not be infringed.

AMENDMENT 3. Quartering Troops 1791 No soldier shall, in time of peace be quartered in any house, without the consent of the owner, nor in time of war, but in a manner to be prescribed by law.

AMENDMENT 4. Search and Seizure 1791 The right of the people to be secure in their persons, houses, papers, and effects, against unreasonable searches and seizures, shall not be violated, and no warrants shall issue, but upon probable cause, supported by oath or affirmation, and particularly describing the place to be searched, and the persons or things to be seized.

AMENDMENT 5. Rights of Accused Persons 1791 No person shall be held to answer for a capital, or otherwise infamous crime, unless on a presentment or indictment of a Grand Jury, except in cases arising in the land or naval forces, or in the militia, when in actual service in time of war or public danger; nor shall any person be subject for the same offense to be twice put in jeopardy of life or limb; nor shall be compelled in any criminal case to be a witness against himself, nor be deprived of life, liberty, or property, without **due process of law**; nor shall private property be taken for public use, without just compensation.

AMENDMENT 6. Right to a Speedy, Public Trial 1791 In all criminal prosecutions, the accused shall enjoy the right to a speedy and public trial, by an impartial jury of the State and district wherein the crime shall have been committed, which district shall have been previously ascertained by law, and to be informed of the nature and cause of the accusation; to be confronted with the witnesses against him; to have **compulsory process** for obtaining witnesses in his favor, and to have the assistance of **counsel** for his defense.

BACKGROUND VOCABULARY

abridging reducing

quartered given a place to stay

due process of law fair treatment under the law

compulsory process required procedure

counsel a lawyer

Legal Rights

In 1966, the Supreme Court made a decision based on the 5th and 6th Amendments. The outcome of this ruling is called "Miranda rights." Miranda rights protect suspects from giving forced confessions. Police must read these rights to a suspect they are questioning. For example:

- "You have the right to remain silent."
- "Anything that you say can and will be used against you in a court of law."
- "You have the right to an attorney."

(*left*) Demonstrators exercise their First Amendment rights of freedom of assembly and of speech at a rally in favor of immigration reform in 2006. (*above*) A journalist, utilizing freedom of the press, interviews a Hispanic family rallying for the same cause.

common law a system of law developed in England, based on customs and previous court decisions

bail money paid by arrested persons to guarantee they will return for trial

equity a system of justice not covered under common law

Members of the jury are expected to determine the guilt or innocence of a defendant in a court proceeding.

AMENDMENT 7. Trial by Jury in Civil Cases 1791 In suits at **common law**, where the value in controversy shall exceed twenty dollars, the right of trial by jury shall be preserved, and no fact tried by a jury, shall be otherwise reexamined in any court of the United States, than according to the rules of the common law.

AMENDMENT 8. Limits of Fines and Punishments 1791 Excessive **bail** shall not be required, nor excessive fines imposed, nor cruel and unusual punishments inflicted.

AMENDMENT 9. Rights of People 1791 The enumeration in the Constitution of certain rights shall not be construed to deny or disparage others retained by the people.

AMENDMENT 10. Powers of States and People 1791 The powers not delegated to the United States by the Constitution, nor prohibited by it to the States, are reserved to the States respectively, or to the people.

States Powers

The 10th Amendment gives the states reserved powers. Any powers not clearly given to the national government by the U.S. Constitution or denied to the states in Article I, Section 10, belong to the states. State constitutions sometimes assume authority in unexpected areas. For example, California's constitution sets rules for governing the use of fishing nets.

18. What are some common areas in which states have authority?

Bill of Rights Assessment

MAIN IDEAS

1. Why do some individual rights need special protection in the Constitution?
2. Which amendment protects your privacy?
3. Which amendments guarantee fair legal treatment?
4. Which amendment prevents the federal government from taking powers away from the states and the people?

CRITICAL THINKING

5. **Form and Support Opinions** The 4th, 5th, 6th, 7th, and 8th Amendments protect innocent people accused of crimes. Do you think these five amendments also favor the rights of actual criminals?

Think about

• criminals who go free if valuable evidence is found after their trials
• criminals released on bail

Amendments 11–27

🔻 **KEY QUESTION** How has the Constitution adapted to social changes and trends?

AMENDMENT 11. **Lawsuits Against States** 1795

Passed by Congress March 4, 1794. Ratified February 7, 1795. Proclaimed 1798.
Note: Article 3, Section 2, of the Constitution was modified by Amendment 11.

The Judicial power of the United States shall not be construed to extend to any suit in law or **equity**, commenced or prosecuted against one of the United States by citizens of another state, or by citizens or subjects of any foreign state.

AMENDMENT 12. **Election of Executives** 1804

Passed by Congress December 9, 1803. Ratified June 15, 1804.
Note: Part of Article 2, Section 1, of the Constitution was replaced by the 12th Amendment.

The electors shall meet in their respective states and vote by ballot for President and Vice-President, one of whom, at least, shall not be an inhabitant of the same state with themselves; they shall name in their ballots the person voted for as President, and in distinct ballots the person voted for as Vice-President, and they shall make distinct lists of all persons voted for as President, and of all persons voted for as Vice-President, and of the number of votes for each, which lists they shall sign and certify, and transmit sealed to the seat of the government of the United States, directed to the President of the Senate;—the President of the Senate shall, in the presence of the Senate and House of Representatives, open all the certificates and the votes shall then be counted;—the person having the greatest number of votes for President, shall be the President, if such number be a majority of the whole number of electors appointed; and if no person have such majority, then from the persons having the highest numbers not exceeding three on the list of those voted for as President, the House of Representatives shall choose immediately, by ballot, the President. But in choosing the President, the votes shall be taken by states, the representation from each state having one vote; a quorum for this purpose shall consist of a member or members from two-thirds of the states, and a majority of all the states shall be necessary to a choice. And if the House of Representatives shall not choose a President whenever the right of choice shall devolve upon them, ~~before the fourth day of March next following~~, then the Vice-President shall act as President, as in the case of the death or other constitutional disability of the President. The person having the greatest number of votes as Vice-President, shall be the Vice-President, if such number be a majority of the whole number of Electors appointed, and if no person have a majority, then from the two highest numbers on the list, the Senate shall choose the Vice-President; a quorum for the purpose shall consist of two-thirds of the whole number of Senators, and a majority of the whole number shall be necessary to a choice. But no

Separate Ballots

The presidential election of 1800 ended in a tie between Thomas Jefferson and (*above*) Aaron Burr. At this time, the candidate with the most votes became president. The runner-up became vice-president. The 12th Amendment calls for separate ballots for the president and vice president. The vice president is specifically elected to the office, rather than being the presidential candidate with the second-most votes.

AMENDMENT 13. Slavery Abolished 1865

Passed by Congress January 31, 1865. Ratified December 6, 1865.

Note: A portion of Article 4, Section 2, of the Constitution was superseded by the 13th Amendment.

Section 1. Neither slavery nor involuntary **servitude**, except as a punishment for crime whereof the party shall have been duly convicted, shall exist within the United States, or any place subject to their jurisdiction.

Section 2. Congress shall have power to enforce this article by appropriate legislation.

AMENDMENT 14. Civil Rights 1868

Passed by Congress June 13, 1866. Ratified July 9, 1868.

Note: Article 1, Section 2, of the Constitution was modified by Section 2 of the 14th Amendment.

Section 1. All persons born or **naturalized** in the United States, and subject to the jurisdiction thereof, are citizens of the United States and of the state wherein they reside. No state shall make or enforce any law which shall abridge the privileges or immunities of citizens of the United States; nor shall any state deprive any person of life, liberty, or property, without due process of law; nor deny to any person within its jurisdiction the equal protection of the laws.

Section 2. Representatives shall be apportioned among the several states according to their respective numbers, counting the whole number of persons in each state, excluding Indians not taxed. But when the right to vote at any election for the choice of electors for President and Vice-President of the United States, Representatives in Congress, the executive and judicial officers of a state, or the members of the legislature thereof, is denied to any of the male inhabitants of such state, being twenty-one years of age, and citizens of the United States, or in any way abridged, except for participation in rebellion, or other crime, the basis of representation therein shall be reduced in the proportion which the number of such male citizens shall bear to the whole number of male citizens twenty-one years of age in such state.

BACKGROUND VOCABULARY

servitude being under the authority of an owner or master

naturalized granted nationality

insurrection revolt against authority

bounties rewards

Civil Rights Laws

The 14th Amendment laid the groundwork for many civil rights laws, such as the Americans with Disabilities Act (1990). This act gave people with mental or physical disabilities "equal protection of the laws." For example, public places had to be designed for wheelchair use. Wider doors and ramps allow people with disabilities to go in and out of buildings, and wheelchair lifts make public buses accessible to people with disabilities.

Section 3. No person shall be a Senator or Representative in Congress, or elector of President and Vice-President, or hold any office, civil or military, under the United States, or under any state, who, having previously taken an oath, as a member of Congress, or as an officer of the United States, or as a member of any state legislature, or as an executive or judicial officer of any state, to support the Constitution of the United States, shall have engaged in **insurrection** or rebellion against the same, or given aid or comfort to the enemies thereof. But Congress may, by a vote of two-thirds of each house, remove such disability.

Section 4. The validity of the public debt of the United States, authorized by law, including debts incurred for payment of pensions and **bounties** for services in suppressing insurrection or rebellion, shall not be questioned. But neither the United States nor any state shall assume or pay any debt or obligation incurred in aid of insurrection or rebellion against the United States, or any claim for the loss or emancipation of any slave; but all such debts, obligations and claims shall be held illegal and void.

Section 5. The Congress shall have power to enforce, by appropriate legislation, the provisions of this article.

AMENDMENT 15. Right to Vote 1870

Passed by Congress February 26, 1869. Ratified February 3, 1870.

Section 1. The right of citizens of the United States to vote shall not be denied or abridged by the United States or by any state on account of race, color, or previous condition of servitude.

Section 2. The Congress shall have power to enforce this article by appropriate legislation.

Voting Rights

The Voting Rights Act of 1965 extended the 15th Amendment. To qualify as voters, African Americans were no longer required to take tests proving that they could read and write. Also, federal examiners could help register voters. As a result, the number of African-American voters rose sharply. (*above*) Federal voter registrars enforce the Voting Rights Act in Canton, Miss. in 1965.

19. What effect do you think the Voting Rights Act had on candidates running for office?

COMPARING Reconstruction Amendments

The 13th, 14th, and 15th Amendments are often called the Reconstruction Amendments. They were passed after the Civil War during the government's attempt to rebuild the Union and to grant rights to recently freed African Americans.

EQUALITY

YES NO

BALLOTS

13th Amendment 1865
• Ended slavery in the United States

14th Amendment 1868
• Defined national and state citizenship
• Protected citizens' rights
• Promised equal protection of the laws

15th Amendment 1870
• Designed to protect African Americans' voting rights

CRITICAL THINKING What problems did these amendments try to solve?

Passed by Congress July 12, 1909. Ratified February 3, 1913.

Note: Article 1, Section 9, of the Constitution was modified by the 16th Amendment.

The Congress shall have power to lay and collect taxes on incomes, from whatever source derived, without apportionment among the several states, and without regard to any census or enumeration.

Income Tax

People below the poverty level, as defined by the federal government, do not have to pay income tax. In 2004, the poverty level for a family of four was $19,307 per year. About 12.7 percent of all Americans were considered poor in 2004.

20. Why do you think people below the poverty level do not pay any income tax?

AMENDMENT 17. **Direct Election of Senators** 1913

Passed by Congress May 13, 1912. Ratified April 8, 1913.

Note: Article 1, Section 3, of the Constitution was modified by the 17th Amendment.

Section 1. The Senate of the United States shall be composed of two Senators from each state, elected by the people thereof, for six years; and each Senator shall have one vote. The electors in each state shall have the qualifications requisite for electors of the most numerous branch of the state legislatures.

Section 2. When vacancies happen in the representation of any state in the Senate, the executive authority of such state shall issue writs of election to fill such vacancies: Provided, that the legislature of any state may empower the executive thereof to make temporary appointments until the people fill the vacancies by election as the legislature may direct.

Section 3. This amendment shall not be so construed as to affect the election or term of any Senator chosen before it becomes valid as part of the Constitution.

AMENDMENT 18. **Prohibition** 1919

Passed by Congress December 18, 1917. Ratified January 16, 1919. Repealed by the 21st Amendment.

Prohibition

Under Prohibition, people broke the law if they made, sold, or shipped alcoholic beverages. Powerful crime gangs turned selling illegal liquor into a big business. This photo shows a federal agent enforcing the 18th Amendment by destroying kegs of illegal beer.

Section 1. After one year from the ratification of this article the manufacture, sale, or transportation of intoxicating liquors within, the importation thereof into, or the exportation thereof from the United States and all territory subject to the jurisdiction thereof for beverage purposes is hereby prohibited.

Section 2. The Congress and the several states shall have concurrent power to enforce this article by appropriate legislation.

Section 3. This article shall be inoperative unless it shall have been ratified as an amendment to the Constitution by the legislatures of the several states, as provided in the Constitution, within seven years from the date of the submission hereof to the states by the Congress.

(*left*) These women are campaigning in favor of the 19th Amendment—woman suffrage. Since winning the right to vote in 1920, women have slowly gained political power.

Connect *to* Today

The Equal Rights Amendment (ERA) In 1920, the 19th Amendment took effect, guaranteeing women the right to vote. Nevertheless, many women have continued to face discrimination in the United States. In 1923, the National Women's Party supported the passage of an equal rights amendment to protect women. Congress did not pass such an amendment until 1972. In 1982, however, the amendment died after it failed to be ratified by enough states to be added to the Constitution. As of the mid-2000s, the ERA was still not part of the U.S. Constitution.

21. Why do you think the 19th Amendment failed to create equality for women?

AMENDMENT 19. **Woman Suffrage** 1920

Passed by Congress June 4, 1919. Ratified August 18, 1920.

Section 1. The right of citizens of the United States to vote shall not be denied or abridged by the United States or by any state on account of sex.

Section 2. Congress shall have power to enforce this article by appropriate legislation.

AMENDMENT 20. **"Lame Duck" Sessions** 1933

Passed by Congress March 2, 1932. Ratified January 23, 1933.

Note: Article 1, Section 4, of the Constitution was modified by Section 2 of this amendment. In addition, a portion of the 12th Amendment was superseded by Section 3.

Section 1. The terms of the President and Vice-President shall end at noon on the 20th day of January, and the terms of Senators and Representatives at noon on the 3rd day of January, of the years in which such terms would have ended if this article had not been ratified; and the terms of their successors shall then begin.

Section 2. The Congress shall assemble at least once in every year, and such meeting shall begin at noon on the 3rd day of January, unless they shall by law appoint a different day.

Section 3. If, at the time fixed for the beginning of the term of the President, the President elect shall have died, the Vice-President elect shall become President. If a President shall not have been chosen before the time fixed for the beginning of his term, or if the President elect shall have failed to qualify, then the Vice-President elect shall act as President until a President shall have qualified; and the Congress may by law provide for the case wherein neither a President elect nor a Vice-President elect shall have qualified, declaring who shall then act as President, or the manner in which one who is to act shall be selected, and such person shall act accordingly until a President or Vice-President shall have qualified.

BACKGROUND VOCABULARY

inoperative no longer in force

primary an election in which registered members of a political party nominate candidates for office

Section 4. The Congress may by law provide for the case of the death of any of the persons from whom the House of Representatives may choose a President whenever the right of choice shall have devolved upon them, and for the case of the death of any of the persons from whom the Senate may choose a Vice-President whenever the right of choice shall have devolved upon them.

Section 5. Sections 1 and 2 shall take effect on the 15th day of October following the ratification of this article.

Section 6. This article shall be **inoperative** unless it shall have been ratified as an amendment to the Constitution by the legislatures of three-fourths of the several states within seven years from the date of its submission.

AMENDMENT 21. Repeal of Prohibition 1933

Passed by Congress February 20, 1933. Ratified December 5, 1933.

Section 1. The eighteenth article of amendment to the Constitution of the United States is hereby repealed.

Section 2. The transportation or importation into any state, territory, or possession of the United States for delivery or use therein of intoxicating liquors, in violation of the laws thereof, is hereby prohibited.

Section 3. This article shall be inoperative unless it shall have been ratified as an amendment to the Constitution by conventions in the several states, as provided in the Constitution, within seven years from the date of the submission hereof to the states by the Congress.

AMENDMENT 22. Limit on Presidential Terms 1951

Passed by Congress March 21, 1947. Ratified February 27, 1951.

Section 1. No person shall be elected to the office of the President more than twice, and no person who has held the office of President, or acted as President, for more than two years of a term to which some other person was elected President shall be elected to the office of the President more than once. But this article shall not apply to any person holding the office of President when this article was proposed by the Congress, and shall not prevent any person who may be holding the office of President, or acting as President, during the term within which this article becomes operative from holding the office of President or acting as President during the remainder of such term.

Term Limits

George Washington set the tradition of limiting the presidency to two terms. Franklin Roosevelt broke this custom when he was elected president four terms in a row—1932, 1936, 1940, and 1944. His record-long presidency led to the 22nd Amendment. A two-term limit, written into the Constitution, checks the president's power.

President Roosevelt (*far right*) campaigns with farmers in Atlanta, Ga. before the 1932 election.

Section 2. This article shall be inoperative unless it shall have been ratified as an amendment to the Constitution by the legislatures of three-fourths of the several states within seven years from the date of its submission to the states by the Congress.

AMENDMENT 23. Voting in District of Columbia 1961

Passed by Congress June 16, 1960. Ratified March 29, 1961.

Section 1. The district constituting the seat of government of the United States shall appoint in such manner as Congress may direct: a number of electors of President and Vice-President equal to the whole number of Senators and Representatives in Congress to which the district would be entitled if it were a state, but in no event more than the least populous state; they shall be in addition to those appointed by the states, but they shall be considered, for the purposes of the election of President and Vice-President, to be electors appointed by a state; and they shall meet in the district and perform such duties as provided by the twelfth article of amendment.

Section 2. The Congress shall have power to enforce this article by appropriate legislation.

AMENDMENT 24. Abolition of Poll Taxes 1964

Passed by Congress August 27, 1962. Ratified January 23, 1964.

Section 1. The right of citizens of the United States to vote in any **primary** or other election for President or Vice-President, for electors for President or Vice-President, or for Senator or Representative in Congress, shall not be denied or abridged by the United States or any state by reason of failure to pay any poll tax or other tax.

Section 2. The Congress shall have power to enforce this article by appropriate legislation.

AMENDMENT 25. Presidential Disability, Succession 1967

Passed by Congress July 6, 1965. Ratified February 10, 1967.

Note: Article 2, Section 1, of the Constitution was affected by the 25th Amendment.

Section 1. In case of the removal of the President from office or of his death or resignation, the Vice-President shall become President.

Section 2. Whenever there is a vacancy in the office of the Vice-President, the President shall nominate a Vice-President who shall take office upon confirmation by a majority vote of both houses of Congress.

Section 3. Whenever the President transmits to the President pro tempore of the Senate and the Speaker of the House of Representatives his written declaration that he is unable to discharge the powers and duties of his office, and until he transmits to them a written declaration to the contrary, such powers and duties shall be discharged by the Vice-President as Acting President.

Poll Tax

The poll tax was aimed at preventing African Americans from exercising their rights. Many could not afford to pay this fee required for voting.

22. How do you think the 24th Amendment affected elections?

Line of Succession

On June 29, 2002, President George W. Bush underwent a medical procedure which required sedation. Bush declared himself temporarily unable to perform the duties of the presidency. Vice-President Dick Cheney acted as President for about two hours that day—until Bush notified in writing that he was resuming the powers and duties of the office.

23. What do you think can happen in a country where the rules for succession are not clear?

Succession

Who takes over if a president dies in office or is unable to serve? The top five in the line of succession follow:

- vice-president
- speaker of the house
- president pro tempore of the Senate
- secretary of state
- secretary of the treasury

24. Why should voters know the views of the vice-president?

Section 4. Whenever the Vice-President and a majority of either the principal officers of the executive departments or of such other body as Congress may by law provide, transmit to the President pro tempore of the Senate and the Speaker of the House of Representatives their written declaration that the President is unable to discharge the powers and duties of his office, the Vice-President shall immediately assume the powers and duties of the office as Acting President. Thereafter, when the President transmits to the President pro tempore of the Senate and the Speaker of the House of Representatives his written declaration that no inability exists, he shall resume the powers and duties of his office unless the Vice-President and a majority of either the principal officers of the executive department[s] or of such other body as Congress may by law provide, transmit within four days to the President pro tempore of the Senate and the Speaker of the House of Representatives their written declaration that the President is unable to discharge the powers and duties of his office. Thereupon Congress shall decide the issue, assembling within forty-eight hours for that purpose if not in session. If the Congress, within twenty-one days after receipt of the latter written declaration, or, if Congress is not in session, within twenty-one days after Congress is required to assemble, determines by two thirds vote of both houses that the President is unable to discharge the powers and duties of his office, the Vice-President shall continue to discharge the same as Acting President; otherwise, the President shall resume the powers and duties of his office.

Amendments Timeline

Use the key below to help you categorize the amendments.

■ **Voting Rights**　　■ **Overturned Supreme Court Decisions**

■ **Social Changes**　　■ **Election Procedures and Conditions of Office**

1791
Bill of Rights
Amendments 1–10

1868
Amendment 14
Defines American citizenship and citizens' rights.

1870
Amendment 15
Stops national and state governments from denying the vote based on race.

1791　　**1800**　　**1850**

1798
Amendment 11
Protects state from lawsuits filed by citizens of other states or countries.

1804
Amendment 12
Requires separate electoral ballots for president and vice-president.

1865
Amendment 13
Bans slavery.

AMENDMENT 26. 18-year-old Vote 1971

Passed by Congress March 23, 1971. Ratified July 1, 1971.

Note: Amendment 14, Section 2, of the Constitution was modified by Section 1 of the 26th Amendment.

Section 1. The right of citizens of the United States, who are eighteen years of age or older, to vote shall not be denied or abridged by the United States or by any state on account of age.

Section 2. The Congress shall have power to enforce this article by appropriate legislation.

AMENDMENT 27. Congressional Pay 1992

Passed by Congress September 25, 1789. Ratified May 7, 1992.

No law, varying the compensation for the services of the Senators and Representatives, shall take effect, until an election of Representatives shall have intervened.

The Youth Vote

Members of the recording industry founded Rock the Vote. They urge young people to vote in elections.

Amendments 11–27 Assessment

MAIN IDEAS

1. How has the Constitution adapted to social changes and trends?
2. Which amendments affected the office of president?
3. Which pair of amendments shows the failure of laws to solve a social problem?
4. Which amendments corrected unfair treatment toward African Americans and women?

CRITICAL THINKING

5. **Summarize** What is the purpose of amending the Constitution?

Think about

• the purpose of the Constitution
• problems and issues that Americans have faced throughout U.S. history

1961
Amendment 23
Gives citizens of Washington, D.C., right to vote in presidential elections.

1964
Amendment 24
Bans poll taxes.

1920
Amendment 19
Extends the vote to women.

1919
Amendment 18
Prohibits making, selling, and shipping alcoholic beverages.

1933
Amendment 21
Repeals Amendment 18.

1971
Amendment 26
Gives 18-year-olds right to vote in federal and state elections.

1900   **1950**   **2000**

1913
Amendment 16
Allows Congress to tax incomes.

Amendment 17
Establishes direct election of U.S. senators.

1933
Amendment 20
Changes date for starting new Congress and inaugurating new president.

1951
Amendment 22
Limits terms president can serve to two.

1967
Amendment 25
Sets procedures for presidential succession.

1992
Amendment 27
Limits ability of Congress to increase its pay.

I'M AGAINST THE 3rd TERM
WASHINGTON WOULDN'T
GRANT COULDN'T
ROOSEVELT SHOULDN'T

Constitution Assessment

Briefly explain the significance of each of the following.

1. electors
2. impeachment
3. naturalization
4. felonies
5. bill of attainder
6. ex post facto law
7. suffrage
8. due process of law
9. servitude
10. primary

KEY IDEAS

1 Article 1 (pages 267–275)

11. What are the requirements for becoming a member of the House of Representatives and the Senate?

12. What are two military powers granted to Congress?

2 Articles 2–3 (pages 276–281)

13. How does the electoral college choose the president?

14. What are three powers of the president?

15. What are the two most important powers of the federal courts?

3 Articles 4–7 (pages 282–285)

16. How can the Constitution be changed?

17. If a state law and a federal law conflict, which law must be obeyed? Why?

18. How was the Constitution ratified?

4 Bill of Rights and Amendments 11–27 (pages 286–297)

19. What five freedoms are guaranteed in the First Amendment?

20. Which amendments extend voting rights to a broader range of Americans?

CRITICAL THINKING

21. **Drawing Conclusions** In a two-column chart, summarize the processes for changing the Constitution. Then use your completed chart to answer the questions below.

Proposing Amendments	Ratifying Amendments
1.	1.
2.	2.

   a. What role can citizens play in proposing amendments?

   b. What do you think are the main reasons for changing the Constitution?

22. **Make Inferences** Explain how the "elastic clause" in Article 1 gives Congress the authority to take action on other issues unknown to the Framers of the Constitution.

23. **Analyze Leadership** Think about the president's roles described in the Constitution. What qualities does a president need to succeed as a leader in so many different areas?

24. **Recognize Effects** How would you describe the impact of the 14th, 15th, and 16th Amendments on life in the United States?

25. **Citizenship** Suppose you and your family go on a road trip across several states. According to Article 4 of the Constitution, what citizens' rights do you have in the states you are visiting?

26. **Interpret Graphs** Read the graph below. What age group scored highest? Which scored lowest?

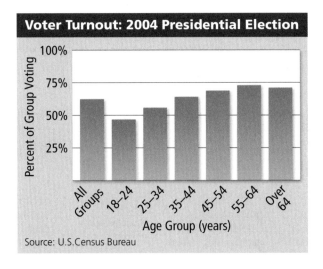

Voter Turnout: 2004 Presidential Election

Percent of Group Voting — Age Group (years): All Groups, 18–24, 25–34, 35–44, 45–54, 55–64, Over 64

Source: U.S. Census Bureau

MEAP PRACTICE

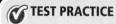

TEST PRACTICE

- Online Test Practice @ ClassZone.com
- Use the **MEAP Strategies & Practice,** pages S1-S27, at the front of this book

MULTIPLE CHOICE

Use the cartoon and your knowledge of U.S. history to answer question 1.

1 This cartoon shows two FBI officers carrying out their duties under the USA Patriot Act of 2001. The cartoon warns of too much power in the hands of

A the government.

B the citizens.

C young people.

D libraries.

Use the quotation and your knowledge of U.S. history to answer question 2.

❝ [The president] shall have power, by and with the advice and consent of the Senate, to make treaties, provided two-thirds of the Senators present concur; and he shall nominate, and by and with the advice and consent of the Senate, shall appoint ambassadors, other public ministers and consuls, judges of the Supreme Court, and all other officers of the United States . . . ❞

—U.S. Constitution, Art. 2, Sec. 2, part 2

2 The passage describes checks on the power of

A the president.

B the judiciary.

C the Senate.

D the states.

YOU BE THE HISTORIAN

27. Make Inferences How does the constitution reflect the fear of too strong a central government?

28. Citizenship Members of the electoral college elect the president. Would you support a campaign to choose the president by direct vote?

29. Evaluate The 15th, 19th, and 26th amendments give voting rights to specific groups. Why was it necessary for Congress to spell out these groups' rights in amendments?

30. WHAT IF? Suppose the 19th Amendment had been defeated. In what ways might this have affected American women?

31. Connect to Today The Bill of Rights guarantees a defendant a speedy, public trial. Do you think this guarantee is being observed today?

32. Writing Report Use the Internet to research the U.S. Supreme Court. Write a brief report explaining the steps necessary towards becoming a Supreme Court justice.

 Answer the

ESSENTIAL QUESTION

How has our 220-year-old Constitution remained a living document?

Written Response Write a two-to three-paragraph response to the Essential Question. Be sure to consider the key ideas of each section as well as the principles of the U.S. Constitution. Use the Response rubric below to guide your thinking and writing.

Response Rubric

A strong response will include:

- discussion of the purpose for extablishing the U.S. Constitution
- analysis of the limits of power within the U.S Constitution
- explanation of the purposes for and the processes of amending the U.S. Constitution.

The Role of the Citizen

Citizens of the United States enjoy many basic rights and freedoms. Freedom of speech and religion are examples. These rights are guaranteed by the Constitution, the Bill of Rights, and other amendments to the Constitution. Along with these rights, however, come **responsibilities**. Obeying rules and laws, voting, and serving on juries are some examples.

Reason and **respect** are also important aspects of citizenship. Reason—considering perspectives, applying logical and analytical thought, and exercising good judgment—is an important part of developing positive character qualities. Respect—for one's self, for other people, and for the community—plays a key role in how you participate in society. These Three R's of Democratic Citizenship are listed below. As you read through this handbook, note how the Three R's impact all aspects of citizenship.

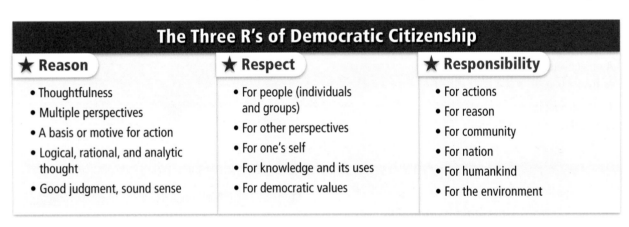

The Three R's of Democratic Citizenship

★ **Reason**

- Thoughtfulness
- Multiple perspectives
- A basis or motive for action
- Logical, rational, and analytic thought
- Good judgment, sound sense

★ **Respect**

- For people (individuals and groups)
- For other perspectives
- For one's self
- For knowledge and its uses
- For democratic values

★ **Responsibility**

- For actions
- For reason
- For community
- For nation
- For humankind
- For the environment

Active Citizenship

Active citizenship is not limited to adults. Younger citizens can help their communities become better places. The following pages will help you to learn about your rights and responsibilities. Knowing them will help you to become an active and involved citizen of your community.

The chart below lists five important ways *you* can be a model citizen. The examples in the pages that follow provide details about the five aspects of citizenship listed here.

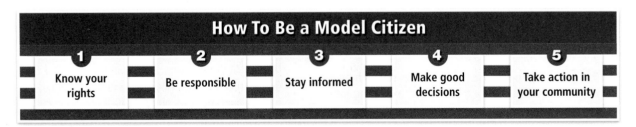

How To Be a Model Citizen

1	2	3	4	5
Know your rights	Be responsible	Stay informed	Make good decisions	Take action in your community

The weather was sunny but cold on January 20, 1961— the day that John F. Kennedy became the 35th president of the United States. In his first speech as president, he urged all Americans to serve their country. Since then, Kennedy's words have inspired millions of Americans to become more active citizens.

> ❝ Ask not what your country can do for you—ask what you can do for your country! ❞
>
> —John F. Kennedy

What Is a Citizen?

A citizen is a legal member of a nation and pledges loyalty to that nation. A citizen has certain guaranteed rights, protections, and responsibilities. A citizen is a member of a community and wants to make it a good place to live.

Today in the United States there are a number of ways to become a citizen. The most familiar are citizenship by birth and citizenship by naturalization. All citizens have the right to equal protection under the law.

President John F. Kennedy urged all Americans to become active citizens and work to improve their communities.

Citizenship by Birth A child born in the United States is a citizen by birth. Children born to U.S. citizens traveling or living outside the country are citizens. Even children born in the United States to parents who are not citizens of the United States are considered U.S. citizens. These children have dual citizenship. This means they are citizens of two countries—both the United States and the country of their parents' citizenship. At the age of 18, the child may choose one of the countries for permanent citizenship.

New U.S. citizens being sworn in on Ellis Island.

Citizenship by Naturalization A person who is not a citizen of the United States may become one through a process called naturalization. To become a naturalized citizen, a person must meet certain requirements.

- Be at least 18 years old. Children under the age of 18 automatically become naturalized citizens when their parents do.
- Enter the United States legally.
- Live in the United States for five years as a permanent resident prior to application.
- Read, write, and speak English.
- Show knowledge of American history and government.

The Naturalization Process

1. File an application.
2. Get fingerprints taken.
3. Be interviewed and take an examination.
4. Take an oath of allegiance.

What Are Your Rights?

Citizens of the United States are guaranteed rights by the U.S. Constitution, state constitutions, and state and federal laws. All citizens have three kinds of rights:

1 **Basic Freedoms** Citizens' basic rights and freedoms are sometimes called **civil rights**. Some of these rights are personal, and others are political.

2 **Protection From Unfair Government Actions** The second category of rights is intended to protect citizens from unfair government actions.

3 **Equal Treatment Under the Law** The third category is the right to equal treatment under the law. The government cannot treat one individual or group differently from another.

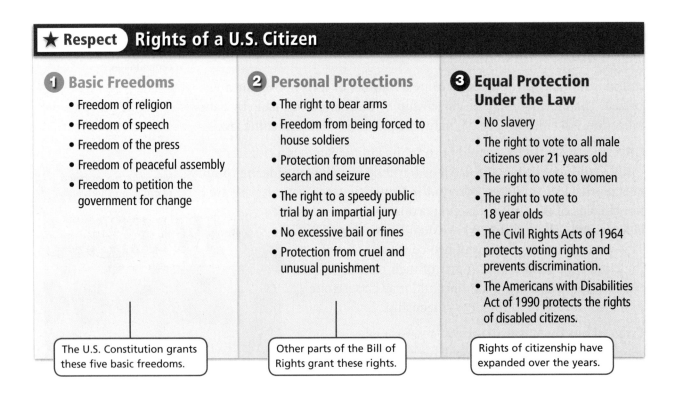

★ Respect **Rights of a U.S. Citizen**

1 **Basic Freedoms**

- Freedom of religion
- Freedom of speech
- Freedom of the press
- Freedom of peaceful assembly
- Freedom to petition the government for change

The U.S. Constitution grants these five basic freedoms.

2 **Personal Protections**

- The right to bear arms
- Freedom from being forced to house soldiers
- Protection from unreasonable search and seizure
- The right to a speedy public trial by an impartial jury
- No excessive bail or fines
- Protection from cruel and unusual punishment

Other parts of the Bill of Rights grant these rights.

3 **Equal Protection Under the Law**

- No slavery
- The right to vote to all male citizens over 21 years old
- The right to vote to women
- The right to vote to 18 year olds
- The Civil Rights Acts of 1964 protects voting rights and prevents discrimination.
- The Americans with Disabilities Act of 1990 protects the rights of disabled citizens.

Rights of citizenship have expanded over the years.

Limits to Rights The rights guaranteed to citizens have sensible limits. For example, the right to free speech does not allow a person to falsely shout, "Fire!" at a crowded concert. The government may place limits on certain rights to protect national security or to provide equal opportunities for all citizens. And rights come with responsibilities.

What Are Your Responsibilities?

For American democracy to work, citizens must carry out important responsibilities. There are two kinds of responsibilities—personal and civic. Personal responsibilities include taking care of yourself, helping your family, knowing right from wrong, and behaving in a respectful way.

Civic responsibilities are those that involve your government and community. They include obeying rules and laws, serving on juries, paying taxes, and defending your country when called upon. One of the most important responsibilities is voting. When you turn 18, you will have that right.

As a young person, you can be a good citizen in a number of ways. You might work with other people in your community to make it a fair and just place to live. Working for a political party or writing to your elected officials about issues that concern you are some other examples.

The chart below shows how responsibilities change with a citizen's age. Notice that all citizens share the responsibility to obey the laws of their communities.

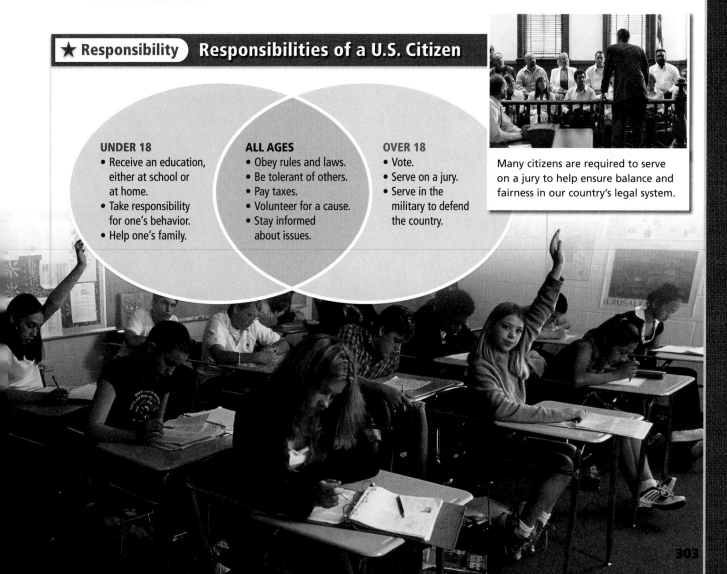

★ **Responsibility** **Responsibilities of a U.S. Citizen**

UNDER 18
- Receive an education, either at school or at home.
- Take responsibility for one's behavior.
- Help one's family.

ALL AGES
- Obey rules and laws.
- Be tolerant of others.
- Pay taxes.
- Volunteer for a cause.
- Stay informed about issues.

OVER 18
- Vote.
- Serve on a jury.
- Serve in the military to defend the country.

Many citizens are required to serve on a jury to help ensure balance and fairness in our country's legal system.

Building Citizenship Skills

Good citizenship skills include staying informed, solving problems or making decisions, and taking action. Every citizen can find ways to build citizenship skills. By showing respect for the law and for the rights of others in your daily life, you promote democracy. You can also work to change conditions in your community to make sure all citizens experience freedom and justice.

How Do You Stay Informed?

Americans can sometimes feel that they have access to too much information. It may seem overwhelming. Even so, you should stay informed on issues that affect your life. Staying informed gives you the information you need to make wise decisions and helps you find ways to solve problems.

★ **Responsibility** **Staying Informed**

1 Watch, Listen, and Read
The first step in practicing good citizenship is to know how to find information that you need.

Sources of information include broadcast and print media and the Internet. Public officials and civic organizations are also good sources for additional information. Remember as you are reading to evaluate your sources.

2 Evaluate
As you become informed, you will need to make judgments about the accuracy of your news sources. You must also be aware of those sources' points of view and biases. (Bias is a one-sided presentation of an issue.)

You should determine if you need more information, and if so, where to find it. After gathering information, you may be ready to form an opinion or a plan of action to solve a problem.

3 Communicate
To bring about change in their communities, active citizens may need to contact public officials. In today's world, making contact is easy.

You can reach most public officials by telephone, voice mail, fax, or letter. Many public officials also have Internet pages or e-mail that encourages input from the public.

Teens from Stand, an Ohio youth group, with Ohio Governor Bob Taft and first lady Hope Taft.

How Do You Make Good Decisions?

Civic life involves making important decisions. As a voter, whom should you vote for? As a juror, should you find the defendant guilty or not guilty? As an informed citizen, should you support or oppose a proposed government action? Unlike decisions about which video to rent, civic decisions cannot be made by a process as easy as tossing a coin. Instead, you should use a problem-solving approach like the one shown in the chart below. Decision making won't always proceed directly from step to step. Sometimes it's necessary to backtrack a little. For example, you may get to the "Analyze the Information" step and realize that you don't have enough information to analyze. Then you can go back a step and gather more information.

★ Reason   Making Good Decisions

Problem-solving and decision-making involves many steps. This chart shows you how to take those steps. Notice that you may have to repeat some steps depending on the information you gather.

1 Identify the Problem
Decide what the main issues are and what your goal is.

2 Gather Information
Get to know the basics of the problem. Find out as much as possible about the issues.

3 Analyze the Information
Look at the information and determine what it reveals about solving the problem.

4 Consider Options
Think of as many ways as possible to solve the problem. Don't be afraid to include ideas that others might think of as unacceptable.

5 Choose a Solution
Choose the solution you believe will best solve the problem and help you reach your goal.

6 Implement the Solution
Take action or plan to take action on a chosen solution.

7 Evaluate the Solution
Review the results of putting your solution into action. Did the solution work? Do you need to adjust the solution in some way?

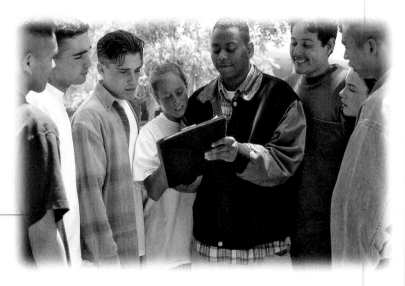

Conducting a survey is one way to gather information.

How Do You Take Action in Your Community?

Across the country many young people have come up with ways to make their communities better places to live. Thirteen-year-old Aubyn Burnside of Hickory, North Carolina, is just one example. Aubyn felt sorry for foster children she saw moving their belongings in plastic trash bags. She founded Suitcases for Kids. This program provides used luggage for foster children who are moving from one home to another. Her program has been adopted by other young people in several states. Below are some ways in which you can participate in your community.

★ Respect Taking Action

1 Find a Cause

How can you become involved in your community? First, select a community problem or issue that interests you. Some ideas from other young people include starting a support group for children with cancer, publishing a neighborhood newspaper with children's stories and art, and putting on performances to entertain people in shelters and hospitals.

2 Develop Solutions

Once you have found a cause on which you want to work, develop a plan for solving the problem. Use the decision-making or problem-solving skills you have learned to find ways to approach the problem. You may want to involve other people in your activities.

3 Follow Through

Solving problems takes time. You'll need to be patient in developing a plan. You can show leadership in working with your group by following through on meetings you set up and plans you make. When you finally solve the problem, you will feel proud of your accomplishments.

Members of Clean & Green, a Los Angeles Conservation Corps program, help to renovate a city building.

Practicing Citizenship Skills

You have learned that good citizenship involves three skills: staying informed, making good decisions, and taking action. Below are some activities to help you improve your citizenship skills. By practicing these skills you can work to make a difference in your own life and in the lives of those in your community.

How To Be a Model Citizen

1. Know your rights
2. Be responsible
3. Stay informed
4. Make good decisions
5. Take action in your community

Stay Informed

▷ *Create a pamphlet or recruiting commercial*

Ask your school counselors or write to your state department of education to get information on state-run colleges, universities, or technical schools. Use this information to create a brochure or recruiting commercial showing these schools and the different programs and degrees they offer.

Keep in mInd

What's there for me?
It may help you to think about what areas students are interested in and may want to pursue after graduation.

Where is it?
You may want to have a map showing where the schools are located in your state.

How can I afford it?
Students might want to know if financial aid is available to attend the schools you have featured.

Make Good Decisions

▷ *Create a game board or skit*

Study the steps on page 305. With a small group, develop a skit that explains the steps in problem solving. Present your skit to younger students in your school. As an alternative, create a game board that would help younger students understand the steps in making a decision.

Keep in mind

What do children this age understand?
Be sure to create a skit or game at an age-appropriate level.

What kinds of decisions do younger students make?
Think about the kinds of decisions that the viewers of your skit or players of the game might make.

How can I make it interesting?
Use visual aids to help students understand the steps in decision making.

Take Action

▷ *Create a bulletin board for your class*

Do some research on the Internet or consult the yellow pages under "Social Services" to find the names of organizations that have volunteer opportunities for young people. Call or write for more information. Then create a bulletin board for your class showing groups that need volunteer help.

Keep in mind

What kinds of jobs are they?
You may want to list the types of skills or jobs that volunteer groups are looking for.

How old do I have to be?
Some groups may be looking for younger volunteers; others may need older volunteers.

How do I get there?
How easy is it to get to the volunteer group's location?

UNIT 4

The Early Republic
1789–1844

Why It Matters Now

It was one thing for the founders to write a Constitution, another to make it work. Every decision made by the president and the Congress in the first 25 years of the Republic established a tradition of governance that continues to influence how we live today.

The history of liberty is a history of resistance. The history of liberty is a history of limitations of governmental power, not the increase of it.
—Woodrow Wilson

Launching a New Republic

1789–1800

ESSENTIAL QUESTION

What political traditions and tensions first appeared in the early years of the new republic?

CONNECT ⟳ **Geography & History**

How might the politics and geography of the United States have affected the choice of a capital?

Think about:

1 why two capitals preceded the final choice of Washington, D.C.

2 why the land forming the District of Columbia came from the states of Virginia and Maryland.

3 the geographic location of early settlement.

Washington's inaugural

Washington's medicine chest

1789

George Washington becomes the first president of the United States.

French Revolution in progress

1795 Pinckney's Treaty ratified.

▼

Effect U.S. southern border set at 31st parallel

1794 Battle of Fallen Timbers takes place.

▼

Effect Treaty of Greenville (1795) is signed.

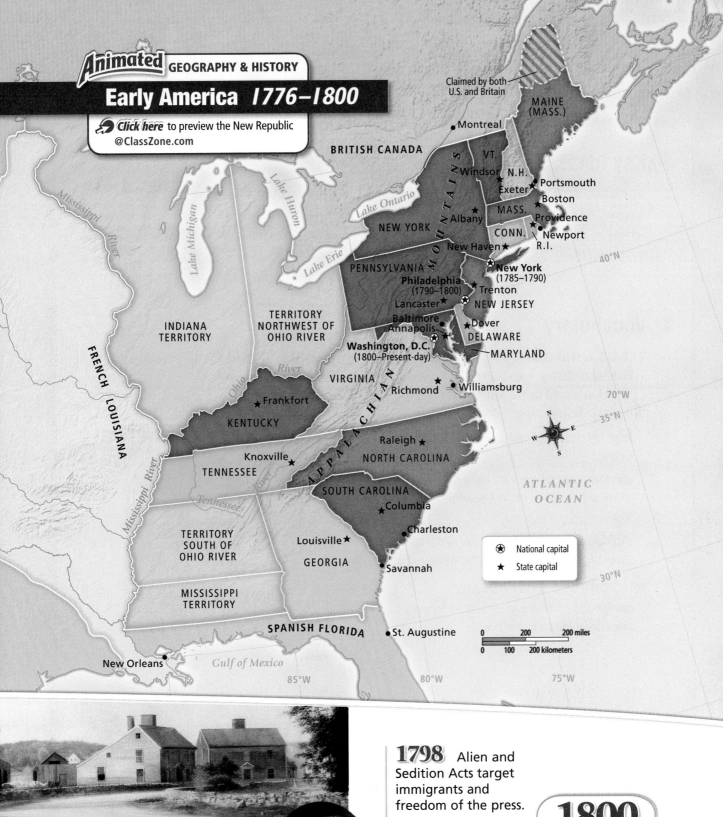

Early America 1776–1800

Click here to preview the New Republic
@ClassZone.com

Claimed by both
U.S. and Britain

BRITISH CANADA

Montreal

MAINE
(MASS.)

VT.

Windsor N.H.

Exeter Portsmouth

Boston

MASS. Providence

Albany CONN. Newport

R.I.

New Haven

New York
(1785–1790)

Trenton

Philadelphia
(1790–1800) NEW JERSEY

Lancaster

Baltimore Dover

Annapolis DELAWARE

Washington, D.C. MARYLAND
(1800–Present-day)

NEW YORK

PENNSYLVANIA

Lake Ontario

Lake Erie

Lake Huron

Lake Michigan

Mississippi River

INDIANA
TERRITORY

TERRITORY
NORTHWEST OF
OHIO RIVER

Ohio River

VIRGINIA

Richmond Williamsburg

FRENCH LOUISIANA

Frankfort

KENTUCKY

Knoxville

TENNESSEE

Tennessee River

TERRITORY
SOUTH OF
OHIO RIVER

Louisville

GEORGIA

Raleigh

NORTH CAROLINA

SOUTH CAROLINA

Columbia

Charleston

Savannah

ATLANTIC
OCEAN

APPALACHIAN MOUNTAINS

MISSISSIPPI
TERRITORY

SPANISH FLORIDA St. Augustine

New Orleans

Gulf of Mexico

40°N

70°W

35°N

30°N

85°W 80°W 75°W

| ★ | National capital |
| ★ | State capital |

0   200   200 miles
0 100 200 kilometers

1798 Alien and
Sedition Acts target
immigrants and
freedom of the press.

1800

1796 Federalists win
presidential election

▼

Effect John Adams
becomes president

(*top left*) John Adams'
birthplace in Braintree, Mass.
(*left*) John Adams

Convention of 1800
Thomas Jefferson is
elected president.

▶ Key Ideas

BEFORE, YOU LEARNED

A new Constitution, approved in 1788, served as a guide for the new republican government.

NOW YOU WILL LEARN

George Washington and his advisers faced many challenges during his Presidency.

▶ Vocabulary

TERMS & NAMES

Federal Judiciary (joo•DISH•ee•AIR•ee) **Act** 1789 law passed by the first Congress that set up lower federal courts

John Jay first chief justice of the U.S. Supreme Court

attorney general nation's top legal officer; today also the head of the Department of Justice

cabinet group of executive department heads that serve as the president's chief advisers

BACKGROUND VOCABULARY

inaugurate (in•AW•gyuh•rate) to formally swear in or induct into office

precedent (PRE•seh•dent) an example that becomes standard practice

tariff tax on imported goods

Visual Vocabulary
cabinet meeting

▶ Reading Strategy

Re-create the diagram shown at right. As you read and respond to the **KEY QUESTIONS**, use the diagram to list members of Washington's cabinet and their responsibilities.

 See Skillbuilder Handbook, page R6.

CATEGORIZE

Cabinet Member	Responsibilities
Hamilton	managed the nation's money
Jefferson	oversaw foreign relations

GRAPHIC ORGANIZERS
Go to **Interactive Review** @ ClassZone.com

Washington's Presidency

8 – U4.1.3.2 Challenge of Political Conflict – foreign relations (e.g., French Revolution, relations with Great Britain)
8 – U4.1.3.3 Challenge of Political Conflict – economic policy (e.g., the creation of a national bank, assumption of revolutionary debt)

One American's Story

Charles Thomson had served as secretary of the Continental Congress in 1774. Now, on April 14, 1789, he came to Mount Vernon in Virginia with a letter for George Washington. Washington knew the reason for the visit. Thomson's letter was to tell him that he had been elected the nation's first president. Before giving Washington the letter, Thomson made a short speech.

PRIMARY SOURCE

❝ I have now Sir to inform you that . . . your patriotism and your readiness to sacrifice . . . private enjoyments to preserve the happiness of your Country [convinced the Congress that you would accept] this great and important Office to which you are called not only by the unanimous votes of the Electors but by the voice of America. ❞

—Charles Thomson, quoted in *George Washington's Papers,*
at the Library of Congress 1741–1799

George Washington— shown in a wax likeness—was a popular choice for first president of the new nation.

Washington accepted the honor and the burden of his new office. He would soon guide the nation through its early years.

Washington's New Government

🔻 **KEY QUESTION** How did Washington's presidency shape new political traditions?

Under the new Constitution, the first presidential election was held in 1789. Washington won, and traveled to New York City, the nation's capital, to be **inaugurated**, or formally sworn in, as president. On April 30, 1789 at Federal Hall, the inauguration took place. The runner-up, John Adams of Massachusetts, became Washington's vice-president. As the nation's first president, Washington knew that his every action would set a **precedent** —an example that becomes standard practice. Under the first president, many political institutions and traditions were established.

Congressional Decisions Washington took charge of a political system that was a bold experiment. No one knew if a government based on the will of the people could really work. The new government began to take shape in the summer of 1789. First, people argued over what to call Washington. Some suggested "His Excellency," but others argued that made the president sound as if he was a king. Finally, in keeping with the simplicity of a republic, Washington agreed to "Mr. President."

The writers of the Constitution had left many matters to be decided by Congress. For example, the Constitution created a Supreme Court but left it to Congress to decide on the details. What type of additional courts should there be and how many? What would happen if federal court decisions conflicted with state laws?

To help answer these questions, Congress passed a federal court system under the **Federal Judiciary** (joo•DISH•ee•AIR•ee) **Act** of 1789. This act gave the Supreme Court six members: a chief justice, or judge, and five associate justices. Over time, that number has grown to nine. The law also provided for less powerful federal courts. Washington appointed **John Jay**, the prominent lawyer and diplomat, as the first chief justice of the Supreme Court.

Assembling a Cabinet The Constitution also gave Congress the task of creating departments to help the president lead the nation. The president had the power to appoint the heads of these departments.

Congress created the departments: state, war, treasury, justice and postal service. The State Department dealt with relations with other countries. The War Department was in charge of the nation's defense. The Treasury Department was in charge of the nation's economy, or financial security.

George Washington's first cabinet

Washington chose talented people to run the departments. For secretary of war, he picked Henry Knox, a trusted general during the Revolution. For secretary of state, Washington chose Thomas Jefferson. He had been serving as U.S. minister to France. Washington chose the brilliant Alexander Hamilton to be secretary of the treasury. Hamilton was to manage the government's money. The secretary's ties to the president began during the war when he had served as one of Washington's aides. To advise the government on legal matters, Washington picked Edmund Randolph as **attorney general**.

These department heads and the attorney general made up Washington's **cabinet**. The Constitution made no mention of a cabinet, but Washington began the practice of calling his cabinet to advise him on official matters. Another high office, that of postmaster general, was not elevated to cabinet status until 1829.

⚠ **EVALUATE** Explain how the decisions made by the first Congress created political traditions.

The Nation's Finances

🔻 **KEY QUESTION** What financial problems faced the new nation?

Washington assigned his secretary of the treasury, Alexander Hamilton, the task of straightening out the nation's finances. The most urgent money issue was the U.S. government's war debts.

War Debts During the Revolution, the United States had borrowed millions of dollars from France, Spain, and the Netherlands. The new nation was also in debt to private citizens, including soldiers who had received bonds—certificates that promised payment plus interest—as compensation for their services during the war. State governments also had wartime debts. By 1789, the national debt—foreign and domestic—totaled more than $52 million.

Most government leaders agreed that the nation must pay its debts to win the respect of both foreign nations and its own citizens. Hamilton saw that the new nation must assure other countries that it was responsible about money. These nations would do business with the United States if they saw that the country would pay its debts.

Hamilton's Political Views Hamilton believed in a strong central government. He thought the power of the national government should be stronger than that of the state governments. Hamilton also believed that government should encourage business and industry and that the nation's prosperity depended on the support of the nation's wealthy merchants and manufacturers. The government owed money to many of these rich men. By paying them back, Hamilton hoped to win their support for the new government.

Hamilton's Proposals In 1790, Hamilton presented his plan to Congress. He proposed three steps to improve the nation's finances and to strengthen the national government: 1) paying off all war debts, 2) raising government revenues, and 3) creating a national bank.

Hamilton also wanted the federal government to pay off the war debts of the states. However, sectional differences arose over repayment of state debts. Many Southern states resisted because they had already gone further

History Makers

Alexander Hamilton   1755–1804

Hamilton was one of the giants of American history. In his early twenties, he was a personal aide to General George Washington during the American Revolution. In the 1780s, he was a signer of the U.S. Constitution. He was one of the authors of a set of essays called *The Federalist* papers that persuaded Americans to ratify the Constitution.

As the first secretary of the treasury, Hamilton helped ensure the economic health of the new republic. His actions helped support his belief in a strong government and helped establish the executive branch as the most powerful branch of the government.

COMPARING *Leaders*

Compare Hamilton's leadership qualities to those of other American leaders mentioned in the chapter.

🔁 **ONLINE BIOGRAPHY** For more on Alexander Hamilton, go to the **Research & Writing Center** @ ClassZone.com

CONNECT Economics and History

HOW BANKS WORK

Hamilton believed that a national bank could help the economy of the new nation. It would be funded by a partnership between the federal government and wealthy private investors. In that way, private money would be tied to the country's welfare.

DEPOSITS

LOANS

LOANS

DEPOSITS

If people want to buy something, like a house or a car, they ask the bank to lend them the money. But they have to pay back the money they borrow, plus interest. The interest rate is higher than the interest rate they get when they make a deposit.

Savers are loaning their money to the bank when they put it in a savings account. The bank pays them interest for using their money. The bank uses their money to make more money.

Businesses use loans to create new products and services. As they sell more, they hire more workers and raise wages.

PURCHASES

CRITICAL THINKING

1. **Analyze Point of View** Do you think that the people who feared a strong central government supported Hamilton's idea of a national bank? Why or why not?

2. **Make Inferences** What are some ways that banks make money?

towards paying off their debts. Hamilton asked Thomas Jefferson of Virginia to help him gain Southern support. They reached a compromise by agreeing that the southern states would support Hamilton's plan and back payment of state debts. In return, northerners would support locating the capital in the South. The location chosen was on the banks of the Potomac River.

Building a Strong Government To raise revenue, the secretary of the treasury favored **tariffs**, which are taxes on imported goods. Tariffs serve two purposes: raising money for the government and encouraging the growth of national business. Americans bought goods from overseas in large quantities, including hemp, steel, and molasses. Tariffs on these goods kept a steady income flowing to the government. Since tariffs made foreign goods more expensive, they encouraged people to buy American goods.

Hamilton also called for the creation of a national bank. It would give the government a safe place to keep money. It would also make loans to businesses and government. Most important, it would issue bank notes—paper money that could be used as currency.

316 Chapter 9

Hamilton's Opponents Overall, Hamilton's plan was to strengthen the national government. Opponents of a national bank, including Jefferson and Madison, claimed that the bank would encourage an unhealthy partnership between the government and wealthy business interests. This angered Jefferson in particular. Those against the bank also argued that, since the Constitution does not mention a national bank, the government cannot create a national bank. They believed in the narrow or "strict" interpretation of the Constitution.

These differences began the debate among those who favored a "strict" interpretation of the Constitution, one in which the federal government has very limited powers, and a "loose" interpretation, which favors greater federal powers. Jefferson favored a strict interpretation, and Hamilton favored a broad or loose interpretation of the Constitution.

Hamilton's group used the so-called "Elastic Clause" of the Constitution (Article 1, Section 8, Number 18) to argue their case. This clause gives Congress the authority to do whatever is "necessary and proper" to carry out its specific powers, such as regulating commerce.

Washington backed Hamilton, and the Bank of the United States was established in 1791. Washington mostly tried to remain above the conflict between Hamilton and Jefferson and to encourage them to work together despite their basic differences. However, the formation of the two political factions, based on Hamilton's and Jefferson's opposing philosophies, laid the foundation for the American political factions that followed.

CATEGORIZE List Hamilton's solutions for the nation's finances.

Michigan Grade Level Content Expectations *Review*

 ONLINE QUIZ
For test practice, go to
Interactive Review @ ClassZone.com

TERMS & NAMES
1. Explain the importance of
- Federal Judiciary Act
- attorney general
- John Jay
- cabinet

USING YOUR READING NOTES
2. Categorize Complete the diagram you started at the beginning of the section.

Cabinet Member	Responsibilities
Hamilton	managed the nation's money
Jefferson	oversaw foreign relations

KEY IDEAS
3. What was the purpose of Washington's cabinet?

4. What were the three steps proposed by Hamilton for helping the nation's finances?

CRITICAL THINKING
5. Compare and Contrast How did Hamilton and Jefferson differ in their interpretation of the Constitution?

6. Make Inferences Why might merchants and manufacturers support a strong central government?

7. Connect to Today What organizational decisions made by the first Congress are still in effect today?

8. Writing Letter Imagine it's the 1790s. Write a letter to the editor that either supports or opposes Hamilton's plan for a national bank.

SECTION 2 Reading for Understanding

▶ Key Ideas

BEFORE, YOU LEARNED
George Washington faced many challenges during his presidency.

NOW YOU WILL LEARN
Washington established central authority at home and avoided war abroad

▶ Vocabulary

TERMS & NAMES

Battle of Fallen Timbers 1794 battle between Native Americans and American forces

Treaty of Greenville 1795 treaty in which 12 Native American tribes ceded control of much of Ohio and Indiana to the U.S. government

Whiskey Rebellion 1794 protest against the government's tax on whiskey by backcountry farmers

French Revolution revolution overthrowing the government in France that began in 1787 and ended in violence and mass executions

Jay's Treaty agreement that ended the dispute with Britain over American shipping during the French Revolution

Pinckney's (PINK•neez) **Treaty** 1795 treaty with Spain allowing U.S. commercial use of the Mississippi River

BACKGROUND VOCABULARY

cede surrender, or give up

REVIEW

Northwest Territory area bounded by the Ohio and Mississippi Rivers and the Great Lakes

neutral (NOO•truhl) not siding with any other country in dispute

▶ Reading Strategy

Re-create the diagram shown at right. As you read and respond to the **KEY QUESTIONS**, use the table to note important challenges and responses of the first U.S. government.

See Skillbuilder Handbook, page R3.

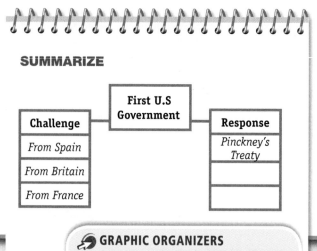

SUMMARIZE

First U.S Government

Challenge		Response
From Spain		Pinckney's Treaty
From Britain		
From France		

GRAPHIC ORGANIZERS
Go to **Interactive Review** @ ClassZone.com

Challenges to the New Government

8 – U4.1.2 Establishing America's Place in the World – Explain the changes in America's relationships with other nations by analyzing treaties with American Indian nations, Jay'Äôs Treaty (1795), French Revolution, Pinckney's Treaty (1795), Louisiana Purchase, War of 1812, Transcontinental Treaty (1819), and the Monroe Doctrine.

8 – U4.1.3.2 Challenge of Political Conflict– foreign relations (e.g., French Revolution, relations with Great Britain)

One American's Story

Settlers moving west often met fierce resistance from Native Americans. In 1790 and 1791, for example, Chief Little Turtle of the Miami tribe of Ohio had won decisive victories against U.S. troops.

In 1794, the Miami again faced attack by American forces. Little Turtle warned his people about the troops led by General "Mad Anthony" Wayne.

PRIMARY SOURCE

❝ We have beaten the enemy twice under separate commanders. . . . The Americans are now led by a chief [Wayne] who never sleeps. . . . We have never been able to surprise him. . . . It would be prudent [wise] to listen to his offers of peace. ❞

—Little Turtle, quoted in *The Life and Times of Little Turtle*

Chief Little Turtle was willing to negotiate with U.S. leaders, but his tribal council voted for war.

While the council members weighed Little Turtle's warning, President Washington was making plans to secure, or to guard or protect, the western borders of the new nation.

Problems at Home

🔻 **KEY QUESTION** How did two crises reveal the power of the national government?

Washington had always supported the idea of a strong national government. During his presidency, the government revealed its strength when dealing with a number of threatening situations.

Competing Claims to Territory Washington knew the nation needed peace to prosper. But trouble brewed in the Trans-Appalachian West, the land between the Appalachian Mountains and the Mississippi River. The source of conflict was competing claims for these lands. The 1783 Treaty of Paris had tried to resolve the claims. And some years later, Spain, Britain, the United States, and Native Americans all claimed parts of the area.

The strongest resistance to white settlement came from Native Americans in the **Northwest Territory**. This territory was bordered by the Ohio River to the south and Canada to the north. Native Americans in that territory hoped to unite to form an independent Native American nation. The British, who still held forts north of the Ohio River, supported Native Americans because they did not want to lose their access to trade in these territories.

Washington sent troops to the Northwest Territory to defend American interests. In 1790 this first federal army was no match for warriors led by Little Turtle. A second American force was defeated in 1791. Washington then formed another army and gave command to Revolutionary hero General Anthony ("Mad Anthony") Wayne.

Native Americans are Defeated On August 20, 1794, a force of around 2,000 Native Americans met Wayne's 1,000 troops near the future site of Toledo, Ohio. The Native Americans were easily defeated. The battlefield was covered with trees that had been struck down in a storm so the Americans called it the **Battle of Fallen Timbers**.

Native Americans were defeated by U.S. troops at the Battle of Fallen Timbers. They were disappointed when the British did not come to their aid.

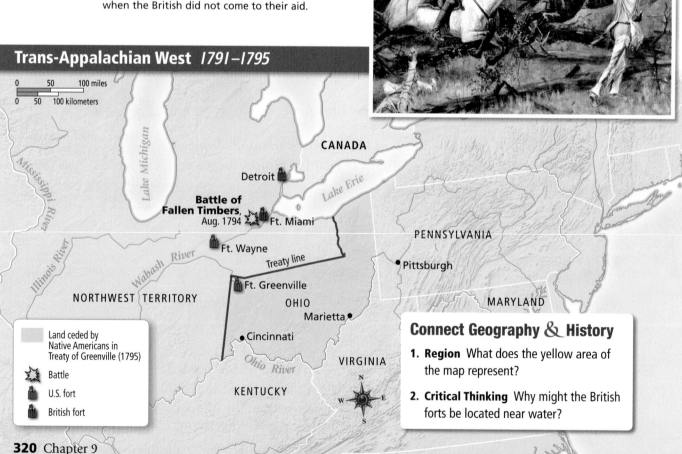

Trans-Appalachian West *1791–1795*

CANADA

Detroit

Battle of Fallen Timbers, Aug. 1794 Ft. Miami

Ft. Wayne

Treaty line

Ft. Greenville

PENNSYLVANIA

Pittsburgh

NORTHWEST TERRITORY

OHIO

Marietta

MARYLAND

Cincinnati

Land ceded by Native Americans in Treaty of Greenville (1795)

Battle

U.S. fort

British fort

VIRGINIA

KENTUCKY

Mississippi River

Lake Michigan

Lake Erie

Illinois River

Wabash River

Ohio River

Connect Geography & History

1. **Region** What does the yellow area of the map represent?

2. **Critical Thinking** Why might the British forts be located near water?

The Native Americans withdrew. The British, not wanting war with the United States, refused to help them. The Battle of Fallen Timbers crushed Native American hopes of keeping their land in the Northwest Territory. Twelve tribes signed the **Treaty of Greenville** in 1795. They agreed to **cede**, or surrender, much of present-day Ohio as well as numerous ports and outposts in Illinois, Michigan, and Indiana to the U.S. government.

Trouble in the Backcountry In spite of the United States' success at the Battle of Fallen Timbers, Washington soon found it necessary to put another army into the field. This was in response to a conflict over a new tax.

To raise revenue, Treasury Secretary Hamilton had pushed through Congress a tax to be levied specifically on the manufacture of whiskey. The tax hit small, backcountry farmers the hardest. One of their major crops was corn. But whiskey made from corn was more profitable than raw grain, so whiskey became central to the Backcountry economy. Having little money with which to buy goods, small farmers used whiskey like money to trade for other goods. As well, whiskey was one of the few local products suitable for transport to markets across the Appalachians. When the whiskey tax was enacted, outraged farmers from Pennsylvania to Georgia resisted.

Farmers Revolt In the summer of 1794, a group of farmers in western Pennsylvania staged the **Whiskey Rebellion** against the tax. One armed group attacked and burned the home of the regional tax collector. Others threatened an armed attack on Pittsburgh.

Most backcountry farmers had a long tradition of independent living and resistance to authority. And backcountry rebelliousness had helped defeat the British. That same rebelliousness was now seen as a threat to the new republic, and Washington and Hamilton needed to keep order. They looked upon the Whiskey Rebellion as an opportunity for the federal government to show it could enforce the law along the western frontier. Hamilton scolded the rebels for resisting the law.

PRIMARY SOURCE

❝ Such a resistance is treason against society, against liberty, against everything that ought to be dear to a free, enlightened, and prudent people. To tolerate it were to abandon your most precious interests. Not to subdue it were to tolerate it. ❞

—Alexander Hamilton, *The Works of Alexander Hamilton*

In October 1794, General Henry Lee, with Hamilton at his side, led an army of 13,000 soldiers into western Pennsylvania to put down the uprising. As news of the army's approach spread, the rebels fled. After much effort, federal troops rounded up a group of about 20 accused leaders. Washington had proved his point. He had shown that the government had the power and the will to enforce its laws. Meanwhile, events in Europe gave Washington a different kind of challenge.

🔺 **SUMMARIZE** Describe how Washington dealt with two early crises.

Connecting History

Individual Rights vs. Majority Rule
The Whiskey Rebellion marked the first major challenge to the authority of the federal government. When the armed rebels gathered in Pittsburgh in 1794, they were angry not only about the whiskey tax but also about their under-representation in the state legislatures.

History *through* **Art**

The Women of Les Halles Marching to Versailles, 5th October 1789

by Jean-Francois Janinet

The work shows hungry, angry French women marching in support of the revolution. They are out to confront the French royal family who live in the palace of Versailles, about 15 miles (24 km) southwest of Paris, the capital of France.

CRITICAL VIEWING Why did the artist choose to portray some ordinary people of the revolution?

Problems Abroad

▼ **KEY QUESTION** Why did events in Europe create problems for America?

The United States was now independent, but it remained tied to European nations by treaty and through trade. Britain was still the United States's biggest trading partner. France was allied with the United States by a treaty of 1778. When European nations went to war, Americans feared being dragged into the conflict.

Trouble in France In 1789, a financial crisis led the French people to rebel against their government. As in the American Revolution, the French revolutionaries demanded liberty and equality. At first, Americans supported the **French Revolution**. By 1792, however, the revolution had become very violent. Thousands were killed. Then, in 1793, the revolutionaries executed both the king and queen of France.

Other European monarchs believed the revolution threatened their own thrones by spreading outside of France. They joined in opposition to the revolution. France soon declared war on Britain, Holland, and Spain. Britain took the lead in the fight against France.

France and Britain at War War between France and Britain put the United States in an awkward position. France had backed America in the Revolution against the British. Also, many ordinary Americans saw France's revolution as proof that the American cause had been just.

Jefferson felt that a move to crush the French Revolution was an attack on liberty everywhere. But Hamilton argued that Britain was the United States' primary trading partner, and British trade was too vital to risk war. In April 1793, Washington declared that the United States would remain **neutral**, meaning it would not take sides. Congress then passed a law forbidding the United States to help either Britain or France.

Hamilton and Jefferson came to agree that entering a war was not in the new nation's interest. But Federalists attacked Jefferson for his support of France anyway. Jefferson was also tired of Washington's support of Hamilton's ideas. In 1793, Jefferson resigned as secretary of state.

Britain made it hard for the United States to remain neutral. The British were seizing the cargoes of American ships carrying goods from the French West Indies. Chief Justice John Jay went to England for talks about the seizure of U.S. ships. Jay also hoped to persuade the British to give up their forts on the northwest frontier.

Jay's Treaty During the talks in 1794, news came of the U.S. victory at the Battle of Fallen Timbers. Fearing another entanglement, the British agreed to leave the Ohio Valley by 1796. In what is called **Jay's Treaty**, the British also agreed to pay damages for U.S. vessels they had seized. Jay failed, however, to open up the profitable British Caribbean trade to Americans. Because of this, Jay's Treaty got through the House and Senate with great difficulty. Western settlers, for example, were angry that the British were still allowed to continue their fur trade on the American side of the U.S.-Canadian border. In spite of criticism, Jay's Treaty did help to reduce frontier tensions.

Like Jay, U.S. diplomat Thomas Pinckney helped reduce tensions along the frontier with the signing of **Pinckney's** (PINK•neez) **Treaty** of 1795. The United States won favorable terms with Spain in the peace treaty.

- Americans had the right to travel freely on the Mississippi River,
- U.S. goods could be stored at the port of New Orleans free of customs duties.
- Spain accepted the 31st parallel as the northern boundary of Florida and the southern boundary of the United States.

Together, Jay's Treaty and Pinckney's Treaty gave Americans a greater sense of security. With far less fear of European hostility, more Americans were moving west. But when Washington announced he would not run again for president, Americans were deeply divided over how the nation should be governed.

 ANALYZE Describe how crises in Europe created challenges for the new American government.

Michigan Grade Level Content Expectations *Review*

ONLINE QUIZ
For test practice, go to
Interactive Review @ ClassZone.com

TERMS & NAMES

1. Explain the importance of:
   - Battle of Fallen Timbers
   - French Revolution
   - Jay's Treaty
   - Treaty of Greenville
   - Pinckney's Treaty
   - Whiskey Rebellion

USING YOUR READING NOTES

2. **Summarize** Complete the diagram you started at the beginning of the section.

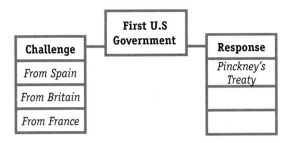

KEY IDEAS

3. Why did Washington consider it important to put down the Whiskey Rebellion?

4. How did the French Revolution create problems for the United States?

CRITICAL THINKING

5. **Evaluate** What were some of the advantages of the new nation remaining neutral?

6. **Connect** *to* **Today** The Whiskey Rebellion threatened civil order. What are some more current example of citizens threatening civil order in the belief that their cause is just?

7. **Connect Economics & History** How did Pinckney's Treaty protect American interests?

8. **Geography/Art** **Map** Make a map that shows a plan of the Battle of Fallen Timbers, or draw a scene from that battle.

American Spirit

NEW STYLES FOR A NEW NATION

The decade of the 1790s is often called the Federal period in the arts. During this time, Americans created art that expressed the attitudes, ideals, and hopes of their new nation.

A REVOLUTION IN FASHION

Clothing styles reflected the revolutionary political changes underway in America and France. Here, the old-style couple on the right is startled by the new fashions of youth. The ornate clothing and wigs of the aristocracy were on their way out, and a more relaxed, plainer style was on its way in.

ACHIEVEMENTS IN ART

Charles Willson Peale was America's greatest artist at this time. His work captured the informality and good humor of American culture. This painting of Peale's sons fooled even George Washington into thinking the stairs were real.

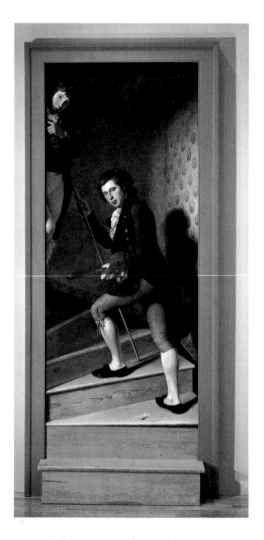

THE MODEL OF LIBERTY

The goddess of Liberty, who appeared on U.S. coins in 1795, was modeled on a famous woman of the Federal period—Anne Willing Bingham. Brilliant and highly educated, Bingham was a friend of Thomas Jefferson. Her world-famous intelligence, independent spirit, and beauty made her the perfect choice to represent liberty on America's new coins.

ABOLISHING SLAVERY

Many Americans in the early republic wanted to make America a place where "All men are created equal." Throughout the 1780s and '90s the Northern states slowly began abolishing slavery. The image shown here became an important symbol for the antislavery movement in America.

BACK TO THE FUTURE

Americans saw a link between their new republic and the ancient republic of Rome. Like the Romans, Americans had rebelled against a king and established a democracy. Architects began designing buildings for their new government using Roman forms to represent the nation's ideals of democracy and justice.

Massachusetts State House 1797

Virginia State Capitol 1789

Now look for pictures of other state capitols and identify the Roman forms you see.

Activity

Reveal the Romans!

Study the architectural forms below. Then identify Roman elements that you find in the American buildings on the left. (Some buildings might combine several Roman forms.)

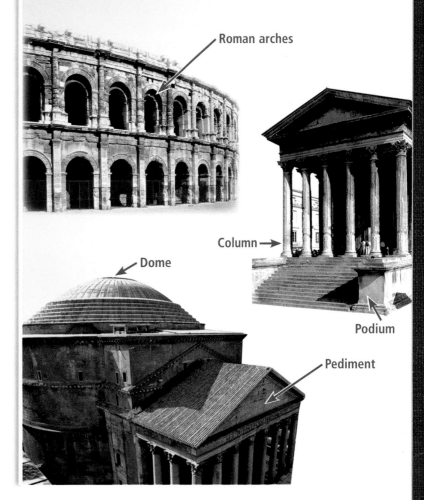

Roman arches

Column →

Podium

Dome

Pediment

▶ Key Ideas

BEFORE, YOU LEARNED
Washington established central authority at home and avoided war overseas.

NOW YOU WILL LEARN
The Federalists dominated politics under the presidency of John Adams.

▶ Vocabulary

TERMS & NAMES

John Adams Second President of the United States

XYZ Affair 1797 incident in which French officials demanded a bribe from U.S. diplomats

Alien and Sedition Acts series of four laws enacted in 1798 to reduce the political power of recent immigrants

states' rights idea that the states have certain rights that the federal government cannot overrule

nullification idea that a state could cancel a federal law within the state

Kentucky and Virginia Resolutions Resolutions passed by Kentucky and Virginia in 1798 giving the states the right to declare acts of Congress null and void

BACKGROUND VOCABULARY

foreign policy relations with the governments of other nations

political party group of people that tries to promote its ideas and influence government

aliens immigrants who are not yet citizens

sedition stirring up rebellion against a government

REVIEW

Federalists people who supported a strong national government; and heirs to the supporters of the ratification of the Constitution

▶ Reading Strategy

Re-create the diagram shown at right. As you read and respond to the **KEY QUESTIONS**, use the diagram to record important events in the new nation.

 See Skillbuilder Handbook, page R4.

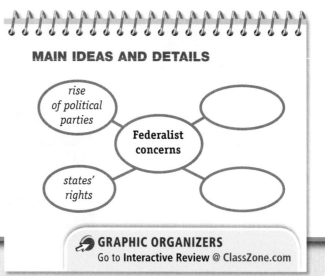

MAIN IDEAS AND DETAILS

rise of political parties

Federalist concerns

states' rights

🔁 **GRAPHIC ORGANIZERS**
Go to **Interactive Review** @ ClassZone.com

The Federalists in Charge

8 – P3.1.1.1 Identify, research, analyze, discuss, and defend a position on a national public policy issue – Identify a national public policy issue.
8 – P3.1.1.7 Identify, research, analyze, discuss, and defend a position on a national public policy issue – Compose a persuasive essay justifying the position with a reasoned argument.

One American's Story

Benjamin Banneker was born a free man at a time when most African Americans were enslaved. Largely self-educated, he became a surveyor, astronomer, and mathematician, and he published a yearly almanac. In 1790 Washington appointed him to the commission planning the new nation's capital.

Banneker was an exceptional example of what African Americans could achieve if released from the bondage of slavery and racism. In a letter to Jefferson, Banneker reminded him that "all men are created equal."

PRIMARY SOURCE

❝ [God] hath not only made us all of one flesh, but that he hath also, without partiality, afforded us all the same sensations and endowed us all with the same faculties; and that however variable we may be in society or religion, however diversified in situation or color, we are all of the same family, and stand in the same relation to him. ❞

—Benjamin Banneker, *letter to Thomas Jefferson 1791*

(*above*) Benjamin Banneker helped to survey the new capital of Washington, D.C.

Despite his efforts, Banneker was unable to change attitudes to slavery. However, Banneker will always be remembered as one of the outstanding Americans who helped launch the new republic.

Washington Retires

🔻 **KEY QUESTION** What dangers did President Washington warn against?

In 1796, President George Washington decided that two terms in office was enough. He wanted to return to Mount Vernon, his estate in Virginia. Throughout his eight years in office (1789–1797), he had tried to serve as a symbol of national unity. In large part, he succeeded.

Washington's Final Concerns During Washington's second term, opponents of Jay's Treaty, and other critics, led attacks on the president's policies. Thomas Paine, for example, called Washington "treacherous in private friendship . . . and a hypocrite in public life" because he failed to support the French Revolution. Washington saw such attacks as the outcome of political disagreements. In his farewell address, he warned that such differences could weaken the nation. Despite this advice, political differences became a part of American politics.

Americans listened more closely to Washington's parting words on **foreign policy**, or relations with the governments of other countries. He urged the nation's leaders to remain neutral and "steer clear of permanent alliances with any portion of the foreign world." He warned that agreements with foreign nations might work against U.S. interests.

Political Differences Continue Despite Washington's warnings against political differences, Americans were deeply divided over how the nation should be run. Hamilton and Jefferson had hotly debated the direction the new nation should take. But, after his frustrated resignation from public office in 1793, Jefferson returned to Virginia. During Washington's second term, Madison replaced Jefferson in the debates with Hamilton.

The two sides disagreed notably on how to interpret the Constitution and on economic policy. Hamilton favored the British and wanted to preserve good relations with them. He opposed the French Revolution. Jefferson and Madison supported it. Hamilton believed in a strong central government. Jefferson and Madison feared such a government might lead to tyranny. Hamilton wanted a United States in which trade, manufacturing, and cities grew. Jefferson and Madison pictured a rural nation of farmers.

Growth of Political Parties These differences on foreign and domestic policy led to the nation's first political parties. A **political party** is a group of people that tries to promote its ideas and influence government. It also backs candidates for office.

Together, Jefferson and Madison founded the Democratic-Republican Party. The party name reflected their strong belief in democracy and the republican system. Their ideas drew farmers' and workers' support to the new political party.

Jefferson and Madison's Democratic-Republican party eventually turned into the Democratic Party that is still active today. Hamilton and his friends formed the Federalist Party which reflected their belief in a strong national government. Many Northern merchants and manufacturers became **Federalists**, following the supporters of the ratification of the U.S. Constitution.

🔺 **SUMMARIZE** List the dangers Washington warned about.

Connecting History

Isolationism
Washington's advice laid the ground for America's policy of isolationism, or steering clear of foreign affairs. This policy lasted through most of the country's history before World War II.

Terence Kennedy's 1847 *Political Banner* combined several symbols of the young nation. **Would the banner have had greater appeal to Jefferson or Hamilton?**

COMPARING ▶ Political Parties

FEDERALISTS

Events in France not only affected politics in the United States, they influenced styles of clothing as well. Political differences could often be detected by observing different styles of dress and appearance.

DEMOCRATIC-REPUBLICANS

LEADERS:
Hamilton, Adams

SUPPORTERS:
lawyers, merchants, manufacturers, clergy

BELIEFS:
• strong national government
• loose construction of the Constitution
• favored national bank
• economy based on trade

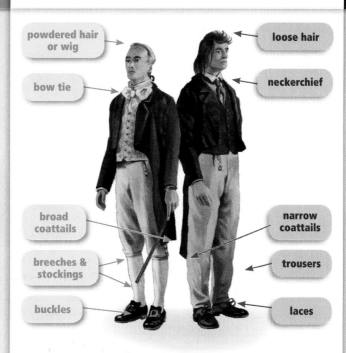

powdered hair or wig

bow tie

broad coattails

breeches & stockings

buckles

loose hair

neckerchief

narrow coattails

trousers

laces

LEADERS:
Jefferson, Madison

SUPPORTERS:
farmers, urban workers

BELIEFS:
• limited national government
• strict construction of the Constitution
• opposed national bank
• agricultural economy

CRITICAL THINKING **Compare and Contrast** Why might the Federalists be considered more supportive of business than the Democratic-Republicans?

John Adams's Administration

🔻 **KEY QUESTION** What issues divided Americans during Adams' presidency?

In 1796, the United States held its first elections in which political parties competed. The Federalists picked vice-president **John Adams** as their candidate for president. The Democratic-Republicans chose Jefferson.

In the Electoral College, Adams received 71 votes and Jefferson 68. The Constitution stated that the runner-up should become vice-president. Therefore, the country had a Federalist president and a Democratic-Republican vice-president. Adams became president in 1797. His chief rival, Jefferson, was his vice-president.

Problems with France When Washington left office in 1797, relations between France and the United States were tense. With Britain and France still at war, the French began seizing and harassing U.S. ships. Within the year, France had looted more than 300 U.S. ships.

Some Federalists called for war with France, but Adams hoped talks would restore calm. He sent Charles Pinckney, Elbridge Gerry, and John

THE XYZ AFFAIR

"The Paris Monster" is the official title of this 1798 political cartoon satirizing the XYZ Affair. On the right, the five members of the French Directory, or ruling executive body, are shown demanding money. On the left, the Americans echo Charles Pinckney's actual reply: "No, no, not a sixpence!"

The French Directory is a five-headed monster demanding "Money, Money, Money!!"

The Americans answer, "Cease bawling, monster! We will not give you sixpence!"

CRITICAL THINKING **Compare and Contrast** How would you contrast the cartoon's depiction of the American representatives with its depiction of the French Directory?

See Skillbuilder Handbook, page R24.

Marshall to Paris. Arriving there, they requested a meeting with the French minister of foreign affairs. For weeks, they were ignored. Then three French agents—later referred to as X, Y, and Z—took the Americans aside to tell them the minister would hold talks. However, the talks would occur only if the Americans agreed to loan France $10 million and to pay the minister a bribe of $250,000. The American representatives refused.

Adams received a full report of what became known as the **XYZ Affair**. After Congress and an outraged public learned of it, "Millions for defense, not one cent for tribute!" became the popular slogan of the day. In 1798, Congress canceled its treaties with France and allowed U.S. ships to seize French vessels. Congress also set aside money to expand the armed forces.

The Alien and Sedition Acts Conflict with France made Adams and the Federalists popular with the public. Many Democratic-Republicans, however, were sympathetic to France. One Democratic-Republican newspaper called Adams "the blasted tyrant of America. Angered by criticism in a time of crisis, Adams blamed the Democratic-Republican newspapers and new immigrants, many of whom were sympathetic to the Democratic-Republicans. To silence their critics, the Federalist Congress passed the **Alien and Sedition Acts** in 1798. These acts targeted **aliens**, or immigrants who were not yet citizens.

One act increased the waiting period for U.S. citizenship from 5 to 14 years. Other acts gave the president the power to arrest suspicious aliens or deport them in wartime. Another act outlawed **sedition**, or stirring up rebellion against a government. Ten Democratic-Republican newspaper editors were convicted of opinions damaging to the government. With these acts, the Federalists clamped down on freedom of speech and the press and tried to silence their opposition.

The Kentucky and Virginia Resolutions Jefferson and Madison looked for a way to fight the Alien and Sedition Acts. They found it in a theory called **states' rights**—the idea that states have certain rights that the federal government cannot overrule. Madison's resolution was approved by the Virginia legislature. Jefferson's resolution was adopted by the Kentucky legislature. This idea of states' rights set a precedent for future conflicts in the nation between the states and the national government.

CONNECT to the Essential Question

What political traditions and tensions first appeared in the early years of the new republic?

PROBLEMS	SOLUTIONS
1789 Washington faces many challenges Authority of state and federal courts is in question	He creates first cabinet members Congress passes Federal Judiciary Act (1789).
1790 Nation's finances are in crisis	Hamilton sets up National bank.
1793 French Revolution in progress: France and Britain at war	U.S. declares neutrality in foreign affairs
1794 Conflict arises in the Northwest Britain seizes American ships.	(1795) Native Americans sign Treaty of Greenville. Jays' Treaty reduces U.S.—Britain border disputes
1795 U.S. challenges Spanish trade restrictions.	Pinckney's Treaty establishes 31st parallel as U.S. southern boundary
1796 Disagreements over interpretation of the Constitution	Two political parties develop: Federalist Party and Democratic-Republican Party.

GEORGE WASHINGTON PRESIDENT 1791

CRITICAL THINKING Draw Conclusions How did the United States manage to stay out of overseas wars during this period?

The Kentucky Resolution, in particular, insisted on the principle of **nullification**, or the idea that a state could nullify, or cancel, any act of Congress that it considered unconstitutional. The **Kentucky and Virginia Resolutions** warned of the dangers that the Alien and Sedition Acts posed to a government of checks and balances as these checks and balances were guaranteed by the Constitution. Jefferson and Madison were not successful in overturning the acts while Adams was President. However, within two years the Democratic-Republicans won control of Congress, and they either reversed the acts or let them expire between 1800 and 1802.

Peace with France While Federalists and Democratic-Republicans battled at home, the United States made peace with France. Although war fever was high, Adams reopened talks with France. This time the two sides quickly signed the Convention of 1800, an agreement to stop all naval attacks. This treaty cleared the way for U.S. and French ships to sail the ocean in peace.

Adams's actions made him enemies among the Federalists. Despite this, he was proud of having saved the nation from bloodshed. In 1800, Adams became the first president to govern from the nation's new capital city, Washington, D.C. In 1800, however, he lost the presidential election to Thomas Jefferson.

 MAIN IDEAS & DETAILS Explain the issues that divided Americans during Adams' presidency.

Michigan Grade Level Content Expectations *Review*

ONLINE QUIZ
For test practice, go to
Interactive Review @ ClassZone.com

TERMS & NAMES

1. Explain the importance of:

- John Adams
- states' rights
- XYZ Affair
- nullification
- Alien and Sedition Acts
- Kentucky & Virginia Resolutions

USING YOUR READING NOTES

2. Main Ideas and Details Complete the diagram you started at the beginning of the section.

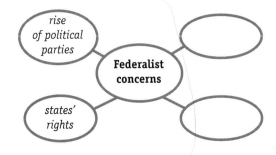

KEY IDEAS

3. What did Washington warn against before he left office?

4. What led to the rise of political parties?

5. Why did Congress pass the Alien and Sedition Acts?

CRITICAL THINKING

6. Evaluate Why was Washington's warning about political parties not heeded?

7. Make Inferences Why do you think so many merchants and manufacturers were Federalists?

8. Draw Conclusions How did the XYZ Affair show the young nation's growing confidence?

9. Synthesize How might the theory of states' rights undermine the federal government?

10. Connect to Today What are some issues that the two leading American political parties disagree on today?

11. Writing Editorial Imagine you are a newspaper editor in 1798. Write an editorial in favor of, or opposed to, the Alien and Sedition Acts.

Chapter Summary

1 **Key Idea**
George Washington and his
advisers faced many challenges
during his presidency.

2 **Key Idea**
Washington established central
authority at home and avoided
war abroad.

3 **Key Idea**
The Federalists dominated
politics under the presidency of
John Adams.

For detailed Review and Study Notes
go to **Interactive Review**
@ ClassZone.com

Name Game

**Use the Terms & Names list to complete each
sentence online or on your own paper.**

1. In 1789, Congress passed the _____ to set up
America's new court system.
    Federal Judiciary Act

2. Fighting over western territory in 1794, American
troops clashed with Native Americans at the _____.

3. America's _____ dictates its relations and interactions
with other countries.

4. _____ was the first chief justice of the United States
Supreme Court.

5. The treaty that allowed Americans to use the
Mississippi River was _____.

6. An exact or literal interpretation of the Constitution
is called a _____.

7. Angry Pennsylvania farmers clashed with the
American government during the _____.

8. The _____ in 1789 ended the monarchy in France.

9. The _____ restricted the political power of immigrants.

10. During the _____, French officials tried to bribe
U.S. diplomats.

A. loose construction
B. Federal Judiciary Act
C. attorney general
D. strict construction
E. Battle of Fallen Timbers
F. Alien and Sedition Acts
G. foreign policy
H. John Jay
I. Whiskey Rebellion
J. Kentucky and Virginia Resolutions
K. French Revolution
L. Pinckney's Treaty
M. XYZ Affair
N. Treaty of Greenville
O. states' rights
P. nullification

Activities

CROSSWORD PUZZLE

Complete the online crossword to show what
you know about the new republic.

ACROSS

1. _____ was the second
American president.

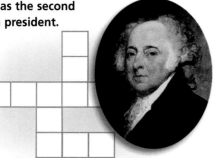

GEOGAME

Use this online map to reinforce your understanding of
early America, incuding the locations of important cities
and geographic features. Drag and drop each place name
in the list at its location on the map. A scorecard helps you
keep track of your progress online.

Philadelphia

New York

District of Columbia

Ohio River

St. Augustine

VOCABULARY

Explain the significance of each of the following.

1. Federal Judiciary Act
2. cabinet
3. nullification
4. Alien and Sedition Acts
5. French Revolution
6. John Jay
7. Attorney General
8. Whiskey rebellion
9. states' rights
10. Treaty of Greenville.

Choose the best answer from each pair.

11. This agreement ended the dispute with Britain over American shipping during the French Revolution. (Jay's Treaty / Pinckney's Treaty)

12. Which treaty ended a war with Native Americans? (Jay's Treaty / Treaty of Greenville)

13. Which law was passed in 1798 to reduce criticism of the government and limit the political activities of recent immigrants? (Alien and Sedition Acts / Federal Judiciary Act)

KEY IDEAS

1 Washington's Presidency (pages 312–317)

14. What questions about the judiciary were left open by the Constitution? How were they answered?

15. What financial problems did the new nation face?

16. How did Hamilton and Jefferson interpret the Constitution differently?

2 Challenges to the New Government (pages 318–323)

17. What did Washington do to secure the West?

18. What were the major arguments regarding taxation under the new government?

19. Why did Washington favor neutrality in the conflict between France and Britain?

3 The Federalists in Charge (pages 326–332)

20. Why did Washington oppose political parties?

21. Why did the Federalists pass the Alien and Sedition Acts?

CRITICAL THINKING

22. **Draw Conclusions** Why did Washington want both Thomas Jefferson and Alexander Hamilton to be among his closest advisers?

23. **Evaluate** Why did the federal government demonstrate its authority during the Whiskey Rebellion?

24. **Problems & Solutions** Create a chart to record the major problems and solutions faced by the leaders of the new nation.

Problems	Solutions
Need for executive aid and advice	Cabinet appointments
Government source of income	
Disputes with foreign nations	

25. **Draw Conclusions** Why do you think John Adams lost the presidential election of 1800?

26. **Causes and Effects** How did the French Revolution affect American politics?

27. **Citizenship** How did Washington's efforts to serve as a symbol of national unity help the new nation?

28. **Interpret Graphs** How much money did the government owe between 1789–1791?

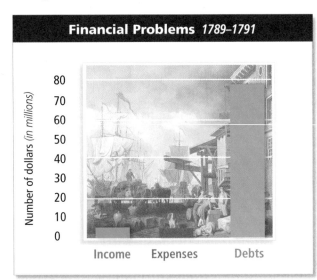

Financial Problems *1789–1791*

Source: *Historical Statistics of the United States*

✓ **TEST PRACTICE**

• **Online Test Practice @ ClassZone.com**
• Use the **MEAP Strategies & Practice,** pages S1-S27, at the front of this book

DOCUMENT-BASED QUESTIONS

Analyze each document and answer the question that follows.

DOCUMENT 1

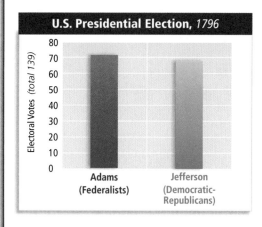

U.S. Presidential Election, *1796*

Electoral Votes *(total 139)*

Adams (Federalists)   Jefferson (Democratic-Republicans)

DOCUMENT 2

PRIMARY SOURCE

❝ Let me now . . . warn you . . . against the harmful effects of the spirit of party. . . . This spirit, unfortunately . . . exists in different shapes in all governments . . . but in those of the popular form, it is seen in its greatest rankness and is truly their worst enemy. ❞

—George Washington, Farewell Address

1 Examine the graph and the quotation. Which statement *best* describes the message of both documents?

  A Political parties can unite a nation.

  B Federalists and Democratic-Republicans have too much political power.

  C Political parties can divide a nation.

  D Democratic-Republicans are more popular than Federalists.

YOU BE THE HISTORIAN

29. Problems and Solutions How might the farmers in the Whiskey Rebellion have expressed their disapproval of the whiskey tax while staying within the law?

30. Compare and Contrast What are some of the similarities and differences between the American Revolution and the French Revolution?

31. Evaluate How did the Virginia and Kentucky Resolutions challenge the authority of the federal government?

32. WHAT IF? What might have happened to immigrants and members of the press if the Alien and Sedition Acts had remained in effect?

33. Draw Conclusions Why did Native Americans demand negotiations with the United States over the Northwest Territory?

34. **Connect *to* Today** What are some examples of how people exercise their rights of free speech today?

Answer the

ESSENTIAL QUESTION

What political traditions and tensions first appeared in the early years of the new republic?

Written Response Write a two or three paragraph response to the Essential Question. Be sure to consider the key ideas of each section, as well significant events that formed the political life of the new nation. Use the Rubric Response below to guide your thinking and writing.

Response Rubric

A strong response will

• discuss the precedents and challenges faced by Washington and Adams

• analyze the differences between Hamilton and Jefferson

• compare and contrast the Federalists and Democratic-Republicans

1. Jeffersonian
   Democracy
2. The Louisiana
   Purchase and
   Exploration
3. The War of 1812

The Jefferson Era

1800–1816

 ESSENTIAL QUESTION

How did the events of the Jefferson Era
strengthen the nation?

CONNECT Geography & History

How might the United States have been changed by the
purchase and exploration of western land?

Think about:

1 the amount of information about **physical features,**
such as hills and lakes, in the West

2 how many **settlements** there were in the East

3 what **challenges** a nation might face in expanding its
territory

George Catlin,
Buffalo Chase

1800

Thomas Jefferson
is elected president.

1803 The United States
purchases the Louisiana Territory.

Marbury v. *Madison* affirms
the Supreme Court's power
of judicial review.

1804 Lewis and Clark explore
the Louisiana Territory.

A page from
Lewis's journal

Effect Expands knowledge
of the American West.

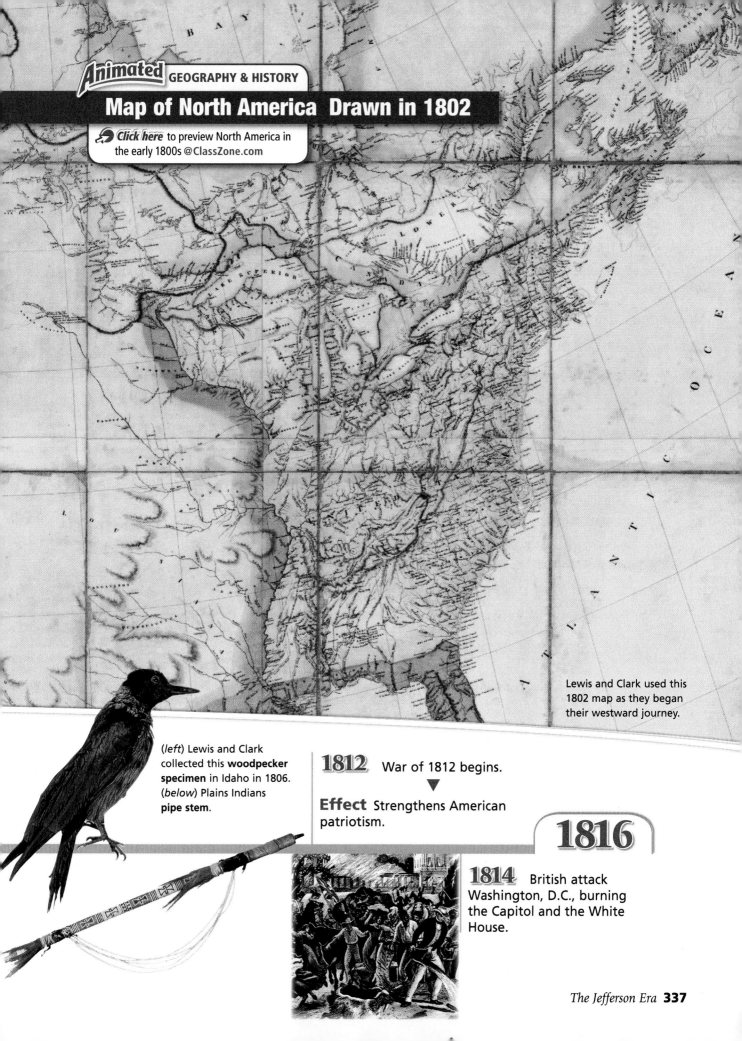

Lewis and Clark used this 1802 map as they began their westward journey.

(*left*) Lewis and Clark collected this **woodpecker specimen** in Idaho in 1806. (*below*) Plains Indians **pipe stem**.

1812 War of 1812 begins.

▼

Effect Strengthens American patriotism.

1816

1814 British attack Washington, D.C., burning the Capitol and the White House.

The Jefferson Era **337**

▶ Key Ideas

BEFORE, YOU LEARNED

The Federalists dominated politics under the presidency of John Adams.

NOW YOU WILL LEARN

After a tied election, Jefferson became president and the Democratic-Republicans reduced the power of the federal government.

▶ Vocabulary

TERMS & NAMES

Thomas Jefferson third president of the United States, elected in 1801

Judiciary Act of 1801 law that let President John Adams fill federal judgeships with Federalists

John Marshall chief justice of the Supreme Court appointed by President John Adams

judicial review principle that states that the Supreme Court has the final say in interpreting the Constitution

BACKGROUND VOCABULARY

radical person who takes extreme political positions

REVIEW

Federalist political party of Hamilton and Adams; supported a strong central government

Democratic-Republican Jefferson's political party; feared a strong central government

▶ Reading Strategy

Re-create the diagram shown at right. As you read and respond to the **KEY QUESTIONS**, use the boxes to show some of the changes made by Jefferson and his party.

 See Skillbuilder Handbook, page R4.

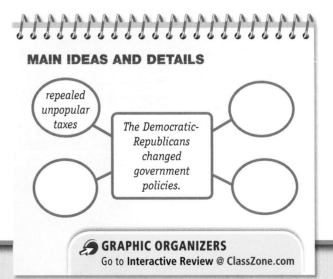

MAIN IDEAS AND DETAILS

repealed unpopular taxes

The Democratic-Republicans changed government policies.

GRAPHIC ORGANIZERS
Go to **Interactive Review** @ ClassZone.com

Jeffersonian Democracy

8 – U4.1.4 Establishing a National Judiciary and Its Power – Explain the development of the power of the Supreme Court through the doctrine of judicial review as manifested in *Marbury* v. *Madison* (1803) and the role of Chief Justice John Marshall and the Supreme Court in interpreting the power of the national government (e.g., *McCullouch* v. *Maryland*, *Dartmouth College* v. *Woodward*, *Gibbons* v. *Ogden*).
8 – P3.1.1.5 Identify, research, analyze, discuss, and defend a position on a national public policy issue – Identify and apply core democratic values or constitutional principles.

One American's Story

During the election of 1800, supporters of President John Adams and challenger **Thomas Jefferson** fought for their candidates with nasty personal attacks. For instance, journalist James Callender published pamphlets that warned voters not to re-elect Adams.

PRIMARY SOURCE

❝ In the fall of 1796 . . . the country fell into a more dangerous juncture than almost any the old confederation ever endured. The tardiness and timidity of Mr. Washington were succeeded by the rancour [bitterness] and insolence [arrogance] of Mr. Adams. . . . Think what you have been, what you are, and what, under [Adams], you are likely to become. ❞

—James Callender, quoted in *American Aurora*

This campaign banner declared: "T. Jefferson President of the United States of America—John Adams no more."

Adams's defenders were just as vicious. Yet, in spite of the campaign's nastiness, the election ended with a peaceful transfer of power from one party to another.

A New Party Comes to Power

▼ **KEY QUESTION** How was the presidential election of 1800 resolved?

The 1800 election was a contest between two parties with different ideas about the role of government.

Election of 1800 The two parties contesting the election of 1800 were the **Federalists**, led by President John Adams, and the **Democratic-Republicans**, represented by Thomas Jefferson. Each party believed that the other was a threat to the Constitution and the American republic.

The Democratic-Republicans thought they were saving the nation from monarchy and oppression. They argued that the Alien and Sedition Acts passed by the Federalist congress in 1798 violated the Bill of Rights.

Meanwhile, the Federalists thought that the nation was about to be ruined by **radicals**—people who take extreme political positions. The Federalists remembered the violence of the French Revolution, in which radicals executed thousands in the name of liberty.

When election day came, the Democratic-Republicans won the presidency. Jefferson received 73 votes in the electoral college, and Adams earned 65. But there was a problem. Aaron Burr, whom the Democratic-Republicans wanted as vice president, also received 73 votes.

Breaking the Tie According to the Constitution, the House of Representatives had to choose between Burr and Jefferson. The Democratic-Republicans clearly wanted Jefferson to be president. However, the new House of Representatives, dominated by Jefferson's party, was not yet in office. Federalists still had a House majority, and their votes would decide the winner.

The Federalists were divided. Some feared Jefferson so much that they decided to back Burr. Others, such as Alexander Hamilton, considered Burr an unreliable man and urged the election of Jefferson.

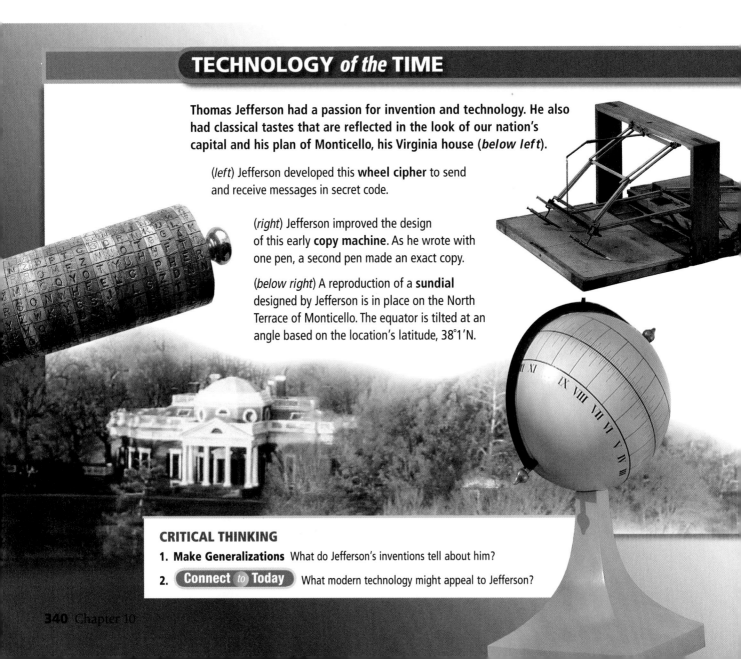

TECHNOLOGY *of the* TIME

Thomas Jefferson had a passion for invention and technology. He also had classical tastes that are reflected in the look of our nation's capital and his plan of Monticello, his Virginia house (*below left*).

(*left*) Jefferson developed this **wheel cipher** to send and receive messages in secret code.

(*right*) Jefferson improved the design of this early **copy machine**. As he wrote with one pen, a second pen made an exact copy.

(*below right*) A reproduction of a **sundial** designed by Jefferson is in place on the North Terrace of Monticello. The equator is tilted at an angle based on the location's latitude, 38°1′N.

CRITICAL THINKING

1. **Make Generalizations** What do Jefferson's inventions tell about him?

2. **Connect** *to* **Today** What modern technology might appeal to Jefferson?

Hamilton did not like Jefferson, but he believed that Jefferson would do more for the good of the nation than Burr. "If there be a man in the world I ought to hate," he said, "it is Jefferson. . . . But the public good must be [more important than] every private consideration."

From February 11 to February 17, the House voted 35 times without a winner. Finally, Alexander Hamilton's friend James A. Bayard persuaded several Federalists not to vote for Burr. On the thirty-sixth ballot, Jefferson was elected president. Aaron Burr became vice president.

People were overjoyed by Jefferson's election. His many achievements and talents went beyond politics. He was a skilled violinist, amateur scientist, and devoted reader. His book collection later became the core of the Library of Congress. In addition, Jefferson's deep interest in the architecture of ancient Greece and Rome is reflected in the architecture of the nation's capital.

▲ **SUMMARIZE** Explain how the election of 1800 was resolved.

Jefferson and Democracy

▼ **KEY QUESTION** How did Jefferson's policies differ from those of the Federalists?

On inauguration day, no guards, no coach, not even a horse waited at the door for Thomas Jefferson. He strolled through Washington, D.C., accompanied by a few friends. As Americans would learn in the months to come, Jefferson's humble behavior on inauguration day reflected his ideas about government.

Jefferson's View of Government The new president's first order of business was to heal political wounds. He urged political enemies to unite as Americans.

PRIMARY SOURCE

❝ Let us, then, fellow-citizens, unite with one heart and one mind. . . . Every difference of opinion is not a difference of principle. . . . We are all Republicans, we are all Federalists. ❞

—Thomas Jefferson, First Inaugural Address

One way Jefferson sought to unify Americans was by promoting a common way of life. He wanted the United States to remain a nation of small independent farmers. Such a nation, he believed, would uphold the strong morals and democratic ideals he associated with country living. Jefferson also hoped that the enormous amount of land available in the United States would prevent Americans from crowding into cities, as so many people had in Europe.

Jefferson wanted to avoid having too much government. He believed that the power of the central government should be limited, and that the people should be enabled to govern themselves. Some of the changes he made during his presidency reflect these beliefs.

Connecting History

Change & Continuity
Americans' concerns about overcrowding grew during the first half of the eighteenth century. You will see this theme develop in later chapters when you study the emergence of industry and the effects of immigration.

Marbury v. Madison (1803)

KEY ISSUE Judicial review

KEY PEOPLE

John Adams	president 1797–1801; appointed Federalists as judges
Thomas Jefferson	president 1801–1809; Democratic-Republican
James Madison	secretary of state to President Jefferson
William Marbury	Federalist financier; appointed as justice by President Adams

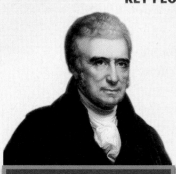

History Makers

John Marshall
1755–1835

John Marshall was the fourth chief justice of the U.S. Supreme Court. Marshall set out to make the judiciary a force to be reckoned with.

In 1803, in the case of *Marbury* v. *Madison*, Marshall upheld the power of judicial review. Many other rulings during Marshall's tenure as chief justice also strengthened federal power over the states.

Jefferson and Madison were angry when Marshall claimed this power for the Court, but they could hardly fight his decision. After all, *Marbury* v. *Madison* was decided in their favor.

ONLINE BIOGRAPHY

For more on John Marshall, go to the **Research & Writing Center** @ ClassZone.com

The Case

President John Adams appointed William Marbury to be a justice of the peace. However, Adams's term as president ended before the appointment papers were delivered to Marbury. After Thomas Jefferson took office, he named James Madison as secretary of state. Normally it would have been Madison's job to deliver appointment papers, but Jefferson ordered Madison not to deliver Marbury's papers.

Marbury then sued. He asked the Supreme Court to order Madison to deliver the papers.

The Court's Decision Marbury based his demand on two sections of the Judiciary Act of 1789. One section of that law created federal judgeships. Another section named the Supreme Court to settle disputes about certain judicial appointments.

The Supreme Court decided that the Judiciary Act was an invalid law. When Congress passed the Judiciary Act it gave a new power to the Supreme Court. But the Constitution does not allow Congress to do that. As Chief Justice John Marshall wrote, if the Constitution is to be the supreme law of the land, then any law contrary to the Constitution "is not law."

Historical Impact This was the first time the Supreme Court exercised the power of judicial review by overruling a law passed by Congress. Until this time, the Supreme Court was thought of as virtually powerless. That changed after Marshall proclaimed, "It is, emphatically, the province and the duty of the judicial department to say what the law is." Marshall's decision strengthened the Constitution's system of checks and balances by affirming an important power of the courts.

By upholding judicial review, Marshall helped to create a lasting balance among the three branches of government. The strength of this balance would be tested as the United States grew.

CRITICAL THINKING **Summarize** Explain how John Marshall strengthened the Supreme Court.

Jefferson and the Federalists Jefferson wanted the government to have less power than it had under the Federalists. He reduced the number of federal employees and the size of the military, and sought to end Federalist programs. Congress, now controlled by Democratic-Republicans, let the Alien and Sedition Acts end. Jefferson released prisoners convicted under the acts. Congress also ended many taxes, such as the unpopular whiskey tax.

Next, Jefferson made changes to Federalist financial policies. Alexander Hamilton had created a system that depended on a certain amount of public debt. Hamilton believed that people who were owed money by their government would make sure the government was run properly. But Jefferson opposed public debt. He used revenues from tariffs and land sales to reduce the amount of money owed by the government.

Conflict with the Courts Although Jefferson ended many Federalist programs, he had little power over the courts. Under the **Judiciary Act of 1801**, Adams had appointed as many Federalist judges as he could between the election of 1800 and Jefferson's inauguration. Because judges were appointed for life, Jefferson could do little about Federalist control of the courts.

Under Chief Justice **John Marshall**, the Supreme Court upheld federal authority and strengthened federal courts. In 1803, in *Marbury* v. *Madison*, Marshall affirmed the principle of **judicial review**—the final authority of the Supreme Court on the meaning of the Constitution. (See page 342.)

 COMPARE AND CONTRAST Explain how Jefferson's policies differed from those of the Federalists.

Michigan Grade Level Content Expectations *Review*

ONLINE QUIZ
For test practice, go to
Interactive Review @ ClassZone.com

TERMS & NAMES

1. Explain the significance of
- Thomas Jefferson
- John Marshall
- Judiciary Act of 1801
- judicial review

USING YOUR READING NOTES

2. Main Ideas and Details Complete the chart you started at the beginning of this section.

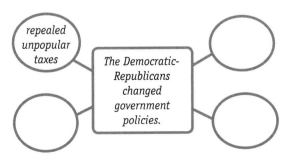

repeated unpopular taxes

The Democratic-Republicans changed government policies.

KEY IDEAS

3. What was unusual about the election of 1800?

4. Why did Jefferson seek unity between political parties?

5. What is the lasting importance of *Marbury* v. *Madison*?

CRITICAL THINKING

6. Compare and Contrast In what ways did the Federalists and Democratic-Republicans differ?

7. Analyze Point of View Why do you think Jefferson wished to promote a modest lifestyle?

8. Causes and Effects How did Adams's last-minute appointments affect the new president?

9. **Technology** Research Thomas Jefferson's interests. Design an Internet page about Jefferson that shows his inventions or a building he designed.

SECTION 2 — Reading for Understanding

▶ Key Ideas

BEFORE, YOU LEARNED
After a tied election, Jefferson became president and the Democratic-Republicans reduced the power of the federal government.

NOW YOU WILL LEARN
The nation doubled in size when Jefferson acquired the Louisiana Purchase.

▶ Vocabulary

TERMS & NAMES

Meriwether Lewis army captain appointed by President Jefferson to explore the Louisiana Territory and lands west to the Pacific Ocean

William Clark co-leader of the Lewis and Clark expedition

Sacagawea (sak•uh•juh•WEE•uh) Shoshone woman who assisted the Lewis and Clark expedition

Louisiana Purchase American purchase of the Louisiana Territory from France in 1803

Lewis and Clark expedition group that explored the Louisiana Territory and lands west; also known as the Corps of Discovery

Zebulon Pike leader of a southern expedition in the Louisiana Territory

BACKGROUND VOCABULARY

corps (kor) a number of people acting together for a similar purpose

Visual Vocabulary
William Clark (*left*) and Meriwether Lewis

▶ Reading Strategy

Re-create the diagram shown at right. As you read and respond to the **KEY QUESTIONS**, use the diagram to record important events and their effects. Add more boxes or start a new diagram as needed.

 See Skillbuilder Handbook, page R7.

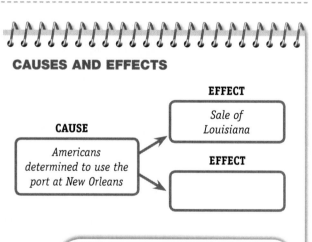

CAUSES AND EFFECTS

CAUSE
Americans determined to use the port at New Orleans

EFFECT
Sale of Louisiana

EFFECT

GRAPHIC ORGANIZERS
Go to **Interactive Review** @ ClassZone.com

The Louisiana Purchase and Exploration

8 – U4.1.2 Establishing America's Place in the World – Explain the changes in America's relationships with other nations by analyzing treaties with American Indian nations, Jay's Treaty (1795), French Revolution, Pinckney's Treaty (1795), Louisiana Purchase, War of 1812, Transcontinental Treaty (1819), and the Monroe Doctrine.

8 – U6.1.1.1 America at Century's End – territory, including the size of the United States and land use

One American's Story

In 1803, an expedition led by explorers **Meriwether Lewis** and **William Clark** set out to explore the American West. As they neared the Rocky Mountains, Lewis and Clark hired a French trapper to act as an interpreter with the Native Americans. He brought along his young wife, **Sacagawea**, a Shoshone Indian. Her knowledge of Native American languages and the land played an essential role in the expedition.

PRIMARY SOURCE

❝ *The sight* of this Indian woman . . . [assured the Native Americans] of our friendly intentions. . . . No woman ever accompanied a war party in this quarter. ❞

—William Clark, journal entry, October 19, 1805

This detail from *Lewis and Clark* by N. C. Wyeth shows Sacagawea with Meriwether Lewis.

Sacagawea did more than enable conversation and trade. Her presence led many tribes to believe that the explorers came in peace.

The Louisiana Purchase

🔻 **KEY QUESTION** How did the United States acquire the Louisiana Purchase?

When Americans talked about the West in 1800, they meant the area between the Appalachian Mountains and the Mississippi River.

The West in 1800 By 1800, thousands of settlers were moving westward across the Appalachians. Many settled on land inhabited by Native Americans. Even so, several U.S. territories soon declared statehood. Kentucky and Tennessee became states by 1800, and Ohio entered the union in 1803.

Although the Mississippi River was then the western border of the United States, there was much activity farther west. France and Spain were negotiating for ownership of the Louisiana Territory—the vast region between the Mississippi River and the Rocky Mountains.

The Mississippi River and New Orleans As the number of westerners grew, so did their political influence. A vital issue for many farmers and merchants was the use of the Mississippi River. They used this highway of commerce to transport their products through the New Orleans port, across the Gulf of Mexico, and then to East Coast markets.

Although originally claimed by France, the port was turned over to Spain after the French and Indian War. In a secret treaty in 1800, Spain returned the port to France's powerful leader, Napoleon. Now Napoleon planned to colonize the American territory. This brought America close to war.

The United States Expands In 1802, before turning Louisiana over to France, Spain closed New Orleans to American shipping. Angry westerners called for war against both Spain and France. To avoid hostilities, Jefferson offered to buy New Orleans from France. He received a surprising answer. The French asked if the United States wanted to buy all of the Louisiana Territory—a tract of land even larger than the entire United States at that time.

A number of factors may have influenced Napoleon's offer. He was probably alarmed by America's determination to keep the port of New Orleans open. Also, his enthusiasm for a colony in America may have been lessened by events in Haiti, a French colony in the West Indies. There, a revolt led by Toussaint L'Ouverture (too•SAN loo•vehr•TOOR) had resulted in disastrous losses for the French. Another factor was France's costly war against Britain. America's money may have been more valuable to Napoleon than land.

Jefferson was thrilled by Napoleon's offer. However, the Constitution said nothing about the president's right to buy land. This troubled Jefferson, who believed in the strict interpretation of the Constitution. But he also believed in a republic of small farmers, and that required land. So, on April 30, 1803, the **Louisiana Purchase** was approved for $15 million—about three cents per acre. The size of the United States doubled. At the time, most Americans knew little about this territory. But that would soon change.

▲ **SUMMARIZE** Explain how the United States acquired the Louisiana Territory.

Exploring the Louisiana Territory

▼ **KEY QUESTION** What were some effects of exploring the Louisiana Territory?

Since 1802, Thomas Jefferson had planned an expedition to the Louisiana country. Now that the Louisiana Purchase had been made, learning about the territory became more important than ever.

The Lewis and Clark Expedition Jefferson chose a young officer, Captain Meriwether Lewis, to lead an exploration of the Louisiana country. Lewis asked Lieutenant William Clark, a mapmaker and outdoorsman, to help him oversee a volunteer force, or **corps**. They called it the Corps of Discovery, but it soon became known as the **Lewis and Clark expedition**.

Clark was accompanied by York, his African-American slave. York's hunting skills won him many admirers. The first black man that many Native Americans had seen, he became something of a celebrity among them.

Connect *to the* **World**

Dissent and Rebellion
Haiti had been a highly profitable French colony that used slave labor. Toussaint L'Ouverture, a former slave, led a 1791 rebellion against French rule. Thirteen bloody years later, Haiti became the first independent black republic in the world.

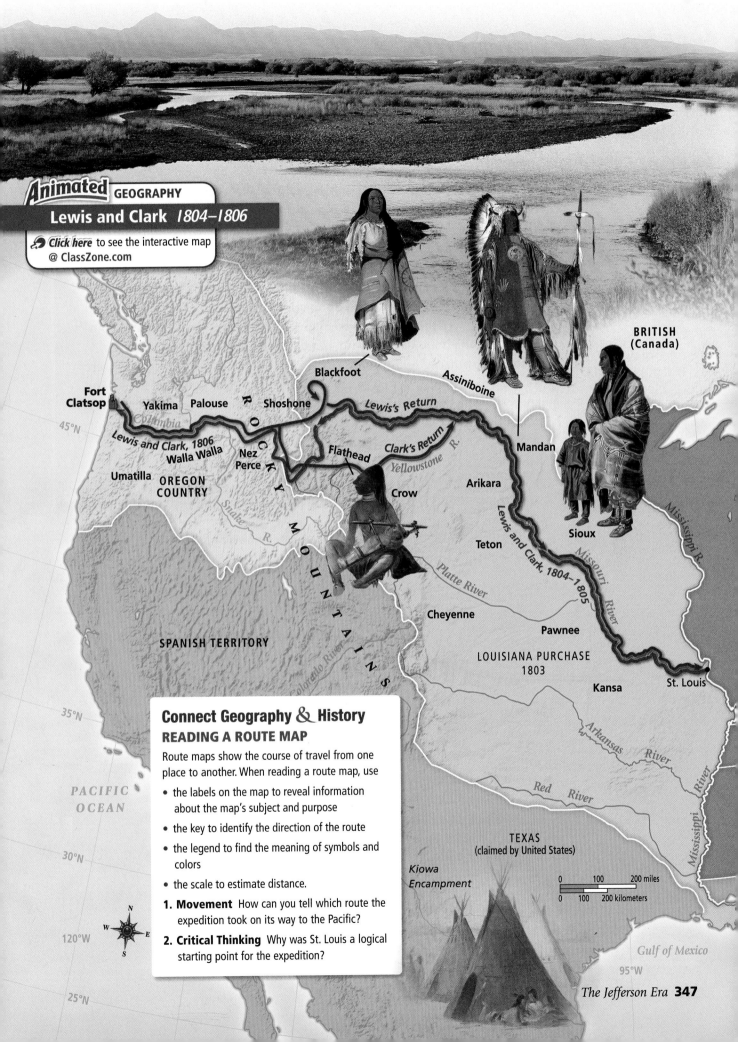

BRITISH
(Canada)

Blackfoot

Assiniboine

Fort
Clatsop

Yakima Palouse Shoshone

R   Lewis's Return

45°N Columbia

Lewis and Clark, 1806

Walla Walla Nez   Flathead Clark's Return

Perce   Yellowstone R.

Mandan

Umatilla OREGON
          COUNTRY

Crow

Arikara

Sioux

R
O
C
K
Y

Snake R.

Teton

Lewis and Clark, 1804–1805

Missouri River

M
O
U
N
T
A
I
N
S

Platte River

Cheyenne

Pawnee

SPANISH TERRITORY

Colorado River

LOUISIANA PURCHASE
1803

Kansa   St. Louis

35°N

Arkansas River

PACIFIC
OCEAN

Red   River

Mississippi R.

30°N

TEXAS
(claimed by United States)

Kiowa
Encampment

Connect Geography & History
READING A ROUTE MAP

Route maps show the course of travel from one place to another. When reading a route map, use

- the labels on the map to reveal information about the map's subject and purpose
- the key to identify the direction of the route
- the legend to find the meaning of symbols and colors
- the scale to estimate distance.

1. Movement How can you tell which route the expedition took on its way to the Pacific?

2. Critical Thinking Why was St. Louis a logical starting point for the expedition?

| 0 | 100 | 200 miles |
| 0 | 100 | 200 kilometers |

Gulf of Mexico

120°W

N
W   E
S

95°W

25°N

The Jefferson Era **347**

The Journey Begins Lewis and Clark set out in the summer of 1803. By winter, they reached St. Louis. Located on the western bank of the Mississippi River, St. Louis would soon become the gateway to the West. But in 1803 it was a sleepy town. Lewis and Clark spent the winter there, waiting for the official transfer of Louisiana to the United States. In March 1804, the American flag flew over St. Louis for the first time.

West to the Ocean The expedition, which numbered about 40, left St. Louis in May of 1804. Jefferson had instructed them to explore the Missouri River in hopes of finding a water route across the continent. He also told them to establish good relations with Native Americans and to describe the landscape, plants, and animals they saw.

After reaching what is now North Dakota, the explorers spent the winter with the Mandan people. They also met British and Canadian trappers and traders, who were not happy to see them. The traders feared American competition in the trade in beaver fur—and they would be proved right.

In the spring of 1805, the expedition set out again. This time they were joined by Sacagawea, who was a Shoshone Indian. Her language skills—she knew sign language and several Native American languages—and her knowledge of geography would be of great value to Lewis and Clark.

ONLINE PRIMARY SOURCE

Hear the perspectives at the **Research & Writing Center** @ ClassZone.com

COMPARING *Perspectives*

President Thomas Jefferson sponsored Lewis and Clark's expedition to the West, where they met almost 50 tribes. In an 1806 speech, Jefferson described his goals for relations between the United States and Native Americans. From the Native American perspective, Kiowa Chief Satanta (c. 1830–1878) later described the impact of Jefferson's policies.

Jefferson Speaks

" My friends and children. We are descended from the old nations which live beyond the great water: but we and our forefathers have been so long here that we seem like you to have grown out of this land . . . you are all my children . . . we wish as a true father should do, that we may all live together as one household. "

—Thomas Jefferson, Speech to a Delegation of Indian Chiefs, January 4, 1806

Satanta Speaks

" I hear a great deal of good talk from the gentlemen the Great Father sends us . . . I have heard you intend to settle us on a reservation near the mountains. I don't want to settle. . . . A long time ago this land belonged to our fathers, but when I go up to the river I see camps of soldiers on its banks. These soldiers cut down my timber, they kill my buffalo and when I see that, my heart feels like bursting. "

—Satanta, Kiowa Chief, September 1876

CRITICAL THINKING

1. **Make Inferences** What did Jefferson want for Native Americans?
2. **Analyze** Why were the Native Americans resentful of the soldiers?

As they approached the Rocky Mountains, Sacagawea pointed out Shoshone lands. Lewis and a small party made their way overland. The chief recognized Sacagawea as his sister and traded horses to Lewis and Clark. This enabled the explorers to cross the mountains. The expedition continued on to the Columbia River, which leads to the Pacific Ocean. The group arrived at the Pacific Coast in November 1805 and returned to St. Louis in 1806.

Lewis and Clark brought back a wealth of valuable information. Though they learned that an all-water route across the continent did not exist, Americans received an exciting report of what lay to the west. More importantly, the expedition produced the first good maps of the Louisiana Territory.

Zebulon Pike and the Southern Route In 1806, an expedition led by explorer **Zebulon Pike** left St. Louis on a southerly route to find the sources of the Arkansas and Red rivers. The group entered Spanish territory and was arrested. The explorers were released in 1807 and returned to the United States.

Pike's group brought back valuable descriptions of the land it explored. Not all these descriptions were accurate, however. For example, Pike described the treeless Great Plains as a desert. This led many Americans to believe, mistakenly, that the Plains region was useless for farming.

Pike's Route 1806–1807

 CAUSES AND EFFECTS Describe some effects of exploring the Louisiana Territory.

Michigan Grade Level Content Expectations *Review*

ONLINE QUIZ
For test practice, go to
Interactive Review @ ClassZone.com

TERMS & NAMES

1. Explain the importance of
- Louisiana Purchase
- Sacagawea
- Meriwether Lewis
- Zebulon Pike
- William Clark

USING YOUR READING NOTES

2. Causes and Effects Complete the diagram you started at the beginning of this section. Then create a diagram for each of the other main events in this section.

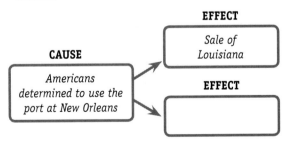

CAUSE

Americans determined to use the port at New Orleans

EFFECT

Sale of Louisiana

EFFECT

KEY IDEAS

3. Why was the Louisiana Purchase important to Jefferson?

4. Why were Lewis and Clark instructed to document the natural resources they found in their travels?

CRITICAL THINKING

5. Evaluate How did the Louisiana Purchase change the United States?

6. Make Inferences How might the information gathered by the explorers be useful to Jefferson?

7. Recognize Bias and Propaganda Read the quote by Jefferson on page 348. Is it propaganda? Explain.

8. Connect *to* Today Explorers still seek government funding for new expeditions. Where might today's explorers want to study?

9. Writing Letter Write a one-page letter from Jefferson to Lewis in which you describe your goals for the exploration of the Louisiana Territory.

American Landscapes

PACIFIC NORTHWEST Damp ocean winds help keep the coastal region green. East of the Cascades lie relatively dry highlands. The mountains of the region include more than a dozen major volcanoes.

SOUTHWEST For thousands of years, Native Americans have lived in the desert Southwest. Spanish settlement began here in 1598 and lasted to the 1840s. Explorer Zebulon Pike was arrested by Spanish authorities in the region in 1807.

ROCKY MOUNTAINS The majestic Rockies form the Continental Divide, which separates east-flowing and west-flowing rivers. Lewis and Clark crossed these mountains with the aid of Sacagawea, who obtained horses for them.

GREAT PLAINS The Plains region stretches from the foothills of the Rocky Mountains to the humid grasslands that lie west of the Mississippi River. It is mostly flat. At the time of the Lewis and Clark expedition, it was home to millions of bison.

GULF COAST The low, marshy region bordering the Gulf of Mexico is known as the Gulf Coast. Riverways and natural ports have long made commerce important here. The United States gained the valuable Lower Mississippi Valley in the 1803 Louisiana Purchase.

Pacific Northwest

Cascade Range

40°N

Sierra Nevada

Great Basin

N
W   E
S

0   100   200 miles
0   100   200 kilometers

Southwest

125°W

PACIFIC OCEAN

CROSS SECTION OF NORTH AMERICA (39°N)

Coast Ranges | Sierra Nevada | Rocky Mts. | Great Plains | Appalachian Mts.

Pikes Peak | Mississippi River

4,000 m	13,100 ft
3,000 m	9,800 ft
2,000 m	6,600 ft
1,000 m	3,300 ft
0 m	0 ft

2,640 mi

115°W

Rocky Mountains

Great Plains

History Makers

Sacagawea c. 1786–1812

A Shoshone Indian, Sacagawea was born in what
is now Idaho. When she was about 12 years old
she was kidnapped by the Hidatsa Sioux and
taken to what is now North Dakota. About four
years later she married a French trader, Toussaint
Charbonneau. Sacagawea and her husband traveled
with Lewis and Clark from 1804 to 1806. Their son
Jean Baptiste was born during the journey. When
the expedition reached Shoshone territory in the
Rocky Mountains, Sacagawea met her brother, Chief
Cameahwait. He agreed to trade the horses that the
explorers needed to cross the mountains.

CRITICAL THINKING Make Inferences How
might living in different cultures have helped
Sacagawea as a guide?

**ONLINE
BIOGRAPHY**
For more on Sacagawea, go to the
Research & Writing Center
@ ClassZone.com

Connect Geography & History

1. **Region** Where are regions connected by water routes?

2. **Make Inferences** Which region would you expect to
be the hardest to cross on foot? Why?

 See Geography Handbook, pages A8–A11.

Gulf Coast

Gulf of
Mexico

▶ Key Ideas

BEFORE, YOU LEARNED

After Jefferson acquired the Louisiana Purchase, the nation doubled in size.

NOW YOU WILL LEARN

The nation gained confidence and worldwide respect as a result of the War of 1812.

▶ Vocabulary

TERMS & NAMES

Embargo Act of 1807 law that forbade American ships from sailing to foreign ports and closed American ports to British ships

Tecumseh (tih•KUM•seh) Shawnee chief who sought to stop the loss of Native American land to white settlers

war hawk westerner who supported the War of 1812

Oliver Hazard Perry naval officer who led the U.S. victory over the British on Lake Erie in 1813

BACKGROUND VOCABULARY

tribute (TRIHB•yoot) payment in exchange for protection

impressment the act of seizing by force; between 1803 and 1812, the British impressed, or kidnapped, about 6,000 American sailors to work on British ships

coercion (ko•ER•shun) practice of forcing someone to act in a certain way by use of pressure or threats

Visual Vocabulary
impressment

▶ Reading Strategy

Re-create the diagram shown at right. As you read and respond to the **KEY QUESTIONS**, use the diagram to record important events in the order in which they occurred.

 See Skillbuilder Handbook, page R5.

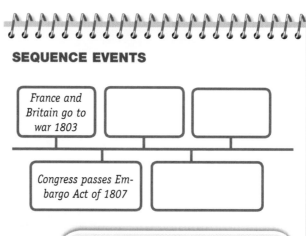

SEQUENCE EVENTS

France and Britain go to war 1803

Congress passes Embargo Act of 1807

GRAPHIC ORGANIZERS
Go to **Interactive Review** @ ClassZone.com

The War of 1812

8 – U4.1.2 Establishing America's Place in the World – Explain the changes in America,'s relationships with other nations by analyzing treaties with American Indian nations, Jay's Treaty (1795), French Revolution, Pinckney's Treaty (1795), Louisiana Purchase, War of 1812, Transcontinental Treaty (1819), and the Monroe Doctrine.
8 – U4.1.3.2 Challenge of Political Conflict – foreign relations (e.g., French Revolution, relations with Great Britain)

One American's Story

From 1801 to 1805, the United States was at war with Tripoli, a state on the Barbary coast of North Africa. The war began because of attacks on American merchant ships by Barbary pirates. The United States had been paying protection money, or **tribute**, but the pasha (ruler) of Tripoli wanted more money.

In February 1804, President Thomas Jefferson sent U.S. Navy Lieutenant Stephen Decatur to destroy the U.S. ship *Philadelphia*, which was in the hands of Barbary pirates. Decatur set fire to the *Philadelphia* and then escaped under enemy fire. Later, he issued this rallying cry.

PRIMARY SOURCE

❝ Our country! In her [relationships] with foreign nations may she always be in the right; but our country, right or wrong. ❞

—Stephen Decatur, 1816

Stephen Decatur was a hero of the war between the United States and the North African state of Tripoli.

The conflict with Tripoli showed how hard it was for the United States to stay out of foreign affairs while its citizens were involved in overseas trade.

The Path to War

▼ **KEY QUESTION** What conflicts with other nations did the United States have in the early 1800s?

Jefferson wanted the United States to seek the friendship of all nations but have "entangling alliances with none." However, his desire to keep the United States out of conflict with other nations was doomed from the start. American merchants were engaged in trade all over the world. Besides, the United States had little control over the actions of foreign powers.

Problems with France and England War broke out between France and Great Britain in 1803. The United States tried to stay out of the war. But many American trading ships made stops in Europe. The British captured any ship bound for France, and the French stopped all ships bound for Britain.

Another conflict grew out of Britain's shortage of sailors. Life in the British navy was so bad at the time that few British citizens chose to join—and many deserted. To fill its need for sailors, Britain used the policy of **impressment**, or kidnapping, of American merchant sailors. Between 1803 and 1812, the British impressed about 6,000 Americans to work on British ships.

No More Trade Instead of declaring war, Jefferson asked Congress to pass legislation that would stop all foreign trade. The president described his policy as "peaceable **coercion**." Coercion means forcing someone to act in a certain way by pressure or threats. Jefferson believed that the legislation would prevent further bloodshed.

In December, Congress passed the **Embargo Act of 1807**, which forbade American ships from sailing to foreign ports. The act also closed American ports to British ships. The policy harmed the United States more than it harmed France or Britain. American farmers lost key markets for their products. Shippers lost income, and many chose to violate the embargo by making false claims about where they were going.

The embargo became an issue in the election of 1808, which James Madison won. By then, Congress had repealed the act. Madison's solution to the problem was a law that allowed merchants to trade with any country except France and Britain. Trade with them would resume when they agreed to respect U.S. ships. This law was no more effective than the embargo.

Tecumseh and Native American Unity British interference with American shipping and impressment of U.S. citizens made Americans angry. Many also believed the British were trying to stop American expansion in the Northwest by stirring up Native American resistance to frontier settlements.

Since the Battle of Fallen Timbers in 1794, Native Americans had continued to lose their land to white settlers. **Tecumseh**, a Shawnee chief, vowed to stop this. He believed that Native American tribes had to unite in order to protect their land. Events in 1809 proved him right. That September, William Henry Harrison, governor of the Indiana Territory, signed the Treaty of Fort Wayne with chiefs of the Miami, Delaware, and Potawatomi tribes. They agreed to sell more than three million acres of land. But Tecumseh declared the treaty void. He believed that the sale could go through only with the agreement of all tribes, not just some.

(*below right*) The Shawnee were defeated at the Battle of Tippecanoe. **How did the Battle of Tippecanoe affect Tecumseh's hopes for unity?**

Chief Tecumseh

Many Native Americans did answer Tecumseh's call for unity. But he was too late. In late 1811, while Tecumseh was away recruiting for his alliance, Harrison's forces defeated the Shawnee at the Battle of Tippecanoe. Following this defeat, Tecumseh sided with the British in Canada. Tecumseh's welcome in Canada increased anti-British feelings in the West.

▲ **SUMMARIZE** Explain what conflicts with other nations the United States had in the early 1800s.

The War of 1812

▼ **KEY QUESTION** What were the effects of the War of 1812?

By 1812, more and more Americans were calling for war against Britain for its role in helping Native Americans and its policy on the high seas. Those who supported war were called **war hawks**. Many of them came from the western part of the country. Those in the Northeast, which had business ties with Britain, were less eager for war. The American government wanted all Americans to feel that their country could protect them. Finally on June 18, 1812, President James Madison asked Congress to declare war on Britain.

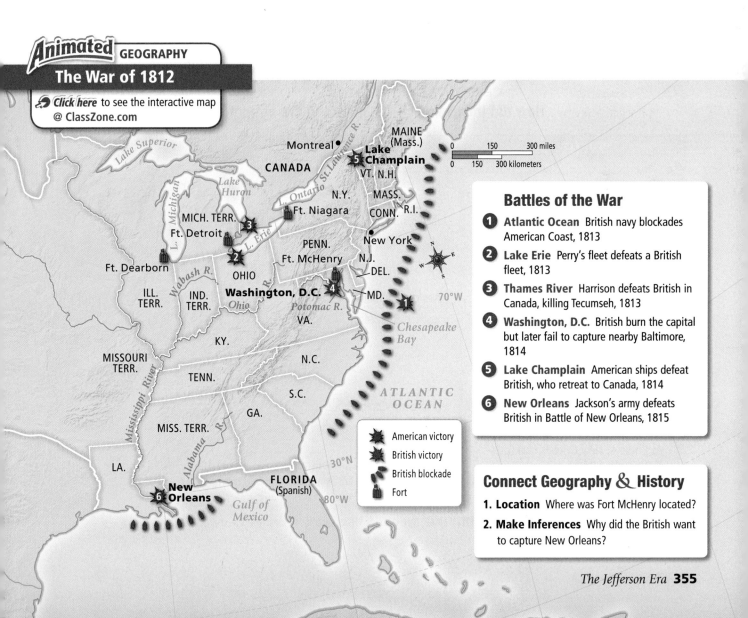

Animated GEOGRAPHY

The War of 1812

🖱 *Click here* to see the interactive map
@ ClassZone.com

Battles of the War

❶ **Atlantic Ocean** British navy blockades American Coast, 1813

❷ **Lake Erie** Perry's fleet defeats a British fleet, 1813

❸ **Thames River** Harrison defeats British in Canada, killing Tecumseh, 1813

❹ **Washington, D.C.** British burn the capital but later fail to capture nearby Baltimore, 1814

❺ **Lake Champlain** American ships defeat British, who retreat to Canada, 1814

❻ **New Orleans** Jackson's army defeats British in Battle of New Orleans, 1815

KEY:
- American victory
- British victory
- British blockade
- Fort

Connect Geography & History

1. **Location** Where was Fort McHenry located?

2. **Make Inferences** Why did the British want to capture New Orleans?

The Jefferson Era **355**

The First Phase of the War The War of 1812 had two main phases. From 1812 to 1814, Britain concentrated on its war with France. It spent little energy on its conflict in North America, although it did send ships to blockade the American coast.

The American military was weak at the beginning of the war. Democratic-Republicans had reduced the size of the American armed forces. The U.S. Navy had only 16 warships. In spite of its small size, the U.S. Navy rose to the challenge. Ships such as the *Constitution* and the *United States* won stirring victories that boosted American confidence.

Triumph on Lake Erie The most important U.S. naval victory took place on Lake Erie. In September 1813, a small British force on the lake set out to attack a new fleet of American ships. Commodore **Oliver Hazard Perry**, who had taken charge of the fleet, sailed out to meet the enemy. Perry's ship, the *Lawrence*, flew a banner reading, "Don't give up the ship."

For two hours, the British and Americans exchanged cannon shots. Perry's ship was demolished and the guns put out of action. Under British fire, Perry grabbed the banner as he and four companions escaped and rowed to another ship. Commanding the second ship, Perry soon forced the British to surrender. In a message to General William Henry Harrison, commander

CONNECT ⤻ *to the Essential Question*

How did the events of the Jefferson Era strengthen the nation?

EVENT	EFFECTS
1801–1804 Jefferson takes office; Democratic-Republicans in power	Many Federalist policies end, though Federalists retain control of Judiciary
Jefferson purchases Louisiana Territory	Doubles size of the United States
Lewis and Clark expedition charts important information about the West	Western settlement fever begins
1807–1812 Congress passes Embargo Act of 1807	American shipping and trade suffer
Shawnee defeated at the Battle of Tippecanoe	Shawnee chief Tecumseh sides with British in Canada
Congress declares war on Britain	Britain and the United States are at war
1814–1815 British defeat Napoleon, turn focus to war with the United States	British burn Capitol building, White House; attack Fort McHenry
Treaty of Ghent is signed	War ends, but news reaches the United States too late to prevent further hostilities
At Battle of New Orleans, Jackson's forces defeat British	Increases American patriotism; weakens Native American resistance; strengthens American manufacturing

CRITICAL THINKING **Synthesize** How would you describe the characteristics of the Jefferson Era?

of the Army of the Northwest, Perry wrote: "We have met the enemy and they are ours."

After General Harrison received Perry's note, he set out to attack the British. But when Harrison transported his army across Lake Erie to Detroit, he discovered that the British already had retreated into Canada. Harrison pursued the British and defeated their forces at the Battle of the Thames in October 1813. This American victory put an end to the British threat to the Northwest—and took the life of Tecumseh, who died in the battle, fighting for the British.

The Second Phase of the War The second phase of the War of 1812 began after the British defeated Napoleon in Europe in April 1814. Britain's army and navy were then free to attack the United States. In August 1814, President Madison and other officials fled Washington, D.C., as British forces neared the nation's capitol. Dolley Madison, the president's wife, stayed behind to rescue important objects from the White House. (See History Through Art at right.) She barely escaped before the British burned the White House and the Capitol building. The British then attacked Fort McHenry at Baltimore.

The commander of Fort McHenry had earlier requested a flag "so large that the British will have no difficulty in seeing it." Detained on a British ship, a Washington lawyer named Francis Scott Key watched the all-night battle. At dawn, Key saw that the flag was still flying. He expressed his pride in a poem that is now known as "The Star-Spangled Banner." It became the American national anthem.

Meanwhile, in the North, the British sent a force from Canada across Lake Champlain. Its goal was to push south and cut off New England. The plan failed when the American fleet defeated the British in the Battle of Lake Champlain in September 1814.

The Battle of New Orleans In the South, the British began to move against the strategically located port of New Orleans, in Louisiana. In December 1814, dozens of ships carrying some 7,500 British troops approached the coastline of Louisiana. To defend themselves, the Americans patched together an army under the

History *through* Art

George Washington, by Gilbert Stuart

As British troops closed in on Washington, D.C., in August 1814, most civilians fled the city. Even the 100 troops guarding the White House and First Lady Dolley Madison left. But Madison herself refused to leave until she had rescued one treasure: this full-length portrait of George Washington by renowned painter Gilbert Stuart. Madison was determined to save the painting or destroy it herself rather than let the British ruin it. When newly elected president James Monroe moved into the rebuilt White House in 1817, he restored this symbol of America to its rightful place.

CRITICAL VIEWING How does the artist show that Washington is an important person?

Connecting History

Leadership

Jackson's heroism at New Orleans helped him to win the presidency in 1828. A self-made man who was known for his toughness, Jackson considered himself a champion of the "common people." You will learn about his presidency in Chapter 12.

command of General Andrew Jackson. The British attacked Jackson's forces on January 8, 1815. American riflemen, who had protected themselves by building defenses out of earth, shot at advancing British troops. It was a great victory for Jackson. American casualties totaled 71, compared to Britain's 2,000.

The Battle of New Orleans made Jackson a hero. Nevertheless, the battle itself did not affect the course of the war. Slow mails from Europe had delayed news of the Treaty of Ghent, which had already ended the war. British and American diplomats had signed this treaty two weeks earlier. Americans, eager for an end to the fighting, welcomed the treaty.

The Legacy of the War The Treaty of Ghent showed that the War of 1812 had no clear winner. No territory changed hands, and trade disputes were left unresolved. Neither side made any significant gains. Still, the war had important consequences for America.

First, heroic exploits of men such as Jackson and Perry increased American patriotism. Second, the war broke the strength of Native Americans, who had sided with the British. Native American resistance was significantly weakened, especially in the South. Finally, when war interrupted trade, Americans were forced to make many of the goods they had previously imported. This encouraged the growth of American manufacturing.

The American victory also increased optimism about the nation's future. The United States had defended itself against one of the mightiest military powers of the era. For perhaps the first time, many Americans believed that their young nation would survive and prosper.

 SYNTHESIZE Explain how the War of 1812 led to changes in America.

Michigan Grade Level Content Expectations *Review*

ONLINE QUIZ
For test practice, go to
Interactive Review @ ClassZone.com

TERMS & NAMES

1. Explain the importance of

- impressment
- war hawk
- Embargo Act of 1807
- Oliver Hazard Perry
- Tecumseh

USING YOUR READING NOTES

2. Sequence Events Complete the diagram you started at the beginning of this section.

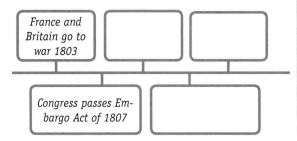

KEY IDEAS

3. How did foreign powers affect American shipping?

4. Why did many Americans in the western part of the country support the war?

CRITICAL THINKING

5. Evaluate How did Jefferson use trade as a weapon prior to the start of the war?

6. Causes and Effects What effects did Native American unity have on the United States?

7. Connect *to* Today How do you think overseas trade affects America's relations with other nations today?

8. Writing Poem Use the Internet to research the U.S.S. *Constitution*. Write a poem or speech to commemorate one of its victories.

CHAPTER 10 Interactive ◀Review

Click here to complete these activities online @ **ClassZone.com**

Chapter Summary

1 Key Idea
After a tied election, Jefferson became president and the Democratic-Republicans reduced the power of the federal government.

2 Key Idea
The nation doubled in size when Jefferson acquired the Louisiana Purchase.

3 Key Idea
The nation gained confidence and worldwide respect as a result of the War of 1812.

For detailed Review and Study Notes go to **Interactive Review** @ ClassZone.com

Name Game

Use the Terms & Names list to identify each sentence online or on your own paper.

1. I helped to guide the Lewis and Clark expedition.
   Sacagawea

2. This doubled the size of the United States.

3. President John Adams appointed me chief justice of the Supreme Court.

4. President Jefferson asked me to lead the Corps of Discovery.

5. This let President John Adams appoint many Federalist judges.

6. I was the third president of the United States.

7. This forbade U.S. ships from sailing to foreign ports.

8. I led the U.S. Navy to victory on Lake Erie.

9. I led a southern expedition in the Louisiana Territory.

10. This says the Supreme Court has the final say in interpreting the Constitution.

A. Thomas Jefferson
B. John Marshall
C. Meriwether Lewis
D. John Clark
E. Sacagawea
F. Zebulon Pike
G. impressment
H. judicial review
I. Oliver Hazard Perry
J. Judiciary Act of 1801
K. Embargo Act of 1807
L. Louisiana Purchase

Activities

CROSSWORD PUZZLE

Complete the online crossword puzzle to show what you know about the Jefferson era.

ACROSS
1. He fought to stop the loss of Native American land

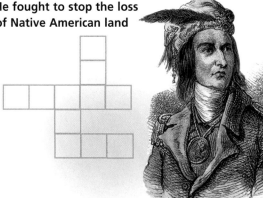

FLIPCARD

Use the online flipcards to quiz yourself on the terms and names introduced in this chapter.

ANSWER
Louisiana Purchase

The United States bought this land from France

VOCABULARY

Explain the significance of each of the following.

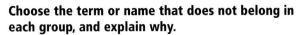

1. Thomas Jefferson
2. Meriwether Lewis
3. Sacagawea
4. John Marshall
5. Tecumseh
6. William Clark
7. Oliver Hazard Perry
8. Zebulon Pike

Choose the term or name that does not belong in each group, and explain why.

9. Tecumseh, war hawk, Lewis and Clark expedition
10. impressment, judicial review, *Marbury* v. *Madison*
11. Judiciary Act of 1801, Embargo Act of 1807, Oliver Hazard Perry

KEY IDEAS

① **Jeffersonian Democracy (pages 338–343)**

12. Following the presidential election of 1800, how was the tie between Thomas Jefferson and Aaron Burr settled?
13. How did Jefferson imagine that Americans would live in the future?

② **The Louisiana Purchase and Exploration (pages 344–349)**

14. What was the extent of U.S. territory after the Louisiana Purchase?
15. What information did Lewis and Clark gain from their expedition?

③ **The War of 1812 (pages 352–358)**

16. What factors contributed to the outbreak of the War of 1812?
17. Where did the key conflicts in the second phase of the war take place?

CRITICAL THINKING

18. **Synthesize** Why did Jefferson take a stance on the issue of public debt?
19. **Analyze Point of View** The case of *Marbury* v. *Madison* was ruled in Jefferson's favor. Why, then, was he upset by the verdict?
20. **Evaluate** How did Jefferson think the American public could benefit from the information to be collected by Lewis and Clark?
21. **Sequence Events** In a chart like the one below, list the progression of the Lewis and Clark expedition.

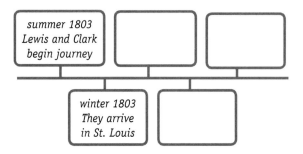

22. **Causes and Effects** How did the expansion of the United States affect its foreign policy?
23. **Make Inferences** How do you think Thomas Jefferson's behavior as president might have affected the way later presidents viewed the office?
24. **Draw Conclusions** In the painting, Andrew Jackson rides a horse into the Battle of New Orleans. Why does the artist show Jackson on horseback?

Andrew Jackson at the Battle of New Orleans, 1815

MEAP PRACTICE

DOCUMENT-BASED QUESTIONS

Study each document carefully and answer the questions that follow.

DOCUMENT 1

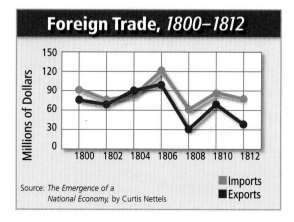

Foreign Trade, 1800–1812

Source: *The Emergence of a National Economy,* by Curtis Nettels

■ Imports
■ Exports

1 Examine the graph above that shows foreign trade between 1800 and 1812. Between what years was the drop in trade *most* dramatic?

  A 1800–1802

  B 1802–1806

  C 1806–1808

  D 1810–1812

DOCUMENT 2

2 Examine the above political cartoon. Based on the clues in the cartoon, what do you think the artist is protesting?

  A the election of 1800

  B the Judiciary Act of 1801

  C the Embargo Act of 1807

  D the War of 1812

YOU BE THE HISTORIAN

25. Make Inferences Based on Zebulon Pike's mistaken descriptions, many Americans believed the Great Plains was a desert and useless for farming. What may have led to the idea that Native Americans east of the Mississippi should be moved to this region?

26. **Connect *to* Today** The Embargo Act of 1807 stopped American ships from going to foreign ports, and closed American ports to British ships. Suppose that an act were passed today that stopped international shipping. How would your life be affected? Use examples of items you use that are manufactured in other countries.

27. Evaluate Do you think that Tecumseh's confederacy helped or hurt the cause of Native Americans?

28. Draw Conclusions After the election of 1800, Congress passed the Twelfth Amendment, which required electors to cast separate ballots for president and vice president. Why was this change important for future elections?

Answer the
ESSENTIAL QUESTION
How did the events of the Jefferson Era strengthen the nation?

Written Response Write a two- to three-paragraph response to the Essential Question. As you consider the key ideas of each section, think about the most significant factors that contributed to the growth of the nation from 1800 to 1816. Use the Response Rubric to guide your thinking and writing.

Response Rubric
A strong response will
- describe Jefferson's views and changes in political policy
- explain the effects of the Louisiana Purchase
- analyze the impact of Jefferson's policies on foreign relations
- analyze the results of the War of 1812

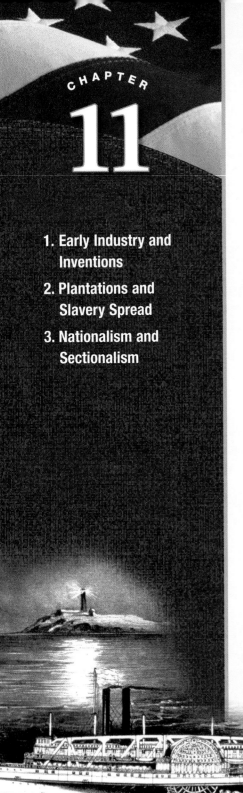

CHAPTER 11

1. Early Industry and Inventions

2. Plantations and Slavery Spread

3. Nationalism and Sectionalism

National and Regional Growth

1800–1844

 ESSENTIAL QUESTION

What forces and events affected national unity and growth?

CONNECT ↻ **Geography & History**

How did geography affect regional growth?

Think about:

1 the rivers in the Northeast that powered the first textile mills

2 how a demand for cotton to supply Northeastern mills led to the spread of plantations in the South

3 how available farmland in the Midwest raised the need for better transportation routes

---

Steamboats speeded transportation on American waterways.

Portrait of Euphemia Toussaint, a free African American, c. 1825

1820 The Missouri Compromise balances the number of slave and free states.

▼

Effect Tension between the North and the South over slavery is temporarily eased.

1800

Gabriel Prosser plans a slave rebellion in Virginia.

1807 Robert Fulton launches the first widely successful steamboat in America.

1812 War of 1812 disrupts U.S. shipping.

▼

Effect Americans start manufacturing more of their own goods.

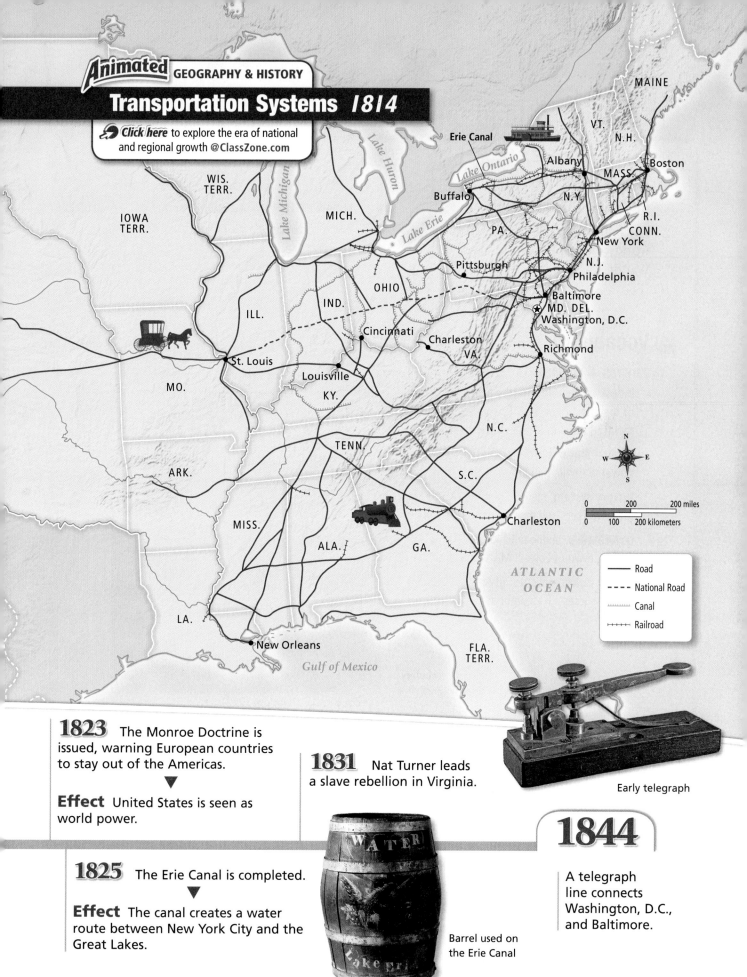

Click here to explore the era of national and regional growth @ClassZone.com

Erie Canal

MAINE

VT.

N.H.

MASS.

Albany

Boston

Buffalo

N.Y.

R.I.

CONN.

New York

WIS. TERR.

Lake Huron

Lake Michigan

MICH.

Lake Ontario

Lake Erie

PA.

Pittsburgh

N.J.

Philadelphia

IOWA TERR.

OHIO

IND.

Baltimore

MD. DEL.

Washington, D.C.

ILL.

Cincinnati

Charleston

VA.

Richmond

St. Louis

Louisville

MO.

KY.

N.C.

TENN.

S.C.

ARK.

Charleston

MISS.

ALA.

GA.

N

W   E

S

0   200   200 miles

0   100   200 kilometers

LA.

New Orleans

ATLANTIC OCEAN

FLA. TERR.

Gulf of Mexico

—— Road

- - - National Road

.... Canal

+++++ Railroad

1823 The Monroe Doctrine is issued, warning European countries to stay out of the Americas.

▼

Effect United States is seen as world power.

1831 Nat Turner leads a slave rebellion in Virginia.

Early telegraph

1825 The Erie Canal is completed.

▼

Effect The canal creates a water route between New York City and the Great Lakes.

WATER

Lake Erie

Barrel used on the Erie Canal

1844

A telegraph line connects Washington, D.C., and Baltimore.

▶ Key Ideas

BEFORE, YOU LEARNED

The nation gained confidence and worldwide respect as a result of the War of 1812.

NOW YOU WILL LEARN

New industries and inventions changed the way people lived and worked in the early 1800s.

▶ Vocabulary

TERMS & NAMES

Industrial Revolution the economic changes of the late 1700s, when manufacturing replaced farming as the main form of work

Samuel Slater builder of the first water-powered textile mill in America

factory system method of production using many workers and machines in one building

Lowell mills textile mills located in the factory town of Lowell, Massachusetts

Robert Fulton inventor of America's first widely successful steamboat

Peter Cooper builder of America's first successful steam-powered locomotive

Samuel F. B. Morse inventor of the telegraph

BACKGROUND VOCABULARY

threshing machine a device that separates kernels of wheat from their husks

mechanical reaper a device that cuts grain

Visual Vocabulary
threshing machine

▶ Reading Strategy

As you read and respond to the **KEY QUESTIONS**, use a graphic organizer like the one shown to record important events in the order in which they occurred.

 See Skillbuilder Handbook, page R5.

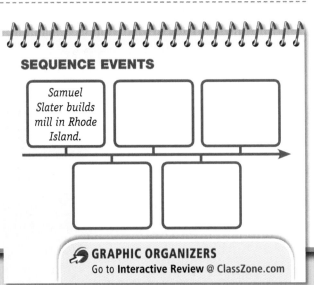

SEQUENCE EVENTS

Samuel Slater builds mill in Rhode Island.

GRAPHIC ORGANIZERS
Go to **Interactive Review** @ ClassZone.com

SECTION 1

Early Industry and Inventions

8 – U4.2.1.1 Comparing Northeast and the South – agriculture, including changes in productivity, technology, supply and demand, and price
8 – U4.2.1.2 Comparing Northeast and the South – industry, including entrepreneurial development of new industries, such as textiles

One American's Story

Harriet Hanson Robinson began working in the textile mills in Lowell, Massachusetts, in 1835, when she was ten years old. At the time, there were few opportunities for girls and women to work outside the home, and Harriet was proud to earn a good wage. As an adult, Harriet described the life of the mill girls.

PRIMARY SOURCE

❝ Though the hours of labor were long, they were not overworked; they were obliged to tend no more looms and frames than they could easily take care of, and they had plenty of time to sit and rest. . . . They were treated with consideration by their employers, and there was a feeling of respectful equality between them. . . . In those days, there was no need of advocating the doctrine of the proper relation between employer and employed. *Help was too valuable to be ill-treated.* ❞

—Harriet Hanson Robinson, from *Loom and Spindle; or, Life Among the Early Mill Girls*

The textile industry employed young workers such as this unidentified mill girl, photographed holding a spindle (for spinning fibers).

Later, when laborers were more plentiful, the mill owners were able to cut wages, and life in the mills became much more difficult.

The Industrial Revolution

🔻 **KEY QUESTION** How did the Industrial Revolution change the way Americans lived and worked?

After the War of 1812, Americans experienced a new kind of revolution. This was not a political revolution, but a change in the way that goods were produced. For centuries, people had made clothing, furniture, and other goods at home. Then, in late-18th-century Britain, factory machines started replacing hand tools. Soon large-scale manufacturing was producing huge quantities of goods. These changes are called the **Industrial Revolution**.

Connect to the World

Child Labor

In the late 1700s, a great many workers in British textile factories were children. Their small, agile fingers were considered well-suited to textile work. Children as young as five years old might work 12 to 16 hours a day.

ONLINE PRIMARY SOURCE

Hear the perspectives at the **Research & Writing Center** @ ClassZone.com

Factories Rise in New England In America, the Industrial Revolution began in 1793, when the Englishman **Samuel Slater** built the first spinning mill in Pawtucket, Rhode Island. The year before, he had sailed to the United States, perhaps under a false name—it was illegal for British textile workers to leave the country. Britain did not want another nation to copy its machines for making thread and cloth. But Slater brought the secrets to America.

At first, Slater hired a small group of children and paid them a low wage. Later, he built a larger mill and employed whole families. As Slater influenced others to start mills, his family system of employment spread through Rhode Island, Connecticut, and southern Massachusetts.

New England was a good place to build factories. The mills needed water power, and New England had many fast-moving rivers. For transportation, it had ships and access to the ocean. The region also had a ready labor force of farmers who were tired of scraping together a living from stony fields.

The **factory system** brought many workers and machines together under one roof. People left their family farms and crowded into cities to take jobs in factories. They worked for wages on a set schedule. Their way of life changed—and not always for the better.

COMPARING *Perspectives*

LIFE IN THE MILLS

The Industrial Revolution swept England in the mid-1700s. Half a century later, America, too, began to be transformed from a land of small farmers to an industrial nation. In these excerpts, observers from America and England described what they saw on visits to America's then-new Lowell mills.

An American Speaks

❝ The din and clatter of these five hundred looms under full operation, struck us . . . as something frightful and infernal . . . The atmosphere of such a room . . . is charged with cotton filaments and dust, which, we were told, are very injurious to the lungs. On entering the room, although the day was warm, we remarked that the windows were down . . . [W]e found ourselves . . . in quite a perspiration. ❞

—*A Description of Factory Life by an Associationist*, 1846

An Englishman Speaks

❝ The rooms in which [the girls] worked were as well ordered as themselves. In the windows of some, there were green plants, which were trained to shade the glass; in all, there was as much fresh air, cleanliness, and comfort, as the nature of the occupation would possibly admit of. . . . I solemnly declare, that from all the crowd I saw . . . I cannot recall . . . one young face that gave me a painful impression . . . ❞

—Charles Dickens, *American Notes*, 1842

CRITICAL THINKING

1. **Make Inferences** What do you think working conditions were like in the mills in England?
2. **Recognizing Bias and Propaganda** Why might the two writers describe the same working conditions in such different ways?

Many Americans, such as Thomas Jefferson, did not want the United States to industrialize. But the War of 1812 brought growth to American industry. Because the British naval blockade kept imported goods from reaching U.S. shores, Americans had to manufacture their own goods. The blockade also stopped investors from spending money on shipping and trade. Instead, they invested in new American industries. Entrepreneurs built factories, starting in New England. These entrepreneurs and their region grew wealthier.

The Lowell Mills Hire Women In 1814, the U.S. textile industry took a leap forward when Francis Cabot Lowell built a factory in eastern Massachusetts. This factory spun raw cotton into yarn, and then wove the yarn into cloth on power looms. Lowell had seen power looms in English mills and had figured out how to build them.

The factory was so successful that Lowell's associates built a new factory town, Lowell, near the Merrimack and Concord rivers. The **Lowell mills**, textile mills in the town, brought another significant change as large numbers of women entered the workforce. Many were farm girls who lived in company-owned boardinghouses. In the early years, the Lowell girls' wages were high—between two and four dollars a week. Older women supervised the girls. Later, falling profits meant that wages dropped and working conditions worsened at the Lowell mills.

The Lowell mills and other early factories ran on water power. Factories built after the 1830s were run by more powerful steam engines. Because steam engines used coal and wood, not fast-moving water, these newer factories could be built away from rivers and beyond New England.

New Manufacturing Methods Spread New manufacturing methods changed work in other industries as well. In 1797, the U.S. government hired the inventor Eli Whitney to make 10,000 muskets for the army. Before this time, guns were made one at a time by a gunsmith. Each gun differed slightly. If a part broke, a new part had to be created to match the broken one.

Whitney sought a better way to make guns. In 1801, he went to Washington and laid out several piles of musket parts. He took a part from each pile and quickly assembled a musket. He had just demonstrated the use of interchangeable parts—parts that are exactly alike.

Machines that produced identical parts soon became standard. Interchangeable parts speeded up production, made repairs easy, and allowed the use of less-skilled workers.

SYNTHESIZE Describe how the Industrial Revolution changed the way Americans lived and worked.

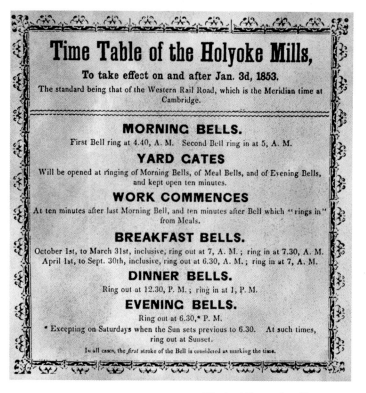

Work at the early mills was guided by a bell schedule such as this one, which begins with a wake-up bell at 4:40 in the morning. **What does this schedule tell you about the workers' daily lives?**

1765

▶ **1769**
Improved
Steam engine,
James Watt

c. 1786
Threshing machine, Andrew Meikle

1793
Cotton gin, Eli Whitney

▲ **c. 1803**
Locomotive,
Richard Trevithick

1807
Steamboat,
◀ Robert Fulton

1834 Reaper, Cyrus McCormick

1837 Telegraph, Samuel F. B. Morse
Steel plow, John Deere

1839
Photography, ▶
Louis Daguerre

1845

CRITICAL THINKING Evaluate Which of these inventions do you think had the greatest impact on life in the middle of the 19th century?

New Inventions Improve Life

▼ **KEY QUESTION** How did new inventions improve American life?

New inventions improved transportation, communication, and production. They also quickened the pace of life.

Transportation and Communication Inventor **Robert Fulton** developed a steamboat that could move against the current or a strong wind. He launched the *Clermont* on the Hudson River in 1807. Its steam engine turned two side paddle wheels, which pulled the boat through the water. Many thought it looked silly and nicknamed it "Fulton's Folly," but it made the 300-mile round-trip from New York to Albany and back in a record 62 hours.

In 1811, a steamship first traveled down the Ohio and Mississippi rivers. However, its engine was not powerful enough to return upriver against the current. Henry Miller Shreve, a trader on the Mississippi, designed a steamship that could be powered up the Mississippi, against the current. In 1816, his boat launched a new era of transportation on the river.

Some cities, however, were not on rivers that could be navigated by steamship. Traders in these cities needed a way to ship goods. Steam-powered trains were the answer. English engineer Richard Trevithick had introduced the locomotive around 1803. In 1830, **Peter Cooper** built America's first successful steam-powered locomotive, called the *Tom Thumb*. By 1833, the 136-mile railroad track connecting Charleston and Hamburg, South Carolina, was the longest in the world.

Around 1837, **Samuel F. B. Morse** first demonstrated his telegraph. This machine sent long and short pulses of electricity along a wire. These pulses could be translated into letters spelling out messages. With the telegraph, it took only seconds to communicate with someone in another city. In 1844, the first long-distance telegraph line carried news from Baltimore to Washington, D.C., about who had been nominated for president. Telegraph lines spanned the country by 1861, bringing people closer as a nation.

Technology Improves Farming Other new inventions increased farm production. In 1837, blacksmith John Deere invented a lightweight plow with a steel cutting edge. Older cast-iron plows were designed for the relatively light and sandy soil of New England. But rich, heavy Midwestern soil clung to the bottom of these plows and slowed down farm work. Deere's new plow made preparing ground to plant crops much less work. As a result, more farmers began to move to the Midwest.

The **threshing machine** and the **mechanical reaper** were other inventions that improved agricultural production by making farm work quicker and more efficient. The threshing machine, which was invented around 1786 by Andrew Meikle of Scotland, mechanically separated kernels of wheat from husks. In 1831, Cyrus McCormick developed a reaper that cut ripe grain quickly and efficiently. McCormick patented his invention in 1834 and brought it to Europe in the 1850s.

New technologies linked regions and contributed to a feeling of national unity. With new farm equipment, Midwestern farmers grew food to feed Northeastern factory workers. In turn, Midwestern farmers became a market for Northeastern manufactured goods. The growth of Northeastern textile mills increased demand for Southern cotton, which, unfortunately, led to the expansion of slavery in the South.

 MAIN IDEAS & DETAILS Explain how new inventions improved American life.

 Michigan Grade Level Content Expectations *Review*

 ONLINE QUIZ
For test practice, go to
Interactive Review @ ClassZone.com

TERMS & NAMES

1. Explain the importance of
   - Industrial Revolution
   - Robert Fulton
   - Samuel Slater
   - Peter Cooper
   - factory system
   - Samuel F. B. Morse
   - Lowell mills

USING YOUR READING NOTES

2. **Sequence Events** Complete the diagram you started at the beginning of this section.

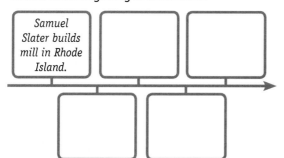

Samuel Slater builds mill in Rhode Island.

KEY IDEAS

3. Why was New England a good place to set up factories?

4. How were different regions of the United States linked economically?

CRITICAL THINKING

5. **Summarize** Explain how the use of interchangeable parts improved the manufacturing process.

6. **Form and Support Opinions** Samuel Slater and Francis Lowell both illegally brought industrial secrets to the United States. Do you think they were wrong to do this? Explain.

7. **Art** Use the library to find an image of one of the early inventions mentioned in this section. Draw a detailed picture of it. Then write a paragraph explaining how the invention worked.

Animated HISTORY
AN AMERICAN TEXTILE MILL

Click here to see an American textile mill in operation
@ ClassZone.com

The first textile mills in America ran on water power. Falling or flowing water powered the machinery through a system of gears and belts. Eventually, however, steam engines replaced water as the source of power for the mills.

Click here Early mills were built on deep, fast-moving rivers in the Northeast.

Click here The mills changed working life by bringing together many workers and machines in the same building.

Click here Many children worked at the early textile mills.

Long shafts distribute power to the machines on each floor.

Yarn is woven into cloth.

Carded fiber can be spun into yarn

Belts and pulleys transmit power to each floor.

Wool or cotton fiber must be carded, or disentangled.

A water turbine—a machine driven by water pressure—provides power to the belts and pulleys above.

Activity

Four Corners

1. Have a volunteer from the class write the following statement on the board: *Working at a textile mill was a good opportunity for young women in the 1800s.*

2. Ask another volunteer to write **Agree**, **Strongly Agree**, **Disagree**, and **Strongly Disagree** on four separate sheets of paper, and then tape each sheet in a different corner of your classroom.

3. Think about what you've read and studied about New England textile mills, including salaries, living quarters, working conditions, and the daily schedules of mill workers. Now go to the corner of the room that best represents your agreement or disagreement with the statement on the board.

4. Be prepared to use information from the chapter and the Animated History feature to defend the position or opinion you represent.

▶ Key Ideas

BEFORE, YOU LEARNED

New industries and inventions changed the way people lived and worked in the early 1800s.

NOW YOU WILL LEARN

The invention of the cotton gin and the demand for cotton caused slavery to spread in the South.

▶ Vocabulary

TERMS & NAMES

cotton gin machine that made cleaning seeds from cotton faster

Eli Whitney inventor of the cotton gin

Nat Turner leader of an 1831 slave rebellion in Virginia

BACKGROUND VOCABULARY

spirituals religious folk songs

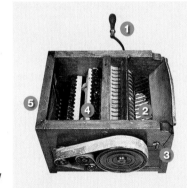

Visual Vocabulary
cotton gin

1 A hand crank turns a series of rollers.

2 A roller with wire teeth pulls the cotton through slots too narrow for the seeds.

3 The cotton seeds fall into a hopper.

4 A roller with brushes removes the cleaned cotton from the first roller.

5 The cleaned cotton leaves the gin.

▶ Reading Strategy

As you read and respond to the **KEY QUESTIONS**, use a graphic organizer like the one shown to note important events and their effects. Add boxes or start a new diagram as needed.

 See Skillbuilder Handbook, page R7.

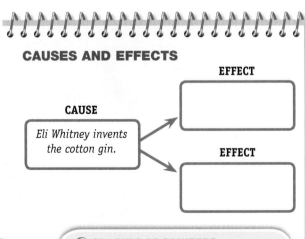

CAUSES AND EFFECTS

CAUSE

Eli Whitney invents the cotton gin.

EFFECT

EFFECT

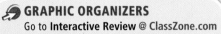

🔁 **GRAPHIC ORGANIZERS**
Go to **Interactive Review** @ ClassZone.com

Plantations and Slavery Spread

8 – U4.2.1.6 Comparing Northeast and the South – race relations
8 – U4.2.2 The Institution of Slavery – Explain the ideology of the institution of slavery, its policies, and consequences.

One American's Story

Catherine Beale was born into slavery in 1838. In 1929, she recalled her childhood on a Southern plantation.

PRIMARY SOURCE

❝ We had to work in the field in the day and at night we had to pick out the seed before we went to bed. And we had to clean the wool, we had to pick the burrs and sticks out so it would be clean and could be carded and spun and wove. ❞

—Catherine Beale, quoted in *Slave Testimony*

Workers picking cotton in Texas

Catherine had to clean cotton by hand, probably because the plantation didn't have a **cotton gin**. This machine made cleaning cotton much faster. As a result, it became more profitable to grow cotton—and to own slaves.

The Cotton Boom

🔻 **KEY QUESTION** How did the invention of the cotton gin change Southern life?

The Industrial Revolution increased the number of goods being produced. It also increased the demand for raw materials. In England, textile mills needed huge quantities of cotton to produce goods to sell throughout the British Empire. Cotton growers in the South wanted to meet this demand.

The Cotton Gin The short-fibered cotton that grew in most parts of the South was hard to clean by hand. A worker could clean just one pound of this cotton in a day. Then, in 1793, **Eli Whitney** invented a machine for cleaning cotton. With the new machine, one worker could clean as much as 50 pounds of cotton a day. The cotton gin helped set the South on a very different course of economic development than the North.

Slavery Expands From 1790 to 1860, cotton production increased more than a thousandfold, thanks in large part to the new cotton gin. Using slave labor, the South raised millions of bales of cotton each year for the textile mills of England and the American Northeast.

As cotton production grew, so did the demand for slavery. In 1808, it became illegal to import Africans for use as slaves. At the same time, however, the birth rate among the enslaved population already in the country began to increase rapidly. Between 1810 and 1840, the enslaved population in the South more than doubled.

Southern Support for Slavery Slavery divided white Southerners into those who held slaves and those who did not. Slaveholders with large plantations were the wealthiest and most powerful people in the South, but they were relatively few in number. Only about one-third of white families owned slaves in 1840. Of these slave-owning families, only about one-tenth had large plantations with 20 or more slaves.

Although most Southern farmers owned few or no slaves, many supported slavery anyway. They hoped to buy slaves someday, which would allow them to raise more cotton and earn more money.

▲ **CAUSES AND EFFECTS** Explain how the cotton gin changed Southern life.

Connecting History

Human Rights
As slavery expanded in the South, an antislavery movement spread in the North. By the 1840s, the movement to abolish slavery had become a political force.
See Chapter 14, pages 465–468

African Americans in the South

▼ **KEY QUESTION** What was life like for African Americans in the South?

By 1840, enslaved people formed about a third of the South's population.

Varied Conditions About half of enslaved people worked on plantations. Conditions could be cruel, as a former slave recalled decades later.

PRIMARY SOURCE

❝ The overseer was 'straddle his big horse at three o'clock in the mornin', roustin' the hands off to the field . . . . The rows was a mile long and no matter how much grass [weeds] was in them, if you [left] one sprig on your row they [beat] you nearly to death. ❞

—Wes Brady, quoted in *Remembering Slavery*

Not all enslaved people labored on plantations. In cities, some worked as domestic servants, skilled craftsmen, factory hands, and day laborers. Some were hired out and allowed to keep part of their earnings. But they were still enslaved—under the law, they were considered property.

In 1840, about 5 percent of African Americans in the South were free. They had either been born free, been freed by an owner, or bought their own freedom. Although they were not enslaved, they still faced many problems. Some states made them leave once they gained their freedom. Most states did not permit them to vote or to be educated. Many employers refused to hire them. But the biggest threat was the possibility of being captured and sold into slavery.

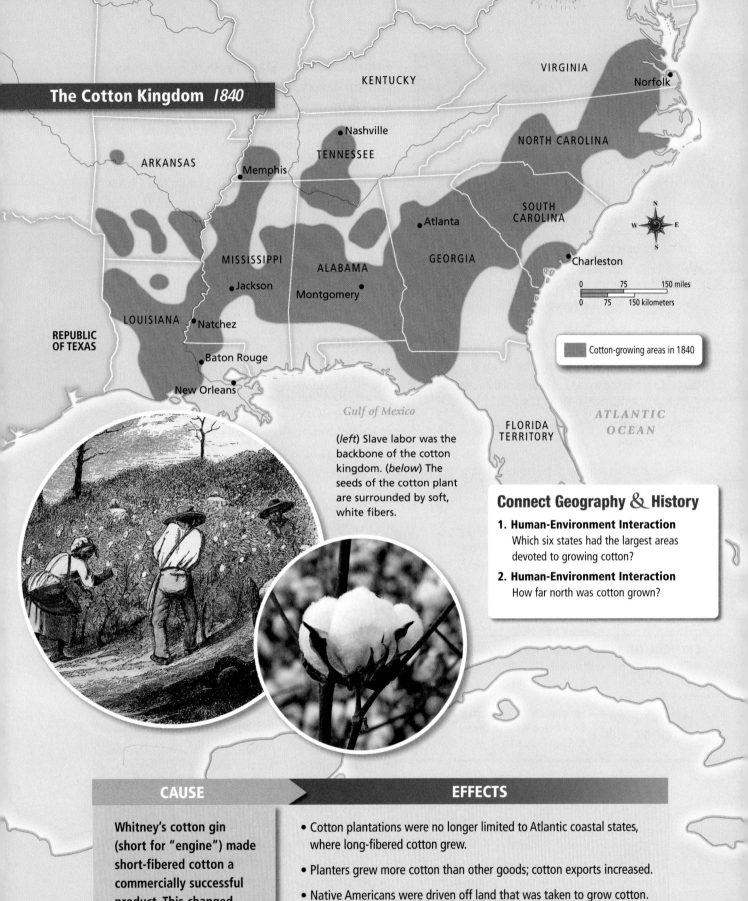

The Cotton Kingdom 1840

KENTUCKY

VIRGINIA

Norfolk

Nashville

TENNESSEE

NORTH CAROLINA

ARKANSAS

Memphis

SOUTH CAROLINA

Atlanta

Charleston

MISSISSIPPI

ALABAMA

GEORGIA

Jackson

Montgomery

LOUISIANA

Natchez

REPUBLIC OF TEXAS

Baton Rouge

New Orleans

Gulf of Mexico

FLORIDA TERRITORY

ATLANTIC OCEAN

0 75 150 miles
0 75 150 kilometers

Cotton-growing areas in 1840

(*left*) Slave labor was the backbone of the cotton kingdom. (*below*) The seeds of the cotton plant are surrounded by soft, white fibers.

Connect Geography & History

1. Human-Environment Interaction
Which six states had the largest areas devoted to growing cotton?

2. Human-Environment Interaction
How far north was cotton grown?

CAUSE	EFFECTS
Whitney's cotton gin (short for "engine") made short-fibered cotton a commercially successful product. This changed Southern life in four important ways.	• Cotton plantations were no longer limited to Atlantic coastal states, where long-fibered cotton grew. • Planters grew more cotton than other goods; cotton exports increased. • Native Americans were driven off land that was taken to grow cotton. • Slavery expanded, especially westward to new cotton plantations.

History Makers

Nat Turner   1800–1831

Nat Turner (above left) was born into slavery in Virginia. He learned to read as a child and became an enthusiastic reader of the Bible. Enslaved people gathered in forest clearings to listen to Turner's powerful sermons.

In 1831, Turner led a group of followers in killing about 55 white Virginians, starting with the family of his former owner. It was the bloodiest slave rebellion in American history. In an account of events that he dictated to Thomas R. Gray before his execution, Turner called himself a "prophet" and said that God had called him to commit his violent acts.

CRITICAL THINKING Analyze Point of View How did Turner justify his use of violence?

 **ONLINE BIOGRAPHY**   For more on Nat Turner, go to the **Research & Writing Center** @ ClassZone.com

Families Under Slavery Perhaps the cruelest part of slavery was the sale of family members away from one another. Although some slaveholders would not part mothers from children, many did, causing unforgettable grief.

When enslaved families could manage to be together, they took comfort in family life. Enslaved people did marry each other, although their marriages were not legally recognized. They tried to raise children, while knowing that their children could be taken from them and sold at any time. Abolitionist Frederick Douglass, who was born into slavery, recalled visits from his mother, who lived 12 miles away.

PRIMARY SOURCE

❝ I do not recollect [remember] ever seeing my mother by the light of day. She was with me in the night. She would lie down with me, and get me to sleep, but long before I waked she was gone. ❞

—Frederick Douglass, *Narrative of the Life of Frederick Douglass*

Douglass's mother resisted slavery by the simple act of visiting her child. Douglass later rebelled by escaping to the North. A small number of enslaved people rebelled in violent ways.

Slave Rebellions Armed rebellion by enslaved persons was an extreme form of resistance to slavery. Gabriel Prosser planned an attack on Richmond, Virginia, in 1800. In 1822, Denmark Vesey planned a revolt in Charleston, South Carolina. Both plots were betrayed and the leaders, as well as numerous followers, were hanged.

The most famous rebellion was led by **Nat Turner** in Southampton County, Virginia, in 1831. Beginning on August 21, Turner and 70 followers killed about 55 white men, women, and children. Most of Turner's men were captured when their ammunition ran out, and some were killed. After Turner was caught, he was tried and hanged.

Turner's rebellion spread fear in the South. Whites killed more than 200 African Americans in revenge. The state of Virginia considered ending slavery because of the upheaval, but the proposal was narrowly defeated. Some state legislatures, however, passed harsh laws that further limited the freedom of both free and enslaved African Americans. For African Americans in the South, the grip of slavery grew even tighter.

A Common Culture By the early 1800s, a distinctive African-American culture had emerged on Southern plantations. This common culture helped enslaved African Americans bond together and endure the brutal conditions of Southern plantation life.

Religion was a cornerstone of African-American culture in the South. Some slaveholders had tried to use religion to force enslaved people to accept mistreatment, emphasizing such Bible passages

as "Servants, obey your masters." But enslaved people took their own messages from the Bible. They were particularly inspired by the book of Exodus, which tells of Moses leading the Hebrews out of bondage in Egypt. Many enslaved African Americans believed that this story offered a message of hope for their own people.

Enslaved people expressed their beliefs in **spirituals**—folk songs that were often religious in nature. Many spirituals voiced the desire for freedom. Sometimes, spirituals contained coded messages about a planned escape or an owner's unexpected return. African-American spirituals later had a strong influence on blues, jazz, and other forms of American music.

▲ **COMPARE AND CONTRAST** Compare the different conditions faced by African Americans in the South.

(*top*) *The Old Plantation*, late 1700s.
(*above*) Enslaved Africans brought the banjo to the American colonies.

Michigan Grade Level Content Expectations *Review*

🖱 **ONLINE QUIZ**
For test practice, go to
Interactive Review @ ClassZone.com

TERMS & NAMES

1. Explain the importance of
- cotton gin
- Eli Whitney
- Nat Turner

USING YOUR READING NOTES

2. Causes and Effects Complete the diagram you started at the beginning of this section.

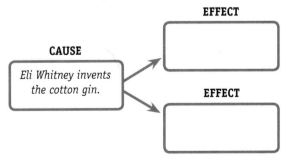

CAUSE

Eli Whitney invents the cotton gin.

EFFECT

EFFECT

KEY IDEAS

3. How did the invention of the cotton gin change Southern life?

4. What forms did resistance to slavery take?

CRITICAL THINKING

5. Analyze Point of View Why did many Southern farmers who owned no slaves support slavery?

6. Connect Economics and History The cotton gin made it possible to clean the same amount of cotton with fewer workers. Why did this result in an increased demand for slaves?

7. **Art** Choose an African-American spiritual. Write down and illustrate the lyrics, drawing any images or symbols used in the spiritual.

▶ Key Ideas

BEFORE, YOU LEARNED

The invention of the cotton gin and the demand for cotton caused slavery to spread in the South.

NOW YOU WILL LEARN

While patriotic pride increased national unity, tensions grew between the North and the South.

▶ Vocabulary

TERMS & NAMES

Henry Clay nationalist Representative from Kentucky

American System plan introduced in 1815 to make America economically self-sufficient

James Monroe fifth president of the United States, who proclaimed the Monroe Doctrine

Erie Canal waterway that connected New York City with Buffalo, New York

Missouri Compromise laws enacted in 1820 to maintain balance of power between slave and free states

Monroe Doctrine U.S. policy opposing European interference in the Western Hemisphere

BACKGROUND VOCABULARY

nationalism a feeling of pride, loyalty, and protectiveness toward one's country

protective tariff a tax on imported goods that protects a nation's businesses from foreign competition

sectionalism loyalty to the interests of one's own region or section of the country

Visual Vocabulary
a contemporary lock
on the Erie Canal

▶ Reading Strategy

As you read and respond to the **KEY QUESTIONS**, use a graphic organizer like the one shown to record main ideas and important details about factors that affected national unity in the early 1800s. Add ovals or start a new diagram as needed.

 See Skillbuilder Handbook, page R4.

MAIN IDEAS AND DETAILS

Nationalist feelings united the states

GRAPHIC ORGANIZERS
Go to **Interactive Review** @ ClassZone.com

Nationalism and Sectionalism

 8 – U4.1.2 Establishing America's Place in the World – Explain the changes in America's relationships with other nations by analyzing treaties with American Indian nations, Jay's Treaty (1795), French Revolution, Pinckney's Treaty (1795), Louisiana Purchase, War of 1812, Transcontinental Treaty (1819), and the Monroe Doctrine.
8 – U5.1.4.1 Describe how the following increased sectional tensions – the Missouri Compromise (1820)

One American's Story

The War of 1812 increased American nationalism. **Nationalism** is a feeling of pride, loyalty, and protectiveness toward your nation. Representative **Henry Clay** was a strong nationalist.

PRIMARY SOURCE

❝ Every nation should anxiously endeavor to establish its absolute independence, and consequently be able to feed and clothe and defend itself. If it rely upon a foreign supply that may be cut off . . . it cannot be independent. ❞

—Henry Clay, *The Life and Speeches of Henry Clay*

Henry Clay, U.S. representative from Kentucky

After the war, President James Madison supported Clay's plan to strengthen the country and unify its regions.

Nationalism Unites the Country

🔻 **KEY QUESTION** What factors helped to promote national unity?

Madison wanted America to prosper by itself, without foreign products.

The American System In 1815, Madison presented a plan to Congress for making America economically self-sufficient. The plan—which Clay promoted as the **American System**—had three main actions.

1. Establish a **protective tariff**, a tax on imported goods that protects a nation's businesses from foreign competition. Congress passed a tariff in 1816. It made European goods more expensive and encouraged Americans to buy cheaper, American-made products.
2. Establish a national bank that would promote a single currency, making trade easier. (Most regional banks issued their own money.) In 1816, Congress set up the second Bank of the United States.
3. Improve the country's transportation systems, which were important for the economy. Poor roads made transportation slow and costly.

The Era of Good Feelings As nationalist feeling spread, people shifted their loyalty away from state governments and toward the federal government. Democratic-Republican **James Monroe** won the presidency in 1816 with a large majority of electoral votes. The Federalist Party provided little opposition to Monroe and soon disappeared. Political differences gave way to what one Boston newspaper called the Era of Good Feelings.

During the Monroe administration, several landmark Supreme Court decisions promoted national unity by strengthening the federal government. For example, in *McCulloch v. Maryland* (1819), the court ruled that a state could not tax a national bank. As Justice Marshall explained, "The power to tax involves the power to destroy."

Gibbons v. *Ogden* (1824) also strengthened the federal government. Two steamship operators fought over shipping rights on the Hudson River in New York and New Jersey. The Court ruled that interstate commerce could be regulated only by the federal government, not the state governments.

Historic Decisions of the SUPREME COURT

McCulloch v. Maryland (1819)

KEY ISSUE   federal supremacy vs. state powers
KEY PEOPLE   James McCulloch   cashier, Bank of the United States
(Maryland branch)

The Case

The Second Bank of the United States was established by the U.S. Congress in 1816. The state of Maryland tried to put the bank out of business: it set a high tax on currency issued by the bank. When James McCulloch, the cashier at the Maryland branch, refused to pay the tax, Maryland sued him and the bank.

The Supreme Court ruled in favor of McCulloch and the Bank of the United States. It ruled that Congress had the right to establish the bank.

The court also ruled that the states do not have the right to tax the federal government. If the tax were allowed, it would give Maryland power over the federal government. In the ruling, John Marshall wrote that the framers of the Constitution did not intend to make the federal government subject to state powers. He cited the Supremacy Clause (Art. 6, Sec. 2): "This Constitution, and the laws of the United States . . . shall be the supreme law of the land."

CRITICAL THINKING

1. **Draw Conclusions** Why did John Marshall say that the power to tax "involves the power to destroy"?

2. **WHAT IF?** What do you think might have happened if *McCulloch* v. *Maryland* had been decided in Maryland's favor?

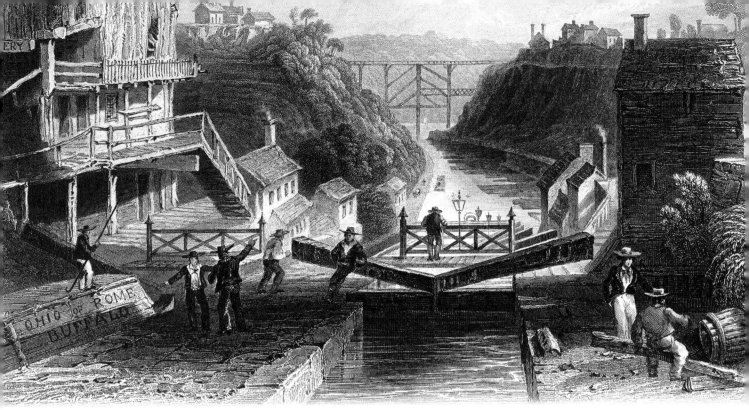

The Erie Canal

Transportation Links Cities In 1806, Congress had funded a road from Cumberland, Maryland, to Wheeling, West Virginia. By 1841, the National Road, the country's main east-west route, extended to Vandalia, Illinois.

Water transportation improved with the building of canals. The period from 1790 to 1855 is often called the Age of Canals. Completed in 1825, the massive **Erie Canal** created a water route between New York City and Buffalo, New York. The Erie Canal allowed farm products from the Great Lakes region to flow east, and people and manufactured goods from the East to flow west. Trade stimulated by the canal helped New York City to become the nation's largest city. Between 1820 and 1830, its population nearly doubled.

Improvements in railroads led to a decline in canal use. In 1830, about 23 miles of train track existed. By 1850, the number had climbed to 9,000.

▲ **SUMMARIZE** Describe the factors that helped to promote national unity.

Sectional Tensions Increase

▼ **KEY QUESTION** What factors increased sectional tension?

While nationalism grew, sectionalism threatened to tear the nation apart.

Sectional Interests Sectionalism is loyalty to the interests of a region or section of the country. By the early 1800s, economic changes had created divisions. The South relied on a plantation economy that used slavery. The Northeast focused on manufacturing and trade. In the West, settlers wanted cheap land. The interests of these sections were often in conflict.

Sectionalism became a major issue when Missouri applied for statehood in 1817. People in Missouri wanted to allow slavery in their state. At the time, the United States consisted of 11 slave states and 11 free states. Adding Missouri as a slave state would upset the balance of power in Congress.

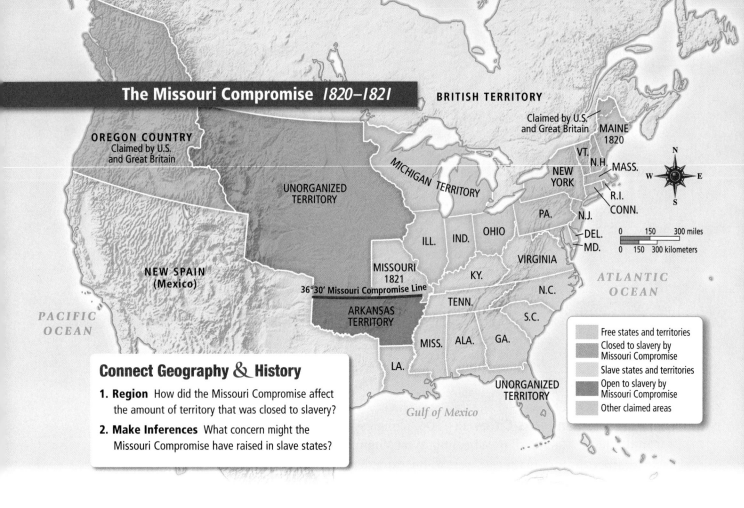

The Missouri Compromise 1820–1821

BRITISH TERRITORY

OREGON COUNTRY
Claimed by U.S.
and Great Britain

Claimed by U.S.
and Great Britain

MAINE
1820

VT.

N.H.

MASS.

R.I.

CONN.

NEW
YORK

MICHIGAN TERRITORY

UNORGANIZED
TERRITORY

PA.

N.J.

DEL.

MD.

NEW SPAIN
(Mexico)

ILL.

IND.

OHIO

VIRGINIA

MISSOURI
1821

KY.

36°30' Missouri Compromise Line

ARKANSAS
TERRITORY

TENN.

N.C.

S.C.

PACIFIC
OCEAN

ATLANTIC
OCEAN

MISS.

ALA.

GA.

LA.

UNORGANIZED
TERRITORY

Gulf of Mexico

N

W

E

S

0   150   300 miles
0   150   300 kilometers

Free states and territories

Closed to slavery by
Missouri Compromise

Slave states and territories

Open to slavery by
Missouri Compromise

Other claimed areas

Connect Geography & History

1. Region How did the Missouri Compromise affect the amount of territory that was closed to slavery?

2. Make Inferences What concern might the Missouri Compromise have raised in slave states?

The Missouri Compromise Representatives in Congress argued over admitting the new state of Missouri as a slave state or a free state. Southerners claimed that the Constitution did not give Congress the power to ban slavery. They worried that if free states formed a majority in Congress, they would ban slavery altogether. Warned Representative Thomas Cobb of Georgia:

PRIMARY SOURCE

❝ If you persist, the Union will be dissolved. You have kindled a fire which . . . seas of blood can only extinguish. ❞

—Thomas Cobb, quoted in *Henry Clay: Statesman for the Union*

Meanwhile, Maine, which had been part of Massachusetts, also wanted statehood. Henry Clay suggested that Missouri be admitted as a slave state and Maine as a free state. Congress passed this plan, known as the **Missouri Compromise**, in 1820. It kept the balance of power in the Senate between the slave states and free states. It also called for slavery to be banned north of the parallel 36° 30′, Missouri's southern border.

Amid these tensions, the Mason-Dixon Line, which formed the Maryland-Pennsylvania border, took on symbolic importance. The term "Mason-Dixon Line" came to be used for the division between slave states and free states, as well as the division between the North and the South.

▲ **SYNTHESIZE** Describe the factors that increased sectional tension.

National Boundaries and Foreign Affairs

▼ **KEY QUESTION** How were U.S. borders made more secure?

Nationalist feeling made Americans want to define the nation's borders. To do this, U.S. leaders had to reach agreements with Britain and Spain.

Settling Boundary Issues Two agreements improved relations between the United States and Britain. The Rush-Bagot Agreement (1817) limited each side's naval forces on the Great Lakes. In the Convention of 1818, the two countries set the 49th parallel as the U.S.-Canadian border as far west as the Rocky Mountains.

But U.S. relations with Spain were tense. The two nations disagreed on the boundaries of the Louisiana Purchase and the ownership of West Florida. Meanwhile, pirates and runaway slaves used Spanish-held East Florida as a refuge. In addition, the Seminoles of East Florida raided white settlements in Georgia to reclaim lost lands.

CONNECT to the Essential Question

What forces and events affected national unity and growth?

STRENGTHENING FORCES	WEAKENING FORCES
The Industrial Revolution fuels economic growth.	New industry and inventions lead to reliance on manufacturing in the North, and increased dependence on cotton and slavery in the South.
The American System encourages economic self-sufficiency.	
Supreme Court decisions strengthen the federal government.	Regional differences divide the nation among Northerners, Southerners, and Westerners.
Improvements in transportation and communication link cities and regions.	Although the Missouri Compromise keeps the balance of free and slave states, the issue of slavery continues to divide the nation.
The United States expands and defines its borders.	

CRITICAL THINKING Compare and Contrast In what ways did economic changes both strengthen and threaten national unity?

In 1817, U.S. General Andrew Jackson followed the Seminoles into Spanish territory and then captured two cities—Pensacola and Saint Marks—for the United States. Monroe ordered Jackson to withdraw but gave Spain a choice. It could either police the Floridas or turn them over to the United States. In the Adams-Onís Treaty of 1819, Spain handed Florida to the United States and gave up claims to the Oregon Country.

Connect *to the* **World**

Latin American Independence
Venezuelan-born Simón Bolívar was popularly known as the "George Washington of Latin America." When the Monroe Doctrine was issued, Bolívar was the dictator of Peru and already had led Venezuela, Colombia, Peru, and Ecuador to independence.

The Monroe Doctrine The nation felt threatened not only by sectionalism, but by other events in the Americas. In Latin America, several countries had successfully fought for independence from Spain and Portugal. Some European monarchies planned to help Spain and Portugal regain their colonies. U.S. leaders feared that this could put their own government in danger.

Russian colonies in the Pacific Northwest also concerned Americans. The Russians entered Alaska in 1784. By 1812, their trading posts reached almost to San Francisco.

In December 1823, Monroe issued a statement that became known as the **Monroe Doctrine**. (See Reading Primary Sources, page 385.) Monroe said that the Americas were closed to further colonization. He also warned that European efforts to reestablish colonies would be considered "dangerous to our peace and safety." Finally, he promised that the United States would stay out of European affairs. The Monroe Doctrine showed that the United States saw itself as a world power and protector of Latin America.

 PROBLEMS AND SOLUTIONS Describe how U.S. borders were made more secure.

Michigan Grade Level Content Expectations *Review*

 ONLINE QUIZ
For test practice, go to
Interactive Review @ ClassZone.com

TERMS & NAMES
1. Explain the importance of
- Henry Clay
- American System
- James Monroe
- Erie Canal
- Missouri Compromise
- Monroe Doctrine

USING YOUR READING NOTES
2. Main Ideas and Details Complete the diagram you started at the beginning of this section.

Nationalist feelings united the states

KEY IDEAS
3. What were the three parts of the American System?

4. What was the main message of the Monroe Doctrine?

CRITICAL THINKING
5. Summarize How did the question of admitting Missouri to the Union divide the nation?

6. **Connect** *to* **Today** Think about the diagram you made of factors that contributed to American national unity in the early 1800s. Which of these factors are still important for national unity?

7. **Writing** **Editorial** Write an editorial giving your opinion of either the Missouri Compromise or the Monroe Doctrine. State how you believe it will affect the nation.

The Monroe Doctrine

SETTING THE STAGE On December 2, 1823, President Monroe gave a State of the Union address, part of which became known as the Monroe Doctrine. The "allied powers" he refers to are European monarchies that were threatening to help Spain regain its Latin American colonies.

The occasion has been judged proper for asserting, as a principle in which the rights and interests of the United States are involved, that the American continents, by the free and independent condition which they have assumed and maintain, are henceforth not to be considered as subjects for future colonization by any European powers. . . .

It was stated at the commencement of the last session that a great effort was then making in Spain and Portugal to improve the condition of the people of those countries, and that it appeared to be conducted with extraordinary moderation. It need scarcely be remarked that the result has been so far very different from what was then anticipated. . . . The citizens of the United States cherish sentiments the most friendly in favor of the liberty and happiness of their fellowmen on that side of the Atlantic. In the wars of the European powers in matters relating to themselves we have never taken any part, nor does it **comport**[1] with our policy so to do. It is only when our rights are invaded or seriously **menaced**[2] that we resent injuries or make preparation for our defense.

With the movements in this hemisphere we are of necessity more immediately connected, and by causes which must be obvious to all enlightened and impartial observers. The political system of the allied powers is essentially different in this respect from that of America. This difference proceeds from that which exists in their respective governments; and to the defense of our own, which has been achieved by the loss of so much blood and treasure, and matured by the wisdom of their most enlightened citizens, and under which we have enjoyed **unexampled felicity**,[3] this whole nation is devoted.

---

1. **comport:** agree with
2. **menaced:** threatened
3. **unexampled felicity:** the greatest happiness

No Future Colonies

Monroe declares that European countries may not start any new colonies in the Americas.

1. Why might it threaten the United States to have new European colonies nearby?

Neutrality Toward Europe

Monroe says that the United States will not take sides in European wars.

2. Why might the United States want to remain neutral toward conflicts in Europe?

A Different System

Monroe says that the United States will defend its republican form of government and would be threatened if Europeans set up monarchies in the Americas.

3. Why would U.S. citizens want their government to be a republic and not an absolute monarchy?

No Interference

Monroe warns that if Europeans invade the newly independent republics in Latin America, this would be considered hostile to the United States as well.

4. What would the United States have to fear if these republics were overthrown?

We owe it, therefore, to **candor**[4] and to the **amicable**[5] relations existing between the United States and those powers to declare that we should consider any attempt on their part to extend their system to any portion of this hemisphere as dangerous to our peace and safety.

With the existing colonies or dependencies of any European power we have not interfered and shall not interfere. But with the Governments who have declared their independence and maintained it, and whose independence we have, on great consideration and on just principles, acknowledged, we could not view any **interposition**[6] for the purpose of oppressing them, or controlling in any other manner their destiny, by any European power in any other light than as the manifestation of an unfriendly disposition toward the United States. In the war between those new Governments and Spain we declared our neutrality at the time of their recognition, and to this we have adhered, and shall continue to adhere, provided no change shall occur which, in the judgment of the competent authorities of this Government, shall make a corresponding change on the part of the United States indispensable to their security.

The late events in Spain and Portugal show that Europe is still unsettled. Of this important fact no stronger proof can be adduced than that the allied powers should have thought it proper, on any principle satisfactory to themselves, to have interposed by force in the internal concerns of Spain. To what extent such interposition may be carried, on the same principle, is a question in which all independent powers whose governments differ from theirs are interested, even those most remote, and surely none more so than the United States.

—James Monroe

- -

4. **candor:** honesty and openness
5. **amicable:** friendly
6. **interposition:** interference

DOCUMENT-BASED QUESTIONS

Short Answer

1. How would staying neutral in European wars protect the United States?

2. How might the U.S. system of government be threatened if Europeans regained control of former colonies in the Americas?

Extended Answer

3. What does the Monroe Doctrine show about how the United States saw itself and wanted to be seen by other nations?

Chapter Summary

1 **Key Idea**
New industries and inventions changed the way people lived and worked in the early 1800s.

2 **Key Idea**
The invention of the cotton gin and the demand for cotton caused slavery to spread in the South.

3 **Key Idea**
While patriotic pride increased national unity, tensions grew between the North and the South.

For detailed Review and Study Notes go to **Interactive Review** @ **ClassZone.com**

Name Game

Use the list of terms and names to identify each sentence online or on your own paper.

1. I led a rebellion against slavery in Virginia in 1831. Nat Turner

2. I built a water-powered textile mill. ____

3. This connected New York City with Buffalo, New York, by water. ____

4. This policy opposed European interference in the Western Hemisphere. ____

5. The invention of this led to the expansion of slavery. ____

6. This was enacted in 1820 to keep a balance of power between slave states and free states. ____

7. I promoted the American System. ____

8. This is a feeling of pride, loyalty, and protectiveness toward one's country. ____

9. The telegraph is my invention. ____

10. I built America's first successful steam-powered locomotive. ____

A. Missouri Compromise
B. Erie Canal
C. Peter Cooper
D. Nat Turner
E. sectionalism
F. Monroe Doctrine
G. Henry Clay
H. nationalism
I. steamboat
J. Samuel F. B. Morse
K. Eli Whitney
L. Samuel Slater
M. cotton gin

Activities

CROSSWORD PUZZLE

Complete the online crossword puzzle to show what you know about the Industrial Revolution.

DOWN
1. The ____ made cleaning cotton faster

FLIPCARD

Use the online flipcards to quiz yourself on the terms and names introduced in this chapter.

Method of production that brought workers and machines together in one building.

ANSWER
factory system

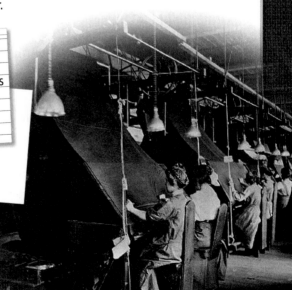

VOCABULARY

Explain the significance of each of the following.

1. Samuel Slater
2. Industrial Revolution
3. Missouri Compromise
4. spirituals
5. cotton gin
6. Nat Turner
7. nationalism
8. sectionalism

Explain how the terms and names in each group are related.

9. Samuel F. B. Morse, Eli Whitney, interchangeable part
10. Monroe Doctrine, James Monroe, nationalism
11. mechanical reaper, threshing machine, cotton gin
12. Robert Fulton, Peter Cooper, Erie Canal
13. Henry Clay, protective tariff, American System
14. factory system, Industrial Revolution, Lowell mills

Robert Fulton

KEY IDEAS

① Early Industry and Inventions (pages 364–369)

15. How did the War of 1812 cause economic changes in the United States?
16. How did interchangeable parts transform the manufacturing process?

② Plantations and Slavery Spread (pages 372–377)

17. How did the rise in cotton production affect slavery?
18. What was family life like for enslaved people?

③ Nationalism and Sectionalism (pages 378–384)

19. How did the Erie Canal help the nation to grow?
20. How did the Missouri Compromise attempt to resolve a conflict between the North and the South?

CRITICAL THINKING

21. **Summarize** How did the Industrial Revolution change the way Americans worked?

22. **Causes and Effects** In a chart like the one shown, note new inventions discussed in the chapter and their effects on the United States. Then explain which inventions helped to link the nation, and how.

Invention	Effects
threshing machine	

23. **Form and Support Opinions** In your opinion, were free African Americans in the South truly free? Explain.

24. **Make Generalizations** What role did religion play in the system of slavery?

25. **Analyze Point of View** Why was it so important to Southerners to admit Missouri as a slave state?

26. **Connect Geography and History** How did geography affect the way each region developed?

27. **Analyze Primary Sources** This political cartoon shows European nations observing a naval blockade. Explain what the blockade represents as well as what nation caused it to exist, and why.

MEAP PRACTICE

☑ **TEST PRACTICE**

• Online Test Practice @ ClassZone.com

• Use the **MEAP Strategies & Practice,** pages S1-S27, at the front of this book

MULTIPLE CHOICE

Use the quotation and your knowledge of U.S. history to answer question 1.

PRIMARY SOURCE

❝ [The Missouri] question, like a fire bell in the night, awakened and filled me with terror. . . . A geographical line . . . once conceived and held up to the angry passions of men, will never be [erased]; and every new irritation will mark it deeper and deeper. ❞

—Thomas Jefferson, April 22, 1820

1 What did Jefferson fear the growth of?

A industry

B national unity

C sectional tensions

D European colonies

Read each question and choose the best answer.

2 Which invention had the *greatest* impact on the spread of slavery?

A cotton gin

B locomotive

C steamboat

D steel plow

3 Which was a result of the Missouri Compromise?

A Congress established a protective tariff.

B The Mason-Dixon Line divided slave states and free states.

C Slavery was banned from the Louisiana Territory.

D Maine was admitted to the Union as a free state.

4 What was the power source for the first textile mills in America?

A slave labor

B water

C coal

D mules and oxen

YOU BE THE HISTORIAN

28. Evaluate How did the Industrial Revolution affect the balance of power among American regions?

29. Connect to Today The steamboat and the telegraph were two of the most significant inventions of the early 1800s. What recent inventions have had a similar impact on life today?

30. Make Inferences What effect do you think armed rebellions by enslaved people, such as the uprising led by Nat Turner, had on the institution of American slavery?

31. Form and Support Opinions Consider what might have happened if the Missouri Compromise had not been passed, and explain whether you think the plan was a wise decision.

32. Analyze Point of View Does Marshall's opinion in *McCulloch* v. *Maryland* reflect a strict or a loose interpretation of the Constitution? Explain.

 Answer the

ESSENTIAL QUESTION

What forces and events affected national unity and growth?

Written Response Write a two- to three-paragraph response to the Essential Question. Be sure to consider the key ideas of each section as well as economic changes in America during the early 1800s. Use the Response Rubric below to guide your thinking and writing.

Response Rubric

A strong response will

• describe the impact of the Industrial Revolution

• explain how new inventions affected the economy in different regions

• analyze the spread of slavery in South

• discuss the impact of nationalism and sectionalism

A Changing Nation

1824–1860

Why It Matters Now

Between 1810 and 1860, the nation had to face difficult questions about expansion, immigration, slavery, and the rights of minorities. America is still wrestling with the imperfect solutions of those crucial years in its early history.

Difficulty is the excuse history never accepts.
—Edward R. Murrow

1. Jacksonian Democracy and States' Rights
2. Jackson's Policy Toward Native Americans
3. Prosperity and Panic

The Age of Jackson

1824–1840

 ESSENTIAL QUESTION
What impact did Andrew Jackson's presidency have on the nation?

CONNECT ↻ Geography & History

How did geography affect the settlement of the United States during this period?

Think about:

1 U.S. population growth

2 reasons why land might be considered valuable

3 the importance of rivers

Jackson's inauguration

1830 Indian Removal Act is passed.
▼
Effect Thousands of Cherokees are forced west on the Trail of Tears.

1824

Sectional interests divide the Democratic-Republican Party in the 1824 election.
▼
Effect John Quincy Adams is elected president.

1828 Andrew Jackson is elected president.

Animated GEOGRAPHY & HISTORY

Settled Areas *1800–1830*

Click here to explore the Age of Jackson
@ClassZone.com

Claimed by both
U.S. and Britain

MAINE

VT.

N.H.

Albany • MASS. • Boston

NEW YORK

CONN. R.I.

New York

MICHIGAN TERRITORY

UNORGANIZED
TERRITORY

Mississippi River

Missouri River

PENNSYLVANIA N.J.

• Pittsburgh • Philadelphia

MD. DEL.

Washington, D.C.

ILLINOIS INDIANA OHIO

• Cincinnati

VIRGINIA

Ohio River

MISSOURI

KENTUCKY

ATLANTIC
OCEAN

TENNESSEE

NORTH
CAROLINA

ARKANSAS
TERRITORY

Mississippi River

SOUTH
CAROLINA

• Charleston

MISS. ALABAMA GEORGIA

MEXICO

Claimed
by U.S.

LOUISIANA

• New Orleans

FLORIDA
TERR.

Gulf of Mexico

| Settled area, 1800 |
| Settled area, 1830 |
| Borders of 1830 |

0   200   200 miles
0 100   200 kilometers

1832 Jackson vetoes charter
of the Bank of the United States.

Jackson is reelected.

Harrison
campaign
poster

Our cause our country
Our champion general

W™ H. HARRISON,
OUR BRAVE DEFENDER

1836 Martin
Van Buren is
elected president.

1840

Western settlers
clearing land

1834 Whig
Party is formed.

1837 Panic of
1837 occurs.

▼

Effect Many people
lose money and jobs.

William Henry
Harrison is elected
president.

▶ Key Ideas

BEFORE, YOU LEARNED

Forces and events in the early 19th century both strengthened and threatened national unity and growth.

NOW YOU WILL LEARN

Andrew Jackson's election to the presidency in 1828 opened a new era of popular democracy.

▶ Vocabulary

TERMS & NAMES

Andrew Jackson U.S. president from 1829–1837

John Quincy Adams 1824 presidential candidate favored by New Englanders

Jacksonian democracy the idea of widening political power to more of the people

spoils system the practice of giving government jobs to political backers

Tariff of Abominations 1828 law that significantly raised tariffs on raw materials and manufactured goods

John C. Calhoun Jackson's vice-president

doctrine of nullification idea that a state had the right to nullify, or reject, a federal law that it considers unconstitutional

BACKGROUND VOCABULARY

secede (SIH•SEED) to withdraw

REVIEW

states' rights the rights of the states to make decisions without interference from the federal government

Visual Vocabulary
John Quincy Adams

▶ Reading Strategy

As you read and respond to the **KEY QUESTIONS**, use a graphic organizer like the one shown to note the main ideas and important details. Create new diagrams as needed.

 See Skillbuilder Handbook, page R4.

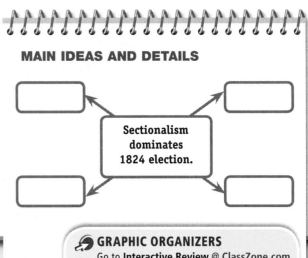

MAIN IDEAS AND DETAILS

Sectionalism dominates 1824 election.

🖱 **GRAPHIC ORGANIZERS**
Go to **Interactive Review** @ ClassZone.com

Jacksonian Democracy and States' Rights

 8 – U5.1.3 Describe the competing views of Calhoun, Webster, and Clay on the nature of the union among the states (e.g., sectionalism, nationalism, federalism, state rights).
8 – U5.2.1 Explain the reasons (political, economic, and social) why Southern states seceded and explain the differences in the timing of secession in the Upper and Lower South.

One American's Story

Margaret Bayard Smith and her husband were central figures in the political and social life of Washington. Here Smith describes the lively scene at the presidential inauguration of **Andrew Jackson** on March 4, 1829.

Margaret Bayard Smith wrote about life in the nation's capital in the first half of the 19th century.

PRIMARY SOURCE

❝ When the speech was over, and the President made his parting bow, the barrier that had separated the people from him was broken down and they rushed up the steps all eager to shake hands with him. . . . Country men, farmers, gentlemen, mounted and dismounted, boys, women, and children, black and white. Carriages, wagons, and carts all pursuing him to the President's house. ❞

—Margaret Bayard Smith, *The First Forty Years of Washington Society*

Jackson's election to the presidency set the stage for an era of greater public involvement in government.

Sectionalism Changes Politics

🔽 KEY QUESTION What political divisions appeared during the election of 1824?

By the 1820s, politics were increasingly dominated by sectionalism, or loyalty to the interests of a particular region of the country. In the election of 1824, these sectional interests tore apart the Democratic-Republican Party (the party of Thomas Jefferson). Four men competed to replace James Monroe as president. Their supporters were divided along sectional lines:

- New Englanders liked **John Quincy Adams**, Monroe's secretary of state.
- Westerners backed Henry Clay, "the Great Compromiser," and Andrew Jackson, a former military hero from Tennessee.
- Southerners supported Jackson and William Crawford of Georgia.

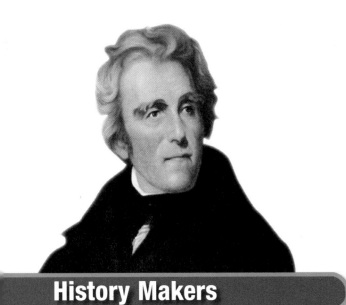

History Makers

Andrew Jackson   1767–1845

The son of Scots-Irish immigrants, Jackson grew up in the Carolina backcountry. Jackson's father died shortly before his birth, and his mother and two brothers died during the Revolutionary War. After the war, Jackson moved to Tennessee, built a successful law practice, and bought and sold land. After the War of 1812 broke out, he was appointed as a general in the army. His decisive win against the British at the Battle of New Orleans in 1815 brought him national recognition. He earned the nickname "Old Hickory" after soldiers claimed that he was "tough as hickory." Jackson's humble background, and his reputation as a war hero, helped make him president. Many saw his rise above hardship as an American success story.

CRITICAL THINKING

Connect *to* Today Do you think Andrew Jackson would be a popular presidential candidate today? Record evidence to support your opinion as you read through this chapter.

 **ONLINE BIOGRAPHY**   For more on Andrew Jackson, go to the **Research & Writing Center** @ ClassZone.com

---

Adams Defeats Jackson in 1824 Jackson won the most popular votes in the election. But no candidate received a majority of electoral votes. According to the Constitution, the House of Representatives must choose the president when this happens.

Clay had come in fourth and threw his support to Adams, who then won. Because Adams later named Clay as his secretary of state, Jackson's supporters claimed that Adams gained the presidency by making a deal with Clay. Charges of a "corrupt bargain" followed Adams throughout his term.

Adams had many plans for his presidency. He wanted to build roads and canals, aid education and science, and regulate the use of natural resources. But Congress, led by Jackson supporters, defeated his proposals.

Jackson felt that the 1824 election had been stolen from him and that the will of the people had been ignored. He immediately set to work on gaining the presidency in 1828.

Over the next four years, the division in the Democratic-Republican Party between the supporters of Jackson and of Adams grew wider. Jackson claimed to represent the "common man." He said Adams represented a group of privileged, wealthy Easterners. This division eventually created two parties. The Democrats came from among the Jackson supporters, while the National Republicans grew out of the Adams camp.

▲ **SUMMARIZE** Describe the political divisions that appeared before and after the 1824 election.

Jackson Redefines "Democracy"

▼ **KEY QUESTION** How did American democracy change during Jackson's presidency?

Although the United States had been founded on democratic principles, only white male landowners could vote in many states. In the face of growing calls for reform, Andrew Jackson helped broaden American democracy by advocating the extension of voting rights to more of the population.

Voting Rights Expand The election of 1828 again matched Jackson against Adams. It was a bitter campaign—both sides made vicious personal attacks. Even Jackson's wife, Rachel, became a target. During the campaign,

EXERCISING THE VOTE

The 1828 presidential election drew more than three times as many voters to the polls as the election of 1824. However, voting was limited to adult white males. Today, all citizens aged 18 and over are eligible to vote.

Citizens under the age of 18 can also participate in the election process. They can educate themselves about the issues, campaign for candidates they support, and practice casting their votes in mock, or pretend, elections. They can also urge eligible voters to cast their ballots, like the student shown here.

Hold a Mock Election.

1 Choose issues and candidates. You may focus on the national, state, or local level.

2 Campaign for the candidates or issues you support.

3 Set up a mock election in your classroom. Create a polling place, ballots, and other needed materials.

4 Prepare mock media reports on the election's outcome.

📖 See Citizenship Handbook, page 303.

Jackson crusaded against control of the government by the wealthy. He promised to look out for the interests of the common people. He also promoted the concept of majority rule. The idea of widening political power to more of the people and ensuring majority rule became known as **Jacksonian democracy**.

Actually, the practice of spreading political power had begun before Jackson ran for office. In the early 1800s, many states reduced restrictions on who could vote. This increased the number of voters. Despite the extension of voting rights, however, large segments of the population were still excluded. Women, the enslaved, and free African Americans still could not vote in most places.

Jackson Wins in 1828 The expansion of voting rights helped Jackson achieve an overwhelming win in the 1828 presidential election. Jackson's triumph was hailed as a victory for the common people. Large numbers of Western farmers as well as workers in the nation's cities supported him. Their vote put an end to the idea that government should be controlled by an educated elite.

Jackson's success in the election came at a high price. Shortly after he won, his wife died of a heart attack. Jackson believed that campaign attacks on her reputation had caused her death. She was a religious person who preferred a more private life. In fact, she had said that she "would rather be a doorkeeper

Views of Democracy

Jackson's presidency marked a dramatic shift in American politics. Although Jackson's Democrats had grown out of Jefferson's Democratic-Republican Party, ideas of democracy had changed.

JEFFERSONIAN DEMOCRACY	JACKSONIAN DEMOCRACY
Government by an educated few	More public involvement in government
Voting restricted to property owners	Voting expanded to all white males
Limited government	Limited government with a stronger executive branch

CRITICAL THINKING

1. **Draw Conclusions** Which president do you think exercised more power? Why?

2. **Compare and Contrast** What ideas did Jeffersonians and Jacksonians share in common?

in the house of God than . . . live in that palace at Washington."

The tragedy of his wife's death overshadowed Jackson's inauguration. But the capital was full of joy and excitement. Thousands of people attended the ceremony.

A throng followed Jackson to the White House. At the reception, people broke china and glasses as they grabbed for the food and drinks. The rowdiness finally drove Jackson to flee the White House. As Supreme Court Justice Joseph Story observed, "The reign of King Mob seemed triumphant."

A New Political Era Begins Jackson's inauguration began a new political era. In his campaign, he had promised to reform government. He started by replacing many government officials with his supporters. This practice of giving government jobs to political backers became known as the **spoils system**. The name comes from the statement "to the victor belong the spoils [possessions] of the enemy." Jackson defended the principle of "rotation in office," noting that it broke up one group's hold on government.

▲ **CAUSE AND EFFECT** Explain how Jackson helped change American democracy.

Rising Sectional Differences

▼ **KEY QUESTION** How did economic issues increase sectional tensions?

At the time of Jackson's inauguration, the country was being pulled apart by conflicts among its three main sections. Legislators from the Northeast, the South, and the West disputed three major economic issues:

- the sale of public lands in the West
- federal spending on internal improvements, such as roads and canals
- rising tariffs

Regional Interests Westerners wanted the federal government to sell public lands at low prices. They hoped to encourage settlement and give the section more political power. Northeasterners feared that cheap Western land might attract workers who were needed in Northeastern factories.

Better transportation routes would help bring food and raw materials to the Northeast and manufactured goods to Western markets. Southerners opposed federal spending on such projects because they were financed through tariffs.

Southerners Against Tariffs Tariffs made imported goods more expensive than American-made goods, which helped protect Northeastern factories from foreign competition. But Southern planters depended on trading cotton in exchange for foreign manufactured goods. Rising tariffs hurt the South's economy.

▲ **MAIN IDEAS AND DETAILS** In what ways did economic issues increase sectional tensions?

Federal Government vs. the States

▼ **KEY QUESTION** What issues were at stake in the debate over states' rights?

The issue of tariffs fueled the fires of a national debate that had been raging ever since the nation was formed. That debate was over the balance of power between federal and state governments. Some supported a strong federal government. Others defended **states' rights**, or the rights of the states to make decisions without interference from the federal government.

COMPARING *Sectional Interests*

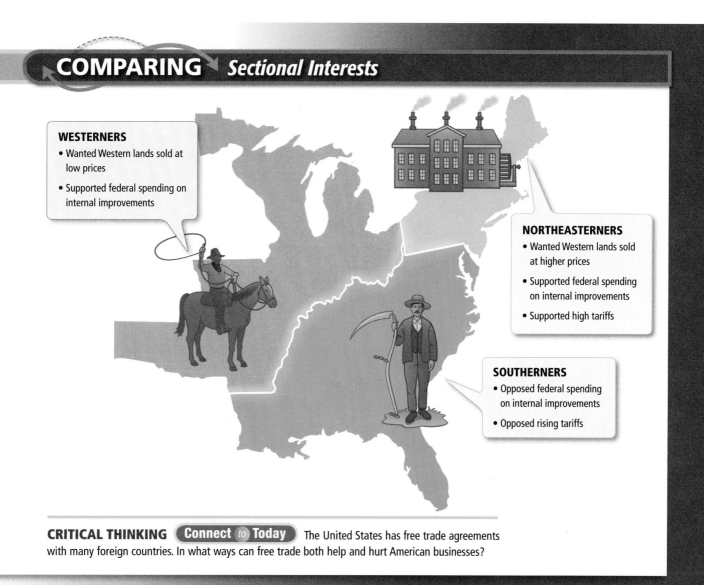

WESTERNERS
• Wanted Western lands sold at low prices
• Supported federal spending on internal improvements

NORTHEASTERNERS
• Wanted Western lands sold at higher prices
• Supported federal spending on internal improvements
• Supported high tariffs

SOUTHERNERS
• Opposed federal spending on internal improvements
• Opposed rising tariffs

CRITICAL THINKING **Connect** *to* **Today** The United States has free trade agreements with many foreign countries. In what ways can free trade both help and hurt American businesses?

The Nullification Crisis In 1828 Congress passed a bill that significantly raised tariffs on raw materials and manufactured goods. Southerners hated the tariff and called it the **Tariff of Abominations** (an abomination is a hateful thing). Southerners felt that the economic interests of the Northeast were determining national policy.

John C. Calhoun led the fight for states' rights.

The Tariff of Abominations hit South Carolina especially hard because the state's economy was in a slump. Some leaders in the state even spoke of leaving the Union over the issue. **John C. Calhoun**, Jackson's vice-president, sympathized with the South Carolinians because he was one himself. However, he wanted to find a way to keep South Carolina from leaving the Union. His solution was the **doctrine of nullification**. A state, he said, had the right to nullify, or reject, a federal law that it considered unconstitutional. He believed that Congress had no right to impose a tariff that favored one section of the country over another.

The States' Rights Debate Calhoun's ideas increased controversy over the nature of the federal union. This would remain a major political issue until the Civil War resolved it almost 30 years later.

Senators Daniel Webster of Massachusetts and Robert Y. Hayne of South Carolina debated the doctrine of nullification. Hayne argued that nullification gave the states a lawful way to protest and maintain their freedom. In words that were printed and spread across the country, Webster argued that freedom and the Union go together.

PRIMARY SOURCE

❝ When my eyes shall be turned to behold for the last time the sun in heaven, may I not see him shining on the broken and dishonored fragments of a once glorious Union. . . . Liberty and Union, now and forever, one and inseparable! ❞

—Daniel Webster, a speech in the U.S. Senate, January 26, 1830

Daniel Webster spoke powerfully in favor of a strong Union.

Jackson States His Position Although Jackson supported states' rights, he did not believe that the states should nullify federal law. But he kept his opinion to himself, until a dinner in honor of Thomas Jefferson's birthday. Jackson had learned that Calhoun planned to use the event to win support for nullification.

After dinner, Jackson was invited to make a toast. He stood up, looked directly at Calhoun, and stated bluntly, "Our Federal Union—it must be preserved." As Calhoun raised his glass, his hand trembled. Called on to make the next toast, Calhoun stood slowly and countered, "The Union—next to our liberty, the most dear; may we all remember that it can only be preserved by respecting the rights of the states and distributing equally the benefits and burdens of the Union." From that day, the two men were political enemies.

Henry Clay earned the nickname the "Great Compromiser" for his efforts to end sectional conflicts.

South Carolina Threatens to Secede Even though Jackson worked to limit the powers of the federal government, he was dedicated to preserving the Union. He asked Congress to reduce the tariffs, and Congress did so in 1832. Unsatisfied, South Carolina nullified the tariff acts of 1828 and 1832 and voted to build its own army. South Carolina's leaders threatened to **secede**, or withdraw from the Union, if the federal government tried to collect tariffs.

Jackson ran for reelection in 1832, this time without Calhoun as his running mate. After he won, he made it clear that he would use force to see that federal laws were obeyed and the Union preserved.

In the Senate, Henry Clay came forward with a compromise tariff in 1833. Congress quickly passed the bill, and the crisis ended. South Carolina remained in the Union.

▲ **SUMMARIZE** Identify the issues at stake in the state's rights debate.

Michigan Grade Level Content Expectations *Review*

 ONLINE QUIZ
For test practice, go to
Interactive Review @ ClassZone.com

TERMS & NAMES

1. Explain the importance of
- Andrew Jackson
- John Quincy Adams
- Jacksonian democracy
- spoils system
- Tariff of Abominations
- John C. Calhoun
- doctrine of nullification

USING YOUR READING NOTES

2. Main Ideas and Details Complete the diagram you started at the beginning of this section. Then create a diagram for each other main idea in this section.

Sectionalism dominates 1824 election.

KEY IDEAS

3. What were the effects of the 1824 election?

4. What factors helped Jackson win the 1828 election?

CRITICAL THINKING

5. Compare and Contrast Why did Northeasterners and Southerners disagree over the issue of tariffs?

6. Problems and Solutions How was the nullification crisis resolved?

7. WHAT IF? What might have happened if states were allowed to nullify federal law?

8. **Connect** *to* **Today** Is the spoils system prevalent in government today?

9. **Math** Research the popular vote totals and percentages of the 1824 and 1828 elections. Then create comparison charts or graphs to display your findings.

▶ Key Ideas

BEFORE, YOU LEARNED

Andrew Jackson's election to the presidency in 1828 opened a new era of popular democracy.

NOW YOU WILL LEARN

During Jackson's presidency, Native Americans were forced to move west of the Mississippi River.

▶ Vocabulary

TERMS & NAMES

Sequoya (sih•KWOY•uh) a brilliant Cherokee who invented a writing system for the Cherokee language

Indian Removal Act 1830 law that called for the government to negotiate treaties requiring Native Americans to relocate west

Indian Territory an area to which Native Americans were moved covering what is now Oklahoma and parts of Kansas and Nebraska

Trail of Tears forced removal of the Cherokee from their homeland to Indian Territory

Osceola (AHS•ee•OH•luh) leader during the Second Seminole War

BACKGROUND VOCABULARY

assimilate to absorb into a culture

REVIEW

literacy the ability to read and write

Visual Vocabulary
Trail of Tears

▶ Reading Strategy

As you read and respond to the **KEY QUESTIONS,** use a graphic organizer like the one shown to list causes and effects of the forced removal of Native Americans from their homeland.

 See Skillbuilder Handbook, page R7.

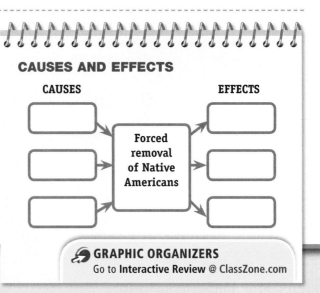

CAUSES AND EFFECTS

CAUSES → Forced removal of Native Americans → EFFECTS

GRAPHIC ORGANIZERS
Go to **Interactive Review** @ ClassZone.com

Jackson's Policy Toward Native Americans

8 – U4.2.3 Westward Expansion – Explain the expansion, conquest, and settlement of the West through the Louisiana Purchase, the removal of American Indians (Trail of Tears) from their native lands, the growth of a system of commercial agriculture, and the idea of Manifest Destiny.
8 – U4.2.4 Consequences of Expansion – Develop an argument based on evidence about the positive and negative consequences of territorial and economic expansion on American Indians. the institution of slavery, and the relations between free and slaveholding states.

One American's Story

In 1821, a brilliant Cherokee named **Sequoya** invented a writing system for the Cherokee language. Using this simple system, the Cherokees soon learned to read and write. A traveler in 1828 marveled at how many Cherokees had learned to read and write without schools or even paper and pens.

PRIMARY SOURCE

❝ I frequently saw as I rode from place to place, Cherokee letters painted or cut on the trees by the roadside, on fences, houses, and often pieces of bark or board, lying about the houses. ❞

—Anonymous traveler, quoted in the *Advocate*

Sequoya invented a writing system of 86 characters for the Cherokee language.

Sequoya hoped that by gaining **literacy**—the ability to read and write—his people could share the power of whites and keep their independence. But even Sequoya's invention could not save the Cherokees from the upheaval to come.

Native Americans Forced West

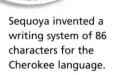 **KEY QUESTION** Why did Jackson want native people moved to the West?

By the early 1800s, there were still many Native Americans living east of the Mississippi, despite the fact that white settlers had been pushing them westward for two hundred years. These remaining tribes were viewed by many whites as an obstacle to progress. They debated what to do with the native population.

Tribes of the Southeast Some whites hoped that Native Americans could **assimilate**, or be absorbed into white culture. Others wanted Native Americans to move. They believed this was the only way to avoid conflict over land. Also, many whites felt that Native Americans were "uncivilized" and did not want to live near them.

The Age of Jackson **403**

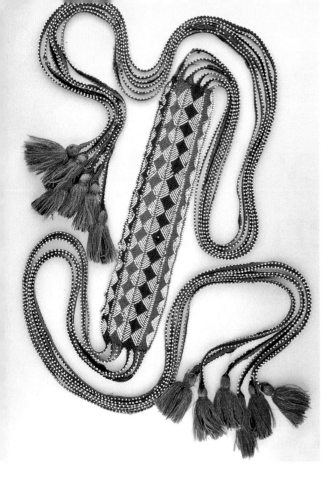

Traditional Creek belt

By the 1820s, about 100,000 Native Americans remained east of the Mississippi River. Most lived in the Southeast. The major tribes were the Cherokee, Chickasaw, Choctaw, Creek, and Seminole. Whites called them the Five Civilized Tribes because they had adopted many aspects of white culture. They held large areas of land in Georgia, the Carolinas, Alabama, Mississippi, and Tennessee.

More than any other Southeastern tribe, the Cherokee had adopted white customs, including their way of dressing. Cherokees owned prosperous farms and cattle ranches. From Sequoya, they acquired a written language, and they published their own newspaper, the *Cherokee Phoenix*. Some of their children attended missionary schools. In 1827, the Cherokees drew up a constitution based on the U.S. Constitution and founded the Cherokee Nation.

Jackson's Removal Policy Andrew Jackson had long supported a policy of moving Native Americans west of the Mississippi. He first dealt with moving the Southeastern tribes after the War of 1812. The federal government had ordered Jackson, then acting as Indian treaty commissioner, to make treaties with the Native Americans of the region.

Jackson believed that the government had the right to regulate where Native Americans could live. He viewed them as conquered subjects who lived within the borders of the United States. He thought Native Americans had two choices. They could either assimilate and become U.S. citizens, or they could move into western territories. They could not, however, have their own government within the nation's borders.

In 1828, gold was discovered on Cherokee land in Georgia. Now, not only settlers but also miners wanted to move the Cherokee. Many whites began to move onto Cherokee land. Georgia and other Southern states passed laws that gave them the right to take over Native American lands. When the Cherokee and other tribes protested, Jackson supported the states.

The Indian Removal Act Jackson asked Congress to pass a law that would require Native Americans to either move west or submit to state laws. Many Americans objected to Jackson's proposal. Massachusetts congressman Edward Everett warned against forcing Native Americans to a distant land, saying that the "inevitable suffering" would be "incalculable." Religious groups such as the Quakers also opposed moving Native Americans against their will. After heated debate, Congress passed the **Indian Removal Act** of 1830. The act called for the government to negotiate treaties that would require Native Americans to relocate west of the Mississippi.

▲ **CLARIFY** Explain why Jackson wanted Native Americans moved to the West.

The Trail of Tears

▼ **KEY QUESTION** What were the effects of the Indian Removal Act?

Jackson immediately set out to enforce the law. He claimed his policy was "just and liberal" and would allow Native Americans to keep their way of life. Instead, his policy caused much hardship and forever changed relations between whites and Native Americans.

The Forced March As whites invaded their homelands, many Native Americans saw no choice but to sign treaties. Under the treaties, Native Americans would exchange their current lands for lands in an area that covered what is now Oklahoma and parts of Kansas and Nebraska. This area came to be called **Indian Territory**.

Beginning in 1831, the Choctaw and other Southeast tribes were moved west. The Cherokees, however, appealed to the U.S. Supreme Court to protect their land from being seized by Georgia. In 1832, the Court, led by Chief Justice John Marshall, ruled that only the federal government, not the states, could make laws governing the Cherokees. This ruling meant that the Georgia laws did not apply to the Cherokee Nation. However, both Georgia and President Jackson ignored the Supreme Court. Jackson said, "John Marshall has made his . . . . let him enforce it."

Connecting History

Westward Expansion
By 1890, the western half of Indian Territory had opened up to white settlement as Oklahoma Territory. Native Americans tried to organize their remaining lands into the state of Sequoya. The federal government rejected this idea, and in 1907 the two territories formed the state of Oklahoma.

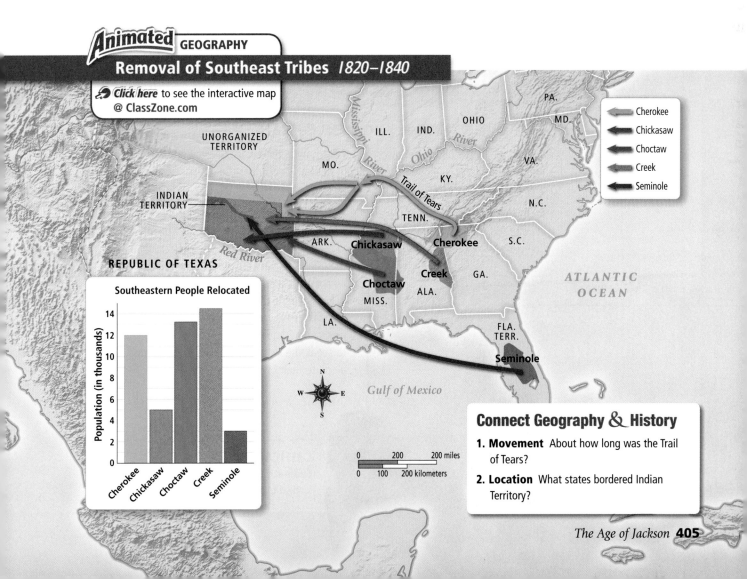

Animated GEOGRAPHY

Removal of Southeast Tribes 1820–1840

↪ **Click here** to see the interactive map @ ClassZone.com

Map legend:
- Cherokee
- Chickasaw
- Choctaw
- Creek
- Seminole

Southeastern People Relocated

(bar chart, Population in thousands)
- Cherokee: 12
- Chickasaw: 5
- Choctaw: 13
- Creek: 14.5
- Seminole: 3

Connect Geography & History

1. **Movement** About how long was the Trail of Tears?

2. **Location** What states bordered Indian Territory?

The Age of Jackson **405**

A small group of Cherokees gave up and signed a treaty. But most Cherokees, led by John Ross, opposed the treaty. Jackson refused to negotiate with these Cherokees.

In 1838, federal troops commanded by General Winfield Scott forced about 16,000 Cherokees into camps. Soldiers took people from their homes with nothing but the clothes on their backs. Over the fall and winter these Cherokees were forced to make the long journey west in the cold, rain, and snow. Many grew weak and ill. A quarter of the Cherokees died. The dead included John Ross's wife. One soldier never forgot what he witnessed.

PRIMARY SOURCE

❝ Murder is murder and somebody must answer. . . . Somebody must explain the four-thousand silent graves that mark the trail of the Cherokees to their exile. I wish I could forget it all, but the picture of six-hundred and forty-five wagons lumbering over the frozen ground with their Cargo of suffering humanity still lingers in my memory. ❞

—John G. Burnett, quoted in *The Native Americans*,
edited by Betty and Ian Ballantine

This harsh journey of the Cherokee from their homeland to Indian Territory became known as the **Trail of Tears**.

CONNECT ↻ To Today

THE CHEROKEE NATION OF OKLAHOMA

As soon as the Cherokees arrived in Indian Territory in the 1830s, they set out to rebuild. They established schools, churches, and businesses. A new constitution was adopted and newspapers and periodicals began circulating.

Today the Cherokee Nation is a leader in education, business, and economic development in Oklahoma. The Cherokee Nation and its agencies employ over 3,000 people. Cherokee history and language continue to be taught in Cherokee schools. Recently, the Cherokee Nation began offering language immersion classes to preschoolers in an effort to preserve the Cherokee language. By teaching the classes in Cherokee at such an early age, many hope that the children will not only learn to speak the language, but will one day pass it along to their own children.

CRITICAL THINKING
Evaluate In what ways have the Cherokees worked to preserve their culture?

Native American Resistance Some Native Americans resisted relocation. In 1838, a Cherokee farmer named Tsali and his family struggled to escape as U.S. soldiers were taking them to a camp. Two soldiers were killed before Tsali fled with his family to the Great Smoky Mountains. There they found other Cherokees. According to Cherokee tradition, Tsali was assured by the U.S. Army that if he and his sons were found, the others could remain. They surrendered or were captured, and all except the youngest son were executed. This sacrifice allowed some Cherokees to stay in their homeland.

In 1835, the Seminoles' refusal to leave Florida led to the Second Seminole War. One of the most important leaders in the war was **Osceola**. Hiding in the Everglades, Osceola and his band used surprise attacks to defeat the U.S. Army in many battles. In 1837, Osceola was tricked into capture when he came to peace talks during a truce. He later died in prison, but the Seminoles continued to fight. Some went deeper into the Everglades, where their descendants live today. Others moved west. The Second Seminole War ended in 1842.

Some Northern tribes also resisted relocation. In 1832, a Sauk chief named Black Hawk led a band of Sauk and Fox from Indian Territory back to their lands in Illinois. In the Black Hawk War, the Illinois militia and the U.S. Army crushed the uprising.

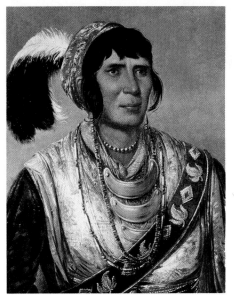

Osceola led the Seminole in the fight against removal.

 CAUSES AND EFFECTS Describe the effects of the Indian Removal Act.

Michigan Grade Level Content Expectations *Review*

ONLINE QUIZ
For test practice, go to
Interactive Review @ ClassZone.com

TERMS & NAMES

1. Explain the importance of

- Sequoya
- Trail of Tears
- Indian Removal Act
- Osceola
- Indian Territory

USING YOUR READING NOTES

2. Causes and Effects Complete the diagram you started at the beginning of this section.

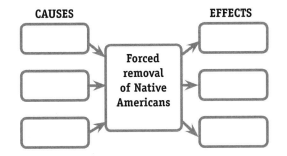

CAUSES   EFFECTS

Forced removal of Native Americans

KEY IDEAS

3. How did Americans react to Jackson's Native American policy?

4. Why were the Cherokees forced to move even though the Supreme Court ruled in their favor?

5. Describe how Native Americans resisted relocation.

CRITICAL THINKING

6. Main Ideas and Details In what ways had the Cherokee adapted to white culture?

7. Connect Geography & History How did the land in Indian Territory differ from the homelands of Southeastern Native Americans?

8. **Writing** **Journal** Write a journal entry as a Cherokee on the Trail of Tears. Include details about the traveling conditions and the people around you.

▶ Key Ideas

BEFORE, YOU LEARNED
During Jackson's presidency, Native Americans were forced to move west of the Mississippi River.

NOW YOU WILL LEARN
After Jackson left office, his policies caused the economy to collapse and affected the next election.

▶ Vocabulary

TERMS & NAMES

Martin Van Buren elected president in 1836 after serving as Jackson's vice-president

Panic of 1837 widespread fear about the state of the economy that spread after Van Buren took office

depression a severe economic slump

Whig Party political party formed by Henry Clay, Daniel Webster, and other Jackson opponents

William Henry Harrison Whig presidential candidate in 1840

John Tyler Harrison's running mate in the 1840 presidential election

BACKGROUND VOCABULARY

inflation an increase in prices and a decrease in the value of money

REVIEW

charter a written grant

Visual Vocabulary
William Henry Harrison

▶ Reading Strategy

As you read and respond to the **KEY QUESTIONS,** use a graphic organizer like the one shown to record important events in the order in which they happened.

 See Skillbuilder Handbook, page R5.

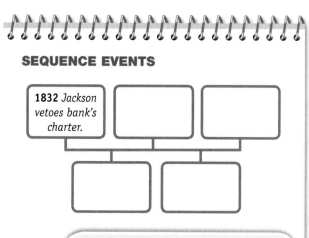

SEQUENCE EVENTS

1832 *Jackson vetoes bank's charter.*

GRAPHIC ORGANIZERS
Go to **Interactive Review** @ ClassZone.com

Prosperity and Panic

8 –U4.1.3.3 Challenge of Political Conflict – economic policy (e.g., the creation of a national bank, assumption of revolutionary debt)
8 – U5.1.4.6 Describe how the following increased sectional tensions – changes in the party system (e.g., the death of the Whig party, rise of the Republican party and division of the Democratic party)

One American's Story

Most of the nation prospered during Jackson's last years in office. However, shortly after his second term ended, the economy took a turn for the worse. Many people wanted the government to step in and help. Jackson's vice-president, **Martin Van Buren**, who succeeded Jackson as president, disagreed.

PRIMARY SOURCE

❝ All communities are apt to look to the Government for too much. . . . especially at periods of sudden embarrassment and distress. But this ought not to be. . . . [The framers of the Constitution] wisely judged that the less Government interferes with private pursuits, the better for the general prosperity. ❞

—Martin Van Buren, from a letter to Congress dated September 4, 1837

Jackson and the Democrats opposed many forms of federal power.

Martin Van Buren served as president from 1837 to 1840. He ran unsuccessfully for reelection in 1840 and again in 1848.

Jackson Targets the National Bank

🔻 **KEY QUESTION** How did Jackson destroy the national bank?

The Second Bank of the United States was the most powerful bank in the country. Jackson declared war on the bank.

Mr. Biddle's Bank The bank's president, Nicholas Biddle, set policies that controlled the nation's money supply. Since the bank made loans to members of Congress, Biddle could influence these lawmakers. Jackson believed that the bank was corrupt and had too much power.

To operate, the bank needed a **charter**, or a written grant, from the federal government. In 1832, Biddle asked Congress to renew the bank's charter, even though it would not expire until 1836. He thought Jackson would agree to the renewal rather than risk angering his supporters. But Jackson took the risk.

THE BUSINESS CYCLE

The pattern of ups and downs in the economy is called the business cycle.

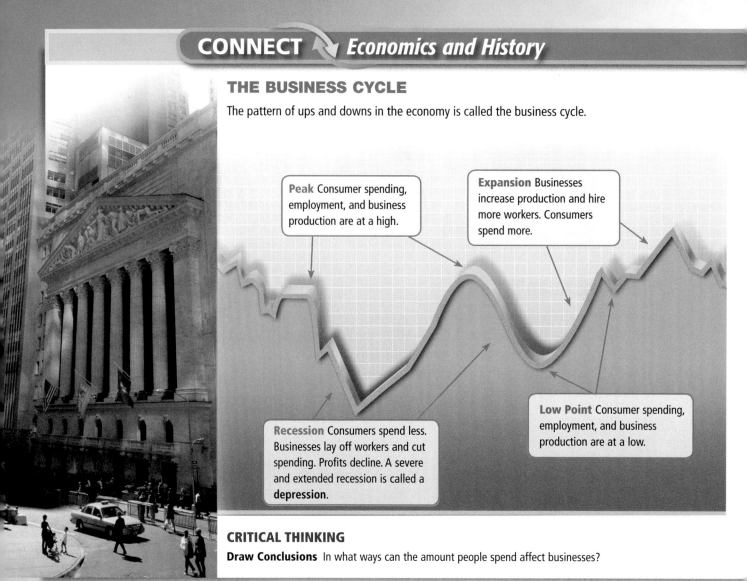

Peak Consumer spending, employment, and business production are at a high.

Expansion Businesses increase production and hire more workers. Consumers spend more.

Recession Consumers spend less. Businesses lay off workers and cut spending. Profits decline. A severe and extended recession is called a depression.

Low Point Consumer spending, employment, and business production are at a low.

CRITICAL THINKING

Draw Conclusions In what ways can the amount people spend affect businesses?

Jackson's War on the Bank When Congress voted to renew the charter, Jackson vetoed the renewal. Although the Supreme Court had ruled that the bank was constitutional, Jackson argued that it was not. He said it was a monopoly that favored the few at the expense of the many.

The bank became the main issue in the presidential campaign of 1832. The National Republican candidate, Henry Clay, called Jackson a tyrant. The Democrats portrayed Jackson as a defender of the people. When he won reelection, Jackson took it as a sign of approval for his war on the bank.

Jackson set out to destroy the bank before its charter ended. He had government funds deposited in state banks. Biddle fought back by making it harder for people to borrow money. He hoped the resulting economic troubles would force Jackson to return government deposits to his bank. Instead, the people supported Jackson. Eventually the bank went out of business. Jackson had won the war, but the economy would suffer for it.

Prosperity to Panic Because Jackson's state banks made it easier to borrow money, many people took out loans. The economy boomed. But the banks issued too much paper money, and the rise in the money supply made each dollar worth less. **Inflation,** or an increase in prices and a decrease in the value of money, was the outcome. To fight inflation, Jackson issued an order that required people to pay in gold or silver for public lands.

Jackson left office proud of the nation's prosperity. But it was puffed-up prosperity. Like a balloon, it had little substance. Jackson's popularity helped Van Buren win the presidency in 1836. A few months after Van Buren took office, a panic, or widespread fear about the state of the economy, spread throughout the country. It became known as the **Panic of 1837**.

People began exchanging paper money for gold and silver. Banks quickly ran out of gold and silver. A **depression**, or severe economic slump, followed. Almost all factories in the East closed. Jobless workers had no way to buy food or pay rent. People went hungry and became homeless.

▲ **SUMMARIZE** Explain how Jackson destroyed the national bank.

CONNECT ⟲ to the Essential Question

What impact did Andrew Jackson's presidency have on the nation?

EVENT	IMPACT
Election of 1828	Voting rights expand; Jackson's win hailed as victory for the common people
Tariff of Abominations	Sectional tensions grow over tariffs and states' rights; Jackson opposes nullification; South Carolina nullifies tariffs and threatens to secede
Indian Removal Act of 1830	Thousands of Native Americans are removed from their homeland; Cherokees suffer on the Trail of Tears
Bank War	Jackson drives the Second Bank out of business; inflation rises
Election of 1836	Jackson's popularity and the nation's prosperity help Vice-President Van Buren win the presidency

CRITICAL THINKING

1. **Form and Support Opinions** What do you think was the most important issue in Jackson's presidency? Why?

2. **Evaluate** In what ways did Jackson continue to affect politics after his presidency had ended?

The Birth of the Whigs

🔻 **KEY QUESTION** In what ways did the Whig Party differ from the Democrats?

Van Buren faced a new political party in his campaign for reelection in 1840. The **Whig Party** had been formed by Henry Clay, Daniel Webster, and other Jackson opponents. It was named after a British party that opposed royal power. The Whigs opposed the concentration of power in the chief executive—whom they mockingly called "King Andrew" Jackson.

This 1840 campaign banner shows a log cabin as a symbol of the frontier. The banner describes Harrison as "The Ohio Farmer" to set him apart from his wealthy opponent, Van Buren.

Political Beliefs The Whigs believed that Congress, not the president, represented the will of the people. They also blamed Van Buren—who objected to government "interference"—for not doing more to help the economy during the panic. In 1840 the Whigs chose **William Henry Harrison** of Ohio as a candidate for president and **John Tyler** as his running mate.

The Election of 1840 The Whigs nominated Harrison, the hero of Tippecanoe and the War of 1812, because of his military record and his lack of strong political views. During the campaign, the Whigs emphasized personalities rather than political issues. They portrayed Harrison as a frontiersman against the wealthy Van Buren. Harrison won the election but he died shortly after his inauguration, and John Tyler became president. The election of 1840 showed the importance of the West in American politics.

🔺 **COMPARE AND CONTRAST** Describe how the Whigs differed from the Democrats.

 Michigan Grade Level Content Expectations *Review*

 ONLINE QUIZ
For test practice, go to
Interactive Review @ ClassZone.com

TERMS & NAMES

1. Explain the significance of
- Martin Van Buren
- Panic of 1837
- depression
- Whig Party
- William Henry Harrison
- John Tyler

USING YOUR READING NOTES

2. Sequence Events Complete the diagram to show the major events of this section.

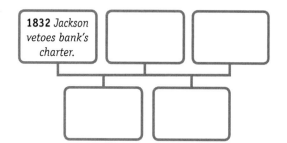

KEY IDEAS

3. Why was Jackson against the Second Bank of the United States?

4. What was Nicholas Biddle's role in the bank war?

CRITICAL THINKING

5. Causes and Effects What role did Jackson's popularity play in the elections of 1836 and 1840?

6. **Connect** *to* **Today** The percentage of eligible voters who participate in elections today is much lower than it was during Jackson's time. In what ways do you think this influences elections today?

7. **Art** **Campaign Poster** Create a campaign poster representing either the Whig Party or the Democrats in the election of 1840.

Chapter Summary

① Key Idea
Andrew Jackson's election to the presidency in 1828 opened a new era of popular democracy.

② Key Idea
During Jackson's presidency, Native Americans were forced to move west of the Mississippi River.

③ Key Idea
After Jackson left office, his policies caused the economy to collapse and affected the next election.

For detailed Review and Study Notes go to **Interactive Review** @ ClassZone.com

Name Game

Use the Terms & Names list to identify each sentence online or on your own paper.

1. People accused me of making a deal with Henry Clay in the 1824 presidential election. John Quicy Adams

2. I felt that the 1824 election was stolen from me. _____

3. I was Jackson's vice president in his first term. _____

4. I invented a writing system for the Cherokee language. _____

5. South Carolina threatened to secede because of this. _____

6. I led the Seminoles in the fight against removal. _____

7. Shortly after Jackson left office, I spread fear about the state of the economy. _____

8. Many people blamed me for the depression during my presidency. _____

9. This name comes from a British party that opposed royal power. _____

10. I succeeded William Henry Harrison after he died in office. _____

A. Osceola
B. John Quincy Adams
C. John Tyler
D. Whig Party
E. Sequoya
F. Martin Van Buren
G. Andrew Jackson
H. Tariff of Abominations
I. inflation
J. Panic of 1837
K. spoils system
L. doctrine of nullification
M. John C. Calhoun

Activities

CROSSWORD PUZZLE

Complete the online crossword puzzle to show what you know about the Age of Jackson.

DOWN
10. 1840 Whig presidential candidate

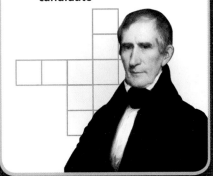

GEOGAME

Use this online map to reinforce your understanding of the settlement of the United States, including the locations of areas settled between 1800 and 1830. Drag and drop each place name in the list at its location on the map. A scorecard helps you keep track of your progress online.

Missouri

Illinois

Indiana

Tennessee

Kentucky

More items online

VOCABULARY

Explain the significance of each of the following:

1. John Quincy Adams
2. Jacksonian democracy
3. spoils system
4. states' rights
5. Sequoya
6. Osceola
7. Whig Party
8. William Henry Harrison

Explain how the terms and names in each group are related.

9. Tariff of Abominations, John C. Calhoun, doctrine of nullification

10. Indian Removal Act, Indian Territory, Trail of Tears

11. Martin Van Buren, Panic of 1837, depression

12. Whig Party, William Henry Harrison, John Tyler

KEY IDEAS

① Jacksonian Democracy and States' Rights (pages 394–401)

13. What changes in American democracy occurred during Jackson's presidency?

14. What issues divided Northeasterners, Southerners, and Westerners in the 1830s?

② Jackson's Policy Toward Native Americans (pages 402–407)

15. Why did many whites want Native Americans to move west?

16. How did the Indian Removal Act affect Native Americans?

③ Prosperity and Panic (pages 408–412)

17. How did Jackson try to destroy the bank before its charter ended?

18. Describe the beliefs of the Whigs.

CRITICAL THINKING

19. **Compare and Contrast** Create a chart like the one below to show how Jackson portrayed himself against Adams in the 1828 election.

Jackson	Adams
Westerner	*Easterner*

20. **Summarize** How did nullification threaten the nation?

21. **Main Ideas and Details** How did the discovery of gold in Georgia affect policies toward Native Americans?

22. **Synthesize** How did Jackson's policy toward Native Americans show his belief in the power of the presidency?

23. **Causes and Effects** What were the effects of Jackson's war on the national bank?

24. **Draw Conclusions** Based on its economic effects, was Jackson's decision to end the national bank a good one?

25. **Evaluate** How does the campaign poster below portray William Henry Harrison?

Harrison campaign poster

✓ **TEST PRACTICE**

• **Online Test Practice @ ClassZone.com**
• Use the **MEAP Strategies & Practice,** pages S1-S27, at the front of this book

MULTIPLE CHOICE

Use the cartoon and your knowledge of U.S. history to answer question 1.

BORN TO COMMAND.

OF VETO MEMORY.

HAD I BEEN CONSULTED.

KING ANDREW THE FIRST.

1 Why do you think Jackson is portrayed as a king?

A He came from a royal family.

B He supported a strong alliance with the British.

C Many people looked up to him.

D His opponents thought he had too much power.

Use the quotation and your knowledge of U.S. history to answer question 2.

PRIMARY SOURCE

❝ All communities are apt to look to the Government for too much. Even in our own country, where its powers and duties are so strictly limited, we are prone to do so, especially at periods of sudden embarrassment and distress. But this ought not to be. . . . [The framers of the Constitution] wisely judged that the less Government interferes with private pursuits, the better for the general prosperity. ❞

—Martin Van Buren, from a letter to Congress dated September 4, 1837

2 Why did Van Buren think the government did **NOT** need to help the economy during the depression?

A It would subject government leaders to embarrassment and distress.

B The economy would be better off without government interference.

C Any action taken should be made by Congress.

D It was the responsibility of the state governments.

YOU BE THE HISTORIAN

26. Form and Support Opinions Do you think Jackson was a champion of the common people? Why or why not?

27. Recognize Bias and Propaganda In what ways did Jackson's policy toward Native Americans reflect bias?

28. Analyze Point of View Do you think Jackson's use of power during his presidency contradicted his views as a proponent of limited government? Why or why not?

29. WHAT IF? What do you think would have happened if Congress had not passed the Indian Removal Act of 1830?

30. **Connect** *to* **Today** **Citizenship** In what ways do you think the changes that have occurred since Jackson's time in voter participation and voter eligibility affect government today?

 Answer the
ESSENTIAL QUESTION
What impact did Andrew Jackson's presidency have on the nation?

Written Response Write a two- or three-paragraph response to the Essential Question. Be sure to consider the key ideas of each section as well as the most significant factors that led to changes in the nation. Use the Response Rubric below to guide your thinking and writing.

Response Rubric
A strong response will

• analyze the democratic and political changes
• describe the relocation of Native Americans
• explain the effects of Jackson's policies

Manifest Destiny

1821–1853

 ESSENTIAL QUESTION

How did westward expansion transform the nation?

CONNECT Geography & History

How might the geography and topography of the United States have affected westward expansion?

Think about:

1 the highest peak of the **Rocky Mountains,** in Central Colorado, is 14,431 feet high

2 how people traveled in the early 1800s

3 the distances covered

This mission, or settlement, is a legacy of Spanish rule.

Oxen yoke

1821

Mexico gains independence from Spain. Stephen Austin starts American settlement in Texas.

▼

Effect Settlers move to Texas from the United States.

1824 Jedediah Smith finds South Pass.

▼

Effect Pioneers move west on faster trails.

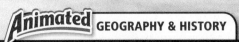

1836 Texas declares independence from Mexico.

▼

Effect Battle of the Alamo; Republic of Texas formed

U.S. military hat

1849 California gold rush

▼

Effect California enters the Union.

1853

This **trunk** was packed with precious possessions. Settlers seeking gold brought it with them to California.

1846 Oregon Territory acquired; war with Mexico begins.

▼

Effect 1848 Treaty of Guadalupe Hidalgo ends war with Mexico.

Reading for Understanding

▶ Key Ideas

BEFORE, YOU LEARNED
President Jefferson moved the border of the United States westward with the purchase of the Louisiana Territory in 1803.

NOW YOU WILL LEARN
Thousands of adventurers and pioneers followed trails to the West to settle the land and make their fortunes.

▶ Vocabulary

TERMS & NAMES

Jedediah Smith explorer who opened up the West with the discovery of the South Pass

mountain men trappers and explorers who opened up the western pioneer trails

Jim Beckwourth legendary trapper who explored the West and opened up the fur trade

Santa Fe Trail trail that began in Missouri and ended in Santa Fe, New Mexico

Oregon Trail trail that ran westward from Independence, Missouri, to the Oregon Territory

Mormon member of a church founded by Joseph Smith in 1830

Brigham Young Mormon leader who moved his followers to Utah to practice their religion in peace

BACKGROUND VOCABULARY

land speculators (SPEC•yuh•LAY•tors) people who buy land in the hope that it will increase in value

converts people who accept a new religious belief

REVIEW VOCABULARY

rendezvous (RAHN•day•voo) meeting; from a French word meaning "present yourselves"

▶ Reading Strategy

Re-create the cluster diagram shown at right. As you read and respond to the **KEY QUESTIONS**, use the outer ovals to record important details about the trails west.

 See Skillbuilder Handbook, page R4.

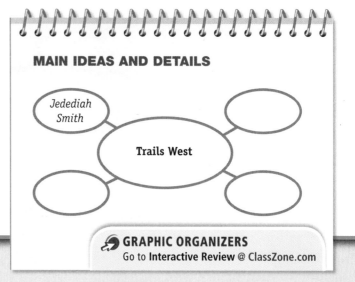

MAIN IDEAS AND DETAILS

Jedediah Smith

Trails West

GRAPHIC ORGANIZERS
Go to **Interactive Review** @ ClassZone.com

Trails West

8 – U4.2.3 Westward Expansion – Explain the expansion, conquest, and settlement of the West through the Louisiana Purchase, the removal of American Indians (Trail of Tears) from their native lands, the growth of a system of commercial agriculture, and the idea of Manifest Destiny.
8 – U4.2.4 Consequences of Expansion – Develop an argument based on evidence about the positive and negative consequences of territorial and economic expansion on American Indians. the institution of slavery, and the relations between free and slaveholding states.

One American's Story

In the 1824–1825 hunting season, trapper **Jedediah Smith** was leading a party through the Rocky Mountains when a grizzly bear attacked. The bear mauled Smith's face and partially tore off one ear. One hunter later remembered.

PRIMARY SOURCE

❝ [Smith] said, '[G]o for water and if you have a needle and thread get it out and sew up my wounds around my head.' . . . I told him I could do nothing for his ear. 'Oh, you must try to stitch it up some way or other,' said he. Then I put in my needle and stitched it through and through. ❞

—Jim Clyman, quoted in *The West*, by Geoffrey C. Ward

(*left*) Jedediah Smith was a true trailblazer, as shown in this desert scene by Frederic Remington. (*above*) Smith was most famous for exploring the Rockies.

Ten days after the attack, Jedediah Smith set out again. This time he found what he was looking for—a pass through the Rocky Mountains. Smith and other daring fur trappers and explorers were known as **mountain men**. They opened up the West by discovering the best trails through the Rockies. These trails were later used by thousands of pioneers who moved west. Smith died while leading a wagon train on the Santa Fe trail in 1831.

The Early Pioneers

🔻 **KEY QUESTION** What motivated early pioneers to journey into the rugged west?

Mountain men were among the early pioneers who journeyed into the vast region, largely wilderness, that lay beyond the Rocky Mountains. These men survived by being tough and resourceful.

Mountain Men Open the West Mountain men roamed the Great Plains and the Far West, the regions between the Mississippi River and the Pacific Ocean, to trap animals for their furs. Some, like Jedediah Smith and

History Makers

James Beckwourth   1798–?1867

Not much is known about Jim Beckwourth's family history. At the age of 25, he joined a group of fur traders going west and in time became a daring mountain man. For several years, he lived with a Crow tribe and earned the warrior name, "Bloody Arm." Later, he worked as an army scout and gold prospector. In 1850, Beckwourth discovered a mountain pass across the Sierra Nevadas that enabled thousands of pioneers and gold seekers to reach northern California. This pass is still called Beckwourth Pass. The Western Pacific Railway later used this route as a gateway to the West.

CRITICAL THINKING Sequence Events How did Beckwourth's discovery of a mountain pass change the future of California and the nation?

 **ONLINE BIOGRAPHY**   For more on on James Beckwourth, go to the **Research & Writing Center @ ClassZone.com**

Jim Beckwourth, became famous for their adventures. Although perceived as rugged loners, the men connected economically to the businessmen who bought their furs.

One businessman, William Henry Ashley, created a trading arrangement called the **rendezvous** system. At a prearranged site, trappers met with traders from the East. There, trappers bought supplies and paid in furs. The rendezvous took place every year from 1825 to 1840, when silk came into fashion and the fur trade died out.

Many animals were killed off at the height of the fur trade. This forced trappers to search for new streams where beaver lived. The mountain men's explorations provided Americans with some of the earliest firsthand knowledge of the Far West. This knowledge, and the trails the mountain men blazed, helped later pioneers moving west.

For example, thousands of pioneers used the wide valley through the Rockies called South Pass. Smith learned of this pass, in present-day Wyoming, from Native Americans. Unlike the high northern passes used by Lewis and Clark, South Pass was low, so it got less snow than the higher passes. Also, because South Pass was wide and less steep, wagon trails could run through it.

The Lure of the West To many the West, with its vast stretches of land, offered a golden chance to make money. The Louisiana Purchase had doubled the size of the United States. Some Americans believed it was their right to take land away from Native Americans who inhabited the territory but did not own it.

People called **land speculators** bought huge areas of land. To speculate means to buy something in the hope that it will increase in value. If land value did go up, speculators divided their holdings into smaller sections. They made great profits by selling those sections to the thousands of settlers who dreamed of owning their own farms. Traders also traveled west. Manufacturers and merchants hoped to earn money by making and selling items to settlers and markets opening up in new communities. Others went to find jobs or to hide from the law.

▲ **SUMMARIZE** Explain what motivated pioneers to undertake the hazardous journey into the rugged west.

Settling the West

▼ **KEY QUESTION** How did settlers make the difficult journey west?

The success of early pioneers convinced thousands of families and individuals to make the dangerous journey west. They traveled along a series of routes that led to New Mexico, Oregon, and Utah. Once in these places, the new pioneers claimed the land and established settlements.

The Santa Fe Trail In 1821, Mexico gained its independence from Spain. Lands in the Southwest that used to belong to Spain now belonged to Mexico. Spain had kept Americans out of these lands, but Mexico opened its borders to American traders.

One adventurer who took advantage of this new policy was Missouri trader William Becknell. In 1821 he left Missouri for the customary route to Santa Fe, capital of the Mexican province of New Mexico. He made a large profit because the New Mexicans were eager for goods. Back in Missouri, news spread that New Mexico was a place where traders could become rich.

The following year, Becknell left Missouri with a group of traders and pioneered a new route that became the **Santa Fe Trail.** Goods were hauled by covered wagons—rather than by pack animals. Becknell knew he could not haul wagons over the mountain pass he had used on his first trip. Instead, he found a cutoff, a shortcut that avoided steep slopes but it passed through a deadly desert to the south. As his traders crossed the burning sands, they ran out of water and were crazed by thirst. Finally, the traders found a stream

Along with tools, cooking supplies, and a hunting rifle, a tin of gunpowder was an essential item on an overland journey to the West.

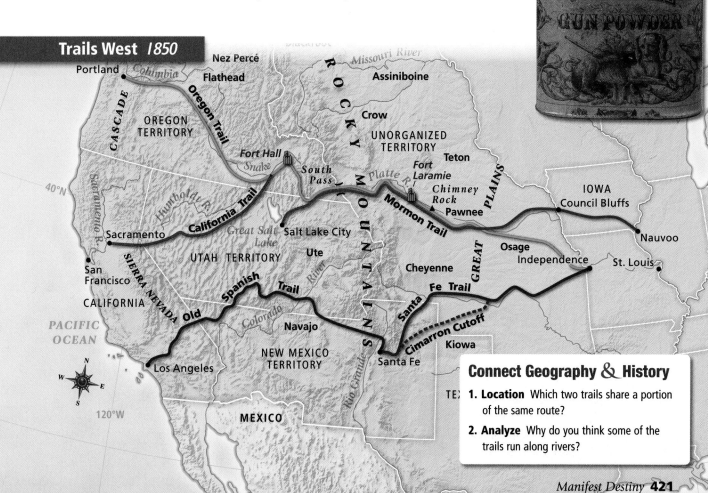

Trails West *1850*

Connect Geography & History

1. **Location** Which two trails share a portion of the same route?

2. **Analyze** Why do you think some of the trails run along rivers?

and pushed on to reach Santa Fe. Becknell returned home with another huge profit. Soon, hundreds of families were braving the cutoff to make the 800-mile journey from Missouri to Santa Fe, New Mexico.

Oregon Fever Hundreds of settlers began migrating west on the **Oregon Trail**, which ran from Independence, Missouri, to the Oregon Territory. Among the first settlers to cross the continent to Oregon were missionaries, such as Marcus and Narcissa Whitman in 1836. The Whitmans made few **converts** among the Native Americans, but their glowing reports of Oregon began to attract other American settlers to the region. American settlement eventually led to conflict between Britain and the United States because Oregon was jointly occupied by those two countries.

Daily Life — *On the Trail*

A Difficult Journey

For pioneers, the western lands held great hope. Following the trails promised new adventures. However, the journey was hazardous and filled with many challenges along the 2,000-mile route.

> " The dust got deeper and deeper . . . Often it would lie in the road fully six inches deep, so fine that a person wading though it would scarcely leave a track. And when disturbed, such clouds! No words can describe it. "
>
> —Ezra Meeker, pioneer

STRANGE BUT TRUE

A glass of water sometimes cost a lot of money on the trail.

Guess How Much!

$1 $5 $10 $20 $50 $100

Data File

WHO   350,000 pioneers between 1841 and 1867

WHAT   2,000 miles of trail across prairies, rivers, and mountains

WHERE   Missouri to Oregon. (There were many other trails including the Santa Fe trail and the Mormon Trail).

WHEN   early spring to avoid harsh winters

WHY   lure of available land and adventure

CHALLENGES OF THE TRAILS

• Wagon trains traveled from dawn to dusk with only a short break for a noontime meal, for nearly six months.

• Wagons were often overloaded with supplies, forcing family members, including children, to travel by foot.

• Children gathered firewood; when none was available they searched for dry buffalo dung.

ANSWER: 001$

Amazing stories spread about Oregon—the sun always shone there and wheat grew as tall as six feet. Such stories lured many people to the 2,000-mile journey to Oregon. In 1843, nearly 1,000 people traveled from Missouri to Oregon. The next year, twice as many came. "The Oregon fever has broken out," observed the *National Intelligencer*, "and is now raging."

The Mormon Trail Most pioneers went west in search of wealth, but one large group migrated for religious reasons. Members of the Church of Jesus Christ of Latter-Day Saints, or **Mormons**, also moved west. The church was founded by Joseph Smith in upstate New York in 1830. The Mormons lived in close communities, worked hard, shared their goods, and prospered.

The Mormons also made enemies. Some saw the Mormon practice of polygamy—allowing a man more than one wife at a time—as immoral. Others objected to their policy of holding property in common.

In 1844, an anti-Mormon mob in Illinois killed Joseph Smith. **Brigham Young**, the next Mormon leader, moved his people out of the United States. His destination was Utah, then part of Mexico, where he hoped his people would be left in peace.

In 1847, about 148 Mormon pioneers followed part of the Oregon Trail to Utah. With about 1,700 who soon joined them, they built a new settlement by the Great Salt Lake called Salt Lake City. Because Utah has little rainfall, the Mormons built dams and canals. These structures caught water in the hills and carried it to the farms in the valleys below. During this same period, American settlers were also changing Texas.

 SUMMARIZE Explain how settlers made the difficult journey west.

Connecting History

Religion in Public Life
Today the Church of Jesus Christ of Latter-Day Saints thrives in Utah, where Mormons make up about 70 percent of the state's population.

Michigan Grade Level Content Expectations *Review*

ONLINE QUIZ
For test practice, go to
Interactive Review @ ClassZone.com

TERMS & NAMES

1. Explain the importance of
   - Jedediah Smith
   - Oregon Trail
   - Jim Beckwourth
   - Mormon
   - Mountain Men
   - Brigham Young
   - Santa Fe Trail

USING YOUR READING NOTES

2. **Main Ideas and Details** Complete the diagram you began at the beginning of this section.

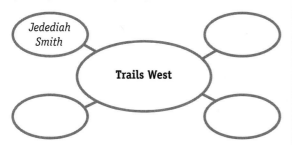

Jedediah Smith

Trails West

KEY IDEAS

3. How did the mountain men open up the West for future settlement?

4. What were some of the reasons settlers chose to live in the West?

CRITICAL THINKING

5. **Draw Conclusions** Of all the hardships faced by people who went west, what do you think was the most challenging?

6. **Analyze Causes and Effects** How do you think the pioneers' needs affected the local economy of Missouri?

7. **Draw Conclusions** How did the early Mormon settlers adapt to the desert?

8. **Writing** **Letter** Research a pioneer from this section and either write a letter from his or her point of view to a friend or write a journal entry and illustrate it with sights from the journey.

Animated HISTORY
AMERICAN TRAILS WEST

Click here to see an animated version of wagon trains @ ClassZone.com

American Trails West

Most of the trails west took pioneers over rugged mountain ranges and across rivers. The settlers often endured hunger and disease. Some Native American groups were friendly toward the settlers, other groups were hostile to settlers.

Click here Pioneers packed carefully for the challenges of the trail.

Click here Pioneers experienced varied climate conditions—such as the stark, dry, terrain of the desert.

Click here Pioneers had to clear the land to build a home for their families.

Activity

Songs on the Trail

1 Research the music and songs sung by the people going west.

2 Study the lyrics to understand what the journey west was like.

3 Divide the class into groups—narrators and performers.

4 Let each group take turns performing a song or playing recordings of ballads or folk songs from the trails west.

▶ Key Ideas

BEFORE, YOU LEARNED

Thousands of adventurers and pioneers followed trails to the West to make their fortunes and settle the land.

NOW YOU WILL LEARN

Conflicts between American settlers and the government of Mexico led Texas to revolt and win independence from Mexico in 1836.

▶ Vocabulary

TERMS & NAMES

Stephen F. Austin founded a colony for Americans in Spanish Texas

Tejanos (tay•HAH•nohs) people of Mexican heritage who consider Texas their home

Antonio López de Santa Anna Mexican president who led an army against Texas

Sam Houston commander of the Texas army at the Battle of San Jacinto; later elected president of the Republic of Texas

Juan Seguín (wahn seh•GEEN) a *Tejano* hero of the Texas Revolution

Battle of the Alamo battle between Texas and Mexico in 1836

Lone Star Republic nickname of the republic of Texas once free from Mexico

BACKGROUND VOCABULARY

Tejas (tay•HAHS) name the Spanish explorers gave present-day Texas

annex join or merge territory into an existing political unit such as a country or state

Visual Vocabulary
Lone Star Republic flag

▶ Reading Strategy

Re-create the diagram at right. As you read and respond to the **KEY QUESTIONS**, use the diagram to show important events leading to Texan independence.

 See Skillbuilder Handbook, page R5.

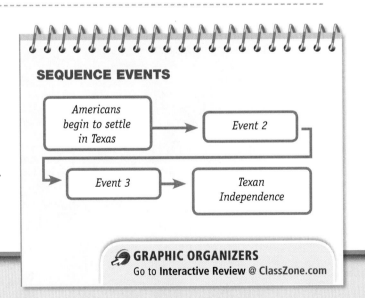

SEQUENCE EVENTS

Americans begin to settle in Texas → Event 2

Event 3 → Texan Independence

GRAPHIC ORGANIZERS
Go to **Interactive Review** @ ClassZone.com

The Texas Revolution

8 – U4.1.2 Establishing America's Place in the World – Explain the changes in America's relationships with other nations by analyzing treaties with American Indian nations, Jay's Treaty (1795), French Revolution, Pinckney's Treaty (1795), Louisiana Purchase, War of 1812, Transcontinental Treaty (1819), and the Monroe Doctrine.

8 – U4.2.3 Westward Expansion – Explain the expansion, conquest, and settlement of the West through the Louisiana Purchase, the removal of American Indians (Trail of Tears) from their native lands, the growth of a system of commercial agriculture, and the idea of Manifest Destiny.

One American's Story

In 1831, Mary Austin Holley visited her cousin Stephen F. Austin in Texas. She decided not to settle there, but published a widely read guide to the territory. Holley's guide was credited with bringing many settlers to Texas territory. Holley wrote approvingly of her cousin's vision.

PRIMARY SOURCE

Mary Austin Holley

❝ When, in the progress of years, the state of Texas shall take her place among the powerful empires of the American continent, her citizens will doubtless regard Col. Austin as their patriarch, and children will be taught to hold his name in reverence. . . . Col. Austin began the work, and was the first to open the wilderness. ❞

—Mary Austin Holley, *Texas: Observations Historical, Geographical and Descriptive* 1833

Stephen F. Austin's father, Moses Austin, had spent the last years of his life chasing a dream. He had hoped to found a colony for Americans in Spanish Texas. A week after his father's death in 1821, Stephen F. Austin was standing on Texas soil. His father's dream would become his destiny. Austin led the surge of American settlement in Texas.

Changes in Spanish Texas

🔻 **KEY QUESTION** How did American settlers cause problems in Texas?

Texas—the land the Spanish explorers called *Tejas* (tay•HAHS)—bordered the Louisiana Territory. *Tejas* had lush forests, plains, and rich soil, but relatively few settlers. When Austin arrived, fewer than 5,000 *Tejanos* (tay•HAH•nohs), people of Spanish heritage who thought of Texas as their home, lived in Texas.

American Settlers in Texas In 1820, to defend the land from hostile Native Americans, the Spanish government offered huge tracts of land to *empresarios*—people who agreed to find settlers for the land. When Spanish settlers did not respond to their offer of land, the Spanish agreed to let American Moses Austin start a colony there, provided the settlers followed Spanish law. Shortly after Stephen F. Austin arrived in Texas in 1821, Mexico successfully gained its independence from Spain. *Tejas* was now a part of the new nation of Mexico. With the change in government, the Spanish land grant given to Austin's father was worthless.

Stephen F. Austin traveled to Mexico City to persuade the new Mexican government to let him start his American colony. The Mexican government would consent only if the new settlers agreed to become Mexican citizens and members of the Roman Catholic Church.

Between 1821 and 1825, Austin attracted about 300 families to his new settlement. These original Texas settler families are known as the "Old Three Hundred." He demanded proof that each family head worked hard and did not use alcohol. The colony attracted more and more settlers. Some were looking for a new life, some were escaping from the law, and others were looking for a chance to grow rich. By 1830, the population had swelled to about 25,000, with Americans outnumbering the *Tejanos* six to one.

Rising Tensions in Texas As more Americans settled in Texas, tensions increased. Americans resented Mexican laws. They were unhappy that offi-

🔊 **ONLINE PRIMARY SOURCE**

Hear the perspectives at the **Research & Writing Center** @ ClassZone.com

COMPARING *Perspectives*

By the 1820s, non-Mexican settlers were a growing presence in Texas. *Tejanos* were quickly outnumbered. Most of the American settlers refused to learn Spanish and resented the Mexican laws they were expected to honor. Different perspectives of the changes in Texas are quoted below.

Against Settlement

❝ The Americans . . . have taken possession of practically all the eastern part of Texas, in most cases without the permission of the authorities. They immigrate constantly, finding no one to prevent them, and take possession of the sitio [site] that best suits them without either asking leave or going through any formality other than that of building their homes.

❞ *attributed to Mexican soldier José María Sánchez, April 1828*

For Settlement

❝ My object, the sole and only desire of my ambitions since I first saw Texas, was to . . . settle it with an intelligent, honorable, and enterprising people. . . . Texas should be effectually, and fully, Americanized—that is—settled by a population that will harmonize with their neighbors on the East, in language, political principles, common origin, sympathy, and even interest. ❞

— *Stephen F. Austin, ca. 1837*

CRITICAL THINKING Make Inferences Why do you think American settlers believed they could Americanize Texas?

cial documents were written in Spanish. Slave owners became angry when Mexico outlawed slavery in 1829. They wanted to maintain slavery so they could grow cotton. Austin persuaded the government to allow slave owners to keep their slaves.

On the other hand, the *Tejanos* found the Americans difficult to live with, too. *Tejanos* thought that the Americans believed they were superior and deserved special privileges. The Americans seemed unwilling to adapt to or to understand Mexican laws.

Responding to warnings of a possible revolution, the Mexican government cracked down on Texas. First, it closed the state to further American immigration. Next, it required Texans to pay taxes for the first time. Finally, to enforce these laws, the government sent more Mexican troops to Texas.

🔺 **ANALYZE CAUSES AND EFFECTS** Explain how American settlers caused problems in Texas.

Texans Revolt Against Mexico

🔻 **KEY QUESTION** What events led to Texas's independence from Mexico?

The actions of the Mexican government caused angry protests from Americans and many *Tejanos*. Some Texans talked about breaking away from Mexico. But Austin remained loyal to Mexico.

(*left*) Mexican general Antonio López de Santa Anna liked to be known as the "Napoleon of the West."

War Begins In 1833, Austin went to Mexico City to present a list of requested reforms to Mexican officials. The most urgent request was that Texas become a self-governing state within Mexico. Mexican president **General Antonio López de Santa Anna** agreed to most of the reforms. But Santa Anna then learned of a letter Austin had written. If his requests weren't met, wrote Austin, he would support breaking away from Mexican rule. This was rebellion! Santa Anna jailed Austin for almost a year. The furious Texans were ready to rebel.

Santa Anna sent more troops to Texas. In October 1835, Mexican soldiers marched to the town of Gonzales. They had orders to seize a cannon used by the Texans for protection against Native Americans. Texas volunteers had hung a flag over the big gun that said, "Come and Take It."

The Mexican troops failed to capture the cannon. In December, Texans drove Mexican troops out of an old mission in San Antonio called the Alamo that was used as a fortress. Angered by these insults, Santa Anna and 6,000 troops headed for Texas.

The Fight for the Alamo On March 1–2, 1836, Texans met at a settlement called Washington-on-the-Brazos to decide what to do about Santa Anna's troops. They decided to declare Texas a free and independent republic. **Sam Houston** was placed in command of the Texas army.

History Makers

Juan Seguín   1806–1890

Juan Seguín was a *Tejano* who wanted Texas to remain independent and not become part of the United States. He was a hero of the Battle of the Alamo. Seguín was elected to the Texas Senate in 1837 and was mayor of San Antonio twice. However, Seguín was often betrayed and harassed by American newcomers who mistrusted *Tejanos*. Finally he was forced to move to Mexico in 1842. In 1846–1848, Seguín fought against Americans in the War with Mexico.

CRITICAL THINKING Compare In what ways did the goals of Seguín and the Americans in Texas differ?

 **ONLINE BIOGRAPHY**   For more on Juan Seguín, go to the **Research & Writing Center** @ ClassZone.com

Juan Seguín (wahn seh•GEEN) led a band of 25 *Tejanos* in support of revolt. Also among the Texas volunteers were free African Americans, but the Texas army hardly existed. There were two small forces ready to stand up to Santa Anna's army. One was a company of some 300 to 400 men, led by James Fannin, stationed at Goliad, a fort in southeast Texas. The second was a company of about 180 volunteers at the Alamo. Headed by James Bowie and William Travis, this small force also included such famous frontiersmen as Davy Crockett.

On February 23, 1836, Santa Anna's troops surrounded San Antonio. The next day, Mexicans began their siege of the Alamo. Two nights later, Travis scrawled a message to the world: "The enemy has demanded surrender. . . . I have answered . . . with a cannon shot. . . . I shall never surrender or retreat." Juan Seguín, a *Tejano*, spoke Spanish, so he was chosen to carry the declaration through enemy lines. Seguín got the message through to other Texas defenders. But when he returned, he saw the Alamo in flames.

The Alamo's defenders held off the Mexican attack for 12 violent days. On the 13th day, Santa Anna ordered over 1,800 men to storm the fortress. The Texans met the attackers with a hailstorm of cannon and gun fire until the Texans ran out of ammunition. At day's end, all but seven Texans were dead and more than 1,000 Mexicans had fallen. The **Battle of the Alamo** was over.

The survivors were executed. A total of 183 Alamo defenders died. Only a few women and children were spared. Hundreds of Mexicans also perished. The slaughter shocked Texans—and showed them how hard they would have to fight for their freedom from Mexico.

Victory at San Jacinto With Santa Anna on the attack, Texans—both soldiers and settlers—fled eastward. Houston sent a message to the troops at Goliad, ordering them to retreat. They were captured by Mexican forces, who executed more than 300. But even in retreat and defeat, Houston's army doubled. Now it was a fighting force of 800 angry men. It included *Tejanos*, American settlers, and many free and enslaved African Americans.

In late April 1836, Houston surprised Santa Anna near the San Jacinto (san juh•SIN•toh) River. The Texans advanced screaming "Remember the Alamo!" and "Remember Goliad!"

In just 18 minutes, the Texans killed more than half of the Mexican army. Santa Anna had to sign a treaty giving Texas its freedom. With the Battle of San Jacinto, Texas was an independent nation.

Republic of Texas In December 1836, Texans raised the official flag of the independent nation of Texas, nicknamed the **Lone Star Republic**. Sam Houston was elected president.

Many Texans wanted to be part of the United States. In 1836 the Texas government asked Congress to **annex**, or join, Texas to the Union. Some Northerners objected. Some feared that Texas would allow slavery and upset the balance between free and slave states. Some opposed any expansion of slavery. Others feared that annexing Texas would lead to war with Mexico. In response Congress voted against annexation.

 SEQUENCE EVENTS Describe the events that led to Texas's independence from Mexico.

Connect Geography & History

1. **Place** What geographic features marked the boundaries of the disputed territory?

2. **Clarify** What does the map show as a major disagreement left unresolved by the war?

Michigan Grade Level Content Expectations *Review*

ONLINE QUIZ
For test practice, go to
Interactive Review @ ClassZone.com

TERMS & NAMES

1. Explain the importance of
   - Stephen F. Austin
   - *Tejanos*
   - Sam Houston
   - Juan Seguín
   - Battle of the Alamo
   - Lone Star Republic
   - Antonio López de Santa Anna

USING YOUR READING NOTES

2. **Sequence** Complete the diagram you started at the beginning of this section. Then expand the diagram for each of the other important events in this section.

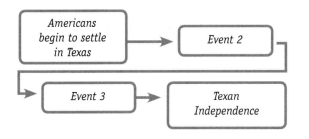

KEY IDEAS

3. How and why did Texas attract American settlers?

4. How did the Mexican government respond to the Texas rebellion?

CRITICAL THINKING

5. **Analyze Motives** Why do you think Stephen F. Austin thought it necessary to demand proof of settlers' high morals for his colony?

6. **Recognize Effects** How did losing the Battle of the Alamo serve as a turning point for Texas independence?

7. **Connect Economics & History** Why was Texas a magnet for land speculators and investors?

8. **Writing** Speech Write a one-page persuasive speech from Stephen F. Austin to the Mexican government asking for permission to form a colony in Texas.

▶ Key Ideas

BEFORE, YOU LEARNED

Conflicts between American settlers and the government of Mexico led Texans to revolt and win independence from Mexico in 1836.

NOW YOU WILL LEARN

Victory in a war with Mexico allowed Americans to expand the nation across the continent.

▶ Vocabulary

TERMS & NAMES

James K. Polk eleventh president of the United States who was committed to westward expansion

manifest destiny belief that the U.S. was meant to expand from coast to coast

Zachary Taylor U.S. general who led the battle over the disputed territory of the Rio Grande

Bear Flag Revolt rebellion by Americans in 1846 against Mexican rule of California

Treaty of Guadalupe Hidalgo (gwah•duh•L OOP•ay hih•DAHL•go) treaty that ended the War with Mexico

Mexican cession Mexican territory surrendered to the United States at the end of the war with Mexico

Visual Vocabulary
(*above left*) Original 1846 bear flag was replaced by (*above right*) state flag of California in 1911.

▶ Reading Strategy

Re-create a diagram like the one shown at right. As you read and respond to the **KEY QUESTIONS**, use boxes to show the sequence of events leading to war with Mexico.

 See Skillbuilder Handbook, page R5.

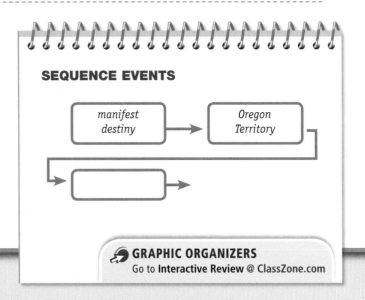

SEQUENCE EVENTS

manifest destiny → Oregon Territory → [ ] →

GRAPHIC ORGANIZERS
Go to **Interactive Review** @ ClassZone.com

The War with Mexico

8 – U4.1.2 Establishing America's Place in the World – Explain the changes in America's relationships with other nations by analyzing treaties with American Indian nations, Jay's Treaty (1795), French Revolution, Pinckney's Treaty (1795), Louisiana Purchase, War of 1812, Transcontinental Treaty (1819), and the Monroe Doctrine.
8 – U4.2.3 Westward Expansion – Explain the expansion, conquest, and settlement of the West through the Louisiana Purchase, the removal of American Indians (Trail of Tears) from their native lands, the growth of a system of commercial agriculture, and the idea of Manifest Destiny.

One American's Story

Henry Clay sneered, "Who is **James K. Polk**?" Clay had just learned the name of the Democratic candidate who would run against him for president in 1844. However, Polk wasn't a complete unknown. He had served seven terms in Congress.

Polk was committed to national expansion. He vowed to annex Texas and take over Oregon. Americans listened and voted. When the votes were counted, Clay had his answer. James Knox Polk was the eleventh president of the United States. On the question of Texas, Polk said:

PRIMARY SOURCE

❝ To Texas, the reunion is important, because the strong protecting arm of our Government would be extended over her, and the vast resources of her fertile soil and genial climate would be speedily developed. ❞

—James K. Polk, *Inaugural Address*, 1845

James Polk's presidential campaign emphasized expansion of the United States.

Polk's ideas about expanding the country captured the attention of Americans. After his election Polk looked for ways to act on his agenda.

Americans Support Manifest Destiny

🔻 **KEY QUESTION** How did belief in manifest destiny lead to friction overseas?

Land in the West held great promise for Americans. Although populated by Native Americans and Mexicans, American settlers viewed those lands as unoccupied. And Americans worried about claims by other nations.

Dispute over Oregon One country with whom the United States faced conflict was Great Britain. The United States and Britain shared control of the northwest Oregon Territory. Many Americans believed that it was their fate, or destiny, to expand the United States across the continent from ocean to ocean. In 1845, a newspaper editor, John O'Sullivan, gave a name to that belief. He called it **manifest destiny.**

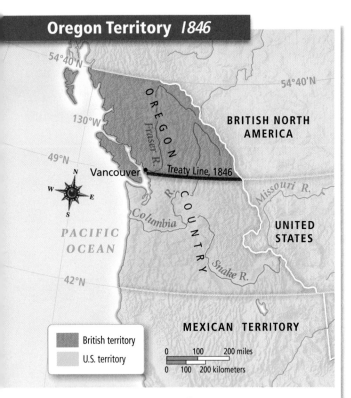

Oregon Territory 1846

BRITISH NORTH AMERICA

54°40'N

130°W

49°N

Vancouver

Treaty Line, 1846

PACIFIC OCEAN

42°N

OREGON COUNTRY

Fraser R.

Columbia

Snake R.

Missouri R.

UNITED STATES

MEXICAN TERRITORY

British territory
U.S. territory

0   100   200 miles
0   100   200 kilometers

Connect Geography & History

1. **Movement** Why was Oregon an attractive destination for settlers moving west?

2. **Compare** Refer to the map of Trails West on p. 421. How did the Oregon Trail contribute to the course of manifest destiny?

John O'Sullivan used the word *manifest* to mean *clear* or *obvious*. The word *destiny* means events sure to happen. Therefore, manifest destiny suggested that expansion was not only good but bound to happen—even if it meant pushing Mexicans and Native Americans out of the way.

PRIMARY SOURCE

❝Our manifest destiny [is] to overspread the continent allotted [given] by Providence [God] for the free development of our yearly multiplying millions.❞

—John 0'Sullivan, *the Annals of America, Vol 7*

Since 1818, Oregon had been occupied jointly by the United States and Britain. By the 1840s, thousands of American settlers had moved into the Oregon Territory. In his campaign, Polk promised to take over all of Oregon. "Fifty-four forty or fight!" was one of his slogans. The parallel of 54°40'N latitude was the northern boundary of the shared Oregon Territory. After Polk's election in 1844, manifest destiny became government policy. The term "manifest destiny" was new, but not the idea.

Rather than fight for all of Oregon, however, Polk settled for half. In 1846, the United States and Great Britain agreed to divide Oregon at the 49th parallel. This agreement extended the boundary line already drawn between Canada and the United States. Today this line still serves as the border between much of the United States and Canada.

Troubles with Mexico Polk had good reason for settling with Britain over Oregon. By 1846, he had bigger troubles brewing with Mexico over Texas. In 1845, Congress admitted Texas as a slave state, despite Northern objections to the spread of slavery. However, Mexico still claimed Texas as its own. Mexico angrily viewed this **annexation**, or attachment, as an act of war.

To make matters worse, Texas and Mexico could not agree on the official border between them. Texas claimed the Rio Grande, a river south of San Antonio, as its southern boundary. Mexico insisted on the Nueces (noo•AY•sis) River (See the map on page 435.) as the Texas border. The difference in the distance between the two rivers was more than 100 miles at some points. Many thousands of square miles of territory were at stake.

Mexico said it would fight to defend its claim. Polk sent John Slidell, a Spanish-speaking ambassador, to offer Mexico up to $30 million for Texas, California, and New Mexico. But Slidell's diplomacy failed.

▲ **SEQUENCE EVENTS** Explain how belief in manifest destiny led to friction overseas.

The War with Mexico

KEY QUESTION What events led to war with Mexico?

Giving up on diplomacy, Polk's next strategy was to force the issue. He purposefully ordered General **Zachary Taylor** to station 3,500 troops on the north bank of the Rio Grande, which was part of the disputed territory.

Polk Urges War On April 25, 1846, a Mexican unit crossed the Rio Grande and ambushed an American patrol. Polk sent a rousing war message to Congress, saying, "Mexico . . . has invaded our territory and shed American blood upon the American soil." Two days later, Congress declared war. The War with Mexico had begun.

Americans had mixed reactions to the war. In general, Southerners wanted to extend the territory open to slavery, while Northeners feared the expansion of slavery. Many also questioned the justice of men dying for territorial gain. Despite opposition, the United States plunged into war. In May 1846, General Zachary Taylor led troops into Mexico.

Capturing New Mexico and California Not long after the war began, U.S. General Stephen Kearny (KAHR•nee) left Kansas with orders to occupy New Mexico. Once there, Kearny persuaded the Mexican troops that he would withdraw. He took New Mexico without firing a shot. Then Kearny marched on to what is now California, which had fewer than 12,000 Mexican residents. The remainder of the force moved south toward Mexico.

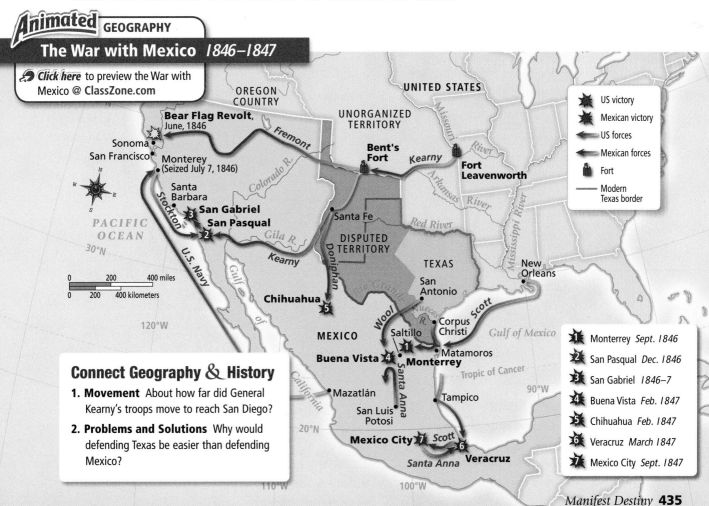

Animated GEOGRAPHY
The War with Mexico 1846–1847

Click here to preview the War with Mexico @ ClassZone.com

Legend:
- US victory
- Mexican victory
- US forces
- Mexican forces
- Fort
- Modern Texas border

1. Monterrey *Sept. 1846*
2. San Pasqual *Dec. 1846*
3. San Gabriel *1846–7*
4. Buena Vista *Feb. 1847*
5. Chihuahua *Feb. 1847*
6. Veracruz *March 1847*
7. Mexico City *Sept. 1847*

Connect Geography & History

1. **Movement** About how far did General Kearny's troops move to reach San Diego?

2. **Problems and Solutions** Why would defending Texas be easier than defending Mexico?

Connecting History

Not all war declarations have been as contentious as the war against Mexico. Representative Jeanette Rankin of Montana, the first woman in Congress and an avowed pacifist, was the only member of the House to vote against World War II.

Meanwhile, Americans in northern California staged a revolt and raised a crude flag featuring a grizzly bear. The revolt, known as the **Bear Flag Revolt**, was joined by explorer John C. Frémont. The rebels declared independence from Mexico and formed the Republic of California. U.S. troops joined forces with the rebels. Within weeks, American forces controlled all of California.

The Fighting in Mexico The defeat of Mexico proved more difficult. American forces invaded Mexico from two directions. Taylor battled his way south from Texas toward Monterrey in northern Mexico. On February 23, 1847, his 4,800 troops met Santa Anna's 15,000 Mexican soldiers near a ranch called Buena Vista. After two bloody days of fighting, Santa Anna retreated. The war in the north of Mexico was over.

In southern Mexico, Winfield Scott's forces landed at Veracruz on the Gulf of Mexico and made for Mexico City. Outside the capital, the Americans met fierce resistance. But Mexico City fell to Scott in September 1847. America had won the War with Mexico.

▲ **SEQUENCE EVENTS** Explain the events that led to the war with Mexico.

Impact of Victory

▼ **KEY QUESTION** What Mexican territory had the United States gained by 1853?

For Mexico, the war marked an ugly milestone in its relations with the United States. For the United States, the end of the war meant the fulfillment of manifest destiny—expansion of the nation from the Atlantic to the Pacific.

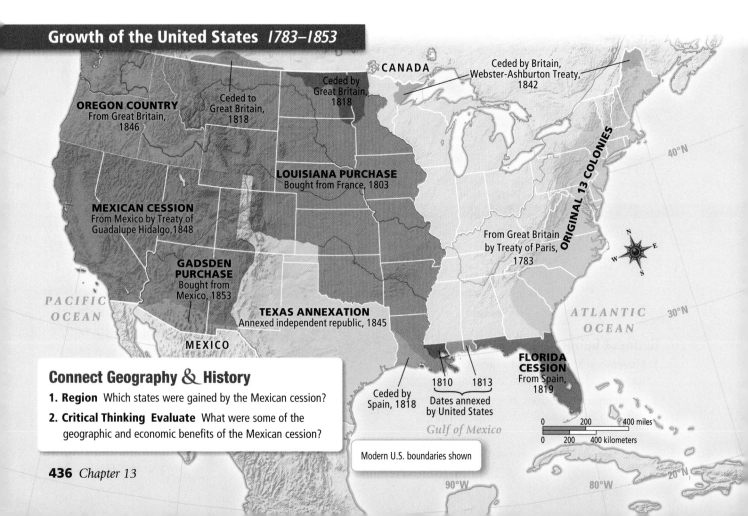

Growth of the United States *1783–1853*

CANADA

Ceded by Britain, Webster-Ashburton Treaty, 1842

OREGON COUNTRY From Great Britain, 1846

Ceded to Great Britain, 1818

Ceded by Great Britain, 1818

LOUISIANA PURCHASE Bought from France, 1803

MEXICAN CESSION From Mexico by Treaty of Guadalupe Hidalgo, 1848

ORIGINAL 13 COLONIES

From Great Britain by Treaty of Paris, 1783

40°N

GADSDEN PURCHASE Bought from Mexico, 1853

PACIFIC OCEAN

TEXAS ANNEXATION Annexed independent republic, 1845

ATLANTIC OCEAN

30°N

MEXICO

FLORIDA CESSION From Spain, 1819

Ceded by Spain, 1818

1810   1813
Dates annexed by United States

Gulf of Mexico

0   200   400 miles
0   200   400 kilometers

Modern U.S. boundaries shown

Connect Geography & History

1. **Region** Which states were gained by the Mexican cession?

2. **Critical Thinking Evaluate** What were some of the geographic and economic benefits of the Mexican cession?

90°W   80°W   20°N

From Sea to Shining Sea In February 1848, the war ended with the **Treaty of Guadalupe Hidalgo** (gwah•duh•LOOP•ay hih•DAHL•go). The loss was a bitter defeat. Many Mexicans felt that the United States had provoked the war in the hope of gaining Mexican territory. In this treaty Mexico

- recognized that Texas was part of the United States
- agreed to the Rio Grande as the border between the two nations
- gave up a vast region known as the **Mexican cession**— including Texas—amounting to almost one-half of present-day Mexico

In return the United States promised to protect the 80,000 Mexicans living in Texas and the Mexican cession. Some Mexicans, however, saw themselves as minorities in a nation with a strange language, culture, and legal system. Others taught new settlers how to develop the land for farming, ranching, and mining. Eventually, a rich new culture resulted from the blend of many cultures.

In 1853, Mexico sold one last strip of land, called the Gadsden Purchase, to the United States for $10 million. The U.S. wanted the land, now part of southern New Mexico and Arizona, for a southern transcontinental railroad. The United States now stretched "from sea to shining sea."

Frederic Remington painted this colorful portrait of a Mexican cowboy, *A Vaquero*, in the late nineteenth century.

 SUMMARIZE Describe the territory the United States gained from Mexico by 1853.

 Michigan Grade Level Content Expectations *Review*

ONLINE QUIZ
For test practice, go to
Interactive Review @ ClassZone.com

TERMS & NAMES

1. Explain the importance of

- James K. Polk
- manifest destiny
- Zachary Taylor
- Bear Flag Revolt
- Treaty of Guadalupe Hidalgo
- Mexican cession

USING YOUR READING NOTES

2. Sequence Events Complete the diagram you started at the beginning of this section.

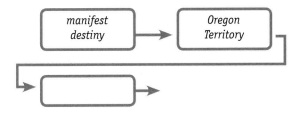

KEY IDEAS

3. Why did Britain and Mexico oppose American expansion?

4. How did the acquisitions of Oregon and the Mexican cession contribute to manifest destiny?

CRITICAL THINKING

5. Analyze Traveling along the Santa Fe Trail, General Kearny and his army sang songs like this one:

❝ Old Colonel Kearny, you can bet
Will keep the boys in motion,
Till Yankee Land include the sand
On the Pacific Ocean. ❞

How does this song support the idea of manifest destiny?

6. (Writing) **Political Cartoon** It is 1853. The Gadsden Purchase has just been completed. Create a political cartoon that comments on America's belief in manifest destiny.

▶ Key Ideas

BEFORE, YOU LEARNED

Victory in a War with Mexico allowed Americans to expand the country across the continent.

NOW YOU WILL LEARN

The discovery of gold in California in 1848 led to a population increase and statehood.

▶ Vocabulary

TERMS & NAMES

forty-niner person who went to California to find gold in 1849

Californios settlers of Spanish or Mexican descent who populated California

Mariano Vallejo a prosperous *Californio* who lost a lot of property after American settlement

James Marshall carpenter who discovered gold in California in 1848

California gold rush migration of thousands of settlers to California in search of gold

BACKGROUND VOCABULARY

migration movement of people from one country or locality to another

Visual Vocabulary
forty-niner

▶ Reading Strategy

Re-create the diagram shown at right. As you read and respond to the **KEY QUESTIONS**, use the chart to note important events and their effects. Add boxes or start a new diagram as needed.

 See Skillbuilder Handbook, page R7.

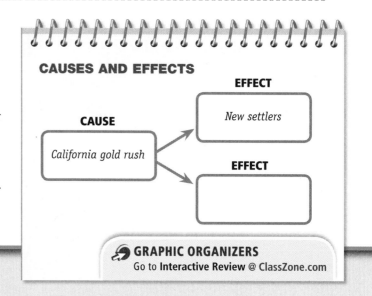

CAUSES AND EFFECTS

CAUSE

California gold rush

EFFECT

New settlers

EFFECT

GRAPHIC ORGANIZERS
Go to **Interactive Review** @ ClassZone.com

The California Gold Rush

8 – U4.2.1.5 Comparing Northeast and the South – immigration and the growth of nativism

8 – U4.2.4 Consequences of Expansion – Develop an argument based on evidence about the positive and negative consequences of territorial and economic expansion on American Indians, the institution of slavery, and the relations between free and slaveholding states.

One American's Story

Luzena Wilson said of the year 1849, "The gold excitement spread like wildfire." That year, **James Marshall** had discovered gold in California. Luzena's husband became a **forty-niner**—someone who went to California to find gold, starting in 1849. Luzena went to California with her husband. She found that women were rare in California. Shortly after she arrived, a miner offered her five dollars for her baked biscuits. Shocked, she just stared at him. He quickly doubled his offer and paid in gold. Finding she could make money by taking care of miners, Luzena opened a hotel.The gold rush boosted California's economy and changed the nation's history.

A Discovery Changes California

🔻 **KEY QUESTION** What led to the rapid settlement in California?

Before the forty-niners came, California was populated by as many as 150,000 Native Americans and 6,000 *Californios*—settlers of Spanish or Mexican descent. Many *Californios* lived on huge cattle ranches.

The Rush for Gold On January 24, 1848, just one month before Mexico lost California to the United States, a carpenter named James Marshall made an important discovery. While building a sawmill in northern California, he saw a shiny stone in the nearby American River. He later said, "My eye was caught by a glimpse of something shining. . . . It made my heart thump for I felt certain it was gold." It was indeed. Marshall's discovery led to one of the greatest **migrations**—movements of persons from one country or locality to another—in American history, as thousands from all over the world poured into California to make their fortunes.

In 1849, people from all over California and the United States raced to the American River—starting the **California gold rush.** A gold rush occurs when large numbers of people move to a site where gold has been found.

These prospectors were residents of a mining camp in Auburn Ravine, California, in the mid-1800s.

Mariano Vallejo (*inset*), a *Californio*, was the proud owner of a large California estate (*top*). **What major migration changed the *Californio* way of life?**

Miners soon found gold in other streams flowing out of the Sierra Nevada. The military governor of California estimated that the region held enough gold to "pay the cost of the present war with Mexico a hundred times over." He sent this news to Washington with a box of gold dust as proof.

The following year thousands of gold seekers set out to make their fortunes. A forty-niner who wished to reach California from the East had a choice of three routes, all of them dangerous. 1) Sail 18,000 miles around South America and up the Pacific coast—enduring storms, seasickness, and spoiled food. 2) Sail to the narrow Isthmus of Panama, cross overland (and risk catching a deadly tropical disease), and then sail to California. 3) Travel the trails across North America—braving rivers, prairies, mountains, and all the hardships of the trail. Because the venture was so hard, most gold seekers were young men.

Changes for *Californios* James Marshall's discovery of gold in 1848 did little to improve the lot of the *Californios*. Before the gold rush, many *Californio* families had prospered when the Mexican government took away the land that once belonged to the Spanish missions in California.

One important *Californio* was **Mariano Vallejo**. He was a member of one of the oldest Spanish families in America, and owned 250,000 acres of land. Vallejo's nephew proudly described the heritage of the *Californios* as "the pioneers of the Pacific coast." The gold rush found *Californios* challenged by a new wave of pioneers.

The Gold Seekers About two-thirds of the forty-niners were Americans. Most of these were white men. However, Native Americans, free blacks, and enslaved African Americans also worked the mines.

Thousands of experienced miners came from Sonora in Mexico. Other foreign miners came from Europe, South America, Australia, and China. Most of the Chinese miners were peasant farmers who fled hardships in China. By the end of 1851, one of every ten immigrants was Chinese.

The Chinese would often take over sites that American miners had left because the easy gold was gone. Through steady, hard work, the Chinese made these "played-out" sites yield profits. Some Americans envied the success of the Chinese and made fun of their different customs. As the numbers of Chinese miners grew, American resentment toward them also increased.

The mining camps began as rows of tents along the streams flowing out of the Sierra Nevada. Gradually the tents gave way to rough wooden buildings that housed stores and saloons. Camp gossip told of miners who got rich overnight by finding eight-pound nuggets, but in reality, few miners got rich. Exhaustion, poor food, and disease all damaged the miners' health. Not only was acquiring gold brutally difficult, but the miners had to pay very high prices for basic supplies.

▲ **EVALUATE** Explain the events that led to fast settlement in California.

Final Impact of the Gold Rush

🔻 **KEY QUESTION** What was the final impact of the gold rush on California?

The gold rush peaked in 1852. While it lasted, about 250,000 people flooded into California. This huge migration caused economic growth that changed California permanently.

Opportunities and Turmoil By 1849, California had enough people to apply for statehood. It was admitted as a free state in 1850. Its constitution banned slavery, but it did not grant African Americans the right to vote.

For some people, California's statehood proved to be the opportunity of a lifetime. An enslaved woman, Nancy Gooch, gained her freedom because of the law against slavery. Then she worked to buy the freedom of her children in Missouri. Eventually, the Gooch family became so prosperous that they bought Sutter's sawmill, where James Marshall first found the gold that started California's gold rush.

The population explosion ruined many *Californios*. The newcomers did not respect *Californios* or their legal rights. In many cases, Americans seized their property. Mariano Vallejo lost all but 300 acres of his huge estate. Yet the Spanish heritage plays a prominent role in California culture today.

CONNECT ➦ *To Today*

ECONOMIC OPPORTUNITY

The discovery of gold brought tens of thousands of settlers west to find prosperity. Many newcomers chose to open businesses to meet the demands of what became a booming region.

Today, economic opportunity doesn't necessarily require people to move to another state, region, or country. Instead, many companies use the Internet to communicate with employees and customers at home and overseas. This practice is known as offshoring or outsourcing.

A number of large corporations outsource some or most of their work. Consequently, many overseas economies have ballooned since going into the offshore business. Huge western investments in outsourcing are bringing new prosperity to many developing nations. India is one example of successful offshoring. (*right*) Indian office workers work in a time zone 10.5 hours ahead of Eastern Standard Time. This means more time to conduct business.

CRITICAL THINKING

1. **Make Inferences** Why might a company hire workers in a different country and/or a different time zone?

2. **Evaluate** How might outsourced programs affect American education and the American workplace?

Native Americans and Foreigners Thousands of Native Americans died from diseases brought by the newcomers. Settlers killed thousands more. The impact on the environment also affected Native Americans' use of the land. Rivers that had been their waterways and fishing sites were diverted and polluted. Hunting grounds were taken over by settlers. By 1870, California's Native American population had fallen from 150,000 to about 58,000.

Once the easy-to-find gold was gone, American miners began to force Native Americans and miners such as Mexicans and Chinese out of the gold fields to reduce competition. This practice increased after California became a state in 1850.

Foreign Miners Tax One of the first acts of the California state legislature was to pass the Foreign Miners Tax, which imposed a tax of $20 a month on miners from other countries. That was more than most could afford to pay. As the tax collectors arrived in the camps, most foreigners left.

Driven from the mines, the Chinese opened shops, restaurants, and laundries. So many Chinese owned businesses in San Francisco that their neighborhood became known as Chinatown, as it still is today.

CONNECT to the Essential Question

How did westward expansion transform the nation?

EVENTS	EFFECTS
1820–1840 Westward trails move thousands to new territories	Native Americans are displaced
Austin and others colonize Texas	Earlier settlers are pushed aside
Texans revolt against Mexico	Republic of Texas is proclaimed
1841–1848 Texas annexed as a slave state	War with Mexico
Mexican cession	Almost 50% of Mexican territory is acquired by United States
1849–1853 California Gold Rush	California enters Union as a free state
U.S. transcontinental railroad planned	Gadsden Purchase completes expansion of the United States

CRITICAL THINKING **Clarify** Which event fulfilled the nation's "manifest destiny"?

Economic Effects of Statehood The port city of San Francisco grew to become a center of banking, manufacturing, shipping, and trade. Its population exploded from around 400 in 1845 to 35,000 in 1850. And, in response to increasing demand for food, Sacramento became the center of a rich farming region.

The population explosion also created a huge demand for water. California's complicated water system is a legacy of the inventiveness and skill of the forty-niners. The miners needed lots of water to pan for gold. (See chart at right.)

On a national level, California's application for statehood created turmoil. Before 1850, there were an equal number of free states and slave states. Southerners feared that because the statehood of California made free states outnumber slave states, Northerners might use their majority to abolish slavery. Conflict over this issue would threaten the very survival of the Union.

▲ **CAUSES AND EFFECTS** Describe the events that led to California statehood.

CALIFORNIA WATER RIGHTS

The forty-niners cleverly diverted water for their needs—laying the groundwork for the complex system of dams and canals serving California today. There are three basic categories of water rights in California: Riparian, Appropriative, and Public Trust uses.

RIPARIAN RIGHTS
allows a landowner to use the water flowing past his or her property; takes priority over other claims.

APPROPRIATIVE RIGHTS
allows use of water channelled well away from its original source; based on forty-niners' "finders keepers" law

PUBLIC TRUST DOMAIN
protects fish and wildlife; public recreation areas— such as parks, streams and lakes.

Michigan Grade Level Content Expectations *Review*

🖱 **ONLINE QUIZ**
For test practice, go to
Interactive Review @ ClassZone.com

TERMS & NAMES
1. Explain the importance of
- forty-niner • *Californio* • Mariano Vallejo
- James Marshall • California Gold Rush

USING YOUR READING NOTES
2. Causes and Effects Complete the diagram you started at the beginning of this section.

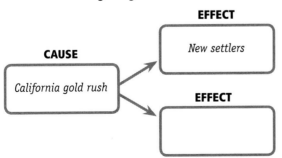

CAUSE
California gold rush

EFFECT
New settlers

EFFECT

KEY IDEAS
3. Why did the gold rush come to an end?

4. Why was California poised to upset the balance of the United States?

CRITICAL THINKING
5. Summarize What were some of the cultural conflicts caused by the influx of new settlers into California?

6. Evaluate What impact did the gold rush have on the people who lived in California before 1849?

7. Recognize Effects What effect did the gold rush have on the growth of California?

8. Writing Report Use the Internet to research women or foreign immigrants during the California gold rush. Write a brief report explaining how they created opportunities and shaped their new communities.

CALIFORNIA'S GOLD RUSH

Discovery of gold brought thousands of settlers to California from all over the world. What were some of the effects of rapid growth?

FORTY-NINERS

Water vastly eased the prospectors' work. At first, they waded in streams sloshing water around dirt and gravel in metal pans. Soon they were shoveling gravel into a sluice—a series of long boxes with ridges on the bottom. Rushing water carried lightweight materials along with it. Heavy gold sank to the bottom and was trapped between the ridges. Within two years, forty-niners were damming rivers and erecting simple storage reservoirs for the water so vital to their existence.

Teens in History

A YOUNG SETTLER

Elizabeth Keegan arrived in Marysville, California, on September 17, 1852. Two months later, she wrote to her brother and sister still back in St. Louis:

"See what gold can do (it) brings men from all nations here to this distance shore to make their fortune [and] many go home worse than when they came [but] others have wealth countless wealth ..."

DIVERSITY

Many of the California migrants came to make their fortunes. Most were disappointed, but they stayed to establish thriving communities.

Chinese miner

Activity

Find the hidden words!

Find the ten words scrambled below—all are connected to the gold rush.

```
B Z R V H B N I H O N B
N T H I P U S V I Y E N
S M Q P V P A N I R G Z
X L M I N E R U L W O X
D A U S M O R G A L A C
C X X I F N E G E C N L
E X V I C O I E X U B O
R E L T T E S T I V N S
S A W M I L L M M I X A
C R O O W B B J U G P O
```

Chapter Summary

① Key Idea
Thousands of adventurers and pioneers followed trails to the West to settle the land and make their fortunes.

② Key Idea
Conflicts between American settlers and the government of Mexico led Texas to revolt and win independence from Mexico in 1836.

③ Key Idea
Victory in a war with Mexico allowed Americans to expand the nation across the continent.

④ Key Idea
The discovery of gold in California in 1848 led to a population increase and statehood.

For detailed Review and Study Notes go to **Interactive Review** @ ClassZone.com

Name Game

Use the Terms & Names list to complete each sentence online or on your own paper.

1. The Mormons settled in Utah for religious reasons.

2. _____ discovered the South Pass through the Rocky Mountains.

3. A person who went to California in search of gold was called a _____ .

4. The _____ was a route across the Rocky Mountains.

5. The victorious general at the Battle of the Alamo. _____

6. The _____ was a nickname for the republic of Texas.

7. _____ commanded the Texas Army at the battle of San Jacinto.

8. In the 1820s, people of Mexican heritage living in Texas were called _____ .

9. _____ was elected the eleventh president of the United States in 1844.

10. _____ was the belief that the United States was meant to expand from coast to coast.

A. Santa Fe Trail
B. *Tejanos*
C. Santa Anna
D. Jedediah Smith
E. Manifest Destiny
F. James K. Polk
G. Mormons
H. Jim Beckwourth
I. Forty-Niner
J. Sam Houston
L. California Gold Rush
M. Oregon Trail
N. Lone Star Republic
O. Zachary Taylor
P. Bear Flag Revolt

Activities

CROSSWORD PUZZLE

Use the online crossword puzzle to show what you know about western expansion.

ACROSS

1. _____ founded American colony in Spanish Texas.

FLIPCARD

Use the online flipcards to quiz yourself on the terms and names introduced in this chapter.

I was a *Tejano* who fought for Texan independence.

ANSWER
Juan Seguín

VOCABULARY

Explain the significance of each of the following.

1. Mexican cession
2. Sam Houston
3. James K. Polk
4. Brigham Young
5. Mariano Vallejo
6. James Marshall
7. Jedediah Smith
8. Stephen Austin
9. Zachary Taylor
10. Antonio López de Santa Anna

Choose the best answer from each pair.

11. Tensions resulted between these people and American settlers in Texas. (*Tejanos/Californios*)

12. This resulted in massive migration to California. (California Gold Rush/Treaty of Guadalupe Hidalgo)

13. American goal reached after post-war settlements with Mexico. (manifest destiny/Mexican cession)

14. William Becknell helped open this trail to pioneers. (Oregon Trail/Santa Fe Trail)

15. This American rebellion was against Mexican rule in California. (Bear Flag Revolt/Gadsden Purchase)

KEY IDEAS

➊ Trails West 1810–1853 (pages 418–423)

16. What were three reasons why people moved west?

17. What were the three main trails that led to the West?

➋ The Texas Revolution (pages 426–431)

18. Why were Texans unhappy with Mexican rule?

19. Why were the Battles of the Alamo and San Jacinto important to the Texas revolution?

➌ The War with Mexico (pages 432–437)

20. What areas did the United States gain as a result of Americans' belief in manifest destiny?

21. What lands did the United States acquire as a result of the Treaty of Guadalupe Hidalgo?

➍ The California Gold Rush (pages 438–443)

22. Who were four groups of forty-niners?

23. What were three ways California changed because of the gold rush?

CRITICAL THINKING

24. **Analyze Causes** How did Mexico's independence from Spain lead to changes in Texas?

25. **Make Inferences** Of the masses of pioneers moving west, in what ways was the Mormon migration unique?

26. **Distinguish Fact from Opinion** How do you think Americans considered Native Americans during the expansion period? How does this relate to the belief in manifest destiny?

27. **Compare and Contrast** Create a table to compare and contrast life in California before and after the Gold Rush.

	Before Gold Rush	**After Gold Rush**
population	*Native Americans & Californians*	*forty-niners & migrants*
economy	*agriculture*	

28. **Make Generalizations** Think about the leaders discussed in this chapter. What characteristics did they have that made them good leaders?

29. **Draw Conclusions** How did the War with Mexico and the California gold rush contributed to the cultural diversity of the United States?

30. **Interpret Graphs** In what year did the population of those living west of the Appalachian Mountains account for about half of the total U.S. population?

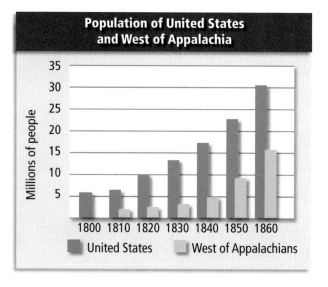

Population of United States and West of Appalachia

Millions of people

35
30
25
20
15
10
5

1800 1810 1820 1830 1840 1850 1860

■ United States   □ West of Appalachians

✓ **TEST PRACTICE**

• **Online Test Practice @ ClassZone.com**
• Use the **MEAP Strategies & Practice,** pages S1-S27, at the front of this book

DOCUMENT-BASED QUESTIONS

Analyze each document, and answer the question that follows.

DOCUMENT 1

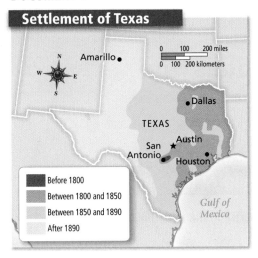

Settlement of Texas

Amarillo •

Dallas •

TEXAS

San Antonio • ★ Austin
• Houston

Gulf of Mexico

0   100   200 miles
0   100   200 kilometers

Before 1800
Between 1800 and 1850
Between 1850 and 1890
After 1890

DOCUMENT 2

PRIMARY SOURCE

❝ The determination of our slaveholding President to prosecute the war, and the probability of his success in wringing from the people men and money to carry it on, is made evident. . . . None seem willing to take their stand for peace at all risks; and all seem willing that the war should be carried on, in some form or other. ❞

—Frederick Douglass in *The North Star*, January 21, 1848

1 Examine the map and the quotation. Both documents illustrate the effects of which U.S. policies?

  A policies toward immigration

  B policies toward manifest destiny

  C policies toward slavery

  D policies toward land speculators

YOU BE THE HISTORIAN

31. Causes & Effects Why, after the gold rush ended, did so many people choose to stay in California rather than return to their home state or country?

32. What If? Suppose the United States had lost the War with Mexico. How might this have changed the history of the territory gained from Mexico?

33. Draw Conclusions How did women and people of different racial, ethnic, or national groups contribute to the California gold rush?

34. Summarize How did the War with Mexico escalate the disagreement over slavery?

35. Connect Geography & History How did the opening of the West affect the economy of that region?

36. Connect *to* Today Large numbers of settlers moved west in the 1840s and after. What factors cause people to move from one part of the country to another today?

Answer the
ESSENTIAL QUESTION
How did westward expansion transform the nation?

Written Response Write a two- to three-paragraph response to the Essential Question. Be sure to consider the key ideas of each section as well as the most important factors that led to the expansion of the United States. Use the Response Rubric below to guide your thinking and writing.

Response Rubric
A strong response will include

• major discoveries and events that led to westward expansion
• discussion of manifest destiny and political issues
• analysis of key leaders
• knowledge of geography and territorial holdings

A New Spirit of Change

1830–1860

ESSENTIAL QUESTION

How did immigration and social reform change the nation in the mid-1800s?

CONNECT Geography & History

How did immigration affect America in the mid-1800s?

Think about:

1 how many immigrants came just from Germany and Ireland

2 the variety of cultures and beliefs they brought to America

3 where most immigrants settled—Northeastern cities and the Midwest

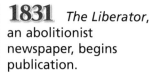

This early-19th-century image shows stagecoaches in lower Manhattan.

An Irish famine memorial in Westchester County, N.Y.

1840 The World Anti-Slavery Convention is held in London.

1830

1831 *The Liberator,* an abolitionist newspaper, begins publication.

1839 Mississippi passes the first U.S. law giving women rights to their own property and wages.

1843 Dorothea Dix asks the Massachusetts legislature to improve care for the mentally ill.

▼

Effect New laws create widespread changes in institutional care.

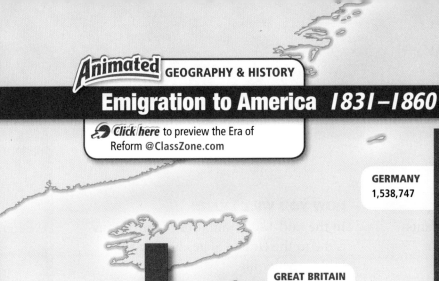

Click here to preview the Era of Reform @ClassZone.com

Animated GEOGRAPHY & HISTORY
Emigration to America 1831–1860

GERMANY
1,538,747

NORWAY and SWEDEN
36,035

IRELAND
940,260

GREAT BRITAIN
339,303

North Sea

ATLANTIC OCEAN

FRANCE
199,195

SWITZERLAND
34,476

A 1978 stamp honoring Harriet Tubman

Harriet Tubman

Black Heritage USA 13c

1848 Women demand rights at the Seneca Falls Convention.

1849 Harriet Tubman escapes from slavery.

▼

Effect Tubman aids runaway slaves on the Underground Railroad.

Women's-rights advocate Amelia Bloomer promoted comfortable clothing for women.

1860

Abraham Lincoln is elected president.

Reading for Understanding

▶ Key Ideas

BEFORE, YOU LEARNED
In colonial times, waves of immigrants created a diverse society in America.

NOW YOU WILL LEARN
In the mid-1800s, millions of Europeans came to the United States hoping to build a better life.

▶ Vocabulary

TERMS & NAMES

"push" factor a reason or force that causes people to leave their native land

"pull" factor a reason or force that causes people to choose to move to a new place

Know-Nothing Party political party in the United States during the 1850s that was against recent immigrants and Roman Catholics

Visual Vocabulary
Know-Nothing Party flag

BACKGROUND VOCABULARY

emigrant person who leaves a country

immigrant person who settles in a new country

steerage the cheapest deck on a ship

famine (FAM•ihn) severe food shortage leading to starvation

prejudice (PREHJ•uh•dihs) a negative opinion that is not based on facts

nativist native-born American who wanted to eliminate foreign influence

▶ Reading Strategy

Re-create the diagram shown at right. As you read and respond to the **KEY QUESTIONS**, use the center oval to record the main idea, and use the outer ovals to note important details. Add ovals or start a new diagram as needed.

 See Skillbuilder Handbook, page R4.

MAIN IDEAS AND DETAILS

abundant land

"pull" factors drew immigrants

GRAPHIC ORGANIZERS
Go to **Interactive Review** @ ClassZone.com

The Hopes of Immigrants

8 – U4.2.1.5 Comparing Northeast and the South – immigration and the growth of nativism
8 – U6.1.1.2 America at Century's End – population, including immigration, reactions to immigrants, and the changing demographic structure of rural and urban America

One American's Story

In 1830, English weaver John Downe became an **emigrant**, or person who leaves a country. Downe left England alone to work in New York, where he awaited his family's arrival.

PRIMARY SOURCE

❝ You will find a few inconveniences in crossing the Atlantic, but it will not be long, and when that is over, all is over, for I know you will like America.

America is not like England, for here no man thinks of himself as your superior. . . . This is a country where a man can stand as a man, and where he can enjoy the fruits of his own exertions [work], with rational liberty to its fullest extent. ❞

—John Downe, letter to his wife, August 12, 1830

The Bay and Harbor of New York, by Samuel B. Waugh

Emigrants—mainly from Europe—flocked to America during the mid-1800s. Like Downe, most left hoping to build a better life. After arrival in America, they became **immigrants**, or people who settle in a new country.

Patterns of Immigration

🔻 **KEY QUESTION** What attracted people to America in the mid-1800s?

Most immigrants endured hardships to reach America. Although some brought their families, many men, like Downe, went through the difficult journey alone. Most immigrants made the ocean voyage in **steerage**, the cheapest deck on a ship. In steerage, conditions were crowded and unhealthy. Many passengers became ill or died on the journey.

Why People Migrated What drew immigrants to America? Historians talk about **"push" factors** and **"pull" factors**. These forces push people out of their native land and pull them toward a new place. One push factor was population growth—a boom in population had made Europe overcrowded. Another push factor was crop failure. Poor harvests brought widespread hunger. Three main pull factors lured people to America:

- freedom
- economic opportunity
- abundant land

Germans Pursue Economic Opportunity The Germans were the largest immigrant group of the 1800s. They settled in cities as well as on farms and the frontier. Many were drawn to the fertile and newly available lands of Wisconsin, which was organized as a territory in 1836. Thousands more formed German-speaking communities in Texas.

Germans opened businesses as bakers, butchers, carpenters, printers, and tailors. Some, like John Jacob Bausch and Henry Lomb, achieved great success. In 1853, they started a firm to make eyeglasses and other lenses. Their company became the world's largest lens maker. Some German immigrants were Jews, many of whom worked as traveling salespeople. They brought pins, needles, pots—and news—to frontier homes and mining camps. In time, some opened their own stores. Many German Jews settled in cities.

German immigrants strongly influenced American culture. Many things we think of as originating in America came from Germany, such as kindergartens, gymnasiums, the Christmas tree, and the hamburger and frankfurter.

COMPARING *Push and Pull Factors*

The "push" factors of immigration pushed millions of people out of Europe and elsewhere in the 1800s. "Pull" factors drew many of them to the United States.

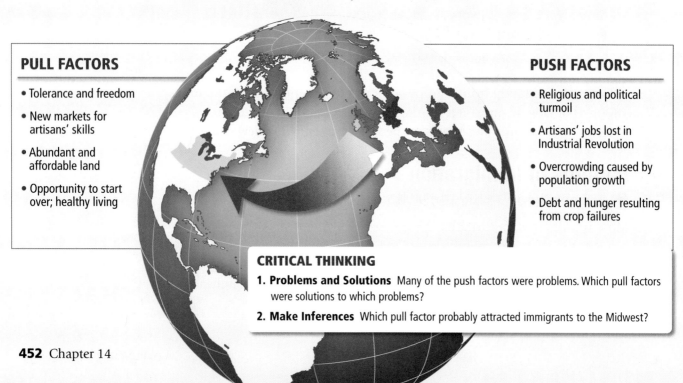

PULL FACTORS

- Tolerance and freedom
- New markets for artisans' skills
- Abundant and affordable land
- Opportunity to start over; healthy living

PUSH FACTORS

- Religious and political turmoil
- Artisans' jobs lost in Industrial Revolution
- Overcrowding caused by population growth
- Debt and hunger resulting from crop failures

CRITICAL THINKING

1. **Problems and Solutions** Many of the push factors were problems. Which pull factors were solutions to which problems?

2. **Make Inferences** Which pull factor probably attracted immigrants to the Midwest?

Immigrants Move Westward In the mid-1800s, public land in America was sold for $1.25 an acre. The promise of cheap land lured thousands of European immigrants, especially to territories in the Midwest.

Thousands of Scandinavians fled poverty in their homeland and moved to Minnesota and Wisconsin. Like Scandinavia, these states had forests, lakes, and cold winters. A high proportion of Scandinavian immigrants became farmers. Meanwhile, land shortages in Great Britain motivated thousands of British farmers to seek new opportunities in America. They, too, helped to make the Midwest a region known for farming. Many British artisans who felt squeezed out by the factory system also chose to emigrate.

The mid-1800s brought another major immigrant group: the Chinese. Most of the first Chinese immigrants went to California after the 1849 gold rush. By 1852, there were an estimated 25,000 Chinese in California. Most were miners, but some worked in agriculture and construction.

The Irish Flee Starvation Most Irish immigrants were Catholic. Protestant Britain had ruled Ireland for centuries—and controlled the Catholic majority by denying them rights. Irish Catholics could not vote, hold office, own land, or go to school. Because of the poverty produced by Britain's rule, some Irish had emigrated to America in the early 1800s.

In 1845, a disease attacked Ireland's main food crop, the potato. This caused a severe food shortage, or **famine** (FAM•in). The Irish Potato Famine killed 1 million people and forced many to emigrate. By 1855, an estimated 1.5 million people had left Ireland. Most went to North America, although some settled in Australia and Great Britain.

Connect *to the* **World**

The Potato Famine
In 1846, an Irish newspaper described famine victims "frantically rushing from their home and country, not with the idea of making fortunes in other lands, but to fly from a scene of suffering and death…"

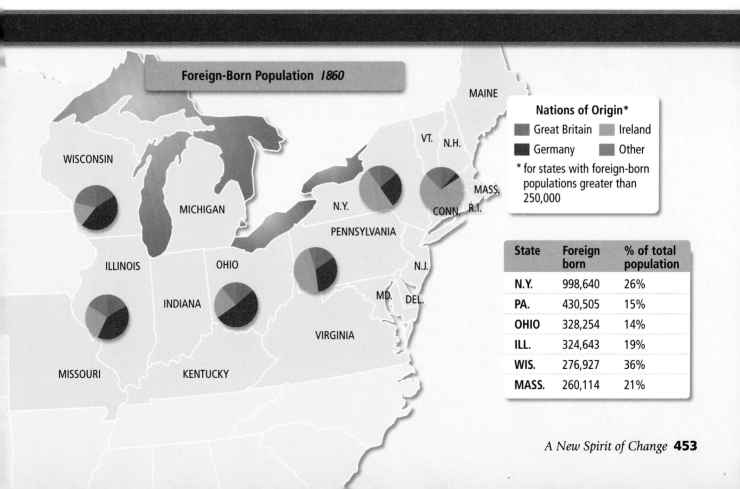

Foreign-Born Population *1860*

Nations of Origin*

- Great Britain
- Ireland
- Germany
- Other

* for states with foreign-born populations greater than 250,000

State	Foreign born	% of total population
N.Y.	998,640	26%
PA.	430,505	15%
OHIO	328,254	14%
ILL.	324,643	19%
WIS.	276,927	36%
MASS.	260,114	21%

In America, Irish farmers became city-dwellers. Arriving with little or no savings, many of these immigrants had to settle in the port cities where their ships had docked. By 1850, the Irish made up one-fourth of the population in Boston, New York, Philadelphia, and Baltimore.

The uneducated Irish immigrants came with few skills and had to take low-paying, back-breaking jobs. Irish women took in washing or worked as servants. The men built canals and railroads across America. So many Irish men died doing this dangerous work that people said there was "an Irish-man buried under every [railroad] tie." The Irish competed with free African Americans for the jobs that nobody else wanted. Both groups had few other choices in America in the 1800s.

▲ **SUMMARIZE** Explain what attracted immigrants to America in the mid-1800s.

During the mid-1800s, thousands of new immigrants settled in the crowded New York City neighborhood known as Five Points.

America Adjusts to Immigrants

▼ **KEY QUESTION** What was life like for the new immigrants?

The huge numbers of immigrants caused overcrowding in the cities. This population explosion alarmed many Americans. However, some formed organizations to help immigrants adapt to their new country. Soon, like all immigrants before them, the new arrivals began to influence American society and culture.

Life for the New Arrivals Immigrants flocked to American cities. So did many native-born Americans, who left rural areas hoping to make a better living in new manufacturing jobs. The North, with its higher wages and greater economic opportunity, attracted many more immigrants than the South. Because the South was a plantation economy based on slave labor, it offered fewer opportunities for free laborers. Between 1800 and 1830, New York's population jumped from 60,489 to 202,589. Both St. Louis and Cincinnati doubled their populations every 10 years between 1800 and 1850.

Rapid urban growth brought problems. Without enough space for newcomers, greedy landlords packed tenants into buildings. Cramped living quarters allowed little sunlight and fresh air, and outdoor toilets overflowed, spreading disease. In such depressing urban neighborhoods, crime flourished. Cities were unprepared for these problems. Most lacked a public police force, fire department, and adequate sewers.

Most immigrant groups set up aid societies to assist newcomers from their country. Many city politicians also offered to help immigrants find housing and work, hoping to earn votes in exchange.

Opposition to Immigration Some native-born Americans believed that immigrants were too foreign to learn American ways. Others feared that immigrants might outnumber natives. Immigrants faced anger and **prejudice**—a negative opinion that is not based on facts. For example, some Protestants believed that Catholics threatened democracy. Those Protestants feared that the Pope, the head of the Roman Catholic Church, was plotting to overthrow democracy in America.

People who want to eliminate foreign influence are known as **nativists**. In the mid-1800s, some American nativists refused to hire immigrants and put up signs like "No Irish need apply." In cities such as New York and Boston, nativists formed a secret society. Members promised not to vote for Catholics or immigrants running for political office. If asked about their society, they said, "I know nothing about it."

In the 1850s, nativists started a political party called the **Know-Nothing Party**. It wanted to ban Catholics and the foreign-born from holding office. It also called for a cut in immigration and a 21-year-wait to become an American citizen. The Know-Nothings did get six governors elected. But their Northern and Southern branches couldn't agree on the issue of slavery, and they disappeared quickly as a national party.

A nineteenth-century advertisement for "Know Nothing Soap" **What might the Native Americans represent?**

 MAKE GENERALIZATIONS Describe what life was like for new immigrants.

Michigan Grade Level Content Expectations *Review*

ONLINE QUIZ For test practice, go to **Interactive Review @ ClassZone.com**

TERMS & NAMES

1. Explain the importance of
- "push" factor
- "pull" factor
- Know-Nothing Party

USING YOUR READING NOTES

2. Main Ideas and Details Use the diagram you started at the beginning of the section to record details about immigration. Note which groups came and why, and where they settled.

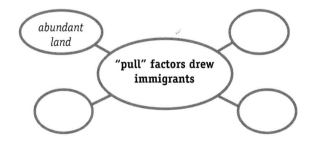

KEY IDEAS

3. What difficulties did immigrants face in the United States?

4. How did the arrival of immigrants affect U.S. cities?

CRITICAL THINKING

5. Make Inferences Why were immigrants willing to endure the hardships of coming to America?

6. Analyze Primary Sources In 1841, British novelist Charles Dickens described the huts in which some Irish railroad workers in New York lived:

❝ The best were poor protection from the weather; the worst let in the wind and rain . . . some had neither door nor window; some had nearly fallen down. ❞

Do you think these immigrants were better off in America than in Ireland? Explain.

7. **Writing** **Letter** Research the Irish Potato Famine. Write a letter to friends in America that describes life in Ireland and why you want to join them in America.

Reading for Understanding

▶ Key Ideas

BEFORE, YOU LEARNED

In the mid-1800s, millions of Europeans came to the United States hoping to build a better life.

NOW YOU WILL LEARN

A 19th-century religious revival launched movements to reform education and society.

▶ Vocabulary

TERMS & NAMES

Second Great Awakening renewal of religious faith in the 1790s and early 1800s

temperance movement campaign to stop the drinking of alcohol

Shaker member of a Christian sect that practiced communal living and did not allow marriage and childbearing

Horace Mann reformer who advocated improving education

Dorothea Dix reformer who was a pioneer in the movement for better treatment of the mentally ill

BACKGROUND VOCABULARY

labor union group of workers who band together to seek better working conditions

strike to stop work to demand better working conditions

REVIEW

evangelicalism the doctrine, or belief, that each person can experience a sudden conversion and experience a new spiritual relationship with God

▶ Reading Strategy

Re-create the problem-solution chart at right. As you read and respond to the **KEY QUESTIONS**, use the chart to organize the problems reformers identified in society and the solutions they proposed.

 See Skillbuilder Handbook, page R9.

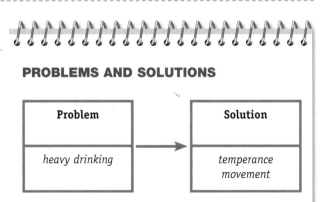

PROBLEMS AND SOLUTIONS

Problem	Solution
heavy drinking →	*temperance movement*

GRAPHIC ORGANIZERS
Go to **Interactive Review** @ ClassZone.com

Reforming American Society

 8 – U4.3.1 Explain the origins of the American education system and Horace Mann's campaign for free compulsory public education.
8 – U4.3.5 Evaluate the role of religion in shaping antebellum reform movements.

One American's Story

In the mid-1800s, many Americans had ideas for creating a better society in their new nation. Mary Lyon, the founder of Mount Holyoke Seminary in Massachusetts, advocated college-level education for women. Seeing the first building go up at her school gave Lyon a sense of awe.

PRIMARY SOURCE

❝ . . . The stones and brick and mortar speak a language which vibrates through my very soul. I have indeed lived to see the time when a body of gentlemen have ventured to lay the corner stone of an edifice [building] which . . . will be an institution for the education of females. . . . This will be an era in female education. ❞

—Mary Lyon, letter, October 7, 1836

Mary Lyon

In this section, you will learn how individuals like Lyon called on Americans to reform, or improve, themselves and their society.

A Spirit of Revival

▼ **KEY QUESTION** How did religion and philosophy encourage people to improve society?

In the early 19th century, a reform movement swept through American society. This movement was inspired mainly by a religious revival, like the one that had changed American life a century before.

The Second Great Awakening The renewal of religious faith in the 1790s and early 1800s is called the **Second Great Awakening**. Unlike Puritans, who believed that only some people would be saved, revivalist preachers insisted that anyone could choose salvation. This idea appealed to Americans' sense of optimism and equality, and offered a new interpretation of Christianity.

Revival meetings—emotionally charged events in which religious leaders hoped to attract followers—spread quickly across the country. Many groups, such as Baptists and Methodists, gained converts during this time. Settlers in the West eagerly awaited revivalist preachers like Peter Cartwright, who spent more than 60 years preaching on the frontier. In Eastern cities, Charles Grandison Finney held large revival meetings. He preached that selfishness was sin and that faith led people to help others.

The spread of evangelical ideas awakened a spirit of reform. Many people began to believe that they could help to right the wrongs of the world.

Temperance pledges often featured inspiring pictures and mottoes. **What does the main picture suggest about the benefits of giving up alcohol?**

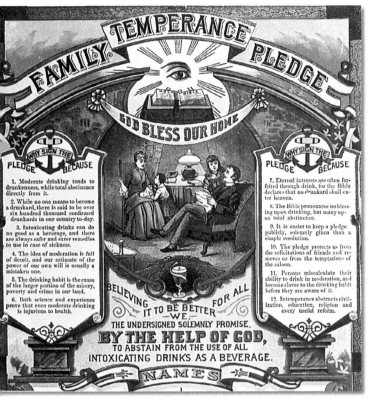

Temperance Heavy drinking was common in the early 1800s. One response to this problem was the **temperance movement**—a campaign to stop the drinking of alcohol. Some men spent most of their wages on alcohol, leaving their families poor. As a result, many women joined the movement.

Temperance workers handed out pamphlets urging people to stop drinking and gave plays dramatizing the evils of alcohol. They asked people to sign a pledge to not use alcohol. By 1838, a million had signed.

In 1851, Maine banned the sale of liquor. By 1855, 13 other states had passed similar laws. Most of these laws were later repealed. Still, the movement to ban alcohol remained strong, even into the 20th century.

Creating Ideal Societies Some people wanted society to start anew. They aimed to build an ideal society, called a utopia.

Religion led to some utopian experiments. The **Shakers** followed the beliefs of English immigrant Ann Lee, who preached that people should live in faith-centered communities. Shakers vowed not to marry or have children. They shared all their goods with each other and treated men and women as equals.

People called them Shakers because they shook with emotion during church services. Shakers set up communities in New York, New England, and on the frontier. Because they did not marry, Shakers depended on converts and adoption to keep their communities going. In the 1840s, Shakers had 6,000 members. In 2005, only four remained.

Not all utopian communities were based on religion. Two well-known experiments in communal living took place in New Harmony, Indiana, and Brook Farm, Massachusetts. However, these communities experienced conflicts and financial difficulties. They ended after only a few years.

▲ **EVALUATE** Explain how religion and philosophy encouraged people to try to improve society.

Workers' Rights

KEY QUESTION How did the labor movement try to improve working conditions?

Factory conditions were often unhealthy, and management could be unjust. By the 1830s, American workers had begun to demand improvements.

Factory Life Most factory workers labored 12 or 14 hours a day for six days a week. A typical workday began at five o'clock in the morning. It was not unusual for workers to spend most of the workday in dark, hot, crowded rooms with air so dirty that it was difficult to breathe. In the 1830s, many workers began to call for a ten-hour workday.

Hoping to increase profits, factory owners sometimes cut workers' pay and forced them to increase their pace. It was also legal to pay women and children lower wages than men in similar jobs. Partly for this reason, the majority of workers at the mills in Lowell, Massachusetts, were young women. Some of these women became active in the fight for workers' rights.

Organizing for Better Conditions The young women mill workers in Lowell, Massachusetts, started a **labor union**—a group of workers who band together to seek better working conditions. In 1836, the mill owners raised the rent of the company-owned boarding houses where the women lived. About 1,500 women went on **strike**, stopping work to demand better conditions. Eleven-year-old Harriet Hanson helped lead the strikers.

> **PRIMARY SOURCE**
>
> 66 I . . . started on ahead, saying, . . . 'I don't care what you do, I am going to turn out, whether anyone else does or not,' and I marched out, and was followed by the others. As I looked back at the long line that followed me, I was more proud than I have ever been since. 99
>
> —Harriet Hanson, quoted in Howard Zinn's *A People's History of the United States*

In 1835 and 1836, 140 strikes took place in the eastern United States alone. Some striking workers compared themselves to the American patriots who had fought for freedom in the Revolutionary War. In 1860, one group of workers began a strike on Washington's birthday.

Then the Panic of 1837 brought hard times economically. Jobs were scarce, and workers were afraid to cause trouble. The young labor movement fell apart. Even so, workers achieved a few goals. For example, in 1840 President Martin Van Buren ordered a ten-hour workday for government workers.

SUMMARIZE Explain how the labor movement tried to improve working conditions.

Connect *to the* **World**

By the 1830s, a labor movement had gathered strength in Great Britain. Like the American labor movement, it sought better conditions and a shorter workday.

About 800 women shoemakers march during a strike in Lynn, Massachusetts, in 1860.

History Makers

Horace Mann 1796–1859

Mann is remembered as "the father of the American common [public] school." He believed that education was "the balance wheel of the social machinery." As secretary of the Massachusetts board of education, Mann advanced his cause by reporting to the state legislature, lecturing widely, and writing for various publications. His efforts raised awareness of the value of public education. They also led to dramatic changes in Massachusetts and across the country, with increased public spending on education, higher teacher salaries, better books for students, advanced teacher training, and—ultimately—a more educated population.

COMPARING Leaders

Compare and Contrast As you read through the chapter, look for other reform leaders. Compare Mann's efforts to promote his cause with those of other leaders in this chapter.

 **ONLINE BIOGRAPHY** For more on Horace Mann, go to the **Research & Writing Center** @ ClassZone.com

Social Reform

🔻 **KEY QUESTION** What aspects of society did reformers try to change?

By the 1830s, the religious revival had sparked the rise of a reform movement. Social reformers campaigned to improve education, establish mental hospitals, and improve prisons.

Improving Education In the 1830s, Americans began to demand better schools. Massachusetts set up the first state board of education in 1837. Its leader, **Horace Mann**, called public education "the great equalizer" and argued for improving public educational opportunities. By 1850, most Northern states had opened public elementary schools.

Boston opened the first public high school in 1821. A few other Northern cities soon did the same. In addition, churches and other groups founded hundreds of private colleges in the following decades. Many were located in states carved from the Northwest Territory. These included Antioch and Oberlin Colleges in Ohio, Notre Dame in Indiana, and Northwestern University in Illinois.

Expanding Opportunities Women could not attend most colleges. An exception was Oberlin—the first college to accept women. From its founding in 1833, Oberlin admitted students regardless of race or sex. Until the late 1800s, however, it was rare for a woman to attend college.

African Americans also faced obstacles to getting an education. This was especially true in the South. Teaching an enslaved person to read was illegal in most of the Southern states. Enslaved African Americans who tried to learn to read were brutally punished. Even in the North, African-American children were barred from most public schools.

Few colleges accepted African Americans. The first African-American man to receive a college degree was Alexander Twilight in 1823. He later became a Vermont state legislator. Mary Jane Patterson was the first African-American woman to earn a college degree. She graduated from Oberlin in 1862 and became a teacher.

Care for the Needy Some reformers sought to improve care for society's most vulnerable members. In 1841 **Dorothea Dix**, a reformer from Boston, was teaching at a women's jail when she discovered that some women were locked up simply because they were mentally ill. Dix learned that the mentally ill often received no treatment, and that some were chained and beaten. Dix lectured widely in the United States and Europe to promote better care. Her efforts led to publicly funded mental hospitals in a number of states.

Some reformers worked to improve life for people with other disabilities. In 1817 in Hartford, Connecticut, educator Thomas H. Gallaudet started the first free school for deaf children in the United States. Reformer Samuel G. Howe directed the New England Asylum for the Blind (now the Perkins School for the Blind), which opened in Boston in 1832.

Reformers also tried to improve prisons. In the early 1800s, debtors, lifelong criminals, and children were put in the same cells. Reformers demanded that children go to special jails. They also called for adult prisoners to be rehabilitated, or prepared to live useful lives after their release.

(*left*) Reading Braille
(*above*) A student reads at the Perkins School for the Blind.

 PROBLEMS AND SOLUTIONS List the problems in society that reformers worked to change.

Michigan Grade Level Content Expectations *Review*

ONLINE QUIZ
For test practice, go to
Interactive Review @ ClassZone.com

TERMS & NAMES

1. Explain the importance of
- Second Great Awakening
- temperance movement
- Shakers
- Horace Mann
- Dorothea Dix

USING YOUR READING NOTES

2. Problems and Solutions Complete the chart you started at the beginning of the section. Show the problems reformers identified in society and the solutions they proposed.

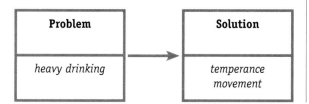

Problem		Solution
heavy drinking	→	*temperance movement*

KEY IDEAS

3. How did the Second Great Awakening influence the reform movement?

4. How did women contribute to social reform?

CRITICAL THINKING

5. Main Ideas and Details How did government work for better schools?

6. Summarize What obstacles faced women and African Americans who wanted an education?

7. Causes and Effects What factors might have caused utopian communities to fail?

8. Art Imagine you are a reformer in the mid-1800s. Choose one of the problems that you read about in this section and make a poster that encourages citizens to become involved and make positive changes.

Report to the Massachusetts Legislature

SETTING THE STAGE After traveling to several places where the mentally ill were kept in terrible conditions, Dorothea Dix wrote a report describing what she had seen. In 1843, she presented her report to lawmakers.

Advocate of the Helpless

In earlier times, the word *idiotic* did not mean "stupid." It was used to describe someone who was mentally disabled.

1. For what groups of people is Dix pleading for help?

History Makers

Dorothea Dix
1802–1887

Dix began teaching at 14 and opened her own school at 19. Later, she turned her skills as an educator toward improving society. Her bold activism earned her the nickname "Dragon Dix."

Gentlemen: . . . I come to present the strong claims of suffering humanity. I come to place before the Legislature of Massachusetts the condition of the miserable, the desolate, the outcast. I come as the **advocate**[1] of helpless, forgotten, insane, and idiotic men and women; of beings sunk to a condition from which the most unconcerned would start with real horror; of beings wretched in our prisons, and more wretched in our **almshouses**.[2] I must confine myself to a few examples, but am ready to furnish other and more complete details, if required.

I proceed, gentlemen, briefly to call your attention to the present state of insane persons confined within this **Commonwealth**,[3] in cages, closets, cellars, stalls, pens! Chained, naked, beaten with rods, and lashed into obedience.

I offer the following extracts from my notebook and journal.

Springfield: In the jail, one lunatic woman, furiously mad, a state **pauper**,[4] improperly situated, both in regard to the prisoners, the keepers, and herself. It is a case of extreme self-forgetfulness and oblivion to all the decencies of life … In the almshouse of the same town is a woman apparently only needing **judicious**[5] care and some well-chosen employment to make it unnecessary to confine her in solitude in a dreary unfurnished room. Her appeals for employment and companionship are most touching, but the mistress replied "she had no time to attend to her."

Lincoln: A woman in a cage. Medford: One idiotic subject chained, and one in a close stall for seventeen years. Pepperell: One often doubly chained, hand and foot; another violent; several peaceable now. Brookfield: One man caged, comfortable. Granville: One often closely confined, now losing the use of his limbs from want of exercise.

---

1. **advocate:** a person who promotes a cause.
2. **almshouses:** homes for poor people.
3. **Commonwealth:** a term used to refer to certain U.S. states; in this case, Massachusetts.
4. **pauper:** a person who lives on the state's charity.
5. **judicious:** wise and careful.

Charlemont: One man caged. Savoy: One man caged. Lenox: Two in the jail, against whose unfit condition there the jailer protests.

Dedham: The insane **disadvantageously**[6] placed in the jail. In the almshouse, two females in stalls, situated in the main building, lie in wooden bunks filled with straw; always shut up. One of these subjects is supposed curable. The overseers of the poor have declined giving her a trial at the hospital, as I was informed, on account of expense.

Besides the above, I have seen many who, part of the year, are chained or caged. The use of cages is all but universal. Hardly a town but can refer to some not distant period of using them; chains are less common; **negligences**[7] frequent; willful abuse less frequent than sufferings proceeding from ignorance, or want of consideration. I encountered during the last three months many poor creatures wandering reckless and unprotected through the country. . . . But I cannot **particularize**.[8] In traversing the state, I have found hundreds of insane persons in every variety of circumstance and condition, many whose situation could not and need not be improved; a less number, but that very large, whose lives are the saddest pictures of human suffering and degradation.

I give a few illustrations; but description fades before reality. . . .
Men of Massachusetts, I beg, I implore, I demand pity and protection for these of my suffering, outraged sex. . . . Become the benefactors of your race, the just guardians of the solemn rights you hold in trust. Raise up the fallen, **succor**[9] the desolate, restore the outcast, defend the helpless, and for your eternal and great reward receive the benediction, "Well done, good and faithful servants, become rulers over many things!"

----

6. **disadvantageously:** harmfully.

7. **negligences:** careless actions.

8. **particularize:** to name in detail.

9. **succor:** to help in a time of need.

I Have Seen Many

Notice that Dix cites evidence from many different towns.

2. Why do you think she includes so many specific details in her report?

Men of Massachusetts

When Dix says "Men of Massachusetts," she is still speaking to the members of the state legislature.

3. What does Dix want the Massachusetts Legislature to do?

DOCUMENT–BASED QUESTIONS

Short Answer

1. On what evidence did Dorothea Dix base her report about "suffering humanity"?

2. Whom did Dix ask to help improve the care of the mentally ill?

Extended Answer

3. What do Dix's efforts have in common with other social reform efforts discussed in this chapter?

▶ Key Ideas

BEFORE, YOU LEARNED

A 19th-century religious revival launched movements to reform education and society.

NOW YOU WILL LEARN

The social campaigns to gain freedom for enslaved persons and equality for women were closely linked.

▶ Vocabulary

TERMS & NAMES

abolition the movement to stop slavery

Frederick Douglass abolitionist and journalist who became an influential lecturer in the North and abroad

Sojourner Truth abolitionist and feminist who spoke against slavery and for the rights of women

Underground Railroad a series of escape routes used by slaves escaping the South

Harriet Tubman conductor on the Underground Railroad who led enslaved people to freedom

Elizabeth Cady Stanton reformer who helped organize the first women's rights convention

Seneca Falls Convention the first women's rights convention, held in Seneca Falls, New York

BACKGROUND VOCABULARY

suffrage the right to vote

Visual Vocabulary
Seneca Falls Convention

▶ Reading Strategy

Re-create the diagram shown at right. As you read and respond to the **KEY QUESTIONS**, use the diagram to note important issues and their effects. Add boxes or start a new diagram as needed.

 See Skillbuilder Handbook, page R7.

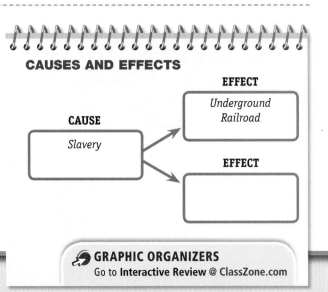

CAUSES AND EFFECTS

CAUSE

Slavery

EFFECT

Underground Railroad

EFFECT

GRAPHIC ORGANIZERS
Go to **Interactive Review** @ ClassZone.com

SECTION 3

Abolition and Women's Rights

8 – U4.3.2 Describe the formation and development of the abolitionist movement by considering the roles of key abolitionist leaders (e.g., John Brown and the armed resistance, Harriet Tubman and the Underground Railroad, Sojourner Truth, William Lloyd Garrison, and Frederick Douglass), and the response of southerners and northerners to the abolitionist movement.
8 – U4.3.3 Analyze the antebellum women's rights (and suffrage) movement by discussing the goals of its leaders (e.g., Susan B. Anthony and Elizabeth Cady Stanton) and comparing the Seneca Falls Resolution with the Declaration of Independence.

One American's Story

African-American poet and reformer Frances Ellen Watkins Harper often wrote about the suffering of enslaved persons, including enslaved mothers.

PRIMARY SOURCE

❝ They tear him from her circling arms,
Her last and fond embrace.
Oh! never more may her sad eyes
Gaze on his mournful face.
No marvel, then, these bitter shrieks
Disturb the listening air:
She is a mother, and her heart
Is breaking in despair. ❞

—Frances Ellen Watkins Harper, "The Slave Mother"

Harper toured the North as an antislavery speaker. She also spoke out for women's rights and against racism. As this section explains, many individuals in the mid-1800s demanded equal rights for African Americans and women.

Frances Ellen Watkins Harper

Abolitionists Protest Slavery

🔻 **KEY QUESTION** What methods did abolitionists use to fight against slavery?

In the late 1600s, the Quakers had been among the first to take a stand against slavery. However, **abolition**, the movement to end slavery, did not begin until the late 1700s. During the Revolution, Northern states began passing antislavery laws. By 1804, almost all the Northern states had abolished slavery, and Congress banned the importation of African slaves into the United States starting in 1807. Abolitionists then demanded a law ending slavery in the South, where the economy depended on slave labor. The stage was set for an emotional debate that would tear the nation apart.

Demanding an End to Slavery Abolitionists were bold in their statements and reactions to their beliefs were just as fierce. David Walker, a free African American in Boston, printed a pamphlet in 1829 urging slaves to revolt. Copies of the pamphlet appeared in the South. This angered slaveholders. Shortly afterward, Walker died; some believed he had been poisoned.

Some Northern whites also fought slavery. In 1831, William Lloyd Garrison began publishing an abolitionist newspaper, *The Liberator,* in Boston. Of his antislavery stand, he wrote, "I will not retreat a single inch—AND I WILL BE HEARD." Many hated his views. In 1835, a mob in Boston grabbed Garrison and dragged him toward a park to hang him. He was rescued by the mayor.

Two famous abolitionists were Southerners who grew up on a plantation. Sisters Sarah and Angelina Grimké believed that slavery was morally wrong. They moved to the North and spoke out against slavery, even though women at the time were not supposed to lecture in public. Theodore Weld, Angelina's husband, led a campaign to send antislavery petitions to Congress. Proslavery congressmen passed a gag rule to prevent the reading of petitions in Congress.

President John Quincy Adams ignored the gag rule and read the petitions. He also introduced an amendment to abolish slavery. Proslavery congressmen tried to stop him. Such efforts, however, weakened the proslavery cause by showing them to be opponents of free speech. Adams also defended a group of enslaved Africans who had rebelled on the slave ship *Amistad.* He successfully argued their case before the U.S. Supreme Court in 1841, and the Africans returned home immediately.

Eyewitness to Slavery Two powerful abolitionist speakers, **Frederick Douglass** and **Sojourner Truth**, spoke from their own experiences of having been enslaved. Douglass had a long career as a lecturer for the Massachusetts Anti-Slavery Society.

People who opposed abolition spread rumors that the brilliant speaker could never have been a slave. To prove them wrong, in 1845 Douglass published an autobiography that vividly narrated his slave experiences. Afterward, he feared recapture by his owner, so he left America for a two-year speaking tour of Great Britain and Ireland. When Douglass returned, he bought his freedom.

History Makers

Frederick Douglass   1818–1895

When lecturing on abolition, Douglass—an escaped slave—was often introduced as "a piece of property." Douglass was a popular and eloquent speaker who had few equals on the lecture circuit. Abolitionists welcomed his graphic descriptions of slave life as a way to publicize the injustice of slavery. As his popularity grew, Douglass began to introduce the topic of racial discrimination in the North. In addition to lecturing, Douglass published his autobiography and an abolitionist newspaper, *The North Star*. He said that in the North, people "are far wealthier than any plantation owner—they are rich with freedom."

CRITICAL THINKING

1. **Draw Conclusions** How might Douglass's life experiences have made him a persuasive speaker?

2. **Make Inferences** What did Douglass mean by Northerners being "rich with freedom"?

ONLINE BIOGRAPHY For more on Frederick Douglass, go to the **Research & Writing Center** @ ClassZone.com

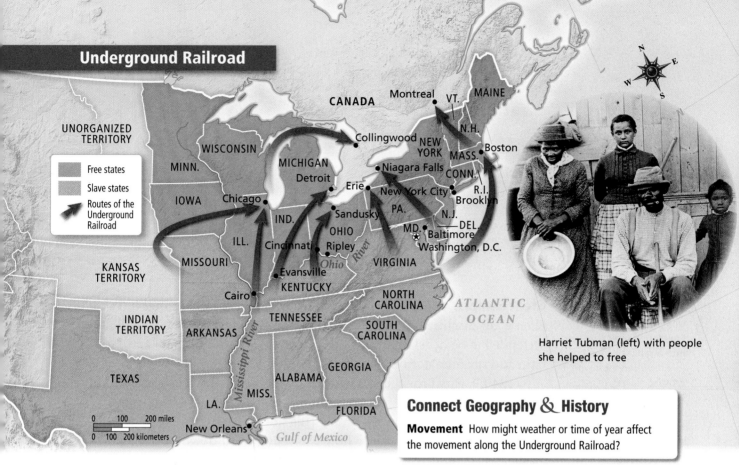

Underground Railroad

UNORGANIZED TERRITORY

Free states

Slave states

Routes of the Underground Railroad

CANADA

Montreal

VT.   MAINE

N.H.

Collingwood NEW MASS. Boston
            YORK

WISCONSIN

MINN.

MICHIGAN   Niagara Falls   CONN.
Detroit   R.I.
        Erie   New York City   Brooklyn
IOWA Chicago   N.J.
            Sandusky   PA.
        IND.   DEL.
ILL.   OHIO   MD.
    Cincinnati Ripley   Baltimore
            Ohio River   Washington, D.C.
KANSAS   MISSOURI   VIRGINIA
TERRITORY   Evansville
            KENTUCKY
        Cairo   ATLANTIC
                    NORTH   OCEAN
INDIAN   TENNESSEE CAROLINA
TERRITORY ARKANSAS
                    SOUTH
                    CAROLINA
TEXAS   GEORGIA
        ALABAMA
    MISS.
    LA.   FLORIDA
0 100 200 miles
0 100 200 kilometers New Orleans
                    Gulf of Mexico

Harriet Tubman (left) with people she helped to free

Connect Geography & History

Movement How might weather or time of year affect the movement along the Underground Railroad?

Sojourner Truth also began life enslaved, in New York State. In 1827, when she was about 30, Truth fled her owners and stayed with a Quaker family. She was originally called Isabella but changed her name in 1843 to reflect her life's work: to sojourn (stay temporarily in a place) and "declare the truth to the people." A bold and captivating speaker, Truth drew huge crowds.

The Underground Railroad Some brave abolitionists helped slaves escape to freedom along the **Underground Railroad**. Neither underground nor a railroad, the Underground Railroad was actually a series of aboveground escape routes from throughout the South up to the free North. On these routes, runaway slaves traveled on foot and by wagons, boats, and trains. They usually journeyed by night and hid by day in places called stations. Stables, attics, and cellars all served as stations. At his home in Rochester, New York, Frederick Douglass once housed 11 runaways at the same time.

The people who led the runaways to freedom were called conductors. The most famous was **Harriet Tubman**, who was born into slavery in Maryland. She escaped in 1849 when she learned that her owner was about to sell her. Tubman later described her feelings as she crossed into the free state of Pennsylvania: "I looked at my hands to see if I was the same person now that I was free. There was such a glory over everything."

After her escape, Harriet Tubman made 19 dangerous journeys to free enslaved persons. She carried medicine to quiet crying babies. Her enemies offered $40,000 for her capture, but no one ever caught her. "I never run my train off the track and I never lost a passenger," she proudly declared. Among the people she saved were her sister, brother, and parents.

(*top left*) In 2004, a visitor to the National Underground Railroad Freedom Center squeezes into a replica of the box in which Henry Brown escaped slavery.
(*top right*) This 19th-century print from Brown's autobiography shows his arrival in Philadelphia. **What dangers did people such as Brown face in trying to escape from slavery?**

Great Escapes Some escapes by enslaved persons became famous. In 1848, Ellen Craft disguised herself as a white man while her husband, William, pretended to be her slave. Together they traveled more than 1,000 miles, by train and steamboat, from slavery in Georgia to freedom in the North.

In 1849, Henry Brown had a white carpenter pack him in a box and ship him to Philadelphia. The box was two and one half feet deep, two feet wide, and three feet long. It bore the label "This side up with care." Nevertheless, Brown spent several miserable hours traveling head down. At the end of about 27 hours, "Box" Brown climbed out a free man in Philadelphia.

▲ **SUMMARIZE** List the methods abolitionists used to fight against slavery.

The Fight for Women's Rights

▼ **KEY QUESTION** What rights were women fighting for in the mid-1800s?

Some white abolitionist women had begun to realize that their own rights were extremely limited. In 1840, an incident at a major antislavery convention in London helped launch the U.S. movement for women's rights.

Women Reformers Face Barriers Lucretia Mott and **Elizabeth Cady Stanton** were two leading women abolitionists. Mott and Stanton were part of an American delegation that attended the World Anti-Slavery Convention in London in 1840. Although the women in the delegation had much to say, they were not allowed to participate in the convention or speak in public. Instead, they had to sit silent behind a heavy curtain.

To show his support, the famed abolitionist William Lloyd Garrison joined them. He said, "After battling so many long years for the liberties of African slaves, I can take no part in a convention that strikes down the most sacred rights of all women."

But most Americans agreed that women should stay out of public life. Women in the 1800s possessed few legal or political rights. Few could vote, sit on juries, or hold public office. Many laws treated women—especially married women—as children. Single women had some freedoms, such as being able to manage their own property. But in most states, a husband controlled any property his wife inherited and any wages she might earn.

The Seneca Falls Convention After the World Anti-Slavery Convention, Stanton and Mott decided it was time to demand not only freedom for enslaved people, but equality for women. They made up their minds to plan a convention for women's rights after they returned to the United States.

On July 19 and 20, 1848, Stanton and Mott headed the **Seneca Falls Convention** for women's rights in Seneca Falls, New York. It was the world's first convention on the rights of women. It attracted about 300 women and men, including the well-known abolitionist Frederick Douglass.

Before the meeting opened, a small group of planners discussed how they would present their ideas. The planners wrote a document modeled on the Declaration of Independence. They called it the Declaration of Sentiments and Resolutions. Just as the Declaration of Independence said that "All men are created equal," the Declaration of Sentiments stated that "All men and women are created equal." It went on to list several statements of opinion, or resolutions. Then it concluded with a demand for rights.

PRIMARY SOURCE

❝ Now, in view of this entire disenfranchisement [denying the right to vote] of one-half the people of this country, their social and religious degradation—in view of the unjust laws above mentioned, and because women do feel themselves aggrieved, oppressed, and fraudulently deprived of their most sacred rights, we insist that they have immediate admission to all the rights and privileges which belong to them as citizens of the United States. ❞

—Declaration of Sentiments and Resolutions, 1848

Every resolution won unanimous approval from the group except **suffrage**, or the right to vote. Some argued that the public would laugh at women if they asked for the vote. But Elizabeth Cady Stanton and Frederick Douglass fought for the resolution. They argued that the right to vote would give women political power that would help them win other rights. The resolution for suffrage won by a slim margin.

History Makers

Elizabeth Cady Stanton   1815–1902

Stanton (pictured with one of her children) had long known that the world could be unfair to women. Her father was a lawyer who had many women clients. Some faced poverty because laws gave a married woman's money to her husband, who could lose it to drink or gambling. Women who divorced often lost the right to see their children. As an adult, Stanton fought to change laws that affected women, and strongly believed that the ability to vote would help women to ensure their rights. Stanton was a persuasive lecturer and writer. During a career that lasted half a century, she recruited many to her cause.

CRITICAL THINKING

1. **Draw Conclusions** Why did Stanton want women to have more legal rights?
2. **Form and Support Opinions** Do you agree with Stanton about the importance of voting? Explain.

 **ONLINE BIOGRAPHY** For more on Elizabeth Cady Stanton, go to the **Research & Writing Center** @ ClassZone.com

Continued Calls for Women's Rights The women's rights movement of the mid-1800s was ridiculed by many people. Newspaper cartoons and editorials often poked fun at women who wanted equal rights, and suffrage seemed far out of reach.

As women's rights activists continued their efforts, however, they began to see results. Susan B. Anthony, a skilled organizer from the temperance and abolitionist movements, played a key part in building the call for women's rights into a national movement. Anthony argued that women's suffrage would be the foundation on which women would achieve other legal rights. She believed that "there never will be complete equality until women themselves help to make laws and elect lawmakers."

Anthony was an outspoken advocate for equal pay for men and women. She also called for laws that would give married women the right to keep their own property and wages. In 1839, Mississippi passed the first such law. New York passed a property law in 1848 and a wages law in 1860. By 1865, 29 states had similar laws.

▲ **CAUSES AND EFFECTS** Explain what rights women fought for in the mid-1800s.

 **CONNECT** to the Essential Question

How did immigration and social reform change the nation in the mid-1800s?

PROBLEM	SOLUTION
Overcrowding and lack of opportunity in Europe and elsewhere	Millions of immigrants settle in the United States
Poor working conditions	Workers form labor unions and go on strikes Schools founded for children with disabilities
Education for only the few	Public schooling becomes more widespread
Slavery in the South	Abolitionists demand an end to slavery Underground Railroad helps some enslaved people escape
Limited rights for women	Women demand rights to vote and to keep their own property and wages

CRITICAL THINKING Causes and Effects What long-term effects did these solutions have on American society?

A Changing Nation

 KEY QUESTION How did immigration, religious revival, and reform change the nation?

In the early and mid–19th century, America experienced dramatic social and cultural changes. These changes came from forces outside the country as well as from the religious and reform movements within its borders.

America Transformed Americans continued to adapt to their growing nation. Immigration had produced a far more diverse population, and cities were dramatically changed in size, culture, and economy. Some people felt threatened by the new face of America and fought to stop immigration. Others launched a reform movement, sparked by the religious revivals, that sought to take control of the forces of change. American reformers advocated such causes as temperance, education, and workers' rights. Soon, some women reformers began to fight for their own rights.

Meanwhile, the issue of slavery continued to tear the nation apart. As the abolitionist movement gathered strength in the North, the economy of the South continued to depend on slave labor—and millions of African Americans remained enslaved.

 CAUSES AND EFFECTS Explain how immigration, religious revival, and reform changed the nation.

Michigan Grade Level Content Expectations *Review*

ONLINE QUIZ
For test practice, go to
Interactive Review @ ClassZone.com

TERMS & NAMES

1. Explain the importance of

- abolition
- Frederick Douglass
- Sojourner Truth
- Underground Railroad
- Harriet Tubman
- Elizabeth Cady Stanton
- Seneca Falls Convention

USING YOUR READING NOTES

2. Causes and Effects Complete the diagram you started at the beginning of this section. Then create a diagram for each of the other main issues in this section.

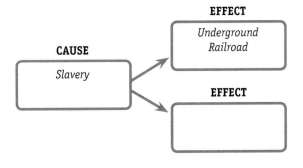

CAUSE

Slavery

EFFECT

Underground Railroad

EFFECT

KEY IDEAS

3. How did formerly enslaved persons participate in the abolitionist movement?

4. What barriers to equality did women face in the mid-1800s?

5. How did women abolitionists help to spark the fight for women's rights?

CRITICAL THINKING

6. Make Inferences Why did the women at the Seneca Falls Convention believe they should have rights?

7. Analyze Point of View Runaway slaves risked their lives for freedom. Why do you think some risked their lives and freedom again to help free others?

8. Draw Conclusions How did the Underground Railroad reflect a geographic division over slavery in America?

9. Computer Science Use the Internet to research the Quakers and their position on slavery. Design a web page that describes their position and how they helped people such as Sojourner Truth.

Connect to Literature

The True Confessions of Charlotte Doyle   by Avi

The period in which *The True Confessions of Charlotte Doyle* takes place was one of significant developments in American literature. In the 1830s, several American thinkers including Ralph Waldo Emerson, a poet and essayist, developed a philosophical and literary movement that rejected traditional beliefs and authority in favor of the individual's intuition and insight. Transcendentalism, as this movement came to be called, was part of the romantic movement prominent in England and Germany at that time—a movement of style, literature, and thought that focused on emotional forms of expression.

Henry David Thoreau, another transcendentalist writer of the period, praised self-reliance and individual decision-making. Thoreau believed that people should reject the materialism and greed that, for many, had come to guide American life. In *Walden*, Thoreau puts his beliefs into practice as he writes of his life alone in the New England woods.

Themes of individualism appeared in the works of other writers of the period as well, including Nathaniel Hawthorne, Henry Wadsworth Longfellow, and later Louisa May Alcott, Herman Melville, and Walt Whitman.

The True Confessions of Charlotte Doyle takes place in this period of change in America and across the seas. Here, Charlotte Doyle, a thirteen-year-old American girl, confronts uncertainty in the dark hold of the ship that carries her across dangerous seas from England to America.

I was too frightened to cry out again. Instead I remained absolutely still, crouching in pitch blackness while the wash of ship sounds eddied about me, sounds now intensified by the frantic knocking of my heart. Then I recollected that Zachariah's dirk was still with me. With a shaking hand I reached into the pocket where I'd put it, took it out, and removed its wooden sheath which slipped through my clumsy fingers and clattered noisily to the floor.

"Is someone there?" I called, my voice thin, wavering.

No answer.

After what seemed forever I repeated, more boldly than before, "*Is someone there?*"

Still nothing happened. Not the smallest breath of response. Not the slightest stir.

Gradually, my eyes became accustomed to the creaking darkness. I could make out the ladder descending from the deck, a square of dim light above. From that point I could follow the line of the ladder down to where it plunged into the hold below. At that spot, at the edge of the hole, I could see the head more distinctly. Its eyes were glinting wickedly, its lips contorted into a grim, satanic smirk.

Horrified, I nonetheless stared back. And the longer I did so the more it dawned on me that the head had not in fact moved—not at all. The features, I saw, remained unnaturally fixed. Finally, I found the courage to edge aside my fear and lean forward—the merest trifle—to try and make out who—or what—was there.

With the dirk held awkwardly before me I began to crawl forward. The closer I inched the more distorted and grotesque grew the head's features. It appeared to be positively inhuman.

When I drew within two feet of it I stopped and waited. Still the head did not move, did not blink an eye. It seemed as if it were *dead*.

ADDITIONAL READING

Two Years Before the Mast Richard Henry Dana chronicles his adventures as a crewmember aboard two ships, the *Pilgrim* and the *Alert*, between 1833 and 1855.

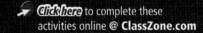

Chapter Summary

1 **Key Idea**
In the mid-1800s, millions of Europeans came to the United States hoping to build a better life.

2 **Key Idea**
A 19th-century religious revival launched movements to reform education and society.

3 **Key Idea**
The social campaigns to gain freedom for enslaved persons and equality for women were closely linked.

For detailed Review and Study Notes go to **Interactive Review** @ ClassZone.com

Name Game

Use the Terms & Names list to identify each sentence online or on your own paper.

1. I lived in a community centered on religion. Shaker 🖐

2. I helped enslaved people reach freedom through the Underground Railroad.

3. This is a work stoppage to demand better conditions.

4. This is the right to vote.

5. I was opposed to recent immigrants.

6. Economic opportunity is an example of this.

7. I was an abolitionist speaker who chose my own name.

8. I worked toward better treatment of the mentally ill.

9. I worked toward improvements in public education.

10. This was the cheapest deck on a ship.

A. Horace Mann
B. Dorothea Dix
C. Elizabeth Cady Stanton
D. steerage
E. suffrage
F. strike
G. nativist
H. Sojourner Truth
I. Harriet Tubman
J. Shaker
K. "push" factor
L. "pull" factor
M. temperance movement

Activities

FLIPCARD

Use the online flip cards to quiz yourself on the terms and names introduced in this chapter.

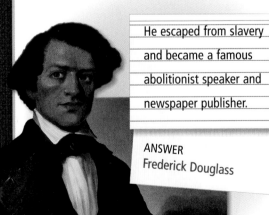

He escaped from slavery and became a famous abolitionist speaker and newspaper publisher.

ANSWER
Frederick Douglass

CROSSWORD PUZZLE

Complete the online crossword puzzle to show what you know about social change in the early 1800s.

ACROSS
1. **Harriet Tubman was a _____ on the Underground Railroad.**

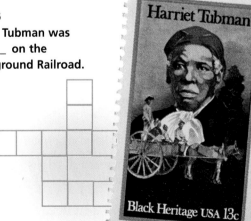

Harriet Tubman

Black Heritage USA 13c

VOCABULARY

Match the term on the left with its description on the right.

1. Know-Nothing Party
2. temperance movement
3. Second Great Awakening
4. Underground Railroad
5. Seneca Falls Convention

A. helped slaves escape
B. called for women's rights
C. opposed immigration
D. revived religious feeling
E. worked to stop the drinking of alcohol

Choose the term or name that does not belong in each group, and explain why.

6. Sojourner Truth, Horace Mann, Frederick Douglass

7. nativism, labor union, strike

8. steerage, suffrage, emigrant

Sojourner Truth

KEY IDEAS

① **The Hopes of Immigrants (pages 450–455)**

9. What factors pushed emigrants out of Europe in the mid-1800s?

10. What was the Know-Nothing Party, and what was its stance on immigration?

② **Reforming American Society (pages 456–461)**

11. What were the goals of people who fought for workers' rights?

12. How did reformers seek to improve educational opportunities?

③ **Abolition and Women's Rights (pages 464–471)**

13. How did the Underground Railroad operate?

14. What were the goals of the women's rights movement in the mid-1800s?

CRITICAL THINKING

15. **Synthesize** Why was America the destination for so many immigrants?

16. **Causes and Effects** How did the rapid increase in immigration during the mid-1800s cause conflicts in society?

17. **Make Generalizations** Why did many factory owners support the temperance movement?

18. **Causes and Effects** Create a chart to show the effects of educational reform in the mid-1800s. After you complete your chart, explain how these efforts have helped to make society more equal.

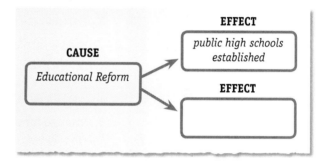

CAUSE

Educational Reform

EFFECT

public high schools established

EFFECT

19. **Compare and Contrast** How were Frederick Douglass and Sojourner Truth similar as abolitionists?

20. **Make Inferences** Why do you think that some of the people who fought for abolition also fought for women's rights?

21. **Draw Conclusions** The cartoon below shows a husband and wife fighting over "who will wear the pants in the family"—that is, who will rule the household. What do the pants symbolize?

MEAP PRACTICE

✓ **TEST PRACTICE**

• **Online Test Practice @ ClassZone.com**

• Use the **MEAP Strategies & Practice,** pages S1–S27, at the front of this book

DOCUMENT-BASED QUESTIONS

Analyze each document and answer the questions that follow.

DOCUMENT 1

1 The above nineteenth-century painting shows a revival meeting. The painting illustrates the influence of which of the following?

   A the Second Great Awakening

   B the temperance movement

   C labor unions

   D abolition

DOCUMENT 2

PRIMARY SOURCE

❝ What, to the American slave, is your Fourth of July? I answer: a day that reveals to him, more than all other days of the year, the gross injustice and cruelty to which he is the constant victim. To him, your celebration is a sham [something false]; . . . your sounds of rejoicing are empty and heartless; . . . ❞

—Frederick Douglass, 1852

2 Frederick Douglass gave this speech at a Fourth of July celebration in New York. Why does he say the sounds of celebration are "empty and heartless"?

   A because women cannot vote

   B because many African Americans are enslaved

   C because immigrants face prejudice

   D because many people oppose temperance

YOU BE THE HISTORIAN

22. **Connect to Today** Which "pull" factors of the mid-1800s still attract new immigrants to the United States today?

23. Analyze Point of View Think of a person in this chapter who exercised leadership by standing up for an unpopular position. Why might this leader have been willing to take such a risk?

24. Causes and Effects What were the long-term effects of the nineteenth-century reform movement?

25. Evaluate How successful was the women's movement of the mid-1800s?

26. Form and Support Opinions Of the reform efforts you learned about in this chapter, which do you consider the most important? Explain.

 Answer the

ESSENTIAL QUESTION

How did immigration and social reform change the nation in the mid-1800s?

Written Response Write a two- to three-paragraph response to the Essential Question. Be sure to consider the key ideas of each section as well as the most significant problems that faced Americans in the mid-1800s. Use the Response Rubric below to guide your thinking and writing.

Response Rubric

A strong response will

• analyze factors that pulled immigrants to America

• evaluate the impact of social reform movements

• discuss the strategies of leading abolitionists

• describe the goals of the women's rights movement

A Nation Divided and Rebuilt

1846–1877

Why It Matters Now

The Civil War represented the greatest threat to the survival of the American republic in our history. Why we fought, how the Union won, and how we rebuilt the nation remain enduring matters of discussion and debate.

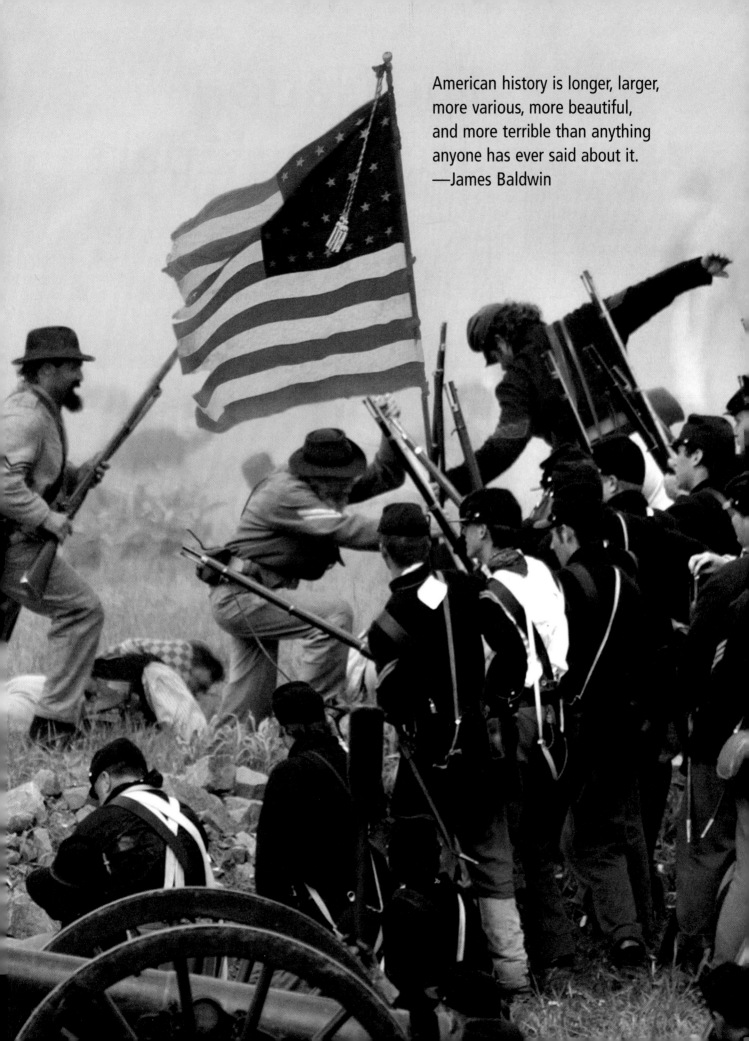

American history is longer, larger,
more various, more beautiful,
and more terrible than anything
anyone has ever said about it.
—James Baldwin

The Nation Breaking Apart

1846–1861

 ESSENTIAL QUESTION

What issues and events shattered the nation's unity and led to civil war?

1. Tensions Rise Between North and South

2. Slavery Dominates Politics

3. Lincoln's Election and Southern Secession

CONNECT ⤸ **Geography & History**

How did geography and climate help create the nation's sectional division?

Think about:

1 the areas where cotton was grown

2 the difference between the climate of the South and that of the North

3 why cotton flourished in the South

Playing cards showing American generals in the War with Mexico

1852 *Uncle Tom's Cabin* published

▼

Effect The novel increases tension between North and South.

1846

War with Mexico

Wilmot Proviso introduced

1850 Compromise of 1850, including the Fugitive Slave Act, is passed.

▼

Effect Abolitionists defy the law by helping slaves escape.

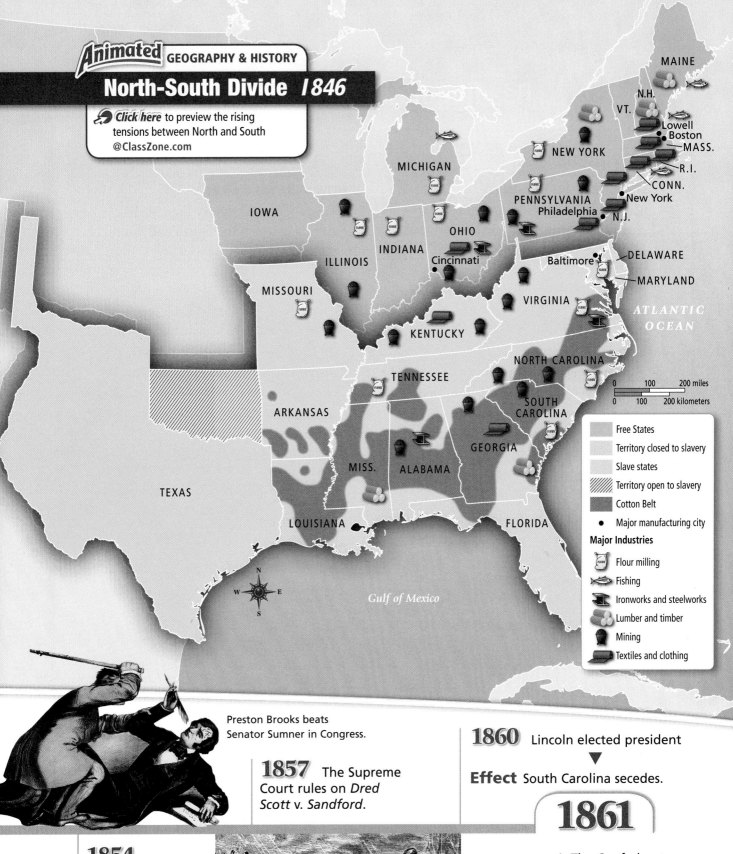

Click here to preview the rising tensions between North and South @ClassZone.com

MAINE

N.H.

VT.

Lowell
Boston
MASS.

NEW YORK

R.I.

CONN.

MICHIGAN

PENNSYLVANIA

New York

Philadelphia

N.J.

IOWA

OHIO

Cincinnati

ILLINOIS

INDIANA

Baltimore

DELAWARE

MARYLAND

MISSOURI

VIRGINIA

ATLANTIC
OCEAN

KENTUCKY

NORTH CAROLINA

TENNESSEE

SOUTH
CAROLINA

ARKANSAS

GEORGIA

MISS.

ALABAMA

TEXAS

LOUISIANA

FLORIDA

Gulf of Mexico

| 0 | 100 | 200 miles |
| 0 | 100 | 200 kilometers |

Free States

Territory closed to slavery

Slave states

Territory open to slavery

Cotton Belt

• Major manufacturing city

Major Industries

Flour milling

Fishing

Ironworks and steelworks

Lumber and timber

Mining

Textiles and clothing

Preston Brooks beats
Senator Sumner in Congress.

1857 The Supreme
Court rules on *Dred
Scott* v. *Sandford*.

1860 Lincoln elected president
▼
Effect South Carolina secedes.

1861

The Confederate
States of America is
formed.

1854
Kansas-
Nebraska Act is
passed.

The Republican
Party is formed.

Fugitive slaves escaping
from Maryland

▶ Key Ideas

BEFORE, YOU LEARNED

The North and South tried to reach a compromise in their disagreements over slavery.

NOW YOU WILL LEARN

Rising anger over slavery increased tensions between the North and South and led to violence.

▶ Vocabulary

TERMS & NAMES

Wilmot Proviso 1846 proposal that outlawed slavery in any territory gained from the War with Mexico

Free-Soil Party political party dedicated to stopping the expansion of slavery

Stephen A. Douglas Illinois senator who backed the Compromise of 1850

Compromise of 1850 series of laws intended to settle the major disagreements between free states and slave states

Fugitive Slave Act 1850 law meant to help slaveholders recapture runaway slaves

Harriet Beecher Stowe abolitionist; author of *Uncle Tom's Cabin*

Uncle Tom's Cabin novel published by Harriet Beecher Stowe in 1852 that showed slavery as brutal and immoral

Kansas-Nebraska Act 1854 law that established the territories of Kansas and Nebraska and gave their residents the right to decide whether to allow slavery

BACKGROUND VOCABULARY

bickering petty quarreling

REVIEW

popular sovereignty a system in which issues are decided by the citizenry or voters

▶ Reading Strategy

Re-create the diagram shown at right. As you read and respond to the **KEY QUESTIONS**, use the diagram to note the difference between the economies of the North and South.

 See Skillbuilder Handbook, page R8.

COMPARE AND CONTRAST

Northern Economy	Southern Economy
	relied on plantation farming

GRAPHIC ORGANIZERS
Go to **Interactive Review** @ ClassZone.com

Tensions Rise Between North and South

8 – U5.1.4.2 Describe how the following increased sectional tensions – the Wilmot Proviso (1846)
8 – U5.1.4.4 Describe how the following increased sectional tensions – the Kansas-Nebraska Act (1854) and subsequent conflict in Kansas

One American Story

During the 1830s, a French government official named Alexis de Tocqueville (TOHK•vihl) traveled along the Ohio River. The river was the border between Ohio, a free state, and Kentucky, a slave state. Tocqueville noted what he saw on both sides of the river.

PRIMARY SOURCE

❝ The State of Ohio is separated from Kentucky just by one river; on either side of it the soil is equally fertile, and the situation equally favourable, and yet everything is different. Here [on the Ohio side] a population devoured by feverish activity, trying every means to make its fortune. . . . There [on the Kentucky side] is a people which makes others work for it and shows little compassion, a people without energy, mettle or the spirit of enterprise. . . . These differences cannot be attributed to any other cause but slavery. ❞

—Alexis de Tocqueville, *Journey to America*

Alexis de Tocqueville

Foreign observers were often surprised by the cultural and political division between North and South. This division was now widening.

North and South Follow Different Paths

🔽 **KEY QUESTION** How did the economies of the North and South differ?

The economies of the North and South had been developing differently ever since colonial times. Although both economies were mainly agricultural, there were more small farms in the North. The North had also developed more industry and commerce. By contrast, the Southern economy relied on plantation farming and slave labor rather than industry. The economic differences between the two sections began to divide the nation politically.

Industry and Immigration in the North The growing industries of the North attracted many immigrants to Northern cities. As the Northern cities grew, immigrants and Easterners were also moving west. They built farms in the new states carved out of the Northwest Territory. Most canals and railroads ran east and west, strengthening ties between Eastern and Midwestern states.

In the North, some abolitionists believed that slavery was immoral and should be ended immediately. But other Northern opponents of slavery took a different position. Some Northern workers opposed slavery because it was an economic threat to them. Because slaves did not work for pay, wage workers feared that enslaved labor would replace them.

Agriculture and Slavery in the South The Southern economy was mostly agricultural. A small class of wealthy planters dominated Southern politics and society. They made great profits from the labor of their slaves. Much of this profit came from trade. Planters relied on exports of cash crops, especially cotton, and invested in land and slaves instead of industry.

Most Southern whites were poor farmers who owned no slaves. Many of these people resented the powerful plantation owners. But some poor whites accepted slavery because it gave them a feeling of social superiority.

Connecting History

Expanding Liberty
In the late 1700s, slavery was gradually outlawed throughout the Northern states. However, as slavery declined in the North, it continued to spread in the South. *See Chapter 8, page 247.*

CONNECT *Economics and History*

INVESTMENT

The sectional differences between North and South increased partly through investment. Investment is when money is committed to a project in order to create a profit.

Northerners invested in new kinds of machinery that might save them money. This helped fuel the industrial boom in the North.

Southerners, in contrast, invested profits back into land and slaves. Thus, investment strengthened sectional differences: the North became more industrial and "modern" while the South remained agricultural.

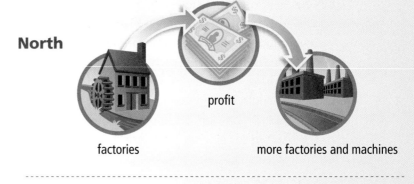

North

factories   profit   more factories and machines

South

land and slaves   profit   more land and slaves

CRITICAL THINKING **Connect *to* Today** If you were an investor, in what new industries would you invest?

When Northern criticism of slavery increased, slaveholders defended their way of life. To justify slavery, most offered the openly racist argument that white people were superior to African Americans. Many also claimed that slavery helped slaves by introducing them to Christianity, as well as providing them with food, clothing, and shelter throughout their lives. In time, different attitudes to slavery brought the North and the South into conflict.

▲ **COMPARE AND CONTRAST** Compare the economies of the North and South.

Slavery and Territorial Expansion

🔻 **KEY QUESTION** How did territorial expansion inflame sectional conflicts?

After the Missouri Compromise in 1820, political disagreements over slavery seemed to fade. However, the War with Mexico in 1846 brought the issue of slavery back to the forefront.

The Wilmot Proviso Many Northerners suspected that Southerners wanted to take territory from Mexico in order to extend slavery. They feared that this would upset the balance between free and slave states. To prevent this, Representative David Wilmot of Pennsylvania proposed a bill, known as the **Wilmot Proviso**, to outlaw slavery in any territory the United States might acquire from the War with Mexico.

But slaveholders believed that Congress had no right to prevent them from bringing slaves into any of the territories. The Constitution, they claimed, gave equal protection to the property rights of all U.S. citizens. The Wilmot Proviso divided Congress along sectional lines. The bill passed the House of Representatives. But Southerners prevented it from passing the Senate.

Even though the Wilmot Proviso never became law, it had important effects. It led to the creation of the **Free-Soil Party**, a political party dedicated to stopping the expansion of slavery. The party's slogan expressed its ideals—"Free Soil, Free Speech, Free Labor, and Free Men." The Free-Soil Party won ten seats in Congress in the election of 1848. More important, the party made slavery a key issue in national politics.

The Compromise of 1850 By 1848, the nation's leaders had begun to debate how to deal with slavery in the lands gained from the War with Mexico. The proposed addition of new states threatened the balance of power in Congress between North and South. Both sides worried about what would happen when California became a state.

The discovery of gold attracted so many people to California that there soon would be enough people to qualify for statehood. Most California residents wanted theirs to be a free state. But this would tip the balance of power in favor of the North. Southerners wanted to divide California in half, making the northern half a free state and the southern half a slave state.

In March 1850, California applied to be admitted as a free state. With California as a free state, slave states would become a minority in the Senate just as they were in the House.

Ribbon of the Free-Soil Party worn on supporters' clothing

IMAGES OF SLAVERY

Supporters of slavery argued that the enslaved were well fed, well clothed, and happy—much as they appear on this tobacco label below. However, the reality of slavery was very different, as the photograph at right reveals. Even the children of the enslaved were forced to labor long hours in dangerous and unhealthy conditions. Slaves suffered violent and cruel punishments. Many enslaved families were broken up when family members were sold to work on distant plantations.

OH CARRY ME BACK

TO OLE VIRGINNY.

CRITICAL THINKING

Connect *to* **Today** Can you describe any modern advertisements that present life in an unrealistic way?

California could not gain statehood, however, without the approval of Congress. And Congress was divided over the issue. But statesmen sought compromise. Senator Henry Clay of Kentucky crafted a plan to settle the problem.

- To please the North, California would be admitted as a free state, and the slave trade would be abolished in Washington, D.C.
- To please the South, Congress would not pass laws regarding slavery for the rest of the territories won from Mexico, and Congress would pass a stronger law to help slaveholders.

People on both sides felt they had to give up too much in this plan. Others, tired of the sectional **bickering**, just wanted to preserve the Union.

The job of winning passage of the plan fell to Senator **Stephen A. Douglas** of Illinois. By the end of September, Douglas succeeded, and the plan, now known as the **Compromise of 1850**, became law.

Some people celebrated the compromise, believing that it had saved the Union. But the compromise would not bring peace. In the years that followed, sectional tensions continued to rise.

▲ **CAUSES AND EFFECTS** Explain how the Wilmot Proviso inflamed debate.

The Crisis Deepens

🔻 **KEY QUESTION** How did the Fugitive Slave Act deepen the crisis?

The Compromise of 1850 was an attempt to calm the political situation. However, it contained one bill that heightened, rather than calmed, the crisis. That bill was called the **Fugitive Slave Act**.

The Fugitive Slave Act Under this law, accused fugitives could be held without an arrest warrant. They had no right to a jury trial. Instead, a federal commissioner ruled on each case.

Southerners backed the Fugitive Slave Act because they considered slaves to be property. But one aspect of the act especially enraged Northerners: it required them to help recapture runaway slaves. It also placed penalties on people who would not cooperate with the law. Southern slave catchers were allowed to roam the North. Sometimes they captured free African Americans.

The act drew more people to the abolitionist cause. Many decided to defy the act, even though this meant breaking the law.

Outrage Over the Act Abolitionist writer **Harriet Beecher Stowe** was outraged by the Fugitive Slave Act. Her anger inspired her to write *Uncle Tom's Cabin* in 1852. The novel presented the cruelty and immorality of slavery. The novel describes the escape of a slave named Eliza and her baby across the Ohio River.

PRIMARY SOURCE

❝ Eliza made her desperate retreat across the river just in the dusk of twilight. The gray mist of evening, rising slowly from the river, enveloped her as she disappeared up the bank, and the swollen current and floundering masses of ice presented a hopeless barrier between her and her pursuer. ❞

—Harriet Beecher Stowe, *Uncle Tom's Cabin*

Stowe's book was popular in the North. But white Southerners argued that the book presented a false picture of the South and slavery.

🔺 **CAUSES AND EFFECTS** Explain how the Fugitive Slave Act affected the country.

History Makers

Harriet Beecher Stowe 1811–1896

Harriet Beecher Stowe came from a family of abolitionists. While Stowe and her family were living in Cincinnati, Ohio, they bravely sheltered slaves fleeing from the neighboring slave state of Kentucky. Outrage at the Fugitive Slave Act of 1850 led Stowe to write *Uncle Tom's Cabin*. This novel, published in 1852, revealed the cruelties of slavery. But it also went a step further—and showed the evil effects that slavery had on slaveholders themselves.

Uncle Tom's Cabin made Stowe famous. It was translated into more than 20 languages. Because of its popularity, it drew the world's attention to the injustice of slavery in the South.

CRITICAL THINKING **Draw Conclusions** Why was the novel so unpopular in the South?

 **ONLINE BIOGRAPHY** For more on Harriet Beecher Stowe, go to the **Research & Writing Center @ ClassZone.com**

Violence Erupts

🔻 **KEY QUESTION** Why did violence erupt in Kansas and Congress?

The Fugitive Slave Act and *Uncle Tom's Cabin* heightened tension between the North and South. As political tensions increased, the issue of slavery in the territories brought bloodshed to the West and even to Congress itself.

The Kansas-Nebraska Act In 1854, Senator Douglas drafted a bill to organize the Nebraska Territory. This bill became known as the **Kansas-Nebraska Act**. It proposed to divide the territory into two parts—Nebraska and Kansas.

To get Southern support for the bill, Douglas suggested that **popular sovereignty** should be used to decide whether a territory becomes either slave or free. Popular sovereignty is a system that allows residents to vote to decide an issue. Southerners liked the bill because people would be able to vote for slavery in territories where it had been banned by the Missouri Compromise. However, if the bill passed, it would mean the destruction of the Missouri Compromise.

The bill angered opponents of slavery, but it passed. Few people realized that the Kansas-Nebraska Act would soon turn Kansas into a violent and bloody battleground over the issue of slavery.

COMPARING *Free States, Slave States, and Territories*

Compromise of 1850

OREGON TERRITORY 1848

MINN. TERR. 1849

UNORGANIZED TERRITORY

CALIFORNIA 1850

UTAH TERRITORY 1850

NEW MEXICO TERRITORY 1850

Kansas-Nebraska Act *1854*

WASH. TERR.

OREGON TERR.

NEBRASKA TERRITORY 1854

KANSAS TERR. 1854

Free States
Territory closed to slavery
Slave states
Territory open to slavery

Senators debate the Compromise of 1850.

Connect Geography & History

1. **Place** How were the political divisions of the East carried into the West?

2. **Evaluate** Why would Northerners believe that slavery was spreading?

Bleeding Kansas During the election of March 1855, there were more proslavery than antislavery settlers in the Kansas Territory. After five thousand residents of neighboring Missouri came and voted illegally, the Kansas legislature was filled with proslavery representatives.

Antislavery settlers rejected the elected government. Settlers on both sides armed themselves. In May, a proslavery mob looted the town of Lawrence, Kansas. This attack was called the Sack of Lawrence.

In response, John Brown, an extreme abolitionist, led seven other men in a massacre of five of his proslavery neighbors. This attack is known as the Potawatomie Massacre, after the creek near where the victims were found. As news of the violence spread, civil war broke out in Kansas. It continued for three years, and the territory came to be called "Bleeding Kansas."

Violence in Congress In May 1856, Senator Charles Sumner of Massachusetts spoke against the proslavery forces in Kansas. In his speech, Sumner insulted A. P. Butler, a senator from South Carolina.

Preston Brooks, a relative of Butler, heard about Sumner's speech. He attacked Sumner, who was sitting at his desk in Congress. Brooks beat Sumner unconscious with his cane, causing severe injuries that disabled him for years.

Brooks was cheered in the South. But Northerners were shocked at the violence in the Senate. "Bleeding Kansas" and "Bleeding Sumner" became rallying cries for antislavery Northerners. In their anger over events, antislavery forces united to create a new political organization—the Republican Party.

▲ **SUMMARIZE** Describe the events that led to violence in Kansas.

Michigan Grade Level Content Expectations *Review*

 ONLINE QUIZ
For test practice, go to
Interactive Review @ ClassZone.com

TERMS & NAMES

1. Explain the importance of
- Wilmot Proviso
- Free-Soil Party
- Stephen A. Douglas
- Compromise of 1850
- Fugitive Slave Act
- Harriet Beecher Stowe
- *Uncle Tom's Cabin*
- Kansas-Nebraska Act

USING YOUR READING NOTES

2. Compare and Contrast Complete the diagram you started at the beginning of this section.

Northern Economy	Southern Economy
	relied on plantation farming

KEY IDEAS

3. What were two ways that the North and the South differed by the 1850s?

4. How did the War with Mexico provoke disagreements between the North and the South?

5. Why was the Kansas-Nebraska Act so controversial?

CRITICAL THINKING

6. Causes and Effects How did *Uncle Tom's Cabin* affect national politics?

7. Problems and Solutions What might have been done to prevent the violence in Kansas?

8. Art Research the architecture of the North and South in the 19th century. Then create a travel poster showing the kinds of houses a visitor might see in each section of the country.

Land Use and Slavery

In 1850 cotton was the main cash crop of the lower South. But there was a problem: cotton exhausts the fertility of the soil. So planters had to abandon farmland and move west into new land. As planters moved west, they brought hundreds of thousands of enslaved people with them to farm the land.

One of the largest concentrations of cotton plantations was along the Mississippi River. The lower Mississippi offered excellent transportation for the crops. It also provided fertile soil for agriculture.

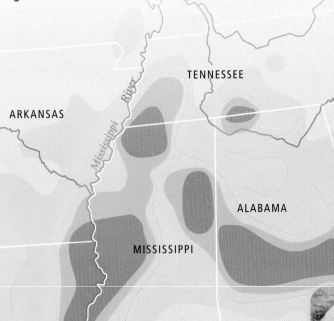

ARKANSAS

TENNESSEE

Mississippi River

ALABAMA

MISSISSIPPI

LOUISIANA

Cotton Production

45
30   In bales
15   per square
5   mile

New Orleans

New Orleans, the main port for shipments of cotton on the Mississippi River

In some places along the river, cranes were used to load cotton onto steamboats.

Enslaved people and their children shown outside the plantation slave cabins

Connect Geography & History

1. **Make Inferences** Why would this region of the South have had such a large African-American population?

2. **Draw Conclusions** Why did New Orleans become such an important city?

See Geography Handbook, pages A1–A17.

▶ Key Ideas

BEFORE, YOU LEARNED

Rising anger over slavery destroyed compromise between the North and South and led to violence.

NOW YOU WILL LEARN

The formation of the antislavery Republican Party further divided the country.

▶ Vocabulary

TERMS & NAMES

Republican Party political party formed in 1854 by opponents of slavery

John C. Frémont Republican presidential candidate in 1856

James Buchanan Democratic presidential candidate in 1856

Dred Scott* v. *Sandford 1856 Supreme Court case in which a slave, Dred Scott, sued for his freedom; the Court ruled against Scott

Roger B. Taney (TAW•nee) Supreme Court chief justice who wrote the majority opinion in the case of *Dred Scott* v. *Sandford*

Abraham Lincoln Illinois Republican who ran against Stephen A. Douglas in 1858

Harpers Ferry federal arsenal in Virginia; captured in 1859 during an antislavery revolt

REVIEW

Whig Party political party organized in 1834 to oppose the policies of Andrew Jackson

Know-Nothing Party anti-immigrant party formed in the 1850s

Visual Vocabulary
Harpers Ferry today

▶ Reading Strategy

Re-create the diagram shown at right. As you read and respond to the **KEY QUESTIONS**, use the center oval to record the main idea; use the outer ovals to note important details.

 See Skillbuilder Handbook, page R4.

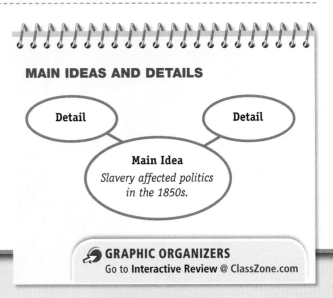

MAIN IDEAS AND DETAILS

Detail

Detail

Main Idea
Slavery affected politics in the 1850s.

GRAPHIC ORGANIZERS
Go to **Interactive Review** @ ClassZone.com

Slavery Dominates Politics

8 – U5.1.4.5 Describe how the following increased sectional tensions – the *Dred Scott* v. *Sandford* decision (1857)
8 – U5.1.5 Describe the resistance of enslaved people (e.g., Nat Turner, Harriet Tubman and the Underground Railroad, John Brown, Michigan's role in the Underground Railroad) and effects of their actions before and during the Civil War.

One American's Story

She was only 13, but her story edged the nation closer to civil war. Emily Edmondson grew up in slavery in Washington, D.C. On April 15, 1848, Emily, her 15-year-old sister Mary, and four of her brothers joined more than 70 other slaves in an escape attempt. Hidden on board a ship, they sailed toward freedom in the North. However, their ship was pursued and captured. Despite a debate in Congress and a public outcry, Emily and her sister were shipped to New Orleans to be resold.

In New Orleans an outbreak of yellow fever forced slave traders to send the girls back to the safety of Virginia. It was then that the girls' parents contacted Harriet Beecher Stowe's brother, who was a famous abolitionist. He raised enough money to buy their freedom. Harriet Beecher Stowe arranged for the girls to attend Oberlin College. (In the photo at right, they appear in plaid dresses.)

Although Mary died young, Emily became a famous abolitionist. Her story motivated various antislavery groups to create the Republican Party—a party dedicated to the elimination of slavery.

Emily Edmondson (standing center behind table) with her sister (in plaid at far left) as well as Frederick Douglass and others at an abolitionist convention, 1850

Slavery and Political Division

KEY QUESTION How did the issue of slavery affect political parties?

As you have read, the Kansas-Nebraska Act allowed residents of a new territory to vote either for or against slavery. This act caused a political crisis for the **Whig Party**. The Whig party had been formed in 1834 to oppose the policies of Andrew Jackson. Now the act began to tear the party apart. Southern

Whigs supported the act. Northern Whigs opposed it. There was no room for compromise. As a result, the Whig Party split into two factions.

The Republican Party Forms Some of the Southern Whigs joined the Democratic Party. Others looked for leaders who supported slavery and the Union. The Northern Whigs, however, joined with other rivals and formed the **Republican Party**.

The Republican Party was both an antislavery party and a sectional party that sought to protect the interests of the North. Republicans not only used moral arguments against slavery, they also looked down on the South's agricultural system based on enslaved labor.

The Republicans quickly gained strength in the North. "Bleeding Kansas" was the key to the Republican rise. Many blamed the violence on the Democrats. With the 1856 elections nearing, Republicans seized the chance to gain seats in Congress and win the presidency.

The Republicans needed a strong presidential candidate in 1856 to strengthen their young party. They nominated **John C. Frémont**. Frémont was a handsome young hero known for his explorations in the West. He was nicknamed "the Pathfinder."

Republicans liked Frémont because he wanted California and Kansas admitted as free states. Also, he did not have a controversial political past. Even so, the Republican position on slavery was so unpopular in the South that Frémont's name did not appear on the ballot there.

Election of 1856 The Democrats nominated **James Buchanan** for the presidency in 1856. As ambassador to Great Britain, he had been in England since 1853 and had spoken neither for nor against the Kansas-Nebraska Act.

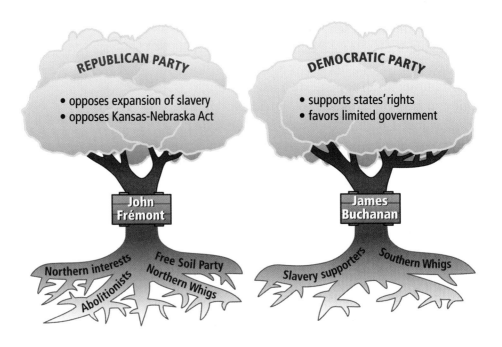

Buchanan said little about slavery and claimed that his goal was to maintain the Union. Buchanan appealed to Southerners, especially to people in the upper South and the border states, and to Northerners who feared that Frémont's election could tear the nation apart.

The American Party, or **Know-Nothing Party**, an anti-immigrant party, nominated Millard Fillmore as presidential candidate in 1856. Fillmore had been president following the death of Zachary Taylor, from 1850 until 1853. But the Know-Nothings were divided over slavery and had little strength.

The 1856 presidential election turned into two separate races. In the North, it was Buchanan against Frémont. In the South, it was Buchanan against Fillmore. Buchanan won. He carried all the slave states except Maryland, where Fillmore claimed his only victory. Buchanan also won several Northern states, such as Pennsylvania and Illinois.

Although he lost the election, Frémont won 11 Northern states. These results showed two things. First, the Republican Party was a major force in the North. Second, slavery was dividing the nation along sectional lines.

▲ **MAIN IDEAS & DETAILS** Explain how the issue of slavery affected political parties.

The Breaking Point

🔻 **KEY QUESTION** What events brought the nation to a crisis?

The argument over slavery was affecting not only Congressional politics. The slavery debate was forcing its way into another branch of government—the judiciary. In the mid-1850s, a legal case involving an enslaved man named Dred Scott reached the Supreme Court. The Supreme Court's decision in this case divided the country even further.

Article covering the Dred Scott case from *Frank Leslie's Illustrated Newspaper*

The Case of Dred Scott Scott had been an enslaved person in Missouri. However, he had lived for a time in free territories before being taken back to Missouri. After his owner's death, Dred Scott argued that he was a free man because he had lived in territories where slavery was illegal. Scott's wife and their two daughters also sued in court for their freedom. Scott's case, **Dred Scott v. Sandford**, reached the Supreme Court in 1856.

In 1857, the Court ruled against Scott. Chief Justice **Roger B. Taney** (TAW•nee) stated that Dred Scott was not a U.S. citizen. As a result, he could not sue in U.S. courts. Taney also ruled that Scott was bound by Missouri's slave code because he had lived in Missouri.

Taney also argued that banning slavery in the territories would violate slaveholders' property rights, protected by the Fifth Amendment. This meant that legislation such as the Missouri Compromise was unconstitutional.

Dred Scott v. Sandford (1857)

KEY ISSUE	citizenship	
KEY PEOPLE	Dred Scott	b. 1795, d. 1858; enslaved to John and Irene Emerson
	John and Irene Emerson	"owners" of Dred and Harriet Scott; residents of Missouri
	John Sanford	executor of the Emersons' estate (Sanford's name was misspelled "Sandford" by a court clerk)
	Roger Taney	Chief justice of the Supreme Court (1836–1864)

History Makers

Roger Taney
1777–1864

Roger Taney was born in Maryland, the son of plantation owners. Personally, he abhorred slavery, and upon inheriting his family's plantation, he freed all his slaves.

In 1831 he became President Andrew Jackson's attorney general. In 1836 Taney was appointed chief justice in the Supreme Court.

ONLINE BIOGRAPHY

For more on the life of Roger Taney, go to the **Research & Writing Center @ ClassZone.com**

The Case

John and Irene Emerson lived in Missouri. John worked for the military, so he traveled, and when he did he brought his slave Dred Scott with him. After the Emersons died, Dred Scott sued their estate for his freedom. Scott's lawyers argued that Scott became free when he lived with Emerson in Illinois—a free state—and in Wisconsin, which was made a free territory by the Missouri Compromise.

The Court's Decision The court protected and even expanded slavery. It said that, as a slave, Dred Scott was property. He was not a citizen; he would not be a citizen even if he were freed. He had no rights; he could not even file a lawsuit. The court also said that the Congress had no power to limit slavery, because any such limits would violate the Constitutional property rights of slaveholders.

Historical Impact The decision meant that the Missouri Compromise was void, because Congress could not limit slavery in the territories. Further, it seemed to imply that no state could be a free state because states could not prohibit their citizens from importing, owning, or buying and selling slaves.

Dred Scott thrilled slaveowners, while it outraged free-soilers and abolitionists. By deepening the sectional divide between North and South, the decision helped bring about the Civil War. Following the Civil War, the 14th Amendment to the U.S. Constitution was passed, undoing the Dred Scott decision.

CRITICAL THINKING

1. **Summarize** What was the basis of Scott's argument, and why did the Taney court disagree?

2. **Make Inferences** How did this decision bring the nation closer to civil war?

The Lincoln-Douglas Debate After the Dred Scott decision, the Republicans charged that the Democrats wanted to legalize slavery not only in all U.S. territories but in all the states. They used this charge to attack individual Democrats. Stephen A. Douglas, sponsor of the Kansas-Nebraska Act, was one of their main targets in 1858. That year, Illinois Republicans nominated **Abraham Lincoln** to challenge Douglas for his U.S. Senate seat. In his first campaign speech, Lincoln expressed the Northern fear that Southerners wanted to expand slavery to the entire nation. He laid the groundwork for his argument by using a phrase from the Bible.

PRIMARY SOURCE

❝ 'A house divided against itself cannot stand.' I believe this government cannot endure, permanently, half slave and half free. I do not expect the Union to be dissolved; I do not expect the house to fall; but I do expect it will cease to be divided. It will become all one thing, or all the other. ❞

—Abraham Lincoln, Springfield, Illinois, June 16, 1858

Later in the year, the two men held debates across Illinois in front of large crowds. The Lincoln-Douglas debates are models of political debate.

CONNECT ⟳ *To Today*

POLITICAL DEBATE

In the mid-19th century, large crowds listened to candidates debate the issues of the day. Lincoln debated Douglas seven times; thousands of people came to listen.

The first televised presidential debate, in 1960, featured candidates John F. Kennedy and Richard Nixon. Today, millions watch televised debates. These debates have strict rules—about the topics, the length of each debate and its closing arguments, and so forth. In contrast to the Lincoln-Douglas debates, today's live audiences are instructed not to applaud or make any noise while the debate is in progress.

Senator John Kerry (*standing*) debates President George W. Bush (*right, seated*) in a 2004 "town meeting" style debate.

CRITICAL THINKING
Make Generalizations What factors might influence your opinion of a candidate during a political debate?

REACHING COMPROMISE

Compromise comes when two people or groups each give way a little to settle their dispute. In the mid-19th century, the failure to compromise led to violence and eventually to a civil war in which hundreds of thousands of Americans died.

Today, negotiation and compromise—whether in government or business or in classrooms and on playgrounds—is just as important as it was in the 19th century. Educational programs under the names of peace education, conflict resolution, and negotiation teach compromising skills. The purpose of these programs is not just to resolve conflicts and prevent violence, but to develop skills for citizenship.

Activity

Discuss how to promote compromise in your school.

1 Respect yourself and encourage your friends to respect others.

2 Encourage your friends to be good observers.

3 Help your friends pause a moment if something angers them.

4 During disagreements, encourage others to keep from shouting.

5 Compromise is a form of bargaining. Next time you overhear a dispute, suggest ways that the two parties might reach an agreement.

CRITICAL THINKING Make Inferences What factors lead to a successful compromise? Give an example of a time when you've compromised.

 See Citizenship Handbook, pages 300–307.

The two men addressed the expansion of slavery. For Lincoln, slavery was "a moral, a social, and a political wrong." But he did not suggest that he wanted to end slavery where it existed. He argued only that slavery should not be expanded.

Douglas agreed that it was the national government's role to prevent the expansion of slavery. But he argued that popular sovereignty was the best way to address the issue because it was the most democratic method of doing so.

Popular sovereignty was a problem for Douglas. The Supreme Court decision in the Dred Scott case had made popular sovereignty unconstitutional. Why? It said that people could not vote to ban slavery, because doing so would take away slaveholders' property rights. (Slaves were considered property.) In a debate at Freeport, Illinois, Lincoln asked Douglas if he thought people in a territory who were against slavery could legally prohibit it—despite the Dred Scott decision.

Douglas replied that it did not matter what the Supreme Court might decide about slavery because "the people have the lawful means to introduce it or exclude it as they please." Douglas won reelection. Lincoln, despite his loss, became a national figure and strengthened his position in the Republican Party.

John Brown's Raid In 1859, John Brown, who had murdered proslavery Kansans three years before, added to the sectional tensions. Brown wanted to provoke a slave uprising. To do this, he planned to capture the weapons in the U.S. arsenal at **Harpers Ferry**, Virginia.

On October 16, 1859, Brown and 18 followers—13 whites and 5 blacks—captured the Harpers Ferry arsenal. Brown then sent out the word to rally and arm local slaves. But no slaves joined the fight. U.S. marines attacked Brown at Harpers Ferry. Some of his men escaped, but Brown and six others were captured, and ten men were killed.

John Brown Going to His Hanging, by Horace Pippin

Brown was tried for murder and betrayal of his country, or treason. He was also accused of conspiracy to cause a slave revolt. Brown was convicted and sentenced to hang. On the day he was hanged, abolitionists tolled bells and fired guns in his honor. Southerners were enraged by Brown's actions and horrified by Northern reactions to his death. As the nation headed toward the election of 1860, the issue of slavery had raised sectional tensions to the breaking point.

▲ **SUMMARIZE** Describe the events that brought the nation to a crisis.

Michigan Grade Level Content Expectations *Review*

🔗 **ONLINE QUIZ**
For test practice, go to
Interactive Review @ ClassZone.com

TERMS & NAMES

1. Explain the importance of
   - Republican Party
   - John C. Frémont
   - James Buchanan
   - *Dred Scott* v. *Sandford*
   - Roger B. Taney
   - Abraham Lincoln
   - Harpers Ferry

USING YOUR READING NOTES

2. **Main Ideas and Details** Complete the diagram you started at the beginning of this section.

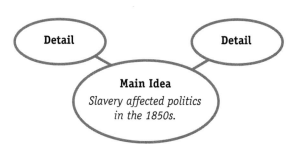

KEY IDEAS

3. Why was the Republican Party created?

4. What were the consequences of the Dred Scott decision for enslaved people?

5. How did John Brown's attack on Harpers Ferry increase tensions between the North and the South?

CRITICAL THINKING

6. **Make Inferences** How did the opinion in the Dred Scott case threaten the idea of popular sovereignty?

7. **Draw Conclusions** What did the Dred Scott decision reveal about Southern attitudes to slavery?

8. **Writing** **Speech** Imagine you are a candidate in the 1856 election. Write a speech explaining your political opinions.

▶ Key Ideas

BEFORE, YOU LEARNED

The formation of the antislavery Republican Party further divided the country.

NOW YOU WILL LEARN

The election of Abraham Lincoln as president in 1860 led seven Southern states to secede from the Union.

▶ Vocabulary

TERMS & NAMES

Confederate States of America confederation formed in 1861 by the Southern states after their secession from the Union

Jefferson Davis first president of the Confederate States of America

Crittenden Compromise compromise introduced in 1861 that might have prevented secession

BACKGROUND VOCABULARY

platform statement of beliefs

secede to withdraw

REVIEW

states' rights idea that the states have certain rights that the federal government cannot overrule

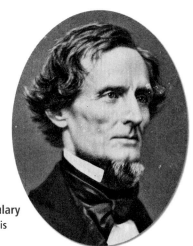

Visual Vocabulary
Jefferson Davis

▶ Reading Strategy

Re-create the diagram shown at right. As you read and respond to the **KEY QUESTIONS**, use the diagram to show why the Democratic Party broke apart.

 See Skillbuilder Handbook, page R6.

CATEGORIZE

Southern Democrats	Northern Democrats
wanted party to defend slavery	

 GRAPHIC ORGANIZERS
Go to **Interactive Review** @ ClassZone.com

Lincoln's Election and Southern Secession

8 – U5.1.4.6 Describe how the following increased sectional tensions – changes in the party system (e.g., the death of the Whig party, rise of the Republican party and division of the Democratic party)

8 – U5.2.1 Explain the reasons (political, economic, and social) why Southern states seceded and explain the differences in the timing of secession in the Upper and Lower South.

One American's Story

Mary Boykin Chesnut was born into wealth but died in poverty, one of the many victims of the political events that tore the nation apart.

Born in South Carolina in 1823, Mary grew up in a world of privilege and political power. At the age of 17 she married James Chesnut, a wealthy lawyer who became a senator. James supported slavery and resigned his senate seat at the news of Lincoln's election in 1860. Mary was also upset by this political event, and recorded the moment when she first heard the news.

PRIMARY SOURCE

❝ CHARLESTON, S.C., November 8, 1860. - Yesterday on the train, just before we reached Fernandina, a woman called out: "That settles the hash." Tanny touched me on the shoulder and said: "Lincoln's elected." "How do you know?" "The man over there has a telegram."

The excitement was very great. Everybody was talking at the same time. One, a little more moved than the others, stood up and said despondently: "The die is cast; no more vain regrets; sad forebodings are useless; the stake is life or death." ❞

—Mary Boykin Chesnut, *A Diary from Dixie*

Wedding photo of Mary and James Chesnut

For Mary Chesnut, Lincoln's election was a threat. Perhaps she foresaw the coming war that would take her from riches to poverty. But like the other Southerners on the train, she knew that Lincoln's election meant there could be no more compromise. Now there was no choice left but to fight.

The Election of 1860

▼ **KEY QUESTION** How did the 1860 election reveal the divisions in the country?

In April, the Democratic convention was held in Charleston, South Carolina. It was clear that Northern and Southern Democrats had very different ideas about slavery. The Democratic Party began to split along sectional lines.

The Split in the Democratic Party The Southerners wanted the party to defend slavery in the party's **platform**, or statement of beliefs. But Northerners wanted the platform to support popular sovereignty as a way of deciding whether a territory became a free state or a slave state. The Northerners won the platform vote, causing many Southern delegates to leave the convention before the Democrats chose a candidate for the presidential election.

The Democrats met again in Baltimore to choose a candidate. Northerners and Southerners remained at odds. Most Southerners left the meeting.

The Northern Democrats backed Stephen A. Douglas and his support for popular sovereignty. Meanwhile, proslavery Southern Democrats nominated vice president John Breckinridge of Kentucky.

The Republicans had already nominated Abraham Lincoln. Also in the race was a fourth party—the Constitutional Union Party. Its members had one aim—to preserve the Union. They nominated John Bell of Tennessee.

Animated GEOGRAPHY

Election of 1860

Click here to preview the Election of 1860 map @ ClassZone.com

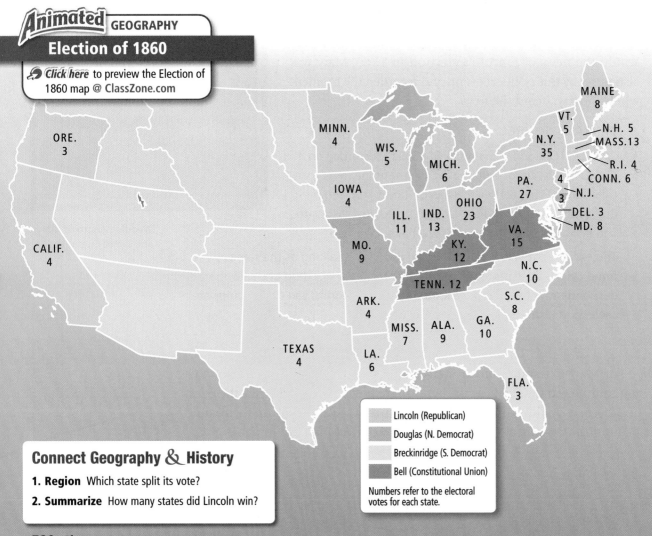

ORE. 3
CALIF. 4
MINN. 4
WIS. 5
IOWA 4
MICH. 6
ILL. 11
IND. 13
OHIO 23
MO. 9
KY. 12
TENN. 12
ARK. 4
MISS. 7
ALA. 9
GA. 10
TEXAS
LA. 6
FLA. 3
S.C. 8
N.C. 10
VA. 15
PA. 27
N.Y. 35
VT. 5
MAINE 8
N.H. 5
MASS. 13
R.I. 4
CONN. 6
N.J.
DEL. 3
MD. 8

Lincoln (Republican)
Douglas (N. Democrat)
Breckinridge (S. Democrat)
Bell (Constitutional Union)

Numbers refer to the electoral votes for each state.

Connect Geography & History

1. Region Which state split its vote?

2. Summarize How many states did Lincoln win?

FOOTRACE TO THE WHITE HOUSE

In this cartoon from 1860, the rival presidential candidates are competing in a footrace. As they race toward the White House, it is obvious which runner is going to win.

Bell:
"Bless my soul . . . I give up."

Breckinridge:
"That long legged Abolitionist is getting ahead of us after all."

Douglas:
"I never run so in my life."

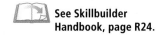

the White House

CRITICAL THINKING

1. **Make Inferences** What common symbol for a political campaign is used in the cartoon?
2. **Synthesize** What is the basic message of the cartoon?

See Skillbuilder Handbook, page R24.

Two Political Races The election of 1860 turned into two different races for the presidency—one in the North and one in the South. Lincoln and Douglas were the only candidates with much support in the North. Breckinridge and Bell competed for Southern votes.

Lincoln and Breckinridge were considered to have the most extreme views on slavery. Lincoln opposed the expansion of slavery into the territories. Breckinridge insisted that the federal government be required to protect slavery in any territory. Douglas and Bell were considered moderates because neither wanted the federal government to pass new laws on slavery.

The outcome of the election made it clear that the nation was tired of compromise. Lincoln defeated Douglas in the North. Breckinridge carried most of the South. Douglas and Bell managed to win only in the border states. Because the North had a larger population, Lincoln won the election.

Despite Lincoln's statements that he would do nothing to abolish slavery in the South, white Southerners did not trust him. Many were sure that he and the other Republicans would move to ban slavery. As a result, white Southerners saw the Republican victory as a threat to their way of life.

▲ **CATEGORIZE** Explain the divisions that affected political parties in 1860.

Southern States Secede

▼ **KEY QUESTION** How did seven Southern states justify their decision to secede?

Connecting History

Federalism
Many Southerners claimed that their fight for independence from the federal government was an echo of America's fight to separate from British tyranny during the Revolutionary War.

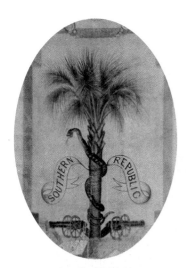

Detail of secession banner with tree representing South Carolina

Even before the election, Southerners had warned that if Lincoln won the presidency, Southern states would **secede**, or withdraw, from the Union.

The Confederate States of America Southerners based their arguments on **states' rights**, the idea that states have certain rights that the federal government cannot overrule. They argued that since the states had voluntarily joined the Union, they could voluntarily leave it.

On December 20, 1860, South Carolina became the first state to secede. Other states in the Deep South, where the economies depended on slavery and cotton production, also considered secession. Shortly after, Mississippi, Florida, Alabama, Georgia, Louisiana, and Texas joined South Carolina.

In early February 1861, the states that had seceded met in Montgomery, Alabama. They formed the **Confederate States of America**. The convention named **Jefferson Davis** president of the Confederacy.

The convention then drafted a constitution. The Confederate Constitution was modeled on the U.S. Constitution. But there were a few important differences. For example, the Confederate Constitution supported states' rights. It also protected slavery in the Confederacy, including any territories it might acquire.

Having formed its government, the Confederate states made plans to defend their separation from the Union. Some believed that war between the states could not be avoided. But everyone waited to see what the Union government would do in response.

The Union's Response Northerners considered the secession of the Southern states was unconstitutional. President James Buchanan argued against secession. He believed that the states did not have the right to withdraw from the Union because the federal government, not the state governments, was sovereign. If secession were permitted, the Union would become weak, like a "rope of sand." He believed that the U.S. Constitution was framed to prevent such a thing from happening.

In addition to these issues, secession raised the issue of majority rule. Southerners complained that Northerners intended to use their majority to force the South to abolish slavery. But Northerners responded that Southerners were not willing to live with the election results. As Northern writer James Russell Lowell wrote, "[The Southerners'] quarrel is not with the Republican Party, but with the theory of Democracy."

The Failure of Compromise With the states in the lower South forming a new government, some people continued to seek compromise. Senator John J. Crittenden of Kentucky proposed that slavery should be protected south of the line established in the Missouri Compromise, that Congress should not abolish slavery in a slave state, and that the federal government should compensate the owners of fugitive slaves. **The Crittenden Compromise** was presented to Congress in early 1861, but it was defeated in the Senate.

With the election of 1860, it was clear that attempts at compromise had failed. The issue of slavery had pulled the nation apart. Every Congressional attempt to reach a compromise only served to enrage one section of the country or the other. The following chart shows how the events and laws of these years brought the nation closer to civil war.

CONNECT to the Essential Question

What issues and events shattered the nation's unity and led to civil war?

	EVENT	NORTHERN REACTION	SOUTHERN REACTION
1846	War with Mexico	fear that slavery would expand into the territories won from Mexico	desire to extend slavery into territory taken from Mexico
1846	Wilmot Proviso proposes that slavery be outlawed in territory taken from Mexico.	support for Wilmot Proviso founding of Free-Soil Party dedicated to stopping expansion of slavery	Southerners fear that more free states will be created and upset the balance of power. Southern senators prevent passage of Wilmot Proviso
1850	Compromise of 1850	relief that California would be a free state outrage over Fugitive Slave Act	relief that Congress would not ban slavery from territories won from Mexico with the exception of California satisfaction with Fugitive Slave Act
1852	*Uncle Tom's Cabin* is published.	The novel becomes highly popular.	Southerners believe the book gives a false impression of the South and slavery.
1854	Kansas–Nebraska Act	anger over repeal of Missouri Compromise, which banned slavery in some territories	support for popular sovereignty, which allowed people to vote for slavery in territories where Missouri Compromise had banned it
1854	Whig Party splits over Kansas–Nebraska Act.	Northern Whigs join other groups to form antislavery Republican Party.	Southern Whigs join Democrats.
1860	Election of 1860	satisfaction with election of Republican candidate Abraham Lincoln	Seven Southern states secede from Union.

CRITICAL THINKING Causes and Effects Why did this series of laws and events shatter the unity of the nation?

Lincoln's Inauguration With the hopes for compromise fading, Americans waited for Lincoln's inauguration. What would the new president do about the crisis? On March 4, Lincoln took the oath of office and gave his First Inaugural Address. He assured the South that he had no intention of abolishing slavery there. But he spoke forcefully against secession. Then he ended his speech with an appeal to friendship.

PRIMARY SOURCE

❝ We are not enemies, but friends. We must not be enemies. Though passion may have strained, it must not break our bonds of affection. The mystic chords of memory, stretching from every battle-field and patriot grave, to every living heart and hearthstone, all over this broad land, will yet swell the chorus of the Union, when again touched, as surely they will be, by the better angels of our nature. ❞

Abraham Lincoln, *First Inaugural Address*

Lincoln did not want to invade the South. But he would not abandon the government's forts that stood on Southern soil. These forts would soon need to be resupplied. Throughout March and into April, Northerners and Southerners waited anxiously to see what would happen next.

 SEQUENCE Explain how the Southern states justified secession.

Michigan Grade Level Content Expectations *Review*

ONLINE QUIZ
For test practice, go to
Interactive Review @ ClassZone.com

TERMS & NAMES

1. Explain the importance of
   - Confederate States of America
   - Jefferson Davis
   - Crittenden Compromise

USING YOUR READING NOTES

2. **Categorize** Complete the diagram you started at the beginning of this section.

Southern Democrats	Northern Democrats
wanted party to defend slavery	

KEY IDEAS

3. Who were the candidates in the 1860 presidential election, and what policies did each candidate support?

4. What attempts did the North and the South make to compromise? What were the results?

CRITICAL THINKING

5. **Analyze Point of View** Do you think the Southern states seceded to protect slavery or states' rights?

6. **Connect to Today** What can the events in this section teach us about compromise in the political process today?

7. **Writing** News Article Imagine you are a newspaper reporter covering the 1860 election. Write a short analysis of the election results for either Northern or Southern readers.

Chapter Summary

① Key Idea
Rising anger over slavery increased tensions between the North and South and led to violence.

② Key Idea
The formation of the antislavery Republican Party further divided the country.

③ Key Idea
The election of Abraham Lincoln as president in 1860 led seven Southern states to secede from the Union.

For detailed Review and Study Notes go to **Interactive Review** @ ClassZone.com

Name Game

Use the Terms & Names list to identify each sentence online or on your own paper.

1. I was the first president of the Confederacy. _____
   Jefferson Davis

2. This compromise of 1861 might have prevented secession. _____.

3. I am the Illinois senator who backed the Compromise of 1850. _____

4. I ran for President as a Democrat in 1856. _____

5. I wrote a novel about slavery. _____

6. I presided in the case of *Dred Scott* v. *Sandford*. _____

7. This party's slogan was "Free Soil, Free Speech, Free Labor, and Free Men." _____

8. This 1850 law was meant to help slaveholders recapture runaway slaves. _____

9. I was the Republican candidate in 1856. _____

10. This proposal was meant to outlaw slavery in new territories. _____

A. Harriet Beecher Stowe
B. Free-Soil Party
C. Roger B. Taney
D. Crittenden Compromise
E. Abraham Lincoln
F. James Buchanan
G. Wilmot Proviso
H. Jefferson Davis
I. Confederate States of America
J. Fugitive Slave Act
K. Stephen A. Douglas
L. John Frémont

Activities

CROSSWORD PUZZLE

Complete the online puzzle to show what you know about the buildup to the Civil War.

ACROSS
1. The election of this man frightened the Southern states.

GEOGAME

Use this online map to reinforce your understanding of the sectional divide. Drag and drop the labels to identify slave states and free states. A scorecard helps you keep track of your progress online.

slave state

free state

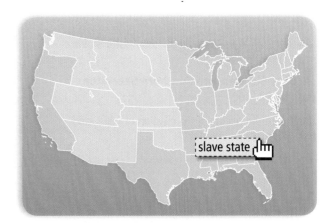

slave state

15 Assessment

VOCABULARY

Explain the significance of each of the following.

1. Harriet Beecher Stowe
2. Stephen A. Douglas
3. Harpers Ferry
4. Jefferson Davis
5. Roger B. Taney
6. Abraham Lincoln
7. *Dred Scott* v. *Sandford*
8. James Buchanan
9. John C. Frémont

Explain how the terms and names in each group are related.

10. Stephen A. Douglas, Compromise of 1850, Kansas-Nebraska Act
11. Compromise of 1850, Fugitive Slave Act
12. James Buchanan, John C. Frémont
13. John Brown, Harpers Ferry
14. Free-Soil Party, Wilmot Proviso

KEY IDEAS

❶ Tensions Rise Between North and South (pages 480–487)

15. In what ways did the North and the South differ in the 1840s?
16. How did Southerners react to the Wilmot Proviso?

❷ Slavery Dominates Politics (pages 490–497)

17. What positions did Lincoln and Douglas take in their debates?
18. Why were Southerners so angry about John Brown's attack on Harpers Ferry?

❸ Lincoln's Election and Southern Secession (pages 498–504)

19. What were the results of the election of 1860, and what did these results show?
20. Why did Southerners want to secede?

CRITICAL THINKING

21. **Compare and Contrast** What did the Compromise of 1850 and the Kansas-Nebraska Act have in common?

22. **Analyze Point of View** Why did Northerners and Southerners disagree about the Kansas-Nebraska Act?

23. **Evaluate** Which event do you think caused the most damage to the relationship between the North and the South?

24. **Compare and Contrast** Make a chart to compare the fears that people in each section of the country had about the other section's intentions.

Northern Fears	Southern Fears
slavery was expanding	

25. **WHAT IF?** What might have been done in the 1850s to prevent the Southern states from seceding?

26. **Draw Conclusions** Which sectional economy was better prepared for war—the industrial North or the agricultural South?

27. **Analyze Primary Sources** What does this poster tell you about how people in the North reacted to the Fugitive Slave Act?

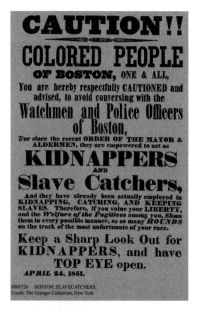

✓ **TEST PRACTICE**

• **Online Test Practice @ ClassZone.com**
• Use the **MEAP Strategies & Practice,** pages S1–S27, at the front of this book

DOCUMENT-BASED QUESTIONS

Study each document carefully and answer the questions that follow.

DOCUMENT 1

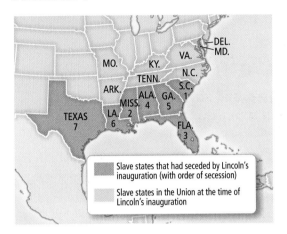

Slave states that had seceded by Lincoln's inauguration (with order of secession)

Slave states in the Union at the time of Lincoln's inauguration

1 At the time of Lincoln's inauguration, which slave states were still in the Union?

A Alabama, Georgia, Florida, and Louisiana

B South Carolina, Arkansas, Missouri, and Texas

C Maryland, Kentucky, Tennessee, and Virginia

D Delaware, Mississippi, Virginia, and Arkansas

DOCUMENT 2

PRIMARY SOURCE

❝ In January next we shall take leave of the Union and shall construct with our Sister Cotton States a government for ourselves. Whether the other Slave States will join seems very uncertain at least for the present. The condition of affairs at the North since the election of an Abolitionist for President makes it necessary for us to get away as quickly as possible. ❞

—E. B. Heyward, South Carolina, Nov. 20, 1860

2 Why does the writer support secession?

A because the Republican Party won the presidency

B because the Whig Party won the presidency

C because the Democratic Party won the presidency

D because the Constitutional Union Party won the presidency

YOU BE THE HISTORIAN

28. Make Inferences Why did the Confederate government's support of states' rights threaten its own unity?

29. WHAT IF? Suppose the Supreme Court had ruled in favor of Dred Scott in *Dred Scott* v. *Sandford*. How might this have changed American history?

30. Make Generalizations How far back in American history can you trace the economic difference between North and South?

31. Draw Conclusions Why do you think so many Americans supported slavery when it seemed to contradict Jefferson's words from the Declaration of Independence that "all men are created equal"?

32. Connect to Today Citizenship What are some of the social, political, and economic trends in modern American life that can traced back to the North-South conflict and secession?

 Answer the
ESSENTIAL QUESTION
What issues and events shattered the nation's unity and led to civil war?

Written Response Write a four-paragraph response to the Essential Question. Be sure to consider the key ideas of each section as well as the most significant factors that led to the split between North and South. Use the Response Rubric below to guide your thinking and writing.

Response Rubric
A strong response will

• analyze the differences between the Northern and Southern states

• discuss the major events that led to the split between North and South

• show why the process of compromise broke down

CHAPTER

16

1. War Erupts

2. Life in the Army

3. No End in Sight

Detail of a painting of Union general McClellan

The Civil War Begins

1861–1862

 ESSENTIAL QUESTION

What events, leaders, and strategies shaped the early years of war?

CONNECT ↻ **Geography & History**

What geographic features would the Union have to seize in order to defeat the Confederacy?

Think about:

1 how goods and weapons were transported in the South, which did not have an extensive railway system

2 the way the Southern economy relied on exporting cotton by ship

3 the position of New Orleans, the South's largest city

1861 July: Confederacy sets up its capital in Richmond.

Recruitment posters

ON TO RICHMOND!
CITIZENS TO THE
LYCEUM HALL, MONDAY EV
AT EIGHT O'
THE PRESEN
PRESIDENT
PUT DOWN TI
READY TO
LIBERTY

Volunteers Wanted!
FOR COMPANY A,
OF THE ORIGINAL
IRISH VOLUNTEERS,
Col. OWEN'S 2d REGIM'T OF
BAKER'S BRIGADE.
Head Quarters, 421 Walnut Street.
PAY AND RATIONS BEGIN WHEN ENROLLED.
JAMES DUFFY, Captain.

1861

April: Confederate attack on Fort Sumter

Detail of a painting of Bull Run

1861 July: First Battle of Bull Run

▼

Effect Lincoln realizes he must raise a national army.

508 Chapter 16

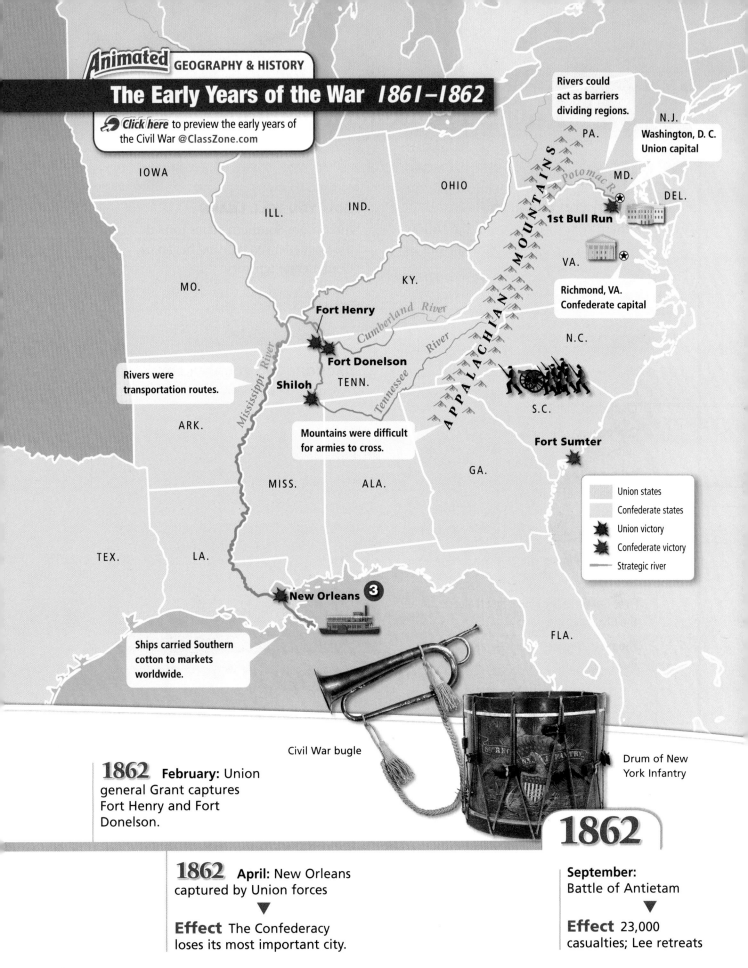

The Early Years of the War *1861–1862*

Click here to preview the early years of the Civil War @ClassZone.com

Rivers could act as barriers dividing regions.

N.J.

PA.

Washington, D. C. Union capital

MD.

DEL.

Potomac R.

IOWA

OHIO

ILL.

IND.

1st Bull Run

VA.

MO.

KY.

Richmond, VA. Confederate capital

Cumberland River

N.C.

Fort Henry

Fort Donelson

Tennessee River

Rivers were transportation routes.

Mississippi River

Shiloh

TENN.

ARK.

S.C.

Mountains were difficult for armies to cross.

APPALACHIAN MOUNTAINS

Fort Sumter

MISS.

ALA.

GA.

Union states

Confederate states

Union victory

Confederate victory

Strategic river

TEX.

LA.

New Orleans ③

Ships carried Southern cotton to markets worldwide.

FLA.

Civil War bugle

Drum of New York Infantry

1862 **February:** Union general Grant captures Fort Henry and Fort Donelson.

1862

1862 **April:** New Orleans captured by Union forces

▼

Effect The Confederacy loses its most important city.

September: Battle of Antietam

▼

Effect 23,000 casualties; Lee retreats

The Civil War Begins **509**

Reading for Understanding

▶ Key Ideas

BEFORE, YOU LEARNED
Southern states seceded from the Union after the election of Abraham Lincoln in 1860.

NOW YOU WILL LEARN
After more Southern states joined the Confederacy, fighting began on Confederate territory.

▶ Vocabulary

TERMS & NAMES

Fort Sumter Union fort in the harbor of Charleston, South Carolina

Confederacy nation formed by Southern states

Robert E. Lee Confederate general, commander of the Army of Northern Virginia

border states slave states that bordered states in which slavery was illegal

Anaconda Plan Union strategy to defeat the Confederacy

First Battle of Bull Run first major battle of the Civil War

Thomas J. Jackson Confederate general at Bull Run

BACKGROUND VOCABULARY

uprising rebellion

populous heavily populated

Visual Vocabulary
Attack on Fort Sumter

▶ Reading Strategy

Re-create the diagram shown at right. As you read and respond to the **KEY QUESTIONS**, use the diagram to note problems faced by the Union and the Southern states and how they were addressed.

 See Skillbuilder Handbook, page R9.

PROBLEMS AND SOLUTIONS

Problem	Solution
What to do about the federal forts located in the Confederacy?	

 GRAPHIC ORGANIZERS
Go to **Interactive Review** @ ClassZone.com

War Erupts

8 – U5.2.2.2 Make an argument to explain the reasons why the North won the Civil War by considering the – the political and military leadership of the North and South
8 – U5.2.2.3 Make an argument to explain the reasons why the North won the Civil War by considering the – the respective advantages and disadvantages, including geographic, demographic, economic and technological

One American's Story

Like other South Carolinians, Emma Holmes got caught up in the passions that led her state to secede. In her diary, she wrote about South Carolina's attack on **Fort Sumter**, a federal fort on an island in Charleston's harbor.

PRIMARY SOURCE

❝ [A]t half past four this morning, the heavy booming of cannons woke the city from its slumbers. . . . Every body seems relieved that what has been so long dreaded has come at last and so confident of victory that they seem not to think of the danger of their friends. . . . With the telescope I saw the shots as they struck the fort and [saw] the masonry crumbling. ❞

—Emma Holmes, *The Diary of Miss Emma Holmes 1861–1866*

Emma Holmes

Many Southerners expected a short war that they would easily win. Northerners expected the same. In this section, you will learn how Americans slowly realized that the war would be long and difficult.

First Shots at Fort Sumter

▼ **KEY QUESTION** What did Lincoln do about the forts in Confederate territory?

As Southern states seceded from the Union, they took control of most of the federal forts located within their borders. President Abraham Lincoln wrestled with a decision that might provoke war—what should he do about the forts that remained under federal control?

Lincoln's Decision In Charleston Harbor, Robert Anderson's garrison in Fort Sumter was running out of supplies.

Lincoln faced a difficult decision. If he sent supplies, he risked war. If he surrendered the fort, he would be giving in to the rebels. Lincoln decided to send supply ships and notified the leaders of the **Confederacy**—the nation formed by Southern states. Confederate leaders decided to attack the fort before the supply ships arrived.

History Makers

Abraham Lincoln   1809–1865

Today Abraham Lincoln, shown above with his son, is regarded as a national hero. Yet when Lincoln became President, many people in the North did not think he was equal to the enormous task before him.

Lincoln surprised his critics with his vision and his ability to organize and lead the war effort. In the nation's worst crisis, he focused on winning the war and preserving the Union. Throughout the war, Lincoln inspired fellow Americans to "dare to do our duty as we understand it."

CRITICAL THINKING **Make Inferences**
Why would the ability to inspire people be important in a wartime leader?

 **ONLINE BIOGRAPHY** For more on Abraham Lincoln, go to the **Research & Writing Center** @ ClassZone.com

On April 12, 1861, the Confederates opened fire. After enduring 34 hours of shelling, Anderson surrendered. No one was killed defending the fort, but the attack on Fort Sumter marked the beginning of the Civil War.

Lincoln Calls Out the Militia Two days after the surrender of Fort Sumter, President Lincoln asked the Union states to provide 75,000 militiamen for 90 days to put down the **uprising**, or rebellion, in the South. Citizens of the North responded with enthusiasm to the call to arms. A New York woman wrote, "it seems as if we never were alive till now; never had a country till now."

In the upper South, however, state leaders responded with defiance. The governor of Kentucky said that the state would "furnish no troops for the wicked purpose of subduing her sister Southern states." In the weeks that followed, Virginia, North Carolina, Tennessee, and Arkansas voted to join the Confederacy.

🔺 **PROBLEMS AND SOLUTIONS** Explain how Lincoln tried to solve the problem of the federal forts.

Preparing For Battle

🔻 **KEY QUESTION** What strategy did each side hope to pursue?

With Virginia on its side, the Confederacy had a better hope of victory. Virginia was rich and **populous**, or heavily populated. In July of 1861, the Confederacy moved its capital to Richmond.

Virginia was also the home of **Robert E. Lee**, a military leader who became the South's greatest general. When Virginia seceded, Lee resigned from the United States army and joined the Confederacy. Lee's support strengthened the Confederacy.

Choosing Sides After Virginia seceded, all eyes turned to the **border states**. The border states—Delaware, Maryland, Kentucky, and Missouri—were slave states that bordered states where slavery was illegal. Their location and resources were important to both sides.

All four states stayed in the Union. Later in the war, the Union gained territory when the western counties of Virginia broke away from the Confederacy and formed the state of West Virginia in 1863. West Virginia supported the Union. In the end, there were 24 states in the Union and 11 in the Confederacy.

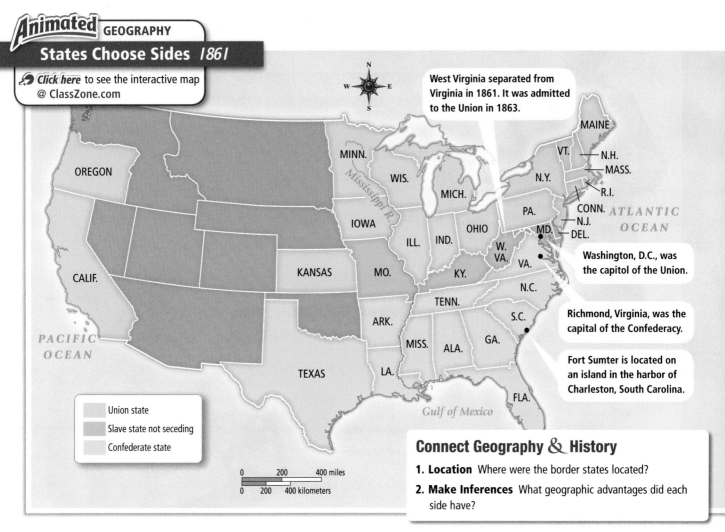

Animated GEOGRAPHY

States Choose Sides 1861

Click here to see the interactive map
@ ClassZone.com

West Virginia separated from Virginia in 1861. It was admitted to the Union in 1863.

Washington, D.C., was the capitol of the Union.

Richmond, Virginia, was the capital of the Confederacy.

Fort Sumter is located on an island in the harbor of Charleston, South Carolina.

Union state
Slave state not seceding
Confederate state

0   200   400 miles
0   200   400 kilometers

Connect Geography & History

1. **Location** Where were the border states located?

2. **Make Inferences** What geographic advantages did each side have?

Planning Strategies The Confederacy started off with a defensive strategy. Confederate leaders knew that support for the war in the North would weaken if the fighting went on for a long time. They also hoped that foreign dependence on their cotton exports would bring military aid from Great Britain and France. But both European nations had sufficient supplies of cotton. The South adopted a mix of defensive and offensive strategy, invading the North several times.

The Northern strategy was to invade and conquer the South. To do this they adopted the **Anaconda Plan**, developed by General Winfield Scott. This plan was designed to strangle the South's economy like a giant anaconda snake squeezing its prey. The plan called for

- a naval blockade of the South's coastline. In a blockade, armed forces block the traffic of goods or people.
- taking control of the Mississippi River. This would split the Confederacy in two.
- capturing Richmond, Virginia—the Confederate capital.

With Richmond only about 100 miles from Washington, Virginia became the site of many battles during the war.

🔺 **CAUSES AND EFFECTS** Explain each side's strategy for winning the war.

The Civil War Begins **513**

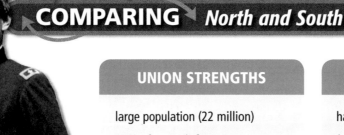

COMPARING › *North and South*

UNION STRENGTHS

large population (22 million)

85% of nation's factories

70% of the nation's railroad mileage

almost all the nation's naval vessels
and shipyards

UNION WEAKNESSES

had to depend on long supply lines

fewer good military leaders

soldiers fighting an offensive war

Union general
McClellan

Confederate
general Lee

CONFEDERATE STRENGTHS

vast size of the Confederacy

good generals

soldiers fighting a defensive war to
protect their homeland

CONFEDERATE WEAKNESSES

smaller population (5.5 million
free; 3.5 million enslaved)

few factories

fewer railroads

no naval power

CRITICAL THINKING **Draw Conclusions** Which strength or weakness
might have had the greatest effects?

First Battle of Bull Run

▼ **KEY QUESTION** Why was the Union surprised by the outcome of Bull Run?

Many people in the North called for an immediate attack on Richmond. But
to take Richmond, the Union army would first have to defeat the Confederate troops stationed at the town of Manassas, Virginia, near Washington,
D.C. Many believed the battle, and the war, would be quickly won.

Intense Fighting On July 16, 1861, Union forces led by General Irvin
McDowell marched to Manassas. They were joined there by hundreds of
spectators from Washington who expected a quick and entertaining battle.
Both soldiers and spectators were totally unprepared for what followed.

Union forces attacked the Confederates near the creek called Bull Run. In
the North this battle is known as the **First Battle of Bull Run**. The Confederates,
led by General Pierre Beauregard, were driven back. However, a regiment led

by **Thomas J. Jackson** stopped the Union advance. Another officer saw Jackson and said, "There is Jackson standing like a stone wall!" From then on, Jackson was known as "Stonewall" Jackson.

Confederate forces launched a counter-charge while letting out a blood-curdling scream that became known as the "rebel yell." Frightened Union soldiers ran for their lives, along with scared and confused spectators.

Fighting at Bull Run

The Confederate victory thrilled the South and shocked the North. Casualty figures reached around 2,700 for the Union and 2,000 for the Confederacy. It was obvious that this would be a deadly war.

Lessons of Bull Run The First Battle of Bull Run made three points clear:

- The fighting would be bloody.
- The war would not be over quickly.
- Southern soldiers would fight fiercely to defend the Confederacy.

After Bull Run, Lincoln realized the 90-day militias were no match for Confederate forces. He sent them home and called for a real army of 500,000 volunteers for three years. He also appointed George McClellan as commander of the Union army in the east.

▲ **SUMMARIZE** Explain why the Union was surprised by the outcome of Bull Run.

Michigan Grade Level Content Expectations *Review*

 ONLINE QUIZ
For test practice, go to
Interactive Review @ ClassZone.com

TERMS & NAMES

1. Explain the significance of

- Fort Sumter
- Confederacy
- Robert E. Lee
- border states
- Anaconda Plan
- First Battle of Bull Run
- Thomas J. Jackson

USING YOUR READING NOTES

2. Problems and Solutions Complete the diagram that you started at the beginning of this section.

Problem	Solution
What to do about the federal forts located in the Confederacy?	

KEY IDEAS

3. What were Lincoln's choices in regard to Fort Sumter?

4. Why were the border states important to both sides in the Civil War?

5. What kind of military strategy did each side develop?

CRITICAL THINKING

6. Evaluate Which side seemed better prepared for the conflict?

7. Draw Conclusions Why did the Confederacy adopt a defensive strategy?

8. Connect Economics and History How did the Union hope to damage the Southern economy?

9. Writing Description Imagine you were a spectator at Bull Run. Describe what you saw and explain how it changed your attitude toward the war.

▶ Key Ideas

BEFORE, YOU LEARNED
The Civil War began on Confederate territory.

NOW YOU WILL LEARN
Army life and new technology brought unexpected hardships to millions of soldiers.

▶ Vocabulary

TERMS & NAMES

the *Monitor* Union ironclad ship

the *Merrimack* Confederate ironclad ship, later renamed the *Virginia*

BACKGROUND VOCABULARY

enlist to join the armed forces

contractor private supplier

hygiene conditions and practices that promote health

Visual Vocabulary
The *Monitor* (*below*) clashes with the *Merrimack,* or *Virginia* (*below left*)

▶ Reading Strategy

Re-create the diagram shown at right. As you read and respond to the **KEY QUESTIONS**, use the boxes to show causes of important events. Create a new diagram for each event.

 See Skillbuilder Handbook, page R7.

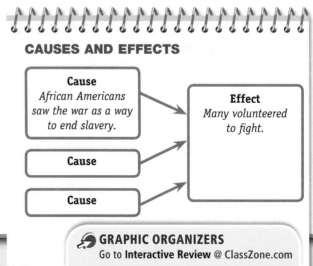

CAUSES AND EFFECTS

| Cause
African Americans saw the war as a way to end slavery. |

| **Cause** |

| **Cause** |

Effect
Many volunteered to fight.

GRAPHIC ORGANIZERS
Go to **Interactive Review** @ ClassZone.com

Life in the Army

8 – U5.2.4 Describe the role of African Americans in the war, including black soldiers and regiments, and the increased resistance of enslaved peoples.
8 – U5.2.5 Construct generalizations about how the war affected combatants, civilians (including the role of women), the physical environment, and the future of warfare, including technological developments.

One American's Story

In 1862, Peter Vredenburgh, Jr., answered President Lincoln's call for an additional 300,000 soldiers. Nearly 26 years old, Vredenburgh became a major in the 14th Regiment New Jersey Volunteer Infantry. Less than two months after joining the regiment, he wrote a letter urging his parents to keep his 18-year-old brother from enlisting.

PRIMARY SOURCE

❝ I am glad that Jim has not joined any [regiment] and I hope he never will. I would not have him go for all my pay; it would be very improbable that we could both go through this war and come out unharmed. Let him come here and see the thousands with their arms and legs off, or if that won't do, let him go as I did the other day through the Frederick hospitals and see how little account a man's life and limbs are held in by others. ❞

—Major Peter Vredenburgh, Jr., quoted in *Upon the Tented Field*

Major Peter Vredenburgh, Jr., was an officer in the Union army.

On September 19, 1864, Vredenburgh was killed in battle. He was only one of many young men unprepared for the horrors of the war.

Civilians Become Soldiers

▼ **KEY QUESTION** Why did so many volunteer to fight?

Like Peter Vredenburgh, the majority of soldiers in the Civil War were between 18 and 30 years of age. But both the Confederate and Union armies had younger and older soldiers, whose ages ranged from 11 to 83. These soldiers came from cities, towns, and farms across America.

Joining Up On both sides volunteers rushed to **enlist**, or join the army. Many were farmers who had never been far from home. Some rode a train for the first time. German and Irish immigrants made up the largest ethnic groups.

(top) Soldiers off duty. (inset) Union jacket and cap.
How does the crisp, new jacket above compare to those in the larger photograph?

At the beginning of the war, African Americans wanted to fight. They saw the war as a way to end slavery. However, neither the North nor the South accepted African Americans into their armies—at first. But as the war dragged on, the North finally took African Americans into its ranks.

In all, about 2 million men served in the Union Army and less than 1 million fought for the Confederacy. Most were volunteers. They enlisted for many different reasons. Some fought out of loyalty to their state or country. They also sought excitement and glory. Some soldiers signed up to escape the boredom of their lives in the factory or on the farm. Still others joined for the money.

Turning Civilians Into Soldiers After enlisting, volunteers were sent to an army camp for training. They lived in tents and had drill sessions. In winter, the soldiers lived in log huts or in heavy tents positioned on a log base.

Union soldiers were issued blue uniforms. Confederate soldiers wore gray or yellowish-brown. Early in the war, Northern soldiers received clothing of very poor quality. **Contractors,** or private suppliers, often supplied shoddy goods. In the Confederacy, some states had trouble providing uniforms at all. Confederate soldiers sometimes lacked shoes. After battles needy soldiers took coats, boots, and other clothing from the dead.

As the war went on, food became scarce. When soldiers were on the march they were sometimes out of reach of supply trains and had to find food on their own.

▲ **CAUSES AND EFFECTS** Explain why men volunteered for the army.

A New Kind of War

🔻 **KEY QUESTION** How was the Civil War different from previous conflicts?

For many soldiers, the experience of army life did not meet their expectations. Advances in military technology brought high casualties. Primitive medical techniques and filthy conditions helped spread disease.

Unhealthy Conditions Military camps were filthy and smelled from the odors of garbage and latrines. One Union soldier described a camp near Washington. In the camp, cattle were killed to provide the troops with meat.

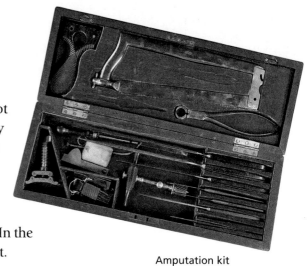

Amputation kit
Why would equipment like this have helped increase casualties?

PRIMARY SOURCE

❝ The hides and [waste parts] of the [cattle] for miles upon miles around, under a sweltering sun and sultry showers, would gender such swarms of flies, armies of worms, blasts of stench and oceans of filth as to make life miserable. ❞

—William Keesy, quoted in *The Civil War Infantryman*

Not only were the camps filthy, but so were the soldiers. They often went weeks without bathing or washing their clothes. Their bodies, clothing, and bedding became infested with lice and fleas. Poor **hygiene**—or conditions and practices that promote health—resulted in widespread sickness. Doctors were unaware that dirt carried germs that caused disease. They performed surgery without washing their hands. Because of these conditions, more soldiers died from disease than on the battlefield.

Andersonville prison camp. A prisoner's meal might be little more than a single cracker.

Civil War Prison Camps The war was difficult for all soldiers, but prisoners had an especially hard time. At prison camps in both the North and the South, prisoners of war faced terrible conditions.

One of the worst prison camps in the North was in Elmira, New York. In just one year, more than 24 percent of Elmira's 12,121 prisoners died of sickness and exposure to severe weather.

Conditions were also horrible in the South. The camp with the worst reputation was in Andersonville, Georgia. Inmates had little shelter from the heat or cold. Drinking water came from a tiny creek that also served as a sewer. As many as 13,000 died at Andersonville from starvation, disease, and exposure.

CIVIL WAR TECHNOLOGY

The American Civil War brought startling changes to military warfare.

Railroads and Cannons

The North's superior railway system gave the Union a distinct advantage. Railways helped move millions of soldiers and supplies quickly and easily to strategic positions. Cannon could also be mounted on railcars, as in the photo above.

Ironclads

The ironclads transformed naval warfare. Powered by steam, and with their sides protected by iron plates, ironclads were fast and deadly. The Union churned them out in order to create an inland navy to control Southern rivers. Union ironclads like the one above played an important role in Grant's capture of Fort Henry.

Rifles and Grenades

The rifle and minié ball increased the range of accuracy from 100 to 400 yards. Defenders could shoot down lines of advancing troops. Grenades were thrown by hand and exploded on impact. The days of formal, linear warfare were over.

Trenches

Soldiers quickly learned to stay low to the ground in order to avoid rifle fire. The new weaponry encouraged soldiers to protect themselves by digging trenches. Massive trench systems were dug by both sides during the war.

CRITICAL THINKING Make Inferences Which aspect of military technology do you think had the most impact on the fighting?

Changes in Military Technology Improvements in the weapons of war had far-reaching effects. The new weaponry increased the number of casualties. It also changed battlefield strategies.

One change was the use of rifles and minié balls. A rifle is a gun with a grooved barrel that spins a bullet through the air. The minié ball is a bullet with a hollow base. The bullet expands upon firing to fit the grooves in the barrel. Rifles with minié balls could shoot farther and more accurately than old-fashioned muskets. As a result, mounted charges and assaults did not work as well. Defenders could shoot more of the attackers before they got close.

New technology also changed naval warfare. Ironclads were naval warships covered with iron. They were a vast improvement over conventional warships. Ironclads were faster and better-protected than wooden ships. A witness reported that an ironclad ship's prow cut through a wooden ship "as a knife goes through cheese."

In March 1862, off the coast of Virginia, a Union ironclad named **the *Monitor***, fought **the *Merrimack***, a Confederate ironclad renamed the *Virginia*. The day-long battle between the *Monitor* and the *Merrimack* ended in a draw. But the event became famous as the first battle in history between two ironclad ships.

Despite new technology and tactics, in the first two years of the war, neither side was able to defeat its enemy.

 SUMMARIZE Describe ways the Civil War differed from previous conflicts.

 Michigan Grade Level Content Expectations *Review*

ONLINE QUIZ
For test practice, go to
Interactive Review @ ClassZone.com

TERMS & NAMES

1. Explain the significance of
- the *Monitor*
- the *Merrimack*

USING YOUR READING NOTES

2. Causes and Effects Complete the diagram that you started at the beginning of this section.

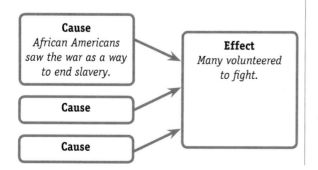

Cause
African Americans saw the war as a way to end slavery.

Cause

Cause

Effect
Many volunteered to fight.

KEY IDEAS

3. What was life like for the volunteers?

4. Why did so many soldiers die of disease?

5. How did the use of the rifle and minié ball change combat tactics in the Civil War?

CRITICAL THINKING

6. Draw Conclusions Why would commanders have to worry about marching too far from supply trains?

7. Causes and Effects What caused the high death rates during the Civil War?

8. Make Inferences Why were ironclads an improvement over wooden ships?

9. Math Research the casualty figures of the Civil War. Make a graph to display the information.

▶ Key Ideas

BEFORE, YOU LEARNED

The Union defeat at the Battle of Bull Run shocked the North.

NOW YOU WILL LEARN

Both the Union and the Confederacy won important victories in the first years of the war.

▶ Vocabulary

TERMS & NAMES

George McClellan commander of Union army in the east

Ulysses S. Grant Union general who won battles in the west

Battle of Shiloh bloody battle in Tennessee won by Grant

William Tecumseh Sherman Union general at Battle of Shiloh

David Farragut Union naval commander who captured New Orleans

Seven Days' Battles Confederate victory in Virginia, during which Lee stopped Union campaign against Richmond

Battle of Antietam battle in Maryland that ended Lee's first invasion of the North

BACKGROUND VOCABULARY

plunder steal from, ransack

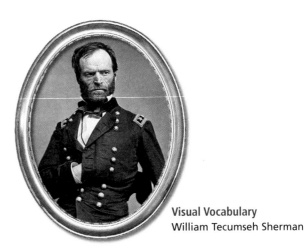

Visual Vocabulary
William Tecumseh Sherman

▶ Reading Strategy

Re-create the diagram shown at right. As you read and respond to the **KEY QUESTIONS**, use the diagram to record the events that support the main idea that the Union was succeeding in splitting the Confederacy in two.

 See Skillbuilder Handbook, page R4.

MAIN IDEA AND DETAILS

Detail

Detail

Main Idea
In 1862, the Union was well on its way to splitting the Confederacy in two.

🖱 **GRAPHIC ORGANIZERS**
Go to **Interactive Review** @ ClassZone.com

No End in Sight

8 – U5.2.2.1 **Make an argument to explain the reasons why the North won the Civil War by considering the** – critical events and battles in the war
8 – U5.2.2.2 **Make an argument to explain the reasons why the North won the Civil War by considering the** – the political and military leadership of the North and South

One American's Story

Twenty-year-old Sarah Morgan was living in the river town of Baton Rouge, Louisiana, when the Yankee gunships arrived. The Union navy had already captured New Orleans. Now Union ships were sailing deep into Confederate territory. When the gunships began shelling the town, the Morgans fled their home.

PRIMARY SOURCE

Sarah Morgan

❝ As we stood in the door, four or five shells sailed over our heads at the same time, seeming to make a perfect corkscrew of the air—for it sounded as though it went in circles. . . . I [stayed] behind to lock the door, with this new music in my ears. . . . I had heard Jimmy laugh about the singular sensation produced by the rifled balls spinning around one's head, and [here] I heard the same peculiar sound, ran the same risk, and was equal to the rest of the boys, for was I not in the midst of flying shells, in the middle of a bombardment? I think I was rather proud of it. ❞

—Sarah Morgan, *The Civil War Diary of a Southern Woman*

Sarah Morgan had rejoiced at the news of Confederate victories in the east. Now she remained defiant as the Union gained control of the Mississippi River in the west.

Union Victories in the West

 **KEY QUESTION** In 1862, how close did the Union come to achieving its goals?

In the summer of 1861, President Lincoln gave **George McClellan** command of the Union army in the East. The army had recently been defeated at Bull Run. Within months, McClellan restored the soldiers' confidence and organized and trained an army that could defeat the Confederates. Although McClellan prepared his army well, he seemed reluctant to attack the Southern capital at

Richmond. Instead, he kept drilling his troops. Lincoln, growing impatient, said that McClellan had "the slows." Meanwhile, another Union general was winning victories in the west.

Grant Opens Up the South That victorious Union general in the west was **Ulysses S. Grant**. In civilian life, he had failed at many things. But Grant had a simple strategy of war: "Find out where your enemy is. Get at him as soon as you can. Strike at him as hard as you can, and keep moving on."

In February 1862, Grant made a bold move to take Tennessee. Using ironclad gunboats, Grant's forces captured two Confederate river forts. These were Fort Henry on the Tennessee and Fort Donelson on the nearby Cumberland. (See map Ⓐ) The seizure of Fort Henry opened up a river highway into the heart of the South. Union gunboats could now travel by river as far as northern Alabama. A week later, Union troops marched into Nashville.

Battle of Shiloh

The Battle of Shiloh After Grant's river victories, Albert S. Johnston, Confederate commander on the Western front, ordered a retreat to Corinth, Mississippi. Grant followed. By early April, Grant's troops had reached Pittsburg Landing on the Tennessee River. There he waited for more troops from Nashville. Johnston, however, decided to attack before Grant gained reinforcements. Marching his troops north

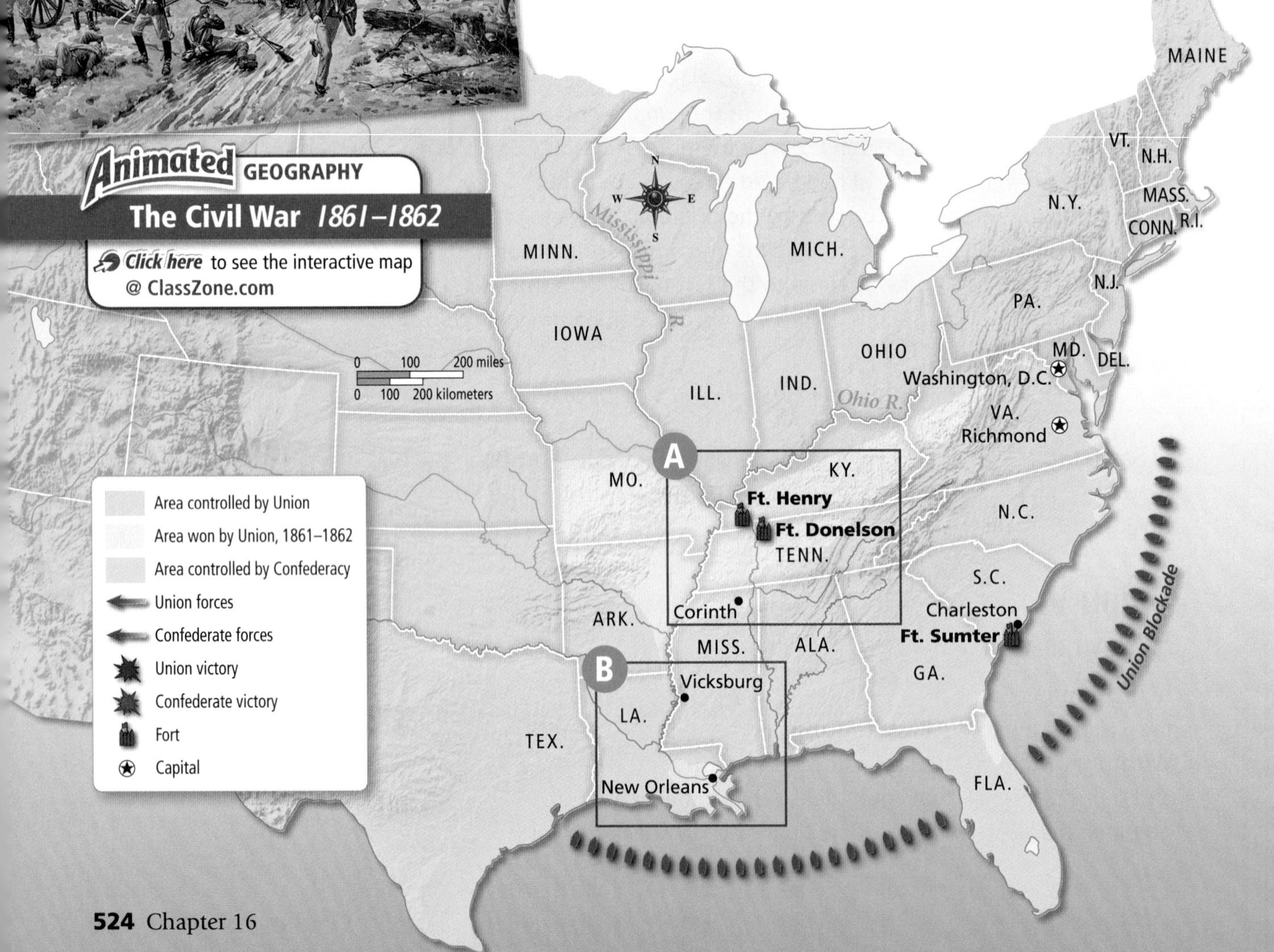

Animated GEOGRAPHY

The Civil War 1861–1862

🔎 *Click here* to see the interactive map @ ClassZone.com

Area controlled by Union
Area won by Union, 1861–1862
Area controlled by Confederacy
Union forces
Confederate forces
Union victory
Confederate victory
Fort
Capital

0   100   200 miles
0   100   200 kilometers

from Corinth on April 6, 1862, Johnston surprised the Union forces near Shiloh Church. The Battle of Shiloh in Tennessee turned into the fiercest fighting the Civil War had yet seen. (See map Ⓑ below.)

Commanders on each side rode into the thick of battle to rally their troops. One Union general, **William Tecumseh Sherman**, had three horses shot out from under him. General Johnston was killed, and the command passed to General Pierre Beauregard. By the end of the day, each side believed that dawn would bring victory.

That night, there was a terrible thunderstorm. Lightning lit up the battlefield, where dead and dying soldiers lay in water and mud. During the night, Union boats ferried fresh troops to Grant's camp. Grant then led an attack at dawn and forced the exhausted Southern troops to retreat.

The cost of the Union victory was staggering. Union casualties at Shiloh numbered over 13,000, about one-fifth of the 65,000 who had fought. The Confederates lost nearly 11,000 out of 41,000 soldiers. Describing the piles of mangled bodies, General Sherman wrote home, "The scenes on this field would have cured anybody of war." In the North, people were horrified at the slaughter. Members of Congress criticized Grant for the high casualties and urged Lincoln to replace him. But Lincoln replied, "I can't spare this man—he fights."

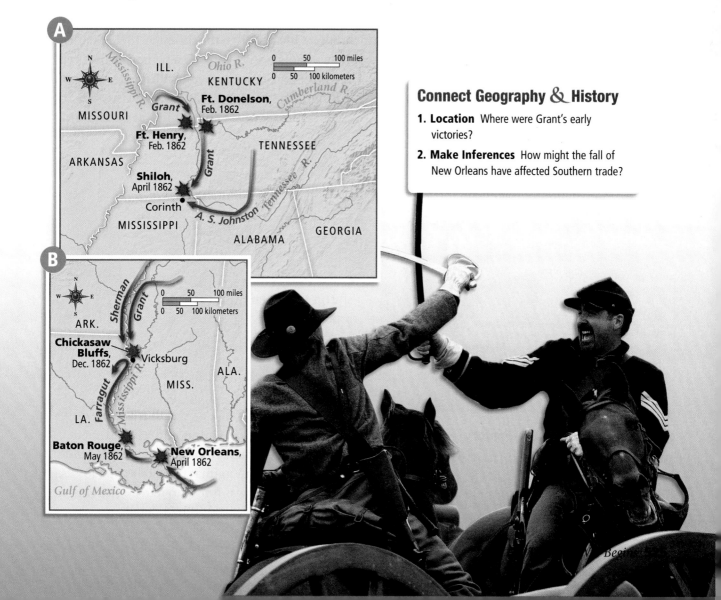

Connect Geography & History

1. **Location** Where were Grant's early victories?
2. **Make Inferences** How might the fall of New Orleans have affected Southern trade?

The Fall of New Orleans The spring of 1862 brought other bad news for the Confederacy. On April 25, a Union fleet led by Admiral **David Farragut** captured New Orleans, the largest city in the South. (See map **B** on page 525.) Rebel gunboats tried to ram the Union warships and succeeded in sinking one. Farragut's ships had to run through cannon fire and then dodge burning rafts in order to reach the city.

The fall of New Orleans was a heavy blow to the South. Mary Chesnut of South Carolina, the wife of an aide to President Davis, wrote in her diary, "New Orleans gone—and with it the Confederacy. Are we not cut in two?" Indeed, after the victories of General Grant and Admiral Farragut, only a 150-mile stretch of the Mississippi remained in Southern hands. The Union was well on its way to achieving its goal of cutting the Confederacy in two. But guarding the remaining stretch of the river was the heavily armed Confederate fort at Vicksburg, Mississippi.

▲ **MAIN IDEAS & DETAILS** Explain how close the Union came to achieving its goals in 1862.

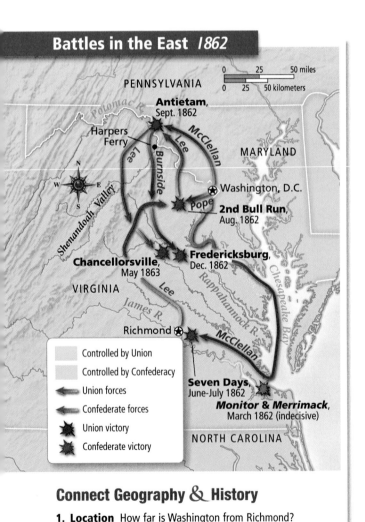

Battles in the East *1862*

Connect Geography & History

1. **Location** How far is Washington from Richmond?
2. **Draw Conclusions** Why was there so much military activity in Virginia?

Southern Success in the East

▼ **KEY QUESTION** In 1862, how close did the South come to victory?

As New Orleans fell in the spring of 1862, McClellan was slowly advancing up a peninsula between the York and James rivers in Virginia. His goal during this Peninsula Campaign was to try to capture the Confederate capital at Richmond. McClellan got so close that his soldiers could see the church steeples in the city. But just as Union forces grew confident of victory, the situation in the East changed dramatically.

Lee's Victories In June 1862, Robert E. Lee took charge of the Army of Northern Virginia and proceeded to turn the situation around. Lee sent Jeb Stuart and his cavalry, or soldiers on horseback, to spy on McClellan. With about 1,200 men, Stuart rode around the whole Union army in a few days and reported its position back to Lee. Lee then attacked McClellan's army. The two sides clashed for a week, from June 25 to July 1, 1862, in what became known as the **Seven Days' Battles**.

Again, the number of casualties was horrific, with 15,849 for the Union and around 20,000 for the Confederacy. Although the Confederate Army of Northern Virginia suffered heavier losses, McClellan's army was forced to retreat. The Union plan to capture Richmond had failed.

In late August, the Confederates won a second victory at Bull Run, and Union troops withdrew to Washington. Within just a few months, Lee had ended the Union threat in Virginia. He had also renewed Confederate hopes of winning the war. After the Confederate defeats in the West, Lee's victories were welcome news for the South.

Lee Invades the North Riding his recent wave of victories, General Lee decided to invade the Union. He wrote to tell President Davis of his plan. Lee thought it was a crucial time, with the North at a low point. Without waiting for Davis's response, Lee crossed the Potomac with his army and invaded Maryland in early September 1862. With this invasion, Lee reversed the previous Southern strategy of fighting a purely defensive war.

Lee had several reasons for taking the war to the North:

- He hoped a victory in the North might force Lincoln into peace talks.
- The invasion would give Virginia farmers a rest from the war during harvest season.
- The Confederates could **plunder**, or steal from, Northern farms for food.
- Lee hoped the invasion would show that the Confederacy could indeed win the war, which might convince European nations to side with the South.

By this time, both Britain and France were leaning toward recognizing the Confederacy as a separate nation. They were impressed by Lee's military successes, and their textile industries needed Southern cotton.

Fighting to a Draw at Antietam Soon after invading Maryland, Lee drew up a plan for his campaign in the North. A Confederate officer accidentally left a copy of Lee's battle plans wrapped around three cigars at a campsite. When Union troops passed by the abandoned campsite, a Union soldier stumbled on the plans. The captured plans gave McClellan a chance to stop Lee and his army.

McClellan went on the attack, though he moved slowly as always. On September 17, 1862, at Antietam Creek near Sharpsburg, Maryland, McClellan's army clashed with Lee's. The resulting **Battle of Antietam** was the bloodiest day in American history. A Confederate officer later described the battle.

History *through* Art

The Peninsula Campaign

Somewhere in Virginia, two soldiers in McClellan's army await orders. A young artist named Winslow Homer caught the moment. Homer was an artist/correspondent for the magazine *Harper's Weekly*. Here he created a different kind of war painting. Instead of showing us a heroic battle scene, Homer gives us a glimpse into the life of ordinary soldiers serving under McClellan during the Peninsula Campaign.

Soldiers in the Peninsula Campaign spent a lot of time waiting for orders. McClellan's reluctance to attack the enemy frustrated Lincoln. This scene captures the endless wait for the fighting to start.

CRITICAL VIEWING

1. **Make Inferences** What does the painting convey about army life?

2. **Draw Conclusions** What does the painting reveal about McClellan's Peninsula Campaign?

CONNECT ⟳ *To The Essential Question*

What events, leaders, and strategies shaped the early years of the war?

Effect on the Union	BATTLE OR EVENT	Effect on the Confederacy
	1861	
	APRIL	
Lincoln calls out the militia.	Fort Sumter in Charlestown harbor surrenders to the Confederacy.	Virginia, North Carolina, Tennessee, and Arkansas join the Confederacy.
Union loses a great military leader.	Robert E. Lee resigns from the Union army and joins the Confederate army.	Confederate army gains its most important general.
	JULY	
Northerners are shocked by the Union defeat. Lincoln realizes that he must raise an army.	First Battle of Bull Run, Virginia: Confederate victory	Southerners are encouraged by their victory.
	1862	
	FEBRUARY	
Grant opens up a river highway into the heart of the South. Over half of Tennessee is now in Union hands.	Union general Ulysses S. Grant captures Fort Henry and Fort Donelson in Tennessee.	Confederate defenses are dramatically weakened.
	APRIL	
Despite the loss of 13,000 men, the Union is now in control of important Confederate territory. Grant continues advance toward the Mississippi River.	Battle of Shiloh in Tennessee: Union victory	Confederacy loses 11,000 men. As Grant marches south, Southerners fear that the Confederacy will be split in two.
Union gets closer to its goal of splitting the Confederacy in two.	New Orleans is captured by Union forces.	South loses its most important city. Only a 150-mile stretch of the Mississippi River remains in Confederate hands.
	JUNE–JULY	
McClellan forced to retreat from his attack on the Confederate capital at Richmond.	During the Seven Days' Battles, Lee attacks Union general McClellan in Virginia.	Lee ends the Union threat to Virginia.
	SEPTEMBER	
Despite the high number of casualties, Northerners are encouraged that Lee's invasion has been stopped.	23,000 Americans die at the Battle of Antietam in Maryland.	Lee is forced to retreat from his invasion of Union territory.

CRITICAL THINKING Compare and Contrast In the first two years of the war, which side seemed closer to achieving its strategic goals?

(*left*) Stereograph image of dead soldiers on the field of Antietam. A stereograph viewer (*inset*) allows the image to appear in 3D.

PRIMARY SOURCE

❝ Again and again . . . by charges and counter-charges, this portion of the field was lost and recovered, until the green corn that grew upon it looked as if it had been struck by a storm of bloody hail. . . . From sheer exhaustion, both sides, like battered and bleeding athletes, seemed willing to rest. ❞

—John B. Gordon, quoted in *Voices of the Civil War*

After fighting all day, neither side had gained any ground by nightfall. The only difference was that about 23,000 men were dead or wounded. Lee, who lost as much as one-quarter of his fighting force, withdrew to Virginia. The cautious McClellan did not follow, missing a chance to finish off the crippled Southern army. Lincoln was so frustrated that he fired McClellan in November 1862.

 CAUSES AND EFFECTS Explain how close the South came to victory in 1862.

Michigan Grade Level Content Expectations *Review*

🖱 **ONLINE QUIZ**
For test practice, go to
Interactive Review @ ClassZone.com

TERMS & NAMES

1. Explain the significance of:
   - George McClellan
   - David Farragut
   - Ulysses S. Grant
   - Seven Days' Battles
   - Battle of Shiloh
   - Battle of Antietam
   - William Tecumseh Sherman

USING YOUR READING NOTES

2. **Main Idea and Details** Complete the diagram that you started at the beginning of this section.

```
  ( Detail )          ( Detail )
          ( Main Idea
   In 1862, the Union was well
   on its way to splitting the
        Confederacy in two. )
```

KEY IDEAS

3. Why were Union victories in the West and the fall of New Orleans significant to the Union cause?

4. Why did Lee go on the offensive against the North?

5. How did the South's fortunes change after Lee took command of the Army of Northern Virginia?

CRITICAL THINKING

6. **Make Inferences** What does Lee's invasion of the North suggest about his qualities as a general and a leader?

7. **Draw Conclusions** Why was Southern cotton not reaching the factories of Europe?

8. **Causes and Effects** Why did Lincoln fire McClellan?

9. (**Writing**) **Letter** Imagine you are a Confederate soldier. Write a letter home about Robert E. Lee and his victories in the east.

Across Five Aprils
by Irene Hunt

Irene Hunt's acclaimed historical novel, *Across Five Aprils*, captures the emotions, events, and people of the Civil War era. The book tells the story of Jethro Creighton, a boy of nine who grows into manhood during the four long years of civil war in the United States. Hunt depicts the savagery of battle as well as the difficulties of those who endure the conflict at home. In this scene, Jethro listens to members of his extended family—Wilse, Matt, John, and Bill—debate the issue of slavery and its effects on the Union. Here Jethro's cousin, Wilse Graham, responds to a question about whether slaves in the South should be freed.

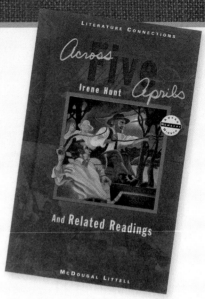

"Well then, I'll ask you this: if tomorrow every slave in the South had his freedom and come up North, would yore abolitionists git the crocodile tears sloshed out of their eyes so they could take the black man by the hand? Would they say, 'We'll see that you git good-payin' work fitted to what you're able to do—we'll see that you're well housed and clothed—we want you to come to our churches and yore children to come to our schools—why, we danged near fergit the difference in the colors of our skins because we air so almighty full of brotherly love!' Would it be like that in yore northern cities, Cousin John?"

"It ain't like that fer the masses of white people in our northern cities—nor in the southern cities either. And yet, there ain't a white man, lean-bellied and hopeless as so many of them are, that would change lots with a slave belongin' to the kindest master in the South."

Then Bill spoke for the first time, his eyes still on the yellow light of the lamp.

"Slavery, I hate. But it is with us, and them that should suffer fer the evil they brought to our shores air long dead. What I want us to answer in this year of 1861 is this, John: does the trouble over slavery come because men's hearts is purer above the Mason-Dixon line? Or does slavery throw a shadder over greed and keep that greed from showin' up quite so bare and ugly?"

Wilse Graham seemed to leap at Bill's question. "You're right, Cousin Bill. It's greed, not slavery, that's stirrin' up this trouble. And as fer human goodness—men's hearts is jest as black today as in the Roman times when they nailed slaves to crosses by the hunderd and left 'em there to point up a lesson."

Matt Creighton shook his head. "Human nature ain't any better one side of a political line than on the other—we all know that—but human nature, the all-over picture of it, *is* better than it was a thousand—five hundred—even a hundred years ago. There is an awakenin' inside us of human decency and responsibility. If I didn't believe that, I wouldn't grieve fer the children I've buried; I wouldn't look for'ard to the manhood of this youngest one."

Jethro felt as if he were bursting with the tumult inside him. The thought of war had given him a secret delight only a matter of hours before . . .

Suddenly he was deeply troubled. He groped towards an understanding of something that was far beyond the excitement of guns and shouting men; but he could not find words to define what he felt, and that lack left him in a turmoil of frustration.

ADDITIONAL READING

Carrying the Flag, by Gordon C. Rhea Mr. Rhea tells the amazing story of Private Charles Whilden, an unlikely hero of the Confederacy.

To Be a Slave, by Julius Lester Julius Lester presents a wealth of slave narratives that provide important insight into the lives of enslaved African Americans in the early years of America. Paintings by Tom Feelings capture the brutality of the slave experience.

Chapter Summary

1 Key Idea
After more Southern states joined the Confederacy, fighting began on Confederate territory.

2 Key Idea
Army life and new technology brought unexpected hardships to millions of soldiers.

3 Key Idea
Both the Union and the Confederacy won important victories in the first years of the war.

For detailed Review and Study Notes go to **Interactive Review @ ClassZone.com**

Name Game

Use the Terms & Names list to identify each sentence online or on your own paper.

1. I was the Confederacy's greatest general.
   Robert E. Lee

2. This Union ironclad fought the *Merrimack*. ____

3. I was a Union general who won battles in the west. ____

4. I was the commander of the Union army in the east. ____

5. This plan was meant to strangle the Confederacy. ____

6. I captured New Orleans. ____

7. This was the first major battle of the Civil War. ____

8. I was a Confederate general at Bull Run. ____

9. During these battles, Lee prevented a Union attack on Richmond. ____

10. The attack on this Union fort marked the beginning of the Civil War. ____

A. Anaconda Plan
B. Thomas J. Jackson
C. *Monitor*
D. George McClellan
E. Seven Days' Battles
F. Fort Sumter
G. Robert E. Lee
H. William Tecumseh Sherman
I. First Battle of Bull Run
J. Ulysses S. Grant
K. Battle of Shiloh
L. David Farragut

Activities

CROSSWORD PUZZLE

Complete the online crossword puzzle to show what you know about the early years of the Civil War.

ACROSS
1. _____ was a very cautious Union general.

GEOGAME

Use this online map to reinforce your understanding of the first years of the Civil War, including the locations of important battles and geographic features. Drag and drop each place name in the list at its location on the map. A scorecard helps you keep track of your progress online.

Mississippi River

Shiloh

New Orleans

Bull Run

Tennessee River

More items online.

New Orleans

16 Assessment

VOCABULARY

Explain the significance of each of the following.

1. William Tecumseh Sherman
2. Battle of Antietam
3. George McClellan
4. Ulysses S. Grant
5. Robert E. Lee
6. the *Monitor* and the *Merrimack*
7. First Battle of Bull Run
8. Fort Sumter
9. Confederacy
10. Anaconda Plan
11. Battle of Shiloh
12. David Farragut

Match each military commander on the left with a battle on the right and explain the role he played in that battle.

13. Grant
14. Sherman
15. Lee
16. McClellan
17. Farragut
18. Jackson
19. Johnston

A. Battle of Shiloh
B. Battle of Antietam
C. Seven Days' Battles
D. New Orleans
E. First Battle of Bull Run

KEY IDEAS

1 War Erupts (pages 510–515)

20. What did the South need to do to win the war?
21. What did the Battle of Bull Run reveal about the future battles of the Civil War?

2 Life in the Army (pages 516–521)

22. Why did so many people volunteer to fight in the Civil War?
23. How did the use of rifles and minié balls change military tactics?

3 No End in Sight (pages 522–529)

24. What part of the Union strategy did Grant accomplish in 1862? How did he do it?
25. Why did Congressmen criticize Grant and why did Lincoln like him?

CRITICAL THINKING

26. **Evaluate** Which side came out of the Battle of Shiloh in worse condition? Explain your answer.
27. **Draw Conclusions** Why do you think Confederate forces attacked Fort Sumter when they did?
28. **Make Inferences** What did the Union hope to gain by damaging the Southern economy?
29. **Compare and Contrast** Compare and contrast the Union with the Confederacy by filling in this chart.

	Union	Confederacy
Reasons for Fighting	*to preserve the Union*	
Advantages		
Disadvantages		
Military Strategy		
Battle Victories		

30. **Causes and Effects** Why did the introduction of ironclad warships have such an impact on naval warfare?
31. **Draw Conclusions** Why did the North have such difficulty in capturing Richmond, Virginia?
32. **Make Inferences** What changes in military technology might have surprised new recruits?
33. **Connect Geography and History** Study the map below. Why didn't McClellan take a land route to attack Richmond?

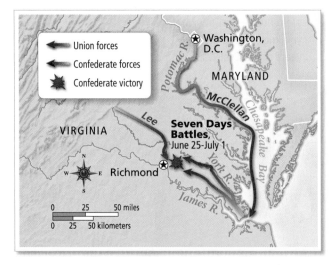

✓ **TEST PRACTICE**

• **Online Test Practice @ ClassZone.com**

• Use the **MEAP Strategies & Practice,** pages S1-S27, at the front of this book

DOCUMENT-BASED QUESTIONS

Analyze each document and answer the questions that follow.

DOCUMENT 1

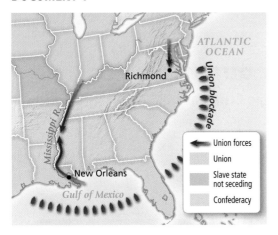

1 Examine this map of the Anaconda Plan. By 1862, which part of the plan had been successful?

   A gaining control of the Mississippi River

   B capturing Richmond, Virginia

   C gaining the support of Great Britain

   D gaining the support of France

DOCUMENT 2

PRIMARY SOURCE

❝ [S]oon as I feel that my army is well organized and well disciplined and strong enough, I will advance and force the Rebels to a battle on a field of my own selection. A long time must elapse before I can do that. ❞

—General George McClellan, quoted in
Civil War Journal: The Leaders

2 Examine the above quotation by General George McClellan. How might McClellan's position affect the Anaconda Plan?

   A help ensure victory of the plan

   B gain support for the plan

   C slow the progress of the plan

   D lower the dollar cost of the plan

YOU BE THE HISTORIAN

34. **WHAT IF?** In what ways might history have been changed if Lincoln had ordered Major Anderson to turn Fort Sumter over to the Confederacy?

35 **Causes and Effects** How do you think the Civil War affected the lives of civilians who were not in the war zone?

36. **Compare and Contrast** In what ways was the South's strategy in 1861–1862 like the American army's strategy during the American Revolution?

37. **Evaluate** What does the presence of picnickers at the Battle of Bull Run reveal about civilians' attitude to the war?

38. **Make Generalizations** Why is an invading army usually at a disadvantage in a conflict?

39. **Analyze Point of View** What does Lincoln's admiration for Grant reveal about Lincoln?

Answer the
ESSENTIAL QUESTION
What events, leaders, and strategies shaped the early years of the war?

Written Response Write a four–paragraph response to the Essential Question. Be sure to consider the key ideas of each section as well as the most significant facts that helped determine your answer. Use the Response Rubric below to guide your thinking and writing.

Response Rubric
A strong response will

• describe each side's strengths and weaknesses

• evaluate how close each side came to achieving its strategic goals

• explain the long-term effects of the events of the first two years of the war

CHAPTER

17

1. The Emancipation Proclamation
2. War Affects Society
3. The North Wins
4. The Legacy of the War

The Freedman by John Quincy Adams Ward

The Tide of War Turns

1863–1865

 ESSENTIAL QUESTION

In what ways did the Civil War transform the nation?

CONNECT 🔄 Geography & History

How did the Union make use of Southern geography in order to defeat the Confederacy?

Think about:

1 Union victories during the first two years of the war

2 the strength of the Union navy

3 the destructive Union march through Georgia

1863 **May**
Siege of Vicksburg begins.

1863

January Lincoln issues the Emancipation Proclamation.

▼

Effect Slaves are declared free in Confederate territory.

1863 **July** Battle of Gettysburg takes place.
July Vicksburg falls.

▼

Effect The tide of war turns in favor of the North.

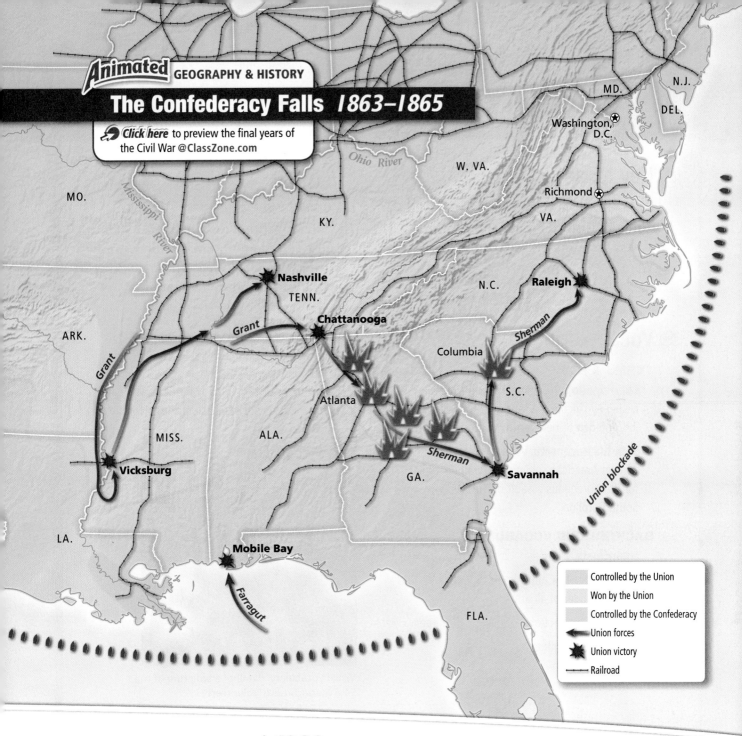

The Confederacy Falls 1863–1865

Click here to preview the final years of the Civil War @ClassZone.com

Ohio River

Mississippi River

MD.
N.J.
DEL.
Washington, D.C.
W. VA.
MO.
Richmond
VA.
KY.
Nashville
TENN.
Grant
Chattanooga
N.C.
Raleigh
Sherman
Columbia
Atlanta
S.C.
ARK.
Grant
MISS.
ALA.
GA.
Sherman
Savannah
Vicksburg
LA.
Mobile Bay
Farragut
FLA.
Union blockade

Legend:
- Controlled by the Union
- Won by the Union
- Controlled by the Confederacy
- Union forces
- Union victory
- Railroad

1864 **March** General Grant is appointed commander of all Union armies.

1864 **November** Union general Sherman begins his March to the Sea.

▼

Effect Southern resources are destroyed; Southern morale sinks.

1865

April Lee surrenders at Appomattox Court House.

Lee Surrendering at Appomattox by Thomas Lovell

The Tide of War Turns **535**

▶ Key Ideas

BEFORE, YOU LEARNED

Abolitionists had been fighting to end slavery for many decades before the Civil War began.

NOW YOU WILL LEARN

The Emancipation Proclamation promised freedom to slaves in the Confederacy and allowed African Americans to join the Union army.

▶ Vocabulary

TERMS & NAMES

Emancipation Proclamation document issued by Lincoln that declared that all slaves in Confederate-held territory were free

54th Massachusetts Volunteers regiment of African-American soldiers that gained fame for its courageous assault on Fort Wagner, South Carolina

BACKGROUND VOCABULARY

emancipate to free

Commander-In-Chief the President in his role as commander of all armed forces

liberation the act of setting someone free

prolong to lengthen (in time)

REVIEW

Battle of Antietam bloody battle in Maryland that ended Lee's first invasion of the North

Visual Vocabulary detail of a sculpture of the 54th Massachusetts Volunteers

▶ Reading Strategy

Re-create the diagram shown at right. As you read and respond to the **KEY QUESTIONS**, use the diagram to note the effects of the Emancipation Proclamation.

 See Skillbuilder Handbook, page R7.

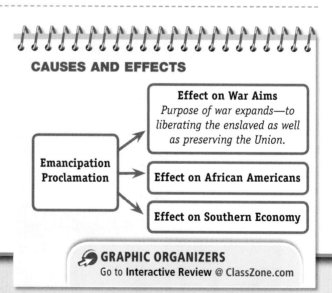

CAUSES AND EFFECTS

Emancipation Proclamation →

Effect on War Aims
Purpose of war expands—to liberating the enslaved as well as preserving the Union.

Effect on African Americans

Effect on Southern Economy

GRAPHIC ORGANIZERS
Go to **Interactive Review** @ ClassZone.com

The Emancipation Proclamation

8 – U5.2.3.2 Examine Abraham Lincoln's presidency with respect to – the evolution of his emancipation policy (including the Emancipation Proclamation)
8 – U5.2.4 Describe the role of African Americans in the war, including black soldiers and regiments, and the increased resistance of enslaved peoples.

One American's Story

During the Civil War, abolitionists such as Frederick Douglass continued their campaign against slavery. Douglass urged President Lincoln to **emancipate**, or free, all enslaved Americans.

Frederick Douglass

PRIMARY SOURCE

❝ To fight against slaveholders, without fighting against slavery, is but a half-hearted business, and paralyzes the hands engaged in it. . . . Fire must be met with water. . . . War for the destruction of liberty [by the South] must be met with war for the destruction of slavery. ❞

—Frederick Douglass, quoted in *Battle Cry of Freedom*

For Douglass there was now a practical as well as a moral purpose for ending slavery. If the Union promised to end slavery, millions of enslaved Americans might help the Union cause. Urged on by Douglass and others, Lincoln decided to act.

A War of Liberation

🔻 **KEY QUESTION** How did the Emancipation Proclamation affect the war effort?

Arguments over the issue of slavery had brought the nation to war. Now the war was forcing Americans to resolve the slavery question once and for all.

Abolitionists Demand Action In parts of the South, slavery began collapsing early in the war. As Union armies swept through Confederate territory, thousands of enslaved people escaped from the plantations.

Meanwhile, abolitionists were pressuring the government to act. They realized that the war provided an opportunity to destroy slavery forever. Lincoln hesitated for several reasons. Although he did not like slavery, he feared that he did not have the constitutional power to abolish slavery in every state.

Most importantly, Lincoln's priority was to preserve the Union. "If I could save the Union without freeing any slave I would do it," he declared. "If I could save it by freeing all the slaves I would do it; and if I could save it be freeing some and leaving others alone, I would also do that."

In his struggle to keep the Union together, Lincoln did not want to anger the border states, the four slave states that remained in the Union. He also knew that many in the North opposed emancipation.

By the summer of 1862, however, Lincoln had decided in favor of emancipation. The war was taking a terrible toll. If freeing the slaves helped weaken the South, then he would do it. Lincoln waited for a moment when the Union was in a position of strength. After General Lee's forces were stopped at the **Battle of Antietam**, Lincoln felt confident enough to act.

The Emancipation Proclamation On January 1, 1863, Lincoln issued the **Emancipation Proclamation**, which declared that all slaves in Confederate-held territory were free.

PRIMARY SOURCE

  " On the first day of January, in the year of our Lord one thousand eight hundred and sixty-three, all persons held as slaves within any State or designated part of a State, the people whereof shall then be in rebellion against the United States, shall be then, thenceforward, and forever free. **"**

—Abraham Lincoln, from the *Emancipation Proclamation*

The proclamation made a great impact on the public, but it freed few slaves. The Union army could enforce the proclamation only in the Confederate territory under its control. Most slaves lived in areas far removed from the Union army and remained under the control of plantation owners.

Scene of the Emancipation Proclamation being read in a slave cabin. **Why didn't the artist show the Proclamation being read outside, in daylight?**

FREEDOM TO THE SLAVE

Political cartoons are images that carry a political message. Older political cartoons, especially those from the 18th and 19th centuries, are often very detailed. First read the words in the banner. Then study the cartoon in order to understand its meaning.

The image shows enslaved African Americans gaining their liberty from a Union soldier as the Union army passes by. On the left-hand side, the cartoonist has imagined what will happen after slavery ends.

freed slaves entering a school

a newspaper, symbolizing literacy

"Freedom to the Slave" printed in Philadelphia 1863

CRITICAL THINKING

1. **Make Inferences** What does the cartoonist suggest will happen after the abolition of slavery?

2. **Synthesize** What is the overall meaning of the cartoon?

 See Skillbuilder Handbook, page R24.

Why, critics asked, did Lincoln free slaves only in the South? Lincoln believed that the Constitution did not give him the authority to free all slaves. But because freeing slaves in the South weakened the Confederacy, the proclamation could be seen as a military action. According to the Constitution, the President is **Commander-in-Chief** of all armed forces. In this role, Lincoln claimed the military authority to issue the proclamation.

Although the Emancipation Proclamation did not free many enslaved people at the time, it added a great moral purpose to the Union cause. The Northern goal was no longer simply to preserve the Union. The Civil War was now being fought to free millions of Americans from slavery. The conflict had become a war of **liberation**.

Response to the Proclamation Abolitionists were thrilled that Lincoln had finally issued the Emancipation Proclamation. "We shout for joy that we live to record this righteous decree," wrote Frederick Douglass. Still, many believed the law should have gone further. They were upset that Lincoln had not freed *all* enslaved people, including those in the border states.

Other people in the North, especially Democrats, were angered by the president's decision. A majority of Northern Democrats opposed emancipat-

Connecting History

Expanding Liberty
During the Revolutionary War, the British had also tried to weaken their opponents by offering to free the enslaved. *See Chapter 7, page 196.*

ing even Southern slaves. They claimed that the proclamation would only **prolong**, or lengthen, the war by further angering the South. A newspaper man in Ohio called Lincoln's proclamation "monstrous, impudent, and heinous . . . insulting to God as to man."

Most Union soldiers welcomed emancipation. One officer noted that, although few soldiers were abolitionists, most were happy "to destroy everything that . . . gives the rebels strength."

White Southerners reacted angrily to the proclamation. Although it had no effect in areas outside the reach of Northern armies, many slaves began escaping to Union lines. At the same time that these slaves deprived the Confederacy of labor, they also began to provide the Union with soldiers.

▲ **CAUSES AND EFFECTS** Describe how the Emancipation Proclamation affected the war.

Fighting for Freedom

🔻 **KEY QUESTION** How did African-American soldiers contribute to the Union cause?

In addition to freeing slaves, the Emancipation Proclamation declared that African-American men willing to fight "will be received into the armed service of the United States." Determined to destroy slavery, African-American soldiers brought renewed intensity to the Union cause.

African-American Soldiers Frederick Douglass had argued for the recruitment of African-American soldiers since the start of the war. He believed that military service would be the first step to full citizenship. Douglass declared, "Once [you] let the black man get upon his person the brass letters, U.S. . . . there is no power on earth which can deny that he has earned the right to citizenship."

Recruitment poster to attract African-American volunteers
Why would an image like this have attracted volunteers?

COME AND JOIN US BROTHERS.

PUBLISHED BY THE SUPERVISORY COMMITTEE FOR RECRUITING COLORED REGIMENTS
1210 CHESTNUT ST. PHILADELPHIA

Before the proclamation, the federal government had discouraged the enlistment of African Americans, and only a few regiments were formed. Once the restriction was lifted, African Americans rushed to join the army. Most of these African Americans came from the South. By war's end, about 180,000 black soldiers wore the blue uniform of the Union army.

African-American soldiers were organized in 166 all-black regiments, usually led by white officers. They were paid less than white soldiers. Despite these obstacles, African Americans showed great courage on the battlefield and wore their uniforms with pride. More than one regiment insisted on fighting without pay rather than accepting lower pay.

African-American soldiers were determined to destroy slavery, gain self-respect, and prove they deserved equal treatment. Many white officers started out with racist views about their soldiers. After seeing these soldiers' determination and courage on the battlefield, many of these officers changed their minds.

Middle school students, dressed in period uniforms, portray life in the 54th Massachusetts Volunteers.

The 54th Massachusetts The **54th Massachusetts Volunteers** was one of the first African-American regiments organized in the North. The soldiers of the 54th—which included two sons of Frederick Douglass—soon made the regiment one of the most famous of the Civil War.

The 54th Massachusetts earned its greatest glory in July 1863, when it led a heroic attack on Fort Wagner in South Carolina. The soldiers' bravery made them famous and increased African-American enlistment.

Soldiers in African-American regiments faced grave dangers if captured. The Confederate government threatened to execute them or return them to slavery rather than make them prisoners of war.

The Emancipation Proclamation was one sign that the war was bringing dramatic change to both North and South. As the fighting continued, it was clear that the war was changing American society in unexpected ways.

 SUMMARIZE Describe the contributions of African-American soldiers to the Union cause.

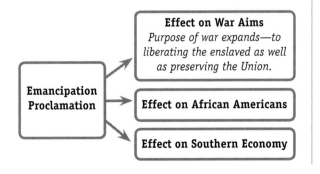 **Michigan Grade Level Content Expectations** *Review*

ONLINE QUIZ
For test practice, go to
Interactive Review @ ClassZone.com

TERMS & NAMES

1. Explain the importance of
- Emancipation Proclamation
- 54th Massachusetts Volunteers

USING YOUR READING NOTES

2. Causes and Effects Complete the chart that you started at the beginning of this section.

Emancipation Proclamation

→ **Effect on War Aims**
Purpose of war expands—to liberating the enslaved as well as preserving the Union.

→ **Effect on African Americans**

→ **Effect on Southern Economy**

KEY IDEAS

3. Why was the Emancipation Proclamation limited in scope?

4. How did African Americans help the Union cause?

CRITICAL THINKING

5. Causes and Effects How did the Emancipation Proclamation change the role of African Americans in the Civil War?

6. Make Inferences Why would African-American Union soldiers face greater danger than white Union soldiers?

7. Draw Conclusions Why do you think that Lincoln waited until the Union was in a position of strength before issuing the Emancipation Proclamation?

8. Math Research the number of free and enslaved people in each Confederate state. Then calculate the percentage of slaves in each of those states.

▶ Key Ideas

BEFORE, YOU LEARNED
The Civil War took millions of men from their homes, disrupting life in both North and South.

NOW YOU WILL LEARN
As the war dragged on, social, economic, and political change affected both the Union and the Confederacy.

▶ Vocabulary

TERMS & NAMES

Copperheads Northern Democrats who favored peace with the South

writ of *habeas corpus* law that prevents the government from holding citizens without formal charges

Clara Barton Civil War nurse who later founded the American Red Cross

BACKGROUND VOCABULARY

conscription military draft

income tax tax on earnings

greenback paper money introduced during the Civil War

REVIEW

inflation increase in prices and decrease in value of money

Visual Vocabulary
greenback

▶ Reading Strategy

Re-create the diagram shown at right. As you read and respond to the **KEY QUESTIONS**, use the center box to record the main idea; use the outer ovals to note important details. Add circles or start a new diagram as needed.

 See Skillbuilder Handbook, page R4.

MAIN IDEAS AND DETAILS

Detail — **Main Idea** *Disagreements emerged in both the Union and the Confederacy.* — Detail

GRAPHIC ORGANIZERS
Go to **Interactive Review** @ ClassZone.com

War Affects Society

 8 – U5.2.2.3 Make an argument to explain the reasons why the North won the Civil War by considering the – the respective advantages and disadvantages, including geographic, demographic, economic and technological
8 – U5.2.5 Construct generalizations about how the war affected combatants, civilians (including the role of women), the physical environment, and the future of warfare, including technological developments.

One American's Story

On April 4, 1863, a Southern woman named Agnes came upon a group of hungry women and children marching through the streets of the Confederate capital of Richmond, Virginia. The crowd was joined by others angered by the shortage of food.

PRIMARY SOURCE

❝ The crowd now rapidly increased, and numbered, I am sure, more than a thousand women and children. It grew and grew until it reached the dignity of a mob—a bread riot. ❞

— Agnes, quoted in *Reminiscences of Peace and War*

The mob broke into shops and stole food and other goods. When President Jefferson Davis appeared, the crowd hissed at him. As the Civil War moved into its third year, American society in both the North and the South began cracking under the strain of war.

A Divisive Time

🔻 **KEY QUESTION** What disagreements emerged inside both the Union and the Confederacy?

The fight between the North and the South was not the only conflict of the Civil War. Even within the Union and the Confederacy, disagreements raged.

Disagreements About the War Some Southern areas opposed secession. The western counties of Virginia had few plantations or slaves. In 1863, these counties seceded from Virginia and formed a new state—West Virginia. West Virginia then joined the Union.

Disagreements over the war also arose in the North. Lincoln's main opponents were the **Copperheads**, Northern Democrats who favored peace with the South. (A copperhead is a poisonous snake that strikes without warning.) Lincoln had protesters arrested. He also suspended the **writ of habeas corpus**, which prevents the government from holding citizens without formal charges.

Illustration of a food riot in the South, from a Northern magazine

The Tide of War Turns **543**

Slaves escaping from Southern plantations. **Why would wartime conditions have allowed enslaved people to escape?**

Slaves Undermine the Confederacy Enslaved people did their best to weaken the Confederacy. Slaves slowed their work or stopped working altogether. When planters fled advancing Union armies, slaves often refused to join their former "masters." In defiance, they stayed behind, waiting to greet or join the Union armies. One Union officer described a common sight.

PRIMARY SOURCE

" It was very touching to see the vast numbers of colored [African-American] women following after us with babies in their arms, and little ones like our Anna clinging to their tattered skirts. One poor creature, while nobody was looking, hid two boys, five years old, in a wagon, intending, I suppose that they should see the land of freedom if she couldn't. **"**

—Union officer, quoted in *Sherman: Fighting Prophet*

After the Emancipation Proclamation, the number of slaves fleeing Southern plantations greatly increased.

The Draft Laws As enthusiasm for the war declined, both the North and the South began passing laws of **conscription**, also known as the draft. These laws required men to serve in the military.

In the South, planters with more than 20 slaves were not required to serve in the army. In both the Union and Confederacy, the rich could pay substitutes to serve in their place. This caused widespread resentment.

The draft was extremely unpopular. In July 1863, anger over the draft and simmering racial tensions led to the four-day-long New York City draft riots. Irish-Americans and others destroyed property and attacked African Americans on the streets. Over 1000 people were killed or wounded. Union troops were brought to the city to put down the uprising.

🔺 **MAIN IDEAS & DETAILS** Describe the disagreements that emerged in both the Union and the Confederacy.

Economic and Social Change

▼ **KEY QUESTION** What economic and social changes were caused by the war?

In the North and the South, the war brought economic and social change. In the North, free African Americans were now serving in the Union military. Women were taking over jobs in factories and hospitals. At the same time, poverty and hunger spread through the Union and the Confederacy. The suffering was worse in the South.

Economic Effects of the War Food shortages were very common in the South. Many farmers were in the army and unable to harvest crops. Transportation was disrupted, preventing food from reaching markets. Additionally, both the Confederate and invading Union armies seized food.

Another problem in the South was **inflation**. Inflation is an increase in the cost of goods and a decrease in the value of money. Over the course of the war, prices rose steadily in the South. Inflation in the North was much lower, but prices still rose faster than wages, making life harder for working people.

During the war, the federal government passed two important economic measures. In 1861, it established the first **income tax**—a tax on earnings. The following year, the government issued a new paper currency, known as

COMPARING *Northern and Southern Inflation*

During the Civil War, inflation affected both the North and the South. Inflation occurs when prices rise and the purchasing power of money falls. Wartime inflation was especially severe in the Confederacy, where basic necessities became outrageously expensive.

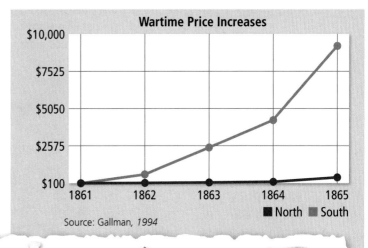

Wartime Price Increases

Source: Gallman, *1994*

■ North ■ South

FOOD PRICES IN THE SOUTH, 1864

| $6.00 | $6.25 | $10.00 | $12.00 | $18.00 |
| Dozen Eggs | Pound of Butter | Quart of Milk | Pound of Coffee | Confederate Soldier's Monthly Pay |

CRITICAL THINKING Draw Conclusions How long would it take a soldier to earn enough to buy some of the items shown above?

greenbacks because of their color. The new currency helped the Northern economy by ensuring that people had money to spend. It also helped the federal government to pay for the war.

Women Aid the War Effort With so many men away at war, women in both the North and the South assumed more responsibilities. Women plowed fields and ran farms and plantations. They also took over office and factory jobs that had previously been done only by men.

Thousands of women, such as **Clara Barton**, served on the front lines as volunteer workers and nurses. Susie King Taylor was an African-American woman who wrote an account of her experiences as a volunteer with an African-American regiment. She asked her readers to remember that "many lives were lost,—not men alone but noble women as well."

Relief agencies allowed women to work gathering supplies, washing clothes, and cooking food for soldiers. Also, nursing became a respectable profession for many women. By the end of the war, around 20,000 nurses had worked in Union and Confederate hospitals. Southern women were also active as nurses and as volunteers on the front.

CONNECTING ⟳ *History*

WARS AND SOCIAL CHANGE

During the Civil War, many people were presented with opportunities for freedom or advancement. This situation was not unique to the Civil War. In fact, throughout American history, long, deadly wars have helped bring about dramatic social change.

1700s

1775–1783
The Revolutionary War allowed African Americans to serve in the military.

1800s

1861–1865
The Civil War freed enslaved people; allowed more women to enter the workforce and take on jobs traditionally done by men.

1900s

1939–1945
World War II helped desegregate some factories and temporarily created more opportunities for women.

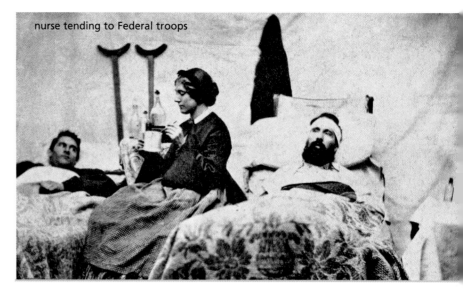

nurse tending to Federal troops

CRITICAL THINKING
1. **Make Inferences** Why would wartime situations offer more opportunities for women?
2. **Summarize** Why do wars help cause social change?

As in the American Revolution, some women on both sides disguised themselves as men and enlisted. One was an Illinois woman named Jennie Hodgers. She served in a Union regiment as Albert Cashier.

Women also played a key role as spies in both the North and the South. Harriet Tubman served as a spy for Union forces in South Carolina. The most famous Confederate spy was Belle Boyd. Although she was arrested six times, she continued her work through much of the war.

War Transforms Society With millions of men absent from their homes and workplaces, the war transformed Northern and Southern societies. In the North, opportunities opened up for those who had traditionally been kept out of public life. Women became active in the war effort and staffed hospitals in large numbers. African Americans gained more rights as several states began repealing discriminatory laws.

In the South, ordinary people began to resent the burden they were forced to bear. Small farmers, reduced to poverty by the war, were growing bitter. Many questioned why they were asked to fight a war for rich slaveowners. As the war dragged on, social resentment, inflation, and food shortages began to destroy Southern morale.

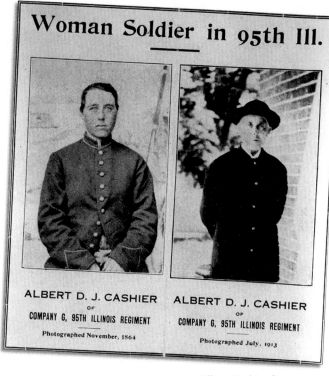

Woman Soldier in 95th Ill.

ALBERT D. J. CASHIER
OF
COMPANY G, 95TH ILLINOIS REGIMENT
Photographed November, 1864

ALBERT D. J. CASHIER
OF
COMPANY G, 95TH ILLINOIS REGIMENT
Photographed July, 1913

Albert Cashier (Jenny Hodgers) was one of hundreds of women who disguised themselves as men in order to fight in the war.

 SUMMARIZE Describe the economic and social changes caused by the war.

Michigan Grade Level Content Expectations *Review*

 ONLINE QUIZ
For test practice, go to
Interactive Review @ ClassZone.com

TERMS & NAMES

1. Explain the importance of
- Copperheads
- Clara Barton
- writ of *habeus corpus*

USING YOUR READING NOTES

2. Main Ideas and Details Complete the diagram that you started at the beginning of this section.

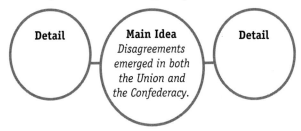

KEY IDEAS

3. Why were people in the western counties of Virginia against secession?

4. What hardships did civilians suffer during the war?

CRITICAL THINKING

5. Connect Economics and History Why do you think the economy of the South suffered more during the war than that of the North?

6. Make Generalizations Why do you think both sides introduced a draft?

7. **Writing** **Newspaper Article** Suppose you are a journalist for a foreign newspaper. Write an article describing war-time conditions in both the Confederacy and the Union.

▶ Key Ideas

BEFORE, YOU LEARNED
General Robert E. Lee caused the Union many difficulties in the east.

NOW YOU WILL LEARN
After a series of Southern victories, the North began winning battles that led to the defeat of the Confederacy.

▶ Vocabulary

TERMS & NAMES

Battle of Gettysburg battle in 1863 in Pennsylvania when Union forces stopped a Confederate invasion of the North

George Pickett Confederate general who fought at Gettysburg

Pickett's Charge failed assault on Union positions on final day of Battle of Gettysburg

Siege of Vicksburg the surrounding of the city of Vicksburg, Mississippi, by Union forces

Sherman's March to the Sea Union general Sherman's destructive march across Georgia

Appomattox Court House town in Virginia where Lee surrendered to Grant

BACKGROUND VOCABULARY
dislodge remove

Visual Vocabulary monument on the site of the Battle of Gettysburg

▶ Reading Strategy

Re-create the diagram shown at right. As you read and respond to the **KEY QUESTIONS**, use the diagram to show the effects of Union victories at Gettysburg and Vicksburg.

 See Skillbuilder Handbook, page R7.

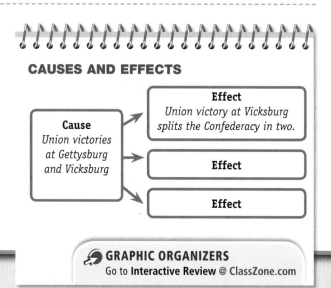

CAUSES AND EFFECTS

Cause
Union victories at Gettysburg and Vicksburg

Effect
Union victory at Vicksburg splits the Confederacy in two.

Effect

Effect

⊛ GRAPHIC ORGANIZERS
Go to **Interactive Review** @ ClassZone.com

The North Wins

 8 – U5.2.2.1 Make an argument to explain the reasons why the North won the Civil War by considering the – critical events and battles in the war
8 – U5.2.2.2 Make an argument to explain the reasons why the North won the Civil War by considering the – the political and military leadership of the North and South

One American's Story

Tillie Pierce was 15 years old when war came to her doorstep in Gettysburg, Pennsylvania. On July 2, 1863, the second day of the battle, Tillie and her family tried to flee. She later wrote about her memories of the epic battle that took place around her home.

PRIMARY SOURCE

Tillie Pierce

❝ Hardly had we arrived at our supposed place of refuge, when we were told to hurry back to where we came from . . . So there was no alternative but to retrace our steps about as fast as we came.

During the whole of this wild goose chase, the cannonading had become terrible! . . . Occasionally a shell would come flying over Round Top and explode high in the air over head. It seemed as though the heavens were sending forth peal upon peal of terrible thunder directly over our heads; while at the same time, the very earth beneath our feet trembled. ❞

—Tillie Pierce, quoted in *War Between Brothers*

Tillie Pierce spent the next few days helping care for wounded Union soldiers. Little did she realize that the battle she had just witnessed would be the turning point of the war.

Union Victories at Gettysburg and Vicksburg

 **KEY QUESTION** Why were the battles of Gettysburg and Vicksburg so significant?

In 1863 the war in the east seemed to be going well for the Confederacy. Confident after a series of victories at Fredericksburg and Chancellorsville, Virginia, General Lee decided to invade the North. It was a fatal mistake.

Lee Invades the North For Lee, the victory at Chancellorsville came at a high price. In the confusion after the battle, Confederate guards accidentally shot Confederate General Stonewall Jackson, who died a week later.

After Chancellorsville, Lee decided to head north once again. He hoped that a victory in Union territory would fuel Northern discontent and bring calls for peace. He also hoped that a Southern victory would lead European nations to recognize the Confederacy as an independent nation.

In late June 1863, Lee crossed into southern Pennsylvania. At the town of Gettysburg the Confederates stumbled upon Union troops. Both sides called for reinforcements, and on July 1, the **Battle of Gettysburg** began.

The Battle of Gettysburg The fighting raged for three days. On the rocky hills and fields around Gettysburg, 90,000 Union troops under the command of General George Meade clashed with 75,000 Confederates.

During the struggle, Union forces tried to hold their ground on Cemetery Ridge, just south of town, while rebel soldiers tried to **dislodge**, or remove, them. (See map on facing page.) At times, the air seemed full of bullets. "The balls [were] whizzing so thick," said one Texan, "that it [looked] like a man could hold out a hat and catch it full."

The turning point came on July 3, when General **George Pickett** mounted a direct attack on the middle of the Union line. It was a deadly mistake. Some 15,000 rebel troops charged up the ridge into heavy Union fire. One soldier recalled "bayonet thrusts, sabre strokes, pistol shots . . . men going down on their hands and knees, spinning round like tops . . . ghastly heaps of dead men."

Pickett's Charge, as this attack came to be known, was a failure. The Confederates retreated and waited for a counterattack. But once again, Lincoln's generals failed to completely defeat Lee's army. The furious Lincoln wondered when he would find a general to defeat Lee once and for all.

Even so, the Union rejoiced over the victory at Gettysburg. Lee's hopes for a Confederate victory in the North were crushed. The North suffered 23,000 casualties, or about one quarter of the army, but Southern losses were even greater. Over one-third of Lee's army, 28,000 men, lay dead or wounded. Sick at heart, Lee led his army back to Virginia.

Although the war would last two years longer, the South never recovered from its defeat at Gettysburg.

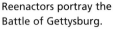

Reenactors portray the Battle of Gettysburg.

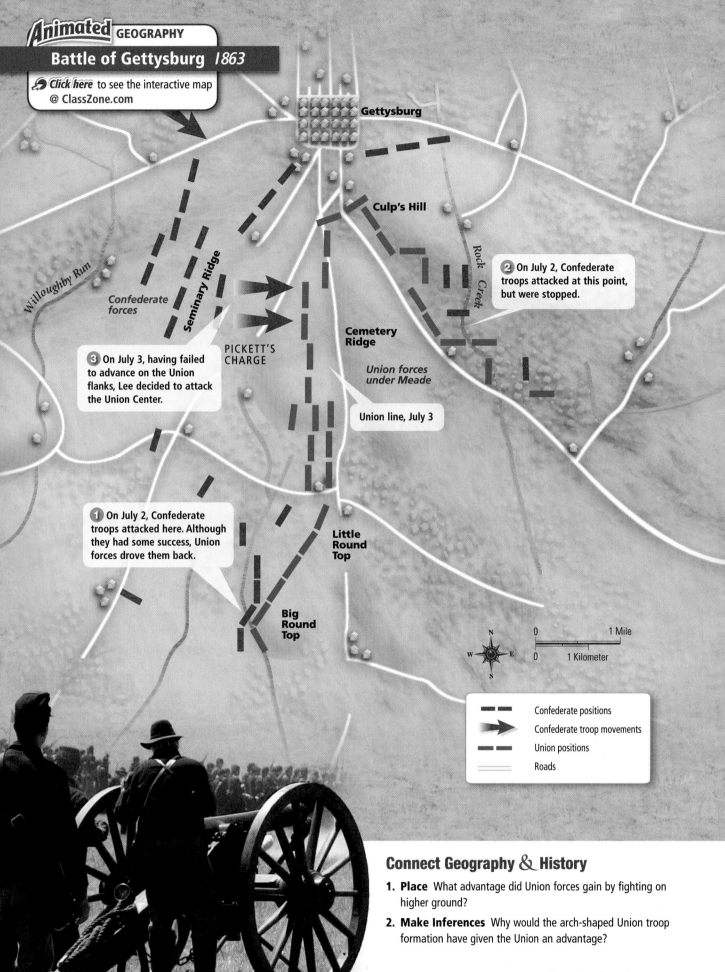

Gettysburg

Culp's Hill

Rock Creek

2 On July 2, Confederate troops attacked at this point, but were stopped.

Willoughby Run

Confederate forces

Seminary Ridge

PICKETT'S CHARGE

Cemetery Ridge

Union forces under Meade

3 On July 3, having failed to advance on the Union flanks, Lee decided to attack the Union Center.

Union line, July 3

1 On July 2, Confederate troops attacked here. Although they had some success, Union forces drove them back.

Little Round Top

Big Round Top

N
W   E
S

0   1 Mile
0   1 Kilometer

- - - - Confederate positions
➤   Confederate troop movements
▬ ▬ Union positions
~~~~ Roads

Connect Geography & History

1. **Place** What advantage did Union forces gain by fighting on higher ground?

2. **Make Inferences** Why would the arch-shaped Union troop formation have given the Union an advantage?

The Siege of Vicksburg On July 4, 1863, the day after Pickett's Charge, the Union received more good news. Confederate troops at Vicksburg in Mississippi had surrendered to General Ulysses S. Grant.

The previous year, Grant had won important victories in the West that opened up the Mississippi River and allowed Union troops to travel deep into the South. Vicksburg was the last major Confederate stronghold on the river. Grant had begun his attack on Vicksburg in May 1863. When direct attacks failed, he settled in for a long siege.

During the **Siege of Vicksburg**, Grant's troops surrounded the city and prevented the delivery of food and supplies. Eventually, the Confederates ran out of food. The civilian population moved into caves to protect themselves from the constant bombardment. After nearly a month and a half, the city surrendered.

The Union victory fulfilled a major part of the Anaconda Plan. The North had taken New Orleans in April 1862. With the Union now in complete control of the Mississippi River, the South was split in two.

With the victories at Vicksburg and Gettysburg, the tide of war turned in favor of the North. In General Grant, President Lincoln found a man who might be able to defeat General Lee.

▲ **CAUSES AND EFFECTS** Explain how the Union victories at Gettysburg and Vicksburg affected the course of the war.

Connect *to the* **World**

Crucial Decisions
After Gettysburg and Vicksburg, the British government dropped discussion of recognizing the Confederacy.

🔍 **ONLINE BIOGRAPHY**

For more on Grant and Lee go to the **Research & Writing Center** @ ClassZone.com

History Makers Civil War Generals

Ulysses S. Grant   1822–1885

When the Civil War broke out, Ulysses S. Grant was quickly promoted through the ranks and proved to be a brilliant general. Highly focused and cool under fire, Grant won the first major Union victories of the war. Grant was willing to attack Lee's army, even if the costs were high. He told one of his generals, "Wherever Lee goes, there you will go also."

Robert E. Lee   1807–1870

In General Robert E. Lee, the Confederacy found an unlikely hero. Lee opposed slavery and secession. He did not want to fight the Union, but felt he had to defend his home state of Virginia. "I did only what my duty demanded," Lee said. "I could have taken no other course without dishonor."

During the Seven Days' Battles Lee forced the Union army away from Richmond. After this, his reputation began to rise. By the end of the war, Lee inspired respect and devotion in the South and fear in the North.

COMPARING *Leaders*

What qualities did Grant have that helped him defeat Lee?

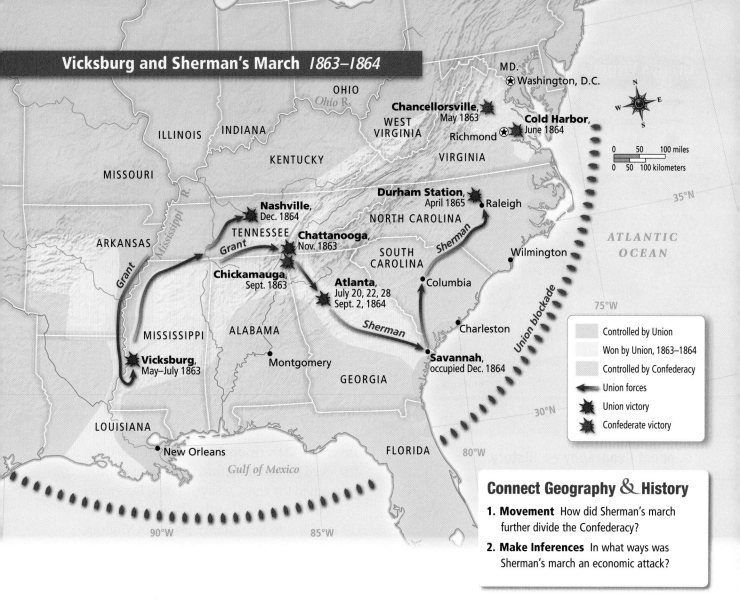

Vicksburg and Sherman's March 1863–1864

Connect Geography & History

1. **Movement** How did Sherman's march further divide the Confederacy?
2. **Make Inferences** In what ways was Sherman's march an economic attack?

Map legend:
- Controlled by Union
- Won by Union, 1863–1864
- Controlled by Confederacy
- Union forces
- Union victory
- Confederate victory

The Confederacy Falls

🔻 **KEY QUESTION** How did Grant's new strategy defeat the Confederacy?

In March 1864, President Lincoln gave General Grant command of all Union armies. Grant then called for all Union forces to coordinate their attacks. Grant would pursue Lee's army in Virginia, while Union forces under General William Tecumseh Sherman pushed through the Deep South.

Sherman Takes Atlanta Battling southward from Tennessee, Sherman took Atlanta in September 1864. Sherman's victory affected the 1864 election. Northerners were tired of war, and Peace Democrats—who had nominated George McClellan—stood a chance of winning on an antiwar platform. But with Sherman's success, Northerners could sense victory. The President won reelection. (See page 564 for Lincoln's Second Inaugural Address.)

In November 1864, Sherman burned Atlanta and set out on a terrifying march to the sea. Sherman's army cut a path of destruction across Georgia that was 60 miles wide and 300 miles long. Sherman waged total war: a war not only against enemy troops, but against everything that supported

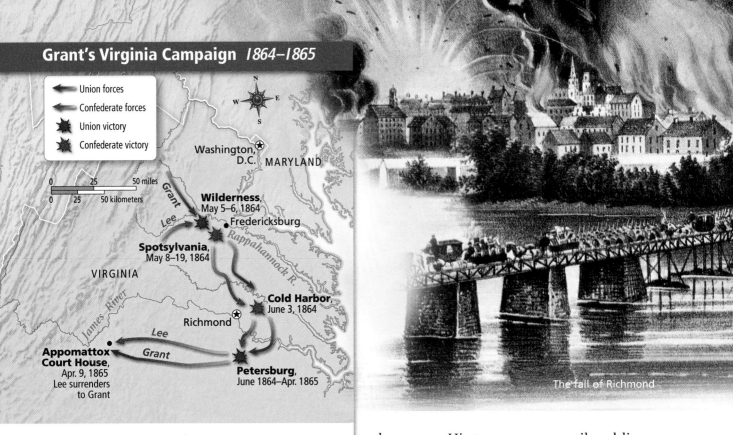

Grant's Virginia Campaign *1864–1865*

Legend:
- ← Union forces
- ← Confederate forces
- ✦ Union victory
- ✦ Confederate victory

0 25 50 miles
0 25 50 kilometers

Washington, D.C.
MARYLAND

Wilderness, May 5–6, 1864
Fredericksburg

Rappahannock R.

Spotsylvania, May 8–19, 1864

VIRGINIA

James River

Cold Harbor, June 3, 1864

Richmond

Appomattox Court House, Apr. 9, 1865 Lee surrenders to Grant

Petersburg, June 1864–Apr. 1865

The fall of Richmond

Connect Geography & History

1. **Movement** Why did the opposing forces circle Richmond?
2. **Make Inferences** Why did Lee turn to the West?

the enemy. His troops tore up railroad lines, destroyed crops, and burned and looted towns. He reached the coast at Savannah in December 1864, then marched north into the Carolinas. His goal was to join Grant's troops in Virginia.

Sherman's March to the Sea, as it was called, tore into the heart of the Confederacy. Sherman's march also increased the size of the Union army—in Georgia alone more than 19,000 former slaves left plantations and followed the Union army to freedom.

Grant's Virginia Campaign In Virginia, Grant pursued Lee's army. Grant had a brutal plan for ending the war: to keep attacking Lee despite the number of casualties that Union forces might suffer. The Union armies could replace fallen soldiers, but the South was running out of men and supplies.

In the Virginia campaign, Lee showed his genius for strategy. Lee's army lacked sufficient manpower and supplies. But Lee excelled at maneuvering his army to fight and then escaping to fight another day. It took Grant a year to corner and defeat Lee.

At the Battle of the Wilderness in May 1864, Union and Confederate forces fought in a tangle of trees and brush so thick that they could barely see each other. Grant suffered over 17,000 casualties, but he pushed on. "Whatever happens," he told Lincoln, "we will not retreat."

At Spotsylvania and Cold Harbor, the fighting continued. Again, the losses were staggering. Grant's attack in June, at Cold Harbor, cost him 7,000 casualties, most in the first few minutes of battle. Some Union troops were so sure they would die in battle that they pinned their names and addresses to their jackets so their bodies could be identified later.

In June 1864, Grant's armies arrived at Petersburg, just south of Richmond. Unable to break through the Confederate defenses, the Union forces dug trenches and settled in for a nine-month-long siege.

Richmond Falls At the beginning of April 1865, Lee realized he could hold out no longer. He sent Davis a note advising the government to leave Richmond. Lee hoped to move his army to food supplies and so prolong the war.

On April 2, the Confederate government fled Richmond. Confederate leaders burnt anything that could be of use to the enemy. The fires spread, and the city was in flames when Union forces arrived on April 3, 1865.

Lincoln visited Richmond to see the prize that the Union had pursued for four years. Most white residents stayed indoors. African Americans cheered the president of the United States who had led the fight for freedom.

Surrender at Appomattox From Richmond and Petersburg, Lee fled west, while Grant followed in pursuit. Lee wanted to continue fighting, but he knew that his situation was hopeless. He sent a message to General Grant that he was ready to surrender.

On April 9, 1865, Lee and Grant met in the small Virginia town of **Appomattox Court House** to arrange the surrender. Grant later wrote that his joy at that moment was mixed with sadness.

Grant offered generous terms of surrender. After laying down their arms, the Confederates could return home in peace, taking their private possessions and horses with them. Grant also fed the hungry Confederate soldiers.

The Civil War was ending. The conflict had changed the country forever.

 SUMMARIZE Explain Grant's strategy for ending the war.

Michigan Grade Level Content Expectations *Review*

 ONLINE QUIZ
For test practice, go to
Interactive Review @ ClassZone.com

TERMS & NAMES

1. Explain the importance of
- Battle of Gettysburg
- George Pickett
- Pickett's Charge
- Siege of Vicksburg
- Appomattox Court House
- Sherman's March to the Sea

USING YOUR READING NOTES

2. Causes and Effects Complete the diagram that you started at the beginning of this section.

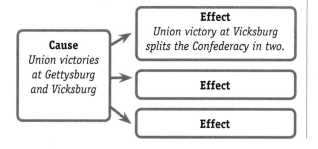

Cause	Effect
Union victories at Gettysburg and Vicksburg	**Effect** *Union victory at Vicksburg splits the Confederacy in two.*
	Effect
	Effect

KEY IDEAS

3. Why was the Battle of Gettysburg important?

4. How did the victory at Vicksburg fulfill a part of the Union strategy?

5. How did Sherman's victory at Atlanta affect the election of 1864?

CRITICAL THINKING

6. Evaluate How was Sherman's March to the Sea different from other military campaigns in the Civil War?

7. Draw Conclusions Why do you think Grant gave generous terms of surrender to Lee?

8. Make Inferences Why was the Confederacy unable to stop Sherman's campaign?

9. Writing Description Suppose that you lived on a farm overlooking the battlefield at Gettysburg. Describe what you saw during the battle.

Animated HISTORY

NAVAL ACTION AT VICKSBURG

 Click here to see an animated version of the Union strategy at Vicksburg @ ClassZone.com

The Struggle for Vicksburg

On April 16, 1863, the Union fleet steamed down the Mississippi past Vicksburg. As the enemy ships sailed south, the Confederate defenders of Vicksburg opened fire. The missiles failed to stop the Union fleet.

General Grant's brilliant strategy to capture Vicksburg had begun.

1 As his fleet sailed south, Grant moved his army down the west bank of the Mississippi.

2 Next, He marched north east. The Confederates could not understand why he was cutting himself off from his supplies on the river.

3 Next, Grant sent forces to conquer Jackson and turned west. He defeated a Confederate force sent from Vicksburg to stop him.

4 Finally, When Grant reached the massive fortifications around Vicksburg, he decided to starve the city into surrender. He surrounded the city with fortifications of his own. The Siege of Vicksburg lasted about six weeks. The city surrendered to the Union on July 4.

Activity

Sharing Perspectives

1. As a class, divide into 2 groups representing (a) the Confederate defenders and civilians of Vicksburg, and (b) the Union attackers.

2. Read about the siege of Vicksburg on pages 552 and 556–557.

3. Discuss how your group would have experienced the siege. For instance: How might a siege affect civilians? In what ways would life be different inside and outside the city?

4. Prepare a brief presentation or skit to present your group's perspective.

CRITICAL THINKING

1. **Draw Conclusions** Why do you think the Confederates in Vicksburg were confused by Grant's strategy?

2. **Make Inferences** How did Grant turn the Vicksburg defenses into a trap for the city's defenders?

▶ Key Ideas

BEFORE, YOU LEARNED

During the Civil War, important social, economic, and political changes took place.

NOW YOU WILL LEARN

The Civil War transformed the nation.

▶ Vocabulary

TERMS & NAMES

Walt Whitman poet who wrote about the Civil War

Ford's Theatre Washington, D.C. theater where Lincoln was shot

John Wilkes Booth Confederate supporter who assassinated Abraham Lincoln

Thirteenth Amendment Constitutional amendment that ended slavery

BACKGROUND VOCABULARY

ratify approve

Visual Vocabulary
Ford's Theatre

▶ Reading Strategy

Re-create the diagram shown at right. As you read and respond to the **KEY QUESTIONS**, use the diagram to categorize what Americans lost and gained because of the war.

 See Skillbuilder Handbook, page R6.

CATEGORIZE

Losses	Gains
	Union preserved

 GRAPHIC ORGANIZERS
Go to **Interactive Review** @ ClassZone.com

The Legacy of the War

8 – U5.2.3.2 Examine Abraham Lincoln's presidency with respect to – the evolution of his emancipation policy (including the Emancipation Proclamation)
8 – U5.2.3.3 Examine Abraham Lincoln's presidency with respect to – the role of his significant writings and speeches, including the Gettysburg Address and its relationship to the Declaration of Independence

One American's Story

Walt Whitman is one of America's greatest poets. Whitman was 41 when the war began, which was too old to serve in the army. Whitman volunteered as a nurse and cared for wounded soldiers at hospitals in Washington, D.C. Whitman wrote many poems about the Civil War. These lines were written after the death of President Lincoln.

Walt Whitman

PRIMARY SOURCE

❝ This dust was once the man,
    Gentle, plain, just and resolute, under whose cautious hand,
    Against the foulest crime in history known in any land or age,
    Was saved the Union of these States. ❞

—Walt Whitman, *This Dust Was Once the Man*

Whitman's poem expresses the grief that followed Lincoln's assassination—five days after Lee's surrender. For many Americans, the terrible costs of the war prevented the celebration of victory.

Costs of the War

🔻 **KEY QUESTION** What were the losses and gains of the war?

With the defeat of the Confederacy, the Union of the United States had been preserved, but at a terrible cost.

Terrible Losses The Civil War was the deadliest war in American history. In four years, around 620,000 soldiers died: 360,000 from the Union and 260,000 from the Confederacy. Another 275,000 Union soldiers and about 100,000 Confederate soldiers were wounded. Many suffered health problems for the rest of their lives.

Both the North and the South spent enormous sums of money. Years later, the government was still paying interest on loans taken out during the war.

COMPARING *Images of Battle*

The photographs of the Civil War altered the way people thought about warfare. For centuries, artists showed battle as a heroic, glorious adventure. The invention of photography changed this misconception. For the first time civilians saw the results of battle. The pictures of contemporary photographers revealed the horrors, rather than the heroism, of war.

Battle of Cedar Creek
by Kurz and Allison

Photograph of Gettysburg by Timothy O'Sullivan

CRITICAL THINKING

1. **Make Inferences** Why did so many traditional images of war show the moment before a battle?

2. **Draw Conclusions** How might photographs have changed civilians' attitudes to war?

The South in Ruins The war brought economic disaster to the South. Farms and plantations were destroyed. About 40 percent of the South's livestock was killed, and 50 percent of its farm machinery was wrecked. Factories were demolished, and thousands of miles of railroad tracks were torn up.

Before the war, the South accounted for 30 percent of the nation's wealth. After the war it accounted for only 12 percent. Long after the Northern economy began to rebound, the South remained locked in poverty. The economic gap between the North and the South would last for decades.

Lincoln's Assassination Although the war was over, one final disaster was yet to come. On April 14, 1865, five days after Lee's surrender, President Lincoln was shot while watching a play at **Ford's Theatre** in Washington, D.C. His attacker was **John Wilkes Booth**, a Confederate supporter. Booth escaped from the theater but was pursued and killed by troops 11 days later.

The wounded Lincoln was carried to a house nearby. Doctors tried to save him, but the bullet in his brain could not be removed. The next morning, April 15, 1865, the president died. He was the first American president to be assassinated. At the news of his death, many Americans wept in the streets.

▲ **CATEGORIZE** List the losses and gains of the war.

The Nation Transformed

KEY QUESTION What changes did the war bring about?

The Civil War brought the most sweeping change to America since the Revolution. Socially and economically, the Civil War created a new nation.

A New Nation The war settled an old argument about states' rights—now it was clear that the states did not have the power to secede. The United States was recognized as a union rather than as a loose federation of states.

The war also caused the national government to expand. Along with a new paper currency and income tax, the government established a new federal banking system. It funded railroads, gave western land to settlers, and provided for state colleges.

CONNECT to the Essential Question

In what ways did the Civil War transform the nation?

Economic Change
- Income tax is introduced.
- New national paper currency is introduced.
- Industry begins to replace farming as the basis of the national economy.
- Southern slavery-based economy is destroyed.
- Factory production increases.

Civil War transforms the nation

Social Change
- Slavery is abolished; millions are freed.
- African Americans serve in the military.
- Conscription is introduced.
- Women become active in nursing.

Political Change
- Federal government grows more powerful.
- Triumph of idea of United States as a union, rather than a loose federation of states.

Changes in Warfare
- Modernized rifle and minié ball gives advantage to defender.
- New weaponry increases number of casualties on battlefield.
- Ironclads make wooden warships obsolete.

CRITICAL THINKING **Draw Conclusions** Which changes continue to affect life today?

The war destroyed a Southern economic system based on slavery and replaced it with paid labor. In the North, industries such as steel, petroleum, food processing, and manufacturing grew rapidly. By the late 1800s, industry had begun to replace farming as the basis of the national economy.

The Thirteenth Amendment But the greatest effect of the war was the freeing of millions of enslaved Americans. One of those was Booker T. Washington, who became a famous educator and reformer. He recalled a Union officer coming to his plantation to read the Emancipation Proclamation.

PRIMARY SOURCE

❝After the reading we were told that we were all free, and could go when and where we pleased. My mother, who was standing by my side, leaned over and kissed her children, while tears of joy ran down her cheeks. She explained to us what it all meant, that this was the day for which she had been so long praying, but fearing that she would never live to see.❞

—Booker T. Washington, *Up from Slavery*

Connect *to the* **World**

Expanding Liberty
In 1861, the Tsar of Russia gave freedom to the Russian serfs, poor farm workers who were treated much like slaves.

In January 1865, Congress passed a constitutional amendment to end slavery. The **Thirteenth Amendment** was **ratified**, or approved, by 27 states, including 8 in the South. Slavery was now banned in the United States.

The country faced difficult challenges after the war. The South had to be brought back into the Union. Four million former slaves had to be integrated into national life. After four years of destruction, Americans turned their energies to rebuilding their nation.

 SUMMARIZE List changes brought about by the Civil War.

 Michigan Grade Level Content Expectations *Review*

ONLINE QUIZ
For test practice, go to
Interactive Review @ ClassZone.com

TERMS & NAMES

1. Explain the importance of
- Walt Whitman
- John Wilkes Booth
- Ford's Theatre
- Thirteenth Amendment

USING YOUR READING NOTES

2. Categorize Complete the diagram you started at the beginning of this section.

Losses	Gains
	Union preserved

KEY IDEAS

3. What long-term effect did the war have on the South?

4. What economic changes did the war bring to the nation?

CRITICAL THINKING

5. Analyze Point of View What do you think former slaveowners thought about the Thirteenth Amendment?

6. Connect *to* **Today** In what ways are the effects of the Civil War still being felt today?

7. Math Graph Research the casualty figures for the Civil War. Make a graph showing the deaths for the North and the South in each year of the war.

The Gettysburg Address (1863)

SETTING THE STAGE On November 19, 1863, officials gathered in Gettysburg, Pennsylvania. They were there to dedicate a national cemetery on the ground where the decisive Battle of Gettysburg had taken place nearly five months earlier. Following the ceremony's main address, which lasted nearly two hours, President Lincoln delivered his Gettysburg Address in just two minutes. In this famous speech, Lincoln expressed his hopes for the nation.

Four**score**[1] and seven years ago our fathers brought forth on this continent a new nation, conceived in liberty, and dedicated to the proposition that all men are created equal.

Now we are engaged in a great civil war, testing whether that nation, or any nation so conceived and so dedicated, can long endure. We are met on a great battlefield of that war. We have come to dedicate a portion of that field as a final resting-place for those who here gave their lives that this nation might live. It is altogether fitting and proper that we should do this.

But, in a larger sense, we cannot dedicate . . . we cannot **consecrate**[2] . . . we cannot hallow . . . this ground. The brave men, living and dead, who struggled here, have consecrated it far above our poor power to add or **detract**.[3] The world will little note nor long remember what we say here, but it can never forget what they did here. It is for us, the living, rather, to be dedicated here to the unfinished work which they who fought here have thus far so nobly advanced. It is rather for us to be here dedicated to the great task remaining before us . . . that from these honored dead we **take increased devotion to**[4] that cause for which they **gave the last full measure of devotion**[5]; that we here highly resolve that these dead shall not have died **in vain**[6]; that this nation, under God, shall have a new birth of freedom; and that government of the people, by the people, for the people, shall not perish from the earth.

Fighting for a Cause

Different people fought for different causes during the Civil War. Sometimes, the causes for which people fought changed over the course of the war.

1. **What cause is Lincoln referring to in the Gettysburg Address?**

Lincoln's Modesty

Lincoln claimed that what he said at Gettysburg would not be long remembered. However, the address soon came to be recognized as one of the best speeches of all time.

2. **What features of Lincoln's address make it so memorable?**

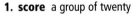

1. **score** a group of twenty
2. **consecrate** declare as sacred
3. **detract** take away from
4. **take increased devotion to** work harder for
5. **gave the last full measure of devotion** sacrificed their lives
6. **in vain** for nothing

Second Inaugural Address (1865)

SETTING THE STAGE President Lincoln delivered his Second Inaugural Address just before the end of the Civil War. In this excerpt, he recalled the major cause of the war and vowed to fight for the restoration of peace and unity.

Slavery in Territories

Before the Civil War, Northern states wanted to prohibit slavery in territories that would eventually become new states. Southern states fought to expand slavery, fearing that outlawing it would threaten slavery where it already existed.

1. **Why did the Southerners fear that prohibiting slavery in new territories might threaten slavery where it already existed?**

Malice Toward None

As Northerners became more confident in victory, many wanted to punish Southerners, whom they blamed for the war. Lincoln, however, urged citizens to care for one another and work for a just and lasting peace.

2. **Why do you think that Lincoln believed it would be wiser for Americans not to place blame or seek revenge on one another?**

One-eighth of the whole population were colored slaves. . . . These slaves constituted a peculiar and powerful interest. All knew that this interest was, somehow, the cause of the war. To strengthen, perpetuate, and extend this interest was the object for which the **insurgents**[1] would rend the Union, even by war; while the government claimed no right to do more than to restrict the territorial enlargement of it. Neither party expected for the war, the magnitude, or the duration, which it has already attained. Neither anticipated that the cause of the conflict might cease with, or even before, the conflict itself should cease. Each looked for an easier triumph, and a result less fundamental and astounding. Both read the same Bible, and pray to the same God; and each invokes His aid against the other. . . . Fondly do we hope—fervently do we pray—that this mighty **scourge**[2] of war may speedily pass away. Yet, if God wills that it continue until all the wealth piled by the **bondsman's**[3] two hundred and fifty years of **unrequited**[4] toil shall be sunk, and until every drop of blood drawn with the lash, shall be paid by another drawn with the sword, as was said three thousand years ago, so still it must be said, "the judgments of the Lord are true and righteous altogether."

With malice toward none; with charity for all; with firmness in the right as God gives us to see the right, let us strive on to finish the work we are in; to bind up the nation's wounds; to care for him who shall have borne the battle, and for his widow, and his orphan—to do all which may achieve and cherish a just and lasting peace, among ourselves and with all nations.

---

1. **insurgents** one that revolts against civil authority
2. **scourge** a source of suffering and devastation
3. **bondsman** enslaved person
4. **unrequited** not paid for

DOCUMENT-BASED QUESTIONS

Short Answer

1. Why might President Lincoln have begun the Gettysburg Address by noting that the country was "dedicated to the proposition that all men are created equal"?

2. According to Lincoln's Second Inaugural Address, why did the Confederacy go to war?

Extended Answer

3. In 1865, if the South had asked to rejoin the Union without ending slavery, do you think Lincoln would have agreed? Use statements from the two documents and your knowledge of U.S. history to support your position.

Chapter Summary

1 **Key Idea**
The Emancipation Proclamation promised freedom to slaves in the Confederacy and allowed African Americans to join the Union army.

2 **Key Idea**
As the war dragged on, social, economic, and political change affected both the Union and the Confederacy.

3 **Key Idea**
After a series of Southern victories, the North began winning battles that led to the defeat of the Confederacy.

4 **Key Idea**
The Civil War transformed the nation.

For detailed Review and Study Notes go to **Interactive Review** @ ClassZone.com

Name Game

Use the list of terms and names to identify each sentence online or on your own paper.

1. I shot Abraham Lincoln. John Wilkes Booth
2. I was a poet who wrote about the Civil War. ____
3. This constitutional amendment ended slavery. ____
4. This was a famous regiment of African Americans. ____
5. I was a nurse who founded the American Red Cross. ____
6. This battle stopped a Confederate invasion of the North. ____
7. We were Northern Democrats who favored peace with the South. ____
8. This document freed all slaves in Confederate territory. ____
9. I was a Confederate general who fought at Gettysburg. ____
10. This law prevents the government from holding citizens without a trial. ____

A. Thirteenth Amendment
B. Clara Barton
C. Emancipation Proclamation
D. John Wilkes Booth
E. writ of habeas corpus
F. Battle of Gettysburg
G. 54th Massachusetts Volunteers
H. Copperheads
I. George Pickett
J. Walt Whitman
K. Siege of Vicksburg
L. Pickett's Charge

Activities

FLIPCARD

Use the online flipcards to quiz yourself on the terms and names introduced in this chapter.

Theater in Washington, D.C., where Lincoln was shot.

ANSWER
Ford's Theatre

GEOGAME

Use this online map to reinforce your understanding of the final years of the Civil War, including the locations of important battles and geographic features. Drag and drop each place name in the list at its location on the map. A scorecard helps you keep track of your progress online.

Nashville

Chattanooga

Richmond

Vicksburg

Raleigh

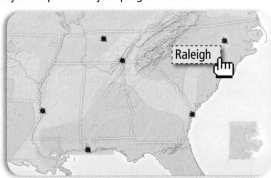

More items online

VOCABULARY

Match the term or name on the left with an item on the right.

1. Clara Barton
2. John Wilkes Booth
3. Copperheads
4. Thirteenth Amendment
5. George Pickett

A. Battle of Gettysburg
B. American Red Cross
C. ended slavery
D. Northern Democrats
E. assassinated President

Explain how the terms in each group are related.

6. Battle of Antietam, Emancipation Proclamation

7. George Pickett, Battle of Gettysburg, Pickett's Charge

8. 54th Massachusetts Volunteers, Emancipation Proclamation

9. Thirteenth Amendment, Emancipation Proclamation

KEY IDEAS

1 The Emancipation Proclamation (pages 536–541)

10. What impact was the Emancipation Proclamation meant to have on the Confederacy?

11. In what ways did African-American soldiers aid the war effort?

2 War Affects Society (pages 542–547)

12. How did enslaved people help undermine the Confederacy?

13. What economic changes did the war bring about?

3 The North Wins (pages 548–555)

14. Why were the Union victories at Gettysburg and Vicksburg a turning point in the war?

15. What was Grant's strategy for defeating Lee?

4 The Legacy of the War (pages 558–562)

16. What were some of the positive results of the war?

17. How did the war change the federal government?

CRITICAL THINKING

18. **Make Inferences** How do you think the assassination of President Lincoln affected the nation?

19. **Categorize** Describe the difference between the tactics of Grant and Lee during the Virginia campaign.

Grant	Lee
determined to keep attacking Lee	

20. **Problems and Solutions** How did Grant help bring the war to an end?

21. **Draw Conclusions** Why do you think Lincoln waited until the Union was in a strong position before he issued the Emancipation Proclamation?

22. **Make Inferences** Why did the federal government expand its powers during the Civil War?

23. **Causes and Effects** How did Sherman's victory in Atlanta affect the election of 1864?

24. **Make Generalizations** At what point did the Civil War become a war of liberation?

25. **Draw Conclusions** Study the casualty charts below. Approximately how many soldiers were wounded in the war?

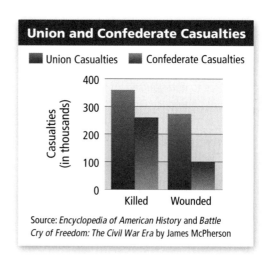

Union and Confederate Casualties

■ Union Casualties ■ Confederate Casualties

Source: *Encyclopedia of American History* and *Battle Cry of Freedom: The Civil War Era* by James McPherson

✔ TEST PRACTICE
- **Online Test Practice @ ClassZone.com**
- Use the **MEAP Strategies & Practice,** pages S1-S27, at the front of this book

DOCUMENT-BASED QUESTIONS

Study each document carefully and answer the questions that follow.

DOCUMENT 1

1 Examine this picture called *A Ride for Liberty* by Eastman Johnson. What message might this painting have conveyed to the people who saw it during the war?

  A that the war was difficult for families

  B that the war was changing life in the South

  C that African Americans helped with the war effort

  D that slavery had come to an end in the South

DOCUMENT 2

PRIMARY SOURCE

❝ The war now being waged in this land is a war for and against slavery; and that it can never be effectually put down till one or the other of these vital forces is completely destroyed. ❞

—Frederick Douglass, quoted in *Passages to Freedom*

2 According to Frederick Douglass, why was the Civil War fought?

  A to preserve the Union

  B to destroy the North

  C to destroy the South

  D to decide the fate of slavery

YOU BE THE HISTORIAN

26. Draw Conclusions Do you think Sherman's tactics were justified? Explain your answer.

27. WHAT IF? How might the course of the Civil War have changed if Lincoln had not issued the Emancipation Proclamation?

28. Causes and Effects Discuss the impact that Grant and Sherman had on the outcome of the Civil War.

29. Connect *to* Today What political, social, and economic issues of the Civil War are still relevant today?

30. Causes and Effects Why did the Union win the war?

31. Problems and Solutions What great national questions were settled by the Civil War?

32. Draw Conclusions Why did Confederates believe they might win the war?

 Answer the
ESSENTIAL QUESTION
In what ways did the Civil War transform the nation?

Written Response Write a four-paragraph response to the Essential Question. Be sure to consider the key ideas of each section as well as the most significant forces that transformed the nation. Use the Response Rubric below to guide your thinking and writing.

Response Rubric
A strong response will
- discuss the social and economic transformation brought by the end of slavery
- analyze the effects of four years of war
- describe the increases in the powers of the federal government

Reconstruction

1865–1877

 ESSENTIAL QUESTION

How did a deeply divided nation move forward after the Civil War?

CONNECT ⟳ **Geography & History**

How might the Civil War have affected the economy of the South?

Think about:

1 how most of the war was fought in the South, including major battles in Virginia, Tennessee, Georgia, and Mississippi

2 how the amount of Southern farmland before the war compares with the amount after the war

3 what happened to the region's main system of labor—slavery

Lincoln's funeral train left Washington, D.C., on April 21, 1865, and arrived in Springfield, Illinois, on May 3.

1868 President Johnson impeached and later acquitted by a single vote

A ticket to Johnson's impeachment proceedings

1865

Lincoln assassinated; Johnson becomes president.

▼

Effect Johnson pardons white Southerners.

1866 Fourteenth Amendment

▼

Effect Former slaves become citizens.

1870 Fifteenth Amendment

▼

Effect African-American men get the vote.

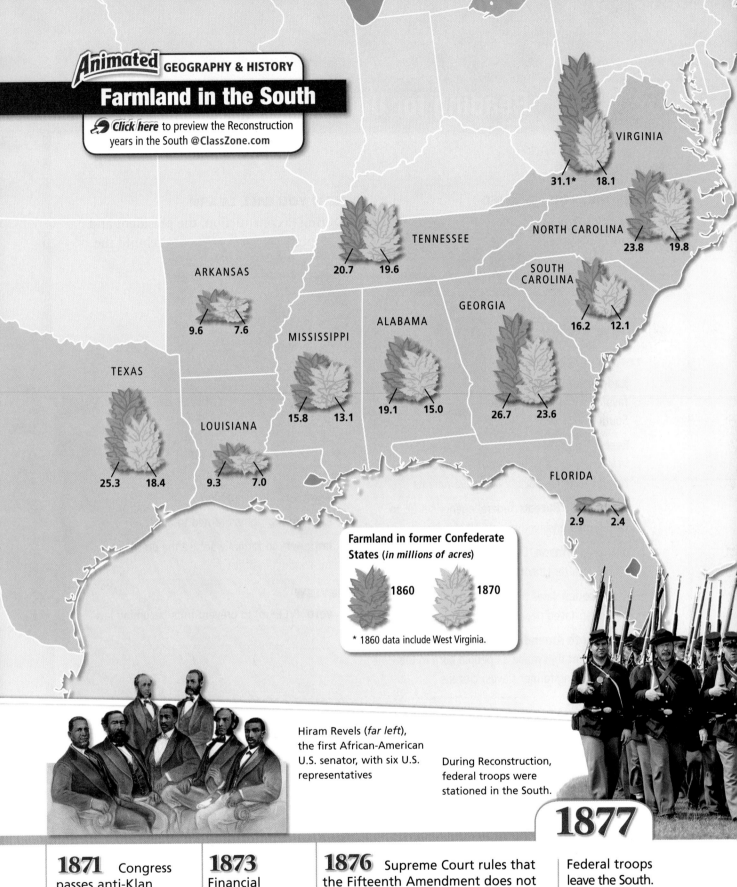

Animated GEOGRAPHY & HISTORY
Farmland in the South

Click here to preview the Reconstruction years in the South @ClassZone.com

VIRGINIA
31.1* 18.1

TENNESSEE
20.7 19.6

NORTH CAROLINA
23.8 19.8

ARKANSAS
9.6 7.6

SOUTH CAROLINA
16.2 12.1

MISSISSIPPI
15.8 13.1

ALABAMA
19.1 15.0

GEORGIA
26.7 23.6

TEXAS
25.3 18.4

LOUISIANA
9.3 7.0

FLORIDA
2.9 2.4

Farmland in former Confederate States (*in millions of acres*)

1860   1870

* 1860 data include West Virginia.

Hiram Revels (*far left*), the first African-American U.S. senator, with six U.S. representatives

During Reconstruction, federal troops were stationed in the South.

1877

1871 Congress passes anti-Klan legislation.

1873 Financial panic begins depression.

1876 Supreme Court rules that the Fifteenth Amendment does not give everyone the right to vote.

▼

Effect Southern states stop African Americans from voting.

Federal troops leave the South.

▼

Effect Reconstruction ends.

▶ Key Ideas

BEFORE, YOU LEARNED

The Civil War promoted industry and economic growth in the North, but left the South in ruins.

NOW YOU WILL LEARN

During Reconstruction, the president and Congress fought over how to rebuild the South.

▶ Vocabulary

TERMS & NAMES

Radical Republican congressman who favored using federal power to rebuild the South and promote African-American rights

Reconstruction period from 1865 to 1877 in which the U.S. government attempted to rebuild Southern society and governments

Freedmen's Bureau federal agency set up to help former enslaved people

Andrew Johnson Democrat who became president after Lincoln was assassinated

black codes laws that limited the freedom of former enslaved people

Fourteenth Amendment constitutional amendment that made all people born in the U.S. (including former slaves) citizens

scalawag white Southerner who supported Radical Reconstruction

carpetbagger Northerner who went to the South after the Civil War to participate in Reconstruction

BACKGROUND VOCABULARY

amnesty official pardon

civil rights rights granted to all citizens

impeach to formally accuse the president of misconduct in office

REVIEW

veto (VEE•to) to prevent from becoming law

▶ Reading Strategy

As you read and respond to the **KEY QUESTIONS**, use a graphic organizer like the one shown to compare presidential and Congressional Reconstruction. Record the goals of each plan in the columns. Circle any shared goals.

 See Skillbuilder Handbook, page R8.

COMPARE AND CONTRAST

Presidential Reconstruction	Congressional Reconstruction
	promote civil rights for freed people

 GRAPHIC ORGANIZERS
Go to **Interactive Review** @ ClassZone.com

Rebuilding the Union

 8 – U5.3.1 Describe the different positions concerning the reconstruction of Southern society and the nation, including the positions of President Abraham Lincoln, President Andrew Johnson, Republicans, and African Americans.
8 – U5.3.2.2 Describe the early responses to the end of the Civil War by describing the – restrictions placed on the rights and opportunities of freedmen, including racial segregation and Black Codes

One American's Story

After the Civil War, Pennsylvania congressman Thaddeus Stevens became a leader of the **Radical Republicans**. This group of congressmen favored using federal power to promote full citizenship for freed African Americans.

PRIMARY SOURCE

❝ We have turned, or are about to turn, loose four million slaves without a hut to shelter them or a cent in their pockets. . . . if we leave them to the legislation of their late masters, we had better have left them in bondage. ❞

—Thaddeus Stevens, the *Congressional Globe*, December 18, 1865

Thaddeus Stevens was a passionate opponent of slavery and a strong supporter of the rights of African Americans.

Radical Republicans wanted to make the South a region of small farms, free schools, and equality for all citizens.

Presidential Reconstruction

🔻 **KEY QUESTION** Why did presidential Reconstruction fail under Johnson?

Soon after the war ended, the nation began a process called **Reconstruction**. It lasted from 1865 to 1877. During Reconstruction, the federal government faced the challenge of rebuilding Southern society and governments.

Reconstruction Under Lincoln In his Second Inaugural Address, in March 1865, President Lincoln promised to reunify the nation "with malice [harm] toward none, with charity for all." Lincoln wanted to treat the South with respect. His plan included pardoning Confederate officials. It also called for allowing the Confederate states to send representatives to Congress.

Congress established the **Freedmen's Bureau**—a federal agency set up to assist former enslaved people. The Freedmen's Bureau set up schools and hospitals for African Americans and distributed clothes, food, and fuel.

Reconstruction Under Johnson When Lincoln was killed, Vice-President **Andrew Johnson** became president. Johnson believed that Reconstruction was the job of the president, not Congress. His policies were based on Lincoln's goals. He insisted that the new state governments ratify the Thirteenth Amendment, which banned slavery in the United States. He also insisted that they accept the supreme power of the federal government.

Johnson offered **amnesty**, or official pardon, to most white Southerners. He promised that their property would be returned to them. However, they had to pledge loyalty to the United States. At first, the large plantation owners, top military officers, and ex-Confederate leaders were not included in this offer. But most of them, too, eventually won amnesty.

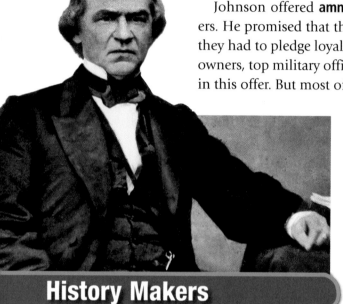

History Makers

Andrew Johnson 1808–1875

Andrew Johnson came from humble beginnings. His first career was as a tailor; his wife taught him to write and do arithmetic. In 1857, he was elected to the U.S. Senate from Tennessee. Although he was a Democrat and a former slaveholder, Johnson remained loyal to the Union. As president, he called for a mild program for bringing the South back into the Union. In particular, he let states decide whether to give voting rights to freed African Americans. Johnson's policies led to a break with the Radical Republicans in Congress and, finally, to his impeachment trial. (See page 575.)

CRITICAL THINKING

1. **Analyze Point of View** Why would many white Southerners have welcomed Johnson's decision on voting rights?

2. **Analyze Point of View** Why might Johnson have chosen not to punish the South?

 **ONLINE BIOGRAPHY** For more on Andrew Johnson, go to the **Research & Writing Center** @ ClassZone.com

Johnson's Failure Congress was not in session when Johnson became president in April 1865. Congress did not reconvene until December. During these eight months, the Southern states rebuilt. As they did so, they set up new state governments that were very much like the old ones. Some states flatly refused to ratify the Thirteenth Amendment. "This is a white man's government," said the governor of South Carolina, "and intended for white men only."

Johnson required only that the Southern states meet the conditions of his Reconstruction plan. His main goal was to have the Southern states readmitted to the Union as quickly as possible. He did not attempt to meet the needs of formerly enslaved people by helping them to gain land, voting rights, or equal protection under the law. Johnson believed the states should have the right to address these matters on their own. This was a relief to many white Southerners.

Southern states passed laws, known as **black codes**, that limited the freedom of formerly enslaved people. These laws were simply updated versions of the rules that had governed Southern African Americans during slavery. In Mississippi, for instance, one law said that African Americans had to have written proof of employment. Anyone without such proof could be arrested or imprisoned. African Americans were forbidden to meet in unsupervised groups or carry guns. Because the black codes were so much like slave codes, many people in the North suspected that white Southerners were trying to bring back the "old South."

▲ **CAUSES AND EFFECTS** Explain what caused the failure of presidential Reconstruction.

Congressional Reconstruction

▼ **KEY QUESTION** What were the goals of Congressional Reconstruction?

When Congress finally met again in December 1865, its members first refused to seat representatives from the South. Many of these Southern representatives had been Confederate leaders only months before.

Congress States Its Intentions Congress exercised its Constitutional right to decide whether its members are qualified to hold office. It set up a committee to study conditions in the South and decide whether the Southern states should be represented. By taking such action, Congress let the president know that it planned to play a major role in Reconstruction.

Republicans outnumbered Democrats in both houses of Congress. Within the Republican Party, however, opinions differed as to how involved Congress should be in Reconstruction. Moderate Republicans supported the states' right to govern themselves. Radical Republicans wanted the federal government to play an active role in remaking Southern politics and society. Led by Thaddeus Stevens and Massachusetts senator Charles Sumner, the group demanded full and equal citizenship for African Americans.

Civil Rights for African Americans Urged on by the Radicals, Congress passed a bill promoting **civil rights**—those rights granted to all citizens. The Civil Rights Act of 1866 said that all people born in the United States (except Native Americans) were citizens. It also stated that all citizens were entitled to equal rights regardless of their race.

"The First Vote," by Alfred R. Waud, appeared on the cover of *Harper's Weekly* on November 16, 1867.

Republicans were shocked when Johnson chose to **veto** the bill, or stop it from becoming law. Johnson argued that federal protection of civil rights would lead to "centralization" of the government. He was also against giving African Americans full citizenship. Two-thirds of the House and two-thirds of the Senate voted to override the veto, and the bill became law.

Republicans wanted equality to be protected by the Constitution itself, and proposed an amendment in 1866. The **Fourteenth Amendment** stated that all people born or naturalized in the United States were citizens, had the same rights, and were to be granted "equal protection of the laws." However, the amendment did not specifically give African Americans the vote. Instead, it declared that any state that kept African Americans from voting would lose representatives in Congress. This meant that the Southern states would have less power if they did not grant black men the vote.

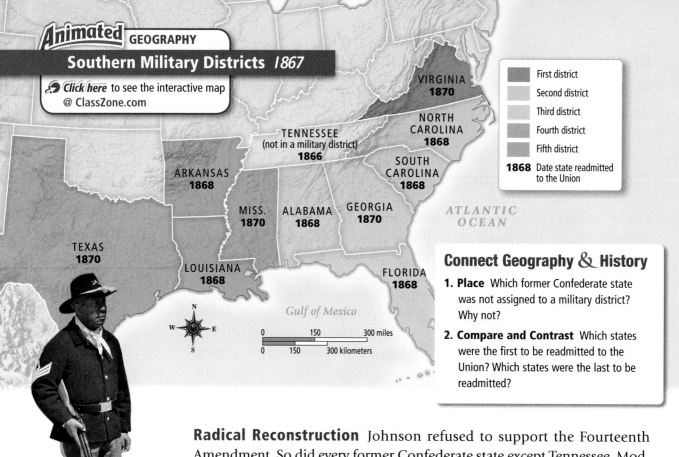

Animated GEOGRAPHY

Southern Military Districts *1867*

Click here to see the interactive map
@ ClassZone.com

VIRGINIA
1870

NORTH
CAROLINA
1868

TENNESSEE
(not in a military district)
1866

SOUTH
CAROLINA
1868

ARKANSAS
1868

	First district
	Second district
	Third district
	Fourth district
	Fifth district
1868	Date state readmitted to the Union

MISS.
1870

ALABAMA
1868

GEORGIA
1870

ATLANTIC OCEAN

TEXAS
1870

LOUISIANA
1868

FLORIDA
1868

Gulf of Mexico

N W E S

| 0 | 150 | 300 miles |
| 0 | 150 | 300 kilometers |

Connect Geography & History

1. **Place** Which former Confederate state was not assigned to a military district? Why not?

2. **Compare and Contrast** Which states were the first to be readmitted to the Union? Which states were the last to be readmitted?

Under the Reconstruction Acts, the U.S. army governed states in the Southern military districts.

Radical Reconstruction Johnson refused to support the Fourteenth Amendment. So did every former Confederate state except Tennessee. Moderate and Radical Republicans were outraged. The two groups joined forces and passed the Reconstruction Acts of 1867. This began a phase, known as Radical Reconstruction, in which Congress controlled Reconstruction.

The Reconstruction Acts divided the South into five military districts. They also said that before Southern states could rejoin the Union, they must:

1. approve new state constitutions that gave the vote to all adult men, including African Americans.
2. ratify the Fourteenth Amendment.

▲ **SUMMARIZE** Summarize Congressional goals for Reconstruction.

The Impact of Reconstruction

▼ **KEY QUESTION** What were the effects of Congressional Reconstruction?

After the Reconstruction Acts, Southern voters chose delegates to draft state constitutions. Delegates—all Republicans—came from three groups.

Constitutional Delegates Many of the Republicans were white farmers, many of them poor, who were angry at planters for starting what they called the "rich man's war." Some Democrats called these delegates **scalawags** (scoundrels) for going along with Radical Reconstruction.

The second group of delegates were known as **carpetbaggers**—white Northerners who rushed to the South after the war. Many Southerners accused them, often unfairly, of seeking only wealth or political power.

African Americans made up the third group of delegates. Of these, half had been free before the war. Most were teachers or other skilled workers.

New Southern Governments The new constitutions written by these delegates gave the vote to all adult males. By 1870, voters in all the Southern states had approved their new constitutions. As a result, former Confederate states were let back into the Union and allowed to send representatives to Congress.

During Reconstruction, nearly 700 African Americans served in Southern state legislatures, and 16 served as Southern U.S. congressmen. These included two senators: Hiram Revels and Blanche Bruce, both of Mississippi.

Johnson Is Impeached Johnson fought many changes made by Radical Republicans. His conflicts with Congress brought a showdown. In 1867, Congress passed the Tenure of Office Act, which prohibited the president from firing government officials without Senate approval. In February 1868, Johnson fired his secretary of war over disagreements about Reconstruction. Three days later, the House **impeached** the president, or formally accused him of improper conduct while in office.

The case moved to the Senate for a trial. If Johnson were convicted, he would have to leave office. In the end, Johnson was acquitted by a single vote. But much work remained to be done in rebuilding the South.

Carpetbaggers— Northerners who went South after the Civil War—were named for a type of luggage, made from old carpet, that was popular at the time.

 CAUSES AND EFFECTS Identify the effects of Congressional Reconstruction.

Michigan Grade Level Content Expectations *Review*

ONLINE QUIZ
For test practice, go to
Interactive Review @ ClassZone.com

TERMS & NAMES

1. Explain the importance of

- Radical Republican
- black codes
- Reconstruction
- Fourteenth Amendment
- Freedmen's Bureau
- scalawag
- Andrew Johnson
- carpetbagger

USING YOUR READING NOTES

2. Compare and Contrast Complete the chart to show the goals of presidential and Congressional Reconstruction.

Presidential Reconstruction	Congressional Reconstruction
	promote civil rights for freed people

KEY IDEAS

3. How did President Andrew Johnson treat the South during Reconstruction?

4. Why did Congress decide to take a larger role in Reconstruction?

5. What conditions did the Southern states meet in order to rejoin the Union?

CRITICAL THINKING

6. Compare and Contrast How were the black codes similar to the old slave codes?

7. Draw Conclusions Did the Fourteenth Amendment truly protect African-American men's right to vote? Explain.

8. Evaluate Do you think the House was justified in impeaching President Johnson? Why or why not?

9. **Writing** Speech Research an African American who served in Congress during Reconstruction. Write a speech about his accomplishments.

Reading for Understanding

▶ Key Ideas

BEFORE, YOU LEARNED

During Reconstruction, the president and Congress fought over how to rebuild the South.

NOW YOU WILL LEARN

As the South rebuilt, millions of freed African Americans worked to improve their lives.

▶ Vocabulary

TERMS & NAMES

freedmen's school school set up to educate newly freed African Americans

sharecropping system under which landowners gave poor farmers seed, tools, and land to cultivate in exchange for part of their harvest

Ku Klux Klan secret group that used violence to try to restore Democratic control of the South and keep African Americans powerless

BACKGROUND VOCABULARY

lynch to kill by hanging without due process of law

REVIEW

plantation large farm that raises cash crops

Visual Vocabulary
freedmen's school

▶ Reading Strategy

Re-create the diagram shown here. As you read and respond to the **KEY QUESTIONS**, use the center box to record the main idea; use the outer ovals to note important details. Add ovals or start a new diagram as needed.

 See Skillbuilder Handbook, page R4.

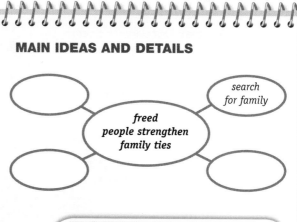

MAIN IDEAS AND DETAILS

freed people strengthen family ties

search for family

GRAPHIC ORGANIZERS
Go to **Interactive Review** @ ClassZone.com

Reconstruction and Daily Life

 8 – U5.3.2.1 Describe the early responses to the end of the Civil War by describing the – policies of the Freedmen's Bureau
8 – U5.3.3 Describe the new role of African Americans in local, state and federal government in the years after the Civil War and the resistance of Southern whites to this change, including the Ku Klux Klan.

One American's Story

After emancipation, many African Americans went in search of family members separated from them by slavery. One observer described a Virginia search party in a letter to an African-American newspaper.

PRIMARY SOURCE

❝ Aged women and grayhaired men journeyed to Virginia from far-off Georgia hoping to . . . meet sons and daughters whom they bade farewell at the auction block. Many had the good fortune to find those they sought, and their greetings were pathetic [heartbreaking] beyond description. ❞

—B., *The New National Era*, July 23, 1874

Freed people on the South Carolina plantation of former Confederate general Thomas Drayton

Some former slaves walked hundreds of miles to find loved ones. Many placed advertisements in newspapers or with the Freedmen's Bureau.

Responding to Freedom

🔻 **KEY QUESTION** How did formerly enslaved people first respond to freedom?

Most African Americans' first reaction to freedom was to leave the **plantations**, the large farms that had raised cash crops using slave labor.

Leaving Plantations Some former slaves went looking for economic opportunity, while others traveled just because they could—they no longer needed passes to travel. Freedom also allowed African Americans to strengthen their family ties. For the first time, they could marry legally and raise families, knowing that their children could not be sold.

Connecting History

Education
American education had boomed in the mid–19th century, thanks to the efforts of reformers in both state governments and private organizations. *See Chapter 14, p. 460.*

Freedmen's Schools With freedom, African Americans no longer had to work for an owner's benefit. They could now work to provide for their families. To reach their goal of economic independence, however, most had to learn to read and write. Children and adults flocked to **freedmen's schools,** which were set up to educate newly freed African Americans.

Such schools were started by the Freedmen's Bureau, Northern missionary groups, and African-American organizations. Freed people in cities held classes in warehouses, billiard rooms, and former slave markets. In rural areas, classes were held in churches and private homes. Children who went to school often taught their parents to read at home.

By 1869, more than 150,000 African-American students were attending 3,000 schools. Almost 20 percent of the South's African-American adults could read. Many white Southerners, however, worked against African Americans' efforts to educate themselves. White racists even killed teachers and burned freedmen's schools in some parts of the South. Despite these violent attacks, African Americans kept working toward an education.

▲ **SYNTHESIZE** Explain how freedom changed the lives of formerly enslaved people.

CONNECT To Today

RICHMOND, VIRGINIA

During the Civil War, Richmond was the capital of the Confederate States of America. In April 1865, the South faced defeat as Union troops approached the city. The retreating Confederates blew up Richmond's gunpowder supplies in a shattering explosion. Most of the business district and many residential areas were destroyed by fire.

Richmond quickly rebuilt after the war, aided by money from the tobacco industry, of which the city was a hub. Today, Richmond is the capital city of Virginia.

(*right*) A statue of Confederate general Robert E. Lee on Richmond's Monument Avenue. The street was built in the 1880s to honor Civil War veterans. (*inset*) Richmond, April 1865

CRITICAL THINKING

1. Make Inferences Why would the Confederates destroy their own supplies?

2. Evaluate What are the advantages and disadvantages of rebuilding a city?

Working the Land

▼ **KEY QUESTION** What prevented formerly enslaved people from making greater economic advances?

More than anything else, freed people wanted land. To them, land meant economic independence. As one freedman said, "Give us our own land and we take care of ourselves, but without land, the old masters can hire us or starve us, as they please."

Forty Acres and a Mule As the Civil War ended, General Sherman suggested that abandoned land in the coastal South be split into 40-acre parcels and given to freedmen. The army also had extra mules that Sherman wanted to loan. The rumor then spread that all freedmen would get 40 acres and a mule. Most freed people thought they deserved at least that much. Said one freedman:

PRIMARY SOURCE

❝ Our wives, our children, our husbands, [have] been sold over and over again to purchase the lands we now [locate] upon; for that reason we have a divine right to the land. . . . And [then] didn't we clear the land, and raise [the] crops [of] corn, of cotton, of tobacco, of rice, of sugar, of everything? And then didn't . . . cities in the North grow up on the cotton and the sugars and the rice that we made! . . . I say they have grown rich, and my people are poor. ❞

—Bayley Wyat, quoted in *Reconstruction: America's Unfinished Revolution*

In the end, however, most freedmen received no land. Those who did often had to return it later to its former owners—planters who were pardoned by President Johnson.

Radical Republicans Thaddeus Stevens and Charles Sumner pushed for land reform. Stevens proposed a plan that would have taken land from plantation owners and given it to freed people. He argued that civil rights meant little without economic independence. But many other Republicans were against the plan. They believed that civil and voting rights for African Americans were enough, and that the plantation owners had the right to keep their land. As a result, Congress did not pass the plan.

Picking cotton on a Southern plantation, 1870

COMPARING *Southern Agriculture*

	Cotton (bales)	Corn (bushels)	Hay (tons)
1850	2.5 million	240 million	718,997
1860	5.3 million	283 million	1.1 million
1870	3.1 million	179 million	474,739
1880	5.9 million	249 million	699,200

(Source: *Historical Statistics of the States of the United States*)

CRITICAL THINKING Make Inferences What effects of the Civil War explain the drop in agricultural production in Southern states?

The Contract System After the Civil War, planters needed workers to raise cotton—still the South's main cash crop. Without their own land, many African Americans accepted contracts for plantation work.

The contract system was far better than slavery. African Americans were paid for their labor and could decide whom to work for. But even the best contracts paid very low wages. Some landowners abused or cheated workers. As a result, many African Americans turned to sharecropping.

The Economics of Sharecropping In the **sharecropping** system, farmers rented land on credit. The landowner provided tools and seed. At harvest time, farmers gave a share of their crops to the landowner as payment.

The sharecropping system had serious problems. Farmers wanted to grow food to feed their families, but landowners forced them to grow cash crops, such as cotton. Meanwhile, most farmers had to buy food, clothing, and other goods on credit—often at inflated prices. By the time they had shared their crops with the landowner and paid their debts, sharecroppers usually had little or no money left. Without money or land of their own, most sharecroppers had no hope of escaping poverty.

▲ **CAUSES AND EFFECTS** Identify the factors that held back the economic advancement of formerly enslaved people.

COMPARING *The Contract System and Sharecropping*

CONTRACT SYSTEM

- earn wages
- choose whom to work for

SHARECROPPING

- earn portion of harvest
- supervise own work

DRAWBACKS

- low wages
- often cheated by landowner

BENEFITS

- families stay together
- landowner provides land, tools, seed

DRAWBACKS

- landowner decides what to grow
- farmers often must buy goods on credit from landowner

CRITICAL THINKING Form and Support Opinions Which do you think offered farmers a better chance of escaping poverty: the contract system or sharecropping? Why?

Violent Racism

▼ **KEY QUESTION** What were the goals of the Ku Klux Klan?

African Americans in the South faced serious problems besides poverty—including violent racism. Many planters and former Confederate soldiers did not want African Americans to have equal rights.

The Ku Klux Klan In 1866, racism in the South spurred the rise of a terrorist group called the **Ku Klux Klan**. Its members came from all walks of life, from poor farmers to former Confederate officers. The Klan's goals were to restore Democratic control of the South and keep former slaves powerless. By 1868, the Klan existed in nearly every Southern state.

The Klan attacked African Americans and white Republicans. Klansmen rode on horseback and dressed in robes and hoods that hid their faces. They beat and tortured people and burned schools, churches, and homes. They even **lynched** some victims—killed them by hanging without a trial as punishment for a supposed crime.

Targets of the Klan had little protection. Military governors in the South often ignored the violence. President Johnson had appointed most of these authorities, and they were against Reconstruction.

The Klan's violence served the Democratic Party. As Klansmen kept Republicans away from the polls, the Democrats' power increased.

▲ **SUMMARIZE** Describe the goals of the Ku Klux Klan.

(*top*) A former slave trader and Confederate general, Nathan Bedford Forrest led the Klan from 1867 to 1869. (*bottom*) an 1866 Klan flag.

Michigan Grade Level Content Expectations *Review*

🔎 **ONLINE QUIZ**
For test practice, go to
Interactive Review @ ClassZone.com

TERMS & NAMES

1. Explain the importance of:
- freedmen's school
- Ku Klux Klan
- sharecropping

USING YOUR READING NOTES

2. Main Ideas and Details Give details about the ways in which newly freed African Americans worked to strengthen family ties.

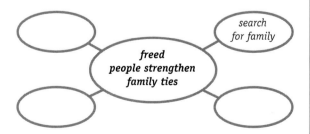

search for family

freed people strengthen family ties

KEY IDEAS

3. How did newly freed African Americans work to improve their lives?

4. Why did many African Americans move from the contract system to sharecropping?

5. How did the Ku Klux Klan benefit the Democratic Party?

CRITICAL THINKING

6. Connect Economics and History How did the sharecropping system affect African Americans' efforts to achieve economic independence?

7. Problems and Solutions What problems did formerly enslaved people face in their efforts to improve their lives?

8. Writing Journal Write a journal entry from the point of view of a sharecropper who was a former contract worker. Describe a day in the life of this person.

▶ Key Ideas

BEFORE, YOU LEARNED

As the South rebuilt, millions of newly freed African Americans worked to improve their lives.

NOW YOU WILL LEARN

As white Southerners regained power in Congress, Reconstruction ended, as did African-American advances toward equality.

▶ Vocabulary

TERMS & NAMES

Fifteenth Amendment constitutional amendment that stated that citizens could not be stopped from voting "on account of race, color, or previous condition of servitude"

Panic of 1873 financial panic in which banks closed and the stock market crashed

Compromise of 1877 agreement that decided the 1876 presidential election

Visual Vocabulary
Panic of 1873

BACKGROUND VOCABULARY

stock market place where shares of ownership in companies are bought and sold

depression time of low business activity and high unemployment

compromise settlement of differences in which each side gives up something it wants

REVIEW

Ulysses S. Grant former Union general

electoral votes votes made by the members of the Electoral College, which elects the president and vice president

amendment formal alteration or addition to the U.S. Constitution

▶ Reading Strategy

Re-create the diagram shown here. As you read and respond to the **KEY QUESTIONS**, use the diagram to note important events and their effects. Add boxes or start a new diagram as needed.

 See Skillbuilder Handbook, page R7.

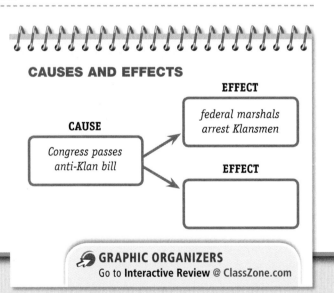

CAUSES AND EFFECTS

CAUSE		EFFECT
Congress passes anti-Klan bill	→	federal marshals arrest Klansmen
	→	EFFECT

GRAPHIC ORGANIZERS
Go to **Interactive Review** @ ClassZone.com

The End of Reconstruction

 8 – U5.3.4 Analyze the intent and the effect of the Thirteenth, Fourteenth, and Fifteenth Amendments to the Constitution.
8 – U5.3.5 Explain the decision to remove Union troops in 1877 and describe its impact on Americans.

One American's Story

Robert B. Elliott was elected to the U.S. Congress from South Carolina in 1871. A brilliant orator, he gave a famous speech to Congress in favor of the Civil Rights Act of 1875, which outlawed racial segregation in public services such as restaurants, hotels, and transportation.

PRIMARY SOURCE

❝ The passage of this bill will determine the civil status, not only of the negro but of any other class of citizens who may feel themselves discriminated against. It will form the capstone of that temple of liberty begun on this continent. ❞

—Robert B. Elliott, quoted in *The Glorious Failure*

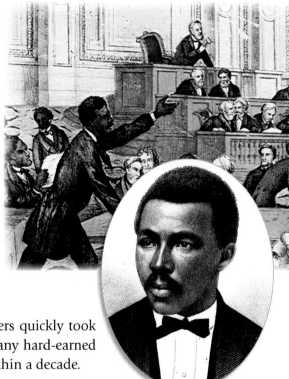

In 1877, federal troops left the South. White Southerners quickly took back control of the region, and African Americans lost many hard-earned gains. Even the Civil Rights Act of 1875 was overturned within a decade.

Protecting African-American Rights

🔻 **KEY QUESTION** How did the Republican Party try to advance civil rights for African Americans?

In 1868, the Republican candidate, former Union general **Ulysses S. Grant**, won the presidency. The Republican Party seemed stronger than ever.

Grant's Victory Grant won with 214 **electoral votes**—votes in the Electoral College, which elects the president and vice president. His Democratic opponent received only 80. In the popular count, however, Grant had a majority of only about 305,000 votes. He would not have had this majority without the freedmen's vote. Despite attacks by the Klan, about 500,000 African Americans voted in the South, and most cast their ballots for Grant.

On January 6, 1874, U.S. Representative Robert B. Elliott argued for "equal rights and equal public privileges for all classes of American citizens." This demand was made law in the Civil Rights Act of 1875.

The Fifteenth Amendment After Grant's win, Radical Republicans feared that Southern states might try to keep African Americans from voting in future elections. In addition, some states outside the South still prohibited African-American men from voting. To protect African-American suffrage, Radical Republican leaders proposed a constitutional **amendment**—a formal change or addition to the U.S. Constitution.

The **Fifteenth Amendment** stated that citizens could not be stopped from voting "on account of race, color, or previous condition of servitude." (This amendment, like the Fourteenth Amendment, did not apply to Native Americans on tribal lands.) The amendment was ratified in 1870.

The amendment did not apply to women. This made many white women angry, especially those who had fought to end slavery. Suffragist Elizabeth Cady Stanton was opposed to the idea of uneducated immigrants and freedmen "who cannot read the Declaration of Independence . . . making laws for . . . women of wealth and education." But most African-American women, including suffragist Frances E. W. Harper, felt it was important for African Americans to gain voting rights, even if that meant only men at first.

COMPARING *Political Representation*

AFRICAN AMERICANS AND WOMEN IN CONGRESS

(*left*) Jeannette Rankin, elected in 1916, and (*right*) Shirley Chisholm, elected in 1968

These graphs show the number of African Americans and women who served in the U.S. Congress from 1866 onward.

Sources: CRS Report for Congress: Black Members of the United States Congress: 1870–2005; *Women of Congress* by Rep. Marcy Kaptur; Center for American Women and Politics

CRITICAL THINKING

1. **Draw Conclusions** What happened to African-American representation in Congress after Reconstruction ended?

2. **Make Generalizations** Who made advances in representation more quickly after 1916, African Americans or women?

Grant Fights the Klan Despite gaining the vote, African Americans in the South continued to be terrorized by the Ku Klux Klan. In 1871, President Grant asked Congress to pass a tough law against the Klan. Joseph Rainey, a black congressman from South Carolina, had received death threats from the Klan. He urged his fellow lawmakers to support the bill.

PRIMARY SOURCE

❝ When myself and colleagues shall leave these Halls and turn our footsteps toward our southern home we know not but that the assassin may await our coming. Be it as it may we have resolved to be loyal and firm, and if we perish, we perish! I earnestly hope the bill will pass. ❞

—Joseph Rainey, quoted in *The Trouble They Seen*

Congress approved the anti-Klan bill. Federal marshals then arrested thousands of Klansmen. Klan attacks on African-American voters declined. As a result, the 1872 presidential election was both fair and peaceful in the South. Grant won a second term.

🔺 **PROBLEMS AND SOLUTIONS** Identify the ways Republicans tried to advance rights for African Americans.

Reconstruction Weakens

🔻 **KEY QUESTION** How did Reconstruction lose its strength?

Under President Grant, support for the Republicans and their pro–African-American attitude toward Reconstruction weakened. One major cause of this loss of support was scandal in Grant's administration.

This cartoon from *Puck* magazine shows Grant weighed down by corruption in his administration. **How was Grant burdened by his employees?**

Scandal in the Republican Party President Grant did not choose his advisers well. He put his former army friends and his wife's relatives in government positions. Many of these people were unqualified. Some Grant appointees took bribes. Grant's private secretary, for instance, was involved with whiskey distillers who wanted to avoid paying taxes. Grant's secretary of war, General William Belknap, left office after people accused him of taking bribes.

Such scandals angered many Republicans. In 1872, some Republican officials broke away and formed the new Liberal Republican Party. The Republicans, no longer unified, became less able to impose tough Reconstruction policies on the South.

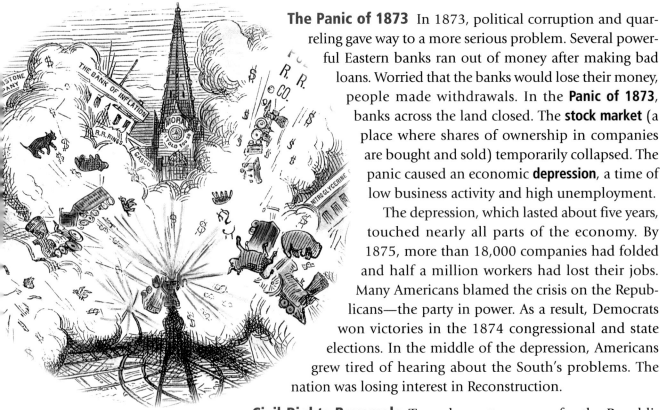

This cartoon by Thomas Nast dramatizes the Panic of 1873: a sudden explosion hits Wall Street, New York's financial center. **What does the image suggest about the effects of the Panic?**

The Panic of 1873 In 1873, political corruption and quarreling gave way to a more serious problem. Several powerful Eastern banks ran out of money after making bad loans. Worried that the banks would lose their money, people made withdrawals. In the **Panic of 1873**, banks across the land closed. The **stock market** (a place where shares of ownership in companies are bought and sold) temporarily collapsed. The panic caused an economic **depression**, a time of low business activity and high unemployment.

The depression, which lasted about five years, touched nearly all parts of the economy. By 1875, more than 18,000 companies had folded and half a million workers had lost their jobs. Many Americans blamed the crisis on the Republicans—the party in power. As a result, Democrats won victories in the 1874 congressional and state elections. In the middle of the depression, Americans grew tired of hearing about the South's problems. The nation was losing interest in Reconstruction.

Civil Rights Reversals To make matters worse for the Republicans, the Supreme Court began to undo some of the progress that had been made for civil rights. In an 1876 case, *U.S.* v. *Cruikshank*, the Court ruled that the federal government could not punish individuals who violated the civil rights of African Americans. Only the states had that power, the Court declared. Southern state officials often would not punish those who attacked African Americans. As a result, violence against them increased.

In the 1876 case *U.S.* v. *Reese*, the Court ruled in favor of white Southerners who barred African Americans from voting. The Court stated that the Fifteenth Amendment did not give everyone the right to vote—it merely listed the grounds on which states could not deny the vote. In other words, states could prevent African Americans from voting for other reasons. States later imposed poll taxes and unfair literacy tests to restrict the vote. These Court decisions weakened Reconstruction and blocked African-American efforts to gain full equality.

▲ **CAUSES AND EFFECTS** Explain what caused Reconstruction to weaken.

Reconstruction Ends

▼ **KEY QUESTION** What finally led to the end of Reconstruction?

The final blow to Reconstruction came with the 1876 presidential election. In the election, the Democrats chose Samuel J. Tilden, governor of New York. The Republicans nominated Rutherford B. Hayes, governor of Ohio. The election's result forced a **compromise**—a settlement in which both parties gave up some things they wanted. The Republicans gave up the most.

Compromise of 1877 Victory in the 1876 presidential election depended on three Southern states—South Carolina, Louisiana, and Florida. The votes in those states were so close that both sides claimed victory. A commission of Republicans and Democrats made a deal. Under the **Compromise of 1877**, Republican Rutherford Hayes became president. But the terms were a blow to Republican Reconstruction in the South:

- The government would remove federal troops from the South.
- The government would provide land grants and loans for the construction of railroads linking the South to the West Coast.
- Southern officials would receive federal funds for construction and improvement projects.
- Hayes would appoint a Democrat to his cabinet.
- The Democrats promised to respect African Americans' rights.

Connecting History

Presidential Elections
The election of 1876 was not the first to be disputed. The election of 1800 had resulted in a tie, which was broken by a compromise in the House of Representatives. *See Chapter 10, pp. 337–339.*

CONNECT *to the Essential Question*

How did a deeply divided nation move forward after the Civil War?

PROBLEM	PRESIDENTIAL SOLUTIONS	CONGRESSIONAL SOLUTIONS
State governments led by former Confederates	Asked Southern states to ratify the Thirteenth Amendment and accept the supreme power of the federal government Offered amnesty and return of property to Confederates who pledged loyalty to the federal government ✓ SUCCESS	Set up commission to study conditions in the South and determine if Southern states should be allowed representation in U.S. Congress ✓ SUCCESS
Resistance to granting civil rights to formerly enslaved people	Asked Congress to pass anti–Ku Klux Klan legislation ✓ SOME SUCCESS	Passed Civil Rights Act of 1866 Proposed Fourteenth and passed Fifteenth Amendments Passed anti–Ku Klux Klan legislation ✓ SOME SUCCESS
Formerly enslaved people needing education and employment	None X FAILURE	Freedmen's Bureau ✓ SOME SUCCESS

CRITICAL THINKING **Make Inferences** Why might Reconstruction be considered a time in which the presidency was weak?

A statue of educator Booker T. Washington at Hampton University, one of several historically black colleges founded during Reconstruction

Abolitionist Wendell Phillips was against the compromise. He doubted that the South would respect African Americans' rights. "The whole soil of the South is hidden by successive layers of broken promises," he said. "To trust a Southern promise would be fair evidence of insanity."

After the 1876 presidential election, Republican Reconstruction in the South collapsed. The Democrats returned to power.

The Legacy of Reconstruction Historians still argue about the success of Reconstruction. The government did achieve its most important goal—the reunification of the nation. However, Reconstruction's effect on African Americans is less straightforward.

African Americans' legal situation changed greatly during Reconstruction. Slavery was outlawed, and African-American men gained the vote and ability to hold office. But the federal government did not enforce the spirit of the Fourteenth and Fifteenth Amendments. In fact, the Supreme Court's rulings in favor of states' rights practically reversed these two amendments. Meanwhile, African Americans continued to face widespread violence and prejudice. White intimidation prevented many African Americans from taking part in politics. Lack of land ownership and economic opportunity meant that most African Americans continued to live in poverty and as second-class citizens.

 SYNTHESIZE Explain how Reconstruction ended.

 Michigan Grade Level Content Expectations *Review*

ONLINE QUIZ
For test practice, go to
Interactive Review @ ClassZone.com

TERMS & NAMES

1. Explain the importance of
- Fifteenth Amendment • Compromise of 1877
- Panic of 1873

USING YOUR READING NOTES

2. Causes and Effects Complete the diagram you started at the beginning of this section. Then create a diagram for each of the other main events in this section.

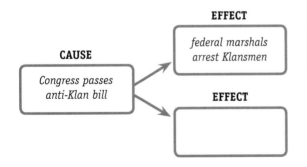

CAUSE

Congress passes anti-Klan bill

EFFECT

federal marshals arrest Klansmen

EFFECT

KEY IDEAS

3. What did the Fifteenth Amendment declare?

4. What effect did scandals in the Grant administration have on the Republican Party?

5. What concessions did the Republicans make in the Compromise of 1877?

CRITICAL THINKING

6. Analyze Point of View Why did the Fifteenth Amendment anger some white women?

7. Causes and Effects Why did the Supreme Court's decisions in favor of states' rights hurt African-American advances toward equality?

8. Draw Conclusions Why do you think the Republicans were willing to agree to the Compromise of 1877, even though they knew it would weaken Reconstruction?

9. Writing Essay Research the presidential election of 2000. Write a one-page essay comparing and contrasting the settlement to that election with that of the presidential election of 1876.

CHAPTER

18 Interactive Review
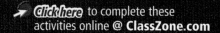
Click here to complete these
activities online @ ClassZone.com

Chapter Summary

1 Key Idea
During Reconstruction, the president and Congress fought over how to rebuild the South.

2 Key Idea
As the South rebuilt, millions of freed African Americans worked to improve their lives.

3 Key Idea
As white Southerners regained power in Congress, Reconstruction ended, as did African-American advances toward equality.

For detailed Review and Study Notes go to **Interactive Review** @ ClassZone.com

Name Game

Use the Terms & Names list to identify each sentence online or on your own paper.

1. I was a farmer who rented land on credit.
   sharecropper

2. I believed in using Congressional power to rebuild the South.

3. This caused high unemployment.

4. This was set up by Congress to help formerly enslaved people.

5. This used violence to try to restore Democratic control of the South.

6. I was a white Southerner who supported Reconstruction.

7. This stated that citizens could not be stopped from voting on the basis of race.

8. This was a reason that formerly enslaved people had limited legal rights.

9. This was a time in which the U.S. government tried to rebuild Southern society.

10. This removed federal troops from the South.

A. Radical Republican
B. Freedmen's Bureau
C. Fourteenth Amendment
D. Fifteenth Amendment
E. Panic of 1873
F. Compromise of 1877
G. carpetbagger
H. Ku Klux Klan
I. black codes
J. scalawag
K. Reconstruction
L. sharecropper

Activities

FLIPCARD

Use the online flip cards to quiz yourself on the terms and names introduced in this chapter.

This president was impeached and later acquitted by a single vote.

ANSWER
Andrew Johnson

CROSSWORD PUZZLE

Complete the online crossword puzzle to show what you know about Reconstruction.

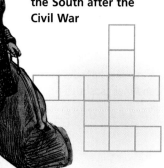

ACROSS
1. Northerner who moved to the South after the Civil War

VOCABULARY

Explain the significance of each of the following.

1. Fifteenth Amendment
2. freedmen's school
3. black codes
4. Fourteenth Amendment
5. amnesty
6. Compromise of 1877
7. carpetbagger

Identify the term that does not belong in each group, and explain why.

8. stock market, Radical Republican, civil rights
9. depression, Panic of 1873, carpetbagger
10. Andrew Johnson, Fifteenth Amendment, amnesty

KEY IDEAS

1 Rebuilding the Union (pages 570–575)

11. Under the Reconstruction Acts of 1867, what was asked of Southern states before rejoining the Union?
12. Why was Andrew Johnson impeached?

2 Reconstruction and Daily Life (pages 576–581)

13. What was a freedmen's school?
14. Why did Congress not pass a land-reform plan?

3 The End of Reconstruction (pages 582–588)

15. Why did Republicans lose power in the government?
16. During Reconstruction, how did the Supreme Court weaken African Americans' civil rights?

CRITICAL THINKING

17. **Synthesize** Why was Reconstruction needed?
18. **Compare and Contrast** How did President Johnson's ideas about Reconstruction differ from those of the Radical Republicans?
19. **Make Inferences** What years included in the chart brought the greatest increase in the national debt? Why might this have been?

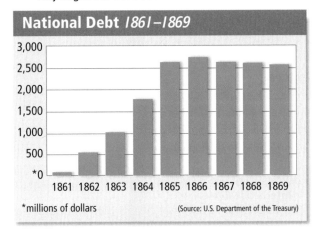

National Debt *1861–1869*

*millions of dollars   (Source: U.S. Department of the Treasury)

20. **Summarize** What impact did the Reconstruction Acts of 1867 have on the South?
21. **Analyze Point of View** Why did African Americans want their own land?
22. **Causes and Effects** How did the Panic of 1873 affect Reconstruction?
23. **Main Ideas and Details** What demands did Southern Democrats make in the Compromise of 1877? What did Republicans gain from the Compromise?
24. **Problems and Solutions** Fill in a table like the one shown to identify the major problems of Reconstruction and how the government attempted to solve them.

PROBLEMS	PROPOSED SOLUTIONS
State governments led by former Confederates	
Resistance to granting civil rights to former enslaved people	
Large numbers of former enslaved people needing education and employment	

✔ **TEST PRACTICE**

• **Online Test Practice @ ClassZone.com**
• Use the **MEAP Strategies & Practice,** pages S1-S27, at the front of this book

MULTIPLE CHOICE

Use the map and your knowledge of U.S. history to answer question 1.

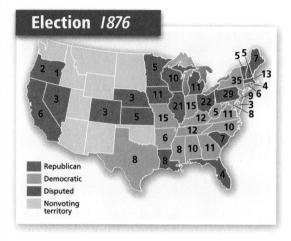

Election *1876*

Republican
Democratic
Disputed
Nonvoting territory

1 What regions voted *mostly* Republican?
  A the North and East
  B the North and West
  C the South and East
  D the South and West

Use the quotation and your knowledge of U.S. history to answer question 2.

PRIMARY SOURCE

❝ It is a matter of regret to me that it is necessary at this day that I should rise in the presence of an American Congress to advocate a bill which simply asserts equal rights and equal public privileges for all classes of American citizens. ❞

—U.S. Representative Robert Elliott of South Carolina

2 Why was it "a matter of regret" to Robert Elliott that he had to speak in support of this bill?
  A He wanted Congress to compromise on the bill.
  B The failures of Reconstruction filled him with regret.
  C Supporting the bill could cause him to lose his job.
  D He believed all Americans should already have equal rights.

YOU BE THE HISTORIAN

25. Make Generalizations How did Reconstruction change the lives of most formerly enslaved people?

26. WHAT IF? If the Ku Klux Klan had not existed, how might Reconstruction have been different?

27. Causes and Effects How did government corruption and misconduct make an impact on Reconstruction?

28. Citizenship How did the Fifteenth Amendment promote citizenship for African Americans? How was the amendment limited?

29. Draw Conclusions What lasting gains did African Americans make during Reconstruction?

30. Form and Support Opinions Do you think African Americans were better off in 1877 than they had been in 1865? Why?

Answer the
ESSENTIAL QUESTION
How did a deeply divided nation move forward after the Civil War?

Written Response Write a two- to three-paragraph response to the Essential Question. Consider the key ideas of each section along with the major successes and failures of Reconstruction. Use the Response Rubric below to guide your thinking and writing.

Response Rubric
A strong response will

• compare presidential and Congressional Reconstruction
• explain the obstacles to Reconstruction
• identify the major successes and failures of Reconstruction
• analyze how those successes and failures affected American society

UNIT 7

America Transformed

1860–1920

Why It Matters Now

The industrialization of the United States in the 60 years after the Civil War made America a world power. But not without a price. The era is also notable for efforts to humanize the U.S. industrial system, to make it work not just for the most privileged members of our society but for everyone.

The history of the past is but one long struggle upward to equality.
—Elizabeth Cady Stanton

COPYRIGHT
BY DETROIT PHOTO

19

1. Railroads Transform the Nation

2. Miners, Ranchers, and Cowhands

3. Native Americans Fight to Survive

4. Farm Economics and Populism

Growth in the West

1860–1900

 ESSENTIAL QUESTION

How did the nation change as a result of westward movement after the Civil War?

CONNECT ⟳ **Geography & History**

How might U.S. geography have affected western settlement?

Think about:

1 the advantages of being on a coastal area or waterway

2 how the population density in desert areas, such as the Southwest, compares with the population density in areas with greater rainfall, such as the Midwest

3 the obstacles presented by mountains in the West

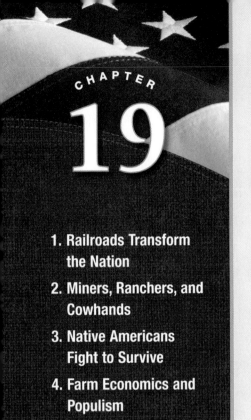

This railroad advertisement shows a route in the outline of a chair.

A replica of a Central Pacific steam engine

1862 Congress passes Homestead Act.

▼

Effect Offer of free land encourages western settlement.

1869 The transcontinental railroad is completed.

▼

Effect Western settlement increases.

1860

Abraham Lincoln is elected president.

1864 Colorado militia kill peaceful Native Americans in Sand Creek Massacre.

1876 Native Americans triumph at Battle of the Little Bighorn.

▼

Effect U.S. steps up military action.

Persons per sq mi

Over 90	
19–90	
2–18	
Under 2	

Cities

■ Over 1 million
◉ 500,000 to 1 million
● 200,000 to 500,000

WASH.

ORE.

IDAHO

MONT.

NORTH
DAKOTA

MINN.

Minneapolis

MAINE

VT. N.H.

N.Y. Boston
MASS.
Buffalo CONN. R.I.

WIS.

MICH.

Detroit

NEV.

San Francisco

CALIF.

UTAH

WYO.

SOUTH
DAKOTA

NEBR.

COLO.

Milwaukee

IOWA Chicago

ILL.

Cleveland
OHIO
IND. Cincinnati

Jersey City New York
PA. Newark N.J.
Pittsburgh Philadelphia
Baltimore
W. DEL.
VA. MD.
Washington, D.C.

St. Louis
MO.

KANS.

ARIZONA
TERR.

NEW MEXICO
TERR.

OKLA.
TERR.

UNORG.
TERR.

ARK.

TEXAS

MISS. ALA.

LA.

New Orleans

KY.

Louisville

VA.

TENN.

N.C.

S.C.

GA.

FLA.

0   150   300 miles

0   150   300 kilometers

A vaquero (cowhand)
in New Mexico Territory

1892 Populist Party is
founded to support rights
of farmers and laborers.

1900

1887 The Dawes Act
distributes reservation land
to individuals.

Sioux moccasins, circa 1895

1896 William McKinley
wins presidential election.

Effect Populist Party
collapses.

Reading for Understanding

▶ Key Ideas

BEFORE, YOU LEARNED

As white Southerners regained power, Reconstruction ended in 1877.

NOW YOU WILL LEARN

A railroad, completed in 1869, spanned the continent and helped to open the way for settlers in the West.

▶ Vocabulary

TERMS & NAMES

transcontinental railroad railroad that spanned the U.S. continent

Great Plains the area from the Missouri River to the Rocky Mountains

frontier parts of the West that were occupied mainly by Native Americans, rather than settlers

BACKGROUND VOCABULARY

solar time time based on calculations of the sun's passage across the sky

standard time the time zones devised by railroad companies

Visual Vocabulary
Great Plains

▶ Reading Strategy

Re-create the diagram shown at right. As you read and respond to the **KEY QUESTIONS**, use the diagram to note the effects of building the transcontinental railroad. Add boxes or start a new diagram as needed.

 See Skillbuilder Handbook, page R7.

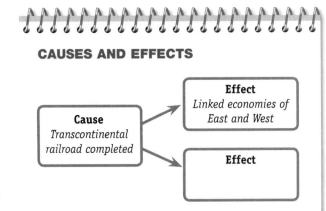

CAUSES AND EFFECTS

Cause
Transcontinental railroad completed

Effect
Linked economies of East and West

Effect

GRAPHIC ORGANIZERS
Go to **Interactive Review** @ ClassZone.com

Railroads Transform the Nation

8 – U6.1.1.1 America at Century's End – territory, including the size of the United States and land use

8 – U6.1.1.3 America at Century's End – systems of transportation (canals and railroads, including the Transcontinental Railroad), and their impact on the economy and society

One American's Story

Ah Goong was one of many Chinese workers on the western railroads in the late 1800s. In some places, workers had to blast rock from a cliff wall. Lightweight Chinese workers were lowered in baskets hundreds of feet to the blasting site. Years later, Ah Goong's granddaughter imagined his work.

PRIMARY SOURCE

❝ Swinging near the cliff, Ah Goong . . . dug holes, then inserted gunpowder and fuses. . . . He struck match after match and dropped the burnt matches over the sides. At last his fuse caught; he waved, and the men above pulled hand over hand hauling him up, pulleys creaking. ❞

—Maxine Hong Kingston, *China Men*

Thousands of Chinese immigrants helped to build the transcontinental railroad.

The building of the transcontinental railroad changed American life. It speeded economic growth and helped open the West to settlers.

Railroads Link East and West

🔻 **KEY QUESTION** How was the first transcontinental railroad built?

For years, Americans had talked about building a **transcontinental railroad**—one that would connect the Atlantic and Pacific coasts. Such a railroad would encourage people to settle in the West and develop its economy.

Help from the Government In 1862, Congress gave the task of building the railroad to two companies: the Union Pacific and the Central Pacific. The Central Pacific was to start in Sacramento, California, and build east. The Union Pacific was to start in Omaha, Nebraska, and build west.

The federal government lent the railroad companies millions of dollars. It also passed legislation that gave them grants of public land along the track. The railroad companies could then sell the land to raise money.

Railroads of the Transcontinental Era 1865–1900

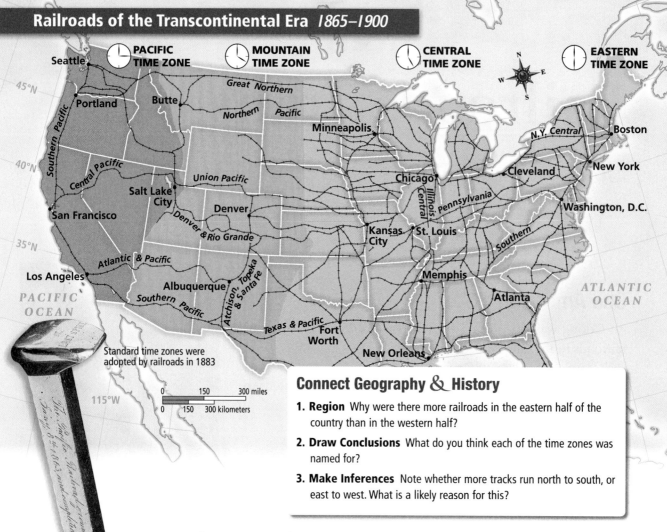

PACIFIC TIME ZONE

MOUNTAIN TIME ZONE

CENTRAL TIME ZONE

EASTERN TIME ZONE

Seattle
45°N
Portland
Butte
Great Northern
Northern Pacific
Minneapolis
N.Y. Central
Boston
Southern Pacific
Central Pacific
40°N
Union Pacific
Chicago
Cleveland
New York
Illinois Central
Pennsylvania
Salt Lake City
Washington, D.C.
San Francisco
Denver
Denver & Rio Grande
Kansas City
St. Louis
35°N
Atlantic & Pacific
Southern
Los Angeles
PACIFIC OCEAN
Albuquerque
Atchison, Topeka & Santa Fe
Memphis
Atlanta
ATLANTIC OCEAN
Southern Pacific
Texas & Pacific
Fort Worth
New Orleans

Standard time zones were adopted by railroads in 1883

115°W

0   150   300 miles
0   150   300 kilometers

Connect Geography & History

1. **Region** Why were there more railroads in the eastern half of the country than in the western half?

2. **Draw Conclusions** What do you think each of the time zones was named for?

3. **Make Inferences** Note whether more tracks run north to south, or east to west. What is a likely reason for this?

Immigrants Lay the Track Building the railroads was hard, dangerous work. Many of the workers hired by the railroad companies were immigrants with few other choices of work. In the West, the Central Pacific railroad hired many Chinese workers, who faced widespread discrimination. More than 10,000 Chinese men worked on the Central Pacific.

The Union Pacific hired workers from a variety of backgrounds. Many of its workers were Irish immigrants. After 1865, many former soldiers from both the North and the South also worked on the railroad.

Joining the Railroads In May 1869, the Central Pacific and the Union Pacific met in Utah at Promontory Summit. The Central Pacific had crossed California's rugged Sierra Nevada Mountains and laid about 700 miles of track. The Union Pacific had laid more than 1,000 miles, mostly across the **Great Plains**—the area from the Missouri River to the Rocky Mountains.

Hundreds of railroad workers, managers, and journalists gathered for a ceremony. A band played and a golden spike was hammered to honor the completion of the railroad. The transcontinental railroad was complete. By 1895, four more railroad lines were built spanning the United States.

▲ **CAUSES AND EFFECTS** Explain the roles of the government and immigrants in building the transcontinental railroad.

This golden spike was used in the ceremony that marked the completion of the railroad.

The Impact of the Railroads

🔻 **KEY QUESTION** How did the transcontinental railroad change America?

The railroads changed many things in people's lives—even timekeeping.

Railroad Time Before the railroads, each community determined its own time, based on calculations about the sun's travels. This system was called "**solar time**." Solar time caused problems for people who scheduled trains crossing a long distance. It also confused railroad travelers, who had to ask, "Is the train arriving at 2:00 our time or their time?" To solve this problem, the railroad companies set up **standard time**. This system divided the United States into four time zones. (See the map on page 598.)

Movement to the Frontier The transcontinental railroad brought settlers to the **frontier**—the parts of the West (mostly in the Great Plains) that were occupied mainly by Native Americans. Trains were a lifeline for settlers. They brought lumber, food, and other necessities. They also brought settlers and miners who laid claim to Native American land. In this way, the railroads helped weaken the Native American hold on the West.

Railroads also linked the nation economically. From the West, trains carried raw materials such as lumber, livestock, and grain eastward. These materials were processed in midwestern cities such as Chicago. From eastern cities, in turn, came manufactured goods, which were sold to westerners.

🔺 **SYNTHESIZE** Explain how the transcontinental railroad changed America.

This nineteenth-century railroad conductor's watch shows the time in different zones.

Michigan Grade Level Content Expectations *Review*

 ONLINE QUIZ
For test practice, go to
Interactive Review @ ClassZone.com

TERMS & NAMES

1. Explain the importance of
- transcontinental railroad
- Great Plains
- frontier

USING YOUR READING NOTES

2. Causes and Effects Complete the diagram you started at the beginning of the section. Then create a diagram for each of the main events in this section.

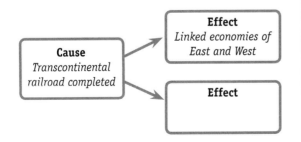

KEY IDEAS

3. How was the transcontinental railroad financed?

4. Why did the country need a standard time?

CRITICAL THINKING

5. Analyze Point of View Why would the federal government have wanted a transcontinental railroad to be built?

6. Synthesize How did the railroads benefit the economy?

7. **Connect to Today** What changes created by the railroads are part of the business world today?

8. **Writing** **Letter** Suppose that you were one of the workers who helped build the railroads. Write a one-page letter to a family member explaining how your work will help to transform the nation.

Reading for Understanding

▶ Key Ideas

BEFORE, YOU LEARNED

A railroad, completed in 1869, spanned the continent and helped to open the way for settlers in the West.

NOW YOU WILL LEARN

The mining and cattle industries contributed to population growth in western territories.

▶ Vocabulary

TERMS & NAMES

vaquero (vah•KAIR•oh) Spanish term for cowhand

long drive journey that takes cattle by foot to a railway

vigilante (vij•uh•LAN•tee) person who takes the law into his or her own hands

buffalo soldier name Native Americans gave to African-American soldiers in the West

Mexicano (may•hi•KAH•noh) Spanish word for a person of Mexican heritage; a Spanish-speaking person in the Southwest whose ancestors had come from Mexico

Anglo English-speaking settler in the Southwest

BACKGROUND VOCABULARY

lode deposit of mineral buried in rock

boomtown town that experiences sudden growth in population or economic activity

REVIEW

black codes laws passed by Southern states that limited the freedom of formerly enslaved people

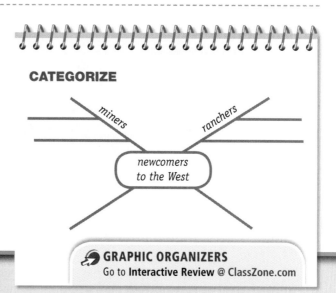

Visual Vocabulary
buffalo soldier

▶ Reading Strategy

Re-create the diagram shown at right. As you read and respond to the **KEY QUESTIONS**, use the main branches to note facts about categories of newcomers in the West. Add stems to record important details in each category.

 See Skillbuilder Handbook, page R6.

CATEGORIZE

miners   ranchers

newcomers
to the West

GRAPHIC ORGANIZERS
Go to **Interactive Review** @ ClassZone.com

Miners, Ranchers, and Cowhands

8 – U6.1.1.1 America at Century's End – territory, including the size of the United States and land use

8 – U6.1.1.3 America at Century's End – systems of transportation (canals and railroads, including the Transcontinental Railroad), and their impact on the economy and society

One American's Story

Nat Love was born into slavery in Tennessee in 1854. After the Civil War, he became one of thousands of African Americans who journeyed west. Love's horse-taming skills landed him a job as a cowhand. He became well known for his expert horsemanship and rodeo riding and roping. In his 1907 autobiography, Love offered a lively but exaggerated account of his life.

PRIMARY SOURCE

❝ I carry the marks of fourteen bullet wounds on different parts of my body, most any one of which would be sufficient to kill an ordinary man. . . . Horses were shot from under me, men killed around me, but always I escaped with a trifling wound at the worst. ❞

—Nat Love, *The Life and Adventures of Nat Love*

Few cowhands led lives as exciting as that described by Love. However, they all helped to open a new chapter in the history of the American West.

This photograph of Nat Love, the most famous African-American cowhand, appeared in his autobiography. He captioned it "In my fighting clothes."

Gold and Silver in the Mountains

🔻 **KEY QUESTION** How did mining affect western settlement during the late 1800s?

The discovery of precious metals in the Rockies helped draw settlers west.

Mining in the West Western gold and silver strikes, or discoveries, brought crowds of fortune seekers. The hope of striking it rich drew Americans from across the nation, as well as prospectors from all over the world. "Gold fever" attracted miners from Europe, South America, Mexico, and China.

In 1859, as many as 100,000 miners raced to what is now Colorado after gold was discovered in the mountains near Pikes Peak. The mining camp that grew up nearby became the town of Denver.

A silver bar

Also in 1859, prospectors hit "pay dirt" in what came to be called the Comstock Lode in western Nevada. (A **lode** is a deposit of valuable mineral buried in layers of rock.) From 1859 to 1880, the Comstock Lode produced at least $300 million in silver and gold.

Bonanza barons, the lucky miners who became instant millionaires, built mansions in nearby Virginia City, Nevada. (The term *bonanza* refers to an especially rich mineral deposit.) Virginia City became a **boomtown**—a town that has a sudden burst of economic activity or population growth. Its population jumped from 3,000 in the 1860s to more than 30,000 in the 1870s. By 1876, the town had an opera house, several theaters, and more than 100 saloons. The writer Mark Twain described the excitement of life there.

PRIMARY SOURCE

❝ The sidewalks swarmed with people. . . . So great was the pack, that buggies frequently had to wait half an hour for an opportunity to cross the principal street. . . . Money was as plenty as dust; every individual considered himself wealthy . . .❞

—Mark Twain, *Roughing It*

Other major strikes took place in the Black Hills of the Dakota Territory in 1874, at Cripple Creek in Colorado in 1891, and in Canada's Yukon Territory in 1896.

The Rush Ends Unfortunately, few prospectors became rich. Most left, disappointed and poor. Large mining companies moved in after surface mines no longer yielded gold and silver. Only they could buy the heavy equipment needed to take the precious metals from underground. Soon, paid workers in company mines replaced independent prospectors. The work was hard and dangerous. Dust caused lung problems, and deadly cave-ins could trap miners hundreds of feet below the surface.

By the 1890s, the mining boom was over. Many mines closed because the costs had become too high, while the precious metals were becoming sparse. Jobless workers moved elsewhere, and once-thriving communities became ghost towns. Still, the mining boom had long-lasting effects in the West. Nevada, Colorado, and South Dakota all grew so rapidly that they soon gained statehood.

▲ **SYNTHESIZE** Describe how mining affected western settlement in the late 1800s.

The Cattle Industry

▼ **KEY QUESTION** What caused the rise and fall of the cattle industry?

While miners searched for gold and silver, a new breed of settler—the rancher—was turning the cattle industry into big business in the West. Before the railroads extended to the Great Plains, most ranchers had small herds and few employees. But rapid growth in the cattle industry greatly increased the need for cowhands, also known as cowboys or "buckaroos."

Vaqueros and Cowhands The first cowhands, or **vaqueros**, as they were known in Spanish, came from Mexico with the Spaniards in the 1500s. They settled in the Southwest. The vaqueros helped Spanish, and later Mexican, ranchers manage their herds.

American cowhands learned how to round up, rope, brand cattle, and ride from the vaqueros. The vaqueros also had a strong influence on how cowhands dressed. American cowhands adapted the vaqueros' saddle, spurs, lariat (which they used to rope a calf or steer), and chaps—seatless leather pants, worn over regular trousers, that protect the legs from scrub brush and cactus. In addition, a number of terms used in American ranching are borrowed from the Spanish, such as *corral*, *rodeo*, and the word *ranch* itself.

A diverse group of men—and a few women—worked as cowhands. About a third of all cowhands in the West were Mexican or African American. Many Mexican cowhands were descendants of the first vaqueros. Like Nat Love, some African-American cowhands had been born into slavery. They came west at the end of Reconstruction in response to the **black codes**—laws in the South that put restrictions on the freedom of formerly enslaved people. Also among the cowhands were large numbers of former Confederate and Union soldiers.

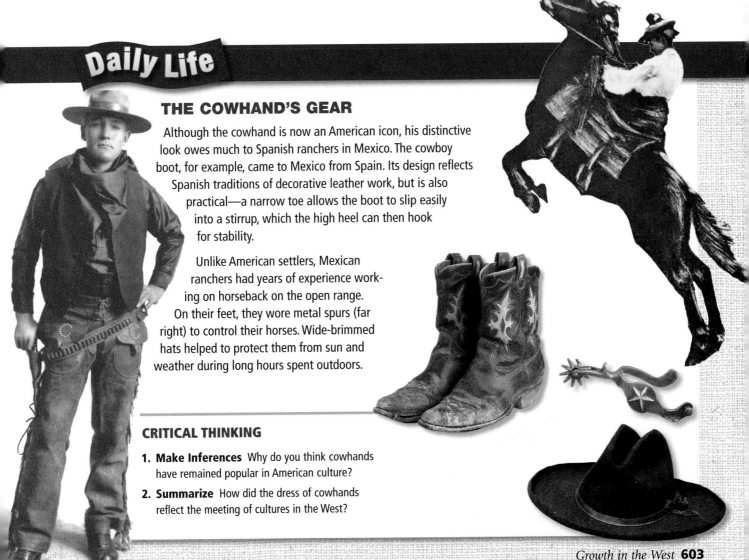

Daily Life

THE COWHAND'S GEAR

Although the cowhand is now an American icon, his distinctive look owes much to Spanish ranchers in Mexico. The cowboy boot, for example, came to Mexico from Spain. Its design reflects Spanish traditions of decorative leather work, but is also practical—a narrow toe allows the boot to slip easily into a stirrup, which the high heel can then hook for stability.

Unlike American settlers, Mexican ranchers had years of experience working on horseback on the open range. On their feet, they wore metal spurs (far right) to control their horses. Wide-brimmed hats helped to protect them from sun and weather during long hours spent outdoors.

CRITICAL THINKING

1. **Make Inferences** Why do you think cowhands have remained popular in American culture?

2. **Summarize** How did the dress of cowhands reflect the meeting of cultures in the West?

The Long Drive In the 1860s, the extension of railroad lines from Chicago and St. Louis into Kansas brought big changes to the cattle industry. A livestock dealer named Joseph McCoy realized that railroads could bring cattle from Texas to cities in the East. All that had to be done was for cowhands to drive Texas cattle to stockyards in Abilene, Kansas. From there, the beef could be shipped by rail. This practice came to be called the **long drive**.

McCoy's plan made cattle ranching very profitable. Cattle fed on the open range for a year or two and cost the rancher nothing. The rancher then hired cowhands to round up the cattle and take them to Abilene. Over time, cowhands followed specific trails. The principal trail was the Chisholm Trail, which stretched from San Antonio, Texas, to Abilene, Kansas. From 1867 to 1884, about 4 million cattle were driven to market on this trail.

The End of the Long Drives For about 20 years, the cattle industry boomed. The long drives grew shorter as the railroads extended farther into Texas. But by 1886, several developments brought the boom to an end.

First, the price of beef dropped sharply as the supply increased in the 1880s. Then came a new invention: barbed wire. As more settlers moved to the Great Plains, they fenced their lands with barbed wire. The open range disappeared, and cowhands could no longer pass freely over trails. Finally, in the harsh winter of 1886–1887, thousands of cattle froze to death. Many ranchers were put out of business or forced to downsize.

▲ **CAUSES AND EFFECTS** Explain why the cattle industry grew and then declined.

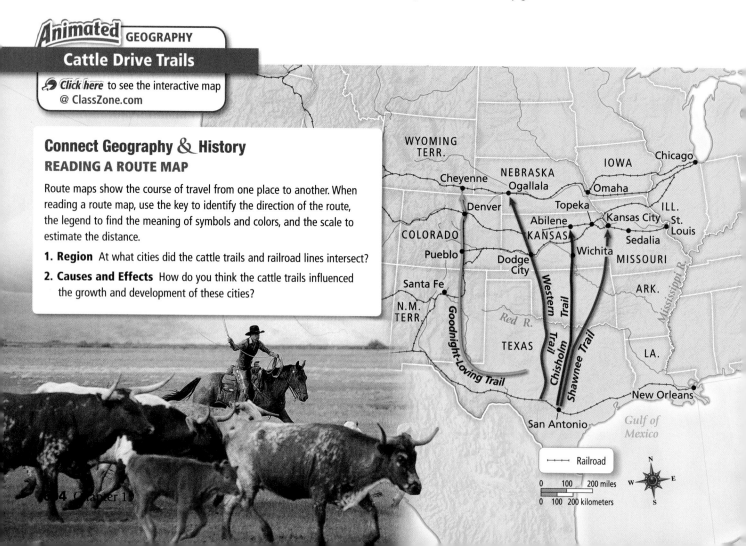

Animated GEOGRAPHY

Cattle Drive Trails

Click here to see the interactive map @ ClassZone.com

Connect Geography & History

READING A ROUTE MAP

Route maps show the course of travel from one place to another. When reading a route map, use the key to identify the direction of the route, the legend to find the meaning of symbols and colors, and the scale to estimate the distance.

1. **Region** At what cities did the cattle trails and railroad lines intersect?

2. **Causes and Effects** How do you think the cattle trails influenced the growth and development of these cities?

Railroad

0   100   200 miles
0   100   200 kilometers

The Myth and Reality of the Wild West

🔻 **KEY QUESTION** How were the myth and reality of the West different?

In American myth, westerners spent their days riding horses on the open range. Popular novels and movies described a world in which white settlers became heroes, often by fighting Native Americans.

The Wild West Legends of the West often suggest that it was lawless. It is true that at first, rapidly growing cow towns had no local governments and no law officers to handle fights that broke out between cowhands.

Outlaws such as John Wesley Hardin, "Billy the Kid," and Jesse James became famous across America. A woman named Belle Starr, the "Bandit Queen," was a legendary horse thief. In some places, citizens formed **vigilante** groups to protect themselves. Vigilantes were people who took the law into their own hands. They caught suspected criminals and punished them without a trial. Vigilante justice sometimes consisted of hanging suspects from the nearest tree or shooting them on the spot.

Reports of this kind of violence gave rise to the idea that the West was a wild place, but the truth was that except for in a few towns at a few times, the West was no wilder than anyplace else. As towns became settled, citizens typically elected a local sheriff.

The "Bandit Queen" Belle Starr, a famous horse thief. Belle once said of herself, "I regard myself as a woman who has seen much of life."

The Real West The myth of the Old West overlooked the contributions of many peoples. Large parts of the region had been Spanish-dominated for centuries, and Hispanic influence helped shape its culture. Native Americans and African Americans played important roles in ranching. Many African Americans also served in the U.S. Army in the West, where Native Americans nicknamed them "**buffalo soldiers**"—a term of honor, inspired by their short, curly hair, that compared their fighting spirit to that of the buffalo. Chinese immigrants were essential to the building of the railroads.

Western legends often emphasized the attacks by Native Americans on soldiers or settlers. But the misunderstandings and broken treaties that led to the conflicts were usually ignored in popular stories.

Historians also note that the image of the self-reliant westerner who tames the wild frontier ignores the important role played by the government in western settlement. Settlers could not have forced Native Americans off the land without the help of the army. The government also aided in the building of the railroads and offered free land that drew settlers to the West.

🔺 **COMPARE AND CONTRAST** Explain how the real West differed from the myth of the Wild West.

Connecting History

American Spirit
Most of the buffalo soldiers were Civil War veterans who had been organized into six all-black regiments in 1866. These regiments had the lowest rates of desertion in the Army and earned the greatest number of Congressional Medals of Honor.

Population Growth

🔻 **KEY QUESTION** What led to population growth in western cities and the Southwest?

Parts of the West seemed to grow overnight. While some cities prospered, however, most of the region remained sparsely settled.

Mining Centers and Railroad Hubs Denver, Colorado, is just one of the western cities that grew up quickly after a gold or silver rush. Miners who flocked to the "Pikes Peak" gold rush of 1859 stopped in Denver to buy supplies. Not even a town in 1857, Denver was the capital of Colorado Territory by 1867. A decade later, it became the capital of the state of Colorado. The decision by Denver citizens to build a railroad to link their city with the transcontinental railroad had contributed to the boom. In 1860, it had about 2,600 residents. By 1890, it had nearly 107,000.

The railroads brought rapid growth to a number of western towns. Omaha, Nebraska, began to flourish as a meat-processing center for cattle ranches in the area. Des Moines grew into a bustling transportation hub in central Iowa. Portland, Oregon, became a regional market for fish, grain, and lumber.

COMPARING *Population of Western Cities*

Some of today's most important western cities sprung up during the last half of the nineteenth century. Others, however, like Virginia City, Nevada (below left), went from boomtown in the 1870s to ghost town by the early 1900s.

CITY	1860	1890
Denver, Colorado	4,749	106,713
Des Moines, Iowa	3,965	50,093
Kansas City, Missouri	4,418	132,716
Omaha, Nebraska	1,883	140,452
Portland, Oregon	2,874	46,385

Sources: *Population Abstract of the United States, 1999*

CRITICAL THINKING

1. **Compare and Contrast** Which city had the largest increase in numbers of people from 1860 to 1890?
2. **Make Generalizations** Which cities had similar rates of growth?

Growth in the Southwest For centuries the Southwest had been home to people of Spanish descent whose ancestors had come from Mexico. These Spanish speakers thought of themselves as Mexican and **Mexicanos**.

In the 1840s, both the annexation of Texas and Mexico's defeat in the Mexican War brought much of the Southwest under the control of the United States. Soon after, many English-speaking white settlers—called **Anglos** by the Mexicanos—began arriving. These settlers were drawn to the Southwest by opportunities in ranching, farming, and mining. Their numbers grew in the 1880s and 1890s, as railroads connected the region with the rest of the country.

Mexicanos in Colorado grinding coffee, c. 1890.

The increase of Anglos in the Southwest caused Mexicanos to lose economic and political power and land. Mexicanos claimed their land through grants from Spain and Mexico. But American courts did not usually recognize these grants. One Mexicano remarked that "the North Americans . . . consider us unworthy to form with them one nation and one society." It was only in New Mexico Territory that Hispanic society survived despite Anglo-American settlement.

 CAUSES AND EFFECTS Explain the causes of population growth in western cities and the Southwest.

 Michigan Grade Level Content Expectations _Review_

ONLINE QUIZ
For test practice, go to
Interactive Review @ ClassZone.com

TERMS & NAMES

1. Explain the importance of
   - vaquero
   - long drive
   - vigilante
   - buffalo soldier
   - Mexicano
   - Anglo

USING YOUR READING NOTES

2. **Categorize** Complete the diagram you started at the beginning of this section.

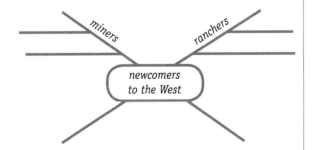

KEY IDEAS

3. What effect did gold and silver strikes have on small towns?
4. What did cowhands learn from vaqueros?
5. What was the purpose of the long drive?

CRITICAL THINKING

6. **Summarize** What role did miners play in the settlement of the West?
7. **Problems and Solutions** Why did vigilante groups arise in some areas?
8. **Causes and Effects** What factors led to the development of western cities?
9. **Science** Use the Internet to research how metallic ore deposits form in rock, and how these deposits are mined. Explain your findings in labeled diagrams.

Reading for Understanding

▶ Key Ideas

BEFORE, YOU LEARNED

The mining and cattle industries contributed to population growth in western territories.

NOW YOU WILL LEARN

Native Americans of the Great Plains fought to maintain their way of life as settlers poured onto their lands.

▶ Vocabulary

TERMS & NAMES

Sand Creek Massacre 1864 attack in which as many as 200 Cheyenne were killed by the Colorado militia

Sitting Bull Sioux chief who led the attack on Custer at the Battle of the Little Bighorn

George A. Custer commander of U.S. troops at the Battle of the Little Bighorn

Battle of the Little Bighorn 1876 battle in which Sioux and Cheyenne killed an entire force of U.S. troops

Dawes Act 1887 law that distributed reservation land to individual Native American owners

Wounded Knee Massacre mass killing by U.S. soldiers of as many as 300 unarmed Sioux at Wounded Knee, South Dakota, in 1890

BACKGROUND VOCABULARY

nomadic characterized by moving from place to place

REVIEW

reservation land set aside by the U.S. government for Native American tribes

Visual Vocabulary
George A. Custer

▶ Reading Strategy

Re-create the diagram shown at right. As you read and respond to the **KEY QUESTIONS**, use the center box to record the main idea, and use the outer ovals to note important details. Add ovals or start a new diagram as needed.

 See Skillbuilder Handbook, page R4.

MAIN IDEAS AND DETAILS

followed the buffalo

Native Americans on the Plains

GRAPHIC ORGANIZERS
Go to **Interactive Review** @ ClassZone.com

Native Americans Fight to Survive

8 – U4.1.2 Establishing America's Place in the World – Explain the changes in America's relationships with other nations by analyzing treaties with American Indian nations, Jay's Treaty (1795), French Revolution, Pinckney's Treaty (1795), Louisiana Purchase, War of 1812, Transcontinental Treaty (1819), and the Monroe Doctrine.
8 – U6.1.1.7 America at Century's End – the policies toward American Indians, including removal, reservations, the Dawes Act of 1887, and the response of American Indians

One American's Story

Buffalo Bird Woman was a Hidatsa who lived almost 100 years. She was born around 1839 in a Native American village on the Knife River. The federal government later forced her family onto a **reservation**—land set aside for Native American tribes. In old age, Buffalo Bird Woman looked back on her early years.

PRIMARY SOURCE

❝Sometimes at evening I sit, looking out on the . . . Missouri [River]. . . . In the shadows I seem . . . to see our Indian village, with smoke curling upward from the earth lodges; and in the river's roar I hear the yells of the warriors, the laughter of . . . children as of old. ❞

—Buffalo Bird Woman, quoted in *Native American Testimony*

Buffalo Bird Woman

As white settlers claimed Native American lands, Plains peoples fought a losing battle to save both their lands and their way of life.

Native Americans on the Plains

🔽 **KEY QUESTION** What was life like for Native Americans on the Great Plains?

Before the arrival of Europeans in the 1500s, most Native American tribes on the Great Plains lived in villages along rivers and streams. They tended crops of beans, squash, and corn. Hunters stalked deer and elk, as well as the vast buffalo herds that inhabited the region.

Horses and Buffalo In the early 1500s, the Spanish brought the first horses to the Great Plains. The arrival of horses changed how the Plains peoples lived. By the late 1700s, most Plains tribes kept their own herds of horses. Hunters traveled far from their villages on horseback in search of buffalo, which were central to the lives of Plains tribes.

Plains tribes ate buffalo meat and used its hide for clothing and tepees. They made its bones and horns into tools. Buffalo chips (dried manure) were used for fuel. Plains tribes followed the buffalo herds, developing a way of life that was **nomadic**—characterized by moving from place to place.

Broken Promises In the 1830s, the U.S. government had forced Native Americans of the Southeast to move onto the Great Plains. White settlers believed the Plains region was too dry for farming. But by the 1850s, some settlers who were crossing the Plains to Oregon and California saw possibilities for farming and ranching there. They pressured the government to take lands from Native Americans and make them available for settlers.

In 1851, the government called the Sioux, Cheyenne, Arapaho, and other Plains tribes together near Fort Laramie in present-day Wyoming. In the First Treaty of Fort Laramie (1851), government officials set boundaries for tribal lands. Many Plains tribes signed the treaty—they saw no other choice.

▲ **SUMMARIZE** Describe Native American life on the Great Plains in the early 1800s.

ONLINE BIOGRAPHY

For more on these leaders, go to the **Research & Writing Center** @ ClassZone.com

History Makers Native American Leaders

Sitting Bull c. 1831–1890

Sitting Bull was a Sioux war chief and spiritual leader. He fought U.S. troops over rights to Sioux land in several battles, most famously at the Little Bighorn. He remained an outspoken critic of the U.S. government until the end of his life.

Chief Joseph 1840–1904

Faced with forced removal, Nez Perce chief Joseph prepared to leave his land peacefully. But three young men massacred a group of whites. Fearing reprisal, Joseph helped lead a legendary retreat over four months and more than 1,000 miles.

Geronimo c. 1829–1909

Apache leader Geronimo fought settlers on his land for more than 25 years—all the while avoiding permanent capture by the U.S. and Mexican armies. In 1886, he became the last Native American leader to formally surrender to the U.S. government.

CRITICAL THINKING

1. **Compare and Contrast** What did these three leaders have in common?

2. **Analyze Point of View** How do you think these three leaders viewed the U.S. government?

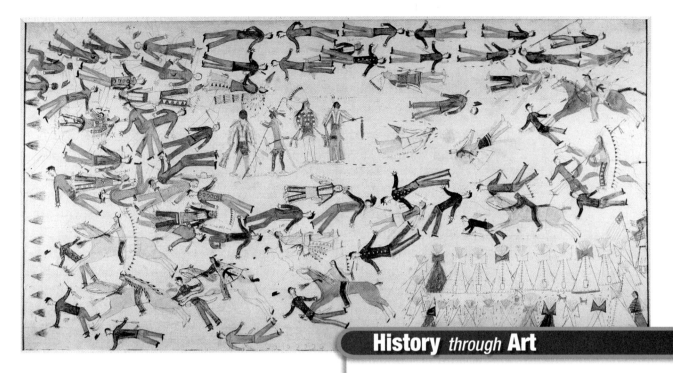

Native Americans Resist

🔻 **KEY QUESTION** How did Native Americans resist white efforts to take their land?

Some Sioux resisted signing the Laramie Treaty. They chose to fight for their land.

Bloodshed on the Plains In 1864, Colorado militia opened fire on a peaceful Cheyenne village along Sand Creek. As many as 200 Cheyenne men, women, and children were killed in what became known as the **Sand Creek Massacre**.

The Plains tribes responded with attacks on settlements and soldiers. The government sought to end the fighting. In 1868, the Second Treaty of Fort Laramie gave tribes a large reservation in the Black Hills of South Dakota. Then, in 1874, white prospectors found gold in the Black Hills. Miners flooded onto Sioux land. Two Sioux chiefs, **Sitting Bull** and Crazy Horse, united to push back the intruders.

Battle of the Little Big Horn

A Lakota Sioux chief, Kicking Bear (c. 1846–1904) fought in the Battle of the Little Bighorn. He made this painting of it more than twenty years later at the request of artist Frederic Remington. White Americans had great curiosity about the battle, but no U.S. soldiers had survived to describe it. In Kicking Bear's painting, Custer is on the left, wearing yellowish buckskins. The ghost-like figures in the upper left, behind the bodies of the soldiers, represent the spirits of the dead. The figures in the middle are the Sioux chiefs Sitting Bull, Rain-in-the-Face, Crazy Horse, and Kicking Bear.

CRITICAL VIEWING How does Kicking Bear's painting show the viewer the result of the battle?

PRIMARY SOURCE

❝ We did not give our country to you; you stole it. You come here to tell lies; when you go home, take them with you. ❞

—Sitting Bull

By the 1870s, the Cheyenne decided to fight back, too. On June 25, 1876, the Seventh Cavalry of the United States, commanded by Lieutenant Colonel **George A. Custer**, confronted several thousand Sioux and Cheyenne near the Little Bighorn River in Montana. In the **Battle of the Little Bighorn**, Custer and all of his men were killed.

In response, the government stepped up military action. Little Bighorn would be the last major Native American victory. In 1877, Crazy Horse surrendered, and Sitting Bull and his followers fled to Canada. In 1881, Sitting Bull surrendered and was eventually sent to a reservation.

Conflict in the Northwest and Southwest The Nez Perce (nehz PURS) lived in Idaho, eastern Oregon, and Washington. In the 1860s, the government took their land and forced them onto a reservation in Idaho. A group of Nez Perce led by Chief Joseph resisted, and in 1877 fled to seek refuge in Canada. Over four months, they crossed more than 1,000 miles with army troops in pursuit. When the army caught up, Chief Joseph was forced to surrender, saying, "I will fight no more, forever."

In the Southwest, both the Navajos and Apaches fought being removed to reservations. U.S. troops ended Navajo resistance in Arizona in 1863 by burning Navajo homes and crops. Most Navajos were forced to take what they called the "Long Walk," a brutal journey of 300 miles to a reservation in eastern New Mexico. Hundreds died on the way.

In the 1870s and 1880s, a group of Apache led by Geronimo resisted being relocated to a reservation. They raided settlements across the Southwest. Geronimo was captured several times but always managed to escape. In 1886, he finally surrendered and was sent to prison. He said, "Once I moved about like the wind. Now I surrender."

🔺 **MAIN IDEAS & DETAILS** Describe how Native Americans resisted white settlement.

A pile of buffalo skulls on the Great Plains, 1870s

A Way of Life Ends

🔻 **KEY QUESTION** What caused the end of Plains peoples' traditional way of life?

While white settlers moved westward, Plains peoples struggled to remain free.

The End of the Buffalo Newcomers threatened the buffalo upon which Plains tribes depended. Once, up to 60 million buffalo had roamed the Plains. But hired hunters killed buffalo to feed railroad crews and supply eastern factories with leather. Beginning in the 1870s, hunters killed at least 1 million buffalo a year. By the 1880s, the buffalo were dying out and most Plains peoples were being forced onto reservations.

Forced Assimilation Some whites believed that assimilation—adopting the dominant culture—was the way for Native Americans to survive. The **Dawes Act** of 1887 was intended to encourage Native Americans to farm alongside settlers. It divided tribal lands into plots for each family.

In the end, the Dawes Act did little to benefit Native Americans. Not all wanted to be farmers. Those who did lacked the tools and money to be successful. Over time, many sold their land for a fraction of its real value to white land promoters or settlers.

The U.S. government also sent many Native American children to boarding schools in an effort to assimilate or "Americanize" them. The children were dressed in European-style clothes, learned English, and typically spent part of the day farming or doing other manual labor. Many were kept away from their families for years at a time. Disease was rampant, and hundreds died.

A shirt worn in the Ghost Dance ceremony

Wounded Knee Massacre With their cultures under attack and their lands disappearing, some Native Americans turned to a prophet named Wovoka. He described a hopeful vision of a new age in which whites would leave the West and the buffalo would return.

A key part of Wovoka's teachings was a ceremony called the Ghost Dance. When Sioux gathered for a Ghost Dance in 1890, white officials thought they were preparing for war. On December 29, at Wounded Knee Creek in South Dakota, troops opened fire, killing more than 200 Sioux men, women, and children in what became known as the **Wounded Knee Massacre**. It was the last armed conflict with Native Americans in the West.

 CAUSES AND EFFECTS Explain the events that ended the Plains Indians' traditional way of life.

Michigan Grade Level Content Expectations *Review*

 ONLINE QUIZ
For test practice, go to
Interactive Review @ ClassZone.com

TERMS & NAMES

1. Explain the importance of
   - Sand Creek Massacre
   - Battle of the Little Bighorn
   - Sitting Bull
   - Dawes Act
   - George A. Custer
   - Wounded Knee Massacre

USING YOUR READING NOTES

2. **Main Ideas & Details** Complete the diagram you started at the beginning of the section. Include key events and note their importance.

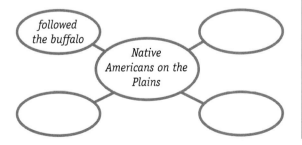

followed the buffalo

Native Americans on the Plains

KEY IDEAS

3. How was the buffalo important to Native Americans on the Great Plains?

4. What caused conflict between Native Americans and settlers on the Great Plains?

CRITICAL THINKING

5. **Causes and Effects** How did the Battle of the Little Bighorn affect U.S. government policy?

6. **Analyze Point of View** Why do you think Chief Joseph, Crazy Horse, Sitting Bull, and Geronimo chose to surrender? What other choices might they have made?

7. **Form and Support Opinions** What do you think was the most important factor in bringing about the end of the Plains peoples' way of life? Explain.

8. **Art** Draw two pictures of Native American life on the Plains that contrast life before and after the flood of settlers.

Native American Land Losses

Native Americans were the sole inhabitants of the Great Plains for thousands of years. In the 1850s, the U.S. government began to take possession of Plains land and set aside specific areas for different tribes. This brought conflicts with Native Americans, who did not believe that the land could be bought and sold. Said Sioux chief Crazy Horse: "One does not sell the land people walk on."

(*clockwise from upper left*) Omaha calumet (ceremonial pipe); Sioux/Arapaho storage bag; Sioux moccasins; Haida basket

Native American Lands *1819*

SPANISH MEXICO

40°N

30°N

90°W   80°W

Land reserved for Native Americans

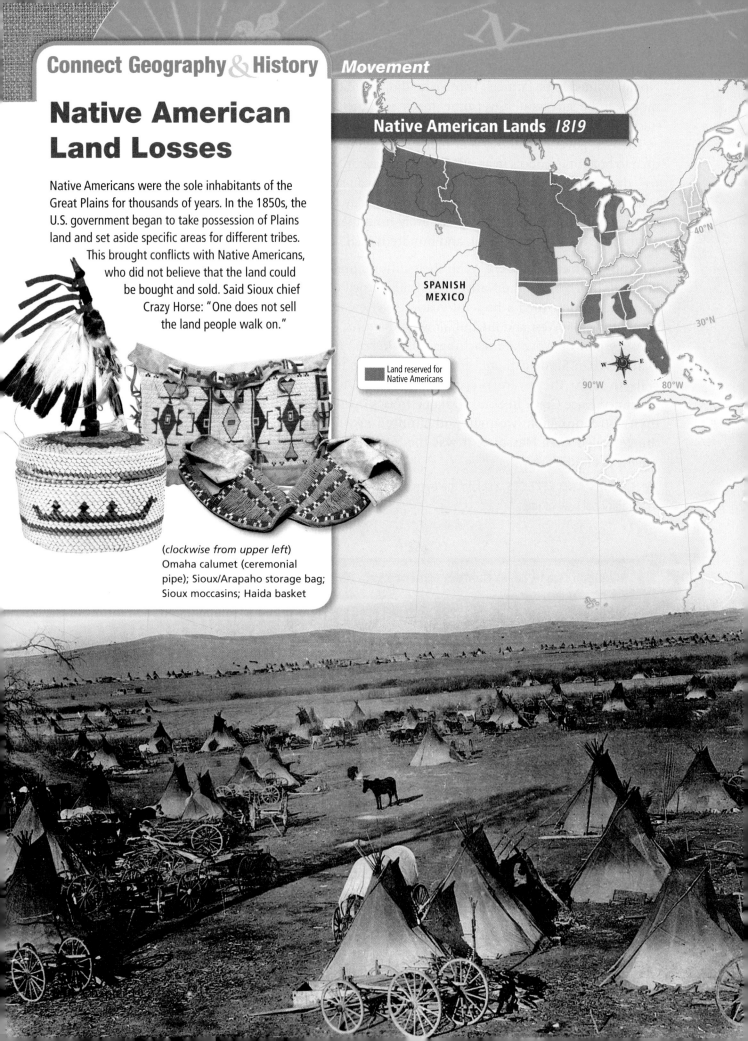

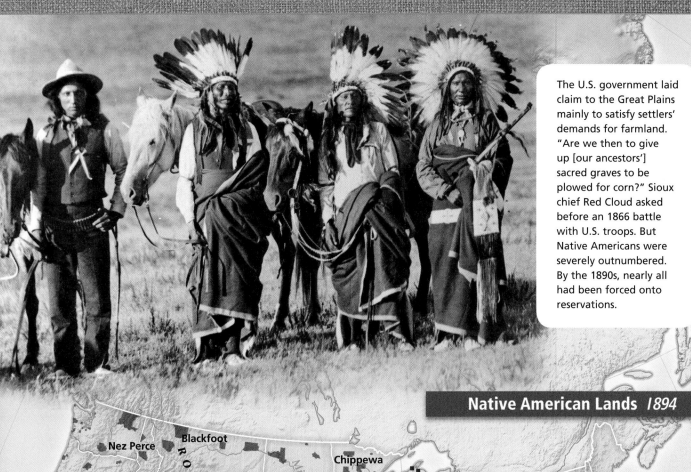

The U.S. government laid claim to the Great Plains mainly to satisfy settlers' demands for farmland. "Are we then to give up [our ancestors'] sacred graves to be plowed for corn?" Sioux chief Red Cloud asked before an 1866 battle with U.S. troops. But Native Americans were severely outnumbered. By the 1890s, nearly all had been forced onto reservations.

Native American Lands 1894

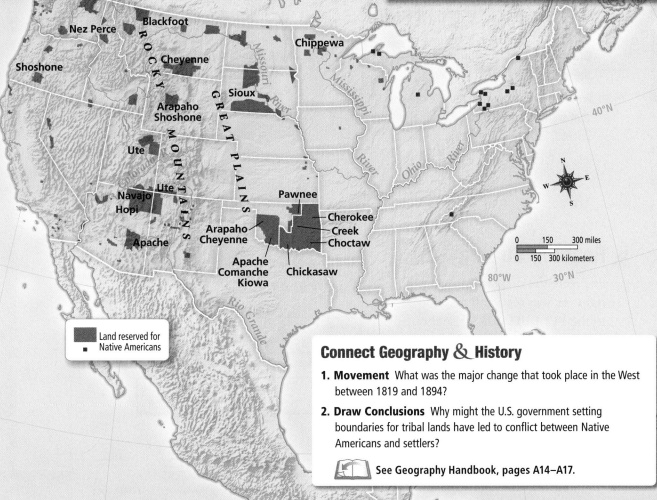

Nez Perce

Blackfoot

Chippewa

Shoshone

ROCKY

Cheyenne

Missouri River

Mississippi

40°N

Sioux

GREAT

Arapaho
Shoshone

MOUNTAINS

PLAINS

Colorado

River

Ohio

River

Ute

Ute

Navajo
Hopi

Pawnee

80°W

30°N

Cherokee

Creek

Choctaw

Apache

Arapaho
Cheyenne

Apache
Comanche
Kiowa

Chickasaw

Rio Grande

0   150   300 miles
0   150   300 kilometers

Land reserved for
Native Americans

Connect Geography & History

1. **Movement** What was the major change that took place in the West between 1819 and 1894?

2. **Draw Conclusions** Why might the U.S. government setting boundaries for tribal lands have led to conflict between Native Americans and settlers?

See Geography Handbook, pages A14–A17.

Reading for Understanding

▶ Key Ideas

BEFORE, YOU LEARNED

Native Americans of the Great Plains fought to maintain their way of life as settlers poured onto their lands.

NOW YOU WILL LEARN

A wave of farmers moved to the Plains in the 1800s and faced many economic problems.

▶ Vocabulary

TERMS & NAMES

Homestead Act 1862 law that offered 160 acres free to anyone who agreed to live on and improve the land for five years

Exodusters name for African Americans who settled on the Great Plains

sodbusters name for pioneer farmers on the Great Plains

Grange organization formed in 1867 to meet the social needs of farm families

Populist Party political party formed in 1890s that wanted a policy that would raise crop prices

gold standard a policy under which the government backs every dollar with a certain amount of gold

William Jennings Bryan Democratic and Populist candidate for President in 1896 who advocated a policy of free silver

BACKGROUND VOCABULARY

sod the top layer of prairie soil that contains thick, tightly tangled grass roots

▶ Reading Strategy

Re-create the diagram shown at right. As you read and respond to the **KEY QUESTIONS**, use the diagram to record significant events in the order in which they occurred.

📖 See Skillbuilder Handbook, page R5.

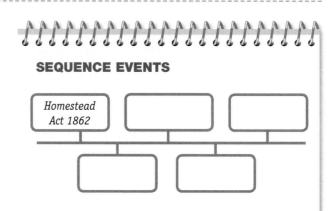

SEQUENCE EVENTS

Homestead Act 1862

GRAPHIC ORGANIZERS
Go to **Interactive Review** @ ClassZone.com

Farm Economics and Populism

8 – U6.1.1.4 America at Century's End – governmental policies promoting economic development (e.g., tariffs, banking, land grants and mineral rights, the Homestead Act)
8 – U6.1.1.5 America at Century's End – economic change, including industrialization, increased global competition, and their impact on conditions of farmers and industrial workers

One American's Story

From 1865 to 1900, about 800,000 Swedes left their homeland in northern Europe. Most, like Olaf Olsson, were drawn to America by the promise of land. Shortly after he arrived in 1869, Olsson wrote home to tell friends and family about the opportunities that awaited them.

PRIMARY SOURCE

❝ We do not dig gold with pocket knives, we do not expect to become . . . rich in a few days or in a few years, but what we aim at is to own our own homes. . . . The advantage which America offers is not to make everyone rich at once, without toil and trouble, but . . . that the poor . . . can work up little by little. ❞

—Olaf Olsson, quoted in *The Swedish Americans*

The hope of land ownership motivated settlers such as the McCarty family in Custer County, Nebraska.

Many immigrants and native-born Americans shared Olsson's optimism about the hope of possessing their own land.

The Great Land Giveaway

🔻 **KEY QUESTION** How did the federal government encourage western settlement?

Millions of farmers saw the Great Plains as an incredible opportunity.

Free Land Attracts Farmers For years, many Americans had been asking their government to make western land available. But people in the South feared that a westward migration would create more nonslave states. In 1862, after the South had left the Union, the government answered the call for free land by passing the **Homestead Act**. This law offered 160 acres of free land to anyone who agreed to live on and improve the land for five years.

Those who took advantage of the Homestead Act were called homesteaders. Many European immigrants became homesteaders. So did some African Americans from the South who went westward to escape violence and poverty, especially after Reconstruction ended in 1877. They compared themselves to the Hebrews in the biblical book of Exodus who escaped slavery in Egypt and called themselves **Exodusters**.

Railroads Profit from Free Land From 1850 to 1871, the government gave millions of acres of public land to the railroads to promote railroad expansion. The railroads resold much of the land to settlers. This made the railroad companies rich and supplied new customers for railroad services. The railroads' sales pitch worked. In the 1860s, so many Swedes and Norwegians settled in Minnesota that a local editor wrote, "It seems as if the Scandinavian Kingdoms were being emptied into this state."

▲ **ANALYZE POINT OF VIEW** Explain the appeal of the Homestead Act.

Connecting History

Expanding Liberty
The Homestead Act was a well-timed opportunity for enslaved African Americans. It took effect the same day President Lincoln issued the Emancipation Proclamation, which abolished slavery: January 1, 1863.

Farm Life on the Frontier

▼ **KEY QUESTION** What was life like for farmers on the frontier?

Farmers on the Plains quickly found that life there was not easy. Winter brought deep snows. In spring, melting snow caused flooding. Then came summer, with its harsh winds and soaring temperatures. To make matters worse, wood and water were in short supply.

A Shortage of Wood and Water Because the Plains were nearly treeless, farmers had to find other building material for their cabins and fuel for their fireplaces. They built homes from blocks of **sod**—the top layer of prairie soil that contains thick, tightly tangled grass roots. These farmers were called **sodbusters**. For fuel, they burned corncobs or "cow chips" (dried manure). In some places, they had to dig wells more than 280 feet deep. Blizzards, prairie fires, tornadoes, grasshoppers, and drought added to the miseries of life.

Lives of Women Women played a central role in settling the frontier. They worked beside men on the farm. They had to make by hand many of the items their families wore, ate, and used. Before schools were established, women taught their children. Many were also skilled in offering medical care—from snakebites to broken limbs.

The Shores family of Custer County, Nebraska, with sod buildings.
What do you think it would be like to live in a sod house?

Although most went west with their families, thousands of women claimed land on their own. Most such women were in their twenties and had never been married, but others were older—even in their sixties. Some women homesteaders were divorced or widowed; some were single mothers. Like the men who homesteaded, many were motivated by the dream of owning their own land. It is estimated that about 5 percent of claims for public land were filed by women, though in some areas the figure was much higher.

Western women gained legal rights more quickly than women in the East. In 1869, Wyoming Territory became the first state or territory to grant women the right to vote. In 1870, it became the first to allow women to serve on juries. By the 1890s, women could vote in Utah, Colorado, and Idaho.

Improvements in Farming New inventions helped Plains farmers meet some of the challenges of frontier life. A steel plow invented by John Deere in 1837 and improved upon by James Oliver in 1868 sliced through the tough sod of the prairie. Windmills adapted to the Plains pumped water from deep wells to the surface. Barbed wire allowed farmers to fence in land and livestock. Reapers made the harvesting of crops much easier, and threshers helped farmers to separate grain or seed from straw.

These inventions also made farm work more efficient. From 1860 to 1890, farmers doubled their production of wheat.

🔺 **MAIN IDEAS & DETAILS** Describe what life was like for frontier farmers.

Connecting History

Rights & Responsibilities
Although some western women could vote in state and local elections, none could vote in federal elections until 1920, when the 19th Amendment secured voting rights for all American women.

CONNECT ↻ *To Today*

FARMING: THEN & NOW

The first settlers struggled to break up the soil of the Great Plains, which was held together by tall prairie grasses. Early farm machinery was pulled by horses or by hand.

Modern-day farming has much more powerful equipment, such as the harvester shown here. Farm machines are often computerized. Sometimes, a worker can remotely operate a plow or tractor.

The agricultural cycle is still reflected in today's nine-month school schedule. This schedule dates from a time when most Americans participated in farming. School was dismissed for the summer so that children could help with farm work.

CRITICAL THINKING

1. **Evaluate** What are some of the advantages of modern-day farming?

2. **Compare and Contrast** What does modern-day farming have in common with farming long ago?

Farmers Organize

KEY QUESTION What economic problems did farmers face?

In the 1870s, farmers in the West and South watched with alarm as prices for their crops dropped lower and lower. One reason for lower prices was overproduction. Farmers were able to grow more food more easily because additional farmland had been opened up, and machines had improved.

The Problems of Farmers Not only were farmers receiving less money for their crops, but they also had to spend more to run a farm. Farming machinery was expensive, and railroads were charging higher rates to ship crops to market. As a result, farmers, angry over lower profits, began to organize to seek solutions to their problems.

In 1867, farmers had formed a group called the **Grange**, officially known as the Patrons of Husbandry. Its main purpose at first had been to meet the social needs of farm families. However, as economic conditions got worse, Grange members, known as Grangers, took action. They formed cooperatives—organizations that are owned and run by their members. The cooperatives bought grain elevators and sold crops directly to merchants. This allowed farmers to keep more of their profits.

CONNECT *Economics and History*

SUPPLY AND DEMAND

In the 1870s, Plains farmers experienced hard times, some of which followed big harvests. How did good harvests create hard times? The answer is the law of supply and demand.

The amount of goods available for sale is the **supply**. The willingness and ability of consumers to spend money for goods is called **demand**. The law of supply and demand says that when supply increases or demand decreases, prices fall. By contrast, when supply decreases and demand rises, prices rise.

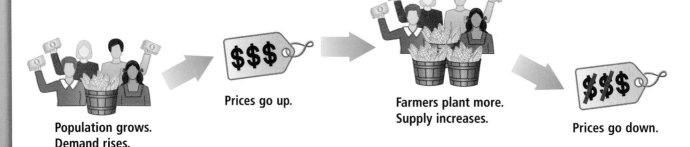

Population grows. Demand rises.

Prices go up.

Farmers plant more. Supply increases.

Prices go down.

CRITICAL THINKING

1. **Summarize** Explain why consumers would buy more of a product when the price is lower, and less when the price is higher.

2. **Causes and Effects** Suppose that in the 1870s, farmers had found an additional new market for their supplies. Would this have been likely to drive prices up or down? Why?

Farmers Demand Action Farmers also began to demand action from the government. Grangers asked states to regulate railroad freight rates and storage charges. Illinois, Minnesota, Wisconsin, Iowa, and Missouri did so. In 1877, the Supreme Court backed the farmers in their fight against the railroads. In *Munn* v. *Illinois*, the Court ruled that states and the federal government could regulate the railroads because this business served the public interest.

The Rise of Populism In the early 1890s, several farm groups joined together to form a new political party called the **Populist Party**, or People's Party.

The Populists wanted the government to adopt a "free silver" policy, or the unlimited coining of silver. Since silver was plentiful, more money would be put in circulation. They believed that increasing the money supply would cause inflation. Inflation, in turn, would result in rising prices. Higher prices for crops would help farmers pay back the money that they had borrowed to improve their farms.

Opponents of free silver wanted to keep the **gold standard**. Under the gold standard, the government backs every dollar with a certain amount of gold. Since the gold supply is limited, fewer dollars are in circulation, and inflation is less likely.

In the 1892 presidential election, the Populist Party called for a free silver policy, government ownership of railroads, and other reforms. The Populist candidate, James B. Weaver, lost to Grover Cleveland. But he won more than a million votes— a good showing for a third-party candidate.

The Election of 1896 Four years later, the Populists joined the Democratic Party in supporting **William Jennings Bryan** for president. Bryan urged the Democratic convention to support free silver.

History Makers

William Jennings Bryan   1860–1925

A Midwest native, William Jennings Bryan was nicknamed "the Great Commoner" because he embraced the causes of farmers and other working people. He championed their interests against the power of big business and the banks.

Bryan served two terms in Congress and made three unsuccessful bids for the presidency. He was an influential speaker and political leader for more than 30 years, even after leaving elective office. Many reforms that he fought for, such as an eight-hour workday and woman suffrage, later became law.

CRITICAL THINKING

1. **Make Inferences** How did the reforms Bryan fought for reflect his concern for working people?

2. **Connect** *to* **Today** What public figures today have some of the same qualities as Bryan?

 **ONLINE BIOGRAPHY**   For more on William Jennings Bryan, go to the **Research & Writing Center** @ ClassZone.com

PRIMARY SOURCE

❝ Burn down your cities and leave our farms, and your cities will spring up again as if by magic; but destroy our farms and the grass will grow in the street of every city in the country. . . . [We] . . . answer . . . their demand for a gold standard by saying . . . : You shall not press down upon the brow of labor this crown of thorns. You shall not crucify mankind upon a cross of gold. ❞

—William Jennings Bryan, "Cross of Gold" speech

In the election of 1896, money issues mattered much more to voters than they had in the previous election. The nation had suffered through an economic crisis—the Panic of 1893. The Republican candidate, William McKinley, favored the gold standard. He warned that "free silver" would mean higher prices for food and other goods.

On election day, farmers in the South and the West voted overwhelmingly for Bryan. But McKinley, who was backed by industrialists, bankers, and other business leaders, won the East and the election by about half a million votes. This election was the beginning of the end for the Populist Party.

▲ **PROBLEMS AND SOLUTIONS** Explain how the Populist Party sought to address the economic problems faced by farmers.

CONNECT to the Essential Question

How did the nation change as a result of westward movement after the Civil War?

Transcontinental railroad built	**Mining and cattle industries develop**	**U.S. government takes Native American lands**	**Congress passes the Homestead Act**
Economies of East and West linked Frontier settlement increases Standard time established	Miners, ranchers, and cowhands settle in the West and Southwest Mexicanos lose economic and political power Mining centers and cow towns grow into western cities	U.S. army and Native Americans clash in bloody battles Buffalo herds are destroyed; nomadic ways of Plains Indians end Native Americans forced onto reservations	Settlers claim western land Plains becomes farming region Farmers become political force

CRITICAL THINKING Summarize How did the population of the West change during the late 1900s? How did the U.S. government help to create this change?

The Closing of the Frontier

🔻 **KEY QUESTION** What events symbolized the frontier's closing?

By 1890, fenced fields had replaced the open frontier.

The Oklahoma Land Rush The last lands not claimed by settlers were in the area called Indian Territory. At the blast of a starting gun on April 22, 1889, thousands rushed to claim 2 million acres that had been inhabited by Native Americans. In May 1890, the area became Oklahoma Territory.

In 1890, 17 million people lived between the Mississippi and the Pacific. That year, the Census Bureau declared that the frontier no longer existed.

Historians' View of the Frontier Many people believed that the frontier was what had made America unique. In 1893, historian Frederick Jackson Turner wrote an influential essay on the frontier, saying "The existence of an area of free land, . . . and the advance of American settlement westward, explain American development." To Turner, the frontier had meant opportunity.

But many historians today think that Turner gave too much importance to the frontier in shaping an American character. They point out that the United States remains a land of opportunity long after the frontier's closing.

🔺 **SUMMARIZE** Describe the events that symbolized the closing of the frontier.

This poster advertised the sale of Native American lands by the U.S. government.

Michigan Grade Level Content Expectations *Review*

ONLINE QUIZ
For test practice, go to
Interactive Review @ ClassZone.com

TERMS & NAMES

1. Explain the importance of
   - Homestead Act
   - Exoduster
   - sodbuster
   - Grange
   - Populist Party
   - gold standard
   - William Jennings Bryan

USING YOUR READING NOTES

2. **Sequence Events** Complete the diagram to show the most important events of this section.

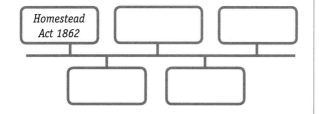

Homestead Act 1862

KEY IDEAS

3. What attracted European immigrants and African Americans to the West?

4. How did new inventions help farmers meet the challenges of the Plains?

5. What were the goals of the Populist Party?

CRITICAL THINKING

6. **Summarize** What steps did farmers take to seek solutions to their problems?

7. **Compare and Contrast** What were the arguments for and against "free silver"?

8. **Evaluate** Reread the quote from the essay by Frederick Jackson Turner, above. What did he mean by "an area of free land"? Was it really free?

9. **Writing** Report Research sod houses. Write a short report that explains how prairie grass held the sod together, and list the advantages and disadvantages of building with sod.

THE WILD WEST

America's fascination with the idea of the "Wild West" began even before the frontier closed. Why did the West capture the popular imagination?

THE PONY EXPRESS

From April 1860 to October 1861, the Pony Express carried mail by relay. Riders switched horses at stations 10 or 15 miles apart on a route covering nearly 2,000 miles. All riders had to weigh less than 125 pounds; the youngest was only 11 years old.

BUFFALO BILL'S WILD WEST

William "Buffalo Bill" Cody (below right), a buffalo hunter turned showman, dramatized legends of the West in his Wild West Show of the 1880s. The show brought reenactments of frontier life across the country and to Europe. Marksman Annie Oakley (above) was a star attraction. She could shoot a dime in the air from 90 feet away.

Make a WANTED poster!

Research one of the outlaws mentioned on page 605, or another outlaw who became part of western legend. Create a WANTED poster for the person. Include images, quotes, and infamous deeds.

CHAPTER 19 Interactive Review

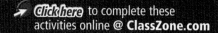 *Click here* to complete these activities online @ ClassZone.com

Chapter Summary

1 Key Idea
A railroad, completed in 1869, spanned the continent and helped to open the way for settlers in the West.

2 Key Idea
The mining and cattle industries contributed to population growth in western territories.

3 Key Idea
Native Americans on the Great Plains fought to maintain their way of life as settlers poured onto their lands.

4 Key Idea
A wave of farmers moved to the Plains in the 1800s and faced many economic problems.

For detailed Review and Study Notes go to **Interactive Review** @ ClassZone.com

Name Game

Use the Terms & Names list to identify each sentence online or on your own paper.

1. In the mid-1800s, this part of the West was occupied mainly by Native Americans.
   frontier

2. I taught American cowhands how to rope and ride.

3. This was invented by the railroad companies.

4. I took the law into my own hands.

5. I was given this nickname by Native Americans in the West.

6. This brought cattle on foot to railway centers.

7. I was an African American who settled on the Great Plains.

8. I built my home from the dense soil of the Plains.

9. This allowed settlers to get free western land.

10. I was defeated at the Battle of the Little Bighorn.

A. vaquero
B. vigilante
C. buffalo soldier
D. Sitting Bull
E. frontier
F. long drive
G. Exoduster
H. sodbuster
I. Dawes Act
J. vaquero
K. standard time
L. George A. Custer
M. Homestead Act

Activities

FLIPCARD

Use the online flipcards to quiz yourself on the terms and names introduced in this chapter.

Native Americans in this region followed the buffalo herds.

ANSWER
Great Plains

GEOGAME

Use this online map to reinforce your knowledge of the locations of western cities, especially railroad hubs that boomed in the late 1800s. Drag and drop each city name in the list at its location on the map. A scorecard helps you keep track of your progress online.

Chicago
Omaha
St. Louis
Kansas City
Minneapolis

More items online

VOCABULARY

Explain the significance of each of the following.

1. transcontinental railroad
2. vaquero
3. boomtown
4. sodbusters
5. Wounded Knee Massacre
6. standard time
7. long drive
8. lode
9. Dawes Act
10. gold standard

Explain how the terms and names in each group are related.

11. Sitting Bull, George Custer, Battle of the Little Bighorn
12. Grange, Populist Party, William Jennings Bryan
13. Homestead Act, frontier, Exodusters

KEY IDEAS

1 Railroads Transform the Nation (pages 596–599)

14. How did the government encourage the building of the first transcontinental railroad?

15. How did the railroad affect the frontier?

2 Miners, Ranchers, and Cowhands (pages 600–607)

16. What economic opportunities drew large numbers of people to the West beginning in the 1860s?

17. What ended the boom in the cattle business?

3 Native Americans Fight to Survive (pages 608–613)

18. Why did the U.S. government take land from Native Americans on the Great Plains?

19. What were the results of the Battle of the Little Bighorn?

4 Farm Economics and Populism (pages 616–623)

20. What problems in the 1890s led farmers to take political action?

21. Why was the Oklahoma Land Rush significant?

CRITICAL THINKING

22. **Causes and Effects** What were the main reasons that settlers moved to the West?

23. **Compare and Contrast** Fill in the chart comparing the building of the Union Pacific and Central Pacific railroads. Which workers do you think had the more difficult route? Why?

Railroad	Route	Workers	Physical Challenges
Union Pacific			
Central Pacific			

24. **Summarize** How did U.S. government policy toward Native Americans change as white settlers moved westward?

25. **Form and Support Opinions** What do you think would be the most difficult challenge in starting a new life on the Great Plains? Explain.

26. **Make Inferences** This image from 1873 depicts the benefits of membership in the Grange. What does the central image suggest about how being part of the Grange might affect an individual farmer?

MEAP PRACTICE

✔ **TEST PRACTICE**

• **Online Test Practice @ ClassZone.com**
• Use the **MEAP Strategies & Practice,** pages S1-S27, at the front of this book

DOCUMENT-BASED QUESTIONS

Analyze each document, and answer the question that follows.

DOCUMENT 1

DOCUMENT 2

PRIMARY SOURCE

❝ Do not misunderstand me, but understand me fully with reference to my affection for the land. I never said the land was mine to do with as I chose. The one who has the right to dispose of it is the one who has created it. I claim a right to live on my land, and accord you the privilege to live on yours. ❞

—Chief Joseph (Nez Perce)

1 Examine the painting and primary source. What is one way that western settlement changed the lives of Native Americans?

  A Many became wealthy selling their land.

  B Most saw the value of farming and decided to stop hunting.

  C Many were forced to move to reservations.

  D Most followed the buffalo to new areas.

YOU BE THE HISTORIAN

27. **Form and Support Opinions** Which groups of people do you think benefited most from western settlement? Which groups did not benefit? Explain.

28. **Analyze Point of View** Chief Joseph said, "It makes my heart sick when I remember all the good words and broken promises." What did he mean by this?

29. **Compare and Contrast** How did the lives of western settlers during the late 1800s compare with the myth of the Wild West?

30. **Make Inferences** Why do you think women in the West were the first women to gain the right to vote?

31. **Connect to Today** Choose a western city from a map of the United States. How might its location have contributed to its growth?

Answer the
ESSENTIAL QUESTION

How did the nation change as a result of westward movement after the Civil War?

Written Response Write a two- or three-paragraph response to the Essential Question. Be sure to consider the key ideas of each section as well as events that encouraged western settlement. Use the Rubric Response below to guide your thinking and writing.

Response Rubric
A strong response will

• discuss events that opened the West to settlers
• explore the role of the mining and cattle industries
• explain how the U.S. government encouraged western settlement
• analyze the effects of settlement on Native Americans

CHAPTER

20

1. **America Enters the Industrial Age**

2. **Immigration and Modern Urban Growth**

3. **Discrimination Against African Americans**

4. **The Labor Movement**

5. **Society and Mass Culture**

Industrialization and Immigration

1860–1914

ESSENTIAL QUESTION

What new problems and opportunities developed as America became an industrial power?

CONNECT ⤹ Geography & History

How did immigration affect industrialization in the United States?

Think about:

1 where immigrants settled

2 the location of the nation's main industrial areas

Immigrants often lived in the same neighborhood as others from their home country.

Statue of Liberty

1860

U.S. population reaches 31,443,321.

Announcement for the demonstration that turned into the Haymarket Affair

Attention Workingmen!
GREAT
MASS-MEETING
TO-NIGHT, at 7.30 o'clock,
AT THE
HAYMARKET, Randolph St. Bet. Desplaines and Halsted.
Good Speakers will be present to denounce
atrocious act of the

1882 Congress passes the Chinese Exclusion Act.

1886 Haymarket Affair occurs.

▼

Effect Opposition to unions increases.

628 Chapter 20

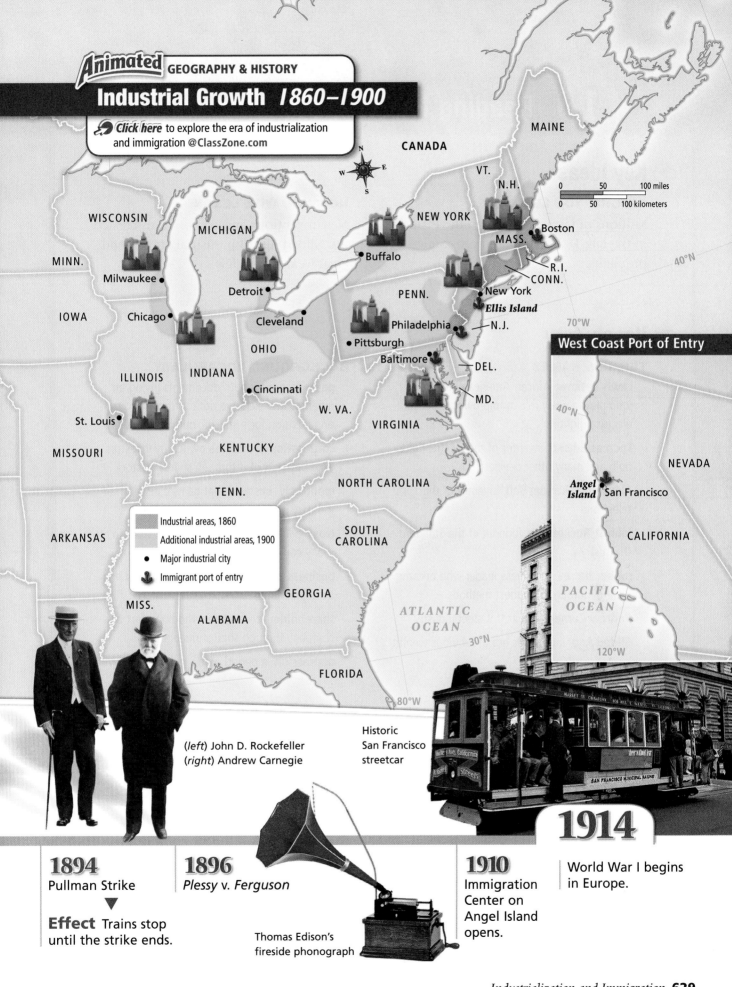

Industrial Growth 1860–1900

Click here to explore the era of industrialization and immigration @ClassZone.com

CANADA

MAINE

WISCONSIN

MICHIGAN

NEW YORK

VT.

N.H.

MASS.

Boston

MINN.

Milwaukee

Detroit

Buffalo

R.I.

CONN.

New York

Ellis Island

N.J.

IOWA

Chicago

Cleveland

PENN.

Philadelphia

70°W

40°N

OHIO

Pittsburgh

Baltimore

DEL.

ILLINOIS

INDIANA

Cincinnati

MD.

St. Louis

W. VA.

VIRGINIA

West Coast Port of Entry

MISSOURI

KENTUCKY

40°N

NEVADA

ARKANSAS

TENN.

NORTH CAROLINA

Angel
Island San Francisco

Industrial areas, 1860

Additional industrial areas, 1900

● Major industrial city

⚓ Immigrant port of entry

SOUTH
CAROLINA

CALIFORNIA

MISS.

GEORGIA

ALABAMA

ATLANTIC
OCEAN

PACIFIC
OCEAN

30°N

120°W

FLORIDA

80°W

(left) John D. Rockefeller
(right) Andrew Carnegie

Historic
San Francisco
streetcar

1914

1894
Pullman Strike

▼

Effect Trains stop
until the strike ends.

1896
Plessy v. *Ferguson*

Thomas Edison's
fireside phonograph

1910
Immigration
Center on
Angel Island
opens.

World War I begins
in Europe.

▶ Key Ideas

BEFORE, YOU LEARNED

Millions of farmers moved to the Plains in the late 1800s and faced economic problems.

NOW YOU WILL LEARN

New inventions and corporations created the Gilded Age of industrial growth and great wealth for a few.

▶ Vocabulary

TERMS & NAMES

Lewis Latimer African-American inventor who played a key role in improving practical electrical lighting

Thomas Edison inventor of the electric light bulb and many other devices

Alexander Graham Bell inventor of the telephone

John D. Rockefeller founder of the Standard Oil Trust

robber baron a business leader who became wealthy through dishonest methods

Andrew Carnegie built U.S. steel industry

Gilded Age late 1800s era of fabulous wealth

BACKGROUND VOCABULARY

patents government documents giving an inventor the exclusive right to make and sell an invention for a specific number of years

corporation a business owned by investors who buy part of it through shares of stock

monopoly business that gains control of an industry by eliminating other competitors

trust a legal body created to hold stock in many companies, often within an industry

business cycle the pattern of good and bad economic times

shareholder an investor who buys part of a company through shares of stock

depression a period of low economic activity

▶ Reading Strategy

Re-create the diagram shown at right. As you read and respond to the **KEY QUESTIONS**, use the diagram to record new inventions and the ways that they changed American life. Add boxes or start a new diagram as needed.

 See Skillbuilder Handbook, page R4.

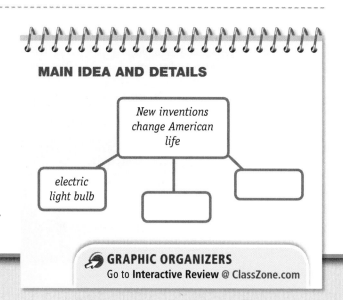

MAIN IDEA AND DETAILS

New inventions change American life

electric light bulb

🔁 **GRAPHIC ORGANIZERS**
Go to **Interactive Review** @ ClassZone.com

America Enters the Industrial Age

8 – U6.1.1.3 America at Century's End – systems of transportation (canals and railroads, including the Transcontinental Railroad), and their impact on the economy and society
8 – U6.1.1.5 America at Century's End – economic change, including industrialization, increased global competition, and their impact on conditions of farmers and industrial workers

One American's Story

Lewis Latimer learned the trade of mechanical drawing after serving in the Union Navy in the Civil War. He worked with inventor Thomas Edison and played a key role in improving practical electric lighting.

Lewis Latimer

PRIMARY SOURCE

❝I had qualified myself to take charge of producing the carbons for the lamps, when I was not drawing, and worked through the day helping to make the lamps and at night locating them in stores and offices... These were strenuous times, and we made long hours each day. At the factory by seven in the morning, and after the day's work somewhere running lamps until twelve o'clock or later at night.❞

—Lewis Latimer, *1911 Logbook*

Latimer held many **patents** as an inventor. A patent is a government document that gives an inventor the exclusive right to make and sell an invention for a number of years. Inventors such as Latimer and Edison developed new technologies during the years of the Industrial Revolution.

The Industrial Revolution Continues

🔻 **KEY QUESTION** What new inventions changed life in the 1800s?

During the early to mid-1800s, an industrial revolution had been underway in America. Factory machines began to replace hand tools. In some parts of the country, large-scale manufacturing began to replace farming. However, it was not until the late 1800s that a surge in industrialization, the process of developing industry, changed the nation dramatically.

Causes of Growth There were many factors that caused industrial growth in the United States after the Civil War.

The New Steel Industry The steel industry contributed to America's industrial growth. In the 1850s, William Kelly in the United States and Henry Bessemer in England independently developed what became known as the Bessemer steel process. This new process used much less coal than the older process used. Because the Bessemer steel process cut the cost of steel, the nation's steel output increased by more than 350 times between 1867 and 1900. Factories began to make plows, barbed wire, nails, and beams for buildings. Throughout the late 1800s, steel was also used for rails to expand the railroads.

Edison and Electricity The electric power industry also grew during the late 1800s. The inventor who found many ways to use electricity was **Thomas Edison**. In 1876, Edison opened a laboratory in Menlo Park, New Jersey. He employed Lewis Latimer and many other assistants. Edison's laboratory invented so many things that Edison received more than 1,000 U.S. patents, more than any other inventor.

One of Edison's most famous inventions was practical electric lighting. Other inventors had already created electric lights, but they were too bright and unstable for home use. Edison figured out how to make a safe, steady light bulb. He also invented a system to deliver electricity to buildings.

(below) Market Street, San Francisco, 1900

Causes of Growth *1860–1900*

Growing Population
The U.S. population more than doubled. Over 14 million immigrants were part of this growth.

Improved Transportation
Raw materials and finished products could be shipped longer distances more quickly with
- steamboats • canals
- railroads

Natural Resources
America was able to produce a variety of goods using its vast resources of
- forests   • copper
- water   • silver
- coal   • gold
- iron

New Inventions
Industry was able to produce goods more efficiently with new machines and processes.

Government Support
States and the federal government used land grants, subsidies, and tariffs to help business grow.

Investment Capital
Hoping to share in the thriving economy, banks and wealthy people lent businesses money.

CRITICAL THINKING **Causes and Effects** How did new technology affect industrial growth?

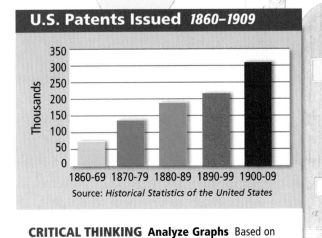

U.S. Patents Issued 1860–1909

Thousands

350
300
250
200
150
100
50
0

1860-69 1870-79 1880-89 1890-99 1900-09

Source: *Historical Statistics of the United States*

CRITICAL THINKING Analyze Graphs Based on the information in the graph, what can you conclude about the process of invention during the late 1800s?

By 1882, Edison had installed the first permanent commercial central power system in New York City. Electric lighting slowly replaced gaslights.

Bell and the Telephone After years of experiments, **Alexander Graham Bell**, an accomplished inventor, invented the telephone in 1876. Bell's breakthrough was the result of an accident. He was adjusting the transmitter in the laboratory and his assistant, Thomas Watson, was in another room with the receiver. Bell reportedly spilled acid on himself and said, "Mr. Watson, come here. I want you." Watson burst into the laboratory, exclaiming that he had heard Bell's words through the receiver.

New Industries New inventions often became the basis of new industries that changed American life. The telephone industry grew rapidly after the invention of the telephone. By 1880, more than 50,000 telephones had been sold. The invention of the switchboard allowed more people to connect to a telephone network. Women commonly worked in the new job of switchboard operator. The typewriter also opened jobs for women. Christopher Latham Sholes helped invent the first practical typewriter in 1867.

The sewing machine created changes in industry, too. Elias Howe first patented the sewing machine in 1846. Isaac Singer also patented a sewing machine in 1851 and continued to improve it. It became a bestseller and led to a new industry. In factories, people produced ready-made clothes. Instead of being fitted to each buyer, clothes came in standard sizes and popular styles. Increasingly, people bought clothes instead of making their own.

Other inventors also helped industry advance. African-American inventor Granville T. Woods patented devices to improve telephone and telegraph systems. Margaret Knight invented machines for the packaging and shoe making industries.

▲ **MAIN IDEAS & DETAILS** Identify new inventions that changed American life.

(*top*) Thomas Edison and his safe, steady light bulb (*bottom*) Alexander Graham Bell and one of his telephones
Why was 1876 an important year for both inventors?

Corporations Gain Power

🔻 **KEY QUESTION** How did corporations affect business competition?

In the decades following the Civil War, the American business world was thoroughly reorganized. This reorganization changed the way businesses were managed and financed. It also appeared to threaten business competition and the free market.

Businesses Become Corporations Until the late 1800s, most businesses were owned directly by one person or by a few partners. Then advances in technology made many business owners want to buy new equipment. To raise money, they turned their businesses into **corporations**. A corporation is a business owned by **shareholders**, investors who buy part of the company through shares of stock. In the late 1800s, few laws regulated corporations. This led to the growth of a few powerful corporations that dominated American industry.

Rockefeller and the Oil Industry The oil industry, led by **John D. Rockefeller**, began to grow in the late 1800s. Rockefeller built his first refinery in 1863. He decided that the best way to make money was to put his competitors

CONNECT — *Economics and History*

THE CORPORATION

The 1882 Supreme Court decision, *San Mateo County* v. *Southern Pacific Railroad*, gave corporations the same rights enjoyed by all people living in the United States. The court based its decision on the Fourteenth Amendment.

Corporations have several advantages over privately-owned businesses:

- Corporations can raise large amounts of money by selling stock.
- A corporation limits the risks to its shareholders.
- A corporation continues to exist after its founders die.
- Corporations are better able to run large operations such as the Standard Oil refinery shown on the right.

SHAREHOLDERS
- Own shares of the corporation
- Elect board of directors
- Vote on corporate policies

BOARD OF DIRECTORS
- Appoints officers
- Sets corporate policies

REPORTS TO SHAREHOLDERS

OFFICERS OF CORPORATION
- Are employees of the corporation
- Manage daily operations

REPORT TO BOARD OF DIRECTORS

REPORT TO SHAREHOLDERS

CRITICAL THINKING

1. **Compare and Contrast** How are corporations different from privately owned businesses?
2. **Draw Conclusions** Which corporate group has the most control over a corporation?

out of business. A company that wipes out its competitors and controls an industry is a **monopoly**. Rockefeller bought other refineries. He made deals with railroads to carry his oil at a lower rate than his competitors' oil. He also built and purchased his own pipelines to carry oil.

One of Rockefeller's most famous moves to end competition was to develop the **trust** in 1882. A trust is a legal body created to hold stock in many companies, often in the same industry. Other oil companies joined Rockefeller's Standard Oil Trust. By 1880, the trust controlled 95 percent of all oil refining in the United States and was able to set a high price for oil. Consumers had to pay Standard Oil's high price because they couldn't buy oil from anyone else. As head of Standard Oil, Rockefeller earned millions of dollars. He became known as a **robber baron**, a business leader who uses dishonest methods to grow rich.

Political cartoons of (*left*) John D. Rockefeller and (*below*) Andrew Carnegie
Why did Rockefeller become known as a robber baron?

Carnegie and the Steel Industry **Andrew Carnegie**, unlike Rockefeller, tried to beat his competition in the steel industry by making the best and cheapest product. To do so, he sought to control all the processes related to the manufacture of steel. He bought iron mines as well as the ships and railroads that carried iron ore to his mills. Carnegie's company dominated the U.S. steel industry from 1889 to 1901, when he sold it to J.P. Morgan, the nation's top banker, for $480 million.

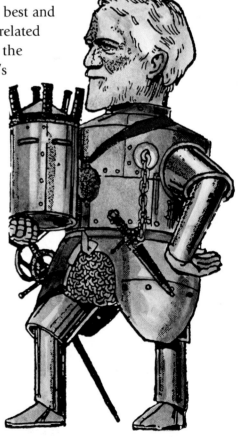

Carnegie and Rockefeller became multimillionaires. They were also philanthropists, or people who give large sums of money to charities. Rockefeller donated money to the University of Chicago and Rockefeller University in New York. Carnegie also gave money to universities, and he built hundreds of public libraries. During his life, Rockefeller gave away more than $500 million. Carnegie gave away more than $350 million.

The Business Cycle In the second half of the 19th century American industry experienced ups and downs. This pattern of good and bad times is called the **business cycle**. During very good times, called booms, people buy more, and some invest in business. As a result, industries and businesses grow. During very bad times, called busts, spending and investing decrease. Industries lay off workers and make fewer goods. Businesses may shrink, or even close. Such a period of extremely low economic activity is a **depression**.

In the late 1800s there were two harsh depressions. The depression of 1873 lasted five years. At its height, three million people were out of work. During the depression that began in 1893, thousands of businesses failed, including more than 150 railroads. Even with these economic lows, industries in the United States grew between 1860 and 1900. The amount of manufactured goods increased six-fold during these years.

▲ **CAUSES AND EFFECTS** Explain how corporations affected business competition.

Economic Growth Brings Wealth and Poverty

▼ **KEY QUESTION** What inequalities emerged in the late 19th century?

Industrialization raised living standards in America and brought great wealth to business owners. The richest Americans celebrated and often flaunted their fortunes by spending them—on mansions filled with fine furniture, antiques, and art. However, the economic growth of this time did little to help minorities, factory workers, and many in the South.

The Gilded Age The rags-to-riches stories of people such as Rockefeller and Carnegie inspired many Americans to believe that they, too, could grow rich. Horatio Alger wrote popular stories about poor boys who worked hard

COMPARING *Life in the Gilded Age*

RICH AND POOR

During the Gilded Age, the wealthiest Americans lived in palace-like mansions, while the poorest families lived in small, cramped apartments.

CRITICAL THINKING Compare and Contrast How do these two images reflect the distance between rich and poor in the United States during the Gilded Age?

and became successful. These stories hid an important truth, however. Most people who made millions had not been raised in poverty. Many belonged to the upper classes, attended college, and began their careers with the advantage of money or family connections.

Writers Mark Twain and Charles Warner named the era the **Gilded Age**. To gild is to coat an object with gold leaf. The name has a deeper meaning, however. Just as gold leaf can disguise an object of lesser value, the wealth of a few masked society's problems, including corrupt politics and widespread poverty. In 1890, the average income for 11 million of the nation's 12 million families was $380, well below the poverty line.

The South Remains Agricultural Most of the industrial growth during the late 1800s took place in the North. Compared with the North's economy, the South's economy grew slowly after the Civil War. Industry did grow in some areas, such as Birmingham, Alabama, and southern Virginia, but most of the South remained agricultural. The price of cotton, the South's main crop, was very low. Sharecroppers made little money from selling cotton and had a hard time paying what they owed. At the same time that southern sharecroppers struggled to break free of debt, workers in the industrial North also faced injustices.

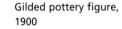

Gilded pottery figure, 1900

 SUMMARIZE Describe the inequalities that emerged during the Gilded Age.

Michigan Grade Level Content Expectations *Review*

ONLINE QUIZ
For test practice, go to
Interactive Review @ ClassZone.com

TERMS & NAMES

1. Explain the importance of
   - Lewis Latimer
   - Thomas Edison
   - Alexander Graham Bell
   - John D. Rockefeller
   - robber baron
   - Andrew Carnegie
   - Gilded Age

USING YOUR READING NOTES

2. **Main Ideas & Details** Complete the diagram you started at the beginning of this section. Then write a one-sentence summary of the most important points.

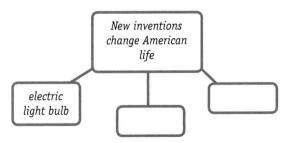

KEY IDEAS

3. How did new inventions change life in the late 1800s?

4. How did John D. Rockefeller become so powerful in the oil industry?

5. Why did Mark Twain and Charles Warner call the late 1800s the Gilded Age?

CRITICAL THINKING

6. **Causes and Effects** How did the growth in population and immigration affect industrial growth in the United States?

7. **Compare and Contrast** How were Rockefeller's methods for building Standard Oil different from Carnegie's in building his steel company?

8. **Connect** *to* **Today** What inventions and industries have done the most to change life in the United States recently?

The Steel Industry

In the late 1800s, the steel and steel-products industries began to boom in the Great Lakes region. The natural resources used to make steel—coal, oil, iron ore, and limestone—were abundant. Trains, rivers, and lakes connected the region to markets in the East and South and brought in raw materials from the West. The map shows the resources of the Great Lakes and how transportation by rail and water joined regions. The steps in the steel production process are shown below.

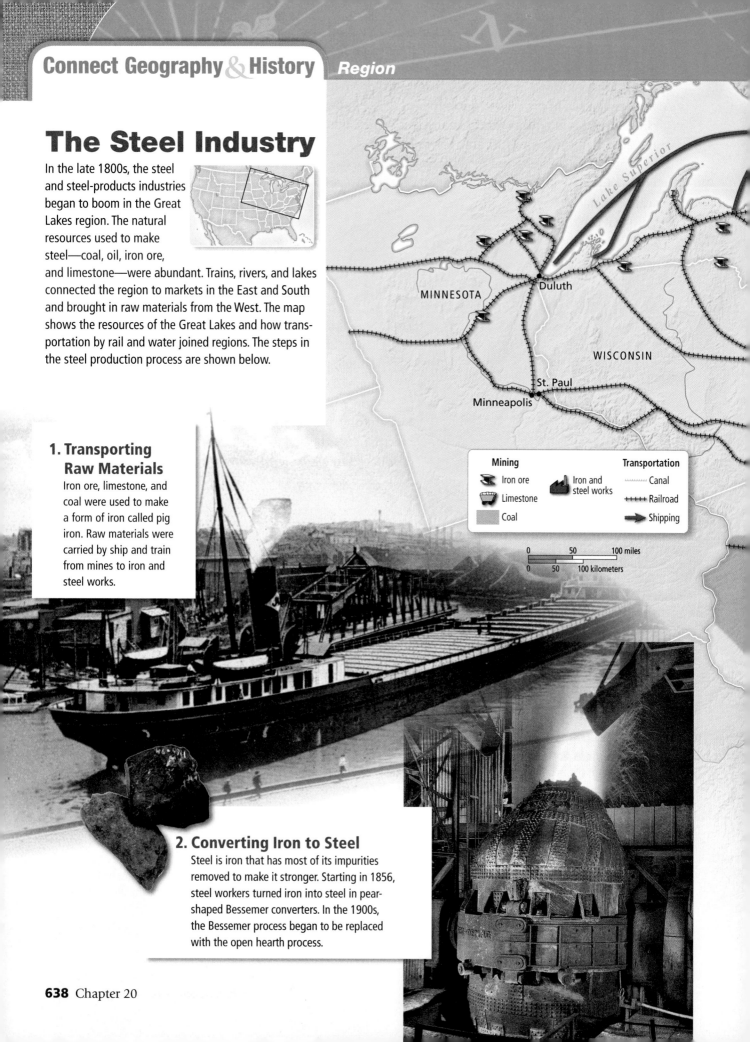

Lake Superior

MINNESOTA

Duluth

WISCONSIN

St. Paul

Minneapolis

Mining

Iron ore

Limestone

Coal

Iron and steel works

Transportation

Canal

Railroad

Shipping

0   50   100 miles

0   50   100 kilometers

1. Transporting Raw Materials

Iron ore, limestone, and coal were used to make a form of iron called pig iron. Raw materials were carried by ship and train from mines to iron and steel works.

2. Converting Iron to Steel

Steel is iron that has most of its impurities removed to make it stronger. Starting in 1856, steel workers turned iron into steel in pear-shaped Bessemer converters. In the 1900s, the Bessemer process began to be replaced with the open hearth process.

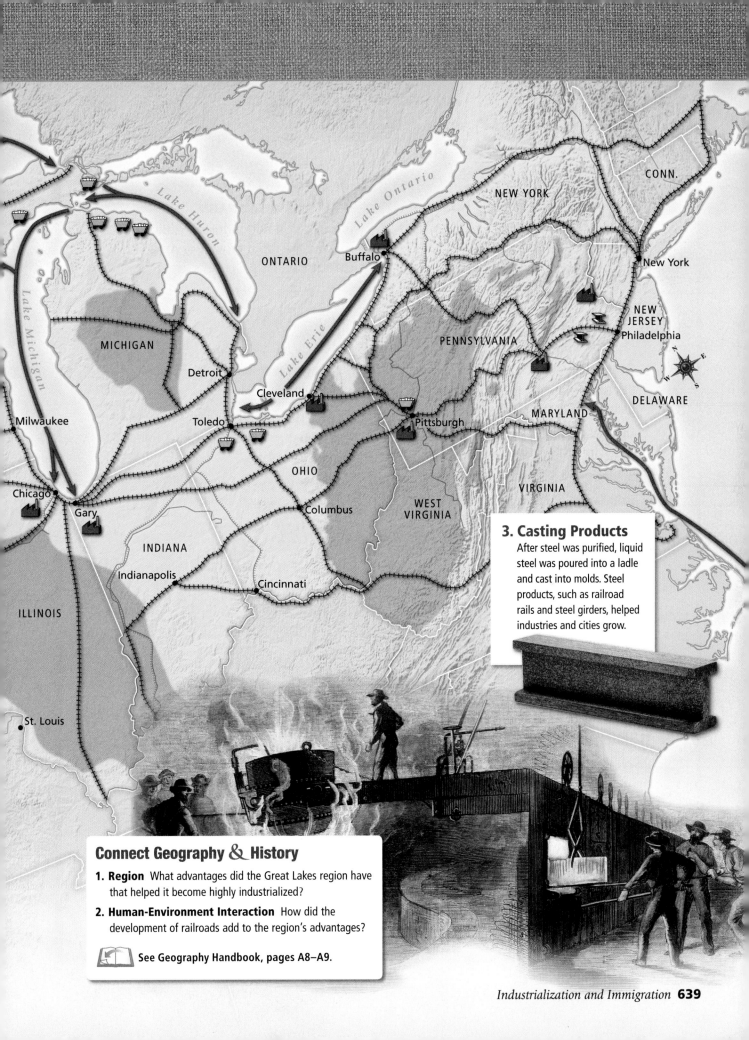

3. Casting Products
After steel was purified, liquid steel was poured into a ladle and cast into molds. Steel products, such as railroad rails and steel girders, helped industries and cities grow.

Connect Geography & History

1. **Region** What advantages did the Great Lakes region have that helped it become highly industrialized?

2. **Human-Environment Interaction** How did the development of railroads add to the region's advantages?

See Geography Handbook, pages A8–A9.

Industrialization and Immigration **639**

▶ Key Ideas

BEFORE, YOU LEARNED
New inventions and corporations created the Gilded Age of industrial growth and great wealth for a few.

NOW YOU WILL LEARN
Immigration and industrialization spurred the rapid growth of America's cities.

▶ Vocabulary

TERMS & NAMES

Ellis Island New York Harbor immigration station for European immigrants

Angel Island San Francisco Bay immigration station for Asian immigrants

melting pot a place where cultures blend

assimilation process of blending into society by adopting the dominant culture

Chinese Exclusion Act 1882 law which banned Chinese immigration

Jane Addams urban reformer

Hull House settlement house founded by Jane Addams in Chicago

social gospel movement reforms based on Christian values

Tammany Hall New York City political machine

BACKGROUND VOCABULARY

urbanization growth of cities resulting from industrialization

sweatshop place where workers labor long hours under poor conditions for low wages

tenements run-down and overcrowded apartment houses

slum neighborhood with overcrowded and dangerous housing

political machine organization that controls a local government

▶ Reading Strategy

Re-create the diagram shown at right. As you read and respond to the **KEY QUESTIONS**, use the diagram to identify causes of urban growth. Add boxes or start a new diagram as needed.

 See Skillbuilder Handbook, page R7.

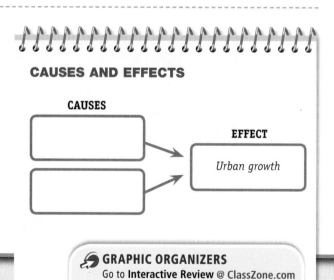

CAUSES AND EFFECTS

CAUSES

EFFECT

Urban growth

⊘ GRAPHIC ORGANIZERS
Go to **Interactive Review** @ ClassZone.com

Immigration and Modern Urban Growth

 8 – U6.1.1.2 America at Century's End – population, including immigration, reactions to immigrants, and the changing demographic structure of rural and urban America
8 – U6.1.1.3 America at Century's End – systems of transportation (canals and railroads, including the Transcontinental Railroad), and their impact on the economy and society

One American's Story

In 1907, 10-year-old Edward Corsi left Italy to come to America. After two weeks at sea, he saw the Statue of Liberty.

PRIMARY SOURCE

❝ This symbol of America . . . inspired awe in the hopeful immigrants. Many older persons among us, burdened with a thousand memories of what they were leaving behind, had been openly weeping. . . . Now somehow steadied, I suppose, by the concreteness of the symbol of America's freedom, they dried their tears. ❞

—Edward Corsi, *In the Shadow of Liberty*

A young immigrant

Edward Corsi was one of millions of immigrants who came to the United States in the years between 1890 and 1920. Most of these immigrants settled in America's growing cities.

Industrialization Changes Cities

🔻 **KEY QUESTION** How did industry and new inventions change society?

New materials and inventions helped speed industrial growth. This growth caused far-reaching changes in American society.

The Population Shifts to Cities The Industrial Revolution changed not just how people worked, but also where they worked. Since colonial days, most Americans had lived and worked in rural areas. In the late 1800s, more and more people moved to cities to find jobs.

Industries were drawn to cities that offered good transportation and plentiful workers. Increasing numbers of factory jobs became available in cities, followed by more workers to fill those jobs. The growth of cities that resulted from these changes is called **urbanization**.

Skyscrapers In the late 1800s, a new type of building called the skyscraper helped cities absorb millions of people. Skyscrapers looked tall enough to scrape the sky. They increased the amount of housing and workspace available within cities.

One invention that made it possible to build skyscrapers was the electric elevator. Before the 1860s, buildings were rarely more than four stories high because many people didn't want to climb more stairs than that. In 1889, Otis Elevator Company installed the first electric elevator. Buildings could now be more than a few stories tall.

The use of steel also helped engineers construct taller buildings. In 1885, the Home Insurance Building in Chicago boasted an iron and steel skeleton that could hold the immense weight of the skyscraper's floors and walls. The building climbed to ten stories. Skyscrapers changed city skylines forever.

Streetcars and Suburbs Just as electricity changed the way people lived inside buildings, it also changed the way they traveled around cities. Before industrialization, people walked or used horse-drawn vehicles to travel over land. But by 1900, electric streetcars in American cities were carrying more than 5 billion passengers a year.

CONNECT To History

CHINESE IMMIGRATION

Between 1849 and 1882, tens of thousands of Chinese immigrants came to America.

San Francisco's Chinatown before 1910

▶ **1849**
California Gold Rush attracts fortune-seekers who have heard that California is a "Gold Mountain."

▶ **1851–1864**
Taiping Rebellion in China causes widespread death, destruction and poverty.

▶ **1877–1878**
Drought in China ruins farms, creating hardship for millions.

▶ **1882**
Chinese Exclusion Act stops immigration of Chinese workers for 10 years; bans Chinese from U.S. citizenship.

CRITICAL THINKING Draw Conclusions Why did Chinese immigrants leave China?

By allowing workers to live further away from their jobs, public transportation helped new suburbs develop. It also helped cities expand. Some suburbs wanted to merge with the city that they bordered in order to be served by the city's transportation system. In 1889, Chicago annexed several suburbs and more than doubled its population and area.

▲ **CAUSES AND EFFECTS** Explain how industry and new inventions changed society.

The New Immigrants

▼ **KEY QUESTION** Who were the new immigrants and where did they settle in the United States?

Until the 1890s, most immigrants to the United States had come from northern and western Europe. But after 1896, immigrants came mainly from southern and eastern Europe, including southern Italy, Poland, and Russia. This later group became known as the "new immigrants."

An Italian immigrant family takes the Ellis Island ferry to Manhattan in 1905. **What process did immigrants go through on Ellis Island?**

New Arrivals For most European immigrants, **Ellis Island** was the first stop. There, they were processed before they could enter the United States. First, they had to pass a physical examination. Those with serious health problems were sent home. Immigrants who passed the physical were then asked for their name, occupation, and financial situation. In 1910, Asian immigrants began to land at **Angel Island** in San Francisco Bay. In Angel Island's filthy buildings, most Chinese immigrants were held for weeks. Many Mexican immigrants entered the United States through Texas.

Finding Work and Housing American cities such as New York, Boston, Philadelphia, and Chicago attracted immigrants with the promise of jobs. Newer immigrants looked for people from the old country to help them find jobs and housing. People with similar ethnic backgrounds often moved to the same neighborhoods. As a result, ethnic neighborhoods with names like "Little Italy" and "Chinatown" became common in American cities.

While European immigrants settled mostly in the East and Midwest, Asian immigrants settled mostly in the West. Many Chinese immigrants worked on the railroads. Others settled in western cities. Japanese immigrants first came to Hawaii in 1868 to work on sugar plantations. Others settled on the mainland where they commonly fished, farmed, or worked in mines.

Immigrants from Mexico came to the Southwest. Mexican immigration increased after 1910 when revolution in that country forced many people to flee. Many Mexican immigrants found work on ranches in California and Texas or in Arizona copper mines.

▲ **MAIN IDEA & DETAILS** Explain where the "new immigrants" came from and where they settled in America.

Reactions to Immigration

🔻 **KEY QUESTION** What did native-born Americans fear about immigration?

Immigrants were eager to become part of their new country. However, many native-born Americans regarded immigrants as a threat.

Americanization and Prejudice Some Americans have described the United States as a **melting pot,** or a place where cultures blend. The new immigrants blended into American society as earlier immigrants had. This process of blending into society is called **assimilation**. To assimilate, new immigrants studied English and how to be American citizens.

Many workers began to assimilate in order to get and retain work. Employers and labor unions both tried to "Americanize" immigrant workers by offering classes in citizenship and English. Yet, at the same time that immigrants were learning about America, they were also changing America. Immigrants did not give up their cultures completely. Bits and pieces of immigrant languages, foods, and music worked their way into the rest of American culture.

Despite their efforts to assimilate, immigrants faced prejudice from native-born Americans. Many Protestants feared the arrival of Catholics and Jews. Other native-born Americans thought immigrants would not fit into demo-

(*below*) New American citizens swear to uphold the Constitution at their citizenship ceremony in New York City, 2005.

CONNECT *Citizenship and History*

BECOMING A CITIZEN

Immigrants to the U.S. in 1900 as today went through the following naturalization process to become citizens:

- Declare an intention to become a U.S. citizen
- Renounce allegiance to foreign country
- Live in the United States for a specified period of time
- Petition the court to become a citizen
- Swear oath to uphold the U.S. Constitution

Today the process is more complex. Applicants need also to be able to read and write English, pass a test about the principles of U.S. government and the Constitution, and undergo a background check, among other requirements.

Activity

How Does Someone Become a Citizen?

1️⃣ In a small group, discuss what questions you would ask those seeking to become U.S. citizens.

2️⃣ Discuss the naturalization process. How has it changed since 1900? Why do you think it has changed?

📖 See Citizenship Handbook, pages 300–301.

cratic society because they would be controlled by politicians. Such prejudices led some native-born Americans to push for restrictions on the numbers of new immigrants.

Restrictions on Immigration Many native-born Americans also feared they would have to compete with immigrants for jobs. Immigrants often took whatever jobs they could get, working for long hours, low wages, and in unsafe conditions. Many found jobs in **sweatshops**—hot, crowded, dangerous factories—for about ten dollars a week.

Some Americans worried that there would not be enough jobs for everyone. These fears led to increased opposition to immigration. In 1882, Congress began to pass laws to restrict immigration. They placed taxes on new immigrants and banned specific groups, such as convicts and people with mental illness. Nonwhites faced deeper prejudice than European immigrants, and Asians faced some of the worst. In 1882, Congress passed the **Chinese Exclusion Act**. It banned Chinese immigration for ten years.

Immigration and Racism The Chinese Exclusion Act was not the only example of prejudice in America around 1900. Chinese immigrants who came to the West in the 1800s also faced severe discrimination. Chinese laborers received lower wages than whites for the same work. Sometimes, Chinese workers faced violence. In 1885, white workers in Rock Springs, Wyoming, refused to work in the same mine as Chinese workers. The whites stormed through the Chinese part of town, killing 28 Chinese people.

At the same time, Mexicans and African Americans who came to the American Southwest were forced into peonage. In this system of labor, people are forced to work until they have paid off debts. Congress outlawed peonage in 1867, but some workers were still forced to work to repay debts. In 1911, the U.S. Supreme Court declared such labor to be the same as peonage. As a result, the Court struck down such forms of labor as a violation of the Thirteenth Amendment.

🔺 **SUMMARIZE** Describe what native-born Americans feared about immigration.

(*top*) Many Jewish immigrants lived on Hester Street on New York's Lower East Side. (*bottom*) A pushcart vendor sells goods on Mulberry Street.
How did immigrants change American culture?

Problems of Urbanization

🔻 **KEY QUESTION** What problems were caused by urbanization?

The growing population of the cities led to overcrowding and disease. Soon political organizations and reformers were working to improve conditions.

History Makers

Jane Addams   1860–1935

Founding Hull House would have assured Jane Addams' place in history. Her remarkable career extended much further, however. She was also a leader in the women's suffrage movement. She was a founder of the National Association for the Advancement of Colored People (NAACP) and the American Civil Liberties Union (ACLU). She also founded the Women's International League of Peace and Freedom and served as its president from 1919 until 1935. In 1931, she became the first American woman to be awarded the Nobel Peace Prize for her work in promoting world peace. (She shared the prize with Nicholas Murray Butler.)

CRITICAL THINKING What obstacles do you think Jane Addams faced in her work promoting justice and peace?

 **ONLINE BIOGRAPHY**   For more on Jane Addams, go to the **Research & Writing Center** @ ClassZone.com

Urban Disasters and Slums   The concentration of people in cities increased the danger of disaster because people and buildings were packed closely together. For example, in 1906, a powerful earthquake rocked San Francisco, destroying the central business district and killing about 700 people.

Natural disasters were not the only danger for city dwellers. Poverty and disease also threatened lives. Many people lived in **tenements,** run-down and overcrowded apartment houses. Old buildings, landlord neglect, poor design, and little government control led to dangerous conditions in many tenements. Inadequate garbage pick-up also caused problems. Tenants sometimes dumped their smelly garbage into the narrow air shafts between tenements.

Many tenements had no running water. Residents had to collect water from a faucet on the street. The water could be heated for bathing, but it was often unsafe for drinking. Sewage flowed in open gutters and threatened to spread disease among tenement dwellers.

A neighborhood with such overcrowded, dangerous housing was called a **slum**. The most famous example was New York City's Lower East Side, but every city had slums.

Reformers Attack Urban Problems   Many Americans were disgusted by poverty and slums. Urban reformers fought for changes that would solve these problems. Some reformers opened settlement houses to help immigrants and the poor improve their lives. Settlement houses offered daycare, education, and health care to needy people in slums.

Many settlement house founders were educated middle-class women. **Jane Addams**, an urban reformer and suffrage leader, founded Chicago's **Hull House** in 1889 with Ellen Gates Starr. Hull House became a model for other settlement houses. In 1893, Lillian D. Wald founded the Henry Street Settlement House in New York.

Some reformers were inspired by the **social gospel movement**, which was based on Christian values and led by Protestant ministers. The movement worked for labor reforms, such as abolishing child labor.

Political Machines Run Cities Political machines were another type of organization that addressed the problems of the city. A **political machine** is an illegal gang that influences enough votes to control a local government. Political machines gained support by trading favors for votes. Machine bosses gave jobs, cash, or food to supporters. In return, supporters voted for the machine. Political machines did many other illegal things. They broke rules to win elections. They demanded bribes and used extortion, or threats, to affect government actions.

The most famous political machine was **Tammany Hall** in New York City. It was led by William Marcy Tweed. Along with his greedy friends, "Boss" Tweed stole enormous amounts of money from the city.

Despite such corruption, political machines did a number of good things. They built parks, sewers, schools, roads, and orphanages in many cities. Machine politicians often helped immigrants get settled by helping them find jobs or homes. Many immigrants gratefully supported the political machine after this kind of help.

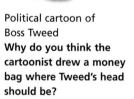

Political cartoon of Boss Tweed
Why do you think the cartoonist drew a money bag where Tweed's head should be?

▲ **PROBLEMS AND SOLUTIONS** Describe the problems caused by urbanization.

Michigan Grade Level Content Expectations *Review*

🖱 **ONLINE QUIZ**
For test practice, go to
Interactive Review @ ClassZone.com

TERMS & NAMES

1. Explain the importance of

- Ellis Island
- Angel Island
- melting pot
- assimilation
- Chinese Exclusion Act
- Jane Addams
- Hull House
- social gospel movement

USING YOUR READING NOTES

2. Causes and Effects Complete the diagram you started at the beginning of this section. Make a new diagram to list other causes and their effects.

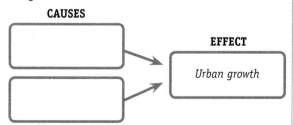

CAUSES

EFFECT

Urban growth

KEY IDEAS

3. How did streetcars change cities?

4. Why did many immigrants move to cities?

5. What was the Chinese Exclusion Act?

6. How did political machines and immigrants help each other?

CRITICAL THINKING

7. Causes and Effects How did industrial growth affect immigration?

8. Draw Conclusions How did urbanization change American society and politics?

9. Compare and Contrast Compare the challenges faced by the new immigrants from Europe to challenges faced by Asian immigrants.

10. Art Political Cartoon Draw a political cartoon that shows a reformer's solution to an urban problem in the late 19th century.

🖱 *Click here* to explore Ellis Island @ ClassZone.com

Gateway to America

Between 1892 and 1954, 12 million immigrants passed through the Ellis Island Immigration Station. Some immigrants stayed on Ellis Island for days or even weeks if they failed their health exams. Others waited for family members or money to arrive before they could travel to the mainland.

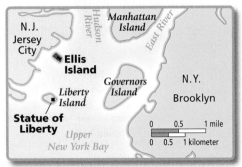

🖱 *Click here* Ferries took immigrants from piers on the mainland to Ellis Island.

🖱 *Click here* In the station cafeteria, immigrants could have their first taste of ice cream and other American dishes.

🖱 *Click here* After waiting for hours to be inspected, immigrants still had to wait in long lines to leave Ellis Island.

❸ After passing the inspections, immigrants were able to exchange money, send mail or telegrams, or buy train tickets.

❹ Immigrants often met relatives and loved ones at what became known as the "kissing post."

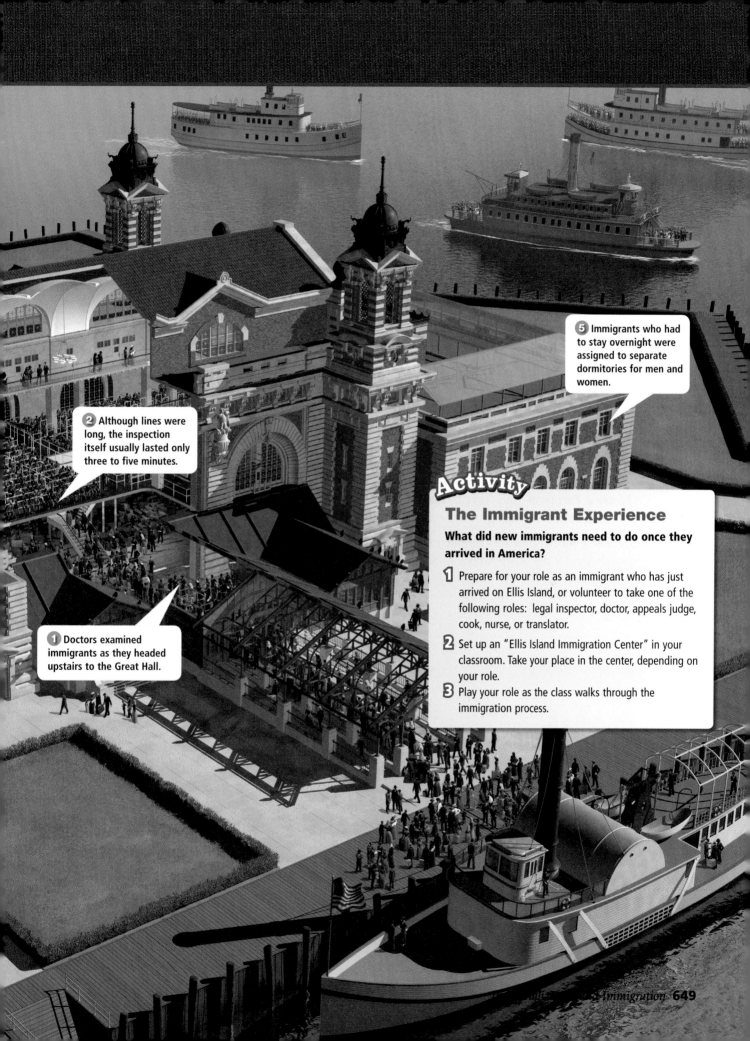

5 Immigrants who had to stay overnight were assigned to separate dormitories for men and women.

2 Although lines were long, the inspection itself usually lasted only three to five minutes.

1 Doctors examined immigrants as they headed upstairs to the Great Hall.

Activity

The Immigrant Experience

What did new immigrants need to do once they arrived in America?

1 Prepare for your role as an immigrant who has just arrived on Ellis Island, or volunteer to take one of the following roles: legal inspector, doctor, appeals judge, cook, nurse, or translator.

2 Set up an "Ellis Island Immigration Center" in your classroom. Take your place in the center, depending on your role.

3 Play your role as the class walks through the immigration process.

▶ Key Ideas

BEFORE, YOU LEARNED

Immigration and industrialization spurred the rapid growth of America's modern cities.

NOW YOU WILL LEARN

Segregation and discrimination against African Americans was commonplace in the years after the Civil War.

▶ Vocabulary

TERMS & NAMES

Jim Crow laws enacted in Southern states designed to separate white and black people

segregation the separation of races

Ida B. Wells African-American journalist who led the fight against lynching

Plessy v. Ferguson 1896 Supreme Court case that upheld the legality of segregation

Booker T. Washington African-American leader who did not believe in challenging segregation

W. E. B. Du Bois African-American leader who fought against segregation and for equal rights and who helped found the NAACP

NAACP National Association for the Advancement of Colored People

REVIEW

literacy the ability to read and write

lynch to kill by hanging without due process of the law

▶ Reading Strategy

Re-create a diagram like the one shown at right. As you read and respond to the **KEY QUESTIONS**, fill in the diagram. Add more fact boxes or create a new diagram as needed.

 See Skillbuilder Handbook, page R3.

SUMMARIZE

Jim Crow laws

Discrimination Against African Americans

GRAPHIC ORGANIZERS
Go to **Interactive Review** @ ClassZone.com

Discrimination Against African Americans

 8 – U6.1.1.6 America at Century's End – the treatment of African Americans, including the rise of segregation in the South as endorsed by the Supreme Court's decision in *Plessy* v. *Ferguson*, and the response of African Americans
8 – P3.1.1.5 Identify, research, analyze, discuss, and defend a position on a national public policy issue – Identify and apply core democratic values or constitutional principles.

An American Story

African-American sisters Sarah and Elizabeth Delany grew up in North Carolina in the early 20th century. Almost 100 years later, they described their first taste of racial discrimination, or different treatment on the basis of race.

Sisters Elizabeth and Sarah Delany

PRIMARY SOURCE

❝ We were about five and seven years old. . . . Mama and Papa used to take us to Pullen Park . . . and that particular day, the trolley driver told us to go to the back. We children objected loudly, because we always liked to sit in the front. . . . But Mama and Papa just gently told us to hush and took us to the back. ❞

—Sarah L. Delany and A. Elizabeth Delany, *Having Our Say*

As you will read in this section, racial discrimination was common throughout the United States in the late 1800s and early 1900s.

Racism Causes Discrimination

🔻 **KEY QUESTION** How did racism affect African Americans?

In America, many whites considered themselves superior to Asians, Native Americans, Latin Americans, and African Americans. Racist beliefs inspired acts of violence and racial discrimination. Some of the most widespread discrimination was directed against African Americans.

A History of Racism Racist attitudes toward African Americans had existed in America since the introduction of slavery. In colonial times, the low social rank held by slaves led many whites to assume that whites were superior to blacks. Reconstruction was a brief period when African Americans began to achieve equal rights in the South. However, when Reconstruction ended in 1877, white Southerners struck back sharply.

Segregation and Jim Crow Laws Whites weakened African-American political power by restricting their voting rights. Southern states passed laws that set up **literacy**, or reading, tests and poll taxes to prevent African Americans from voting. White officials made sure that blacks failed literacy tests by giving unfair exams. For example, white officials sometimes gave blacks tests written in Latin. Poll taxes kept many blacks from voting because they didn't have enough money to pay the tax.

Such laws threatened to prevent poor and uneducated whites from voting, too. To keep them from losing the vote, several Southern states added grandfather clauses to their constitutions. Grandfather clauses stated that a man could vote if he or an ancestor, such as a grandfather, had been eligible to vote before 1867. Before that date, most African Americans, free or enslaved, did not have the right to vote. Whites could use the grandfather clause to protect their voting rights. Blacks could not.

In addition to voting restrictions, African Americans faced **Jim Crow** laws. "Jim Crow" was a character in minstrel shows that made fun of African Americans. Jim Crow laws were meant to enforce **segregation**, or separation, of white and black people in public places. As a result, separate schools, trolley seats, and rest rooms were common in the South.

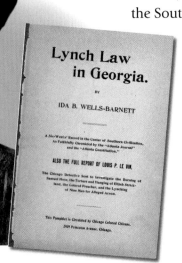

Journalist Ida B. Wells worked to end lynching. **Besides lynching, what else did whites do to keep African Americans from challenging segregation?**

Violence Increases Besides discrimination, African Americans in the South also faced violence. The Ku Klux Klan, which first appeared during Reconstruction, used terror and violence to keep blacks from challenging segregation. Between 1885 and 1900, more than 1,500 African Americans were **lynched**, or hanged without due process of the law.

Ida B. Wells, an African-American journalist from Memphis, led the fight against lynching. After three of her friends were lynched in 1892, she mounted an antilynching campaign in her newspaper. When whites called for Wells herself to be lynched, she moved to Chicago and continued her work against lynching.

Like Wells, some blacks moved north to escape discrimination. Although public facilities there were not segregated by law, Northern whites still discriminated against blacks. Blacks could not get housing in white neighborhoods and usually were denied good jobs. Anti-black feelings among whites sometimes led to violence. In 1908, whites in Springfield, Illinois, attacked blacks who had moved there. The whites lynched two blacks within a half mile of Abraham Lincoln's former home.

Plessy v. Ferguson African Americans resisted segregation, but they had little power to stop it. In 1892, Homer Plessy, an African American, sued a railroad company, arguing that segregated seating violated his Fourteenth Amendment right to "equal protection of the laws." The Supreme Court ruled that "separate but equal" facilities did not violate the Fourteenth Amendment. This decision allowed Southern states to maintain segregated institutions. The separate facilities were not equal. White-controlled governments and companies allowed the facilities for African Americans to decay. African Americans would have to organize to fight for equality.

▲ **CAUSES AND EFFECTS** Explain how racism affected African Americans.

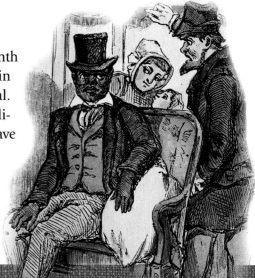

A white train passenger harasses an African-American passenger for sitting in the white section of the train.

Historic Decisions of the SUPREME COURT

Plessy v. Ferguson (1896)

KEY ISSUE Segregation in public facilities
KEY PEOPLE Homer Plessy   African-American shoemaker and activist
             John Ferguson   district court judge

The Case

In 1892, a group of African Americans arranged to challenge Louisiana's Separate Car Act, which legalized segregated seating on trains. They asked African-American shoemaker Homer Plessy to sit in a whites-only train car. As the challengers had expected, railroad officials arrested Plessy. In district court, Plessy's lawyer argued that segregated seating violated Plessy's rights to equal protection. Judge Ferguson ruled against Plessy, stating that Louisiana had the right to make its own laws for railroad travel within the state. Plessy appealed the decision to the U.S. Supreme Court.

The Court's Decision In 1896, the Supreme Court upheld Judge Ferguson's original ruling. Justice Henry B. Brown wrote that although segregation treated the races differently, it did not treat one race as legally inferior or unequal.

Historical Impact The *Plessy* ruling made "separate but equal" the law of the land. In fact, separate facilities were never equal. African Americans received inferior treatment. African-American school buildings were often poorly maintained. Teachers were not paid the same as teachers in white schools. There were fewer books and materials for students. Supreme Court Justice John Marshall Harlan wrote the only dissenting opinion in *Plessy v. Ferguson*. He warned that the "thin disguise" of separate but equal facilities would fool no one, "nor atone for the wrong this day done."

CRITICAL THINKING

1. **Causes and Effects** What effect did the Supreme Court's ruling on *Plessy* v. *Ferguson* have on segregation laws?

2. **Analyze Point of View** What do you think Justice Harlan meant when he said that the "thin disguise" of separate-but-equal facilities would fool no one?

African Americans Organize

▼ **KEY QUESTION** What two approaches did African-American leaders take in the face of segregation?

African Americans faced discrimination and violence with determination and courage. Two different leaders emerged from the African-American community. They had different ideas about how to respond to the problems faced by African Americans.

Two Leaders Booker T. Washington was an early leader in the effort to achieve equality. In 1881, he founded the Tuskegee Institute in Alabama to help African Americans learn teaching or trades as well as patience, enterprise, and thrift. Washington believed that this type of education would help African Americans gain their advancement through economic security. In

ONLINE BIOGRAPHY

For more on Washington and Du Bois go to the **Research & Writing Center** @ ClassZone.com

History Makers African-American Leaders

Booker T. Washington   1856–1915

Between 1895 and 1915, Washington was one of the nation's most prominent African-American educators and reformers. His position of compromise on segregation, known as the Atlanta Compromise, was embraced by moderate whites and most African Americans at the time. Many African Americans considered Washington their unofficial spokesperson. They looked to his self-help autobiography, *Up from Slavery*, as a guide for their own advancement.

W. E. B. Du Bois   1868–1963

In his 1903 essay collection, *The Souls of Black Folk*, Du Bois criticized the principles of the Atlanta Compromise and challenged Washington's leadership. Du Bois helped form the Niagara Movement, and in 1909, the National Association for the Advancement of Colored People (NAACP). Both groups demanded full civil and political rights for African Americans. As an NAACP board member and editor of its magazine, *The Crisis*, Du Bois was able to shape public opinion in the African-American community.

COMPARING *Leaders*

Draw Conclusions Which leader was more effective in advancing African-American civil rights? Explain your answer.

exchange for economic security, he thought that African Americans should not openly challenge segregation. He thought that whites and blacks could work together yet live separate social lives. Washington's position on segregation became known as the Atlanta Compromise.

W. E. B. Du Bois, a sociology professor, disagreed strongly with Booker T. Washington. He believed African Americans should fight against segregation. He also thought that industrial training would limit African Americans to inferior jobs. Instead, he pushed for higher education for the most able African Americans, which he called the "Talented Tenth." They were teachers, ministers, and professionals who would lead the struggle for equal rights.

In 1909, Du Bois, Jane Addams, and other reformers founded the National Association for the Advancement of Colored People, or the **NAACP**. The NAACP played a major role in ending segregation in the 20th century.

NAACP members march in Greenville, South Carolina, 2003.

 SUMMARIZE Explain why Du Bois and Washington disagreed about segregation.

Michigan Grade Level Content Expectations *Review*

ONLINE QUIZ For test practice, go to **Interactive Review** @ ClassZone.com

TERMS & NAMES

1. Explain the importance of

- Jim Crow
- Booker T. Washington
- segregation
- W. E. B. Du Bois
- Ida B. Wells
- NAACP
- *Plessy* v. *Ferguson*

USING YOUR READING NOTES

2. Summarize Complete the diagram you started at the beginning of the section. Add more fact boxes or create a new diagram as needed.

KEY IDEAS

3. How did Southerners keep African Americans from political power?

4. How did Ida Wells lead the fight against lynching?

5. What was the Atlanta Compromise?

CRITICAL THINKING

6. Make Inferences How do you think Jim Crow laws and the Ku Klux Klan kept African Americans from claiming their rights as American citizens?

7. Draw Conclusions Why did reformers form the NAACP?

8. **Connect** *to* **Today** Even though racial discrimination is against the law, do you think it is still a part of American society today? Explain.

▶ Key Ideas

BEFORE, YOU LEARNED

Segregation and discrimination against African Americans was commonplace in the years after the Civil War.

NOW YOU WILL LEARN

As business leaders guided industrial expansion, workers organized to gain their rights.

▶ Vocabulary

TERMS & NAMES

Knights of Labor an organization of workers from all trades formed after the Civil War

socialism system in which the state controls the economy

Haymarket Affair 1886 union protest

Samuel Gompers labor leader, founder of the American Federation of Labor (AFL)

American Federation of Labor (AFL) a national organization of labor unions founded in 1886 by Samuel Gompers

Homestead Strike violent strike at Andrew Carnegie's Homestead, Pennsylvania, steel mills in 1892

Pullman Strike nationwide railway strike that spread throughout the rail industry in 1894

Eugene V. Debs American Railway Union leader jailed in Pullman strike in 1894

BACKGROUND VOCABULARY

anarchist person who believes in a society that has no government at all

Visual Vocabulary
Haymarket Affair

▶ Reading Strategy

Re-create the diagram shown at right. As you read and respond to the **KEY QUESTIONS**, use the diagram to note major events in the labor movement between the Civil War and the 1900s. Add more boxes as needed.

 See Skillbuilder Handbook, page R5.

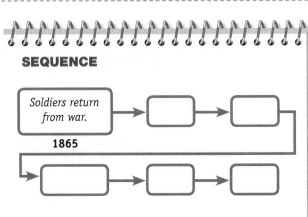

SEQUENCE

Soldiers return from war.

1865

GRAPHIC ORGANIZERS
Go to **Interactive Review** @ ClassZone.com

The Labor Movement

8 – U6.1.1.5 America at Century's End – economic change, including industrialization, increased global competition, and their impact on conditions of farmers and industrial workers

8 – U6.1.1.6 America at Century's End – the treatment of African Americans, including the rise of segregation in the South as endorsed by the Supreme Court's decision in *Plessy* v. *Ferguson*, and the response of African Americans

One American's Story

In 1867, Mary Harris Jones lost her husband and four children to yellow fever. Moving to Chicago, Jones started a dressmaking business. When she lost all she owned in the great Chicago fire of 1871, she found a cause to fight for.

PRIMARY SOURCE

❝From the time of the Chicago fire I . . . decided to take an active part in the efforts of the working people to better the conditions under which they worked and lived.❞

— Mary Harris Jones, *Autobiography of Mother Jones*

Jones became an effective labor leader who organized meetings, gave speeches, and helped strikers. Workers loved her so much that they called her Mother Jones.

Mother Jones won the love of working people by fighting for their rights.

Workers Organize

🔻 **KEY QUESTION** Why did workers organize?

As industrialization expanded, standards of living generally improved. However, workers suffered from dangerous conditions in the factories, low wages, and long hours. To improve conditions, workers began to organize.

Poor Working Conditions Workers faced a long list of problems. Among them were:

- 10–12-hour days
- no sick days
- unsafe and unhealthy working conditions
- low pay
- dull, repetitive jobs

Many business owners of the late 1800s ran their factories as cheaply as possible. Many omitted safety equipment to save money. For example, railroads would not buy air brakes or automatic train-car couplers even though about 30,000 railroad workers were injured and 2,000 killed every year.

Adults and children work in a food-processing factory.

In the 1880s, the average weekly wage was less than ten dollars. This barely paid a family's expenses. To get by, whole families worked, including young children. If a worker missed work due to illness or had unexpected bills, the family usually went into debt.

Workers often had little direct contact with business owners, who kept their distance from workers and their grievances. Workers began to feel that only other working people could understand their troubles. Discontented workers formed labor unions—groups of workers that negotiated with business owners to obtain better wages and working conditions.

Early Unions The first labor unions began in the mid-1800s but did not win many improvements for workers. After the Civil War, some unions formed national organizations such as the **Knights of Labor**. This was a loose federation of workers from different trades. Unlike many unions, the Knights of Labor allowed women and, after 1878, African-American workers to join.

Beginning in 1873, the United States fell into an economic depression. Over the next four years, millions of workers took pay cuts, and about one-fifth lost their jobs. In July 1877, the Baltimore and Ohio (B & O) Railroad declared a 10 percent wage cut. In response, B & O workers in Martinsburg, West Virginia, refused to run the trains. Workers in other cities joined in, throwing the country into turmoil. This work stoppage grew into the Railroad Strike of 1877. President Rutherford B. Hayes called out federal troops. Before the two-week strike ended, dozens of people had been killed.

The strike did not prevent the railroad pay cut, but it showed how angry American workers had become. In 1884–1885, railroaders went on strike again, this time against the Union Pacific and two other railroads. The strikers, members of the Knights of Labor, gained nationwide attention when they won their strike. Hundreds of thousands of workers joined the union.

Racism and the Unions Unions and industry leaders alike had racist policies. Many unions tried to exclude African-American workers from joining. Chinese laborers received lower wages than whites for the same work and sometimes faced violence from white coworkers. During strikes, industry leaders hired Chinese workers and other minorities who would work for less money than white workers.

▲ **SUMMARIZE** Explain why workers organized.

The Struggle Between Business and Labor

🔻 **KEY QUESTION** How did business leaders react to workers' demands?

The growth of labor unions frightened many business leaders. In the last decades of the 1800s, conflicts between business and labor grew bitter.

Union Setbacks Powerful unions could threaten business leaders' profits and their near-complete control of industry. In business leaders' fights with unions, they tried to portray union leaders as people with extreme, un-American ideas. They blamed the labor movement on socialists and anarchists. Socialists believe in **socialism**, a social system in which the means of producing and distributing goods is owned collectively or by a centralized government. **Anarchists** believe in anarchy, the abolition of all governments.

Business and government leaders tried to break union power. In Chicago in 1886, the McCormick Harvester Company locked out striking union members and hired strikebreakers to replace them. On May 3, union members, strikebreakers, and police clashed. One union member died.

The next day, union leaders called a protest meeting at Haymarket Square. As police moved in to end the meeting, an unknown person threw a bomb.

ANALYZING *Political Cartoons*

This cartoon, which appeared in 1883 before the Union Pacific strike of 1884–1885, draws a sharp comparison between powerful monopolies and the lowly working man.

Capitalists cheer for Monopoly.

Monopoly wears armor and wields a lance.

Monopoly's horse has train wheels instead of legs.

Workers cheer on Labor.

Labor rides a scrawny horse and has only a short hammer for a weapon.

"THE TOURNAMENT OF TODAY—A SET-TO BETWEEN LABOR AND MONOPOLY."

CRITICAL THINKING

1. **Draw Conclusions** Which side seems more likely to win? Explain your answer.

2. **Analyze** What point is the cartoonist trying to make about monopolies?

See Skillbuilder Handbook, page R24.

It killed 7 police and wounded about 60 people. The police then fired on the crowd, killing several people and wounding about 100 people. This conflict was called the **Haymarket Affair**. Afterward, the Chicago police arrested hundreds of union leaders, socialists, and anarchists. Opposition to unions increased and union membership dropped rapidly.

The Homestead and Pullman Strikes In 1886, the same year as the Haymarket Affair, **Samuel Gompers**, a labor leader, helped found a national organization of unions called the **American Federation of Labor** (AFL). He served as AFL president for 37 years. The AFL used negotiations, strikes, and boycotts to achieve its aims. By 1904 it had about 1.7 million members.

CONNECT to the Essential Question

What new problems and opportunities developed as America became an industrial power?

DEVELOPMENT	OPPORTUNITIES	PROBLEMS
Industrialization	• Provided job opportunities • Modern and efficient products • Leisure	• Pollution • Unhealthy, unsafe working conditions • Dull, repetitive jobs
Urban growth	• New leisure activities • People from different cultures lived in same communities	• Tenements and slums • Corruption and political machines
Segregation and discrimination	• Greater perceived opportunities for whites	• Injustice against African Americans and other non-whites • Betrayal of the promise of equality and freedom for all Americans
Immigration	• Cultural diversity • Millions of people took jobs and purchased goods in a growing economy	• Discrimination • Corruption from political machines
Corporations gain power	• Corporations raised large amounts of money by selling stock • Corporations turned inventions into new products	• Corporations turned into monopolies • Labor conflicts and strikes

CRITICAL THINKING Analyze What were some of the benefits of immigration?

Gompers' AFL had success, but national labor conflicts grew more bitter. In 1892 Andrew Carnegie reduced wages at his steel mills in Homestead, Pennsylvania. The union organized what became known as the **Homestead Strike**, so the company locked union workers out of the mills and hired nonunion labor as well as 300 armed guards. On July 6, a battle between the guards and the locked-out workers left ten people dead. The Pennsylvania state militia escorted the nonunion workers to the mills. After four months, the strike collapsed, breaking the union.

Workers lost another dispute in 1894. In that depression year, many railroad companies went bankrupt. To stay in business, the Pullman Palace Car Company cut workers' pay 25 percent. However Pullman did not lower the rent it charged workers to live in company housing. After rent was deducted from their pay, many Pullman workers took home almost nothing.

The Pullman workers began the **Pullman Strike**, a strike which spread throughout the rail industry in 1894. When the Pullman Company refused to negotiate, American Railway Union president **Eugene V. Debs** called on all U.S. railroad workers to refuse to handle Pullman cars. Rail traffic in much of the country stopped. President Grover Cleveland called out federal troops, which ended the strike. Debs was put in jail.

Political cartoon of Eugene V. Debs, American Railway Union President and leader of the Pullman Strike.

 CAUSES AND EFFECTS Describe how business leaders reacted to workers' demands.

Michigan Grade Level Content Expectations *Review*

 ONLINE QUIZ
For test practice, go to **Interactive Review @ ClassZone.com**

TERMS & NAMES

1. Explain the importance of the following

- Knights of Labor
- American Federation of Labor (AFL)
- socialism
- Homestead Strike
- Haymarket Affair
- Pullman Strike
- Samuel Gompers
- Eugene V. Debs

USING YOUR READING NOTES

2. Sequence Complete the diagram you started at the beginning of the section. Which events were setbacks for labor?

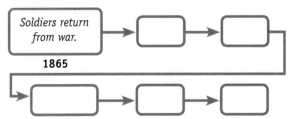

KEY IDEAS

3. What injustices did American workers face in the last decades of the 1800s?

4. What happened in the Pullman Strike?

5. What organization did Samuel Gompers lead?

CRITICAL THINKING

6. Main Idea & Details What was significant about the Railroad Strike of 1877?

7. Draw Conclusions Why do you think the government usually sided with industry in its struggle with early labor unions?

8. Problems and Solutions What were some of the ways that the American Federation of Labor tried to solve workers' problems?

9. Writing Article Write a newspaper article that tells the story of the Haymarket Affair in your own words.

Reading for Understanding

▶ Key Ideas

BEFORE, YOU LEARNED

As business leaders guided industrial expansion, workers organized to gain rights.

NOW YOU WILL LEARN

Industrialization and new technology created a mass culture in the United States.

▶ Vocabulary

TERMS & NAMES

mass culture common culture experienced by a large number of people

Joseph Pulitzer newspaper publisher, owner of the *New York World*

William Randolph Hearst newspaper publisher, owner of *New York Morning Journal*

vaudeville live entertainment that featured song, dance, and comedy

ragtime type of music that blended African-American songs and European musical forms

BACKGROUND VOCABULARY

leisure freedom from time-consuming duties

consumer person who buys something

Visual Vocabulary
vaudeville

▶ Reading Strategy

Re-create the diagram shown at right. As you read and respond to the **KEY QUESTIONS**, use the diagram to identify the effect of immigration on publishing and education. Add more boxes or create a new diagram as needed.

 See Skillbuilder Handbook, page R7.

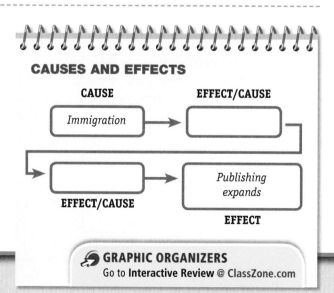

CAUSES AND EFFECTS

CAUSE → EFFECT/CAUSE

Immigration →

→

Publishing expands

EFFECT/CAUSE

EFFECT

🐭 **GRAPHIC ORGANIZERS**
Go to **Interactive Review** @ ClassZone.com

Society and Mass Culture

8 – U4.3.1 Explain the origins of the American education system and Horace Mann's campaign for free compulsory public education.

One American's Story

Schools around 1900 were very different from present-day schools. Classes were large. Most learning was done by memorization and repetition.

PRIMARY SOURCE

A student in the back row stands to recite a lesson at a New York City grammar school, c. 1870.

❝ I learned arithmetic and penmanship and spelling—every misspelled word written ten times or more, traced painfully and carefully in my blankbook . . . In this same way I learned how to read in English, learned geography and grammar . . . Most learning was done in unison. You recited to the teacher standing at attention. ❞

— Leonard Covello, *The Heart Is the Teacher*

Discipline was a key goal of education in the 1800s. In this section, you will learn how education also helped create an American **mass culture**—a common culture experienced by large numbers of people.

Education and Publishing Expand

🔽 **KEY QUESTION** What caused education and publishing to expand?

In the late 19th century, industrialization and urbanization created a new kind of society. Urban populations grew, and industrialization helped create cheaper goods and more **leisure**, or freedom from time-consuming duties. Public education also expanded and more students learned to read.

Changes in Schooling Immigration caused enormous growth in American schools. To teach citizenship and English to immigrants, new city and state laws required children to attend school. Between 1880 and 1920, the number of children attending school more than doubled.

Literacy Increases The growth of education increased the number of American readers. Reading became more popular and led to the growth of publishing, the industry that produces books, magazines, and newspapers. Americans read large numbers of novels. Dime novels were especially popular. They sold for ten cents each and told exciting tales.

Americans also read more newspapers. Tough competition pushed newspaper publishers to try all sorts of gimmicks to outsell their rivals. For example, **Joseph Pulitzer**, owner of the *New York World*, and **William Randolph Hearst**, owner of the *New York Morning Journal*, were fierce competitors. They filled their pages with dramatic stories and special features, such as comics.

🔺 **CAUSES AND EFFECTS** Explain why education and publishing expanded in the late 19th century.

Pleasures of the Consumer Society

🔻 **KEY QUESTION** How did Americans spend their leisure time in the late 1800s?

In the late 1800s, American **consumers** could buy new products and experience new forms of entertainment. Movies, music, sports, and advertising combined to shape modern American mass culture.

Daily Life

Fun at Coney Island

In the late 19th century, New York City's Coney Island was the nation's most famous amusement park. It was known for its plush seaside hotels, boardwalk, hot dogs, roller coasters, rides, and many other amusements. In 1884, fun seekers could ride the nation's first roller coaster, the Switchback Railway, for a nickel. One immigrant woman said Coney Island "is just like what I see when I dream of heaven!" Indeed, Coney Island's Dreamland park opened in 1904.

CRITICAL VIEWING Analyze Based on the pictures above, what kind of leisure activities did people take part in when they went to Coney Island?

Modern Advertising and New Products The rise of modern advertising in newspapers had a wide influence on American life. Advertising made people aware of new products and of places where they could buy them. Department stores were a new type of store that sold everything from clothing to furniture to hardware. People who did not live near a department store could use mail-order catalogs to order goods.

Mass Culture Leisure activities also changed. Cities had new parks, where city dwellers could stroll wooded walkways, ride bikes, and play sports. Amusement parks had shops, food vendors, and exciting rides such as roller coasters. Between 1876 and 1915, Philadelphia, Chicago, St. Louis, and San Francisco hosted world's fairs. Visitors were drawn to foods, shows, and amusements.

Ragtime music program

Baseball was the most popular sport, but racial discrimination kept African-American baseball players out of baseball's American and National Leagues. African Americans formed their own teams in the Negro leagues. Other forms of live entertainment included **vaudeville**, a mixture of song, dance, and comedy. **Ragtime**, a type of music that blended African-American songs and European musical forms, also became popular.

 MAIN IDEAS & DETAILS Describe how Americans spent their leisure time in the late 1800s.

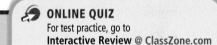

Michigan Grade Level Content Expectations *Review*

ONLINE QUIZ
For test practice, go to
Interactive Review @ ClassZone.com

TERMS & NAMES

1. Explain the importance of:
- mass culture
- Joseph Pulitzer
- William Randolph Hearst
- vaudeville
- ragtime

USING YOUR READING NOTES

2. Analyzing Causes Complete the diagram you started at the beginning of this section. Add more boxes or start a new diagram as needed.

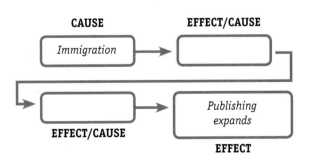

CAUSE

Immigration

EFFECT/CAUSE

EFFECT/CAUSE

Publishing expands

EFFECT

KEY IDEAS

3. What were the connections between newspapers, advertising, and mass culture?

4. What were some of the new forms of entertainment that Americans began to enjoy in the late 1800s?

CRITICAL THINKING

5. Compare and Contrast What is the difference between vaudeville and ragtime?

6. Cause and Effect How did urbanization change leisure activities?

7. Connect to Today What leisure activities from the end of the 1800s are still popular today?

8. Writing Postcard Write a postcard to a friend describing some of the amusements at Coney Island in the late 1800s.

Dragonwings by Laurence Yep

From 1900 to 1914, close to 30,000 Chinese immigrants made the difficult journey to the United States to seek employment and a new life. In *Dragonwings*, Laurence Yep brings that era to life through the experiences of Moon Shadow, a young Chinese boy new to America. As Moon Shadow struggles to find his place in the new land, he grapples with conflicts involving traditional Chinese values, the authority of the police, and mainstream American culture. In this scene, Moon Shadow recalls his early desire to know more about America, where his father has gone to seek work. Based on what he has heard of this distant country, Moon Shadow describes America as both "the land of the Golden Mountain" and "the demon land."

Ever since I can remember, I had wanted to know about the Land of the Golden Mountain, but my mother had never wanted to talk about it. All I knew was that a few months before I was born, my father had left our home in the Middle Kingdom, or *China*, as the white demons call it, and traveled over the sea to work in the demon land. There was plenty of money to be made among the demons, but it was also dangerous. My own grandfather had been lynched about thirty years before by a mob of white demons almost the moment he had set foot on their shores.

Mother usually said she was too busy to answer my questions. It was a fact that she was overworked, for Grandmother was too old to help her with the heavy work, and she had to try to do both her own work and Father's on our small farm. The rice had to be grown from seeds, and the seedlings transplanted to the paddies, and the paddies tended and harvested. Besides this, she always had to keep one eye on our very active pig to keep him from rooting in our small vegetable patch. She also had to watch our three chickens, who loved to wander away from our farm.

Any time I brought up the subject of the Golden Mountain, Mother suddenly found something going wrong on our farm. Maybe some seedlings had not been planted into their underwater beds properly, or perhaps our pig was eating the wrong kind of garbage, or maybe one of our chickens was dirtying our doorway. She always had some good excuse for

not talking about the Golden Mountain. I knew she was afraid of the place, because every chance we got, she would take me into the small temple in our village and we would pray for Father's safety, though she would never tell me what she was afraid of. It was a small satisfaction to her that our prayers had worked so far. Mother was never stingy about burning incense for Father.

I was curious about the Land of the Golden Mountain mainly because my father was there. I had, of course, never seen my father. And we could not go to live with him for two reasons. For one thing, the white demons would not let wives join their husbands on the Golden Mountain because they did not want us settling there permanently. And for another thing, our own clans discouraged wives from leaving because it would mean an end to the money the husbands sent home to their families—money which was then spent in the Middle Kingdom. The result was that wives stayed in the villages, seeing their husbands every five years or so if they were lucky—though sometimes there were longer separations, as with Mother and Father.

- -

ADDITIONAL READING

The Chinese American Family Album, by Dorothy and Thomas Hoobler. Period photos and original documents let Chinese immigrants speak for themselves.

To the Golden Mountain: The Story of the Chinese Who Built the Transcontinental Railroad, by Lila Perl. Chinese immigrants join the gold rush, build a railroad, and endure the Exclusion Act.

Chapter Summary

① Key Idea
New inventions and corporations created the Gilded Age of industrial growth and great wealth for a few.

② Key Idea
Immigration and industrialization spurred the rapid growth of America's cities.

③ Key Idea
Segregation and discrimination against African Americans was commonplace in the years after the Civil War.

④ Key Idea
As business leaders guided industrial expansion, workers organized to gain their rights.

⑤ Key Idea
Industrialization and new technology created a mass culture in the United States.

For detailed Review and Study Notes go to **Interactive Review** @ ClassZone.com

Name Game

Use the Terms & Names list to complete each sentence online or on your own paper.

1. I invented the telephone. ____
   Alexander Graham Bell

2. Standard Oil was my company. ____

3. ____ looked tall enough to scrape the sky.

4. In 1910, Asian immigrants began to land on ____ in San Francisco.

5. I was a journalist who worked to end lynching. ____

6. I challenged Louisiana's Separate Cars Act. ____

7. I founded the American Federation of Labor. ____

8. The ____ was an 1886 union protest.

9. ____ featured a popular mixture of song, dance, and comedy.

10. I disagreed with Booker T. Washington about segregation. ____

A. Ida B. Wells
B. Homer Plessy
C. W. E. B. Du Bois
D. Alexander Graham Bell
E. Ellis Island
F. Skyscrapers
G. Vaudeville
H. Joseph Pulitzer
I. Angel Island
J. Ragtime
K. John D. Rockefeller
L. Mother Jones
M. Samuel Gompers
N. Haymarket Affair
O. Thomas Edison

Activities

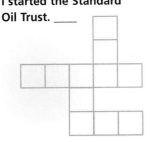

CROSSWORD PUZZLE

Complete the online puzzle to show what you know about industrialization and immigration.

ACROSS
1. I started the Standard Oil Trust. ____

FLIPCARD

Use the online flipcards to quiz yourself on the terms and names introduced in this chapter.

Ellis Island was our first
stop before entering
the United States.

ANSWER
The new immigrants

VOCABULARY

Match the name in the left-hand column with a phrase on the right.

1. Lewis Latimer
2. Jane Addams
3. Booker T. Washington
4. Samuel Gompers
5. Joseph Pulitzer

a. labor leader
b. African-American inventor
c. social reformer, founder of Hull House
d. newspaper owner
e. African-American educator

Explain how the terms and names in each group are related.

6. Ida B. Wells, W. E. B. Du Bois, NAACP
7. Ellis Island, Angel Island, Chinese Exclusion Act
8. Knights of Labor, Haymarket Affair, Homestead Strike

Ida Wells

KEY IDEAS

1 **America Enters the Industrial Age (pages 630–637)**

9. How did Edison's inventions change industry?
10. What advantages does a corporation have over a privately owned business?

2 **Immigration and Modern Urban Growth (pages 640–641)**

11. What causes led to urbanization in the late 1800s?
12. Why were many Americans opposed to immigration?

3 **Discrimination Against African Americans (pages 650–655)**

13. How did Southern whites keep African Americans from voting?
14. What was decided in the case of *Plessy* v. *Ferguson*?

4 **The Labor Movement (pages 656–661)**

15. Why did business owners resist the growth of unions?
16. What was the American Federation of Labor (AFL)?

5 **Society and Mass Culture (pages 662–665)**

17. How did immigration affect American education?
18. How did Americans use leisure in the years around 1900?

CRITICAL THINKING

19. **Causes and Effects** How did abundant natural resources and new means of transportation affect the growth of industry in the United States?

20. **Make Generalizations** What obstacles did immigrants face in trying to make a life in the United States?

21. **Analyze Point of View** What social and historical factors do you think caused Booker T. Washington to take the approach to segregation that he did?

22. **Draw Conclusions** How did the great wealth of some business leaders affect workers' attitudes towards joining unions?

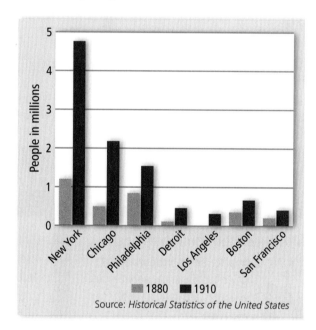

Source: *Historical Statistics of the United States*

23. **Analyze Graphs** Use the graph and your knowledge of American history to explain why most cities more than or nearly doubled in population between 1880 and 1910.

MEAP PRACTICE

✓ TEST PRACTICE
• Online Test Practice @ ClassZone.com
• Use the **MEAP Strategies & Practice,**
pages S1–S27, at the front of this book

DOCUMENT-BASED QUESTIONS

Analyze each document, and answer the question that follows.

DOCUMENT 1

DOCUMENT 2

PRIMARY SOURCE

❝ . . . I believe it is my duty to make money and still more money and to use the money I make for the good of my fellow man according to the dictates of my conscience. ❞

—John D. Rockefeller

1 Examine the cartoon and primary source. Some people did **NOT** like John D. Rockefeller's way of doing business because

  A he wiped out his competition.

  B he gave away too much of his money.

  C he lowered the price of oil.

  D he opposed trusts.

YOU BE THE HISTORIAN

24. Causes and Effects How did the growth of public transportation in cities lead to the leisure activities that became popular in American cities?

25. Draw Conclusions How did inventions in the period from 1870–1910 change American life?

26. Causes and Effects Why did immigrants settle in cities?

27. Compare and Contrast Compare and contrast the experiences of newly arrived immigrants in American cities with the experiences of African Americans who moved to northern cities in the Great Migration.

28. **Connect** *to* **Today** What political changes have improved working conditions for American workers over the last 100 years?

 Answer the

ESSENTIAL QUESTION

What new problems and opportunities developed as America became an industrial power?

Written Response Write a two- to three-paragraph response to the Essential Question. Consider the key ideas of each section and the impact that industrial growth had on workers. Use the rubric below to guide your writing.

Response Rubric
A strong response will

• discuss the struggle for power between business owners and workers

• evaluate the impact of industrialization on immigration

• analyze the way inventions and industry changed American life

The Progressive Era

1890–1920

 ESSENTIAL QUESTION

How did Americans benefit from progressive reforms?

CONNECT Geography & History

Why do you think some states allowed woman suffrage before other states?

Think about:

1 the location of most of the states that did not have woman suffrage

2 what the Western states have in common

Suffragist marching

Theodore Roosevelt helped preserve the wilderness in the West.

1890

Congress passes Sherman Antitrust Act.

▼

Effect Enables government to prevent one company from controlling an entire industry.

1901 President William McKinley is assassinated.

▼

Effect Vice President Theodore Roosevelt becomes president.

1903 Wisconsin becomes the first state to have a direct primary.

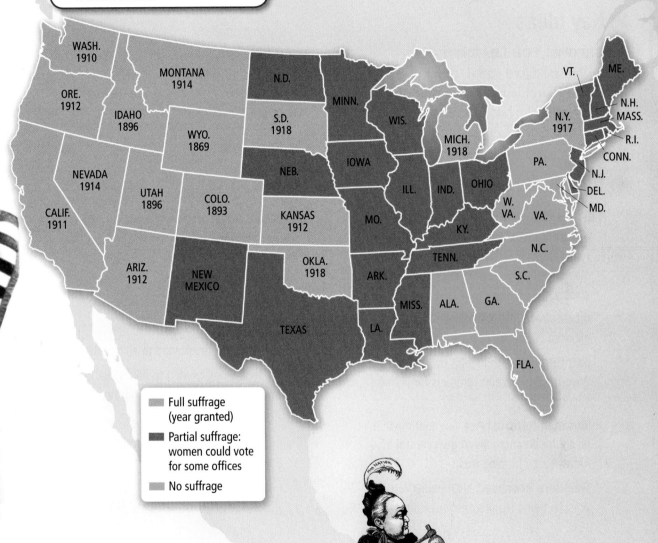

Animated GEOGRAPHY & HISTORY
Woman Suffrage *1919*

Click here to preview the Progressive Era
@ClassZone.com

WASH.
1910

ORE.
1912

IDAHO
1896

MONTANA
1914

N.D.

S.D.
1918

WYO.
1869

NEVADA
1914

UTAH
1896

COLO.
1893

NEB.

KANSAS
1912

CALIF.
1911

ARIZ.
1912

NEW
MEXICO

OKLA.
1918

TEXAS

MINN.

WIS.

IOWA

MICH.
1918

ILL.

IND.

OHIO

MO.

W.
VA.

KY.

ARK.

TENN.

MISS.

ALA.

GA.

LA.

PA.

VT.

N.Y.
1917

N.J.

DEL.

MD.

VA.

N.C.

S.C.

FLA.

ME.

N.H.

MASS.

R.I.

CONN.

■ Full suffrage
(year granted)

■ Partial suffrage:
women could vote
for some offices

■ No suffrage

Prohibitionist Carry Nation

1906 Roosevelt
signs the Pure Food
and Drug Act.

The Pure Food and
Drug Act made it
illegal for advertisers
to make false claims
about food and drugs.

1912 Woodrow
Wilson is elected
president.

1914 Congress passes
Clayton Antitrust Act.
▼
Effect Encourages
competition among businesses.

1919 Eighteenth
Amendment outlaws
alcohol.

1920

Nineteenth
Amendment
grants women
the right to vote.

The Progressive Era **671**

Reading for Understanding

▶ Key Ideas

BEFORE, YOU LEARNED

Americans faced social, economic, and political problems as the result of rapid changes in the last half of the 1800s.

NOW YOU WILL LEARN

Progressive reformers promoted social welfare, expanded democracy, and created economic reform.

▶ Vocabulary

TERMS & NAMES

progressivism (pruh•GREHS•ih•VIHZ•uhm) reform movements that sought to raise living standards and correct wrongs in American society

muckraker (MUHK•RAYK•er) writer who exposed corruption in American society

patronage (PA•truh•nihj) exchanging government jobs and contracts for political support

Sherman Antitrust Act law that made it illegal for corporations to gain control of industries by forming trusts

Theodore Roosevelt (ROH•zuh•VEHLT) president who led progressive reforms

BACKGROUND VOCABULARY

direct primary primary in which voters, not party conventions, choose candidates to run for public office

conservation controlling resource usage

REVIEW

civil rights rights granted to all citizens

trust legal body created to hold stock in many companies in the same industry

▶ Reading Strategy

Re-create the diagram shown here. As you read and respond to the **KEY QUESTIONS**, use the diagram to list details about each type of progressive reform. Add ovals or start a new diagram as needed.

 See Skillbuilder Handbook, page R4.

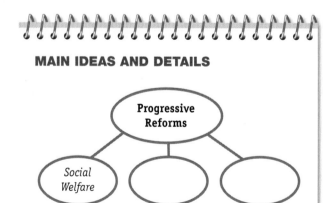

MAIN IDEAS AND DETAILS

Progressive Reforms

Social Welfare

GRAPHIC ORGANIZERS
Go to **Interactive Review** @ ClassZone.com

Roosevelt and Progressivism

8 – P3.1.1.1 Identify, research, analyze, discuss, and defend a position on a national public policy issue – Identify a national public policy issue.
8 – P3.1.1.2 Identify, research, analyze, discuss, and defend a position on a national public policy issue – Clearly state the issue as a question of public policy orally or in written form.

One American's Story

Nellie Bly worked as a reporter. In 1887, she faked mental illness so that she could become a patient at a women's asylum (uh•SY•luhm) in New York. Afterward, Bly wrote a newspaper article about what she had witnessed. She described being forced to take ice cold baths.

PRIMARY SOURCE

❝ My teeth chattered and my limbs were goose-fleshed and blue with cold. Suddenly I got, one after the other, three buckets of water over my head—ice-cold water, too, into my eyes, my ears, my nose, and my mouth. **❞**

—Nellie Bly, quoted in *Nellie Bly: Daredevil, Reporter, Feminist*

Bly reported that nurses choked and beat patients. Shortly after her stories appeared, conditions at the asylum improved.

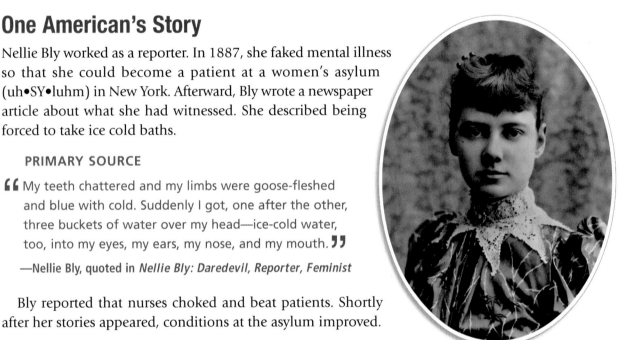

Nellie Bly

The Rise of Progressivism

🔽 **KEY QUESTION** What problems did reformers seek to solve?

Bly was not the only one who wanted to correct society's wrongs. By the end of the 19th century and the beginning of the 20th century, Americans faced many problems as a result of the rapid growth of cities and industry. To attack these problems, some Americans organized political and social reform movements that came to be grouped under the label **progressivism**. Progressive reformers shared at least one of three basic goals: to promote social welfare; to expand democracy; and to create economic reform.

Writers Expose Corruption The progressive movement was helped by a new group of journalists who emerged around 1900. These journalists were called **muckrakers** because they tried to discover muck, or corruption, in society. The muckrakers fueled public demand for reform.

Promoting Social Reform Social reformers wanted to help the poor, the unemployed, immigrants, and workers. Some reformers started community centers that provided educational and employment services to immigrants and the poor. They also promoted minimum wage laws, limits on working hours, and help for the unemployed. Prohibitionists were reformers who worked to prevent the manufacture, sale, and transport of alcohol. The prohibitionists expanded the temperance movement of the 1800s.

Expanding Democracy Progressives wanted qualified workers to get government jobs based on their merits. Instead, officials often handed out jobs in exchange for political support. This practice was called **patronage**. The Pendleton Civil Service Act of 1883 forced candidates for some government jobs to pass an exam. The act also prevented officials from firing workers for political reasons.

Progressives thought officials would be more responsive to voters' interests if voters were directly involved in the government. In 1903, Wisconsin became the first state to have a **direct primary**, in which voters could choose candidates for public office. In Oregon, progressives pushed for direct primaries and three other democratic reforms:

- **Initiative** Voters may directly propose laws.
- **Referendum** Voters can approve proposed laws.
- **Recall** Elected officials can be voted out of office.

CONNECT ⟳ *Citizenship and History*

COMMUNITY SERVICE

Since the United States began, citizens have shared concerns about their communities. Many citizens, such as Jane Addams, have identified problems and helped to solve them.

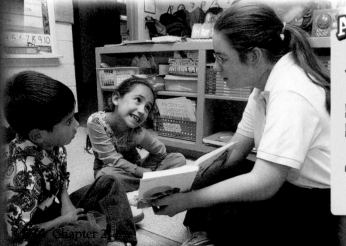

Eighth-grader Kelli Collins reads to first graders as part of National Youth Service Day, 2004.

Young citizens help their communities solve problems, too. National and Global Youth Service Day is a yearly event during which millions of students around the world design and lead service projects. Projects have included helping the elderly, protecting the environment, and providing food for the hungry. In Roswell, New Mexico, Kelli Collins and other middle school students read to first-graders regularly as part of a literacy project.

Activity

How do you help your community?

1 In a small group, think about needs within your community. Make a list of those needs and choose one need to work on.

2 Gather information about the need.

3 After you gather information, brainstorm solutions. Create a plan to carry out one solution.

4 Present the need and your plan to the class.

 See Citizenship Handbook, page 306.

Creating Economic Reform Progressive reformers wanted to limit the power of big business and regulate its activities. By the late 1800s, business leaders in some major industries had formed **trusts**. The businesses in a trust worked together to cut prices and squeeze out competitors. Then the trust would raise prices and make larger profits.

The **Sherman Antitrust Act** of 1890 made it illegal for corporations to gain control of industries by forming trusts. However, the government did not enforce the law at first. Enforcement required a strong president.

▲ **PROBLEMS AND SOLUTIONS** Identify problems that progressive reformers wanted to solve.

Theodore Roosevelt's Square Deal

▼ **KEY QUESTION** What was Roosevelt's square deal?

Young **Theodore Roosevelt** led daring exploits in Cuba during the Spanish-American War. He returned a hero and became governor of New York in 1898. Only two years later, in 1900, Roosevelt became vice-president under William McKinley during McKinley's second term as president. However, McKinley died just six months later. In 1901, at the age of 42, Roosevelt became the youngest president the nation had ever had.

Roosevelt—A Born Reformer Roosevelt entered politics when he was just 23 years old and quickly became known for fighting corrupt political machines in New York. When Roosevelt became president, he turned his fight against corruption into a policy. Roosevelt felt government's purpose was to ensure fairness, or a "square deal," for workers, consumers, and big business.

PRIMARY SOURCE

❝ When I say I believe in a square deal I do not mean, and nobody who speaks the truth can mean, that he believes it possible to give every man the best hand. . . . All I mean is that there shall not be any crookedness in the dealing. ❞

—Theodore Roosevelt, speech on April 5, 1905

History Makers

Theodore Roosevelt 1858–1919

Theodore Roosevelt was one of the most popular, controversial, and important presidents of the United States. Roosevelt was the first reformer president of the modern era. Many Americans, politicians and citizens alike, were afraid of the federal government gaining too much power. Not Roosevelt—he said, "I believe in a strong executive; I believe in power." He used the power of the presidency to strengthen business regulation, support labor unions, promote social welfare, and conserve natural resources and wilderness. He also made the United States a major force in international affairs in the Western Hemisphere, Europe, and the Far East.

CRITICAL THINKING

Connect *to* **Today** How do you think Theodore Roosevelt would address today's problems with the environment and conservation?

ONLINE BIOGRAPHY For more on Theodore Roosevelt, go to the **Research & Writing Center** @ ClassZone.com

Roosevelt began his reforms against "crookedness" by enforcing the Sherman Antitrust Act. Roosevelt was not against big business. However, he thought that industries should be regulated for the public good and he opposed any trust that he thought worked against the national interest.

At the end of 1901, the nation's railroads were run by only a few companies. The power of railroads continued to grow. It was not surprising, therefore, that one of Roosevelt's first targets was the railroads. He used the Sherman Antitrust Act to dissolve a railroad trust. Roosevelt also broke up the Standard Oil Company and a tobacco trust. During Roosevelt's presidency, the government filed suit against 44 corporations for antitrust violations.

Protecting Consumers Roosevelt became concerned about the meat-packing industry after reading Upton Sinclair's (UHP•tuhn sihn•KLAIR) *The Jungle*. The novel describes a packing plant in which dead rats end up in the sausage. Sinclair originally wanted to expose the poor sanitary conditions in which the meat-packers worked. Roosevelt launched an investigation of the meat-packing industry. In 1906, he signed the Meat Inspection Act. This act created a government meat inspection program. Roosevelt also signed the Pure Food and Drug Act. This law banned the sale of impure foods and medicines.

Conserving Natural Resources Roosevelt was a strong crusader for **conservation**—controlling how America's natural resources were used. Roosevelt preserved 194 million acres of public lands, including the Grand Canyon in Arizona, California's Muir Woods, and the country's first wildlife refuge at Pelican Island, Florida. He also created the U.S. Forest Service.

🔺 **EVALUATE** Name the accomplishments of Roosevelt's square deal.

Grand Canyon National Park, Arizona
What effect did Roosevelt's conservation policies have on the Grand Canyon?

Roosevelt's Civil Rights Dilemma

🔻 **KEY QUESTION** What was Roosevelt's civil rights dilemma?

While Roosevelt tried to win a square deal for most Americans, he did not push for civil rights for African Americans. However, he personally felt that everyone should be treated fairly based on merit, regardless of race.

A Man of His Time Roosevelt, like other people of his time, did not believe in African-American suffrage. Yet some of his views on race relations were different from those of the average American. He believed that given the same opportunities as white Americans, African Americans would achieve equality. During Roosevelt's first term as president, he appointed African Americans to Southern political offices, and denounced lynching.

Fierce Opposition On October 16, 1901, Roosevelt invited Booker T. Washington, founder of the Tuskegee (tuhs•KEE•gee) Institute, to stay for dinner after meeting at the White House. No other president had invited an African American to the White House. But Roosevelt decided to break precedent.

While African Americans saw the dinner as a great step towards racial equality, it angered many Southerners. Many Northern newspapers supported the dinner, while a newspaper in Memphis, Tennessee called the dinner an "outrage." Roosevelt told Washington that he did not care what his critics said. Privately, the president worried that the dinner had hurt his chances for re-election. He never asked an African American to a White House dinner again.

Although Roosevelt was re-elected, he did no more to advance civil rights for African Americans. Roosevelt made no statement on the Atlanta race riot of 1906. He also discharged a large group of African American soldiers for allegedly conspiring to protect fellow African American soldiers wrongly accused of murder in Brownsville, Texas.

Booker T. Washington dined with President Theodore Roosevelt at the White House. **Why was the dinner supported by some people and condemned by others?**

 MAIN IDEAS & DETAILS Explain Roosevelt's civil rights dilemma.

Michigan Grade Level Content Expectations *Review*

 ONLINE QUIZ
For test practice, go to
Interactive Review @ ClassZone.com

TERMS & NAMES

1. Explain the importance of

- progressivism
- Sherman Antitrust Act
- muckraker
- Theodore Roosevelt
- patronage

USING YOUR READING NOTES

2. Main Ideas and Details Complete the diagram you started at the beginning of this section. Then write a one-sentence summary of the most important points of this section.

KEY IDEAS

3. How did progressives seek to expand democracy?

4. Explain how Theodore Roosevelt used his presidential power to further progressive reforms.

CRITICAL THINKING

5. Analyze Primary Sources What did Theodore Roosevelt mean when he said he believed in a "square deal"?

6. **Connect** *to* **Today** In what ways do the reforms that President Roosevelt promoted affect your life today?

7. **Writing** News Story In the role of a muckraker, write a short news story about a need in your community.

▶ Key Ideas

BEFORE, YOU LEARNED
Progressive reformers promoted social welfare, expanded democracy, and created economic reform.

NOW YOU WILL LEARN
Progressive reforms continued under Presidents William Howard Taft and Woodrow Wilson.

▶ Vocabulary

TERMS & NAMES

William Howard Taft Republican elected president in 1908

Sixteenth Amendment amendment that gave Congress the power to create income taxes

Seventeenth Amendment amendment that provided for direct election of U.S. senators

Bull Moose Party progressive political party in 1912 presidential election

Clayton Antitrust Act legislation that strengthened the Sherman Antitrust Act's power

Federal Reserve Act law that created the modern banking system

BACKGROUND VOCABULARY

revenue income

REVIEW

socialism system in which the state controls the economy

William Jennings Bryan Democratic candidate in 1908 presidential election

segregation racial separation

Visual Vocabulary
Bull Moose
Party buttons

▶ Reading Strategy

Re-create the diagram shown here. As you read and respond to the **KEY QUESTIONS**, use the diagram to compare and contrast the progressive reform efforts of Presidents Taft and Wilson.

 See Skillbuilder Handbook, page R8.

COMPARE AND CONTRAST

Taft	Wilson
• antitrust	• antitrust

 GRAPHIC ORGANIZERS
Go to **Interactive Review** @ ClassZone.com

Taft and Wilson As Progressives

 8 – U6.6.1.6 America at Century's End – the treatment of African Americans, including the rise of segregation in the South as endorsed by the Supreme Court's decision in *Plessy* v. *Ferguson*, and the response of African Americans
8 – P3.1.1.7 Identify, research, analyze, discuss, and defend a position on a national public policy issue – Compose a persuasive essay justifying the position with a reasoned argument.

One American's Story

During the Progressive Era, many Americans became disturbed by the problems caused by capitalism. Some even turned to **socialism**. This is a system in which the state controls the economy. Labor leader Eugene V. Debs (See Chapter 20, page 661) became a socialist while serving time in prison for his role in an 1894 labor strike.

Debs ran for president in 1900, 1904, 1908, 1912, and 1920. In his 1908 campaign, he urged American workers to consider what competition was like in a capitalist system.

Eugene V. Debs (*right*) was the Socialist candidate for president five times. This button is from his 1912 campaign.

PRIMARY SOURCE

❝ Competition was natural enough at one time, but do you think you are competing today? . . . Against whom? Against Rockefeller? About as I would if I had a wheelbarrow and competed with the Santa Fe [railroad] from here to Kansas City. ❞

—Eugene V. Debs, from a speech given in Girard, Kansas

Taft and Progressivism

🔻 **KEY QUESTION** How did Taft continue Roosevelt's progressive policies?

In the 1908 election, Debs and Democrat **William Jennings Bryan** ran against Republican **William Howard Taft**. Neither candidate stood much of a chance against Taft. Roosevelt had handpicked Taft to carry on his own progressive policies.

Taft As Roosevelt's Heir Taft continued Roosevelt's attack on trusts. During four years in office, Taft pursued almost twice as many antitrust suits as Roosevelt had in nearly eight years. Although Taft's policies angered conservationists, he made democratic, social welfare, and economic reforms.

Connecting History

Judicial Power
During the Civil War era, Congress instituted temporary federal income taxes until 1872. In 1894, the Supreme Court ruled that aspects of federal income taxes were unconstitutional.

Two Progressive Amendments Two of the major progressive achievements under President Taft were constitutional amendments. The **Sixteenth Amendment** was passed in 1909 and ratified in 1913. It gave Congress the power to create federal income taxes. Before this, the Constitution did not allow federal taxes on an individual's income. This amendment was intended to spread the cost of running the government among more people. The income tax soon became an important source of federal revenue.

The **Seventeenth Amendment** gave voters the right to elect senators directly. Formerly, state legislatures had chosen U.S. senators. Under this system, many senators gained their positions through corrupt bargains. The Seventeenth Amendment gave people a more direct voice in the government.

▲ **SUMMARIZE** Summarize the progressive policies achieved under President Taft.

Wilson and Progressivism

▼ **KEY QUESTION** What did Wilson contribute to the progressive movement?

During Taft's presidency, a split developed between Taft and other progressive Republican leaders. Many of these leaders supported Theodore Roosevelt, who entered the 1912 presidential race as a candidate for the new, progressive **Bull Moose Party**. The Democrats chose Woodrow Wilson (WUD•roh WIHL•suhn), governor of New Jersey, as their candidate. With Republicans deeply divided, Wilson won the election.

CONNECT — Economics & History

TYPES OF TAXES

Today, federal, state, and local governments use tax revenues to pay for the services that they provide. The income tax is only one of several taxes governments use to raise money.

SALES TAXES
Sellers collect state sales taxes from consumers when they buy retail goods and services.

INCOME TAXES
Individuals pay a percentage of their earnings, and corporations pay a percentage of their profits. With a graduated income tax, larger incomes are taxed at higher rates than smaller incomes.

PROPERTY TAXES
People who own property, such as a house or land, pay property taxes. Governments often use property taxes to pay for services such as schools.

ESTATE TAXES
When a person dies and leaves behind property, taxes are charged against part of the value of the dead person's property, or estate, before it passes on to heirs.

CRITICAL THINKING

1. **Categorize** What kinds of taxes do businesses pay?

2. **Compare and Contrast** How do sales taxes differ from income taxes?

Wilson's Economic Reforms At Wilson's urging, Congress passed the **Clayton Antitrust Act** of 1914. The new law further prohibited monopolies and business practices that lessened competition. A business, for example, could no longer buy a competitor's stock. The Clayton Act gave the government more power to regulate trusts. In addition, the Clayton Act allowed labor unions to expand and legalized strikes.

Under Wilson, Congress also reformed the nation's financial system. In 1913, the **Federal Reserve Act** created the modern banking system, led by the Federal Reserve Board (the "Fed"). The Fed oversees 12 regional Federal Reserve Banks and makes sure that money is distributed where it is most needed. These are bankers' banks that serve consumer banks. The Federal Reserve Act created a more flexible currency system by allowing banks to control the money supply. To raise money, the Fed lowers the interest rate that it charges member banks. These banks then borrow more from the Fed, and thus have more money to lend to people and businesses.

Wilson's Failure in Civil Rights While Roosevelt's attitude toward African Americans was progressive for his time, Wilson's was not. Wilson was from the South. He personally believed in **segregation**—the practice of keeping whites and African Americans apart. In his presidential campaign, Wilson spoke of his "willingness and desire to deal with [African Americans] fairly and justly." After he was elected, however, Wilson approved segregation in the federal government. During his presidency, white Southerners gained the most federal support they had had since the Civil War.

 COMPARE AND CONTRAST Compare Wilson and Roosevelt as progressives.

Michigan Grade Level Content Expectations *Review*

🔊 **ONLINE QUIZ**
For test practice, go to
Interactive Review @ ClassZone.com

TERMS & NAMES

1. Explain the importance of
- William Howard Taft
- Sixteenth Amendment
- Seventeenth Amendment
- Bull Moose Party
- Clayton Antitrust Act
- Federal Reserve Act

USING YOUR READING NOTES

2. Compare and Contrast Complete the diagram you started at the beginning of the section. Then answer the following question: Who was more effective at reforming society, Taft or Wilson?

Taft	Wilson
• *antitrust*	• *antitrust*

KEY IDEAS

3. What was the purpose of the Sixteenth Amendment?

4. How did the Clayton Antitrust Act change business?

CRITICAL THINKING

5. Make Inferences Why did progressive presidents do little to advance African Americans' civil rights?

6. Evaluate What was the most important progressive reform achieved under Presidents Taft and Wilson? Explain.

7. Writing Speech Use the library or the Internet to learn more about the Bull Moose Party. Then write a presidential campaign speech from the point of view of a Bull Moose Party member endorsing Theodore Roosevelt in the 1912 election.

▶ Key Ideas

BEFORE, YOU LEARNED

Progressive reforms continued under Presidents William Howard Taft and Woodrow Wilson.

NOW YOU WILL LEARN

During the Progressive Era, women became leaders in reform movements and won the right to vote.

▶ Vocabulary

TERMS & NAMES

Carry A. Nation fought for prohibition

prohibition (PROH•uh•BIHSH•uhn) legal ban on the production, possession, and sale of alcohol

Eighteenth Amendment constitutional amendment enacting Prohibition

Susan B. Anthony fought for woman suffrage

Carrie Chapman Catt president of National American Woman Suffrage Association

Nineteenth Amendment constitutional amendment that gave women the vote

BACKGROUND VOCABULARY

settlement house community center providing help to immigrants and the poor

REVIEW

Jane Addams founded Hull House

suffrage right to vote

Visual Vocabulary Carry Nation cartoon

▶ Reading Strategy

Re-create the diagram shown here. As you read and respond to the **KEY QUESTIONS**, use the diagram to record the causes and effects of women's changing roles in society.

 See Skillbuilder Handbook, page R7.

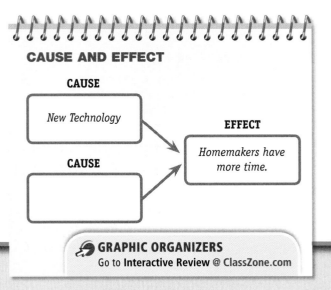

CAUSE AND EFFECT

CAUSE

New Technology

CAUSE

EFFECT

Homemakers have more time.

GRAPHIC ORGANIZERS
Go to **Interactive Review** @ ClassZone.com

SECTION 3

Women Win New Rights

8 – U6.2.1 United States History Investigation Topic and Issue Analysis, Past and Present – Use historical perspectives to analyze issues in the United States from the past and the present; conduct research on a historical issue or topic, identify a connection to a contemporary issue, and present findings (e.g., oral, visual, video, or electronic presentation, persuasive essay, or research paper); include causes and consequences of the historical action and predict possible consequences of the contemporary action.
8 – P3.1.1.3 Identify, research, analyze, discuss, and defend a position on a national public policy issue – Use inquiry methods to trace the origins of the issue and to acquire data about the issue.

One American's Story

In the 1890s, Lillian Wald was teaching a home nursing class at a school for immigrants in New York City. One day a child asked Wald to help her sick mother. Following the child home, Wald was shocked by what she saw.

PRIMARY SOURCE

❝ Over broken asphalt, over dirty mattresses and heaps of refuse we went. The tall houses reeked with rubbish. . . . There were two rooms and a family of seven not only lived here but shared their quarters with boarders. ❞

—Lillian Wald, quoted in *Always a Sister*

Lillian Wald

Inspired to help such poor immigrants, Wald founded the Nurses' Settlement. This was later called the Henry Street Settlement. The Settlement aimed to help children, families, and the poor by providing nurses' training, educational programs for the community, youth clubs, and children's summer camps. It also opened one of New York City's earliest playgrounds.

New Roles for Women

🔽 **KEY QUESTION** How did women's lives change in the late 1800s?

At the turn of the century, middle-class women were looking for new roles outside the home. At the same time, middle-class homes were changing. Families were becoming smaller as women had fewer children. New products and inventions reduced some of the work of homemaking, which was done mostly by women and servants.

New Industries and Technology Factories now produced soap, clothing, canned food, and other goods that had been homemade. New technology, such as indoor running water and vacuum cleaners, made it possible for homemakers to wash clothes, clean, and cook in less time and with less effort than before.

New Opportunities Charlotte Perkins Gilman was an influential writer on women's rights. She wanted to free women from housework to pursue new opportunities. In *Concerning Children* (1900) and *The Home* (1903), she proposed that families live in large apartments. These would have centralized nurseries and a staff devoted to cooking, cleaning, and child-care. According to Gilman, this support would free women to work outside the home.

Some women who took jobs outside of the home worked as telephone operators, store clerks, and typists. Those with a college education could enter fields such as teaching and nursing. Women who could afford to were expected to quit their jobs when they married. In 1890, approximately 30 percent of women between the ages of 20 and 24 worked outside the home. However, only about 15 percent between the ages of 25 and 44 did so.

▲ **CAUSES AND EFFECTS** Explain what led middle-class women's lives to change in the Progressive Era.

COMPARING *The Growth of Women's Rights*

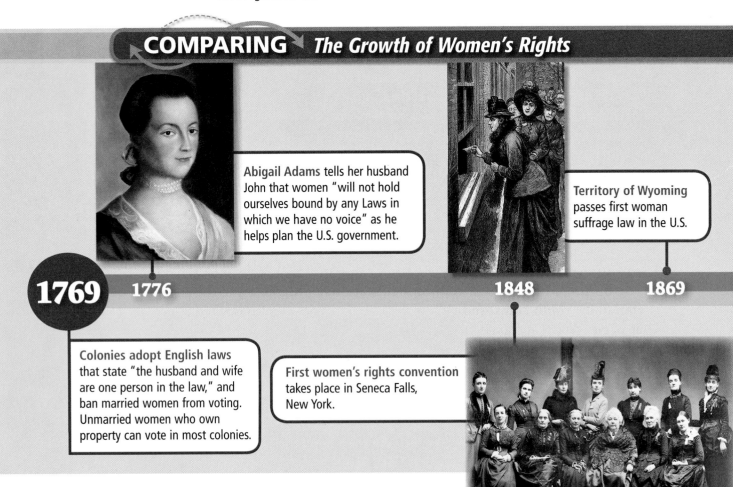

Abigail Adams tells her husband John that women "will not hold ourselves bound by any Laws in which we have no voice" as he helps plan the U.S. government.

Territory of Wyoming passes first woman suffrage law in the U.S.

1769 **1776** **1848** **1869**

Colonies adopt English laws that state "the husband and wife are one person in the law," and ban married women from voting. Unmarried women who own property can vote in most colonies.

First women's rights convention takes place in Seneca Falls, New York.

Women and Progressivism

KEY QUESTION On what social problems did Jane Addams and other women work?

The social reforms that many middle-class, college-educated women took part in were focused on helping people. These reforms included the establishment of **settlement houses**—community centers that provided help to immigrants and the poor—and working to pass prohibition.

Jane Addams and Hull House Jane Addams (See History Maker on page 646) was a good example of a progressive female leader. After graduating from college, Addams sought a meaningful way to participate in society. A visit to a settlement house in a London slum inspired her to start a similar program in Chicago aided by her friend Ellen Gates Starr.

With donations from wealthy Chicagoans, Addams and Starr opened Hull House in a poor, immigrant neighborhood. Hull House served as an information bureau for new immigrants. It also helped the unemployed find jobs. It offered a kindergarten, a day nursery, after-school youth clubs, health clinics, and citizenship classes. Many of the programs were run by the young women residents. Hull House workers also pressured politicians for improved city services for the neighborhood.

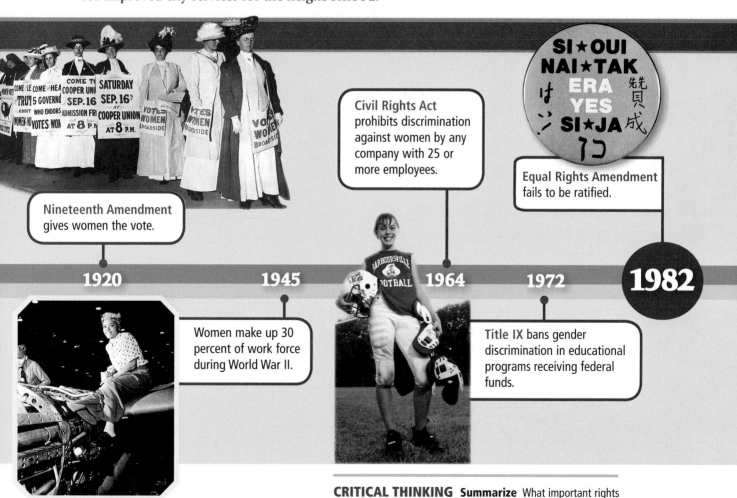

Civil Rights Act prohibits discrimination against women by any company with 25 or more employees.

Equal Rights Amendment fails to be ratified.

Nineteenth Amendment gives women the vote.

1920   **1945**   **1964**   **1972**   **1982**

Women make up 30 percent of work force during World War II.

Title IX bans gender discrimination in educational programs receiving federal funds.

CRITICAL THINKING **Summarize** What important rights have women gained in America?

History Makers

Susan B. Anthony   1820–1906

Susan B. Anthony was born into a Quaker family in Massachusetts. Quakers believe in the equality of men and women, and Anthony's father made sure his daughters received the same education as his sons. Anthony became a teacher. She was once fired for complaining about earning less than a man was paid for the same work. Anthony left teaching to focus full-time on women's rights and other reform efforts.

Anthony noticed that the Fourteenth Amendment referred to citizens as persons, not just men. She thought this could mean that women had the right to vote. In 1872, Anthony voted in the presidential election. She was arrested, tried, and found guilty. Her punishment was a large fine, which she refused to pay. Anthony fought for woman suffrage for over 45 years. At times she despaired that the movement would ever succeed. But she never gave up hope. In her last speech, she said, "Failure is impossible." The Nineteenth Amendment was ratified 14 years after Anthony's death.

CRITICAL THINKING

Connect to Today   What social issues do you think Susan B. Anthony would be concerned about today? Why?

 **ONLINE BIOGRAPHY**   For more on Susan B. Anthony, go to the **Research & Writing Center** @ ClassZone.com

These programs were run by a group of young men and women residents and volunteers. The residents of Hull House received no salary and had to pay for their room and board.

Prohibition   Another prominent, but controversial, progressive leader was **Carry A. Nation**. She campaigned for **prohibition**—a ban on the production and sale of alcohol. Nation had once been married to an alcoholic. Tall and strong, she adopted dramatic methods in her opposition to alcoholic beverages. In the 1890s, she smashed saloons with a hatchet. She was often arrested. Although some people criticized Nation, her efforts helped bring about passage in 1919 of the **Eighteenth Amendment**, which made Prohibition the law of the land.

▲ **MAIN IDEAS & DETAILS** Name the social problems on which progressive women worked.

Suffrage for Women

▼ **KEY QUESTION** How did women finally obtain the right to vote?

Many women progressives were active in the struggle for woman **suffrage**, or the right to vote. American women fought longer for the right to vote than they did for any other reforms.

Women Unite   In 1890, two separate woman suffrage groups merged to form the National American Woman Suffrage Association (NAWSA). Elizabeth Cady Stanton served as its first president. Two years later, in 1892, **Susan B. Anthony** became president. She held the position until 1900. Expressing their frustration over the difficulty of gaining suffrage, Stanton and Anthony wrote, "Words can not describe the indignation… a proud woman feels for her sex in [being deprived of the right to vote]."

NAWSA at first focused on state campaigns to win the right to vote, since earlier efforts at passing a federal amendment had failed. But by 1896, only four states allowed women to vote. These were Wyoming, Utah, Idaho, and Colorado. Between 1896 and 1910, women did not gain the right to vote in a single state. Then, between 1910 and 1914, seven more Western states approved full suffrage for women (See suffrage map on page 671).

The Nineteenth Amendment The Western successes turned the tide in favor of woman suffrage. The United States' entry into World War I in 1917 pushed the nation to take the final step. During the war, membership in NAWSA reached 2 million. **Carrie Chapman Catt**, president of NAWSA, supported President Wilson and volunteered NAWSA's services to the government in case it entered the war. She may have believed

CONNECT to the Essential Question

How did Americans benefit from progressive reforms?

PROBLEM	SOLUTION
POLITICAL	
Government officials respond to special interests instead of public interests	direct primary, initiative, referendum
Corrupt politicians	recall, Pendleton Civil Service Act, Seventeenth Amendment
Women lack equal rights	Nineteenth Amendment grants women the right to vote
ECONOMIC	
Unfair business practices	Sherman Antitrust Act, Clayton Antitrust Act
Unhealthy food and medicines	Meat Inspection Act, Pure Food and Drug Act
Loss of wilderness and nature due to the spread of industry	T. Roosevelt creates Forest Service, establishes wildlife refuges, national parks, and national monuments
Lack of government funds	Sixteenth Amendment creates income tax
Unstable banking system	Federal Reserve Act
SOCIAL	
Alcoholism	Eighteenth Amendment bans production and sale of alcohol
Poverty, poor healthcare, and lack of education among immigrants and the working class	settlement houses

Ayer's Sarsaparilla
Has Cured Others
Will Cure You!
The Superior Medicine

CRITICAL THINKING **Evaluate** Which progressive reform produced the greatest benefit for Americans?

The Progressive Era **687**

Progressive Amendments

16th	Federal income tax
17th	Senators elected by people rather than state legislatures
18th	Manufacture, sale, or transport of alcohol prohibited
19th	Woman suffrage

that by helping President Wilson with the war effort, she could ask for his support of woman suffrage. President Wilson urged the Senate to pass a woman suffrage amendment. He called its passage "vital to the winning of the war."

In 1918, the House gave women full voting rights by passing the **Nineteenth Amendment**. The Senate approved the amendment in 1919. For the final state campaigns, women staged marches, parades, and rallies. In 1920, the states ratified the Nineteenth Amendment and made it law.

PRIMARY SOURCE

❝ The right of citizens of the United States to vote shall not be denied or abridged by the United States or by any State on account of sex. ❞

—The Nineteenth Amendment to the U.S. Constitution

Charlotte Woodard had attended the first women's rights convention in 1848 at Seneca Falls as a teenager. In 1920, the 91-year-old Woodard voted in a presidential election for the first time.

 SEQUENCE EVENTS List the order of events that led to woman suffrage.

 Michigan Grade Level Content Expectations *Review*

ONLINE QUIZ
For test practice, go to
Interactive Review @ ClassZone.com

TERMS & NAMES

1. Explain the importance of

- Carry A. Nation
- Susan B. Anthony
- prohibition
- Carrie Chapman Catt
- Eighteenth Amendment
- Nineteenth Amendment

USING YOUR READING NOTES

2. Causes and Effects Complete the diagram of causes and effects you started at the beginning of this section. Then decide which cause had the greatest impact on women's lives.

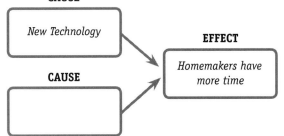

KEY IDEAS

3. How did women's roles in society expand in the Progressive Era?

4. In what ways did settlement houses serve their communities?

5. What voting rights did women have prior to 1920?

CRITICAL THINKING

6. Compare and Contrast Compare the struggle for woman suffrage to African Americans' struggle for equal rights.

7. Make Inferences How did technological advances and social reform movements affect poor women?

8. **Report** Research the history of woman suffrage in a country such as Australia, India, or South Africa. Write a brief report on your findings.

Chapter Summary

1 **Key Idea**
Progressive reformers promoted social welfare, expanded democracy, and created economic reform.

2 **Key Idea**
Progressive reforms continued under Presidents William Howard Taft and Woodrow Wilson.

3 **Key Idea**
During the Progressive Era, women became leaders in reform movements and won the right to vote.

For detailed Review and Study Notes go to **Interactive Review** @ ClassZone.com

Name Game

Use the Terms & Names list to complete each sentence online or on your own paper.

1. As president, I was a strong supporter of conserving natural resources. Theodore Roosevelt.

2. The 20th century movement to correct societal problems was called ____.

3. Ratified in 1913, the ____ enabled Congress to levy and collect income taxes.

4. In the 1912 election, progressive Republican leaders formed the ____.

5. Writers who exposed corruption and wrong-doing were known as ____.

6. As Roosevelt's successor as president, I continued to challenge big business in America. ____

7. Exchanging jobs for political support, or ____, was popular during the 1870s and 1880s.

8. As an advocate for equality between men and women, I fought for women's suffrage for over 45 years. ____

9. Passed by the House in 1918, the ____ gave women in America the right to vote.

10. The ____ made it illegal for corporations to control industries.

A. Sherman Antitrust Act
B. Theodore Roosevelt
C. Seventeenth Amendment
D. Progressivism
E. William Howard Taft
F. Sixteenth Amendment
G. Clayton Antitrust Act
H. muckrakers
I. Federal Reserve Act
J. Patronage
K. Susan B. Anthony
L. Carrie Chapman Catt
M. Bull Moose Party
N. Prohibition
O. Nineteenth Amendment

Activities

CROSSWORD PUZZLE

ACROSS
1. I helped improve conditions at a women's asylum (two words).

FLIPCARD

Use the online flip cards to quiz yourself on the terms and names introduced in this chapter.

I signed the Pure Food and Drug Act of 1906 while I was president.

ANSWER
Theodore Roosevelt

VOCABULARY

Write the term or name that correctly fills in the blank in each of the following sentences.

1. Upton Sinclair wrote a novel describing the _____ industry.

2. _____ was the first state to establish a direct primary.

3. In 1914 Congress passed the _____ to regulate trusts and help organized labor.

4. _____ was the second president of the National American Woman Suffrage Association.

5. The states ratified the _____ in 1920, giving women the vote.

For each of the following pairs, explain the impact that the person had on the event.

6. Theodore Roosevelt; Meat Inspection Act
7. Woodrow Wilson; Federal Reserve Act
8. Carry A. Nation; prohibition

KEY IDEAS

1 Roosevelt and Progressivism (pages 672–677)

9. What were three goals that progressive reformers shared?

10. What reforms were part of Roosevelt's square deal?

2 Taft and Wilson As Progressives (pages 678–681)

11. In what areas did Taft achieve a more progressive record than Roosevelt?

12. What happened to African Americans' civil rights during Wilson's presidency?

3 Women Win New Rights (pages 682–688)

13. How did women work for change in the late 1800s?

14. What organization played an important role in obtaining woman suffrage?

CRITICAL THINKING

15. **Make Inferences** How might the 1912 presidential election have been different if some Republicans had not left their party to form the Progressive Party?

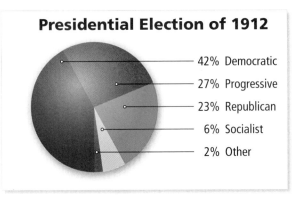

Presidential Election of 1912

- 42% Democratic
- 27% Progressive
- 23% Republican
- 6% Socialist
- 2% Other

16. **Evaluate** Which president do you think was most effective—Roosevelt, Taft, or Wilson? Why?

17. **Analyze Point of View** Why might women at the turn of the century have considered suffrage a cause worth devoting their lives to?

18. **Problems and Solutions** Explain whether you think Hull House was an effective solution to poverty.

19. **Analyze Political Cartoons** Look at the political cartoon below. The words on the peoples' chests read "R.R. Trust," "Oil Trust," and "Everything in General." Explain what Roosevelt is doing in the cartoon below.

NO MOLLY-CODDLING HERE

TEST PRACTICE

• **Online Test Practice @ ClassZone.com**

• Use the **MEAP Strategies & Practice,** pages S1-S27, at the front of this book

DOCUMENT-BASED QUESTIONS

Analyze each document, and answer the question that follows.

DOCUMENT 1

TO THE RUSSIAN ENVOYS

President Wilson and Envoy Root are deceiving Russia. They say we are a democracy. Help us win a world war so that democracies may survive".

We, the Women of America, tell you that America is not a democracy. Twenty million American Women are denied the right to vote. President Wilson is the chief opponent of their national enfranchisement.

Help us make this nation really free. Tell our government that it must liberate its people before it can claim free Russia as an ally.

DOCUMENT 2

PRIMARY SOURCE

 The Settlement . . . is an experimental effort to aid in the solution of the social and industrial problems which are engendered by the modern conditions of life in a great city. . . . It is an attempt to relieve, at the same time, the over accumulation at one end of society and the destitution at the other . . . **"**

—Jane Addams, quoted in *Twenty Years at Hull House*

1 Examine the photograph and primary source. Which of the following is **NOT** true of women reformers during Progressive Era?

A They worked for passage of the Nineteenth Amendment.

B They tried to help immigrants and the poor.

C They opposed woman suffrage.

D They focused on social problems such as alcohol abuse.

YOU BE THE HISTORIAN

20. WHAT IF? How do you think the United States might be different today if Theodore Roosevelt had not made the conservation efforts he did?

21. Causes and Effects Susan B. Anthony never married, and disapproved of suffragist leaders who did. Why do you think Anthony saw marriage as incompatible with the cause of woman suffrage?

22. Analyze Point of View Prior to the Sixteenth Amendment, the federal government was financed by taxes on imports, inheritances, and the sale of various goods. How do you think Americans reacted to the income tax?

23. Predict Do you think prohibition had the potential to succeed? Why or why not?

24. Make Inferences Why did the fight for woman suffrage last so long?

Answer the
ESSENTIAL QUESTION
How did Americans benefit from Progressive reforms?

Written Response Write a two- or three-paragraph response to the Essential Question. Be sure to consider the key ideas of each section as well as the most significant changes in the lives of Americans at the turn of the century. Use the Response Rubric below to guide your thinking and writing.

Response Rubric
A strong response will

• describe the three basic goals of progressives

• explain how changes affected Americans of differing social classes

• discuss contributions by specific individuals

• analyze the role of government in reform

1. Imperialism in the Pacific

2. The Spanish-American War

3. Expanding Interests in Asia and Latin America

Becoming a World Power

1880–1914

 ESSENTIAL QUESTION

How did America's growing power affect its relationships with other nations?

CONNECT ↻ **Geography & History**

How might the geography of the United States have affected its desire to become a world power?

Think about:

1 the location of the newly acquired territory of Alaska

2 the continent on which most European colonies were located

3 the country with the largest expanse of colonial territory

Alaskan totem pole

sugar cane

1880

1884
Congress officially makes Alaska U.S. territory (following U.S. purchase of Alaska from Russia in 1867).

1893
American planters overthrow Hawaii's Queen Liliuokalani.

▼

Effect U.S. annexes Hawaii.

1898 Spanish-American War begins.

▼

Effect Spain cedes Puerto Rico, Guam, and the Philippines.

ASIA   ALASKA   NORTH
                                          AMERICA

                                                  UNITED
                                                  STATES

CHINA   JAPAN

                    PACIFIC OCEAN

        FRENCH
        INDOCHINA   Midway Is.

Philippine   Wake I.   Johnston
Is.   Atoll   Hawaii
        Guam

                              Howland
                              I.   Palmyra Atoll

                              Baker I.   Jarvis I.

AUSTRALIA
                              American
                              Samoa

                                        ← Route of "The
                                          Great White Fleet"

        NEW ZEALAND

1904
Roosevelt Corollary is established.

▼

Effect Allows U.S. interference in
Latin American domestic affairs.

Ship going
through the
Panama Canal

1914

1899   U.S. Open Door Policy
favors foreign traders in China.

▼

Effect 1900 Boxer Rebellion
breaks out in China.

Panama Canal
opens.

Detail of Chinese print
of Boxer Rebellion.

Becoming a World Power **693**

▶ Key Ideas

BEFORE, YOU LEARNED

In the Progressive era, Americans reformed government and expanded rights for women.

NOW YOU WILL LEARN

The United States took its first steps in becoming a world power by acquiring Alaska and Hawaii.

▶ Vocabulary

TERMS & NAMES

Queen Liliuokalani (lee•LEE•oo•oh•kah•LAH•nee) first and only reigning Hawaiian queen

imperialism policy by which stronger nations extend their economic, political, or military control over weaker nations

William Seward Secretary of State under presidents Lincoln and Andrew Johnson; purchased Alaska from Russia in 1867

Pearl Harbor Hawaiian port; granted by 1887 treaty to the United States for use as a refueling station for U.S. ships

REVIEW VOCABULARY

manifest destiny belief that the United States was meant to expand from coast to coast

missionary person sent to another country by a church to spread its faith

Visual Vocabulary
William Seward

▶ Reading Strategy

Re-create the diagram at right. As you respond to the **KEY QUESTIONS**, use the outer boxes to fill in details that support the main idea.

 See Skillbuilder Handbook, page R4.

MAIN IDEA AND DETAILS

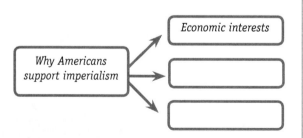

Why Americans support imperialism → *Economic interests*

GRAPHIC ORGANIZERS
Go to **Interactive Review** @ ClassZone.com

Imperialism in the Pacific

8 – U6.2.1 United States History Investigation Topic and Issue Analysis, Past and Present – Use historical perspectives to analyze issues in the United States from the past and the present; conduct research on a historical issue or topic, identify a connection to a contemporary issue, and present findings (e.g., oral, visual, video, or electronic presentation, persuasive essay, or research paper); include causes and consequences of the historical action and predict possible consequences of the contemporary action.

One American's Story

In 1893, American sugar planters in Hawaii, supported by a U.S. naval gunboat, overthrew the Hawaiian government of **Queen Liliuokalani** (lee•LEE•oo•oh•kah•LAH•nee). The proud monarch was forced to surrender.

PRIMARY SOURCE

❝ I had informed President Harrison ...of the ... assistance given by the forces of the United States ship *Boston* ... through which ... my government had been overthrown. I had asked that justice should be done, and that the rights of my people should be restored. President Harrison chose to set aside my statement and petition. ❞

— Queen Liliuokalani, *Hawaii's Story by Hawaii's Queen (1898)*

The U.S. ambassador to Hawaii reported that "The Hawaiian pear is now fully ripe, and this is the golden hour for the United States to pluck it." The annexation of Hawaii was only one of the goals of America's empire builders in the late 19th century.

Queen Lydia Liliuokalani was the first and only reigning queen of Hawaii.

America Becomes an Imperial Power

🔽 **KEY QUESTION** Why did some Americans support imperialist policies?

Americans had always sought to expand the size of their nation. Throughout the 19th century, they believed it was their **manifest destiny** to push American control westward to the Pacific coast. Once this goal had been achieved, Americans began to look overseas for additional sources of wealth.

Reasons for U.S. Expansion By the late 1800s, many American leaders wanted the United States to join the imperialist powers of Europe and establish colonies overseas. **Imperialism** is the policy by which stronger nations extend their economic, political, or military control over weaker nations.

COMPARING *Characteristics of American Imperialism*

ECONOMIC	MILITARY	CULTURAL
Maintain industrial prosperity	Show foreign powers the strength of U.S. power	Belief in cultural superiority of industrialized nations
Acquire raw materials from new markets	Build strong U.S. navy to protect shipping lanes.	Belief in cultural inferiority of nonindustrial societies
Find new markets for sale of American goods.	Establish U.S. military bases overseas	Belief in need to spread democracy and Christianity

CRITICAL THINKING Make Inferences Why might economic and military interests go hand in hand?

European nations had been establishing colonies for centuries. In the late 19th century, for example, Africa became a major area of European expansion. Most Americans gradually came to approve of the idea of expansion overseas (See the chart above).

Supporters of expansionism argued that it would increase the nation's financial prosperity, strengthen the nation militarily, and spread democratic ideas. They also firmly believed in the superiority of western culture.

▲ **MAIN IDEAS & DETAILS** List the main reasons that American leaders supported imperialism.

American Expansionism

▼ **KEY QUESTION** Why did America want to acquire Alaska and Hawaii?

With American territory now stretching between two oceans, America was well placed to extend its influence in the Pacific. Through purchase and annexation, the nation began expanding beyond its shores.

America Acquires Alaska A strong backer of expansion was **William Seward**, Secretary of State under Abraham Lincoln and Andrew Johnson. Seward made his biggest move in 1867 when he arranged for the purchase of Alaska from Russia. Congress officially annexed Alaska in 1884.

Seward was widely criticized for the $7.2-million deal. Newspapers called Alaska "Seward's Icebox." Even so, the purchase of the territory turned out to be a bargain. For about two cents an acre, the United States had acquired a land rich in timber, minerals and, as it turned out, oil.

The Annexation of Hawaii In the early 1800s, American **missionaries** had moved to Hawaii to convert the local population to Christianity. Some of the missionaries' descendants started sugar plantations. By the late 1800s, wealthy American planters dominated Hawaii's economy.

In 1891, Queen Liliuokalani became the leader of Hawaii. Believing that American planters had too much influence, she moved to limit their power. Around the same time, U.S. trade laws changed to favor sugar grown in the United States.

Connecting History

Imperialism
Throughout his career, William Seward continued to pursue new territory. Before he retired in 1869, he considered acquiring the Hawaiian Islands, although that did not happen until 1898.

American planters in Hawaii were upset by these threats to their political and economic interests. As a result, in 1893, the planters staged a revolt. With the help of U.S. Marines, they overthrew the queen and set up their own government. They then asked to be annexed by the United States.

U.S. leaders already understood the value of the islands. In 1887, they had pressured Hawaii to allow a U.S. base at **Pearl Harbor,** the kingdom's best port. The base became an important refueling station for American merchant and military ships bound for Asia.

Thus, when President Benjamin Harrison received the planters' request, he gave his approval. But before the Senate could act on the issue, Grover Cleveland became president. He did not approve of the planters' actions and withdrew the treaty. Hawaii would not be annexed until 1898.

(*above*) Workers harvest sugar cane in Hawaii around 1900, set against a landscape of sugar cane fields today.

 SUMMARIZE Explain the U.S. acquisition of Alaska and interest in Hawaii.

Michigan Grade Level Content Expectations *Review*

 ONLINE QUIZ
For test practice, go to
Interactive Review @ ClassZone.com

TERMS & NAMES

1. Explain the importance of
- Queen Liliuokalani
- imperialism
- William Seward
- Pearl Harbor

USING YOUR READING NOTES

2. Main Ideas and Details Complete the chart you started at the beginning of this section.

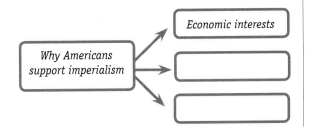

Why Americans support imperialism → Economic interests

KEY IDEAS

3. How did William Seward contribute to U.S. expansion?

4. Why did American planters in Hawaii stage a revolt in 1893?

CRITICAL THINKING

5. Make Inferences How did time prove that the purchase of Alaska was farsighted?

6. WHAT IF? What might have happened to Hawaii if President Cleveland's wishes had been respected by subsequent U.S. administrations?

7. Writing **Diary** Imagine that you are a native Hawaiian in the 1890's. Write a one-or-two-paragraph entry in your diary about the actions of the United States.

Becoming a World Power **697**

▶ Key Ideas

BEFORE YOU LEARNED

The United States took its first steps in becoming a world power by acquiring Alaska and Hawaii.

NOW YOU WILL LEARN

The United States went to war with Spain and gained colonies in the Caribbean and the Pacific.

▶ Vocabulary

TERMS & NAMES

yellow journalism style of journalism that exaggerates and sensationalizes the news

U.S.S. *Maine* U.S. warship that exploded off Havana, Cuba, on February 15, 1898

Spanish-American War 1898 war that began when the United States demanded Cuba's independence from Spain

George Dewey U.S. naval officer who defeated the Spanish fleet during the Spanish-American War

Rough Riders members of the First U.S. Volunteer Cavalry, organized by Theodore Roosevelt during the Spanish-American War

Platt Amendment agreement claiming the United States' right to intervene in Cuban affairs

Anti-Imperialist League group of influential Americans who believed the United States should not deny other people the right to govern themselves

Visual Vocabulary explosion of the U.S.S. *Maine*

▶ Reading Strategy

Re-create the diagram shown at right. As you respond to the **KEY QUESTIONS**, use the diagram to show the important events of the Spanish-American War.

 See Skillbuilder Handbook, page R7.

CAUSES AND EFFECTS

CAUSE	EFFECT
Spain treats Cuba harshly	*U.S.S. Maine to Havana*

GRAPHIC ORGANIZERS
Go to **Interactive Review** @ ClassZone.com

The Spanish-American War

8 – U6.2.1 United States History Investigation Topic and Issue Analysis, Past and Present – Use historical perspectives to analyze issues in the United States from the past and the present; conduct research on a historical issue or topic, identify a connection to a contemporary issue, and present findings (e.g., oral, visual, video, or electronic presentation, persuasive essay, or research paper); include causes and consequences of the historical action and predict possible consequences of the contemporary action.

One American's Story

José Martí, a poet and journalist, was forced to leave Cuba in the 1870s. In those years, Cuba was a Spanish colony, and he had spoken out for independence. Martí later described the terrible conditions the Cuban people suffered under Spanish rule.

PRIMARY SOURCE

❝ Cuba's children . . . suffer in indescribable bitterness as they see their fertile nation enchained and also their human dignity stifled . . . all for the necessities and vices of the [Spanish] monarchy. ❞

— José Martí quoted in *José Martí, Mentor of the Cuban Nation*

Sculpture of José Marti in Central Park, New York City.

In New York City, Martí began to plan a Cuban revolt against Spain that began in 1895. Martí's lifelong struggle for Cuban independence made him a symbol of liberty throughout Latin America. But U.S. disapproval of Spain's treatment of Cubans led to the Spanish-American War.

American Interests in Cuba

🔻 **KEY QUESTION** How did Americans respond to the Cuban Revolution?

When the first English colonies were established in America, Spain had a worldwide empire. This empire grew until it covered most of the Americas, including land that became part of the United States. But, by the 1890's, Spanish power was crumbling, and only a few of its colonies remained. Among them were the Philippine Islands in the Pacific and the Caribbean islands of Cuba and Puerto Rico. (See the maps on pages 701 and 702.) Many of the inhabitants of these colonies had begun to demand independence.

Cubans Rebel Against Spain

Cubans had unsuccessfully revolted against Spain several times. In 1895, anger over poor economic conditions came to a boiling point, and the Cubans rebelled again against Spanish rule. José Martí, who helped to organize the rebellion from New York, went back to Cuba. He was killed in a skirmish with Spanish troops shortly after his return, but the revolt continued.

Spain treated the rebels and other Cubans harshly. Many Cubans were forced from their homes and placed in camps guarded by Spanish troops. Thousands died of starvation and disease.

The Yellow Kid was the first comic strip in America. This edition was published in 1897.

Yellow Journalism

The revolt in Cuba caused alarm in the United States. Business leaders were concerned because the fighting disrupted U.S. trade with Cuba. Most Americans, however, became outraged when the press began to describe the brutality of Spanish officials. Two New York City newspapers, in particular, stirred up people's emotions.

The New York *World*, owned by Joseph Pulitzer, and the New York *Journal*, owned by William Randolph Hearst, were battling for customers. Both owners were able to attract readers by printing stories that described—and often exaggerated—news about Spanish cruelty. This sensational style of writing was known as **yellow journalism**. It was named after *The Yellow Kid*, a popular comic strip that ran in both newspapers.

America Declares War

William McKinley, the U.S. president in 1898, did not want war. "I have been through war," he told a friend. "I have seen the dead piled up, and I do not want to see another." But American public opinion forced McKinley to take action. He demanded that Spain halt its harsh treatment of Cubans.

Riots had broken out in Havana, the Cuban capital. In January 1898, McKinley sent the battleship, **U.S.S.** *Maine* to Havana to protect U.S. citizens. On February 15, the *Maine* exploded and sank. Two hundred and sixty-six American sailors died. No one knows what caused the explosion. Many historians today believe that it was an accident. Most Americans blamed Spain. "Remember the *Maine*!" became a call to arms.

On April 20, 1898, President McKinley signed a congressional resolution that called for Cuba's independence and demanded a withdrawal of Spanish forces. Spain responded by breaking off diplomatic relations with the United States. The stage was set for war.

▲ **CAUSES AND EFFECTS** Explain the American response to the Cuban Revolution.

This photo shows several cannons overlooking the Bay of Havana on the coast of Cuba.

The Battles for the Philippines and Cuba

▼ **KEY QUESTION** What was the outcome of the Spanish-American War?

In 1898, America went to war against Spain to fight for Cuban freedom. But the first major battle of the **Spanish-American War** took place in the Philippine Islands—a Spanish colony in the Pacific Ocean—on the other side of the world. Many Filipinos, as the inhabitants of the islands are called, had also revolted against Spanish rule in the 1890's.

The War in the Philippines On April 30, 1898 the American fleet in the Pacific steamed to the Philippines. American Commodore **George Dewey** had the support of the head of the Filipino rebel forces, Emilio Aguinaldo (eh•MEE•lyoh AH•gee•NAHL•doh).

The next morning, May 1, Dewey gave the command to open fire on the Spanish fleet at Manila, the Philippine capital. In seven hours, Dewey's men had destroyed the Spanish fleet. About 380 Spanish sailors were dead or wounded. No Americans died. U.S. troops, aided by Filipino rebels, took control of Manila in August.

Dewey became an instant hero in the United States. Some babies born at the time of the victory in Manila Bay were named for him, and a chewing gum called "Dewey's Chewies" became popular.

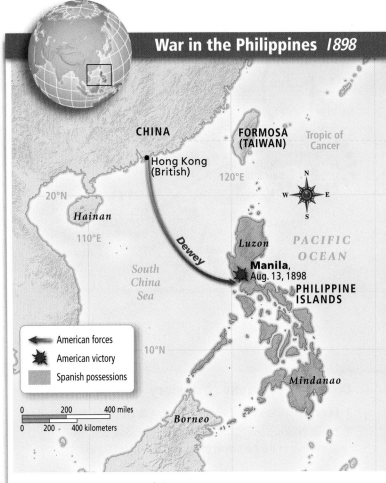

War in the Philippines *1898*

American forces →
★ American victory
Spanish possessions

0   200   400 miles
0 200   400 kilometers

Connect Geography & History

1. **Movement** Where was Dewey's fleet before it steamed toward the Philippines?
2. **Make Inferences** Why might the geographic location of the Philippines be of interest to American imperialists?

The War in the Caribbean When the Spanish-American War began, the U.S. Army had only 28,000 men. Within four months, over 200,000 more joined up. Among the new recruits was Theodore Roosevelt, who had resigned from the U.S. Navy Department to volunteer.

Roosevelt helped to organize the First U.S. Volunteer Cavalry. This unit was nicknamed the **Rough Riders**. Its recruits included cowboys, miners, college students, New York policemen, athletes, and Native Americans.

In June, the Rough Riders and about 15,000 other soldiers, including four regiments that were African American, gathered in Tampa, Florida. They then set out for Santiago, a Spanish stronghold in southern Cuba. (See the map on page 702.) When the Rough Riders arrived, their dark-blue wool uniforms were too hot for the Cuban climate. Also, many of the soldiers came down with tropical diseases. Even so, they fought their way toward Santiago.

American forces

Spanish forces

American victory

U.S. naval blockade

Spanish possessions

| 0 | 150 | 300 miles |
| 0 | 150 | 300 kilometers |

Gulf of Mexico

Tampa

ATLANTIC OCEAN

30°N

FLORIDA

U.S.S. Maine sunk, Feb. 1898

BAHAMAS (Br.)

Havana

CUBA

San Juan Hill, July 1

Santiago

Guantánamo

PUERTO RICO

20°N

JAMAICA (Br.)

Spanish fleet destroyed, July 3

HAITI

DOMINICAN REPUBLIC

Caribbean Sea

Guanica, July 25

From Spain, May 19

70°W

80°W

N W E S

Connect Geography & History

1. **Location** Where does Cuba lie in relation to the United States?

2. **Draw Conclusions** Given its geographic location, why were the islands of the Caribbean of value to the United States?

In order to gain control of Santiago's port, American troops had to capture San Juan Hill. (See map on this page.) They attacked the Spanish on July 1. African-American soldiers from the Tenth Cavalry began to drive the Spanish back. Roosevelt and the Rough Riders joined them as they rushed forward and captured the hill.

Two days later, American ships destroyed Spain's fleet as it tried to escape Santiago Harbor. On July 17, the city surrendered. A week later, U.S. forces took Puerto Rico. Finally, on August 12, 1898, Spain signed a truce. To U.S. Secretary of State John Hay, it had been "a splendid little war." For Spain, four centuries of glory had come to an end.

Although Americans had declared war to secure Cuba's independence, U.S. leaders began demanding that Spain also give up its other colonies. At the Treaty of Paris in 1898, the former Spanish colonies of Cuba, Puerto Rico, Guam, and the Philippines came under U.S. control. Now the United States had to decide how much independence it would allow its new territories.

▲ **SUMMARIZE** Explain the outcome of the Spanish-American War.

The New American Empire

🔻 **KEY QUESTION** How did Americans view their nation's new power?

One of the most challenging questions for U.S. leaders after the war was what to do with the Philippines. Filipinos had fought alongside Americans during the Spanish-American War and believed that Spain's defeat would bring them independence. But President McKinley, in the spirit of imperialism, decided that the Philippines should become an American colony. Disappointed, Filipinos, led by Emilio Aguinaldo, began to fight against their new colonial rulers. American troops were not able to put down the Filipino rebellion until 1902.

Cuba and Puerto Rico Cuban independence was granted by the Treaty of Paris, but Cuba remained under the control of the U.S. military. The American position was that rapid withdrawal might jeopardize Cuban stability.

Cuba was forced to add the **Platt Amendment** to its constitution. This gave the United States the right to intervene in Cuban affairs anytime there was a threat to "life, property, and individual liberty." Cuba also had to allow a U.S. naval base at Guantánamo Bay.

Puerto Rico became an American territory. The United States set up a government and appointed the top officials. Puerto Ricans were allowed little say in their own affairs. In 1917 the United States would agree to make Puerto Rico a self-governing territory and grant U.S. citizenship to all Puerto Ricans.

The Anti-Imperialist League U.S. treatment of Spain's former colonies after the Spanish-American War disappointed many people in the United States. Several influential Americans, including former president Grover Cleveland, businessman Andrew Carnegie, reformer Jane Addams, and writer Mark Twain, joined with others to form the **Anti-Imperialist League**. Members of the League believed that Americans should not deny other people the right to govern themselves.

PRIMARY SOURCE

❝ We hold that the policy known as imperialism is hostile to liberty. . . .
We regret that it has become necessary in the land of Washington and Lincoln to reaffirm that all men, of whatever race or color, are entitled to life, liberty, and the pursuit of happiness. ❞

—from the Platform of the *American Anti-Imperialist League*

The voice of the Anti-Imperialist League was lost, however, in the roar of popular approval of the Spanish-American War. Many Americans hoped that their nation would surpass the glory of the old Spanish empire.

🔺 **COMPARE AND CONTRAST** Explain the different sides Americans took regarding the nation's new power.

Michigan Grade Level Content Expectations *Review*

 ONLINE QUIZ
For test practice, go to
Interactive Review @ ClassZone.com

TERMS & NAMES

1. Explain the importance of:
- U.S.S. *Maine*
- yellow journalism
- Spanish-American War
- George Dewey
- Rough Riders
- Platt Amendment
- Anti-Imperialist League

USING YOUR READING NOTES

2. Causes and Effects Re-create the cause-and-effect diagram from the beginning of this section.

CAUSE	EFFECT
Spain treats Cuba harshly	*U.S.S.* Maine *to Havana*

KEY IDEAS

3. What role did New York City newspapers play in the outbreak of the Spanish-American War?

4. What happened to the Philippines after the war?

CRITICAL THINKING

5. Make Inferences How did the United States betray its democratic principles by adding the Platt Amendment to Cuba's constitution?

6. **Connect** *to* **Today** Give examples of how modern newspapers might impact political events by using "yellow journalism" tactics.

7. **Writing** **Script** Research the Rough Riders. Write a television news script covering a major Rough Rider battle.

Global Expansion

By the end of the nineteenth century, many European powers had established prosperous settlements along the coast of China. They also had carved out spheres of influence—areas where each nation claimed special rights and economic privilege. As a result, American leaders adopted these ideas as the bedrock of U.S. foreign policy:

• the growth of the U.S. economy depended on exports

• the United States had a right to intervene abroad to keep foreign markets open

• the closing of an area to American products, citizens, or ideas threatened U.S. survival

• refueling posts in the Pacific for the U.S. Navy were essential to U.S. security

These goals led to the establishment of U.S. military bases in the Pacific.

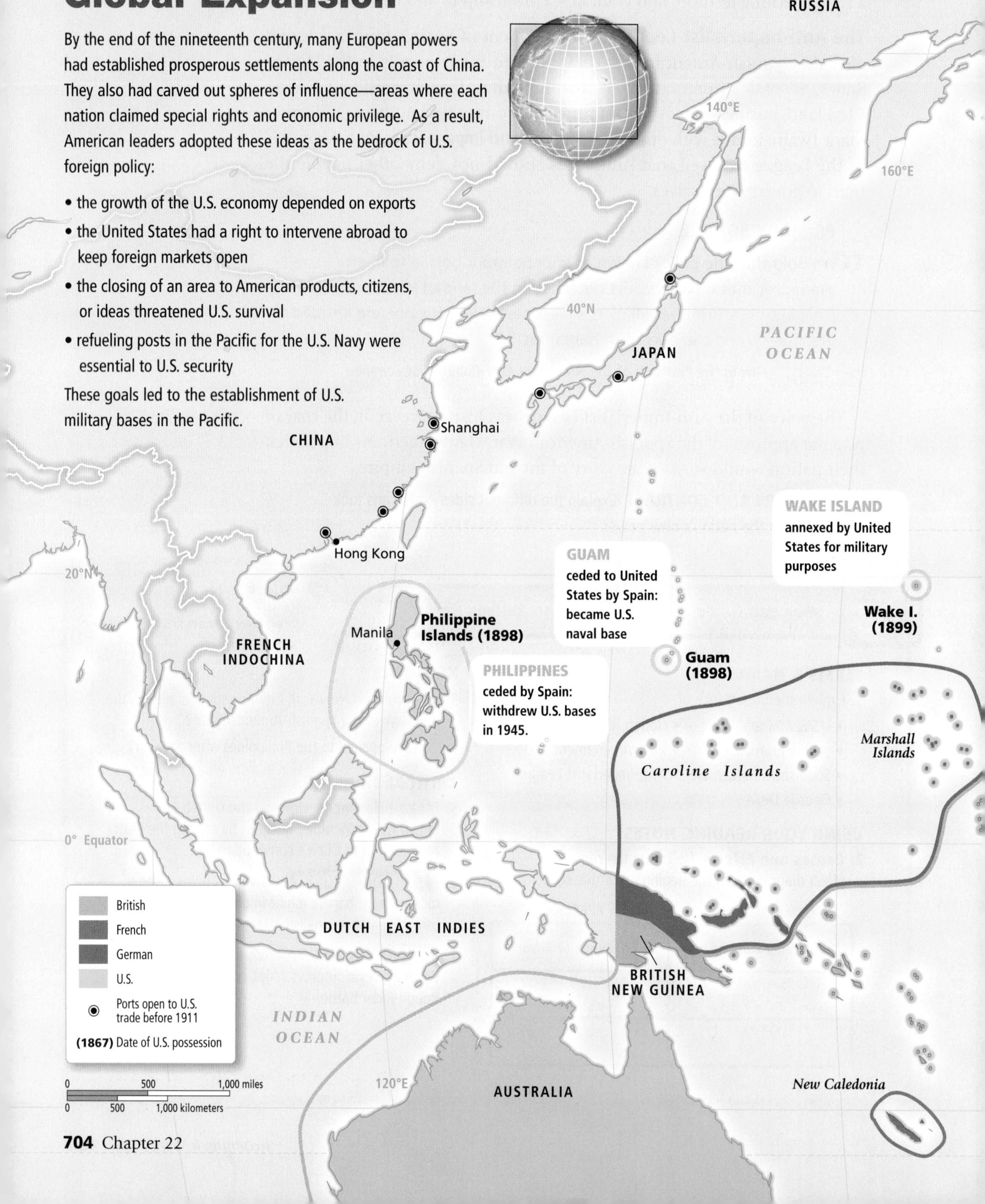

RUSSIA

140°E

160°E

40°N

JAPAN

PACIFIC OCEAN

CHINA

Shanghai

WAKE ISLAND
annexed by United States for military purposes

GUAM
ceded to United States by Spain: became U.S. naval base

Hong Kong

Wake I. (1899)

Manila

Philippine Islands (1898)

FRENCH INDOCHINA

PHILIPPINES
ceded by Spain: withdrew U.S. bases in 1945.

Guam (1898)

Marshall Islands

20°N

Caroline Islands

0° Equator

British

French

German

U.S.

Ports open to U.S. trade before 1911

(1867) Date of U.S. possession

DUTCH EAST INDIES

BRITISH NEW GUINEA

INDIAN OCEAN

| 0 | 500 | 1,000 miles |
| 0 | 500 | 1,000 kilometers |

120°E

AUSTRALIA

New Caledonia

704 Chapter 22

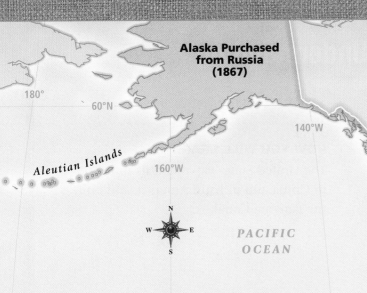

Alaska Purchased
from Russia
(1867)

180°

60°N

Aleutian Islands

160°W

140°W

PACIFIC
OCEAN

UNITED STATES

• San Francisco

Midway I.
(1867)

HAWAIIAN ISLANDS
Hawaii gives U.S. exclusive
rights to build a base in
Pearl Harbor.

Tropic of Cancer

Hawaiian Islands
(1898)

*Johnston
Atoll*

**"Guano Act"
Islands (1856)**

Palmyra Atoll

Howland I.
Baker I.

Jarvis I.

AMERICAN SAMOA
U.S. coaling station and
naval base.

P   o   l   y   n   e   s   i   a

*Western
Samoa*

**American
Samoa (1899)**

French Polynesia

In 1907, Theodore Roosevelt sent a fleet of 16 battleships on
a 14-month long voyage around the world to demonstrate
that the United States was a world-class naval power. Since
the voyage of this "Great White Fleet," U.S. Navy ships have
been painted gray.

0° Equator

Connect Geography & History

1. **Location** What geographic features of the
   Pacific Islands would make them of particular
   interest to the U.S. Navy?

2. **Evaluate** Why do you think American bases
   in the Pacific would be beneficial to the
   United States?

 See Geography Handbook, page A2.

Reading for Understanding

▶ Key Ideas

BEFORE, YOU LEARNED

The United States went to war with Spain and won colonies in the Caribbean and the Pacific.

NOW YOU WILL LEARN

The United States expanded its influence in China and in Latin America, and built the Panama Canal.

▶ Vocabulary

TERMS & NAMES

sphere of influence areas where foreign nations claimed special rights and economic privileges

Open Door Policy U.S. policy proposed in 1899 which stated that no single country should have a monopoly on trade with China

Boxer Rebellion 1900 nationalist uprising in China

Panama Canal canal through the Isthmus of Panama that connects the Atlantic and Pacific

Roosevelt Corollary United States claim of right to interfere in the affairs of Latin American countries

BACKGROUND VOCABULARY

malaria infectious disease spread by mosquitoes

REVIEW

Monroe Doctrine policy of U.S. opposition to any European interference in the Western Hemisphere

Visual Vocabulary
member of Boxer Rebellion

▶ Reading Strategy

Re-create the diagram shown at the right. As you respond to the **KEY QUESTIONS**, use the diagram to record the important events in the order in which they occurred.

 See Skillbuilder Handbook, page R5.

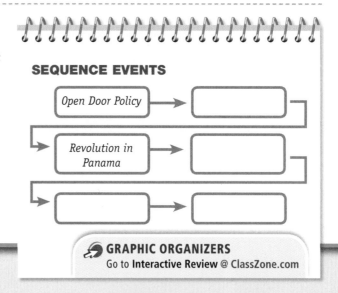

SEQUENCE EVENTS

Open Door Policy → ☐

Revolution in Panama → ☐

☐ → ☐

GRAPHIC ORGANIZERS
Go to **Interactive Review** @ ClassZone.com

Expanding Interests in Asia and Latin America

8 – U6.2.1 United States History Investigation Topic and Issue Analysis, Past and Present – Use historical perspectives to analyze issues in the United States from the past and the present; conduct research on a historical issue or topic, identify a connection to a contemporary issue, and present findings (e.g., oral, visual, video, or electronic presentation, persuasive essay, or research paper); include causes and consequences of the historical action and predict possible consequences of the contemporary action.
8 – P3.1.1.3 Identify, research, analyze, discuss, and defend a position on a national public policy issue – Use inquiry methods to trace the origins of the issue and to acquire data about the issue.

One American's Story

In 1852, President Millard Fillmore sent Commodore Matthew Perry on a mission to open Japan to U.S. trade. For over two centuries, Japan's rulers had kept the country closed to most foreigners. Perry wanted to break Japan's traditional policy.

PRIMARY SOURCE

❝ [I was determined] to adopt an entirely contrary plan of proceedings from that of all others who had . . . visited Japan on the same errand [to open up trade]: to demand as a right and not to [ask] as a favor those acts of courtesy which are due from one civilized nation to another. ❞

—Commodore Matthew Perry, *Personal Journal*

Under the threat of force, Japan signed a treaty in 1854 giving American ships access to its ports. This was the start of U.S. involvement in Asia.

Commodore Matthew Perry as portrayed by a 19th century Japanese artist

A Power in the Pacific

🔻 **KEY QUESTION** What steps increased American influence in East Asia and the Pacific?

When Commodore Perry opened Japan to U.S. trade in the 1850s, he also opened the nation to Western ideas. Because of this, Japan began to modernize and soon emerged as a world power. In the 1890s, Japan demonstrated its strength in a successful war against China. After the war, Japan as well as the major European powers expanded their **spheres of influence**. These were areas where foreign nations claimed special rights and economic privileges. Like other Western nations, the United States also wanted to trade with China.

The United States and China By the late 1890s, France, Germany, Britain, Japan, and Russia had established prosperous settlements along the coast of China. They also claimed exclusive rights to railroad construction and mining development in the nation's interior.

The competition for spheres of influence worried U.S. leaders who wanted access to China's markets and resources. In 1899, Secretary of State John Hay asked nations involved in the region to follow an **Open Door Policy.** This policy stated that no single country should have a monopoly on trade with China. Eventually, most of the nations accepted Hay's proposal.

Many Chinese people were not pleased by the presence of foreigners. One group, called the "Boxers," was angered by the privileges given to foreigners and the disrespect they showed toward Chinese traditions. In 1900, Chinese resentment led to a violent uprising known as the **Boxer Rebellion.** The rebellion was put down by an international force from eight nations, including Americans. About 230 foreigners and thousands of Chinese Christians and rebels were killed as a result of the Boxer Rebellion.

Connect to the World

Imperialism
The Boxers' real name was I-ho ch'üan, or "Righteous and Harmonious fists," from which the term "Boxers" came. The Boxers opposed Christianity, the Chinese power structure, and foreigners. Most of its members were young peasant men.

America Secures the Philippines As the Boxer Rebellion raged in China, American forces were still struggling to put down the independence movement in the Philippines. In 1902, they succeeded. Senator Albert Beveridge from Indiana, a supporter of imperialism boasted, "The Philippines are ours forever. And just beyond the Philippines are China's [unlimited] markets. We will not retreat from either. . . . The power that rules the Pacific is the power that rules the world."

Many Americans looked forward to the profits promised by Asian markets and resources. Others saw a chance to extend U.S. democracy in the region. The Philippines would provide a base for these activities.

Now that the Philippines were firmly under American control, the United States possessed a chain of islands in the Pacific that included Hawaii and Guam. Never before had America owned territories in such distant regions. The United States now had to find a way to help protect its Pacific empire, and allow ships from its east coast to gain easier access to the Far East.

▲ SEQUENCE List in chronological order the events that led to increasing U.S. influence in East Asia and the Pacific.

U.S. Interests in Latin America

▼ KEY QUESTION Why did the United States get involved in Latin America?

As the U.S. economy continued to grow, easy access to the Pacific became vital. For that reason, U.S. leaders proposed a canal to connect the Pacific and Atlantic oceans.

The Panama Canal A canal connecting the Atlantic and Pacific would mean that U.S. ships would not have to travel around the coast of South America. Such a canal would greatly reduce travel time for commercial and military transport. The Spanish-American War, fought in both oceans, also made clear the need for such a shortcut.

Animated HISTORY

TECHNOLOGY *of the* PANAMA CANAL

🖱 *Click here* to explore the technology of the Panama Canal @ ClassZone.com

The Panama Canal begins and ends at sea level but rises to 85 feet above sea level at Panama's Gatun Lake. (See inset map.) Why doesn't the lake empty into the sea?

NORTH AMERICA

N W E S

Gulf of Mexico

BAHAMAS

ATLANTIC OCEAN

CUBA

MEXICO

HAITI

PACIFIC OCEAN

JAMAICA

BELIZE

HONDURAS

Caribbean Sea

GUATEMALA
EL SALVADOR

NICARAGUA

0   250   500 miles
0   250   500 kilometers

COSTA RICA

PANAMA

Caribbean Sea   Colón
Cristóbal
0   5   10 miles
0   5   10 kilometers

Gatun Locks

Madden Lake

Gatun Lake

Pedro Miguel Locks

Miraflores Locks
Panama City
Balboa

← Canal route
☐ Canal Zone, 1903

Gulf of Panama

SOUTH AMERICA

1. With the left gate open and the right gate closed, a ship enters the lock.

2. The gate closes and water is pumped out. As the water level lowers, the ship is lowered with it. When the water level in the chamber reaches the level of the canal, the right gate opens.

3. The ship can also be raised by pumping water into the lock.

CRITICAL THINKING

1. Draw Conclusions Why did the United States want a shorter route between the Atlantic and Pacific oceans?

2. Connect to Today
Why is there less need for the Panama Canal today?

The best spot for a canal was the Isthmus of Panama. It was part of Colombia, but Colombia was unwilling to give up this land. Ignoring Colombia's right to control its territory, President Roosevelt sent the U.S. Navy to support a revolution on the isthmus. Out of this revolution the new nation of Panama was created in 1903.

The Panamanian leaders granted the United States rights to a ten-mile-wide strip of land called the Canal Zone. There the United States would build the **Panama Canal**, the shortcut that would connect the Atlantic and Pacific.

Some people in Latin America and the United States opposed Roosevelt's actions. They believed that he had interfered in Colombia's affairs in order to cheat it out of land. In 1921, the U.S. finally paid Colombia $25 million for the loss of Panama.

Theodore Roosevelt (in white suit) operates a steamshovel during the construction of the Panama Canal.
Why was Roosevelt's visit important?

Building the Panama Canal Building the canal was a huge challenge. The land was swampy and full of mosquitoes that carried the organism that causes **malaria**—an infectious disease marked by cycles of chills and fever.

In spite of the challenges, the project moved forward. When Roosevelt visited Panama in 1906, he described the building of the canal.

PRIMARY SOURCE

❝ Steam shovels are hard at it; scooping huge masses of rock and gravel and dirt previously loosened by the drillers and dynamite blasters, loading it on trains which take it away. . . . They are eating steadily into the mountain cutting it down and down. . . . It is an epic feat. ❞

—Theodore Roosevelt, *from a letter sent to his son*

More than 44,000 workers, including many black West Indians, labored on the canal. The Panama Canal opened in 1914. It cost between $350–$380 million to build, and was then the most expensive construction project in the world. More than 5,500 canal workers died from diseases or accidents.

U.S. Involvement in Latin America The Panama Canal was only one sign of U.S. involvement in Latin America. As the U.S. economy continued to grow, so did U.S. interest in the resources of their southern neighbors.

Businesses in the United States found that they could cheaply buy food and raw materials, such as bananas, coffee, and copper from Latin America. They shipped these goods to the United States and sold them for higher prices.

U.S. companies also bought large amounts of land in the region for farming and mining. As economic interests drew the United States deeper into Latin American affairs, U.S. leaders became concerned about political stability in the region. They worried that instability might tempt European nations to intervene in the region.

Policing the Hemisphere During his presidency, Theodore Roosevelt made it clear that the United States would remain the dominant power in the Western Hemisphere. He summed up his foreign policy toward the region when he said: "Speak softly and carry a big stick." Roosevelt was warning that the United States would use military force if its interests were threatened.

Roosevelt reminded European powers of the **Monroe Doctrine**—the policy that barred European nations from intervening in Latin America. In 1905, he added the **Roosevelt Corollary.** It authorized the United States to act as a "policeman" in the region. That is, U.S. leaders would now intervene in Latin America's domestic affairs when they believed that such action was necessary to maintain stability.

CONNECT to the Essential Question

How did America's growing power affect its relationships with other nations?

1867
U.S. Purchases Alaska

1898
U.S. Annexes Hawaii

1914
Panama Canal Opens
Improves international commerce. Increases U.S. naval power.

IMPERIALISM
○ **Economic Competition**
○ **Belief in Cultural Superiority**
○ **Military Competition**

1898
Spanish–American War
Cuba gains independence from Spain.
U.S. gains Puerto Rico, Guam, and the Philippine islands.

1905
Roosevelt Corollary
Asserts right of the U.S. to exercise police power in the Western Hemisphere.

1899
Open Door Policy
U.S. secures trading rights in China.

> **CRITICAL THINKING Causes and Effects**
> What were some of the long-term effects of U.S. overseas expansion?

Becoming a World Power **711**

In 1905, the United States used the Roosevelt Corollary to justify taking control of the Dominican Republic's finances. This was after the Dominican Republic failed to pay its foreign debts. A year later, when a revolt threatened Cuba's government, the policy was used to send troops there.

Later presidents expanded on Roosevelt's "big stick diplomacy." William Howard Taft urged American businesses to invest in Latin America. Taft promised military action if anything or anyone threatened these investments. He kept his word. In 1912, when Nicaraguan citizens revolted against their leader, Taft sent marines to Nicaragua to put down a revolt against the pro-American president.

President Taft's successor, Woodrow Wilson, also intervened in Latin America. In 1914 a revolution in Mexico began to threaten U.S. interests, Wilson sent a fleet to Veracruz after American sailors were arrested. Two years later, in 1916, he sent troops to Mexico when a Mexican revolutionary named Pancho Villa (PAHN•choh VEE•yah) raided New Mexico and killed 17 Americans in the town of Columbus.

Americans rarely questioned U.S. actions in Latin America. They saw their nation as a good police officer maintaining peace and preventing disorder. However, many Latin Americans did not agree. They saw the United States as a greedy imperial power that cared only about its own interests. This mistrust continues to trouble U.S. relations with its neighbors.

▲ **ANALYZE CAUSES** Why did America expand its involvement in Latin America?

 Michigan Grade Level Content Expectations *Review*

 ONLINE QUIZ
For test practice, go to
Interactive Review @ ClassZone.com

TERMS & NAMES

1. Explain the importance of
- sphere of influence
- Panama Canal
- Open Door Policy
- Roosevelt Corollary
- Boxer Rebellion

USING YOUR READING NOTES

2. Sequence Events Complete the diagram that you started at the beginning of this section.

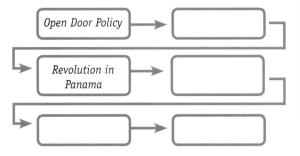

KEY IDEAS

3. What caused the Boxer Rebellion?

4. What events made the building of the Panama Canal so important to the United States?

CRITICAL THINKING

5. Make Inferences Why was the United States interested in the political stability of Latin America?

6. **Connect** *to* **Today** Why do you think the Panama Canal has more commercial than military importance today?

7. **Math** Using the Internet or library resources, find out the dimensions of the Panama Canal. Then write a short report on how much time and distance was saved by ships after the construction of the canal.

Chapter Summary

1 Key Idea
The United States took its first steps in becoming a world power by acquiring Alaska and Hawaii.

2 Key Idea
The United States went to war with Spain and won colonies in the Caribbean and the Pacific.

3 Key Idea
The United States expanded its influence in China and in Latin America, and built the Panama Canal.

For detailed Review and Study Notes go to **Interactive Review** @ ClassZone.com

Name Game

Use the Terms & Names list to complete each sentence online or on your own paper.

1. _____ is the policy by which strong nations extend control over weaker territories. imperialism

2. _____ was responsible for America's acquisition of Alaska in 1867.

3. In 1898, the _____ exploded and sank off the coast of Cuba.

4. The _____ was opposed to foreign presence in China.

5. _____ were members of the first U.S. Volunteer Cavalry.

6. The _____ was fought over Cuba's right to independence.

7. Construction of the _____ facilitated trade between the U.S. and Latin America.

8. In 1902, the U.S. insisted that Cuba add the _____ to its new constitution.

9. Reporting that sensationalized the news was known as _____

10. In 1898, the U.S. proposed an _____ to promote unrestricted trade with China.

A. U.S.S *Maine*
B. Boxer Rebellion
C. Open Door Policy
D. George Dewey
E. William Seward
F. Anti-Imperialist League
G. Roosevelt Corollary
H. Platt Amendment
I. Rough Riders
J. Panama Canal
K. Imperialism
L. Yellow Journalism
M. Sphere of Influence
N. Spanish-American War
O. Queen Liliuokalani

Activities

CROSSWORD PUZZLE

Complete the online crossword to show what you know about American imperialism.

ACROSS

1. _____ _____ is grown on Hawaiian plantations.

FLIPCARD

Use the online flip cards to quiz yourself on the terms and names introduced in this chapter.

Led U.S. trade expedition to Japan in 1850s.

ANSWER: Matthew Perry

VOCABULARY

Choose the correct answer.

1. Commodore George Dewey was (the leader of the Rough Riders/the hero of the Battle of Manila Bay).

2. Queen Liliuokalani was the ruler of (Alaska/Hawaii).

3. William Seward purchased (Alaska/Hawaii) from Russia.

4. The Rough Riders fought in (Cuba/Panama).

5. The Boxer Rebellion took place in (China/the Philippines).

Explain how the terms and names in each group are related.

6. yellow journalism, U.S.S. *Maine*, Spanish-American War

7. Platt Amendment, Panama Canal, Roosevelt Corollary

8. sphere of influence, William Seward, imperialism

KEY IDEAS

1 **Imperialism in the Pacific (pages 694–697)**

9. Why did Americans become interested in overseas expansion in the late 1800s?

10. How did the public react when William Seward negotiated the purchase of Alaska in 1867?

11. Why did the United States take an interest in Hawaii?

2 **The Spanish-American War (pages 698–703)**

12. How did the Spanish-American War begin?

13. What territories did the United States take as a result of its victory over the Spanish?

3 **Expanding Interests in Asia and Latin America (pages 706–712)**

14. Why did U.S. leaders want access to Asian markets after the Spanish-American War?

15. Why was there an interest in building a canal across Latin America?

16. How were the Latin American policies of Roosevelt, Taft, and Wilson similar?

CRITICAL THINKING

17. **Draw Conclusions** How did U.S. economic interests in Latin America influence the foreign policy of the United States?

18. **Form and Support Opinions** How did the presence of foreigners in China contribute to the Boxer Rebellion?

19. **Categorize** Use a chart like the one below to record details about U.S. involvement in Asia and Latin America.

Asia	Latin America
Filipino independence defeated	*Panama Canal constructed*

20. **Summarize** What political difficulty faced U.S. leaders who wanted to build the Panama Canal?

21. **Evaluate** Do you think the United States was justified in going to war with Spain? Explain your answer.

22. **Synthesize** How did the building of the Panama Canal support United States efforts to become a world power?

23. **Analyze Leadership** What qualities made Theodore Roosevelt an effective leader?

24. **Interpret Graphs** Read the graph below. When did U.S. exports first outnumber U.S. imports?

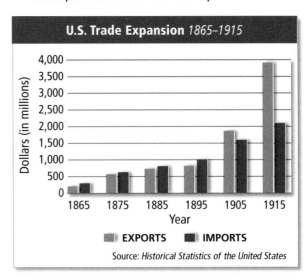

U.S. Trade Expansion *1865–1915*

Dollars (in millions) / Year

■ EXPORTS   ■ IMPORTS

Source: *Historical Statistics of the United States*

✓ **TEST PRACTICE**

• **Online Test Practice** @ ClassZone.com
• Use the **MEAP Strategies & Practice,** pages S1-S27, at the front of this book

DOCUMENT-BASED QUESTIONS

Analyze each document, and answer the question that follows.

DOCUMENT 1

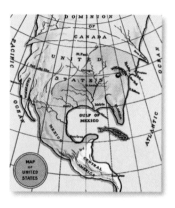

DOCUMENT 2

❝ How long are the Spaniards to drench Cuba with the blood and tears of her people? . . . How long shall American citizens, arbitrarily arrested while on peaceful and legitimate errands, be immured [held] in foul Spanish prisons without trial? . . . How long shall the United States sit idle and indifferent within sound and hearing of . . . murder? How long? ❞

—Joseph Pulitzer, New York *World*, February 13, 1897

1 Examine the cartoon and primary source. How did "yellow journalism" help gain support for the Spanish-American War?

   A by portraying the Spanish as victims of cruelty

   B by writing articles against Cuban rebels

   C by exaggerating news about Spanish cruelty in Cuba

   D by arguing against U.S. imperialism

YOU BE THE HISTORIAN

25. **Draw Conclusions** How do you think manifest destiny set the stage for American imperialism at the end of the 19th century?

26. **Compare and Contrast** How did U.S. expansion at the end of the 19th century compare and contrast with expansion that occurred earlier?

27. **Connect Economics & History** How did the U.S. purchase of Alaska protect America's future interests?

28. **WHAT IF?** How might history have been different if the United States had given the Philippines its independence after the Spanish-American War?

29. **Citizenship** How might the activities of the Anti-Imperialist League have helped to remind citizens of their democratic responsibilities?

30. **Connect** *to* **Today** The "yellow journalism" of major newspapers influenced U.S. foreign policy at the turn of the century. How does modern media, such as television, shape public opinion today?

Answer the
ESSENTIAL QUESTION
How did America's growing power affect its relationships with other nations?

Written Response Write a two-to-three-paragraph response to the Essential Question. Be sure to consider the key ideas of each section as well as the most significant factors that affected America's relationships with other nations.

Response Rubric
A strong response will

• discuss major events that led to the growth of American power

• explain the importance of strong leadership

• evaluate how the use of American power impacted other nations

• analyze how the use of American power influenced public opinion in America

World War I & Its Legacy

1914–1929

War in Europe

Key Idea: World War I devastated Europe and drew America into a global conflict.

The assassination of Austro-Hungarian Archduke Franz Ferdinand in 1914 ignited the underlying causes of World War I—European imperialism, nationalism, militarism, and alliances between nations. Most of the fighting took place in Europe, although nations from every part of the globe became involved in the war. The United States joined the Allies in 1917 and eventually helped them to defeat Germany in 1918.

British soldiers during the Battle of the Lys, April 29, 1918

World War I recruiting poster

1914
World War I begins.

1915 German U-boat sinks Lusitania.

1916 The battles of Verdun and the Somme claim millions of lives.

1917 The United States declares war against Central Powers; Revolution brings Communists to power in Russia.

1918 Wilson's Fourteen Points; Armistice is declared on November 11, 1918. World War I ends.

1919 The Treaty of Versailles is signed; the 18th Amendment establishes Prohibition.

1920 The 19th Amendment grants women the right to vote.

The Home Front

Key Idea: Americans united and made many sacrifices to help the war effort.

Once the United States entered World War I, the federal government built up the military with a draft and sought to control the wartime economy, information, and public opinion. American civilians bought war bonds and economized to help the war effort. Women served in the military and worked in wartime industries, as did African Americans, whose movement to northern cities at this time became known as the Great Migration.

(*above*) Segregated waiting room in train station at Jacksonville, Florida
(*right*) a liberty bond from 1917

The Roaring Twenties

Key Idea: American society changed during the 1920s.

After World War I, most Americans were eager for a "return to normalcy" and prosperity, but were divided over foreign policy and domestic issues such as Prohibition. Women won the right to vote, yet their growing independence often clashed with traditional society. African Americans faced new challenges but made great contributions to American culture during the Jazz Age and the Harlem Renaissance.

Magazine cover from 1926

Louis Armstrong, jazz musician

1923 Calvin Coolidge becomes president; U.S. economy booms during his administration.

1925 The Jazz Age and Harlem Renaissance are in full swing; Scopes "Monkey Trial"

1927 Charles Lindbergh makes first solo flight across the Atlantic.

1927 *The Jazz Singer*: first commercial "talking" motion picture

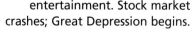
1929

Americans spend $4 billion on entertainment. Stock market crashes; Great Depression begins.

Depression, War, & Recovery
1929–1960

The Great Depression and the New Deal

Key Idea: The government enacted various programs to end the Great Depression.

When the prosperity of the 1920s collapsed, President Herbert Hoover struggled to address the country's economic problems. After becoming president in 1933, Franklin D. Roosevelt launched an aggressive program to fight the Great Depression. The hardships of the Great Depression and the policies of the New Deal forever changed American society and government.

Migrant worker and her children in California during the Great Depression

Man trying to sell his car after the stock market crash

1929

1930 Dust Bowl conditions

1932 Bonus Army; FDR elected

1935 Italy invades Ethiopia.

1940 Germany conquers France; Battle of Britain begins.

Oct. 29: Black Tuesday— Great Depression begins.

1931 Japan invades Manchuria.

1933 Roosevelt's Hundred Days: New Deal begins

1939 Germany invades Poland, starting WWII.

1941 U.S. enters WWII after Japan attacks Pearl Harbor.

The Rise of Dictators and World War II

Key Idea: World War II Transformed America and the World.

The rise of dictators in Europe in the 1930s led to World War II. As the war raged in Europe, Americans at home made great contributions to the Allied cause. After five long years of world conflict, the Allies finally defeated the Axis powers in Europe and Africa. Following victory in Europe, and despite early losses in the Pacific, the Allies eventually defeated the Japanese. During the course of the war, America emerged as a major power in the western hemisphere.

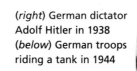

(*right*) German dictator Adolf Hitler in 1938
(*below*) German troops riding a tank in 1944

The Cold War and the American Dream

Key Idea: In the years after World War II, America faced Cold War tensions as well as significant domestic changes.

The end of World War II led to prosperity as well as a new kind of war against Communism. The Cold War led to the Korean War, which produced an intense anti-Communism movement in America. From 1945 to the 1960s, economic growth and Cold War tensions caused many changes in American society.

Hydrogen bomb test in 1957

Rock 'n' roll pioneer Chuck Berry

1942 Battle of Midway; Japanese-American internment begins.

1944 D-Day: Allied invasion of Europe

1945 Yalta Conference; Atomic bombs dropped on Hiroshima and Nagasaki; Germany & Japan surrender; Roosevelt dies, Truman becomes president; United Nations created; Nuremburg trials

1947 HUAC targets communists.

1948 Marshall Plan begins; Israel created; Berlin airlift begins.

1949 Communist revolution in China

1950 Korean War begins.

1957 Soviet Union launches Sputnik.

1960

▼ JFK elected

Depression, War, & Recovery **719**

EPILOGUE 3

Civil Rights, Vietnam, & Watergate
1954–1975

The Struggle for Civil Rights

Key Idea: Americans responded to discrimination during the civil rights era.

Between the 1870s and World War II, African Americans lost many of the civil rights they had gained during Reconstruction. Their long struggle to regain these rights began in the early 20th century as African-American leaders and white activists organized to fight segregation, voting restrictions, and lynching. In the 1950s and 1960s, Supreme Court rulings against segregation and effective protests by the African-American civil rights movement inspired Hispanics, Native Americans, and women to fight for and win increased civil rights.

Martin Luther King, Jr., and his wife, Coretta, lead a civil rights march in 1965.

Leaders of the United Farm Workers, Dolores Heurta and César Chávez, discuss events during grape pickers' strike.

1965 Congress passes the Voting Rights Act; many more African Americans register to vote.

1955 Rosa Parks arrested for refusing to give up her bus seat for a group of white passengers. The Montgomery bus boycott begins.

1962 Cuban Missile Crisis increases fear that communism might spread.

1964 Congress passes Civil Rights Act of 1964.

1954

▼ *Brown* v. *Board of Education* decided by Supreme Court.

1960 John F. Kennedy is elected president.

1963 Lyndon B. Johnson becomes president after Kennedy's assassination; the March on Washington unites the civil rights movement.

The Vietnam War

Key Idea: U.S. involvement in the Vietnam War had lasting effects on America and Southeast Asia.

Fearing the spread of Communism, the U.S. government intensified its military and political interests in Vietnam between 1950 and 1973. Americans expected a quick victory, but soldiers soon grew frustrated by the elusive Viet Cong. As the conflict escalated and dragged on, more Americans protested the war and government misconduct. After the United States pulled out of the war, the Viet Cong gained complete control of Vietnam and Congress limited the president's war-making powers.

American soldiers in Vietnam, 1968

Tourists reading headlines outside the White House in 1974. Richard Nixon is the only U.S. president to resign from office.

Watergate Changes Politics

Key Idea: The Watergate scandal weakened the United States government.

In 1972, President Nixon and his aides illegally tried to cover up a break-in at Democratic Party Headquarters in the Watergate complex in Washington, D.C. The Watergate scandal, as it became known, caused Americans to lose confidence in elected officials and weakened the government, especially the presidency. Facing impeachment, Nixon resigned from office on August 9, 1974.

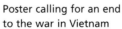

Poster calling for an end to the war in Vietnam

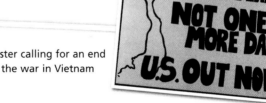

1968 Martin Luther King, Jr., is assassinated; the Tet offensive causes Americans to question the war in Vietnam.

1970 La Raza Unida is founded.

1972 Members of AIM occupy and Bureau of Indian Affairs. Congress passes the Equal Rights Amendment, but it fails to get ratified.

1974 Nixon resigns as a result of the Watergate scandal

1975

1969 Richard M. Nixon becomes president.

1971 The 26th Amendment lowers the voting age from 21 to 18.

1973 United States withdraws from Vietnam.

The Vietnam War ends after Communists take over South Vietnam.

America in a Changing World
1976–2006

The Late 1970s

Key Idea: The late 1970s were years of doubt for many Americans.

In 1976 it seemed that celebrating the bicentennial of American independence would help the nation to recover from the turmoil of Vietnam, assassinations, the civil rights struggles, and Watergate. But like President Ford, Carter also had little success: while he was able to negotiate peace in the Middle East, his presidency was troubled by an oil shortage, a recession, and the hostage crisis in Iran.

Jimmy and Rosalynn Carter on Inauguration Day, 1977

America's bicentennial was celebrated around the world with fireworks, parades, and many other events.

1976 American bicentennial celebrations

1978 Camp David Peace Accords between Egypt and Israel

1979 Americans taken hostage in Iran

1980 Ronald Reagan elected president

1983 IBM releases first desktop "personal computer"

1986 Iran-Contra affair discovered

1989 World Wide Web protocol created; Exxon Valdez oil spill

1990 End of Cold War

1991 Soviet Union breaks apart; Persian Gulf War

1992 Bill Clinton elected president

Conservatives Reshape Politics

Key Idea: During the 1980s, conservatives reshaped U.S. politics.

Republican President Ronald Reagan pursued conservative goals by increasing military spending. By the time Reagan left office, the economy was growing, and soon thereafter Eastern Europe became free of Soviet control. President Bush won a decisive victory in the Persian Gulf War but could not win re-election. Under President Clinton the nation saw reductions in the federal deficit, inflation, crime, and unemployment.

East and West Berlin reunited in 1989.

Challenges to Face, Strengths to Build On

Key Idea: America's strengths have helped us face the challenges of the past four decades and will help us in the 21st century.

Recent events have tested America's strengths—economic and military leadership, enviable technologies, abundant resources, a robust democracy, and a diverse, educated citizenry. Today the nation faces many complex issues, including growing health care costs, jobs moving overseas, global warming, terrorism, and a changing population. How Americans address these challenges will shape the lives of future generations.

America's future lies in the strengths of its young people.

Hours after this photograph was taken on Sept. 11, 2001, both towers of the New York World Trade Center collapsed.

1995 Terrorists blow up Federal Building in Oklahoma City

2000 George W. Bush declared winner of disputed election; More than half of American households have cell phones.

2002 U.S. leads invasion of Afghanistan

2004 George W. Bush wins disputed election

2006

1993 NAFTA lowers tariffs; European Union created

1996 Taliban captures Kabul, Afghanistan; President Clinton impeached, found not guilty

2001 Sept. 11 attacks; first artificial heart

2003 Iraq war begins.

2005 Hurricane Katrina devastates New Orleans

Reference Section

American HISTORY

Table of Contents

Reading and Critical Thinking

Reading Maps, Graphs, and Other Visuals

Research, Writing, and Presentation Skills

Using the Internet

1.1 Taking Notes with Graphic Organizers

Defining the Skill

When you **take notes,** you write down the important ideas and details of a paragraph, passage, or chapter. A chart or an outline can help you organize your notes to use in the future.

Applying the Skill

The following passage describes President Washington's cabinet. Use the strategies listed below to help you take notes on the passage.

How to Take and Organize Notes

Strategy ❶ Look at the title to find the main topic of the passage.

Strategy ❷ Identify the main ideas and details of the passage. Then summarize the main idea and details in your notes.

Strategy ❸ Identify key terms and define them. The term *cabinet* is shown in boldface type and highlighted; both techniques signal that it is a key term.

Strategy ❹ In your notes, use abbreviations to save time and space. You can abbreviate words such as *department (dept.), secretary (sec.), United States (U.S.),* and *president (pres.)* to save time and space.

---

❶ **WASHINGTON'S CABINET**

❷ The Constitution gave Congress the task of creating departments to help the president lead the nation. The ❷ president had the power to appoint the heads of these departments, which became his ❸ **cabinet.**

Congress created three departments. Washington chose talented people to run them. ❷ For secretary of war, he picked Henry Knox, a trusted general during the Revolution. ❷ For secretary of state, Washington chose Thomas Jefferson. He had been serving as ambassador to France. The State Department oversaw U.S. foreign relations. For secretary of the treasury, Washington turned to the brilliant ❷ Alexander Hamilton.

Make a Chart

Making a chart can help you take notes on a passage. The chart below contains notes from the passage you just read.

Item	Notes
1. ❸ cabinet	heads of ❹ depts; ❹ pres. appoints heads
a. War Dept.	Henry Knox; ❹ sec. of war; former Revolutionary War general
b. State Dept.	Thomas Jefferson; sec. of state; oversees relations between ❹ U.S. and other countries
c. Treasury Dept.	Alexander Hamilton; sec. of the treasurey

Practicing the Skill

Turn to Chapter 3, Section 3, "The Southern Colonies." Read "The Region of the South" on page 81, and use a graphic organizer to take notes on the passage.

1.2 Summarizing

Defining the Skill

When you **summarize**, you restate a paragraph, passage, or chapter in fewer words. You include only the main ideas and most important details. It is important to use your own words when summarizing.

Applying the Skill

The passage below tells about Harriet Tubman, a prominent member of the Underground Railroad. She helped runaway slaves to freedom. Use the strategies listed below to help you summarize the passage.

How to Summarize

Strategy 1 Look for topic sentences stating the main idea. These are often at the beginning of a section or paragraph. Briefly restate each main idea—in your own words.

Strategy 2 Include key facts and any numbers, dates, amounts, or percentages from the text.

Strategy 3 After writing your summary, review it to see that you have included only the most important details.

HARRIET TUBMAN

1 One of the most famous conductors on the Underground Railroad was Harriet Tubman. **2** Born into slavery in Maryland, the 13-year-old Tubman once tried to save another slave from punishment. The angry overseer fractured Tubman's skull with a two-pound weight. She suffered fainting spells for the rest of her life but did not let that stop her from working for freedom. When she was 25, Tubman learned that her owner was about to sell her. Instead, **2** she escaped.

After her escape, **2** Harriet Tubman made 19 dangerous journeys to free enslaved persons. The tiny woman carried a pistol to frighten off slave hunters and medicine to quiet crying babies. Her enemies offered $40,000 for her capture, but **2** no one caught her. "I never run my train off the track and I never lost a passenger," she proudly declared. Among the people she saved were her parents.

Write a Summary

You can write your summary in a paragraph. The paragraph at right summarizes the passage you just read.

3 Harriet Tubman was one of the most famous conductors on the Underground Railroad. She had been a slave, but she escaped. She later made 19 dangerous journeys to free other slaves. She was never captured.

Practicing the Skill

Turn to Chapter 6, Section 2, "Colonial Resistance Grows." Read "The Boston Massacre" on pages 163–164, and write a paragraph summarizing the passage.

1.3 Finding Main Ideas

Defining the Skill

The **main idea** is a statement that summarizes the main point of a speech, an article, a section of a book, or a paragraph. Main ideas can be stated or unstated. The main idea of a paragraph is often stated in the first or last sentence. If it is the first sentence, it is followed by sentences that support that main idea. If it is the last sentence, the details build up to the main idea. To find an unstated idea, you must use the details of the paragraph as clues.

Applying the Skill

The following paragraph describes the role of women in the American Revolution. Use the strategies listed below to help you identify the main idea.

How to Find the Main Idea

Strategy 1 Identify what you think may be the stated main idea. Check the first and last sentences of the paragraph to see if either could be the stated main idea.

Strategy 2 Identify details that support that idea. Some details explain the main idea. Others give examples of what is stated in the main idea.

> **WOMEN IN THE REVOLUTION**
>
> 1 Many women tried to help the army. Martha Washington and other wives followed their husbands to army camps. 2 The wives cooked, did laundry, and nursed sick or wounded soldiers. 2 A few women even helped to fight. 2 Mary Hays earned the nickname "Molly Pitcher" by carrying water to tired soldiers during a battle. 2 Deborah Sampson dressed as a man, enlisted, and fought in several engagements.

Make a Chart

Making a chart can help you identify the main idea and details in a passage or paragraph. The chart below identifies the main idea and details in the paragraph you just read.

Main Idea: Women helped the army during the Revolution.

Detail: They cooked and did laundry
Detail: They nursed the wounded and sick soldiers
Detail: They helped to fight.
Detail: One woman, Molly Pitcher, carried water to soldiers during battles.

Practicing the Skill

Turn to Chapter 5, Section 2, "Roots of American Democracy." Read "Parliament and Colonial Government" on page 139, and create a chart that identifies the main idea and the supporting details.

1.4 Sequencing Events

Defining the Skill

Sequence is the order in which events follow one another. By being able to follow the sequence of events through history, you can get an accurate sense of the relationships among events.

Applying the Skill

The following passage describes the sequence of events involved in Britain's plan to capture the Hudson River valley during the American Revolution. Use the strategies listed below to help you follow the sequence of events.

How to Find the Sequence of Events

Strategy 1 Look for specific dates provided in the text. If several months within a year are included, the year is usually not repeated.

Strategy 2 Look for clues about time that allow you to order events according to sequence. Words such as *day*, *week*, *month*, or *year* may help to sequence the events.

> **BRITAIN'S STRATEGY**
>
> Burgoyne captured Fort Ticonderoga in **1** July 1777. From there, it was 25 miles to the Hudson River, which ran to Albany. **2** Burgoyne took three weeks to reach the Hudson. On **1** August 3, Burgoyne received a message from Howe. He would not be coming north, Howe wrote, because he had decided to invade Pennsylvania to try to capture Philadelphia and General Washington. "Success be ever with you," Howe's message said. But General Burgoyne needed Howe's soldiers, not his good wishes. Howe did invade Pennsylvania. In **1** September 1777, he defeated —but did not capture—Washington at the Battle of Brandywine.

Make a Time Line

Making a time line can help you sequence events. The time line below shows the sequence of events in the passage you just read.

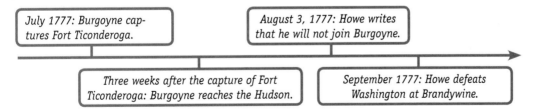

July 1777: Burgoyne captures Fort Ticonderoga.

August 3, 1777: Howe writes that he will not join Burgoyne.

Three weeks after the capture of Fort Ticonderoga: Burgoyne reaches the Hudson.

September 1777: Howe defeats Washington at Brandywine.

Practicing the Skill

Turn to Chapter 8, Section 1, "The Confederation Era." Read "The Articles Are Ratified" on page 237, and make a time line showing the sequence of events in that passage.

1.5 Categorizing

Defining the Skill

To **categorize** is to sort people, objects, ideas, or other information into groups, called categories. Historians categorize information to help them identify and understand patterns in historical events.

Applying the Skill

The following passage contains information about the reasons people went west during the mid-1800s. Use the strategies listed below to help you categorize information.

How to Categorize

Strategy ① First, decide what kind of information needs to be categorized. Decide what the passage is about and how that information can be sorted into categories. For example, find the different motives people had for moving west.

Strategy ② Then find out what the categories will be. To find why many different groups of people moved west, look for clue words such as *some*, *other*, and *another*.

Strategy ③ Once you have chosen the categories, sort information into them. Of the people who went west, which ones had which motives?

THE LURE OF THE WEST

① People had many different motives for going west. ② One motive was to make money. ② *Some* people called speculators bought huge areas of land and made great profits by selling it to thousands of settlers. ② *Other* settlers included farmers who dreamed of owning their own farms in the West because land was difficult to acquire in the East. ② *Another* group to move west was merchants. They hoped to earn money by selling items that farmers needed. Finally, ② *some* people went west for religious reasons. These people included ② missionaries, who wanted to convert the Native Americans to Christianity, and Mormons, who wanted a place where they could practice their faith without interference.

Make a Chart

Making a chart can help you categorize information. You should have as many columns as you have categories. The chart below shows how the information from the passage you just read can be categorized.

③

Motives	Money	Land	Religion
Groups	• speculators • merchants	• farmers	• missionaries • Mormons

Practicing the Skill

Turn to Chapter 14, Section 3, "Reforming American Society." Read "Social Reform" on page 460, and make a chart in which you categorize the changes happening in elementary, high school, and college education.

1.6 Analyzing Causes and Effects

Defining the Skill

A **cause** is an action in history that makes something happen. An **effect** is the historical event that is the result of the cause. A single event may have several causes. It is also possible for one cause to result in several effects. Historians identify cause-and-effect relationships to help them understand why historical events took place.

Applying the Skill

The following paragraph describes events that caused changes in Puritan New England. Use the strategies listed below to help you identify the cause-and-effect relationships.

How to Analyze Causes and Recognize Effects

Strategy 1 Ask why an action took place. Ask yourself a question about the title and topic sentence, such as, "What caused changes in Puritan society?"

Strategy 2 Look for effects. Ask yourself, "What happened?" (the effect). Then ask, "Why did it happen?" (the cause). For example, What caused the decline of Puritan religion in New England?

Strategy 3 Look for clue words that signal causes, such as *cause* and *led to*.

Strategy 4 One way to practice recognizing effects is to make predictions about the consequences that will result from particular actions. Then, as you read, look to see if your predictions were accurate.

> **1** CHANGES IN PURITAN SOCIETY
>
> **1** The early 1700s saw many changes in New England society. **2** One of the most important changes was the gradual decline of the Puritan religion in New England. There were a number of reasons for that decline. **3** One *cause* of this decline was the increasing competition from other religious groups. Baptists and Anglicans established churches in Massachusetts and Connecticut, where Puritans had once been the most powerful group. **3** Political changes also *led to* a weakening of the Puritan community. In 1691, a new royal charter for Massachusetts granted the vote based on property ownership instead of church membership.

Make a Diagram

Using a diagram can help you understand causes and effects. The diagram below shows two causes and an effect for the passage you just read.

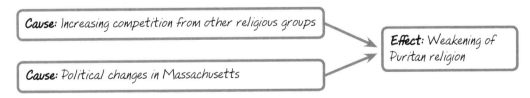

Cause: *Increasing competition from other religious groups*

Cause: *Political changes in Massachusetts*

Effect: *Weakening of Puritan religion*

Practicing the Skill

Turn to Chapter 4, Section 2, "The Southern Colonies: Plantations and Slavery." Read "Expansion of Plantations Brings Resistance" on pages 106–107, and make a diagram about the causes and effects of slave resistance.

1.7 Comparing and Contrasting

Defining the Skill

Comparing means looking at the similarities and differences between two or more things. **Contrasting** means examining only the differences between them. Historians compare and contrast events, personalities, behaviors, beliefs, and situations in order to understand them.

Applying the Skill

The following paragraph describes the American and British troops during the Revolutionary War. Use the strategies listed below to help you compare and contrast these two armies.

How to Compare and Contrast

Strategy ① Look for two aspects of the subject that may be compared and contrasted. This passage compares the British and American troops to show why the Americans won the war.

Strategy ② To contrast, look for clue words that show how two things differ. Clue words include *by contrast*, *however*, *except*, and *yet*.

Strategy ③ To find similarities, look for clue words indicating that two things are alike. Clue words include *both*, *like*, *as*, and *similarly*.

> ### WHY THE AMERICANS WON
>
> ① By their persistence, the Americans defeated the British even though they faced many obstacles. The Americans lacked training and experience. They were often short of supplies and weapons. ② *By contrast*, the British forces ranked among the best trained in the world. They were experienced and well-supplied professional soldiers. ② *Yet*, the Americans also had advantages that enabled them to win. These advantages over the British were better leadership, foreign aid, a knowledge of the land, and motivation. Although ③ *both* the British and the Americans were fighting for their lives, ② the Americans were also fighting for their property and their dream of liberty.

Make a Venn Diagram

Making a Venn diagram will help you identify similarities and differences between two things. In the overlapping area, list characteristics shared by both subjects. Then, in the separate ovals, list the characteristics of each subject not shared by the other. This Venn diagram compares and contrasts the British and American soldiers.

American Soldiers:
- lacked experience and training
- short of supplies and weapons
- had better leadership
- received foreign aid
- had knowledge of the land
- fought for liberty and property

Both: fought for their lives

British Soldiers:
- best trained in the world
- experienced
- well-supplied

Practicing the Skill

Turn to Chapter 5, Section 1, "Early American Culture." Read "Life of the Young" on pages 129–130, and make a Venn diagram showing the similarities and differences between the roles of boys and girls in colonial America.

1.8 Identifying Problems and Solutions

Defining the Skill

Identifying problems means finding and understanding the difficulties faced by a particular group of people during a certain time. **Solutions** are the actions people took to remedy those problems. By studying the solutions to problems in the past, you can learn ways to solve problems today.

Applying the Skill

The following paragraph describes problems that the Constitutional Convention faced on the issues of taxation, representation, and slavery. Use the strategies listed below to help you identify the Founders' solutions to these problems.

How to Identify Problems and Solutions

Strategy ❶ Look for the difficulties, or problems, people faced.

Strategy ❷ Consider how the problem affected people with different points of view. For example, the main problem described here was how to count the population of each state.

Strategy ❸ Look for solutions people tried to deal with each problem. Think about whether the solution was a good one for people with differing points of view.

SLAVERY AND THE CONSTITUTION

Because the House of Representatives would have members based on the population of each state, ❶ the delegates had to decide who would be counted in that population. The Southern states had many more slaves than the Northern states. ❷ Southerners wanted the slaves to be counted as part of the general population for representation but not for taxation. ❷ Northerners argued that slaves were not citizens and should not be counted for representation but should be counted for taxation. ❸ The delegates decided that three-fifths of the slave population would be counted for both purposes: representation and taxation.

Make a Chart

Making a chart will help you identify and organize information about problems and solutions. The chart below shows problems and solutions included in the passage you just read.

❶ Problem	❷ Differing Points of View	❸ Solution
Northerners and Southerners couldn't agree on how to count population because of slavery in the South.	*Southerners wanted slaves counted for representation but not for taxation. Northerners wanted slaves counted for taxation but not for representation.*	*Delegates decided that three-fifths of the slave population should be counted.*

Practicing the Skill

Turn to Chapter 8, Section 2, "Creating the Constitution." Read "Some Challenges of the Convention" on pages 245–246, and make a chart that details the problems faced by the delegates at the Constitutional Convention and the solutions they agreed on.

1.9 Making Inferences

Defining the Skill

Inferences are ideas that the author has not directly stated. **Making inferences** involves reading between the lines to interpret the information you read. You can make inferences by studying what is stated and using your common sense and previous knowledge.

Applying the Skill

The passage below describes the strengths and weaknesses of the North and the South as the Civil War began. Use the strategies listed below to help you make inferences from the passage.

How to Make Inferences

Strategy 1 Read to find statements of facts and ideas. Knowing the facts will give you a good basis for making inferences.

Strategy 2 Use your knowledge, logic, and common sense to make inferences that are based on facts. Ask yourself, "What does the author want me to understand?" For example, from the facts about population, you can make the inference that the North would have a larger army than the South. See other inferences in the chart below.

> ### ADVANTAGES OF THE NORTH AND THE SOUTH
>
> The North had more people and resources than the South. **1** The North had about 22 million people. **1** The South had roughly 9 million, of whom about 3.5 million were slaves. In addition, **1** the North had more than 80 percent of the nation's factories and almost all of the shipyards and naval power. The South had some advantages, too: **1** able generals, such as Robert E. Lee, **1** and the advantage of fighting a defensive war. Soldiers defending their homes have more will to fight than invaders do.

Make a Chart

Making a chart will help you organize information and make logical inferences. The chart below organizes information from the passage you just read.

1 Stated Facts and Ideas	**2** Inferences
The North had about 22 million people. The Confederacy had about 9 million.	The North would have a larger army than the South.
The North had more factories, naval power, and shipyards.	The North could provide more weapons, ammunition, and ships for the war.
The Confederacy had excellent generals.	The Confederacy had better generals, which would help it overcome other disadvantages.
The Confederacy was fighting a defensive war	Confederate soldiers would fight harder because they were defending their homes and families.

Practicing the Skill

Turn to Chapter 12, Section 1, "Jacksonian Democracy and States' Rights." Read "Voting Rights Expand" on pages 396–397, and use a chart like the one above to make inferences about Jacksonian democracy.

1.10 Making Generalizations

Defining the Skill

To **make generalizations** means to make broad judgments based on information. When you make generalizations, you should gather information from several sources.

Applying the Skill

The following three passages contain different views on George Washington. Use the strategies listed below to make a generalization about these views.

How to Make Generalizations

Strategy ① Look for information that the sources have in common. These three sources all discuss George Washington's ability as a military leader.

Strategy ② Form a generalization that describes Washington in a way that all three sources would agree with. State your generalization in a sentence.

WASHINGTON'S LEADERSHIP

① Washington learned from his mistakes. After early defeats, he developed the strategy of dragging out the war to wear down the British. ① Despite difficulties, he never gave up.

—Creating America

① [Washington] was no military genius. . . . But he was a great war leader. Creating an army out of unpromising material, he kept it in being against great odds.

—The Limits of Liberty

① [Washington] certainly deserves some merit as a general, that he . . . can keep General Howe dancing from one town to another for two years together, with such an army as he has.

—The Journal of Nicholas Cresswell, July 13, 1777

Make a Chart

Using a chart can help you make generalizations. The chart below shows how the information you just read can be used to generalize about people's views of Washington.

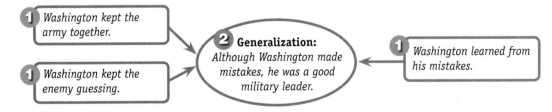

① *Washington kept the army together.*

① *Washington kept the enemy guessing.*

② **Generalization:** *Although Washington made mistakes, he was a good military leader.*

① *Washington learned from his mistakes.*

Practicing the Skill

Turn to Chapter 16, Section 1, "War Erupts." Read "Planning Strategies" on page 513. Also read "Comparing North and South" on page 514. Then, use a chart like the one above to make generalizations about the two sides on the eve of the Civil War.

1.11 Drawing Conclusions

Defining the Skill

Drawing conclusions means analyzing what you have read and forming an opinion about its meaning. To draw conclusions, look at the facts and then use your own common sense and experience to decide what the facts mean.

Applying the Skill

The following passage presents information about the Intolerable Acts and the colonists' reactions to them. Use the strategies listed below to help you draw conclusions about those acts.

How to Draw Conclusions

Strategy ① Read carefully to identify and understand all the facts, or statements, that can be proven true.

Strategy ② List the facts in a diagram and review them. Use your own experiences and common sense to understand how the facts relate to each other.

Strategy ③ After reviewing the facts, write down the conclusion you have drawn about them.

THE INTOLERABLE ACTS

① In 1774, Parliament passed a series of laws to punish the Massachusetts colony and serve as a warning to other colonies.

① These laws were so harsh that colonists called them the **Intolerable Acts**. One of the acts closed the port of Boston. Others banned committees of correspondence and allowed Britain to house troops wherever necessary.

In 1773, Sam Adams had written, "I wish we could arouse the continent." ① The Intolerable Acts answered his wish. Other colonies immediately offered Massachusetts their support.

Make a Diagram

Making a diagram can help you draw conclusions. The diagram below shows how to organize facts and inferences to draw a conclusion about the passage you just read.

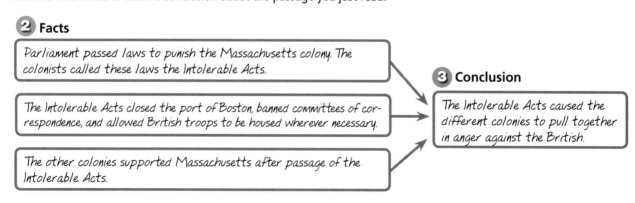

② **Facts**

Parliament passed laws to punish the Massachusetts colony. The colonists called these laws the Intolerable Acts.

The Intolerable Acts closed the port of Boston, banned committees of correspondence, and allowed British troops to be housed wherever necessary.

The other colonies supported Massachusetts after passage of the Intolerable Acts.

③ **Conclusion**

The Intolerable Acts caused the different colonies to pull together in anger against the British.

Practicing the Skill

Turn to Chapter 3, Section 2, "New England Colonies." Read "Puritans Persecute Quakers" on page 71, and use the diagram above as a model to draw conclusions about Puritans' beliefs.

1.12 Making Decisions

Defining the Skill

Making decisions involves choosing between two or more options or courses of action. In most cases, decisions have consequences, or results. Sometimes decisions may lead to new problems. By understanding how historical figures made decisions, you can learn how to improve your decision-making skills.

Applying the Skill

The following passage describes Lincoln's decisions regarding federal forts after the Southern states seceded. Use the strategies listed below to help you analyze his decisions.

How to Make Decisions

Strategy 1 Identify a decision that needs to be made. Think about what factors make the decision difficult.

Strategy 2 Identify possible consequences of the decision. Remember that there can be more than one consequence to a decision.

Strategy 3 Identify the decision that was made.

Strategy 4 Identify actual consequences that resulted from the decision.

FIRST SHOTS AT FORT SUMTER

1 Lincoln had to decide what to do about the forts in the South that remained under federal control. A Union garrison still held Fort Sumter, but it was running out of supplies. **2** If Lincoln supplied the garrison, he risked war. **2** If he withdrew the garrison, he would be giving in to the rebels. **3** Lincoln informed South Carolina that he was sending supply ships to Fort Sumter. **4** Confederate leaders decided to prevent the federal government from holding on to the fort by attacking before the supply ships arrived. No one was killed, but **4** the South's attack on Fort Sumter signaled the beginning of the Civil War.

Make a Flow Chart

A flow chart can help you identify the process of making a decision. The flow chart below shows the decision-making process in the passage you just read.

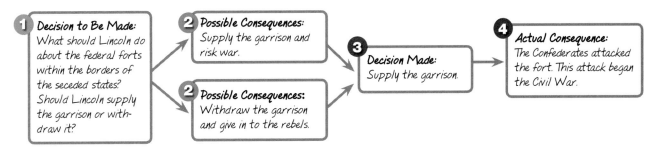

1 Decision to Be Made: What should Lincoln do about the federal forts within the borders of the seceded states? Should Lincoln supply the garrison or withdraw it?

2 Possible Consequences: Supply the garrison and risk war.

2 Possible Consequences: Withdraw the garrison and give in to the rebels.

3 Decision Made: Supply the garrison.

4 Actual Consequence: The Confederates attacked the fort. This attack began the Civil War.

Practicing the Skill

Turn to Chapter 12, Section 2, "Jackson's Policy Toward Native Americans." Read "Native American Resistance" on page 407, and make a flow chart to identify a decision and its consequences described in that section.

1.13 Evaluating

Defining the Skill

To **evaluate** is to make a judgment about something. Historians evaluate the actions of people in history. One way to do this is to examine both the positives and negatives of a historical action, then decide which is stronger—the positive or the negative.

Applying the Skill

The following passage describes Susan B. Anthony's fight for women's rights. Use the strategies listed below to evaluate how successful she was.

How to Evaluate

Strategy 1 Before you evaluate a person's actions, first determine what that person was trying to accomplish.

Strategy 2 Look for statements that show the positive, or successful, results of Anthony's actions. Did she achieve her goals?

Strategy 3 Also look for statements that show the negative, or unsuccessful, results of her actions. Did she fail to achieve something she tried to do?

Strategy 4 Write an overall evaluation of the person's actions.

SUSAN B. ANTHONY

1 Susan B. Anthony was a skilled organizer who fought for women's rights. **2** She successfully built the women's movement into a national organization. An outspoken advocate for equal pay for men and women, she called for laws that would give married women the right to keep their own property and wages. **2** Mississippi passed the first such law in 1839. New York passed a property law in 1848 and a wages law in 1860. **3** Anthony also wanted to win the vote for women but failed to convince lawmakers to pass this reform in her lifetime. This reform did go through in 1920, 14 years after her death.

Make a Diagram for Evaluating

Using a diagram can help you evaluate a person's actions and decisions. The diagram below shows how the information from the passage you just read can be organized.

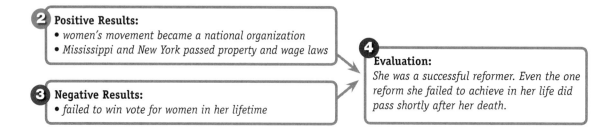

2 Positive Results:
- *women's movement became a national organization*
- *Mississippi and New York passed property and wage laws*

3 Negative Results:
- *failed to win vote for women in her lifetime*

4 Evaluation:
She was a successful reformer. Even the one reform she failed to achieve in her life did pass shortly after her death.

Practicing the Skill

Turn to Chapter 2, Section 3, "The Spanish and Native Americans." Read "The Columbian Exchange" on pages 44–45, and make a diagram in which you evaluate whether the Columbian Exchange had mainly a positive or negative impact on the world.

1.14 Analyzing Point of View

Defining the Skill

Analyzing point of view means looking closely at a person's arguments to understand the reasons behind that person's beliefs. The goal of analyzing a point of view is to understand a historical figure's thoughts, opinions, and biases about a topic.

Applying the Skill

The following passage describes the Panic of 1837 and two politicians' points of view about it. Use the strategies listed below to help you analyze their points of view.

How to Analyze Point of View

Strategy 1 Look for statements that show you a person's view on an issue. Van Buren said he believed the economy would improve if he took no action. Clay thought the government should do something.

Strategy 2 Use information about people to validate them as sources and understand their differences. What do you know about Clay and Van Buren that might explain their biases and disagreements?

Strategy 3 Write a summary that explains why different people took different positions on the issue.

THE PANIC OF 1837

The Panic of 1837 caused severe hardship. People had little money, so manufacturers had few customers for their goods. Almost 90 percent of factories in the East closed. Jobless workers could not afford food or rent. Many people went hungry.

1 Whig senator Henry Clay wanted the government to do something to help the people. **1** President Van Buren, a Democrat, disagreed. He believed that the economy would improve if left alone. He argued that "the less government interferes with private pursuits the better for the general prosperity." Many Americans blamed Van Buren for the Panic, though he had taken office only weeks before it started.

Make a Diagram

Using a diagram can help you analyze points of view. The diagram below analyzes the views of Clay and Van Buren in the passage you just read.

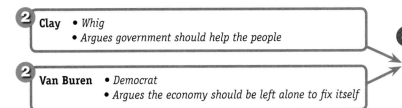

2 Clay
  • *Whig*
  • *Argues government should help the people*

2 Van Buren
  • *Democrat*
  • *Argues the economy should be left alone to fix itself*

3 *Clay is attacking Van Buren because he's in a different party. He does not want Van Buren reelected in 1840.*

Practicing the Skill

Turn to the Reading Primary Sources on pages 255 and 256. Read the selections by James Madison and George Mason. Use their language, information from other sources, and information about each man to validate them as sources. Then make a diagram to analyze their different points of view on the Constitution.

1.15 Distinguishing Fact from Opinion

Defining the Skill

Facts are events, dates, statistics, or statements that can be proved to be true. **Opinions** are the judgments, beliefs, and feelings of a writer or speaker. By distinguishing fact from opinion, you will be able to think critically when a person is trying to influence your own opinion.

Applying the Skill

The following passage tells about the Virginia Plan for legislative representation offered at the Constitutional Convention of 1787. Use the strategies listed below to help you distinguish facts from opinions.

How to Recognize Facts and Opinions

Strategy ① Look for specific information that can be proved or checked for accuracy.

Strategy ② Look for assertions, claims, and judgments that express opinions. In this case, one speaker's opinion is expressed in a direct quotation.

Strategy ③ Think about whether statements can be checked for accuracy. Then, identify the facts and opinions in a chart.

> **ANTIFEDERALIST VIEWS**
>
> ① Antifederalists published their views about the Constitution in newspapers and pamphlets. ① They thought the Constitution took too much power away from the states and did not protect the rights of the people. They charged that the Constitution would destroy American liberties. As one Antifederalist wrote, ② "It is truly astonishing that a set of men among ourselves should have had the [nerve] to attempt the destruction of our liberties."

Make a Chart

The chart below analyzes the facts and opinions from the passage above.

Statement	③ Can It Be Proved?	③ Fact or Opinion
Antifederalists published their views in newspapers and pamphlets.	*Yes. Check newspapers and other historical documents.*	*Fact*
They thought the Constitution took too much power away from the states.	*Yes. Check newspapers and other historical documents.*	*Fact*
It is astonishing that some Americans would try to destroy American liberties.	*No. This cannot be proved. It is what one speaker believes.*	*Opinion*

Practicing the Skill

Turn to Chapter 11, Section 3, "Nationalism and Sectionalism." Read "The Missouri Compromise" on page 382, and make a chart in which you analyze key statements to determine whether they are facts or opinions.

1.16 Analyzing Primary Sources

Defining the Skill

Primary sources are materials written or made by people who lived during historical events and witnessed them. When you **analyze** primary sources, you interpret them, or decide what they tell you about history. Analyzing primary sources will help deepen your understanding of historical events.

Applying the Skill

The following passage is from a magazine article written by an African American who taught formerly enslaved persons in South Carolina. Use the strategies listed below to analyze it.

How to Analyze Primary Sources

Strategy **1** Use the information in the document to make inferences about daily life at the time it was written.

Strategy **2** Look for evidence that will tell you what the author's purpose may have been, and who was her intended audience.

Strategy **3** Identify the author of the primary source and note when it was written. Consider what important historical events were occurring at this time.

> **PRIMARY SOURCE**
>
> **1** Many of the grown people are desirous of learning to read. It is wonderful how a people who have been so long crushed to the earth, so imbruted [treated cruelly] as these have been . . . can have so great a desire for knowledge, and such a capability for attaining it. **2** One cannot believe that the haughty Anglo Saxon race, after centuries of such an experience as these people have had, would be very much superior to them.
>
> **3** —Charlotte Forten, "Life on the Sea Islands," 1864

Make a Chart

Making a chart will help you analyze information from primary sources. The chart below provides an analysis of the passage you just read.

Author: Charlotte Forten	
Type of source: magazine article	**Title:** "Life on the Sea Islands"
Date: 1864	**Historical events:** Civil War
Author's purpose: Gain support for education of former enslaved persons	
Audience: Whites, free African Americans	
What it tells you about history: Enslaved African Americans were prevented from getting an education, but after they were freed, they eagerly pursued education.	

Practicing the Skill

Turn to Chapter 11, Section 1, "Early Industry and Inventions." Read "Time Table of the Holyoke Mills" on page 367, and analyze the poster to understand the historical context in which it was written.

1.17 Recognizing Bias and Propaganda

Defining the Skill

Bias is a one-sided presentation of an issue. **Propaganda** is communication that aims to influence people's opinions, emotions, or actions. Propaganda is not always factual. Rather, it uses prejudicial language or striking symbols to sway people's emotions. Modern advertising often uses propaganda. By thinking critically, you can avoid being swayed by bias and propaganda.

Applying the Skill

The following political cartoon shows Andrew Jackson dressed as a king. Use the strategies listed below to help you understand how it works as propaganda.

How to Recognize Bias and Propaganda

Strategy ❶ Identify the aim, or purpose, of the cartoon. Point out the subject and explain the point of view.

Strategy ❷ Identify those images on the cartoon that viewers might respond to emotionally and identify the emotions.

Strategy ❸ Think critically about the cartoon. What facts has the cartoon ignored?

BORN TO COMMAND.

OF VETO MEMORY.

HAD I BEEN CONSULTED.

KING ANDREW THE FIRST.

Make a Chart

Making a chart will help you think critically about a piece of propaganda. The chart below summarizes the information from the anti-Jackson cartoon.

❶ Identify Purpose	*The cartoon portrays Jackson negatively by showing him as a king.*
❷ Identify Emotions	*The cartoonist knows that Americans like democracy. So he portrays Jackson as a king because kings are not usually supporters of democracy. He also shows Jackson standing on a torn U.S. Constitution—another thing that Americans love.*
❸ Think Critically	*The cartoon shows Jackson vetoing laws. But it ignores the fact that those actions were not against the Constitution. The president has the power to veto legislation. In this case, Jackson was exercising the power of the presidency, not acting like a king.*

Practicing the Skill

Turn to Chapter 6, Section 2, "Colonial Resistance Grows," and look at Paul Revere's etching of the Boston Massacre on page 164. Use a chart like the one above to think critically about the etching as an expression of bias or as an example of propaganda.

1.18 Synthesizing

Defining the Skill

Synthesizing means bringing together information to create an overall picture of a topic. Historians use synthesis to understand the importance of historical events. Like detectives, they look for "clues" such as facts, explanations, and conclusions. The historian then combines this information with his or her own knowledge to understand the event.

Applying the Skill

The following passage presents information about agriculture in the Americas prior to 1500. Use the strategies listed below to help you synthesize the information.

How to Synthesize

Strategy 1 Read the entire passage carefully. Then reread, looking for facts, explanations, conclusions, and other important clues.

Strategy 2 Record the important information in a web. Then review the evidence, looking for the larger idea that ties these pieces of information together.

Strategy 3 Bring together the information you have gathered to create an overall picture of the subject.

AGRICULTURE IN THE AMERICAS

1 The first Americans hunted animals and gathered wild seeds, nuts, and berries. **1** In time, people started to plant the seeds they found. This was the beginning of agriculture. By trial and error, people learned which seeds grew the best crops.

Knowledge of agriculture spread throughout the Americas. **1** Having a stable food supply changed the way people lived. **1** Once they no longer had to travel to find food, they built permanent villages. **1** Farmers were able to produce large harvests, so that fewer people needed to farm. Some people began to practice other crafts, such as weaving or making pottery. A few people became religious leaders. Slowly, some cultures grew complex and became civilizations.

Make a Web

Making a web can help you synthesize. The web at the right shows how to organize the facts, examples, and conclusions needed to synthesize the information in the above passage.

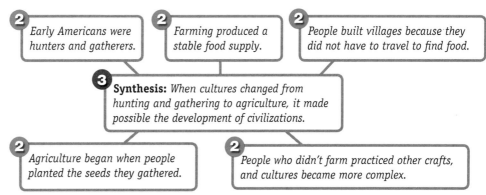

Practicing the Skill

Turn to Chapter 15, Section 1, "Tensions Rise Between North and South." Read "North and South Follow Different Paths" on page 481, and make a web to synthesize the economic factors that contributed to the division between North and South.

Skillbuilder Handbook **R19**

2.1 Reading Maps

Defining the Skill I

Maps are representations of features on the earth's surface. Historical maps often show political features, such as national borders, and physical features, such as bodies of water. Reading maps requires identifying map elements and using math skills.

Applying the Skill

The following map shows the Battle of Yorktown during the Revolution. Use the strategies listed below to help you identify the elements common to most maps.

How to Read a Map

Strategy ❶ Read the title. This identifies the main idea of the map.

Strategy ❷ Look for the grid of lines on the map. These numbered lines are the lines of latitude (horizontal) and longitude (vertical). They indicate the location of the area on the earth.

Strategy ❸ Read the map key. It is usually in a box. This will give you the information you need to interpret the symbols or colors on the map.

Strategy ❹ Use the scale and the pointer, or compass rose, to determine distance and direction.

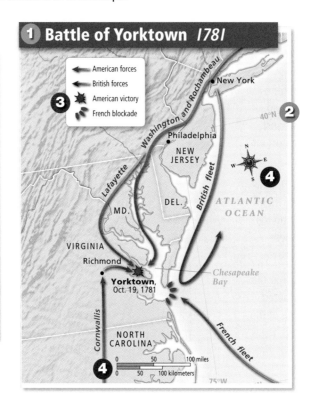

❶ **Battle of Yorktown** *1781*

Make a Chart

A chart can help you organize information given on maps. The chart below summarizes information about the map you just studied.

Title	Battle of Yorktown, 1781
Location	between latitude 40°N and 35°N, just east of longitude 80°W
Map Key Information	blue = American forces, red = British forces
Scale	approx. 3/4 in. = 100 miles; approx. 1/2 in. = 100 km
Summary	British forces led by Cornwallis were trapped by American troops and a French naval blockade.

Practicing the Skill

Turn to Chapter 3, Section 4, "The Middle Colonies." Read the map entitled "American Colonies, 1740" on page 86, and make a chart to identify information on the map.

Defining the Skill II

Special-purpose maps help people focus on a particular aspect of a region, such as economic development in the South. These kinds of maps often use symbols to indicate information.

Applying the Skill

The following special-purpose map indicates the exports of the Southern colonies. Use the strategies listed below to help you identify the information shown on the map.

How to Read a Special-Purpose Map

Strategy ① Read the title. It tells you what the map is intended to show.

Strategy ② Read the legend. This tells you what each color and symbol stands for. This legend shows the exports that were produced in various Southern colonies.

Strategy ③ Look for the places on the map where the symbol appears. These tell you the places where the goods were produced.

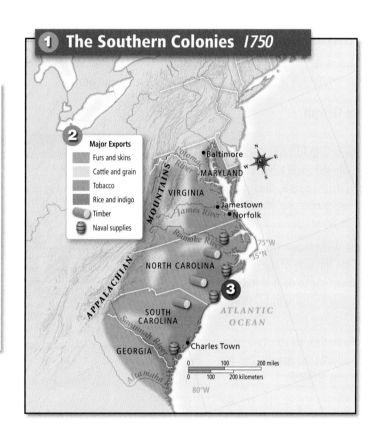

① The Southern Colonies *1750*

② Major Exports
- Furs and skins
- Cattle and grain
- Tobacco
- Rice and indigo
- Timber
- Naval supplies

Make a Chart

A chart can help you understand special-purpose maps. The chart below shows information about the special-purpose map you just studied.

	Furs and skins	Cattle and grain	Tobacco	Rice and indigo	Timber	Naval stores
Maryland	x	x	x			
Virginia	x	x	x			
North Carolina	x	x	x	x	x	x
South Carolina	x	x		x	x	x
Georgia	x			x		

Practicing the Skill

Turn to Chapter 8, Section 2, "Creating the Constitution." Look at the special-purpose map entitled "Slave Popluation, 1790" on page 246, and make a chart that shows information about the population of slaves soon after the Constitution was ratified.

2.2 Reading Graphs and Charts

Defining the Skill I

Graphs use pictures and symbols, instead of words, to show information. Graphs are created by taking information and presenting it visually. The graph on this page takes numerical information on the national debt and presents it as a bar graph. There are many different kinds of graphs. Bar graphs, line graphs, and pie graphs are the most common. Bar graphs compare numbers or sets of numbers. The length of each bar shows a quantity. It is easy to see how different categories compare on a bar graph.

Applying the Skill

The bar graph below shows the amount of the national debt in the United States between 1861 and 1869. Use the strategies listed below to help you interpret the graph.

How to Interpret a Graph

Strategy **1** Read the title to identify the main idea of the graph. Ask yourself what kinds of information the graph shows. For example, does it show chronological information, geographic patterns and distributions, or something else?

Strategy **2** Read the vertical axis (the one that goes up and down) on the left side of the graph. This one shows the amount of the debt in millions of dollars. Each bar represents the national debt during a particular year.

Strategy **3** Read the horizontal axis (the one that runs across the bottom of the graph). This one shows each year from 1861 to 1869.

Strategy **4** Summarize the information shown in each part of the graph. Use the title to help you focus on what information the graph is presenting.

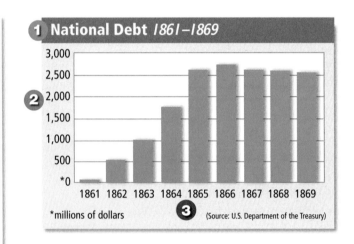

1 National Debt *1861–1869*

*millions of dollars   **3** (Source: U.S. Department of the Treasury)

Write a Summary

Writing a summary will help you understand the information in the graph. The paragraph to the right summarizes the information from the bar graph.

4 The national debt of the United States rose sharply during the years of the Civil War. In 1861 the country owed about $100 million, but by 1865 its debt had surpassed $2.5 billion. The debt peaked in 1866, when it totalled approximately $2.75 billion. By 1869, the U.S. had decreased the national debt by about $200 million.

Practicing the Skill

Turn to Chapter 4, Section 2, "The Southern Colonies: Plantations and Slavery." Look at the graph entitled "Slave Populations" on page 105, and write a paragraph in which you summarize what you learned from it.

Defining the Skill II

Charts, like graphs, present information in a visual form. Charts are created by organizing, summarizing, and simplifying information and presenting it in a format that makes it easy to understand. Tables and diagrams are examples of commonly used charts.

Applying the Skill

The chart below shows a comparison between the Virginia and New Jersey plans for government. Use the strategies listed below to help you interpret the information in the chart.

How to Interpret a Chart

Strategy 1 Read the title. It will tell you what the chart is about. Ask yourself what kinds of information the chart shows. For example, does it show chronological information, geographic patterns and distributions, or something else?

Strategy 2 Read the labels to see how the information in the chart is organized. In this chart, it is organized by plan and branch of government.

Strategy 3 Study the data in the chart to understand the facts that the chart intends to show.

Strategy 4 Summarize the information shown in each part of the chart. Use the title to help you focus on what information the chart is presenting.

COMPARING Plans for Government

	VIRGINIA PLAN	NEW JERSEY PLAN
Legislative branch	Two (branches) houses: representation determined by state population or wealth	One house: one vote for each state, regardless of size
	Lower House: elected by the people Upper House: elected by lower house	Elected by state legislatures
Executive branch	Appointed by Legislature	Appointed by Legislature
Judicial branch	Appointed by Legislature	Appointed by Executive

Write a Summary

Writing a summary can help you understand the information given in a chart. The paragraph to the right summarizes the information in the chart "Comparing Plans for Government."

4 The chart compares the Virginia Plan for government with the New Jersey Plan. It focuses on each plan's approach to how the three branches of government should be formed. The main difference between them was in the legislature, with the Virginia Plan calling for two houses and the New Jersey Plan arguing for one house.

Practicing the Skill

Turn to Chapter 8, Section 1, "The Confederation Era." Study the chart entitled "Powers Granted and Denied Congress" on page 236, and write a paragraph in which you summarize what you learned from it.

2.3 Analyzing Political Cartoons

Defining the Skill

Political cartoons are cartoons that use humor to make a serious point. Political cartoons often express a point of view on an issue better than words do. Understanding signs and symbols will help you to interpret political cartoons.

Applying the Skill

The cartoon below shows Abraham Lincoln and the other candidates running for the presidency in 1860. Use the strategies listed below to help you understand the cartoon.

How to Interpret a Political Cartoon

Strategy ① Identify the subject by reading the title of the cartoon and looking at the cartoon as a whole.

Strategy ② Identify important symbols and details. The cartoonist uses the image of a running race to discuss a political campaign. The White House is the finish line.

Strategy ③ Interpret the message. Why is Lincoln drawn so much taller than the other candidates? How does that make him the fittest candidate?

Make a Chart

Making a chart will help you summarize information from a political cartoon. The chart below summarizes the information from the cartoon above.

Subject	*"A Political Race" (The Election of 1860)*
Symbols and Details	*Running is a symbol for a political campaign. Lincoln is the tallest and fastest candidate.*
Message	**③** *Lincoln is pulling ahead of the other candidates in the campaign for the presidency.*

Practicing the Skill

Turn to Chapter 18, Section 3, "The End of Reconstruction." Look at the political cartoon on page 585 showing a cartoonist's view of corruption in the Grant administration. Use a chart like the one above and the strategies outlined to interpret the cartoon.

2.4 Creating a Map

Defining the Skill

Creating a map involves representing geographical information. When you draw a map, it is easiest to use an existing map as a guide. On the map you draw, you can show geographical information. You can also show other kinds of information, such as data on climates, population trends, resources, or routes. Often, this data comes from a graph or a chart.

Applying the Skill

Below is a map that a student created to show information about the number of slaves in 1750. Read the strategies listed below to see how the map was created.

How to Create a Map

Strategy ① Select a title that identifies the geographical area and the map's purpose. Include a date in your title.

Strategy ② Draw the lines of latitude and longitude using short dashes.

Strategy ③ Create a key that shows the colors.

Strategy ④ Draw the colors on the map to show information.

Strategy ⑤ Draw a compass rose and scale.

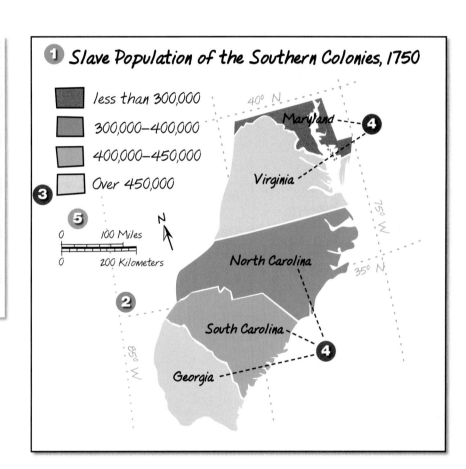

① Slave Population of the Southern Colonies, 1750

less than 300,000
300,000–400,000
400,000–450,000
Over 450,000

③

⑤
0   100 Miles
0   200 Kilometers

N

40° N
Maryland ④
Virginia
75° W
35° N
North Carolina
②
South Carolina ④
85° W
Georgia

Practicing the Skill

Make your own map. Turn to page 90 in Chapter 3 and study the graph entitled "Population of the 13 Colonies, 1650–1750." Use the strategies described above to create a map that shows population growth in the three colonial regions between 1650 and 1750. You can use the map on page 86 of that chapter as a guide.

2.5 Creating a Model

Defining the Skill

When you **create a model**, you use information and ideas to show an event or a situation in a visual way. A model might be a poster or a diagram that explains how something happened. Or, it might be a three-dimensional model, such as a diorama, that depicts an important scene or situation.

Applying the Skill

The following sketch shows the early stages of a model of three ways that people could have traveled from the eastern United States to California during the gold rush. Use the strategies listed below to help you create your own model.

How to Create a Model

Strategy ① Gather the informa-
tion you need to understand the situation or event. In this case, you need to be able to show the three routes and their dangers.

Strategy ② Visualize and sketch
an idea for your model. Once you have created a picture in your mind, make an actual sketch to plan how it might look.

Strategy ③ Think of symbols you
may want to use. Since the model should give information in a visual way, think about ways you can use color, pictures, or other visuals to tell the story.

Strategy ④ Gather the supplies
you will need and create the model. For example, you will need a globe and art supplies, such as yarn, for this model.

Strategy ⑤ Write and answer a
question about the California gold rush, as shown in the model.

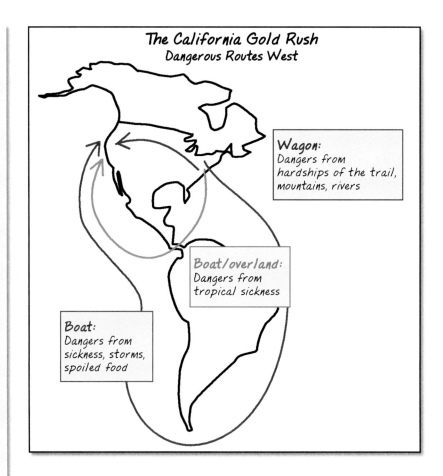

The California Gold Rush
Dangerous Routes West

Wagon: Dangers from hardships of the trail, mountains, rivers

Boat/overland: Dangers from tropical sickness

Boat: Dangers from sickness, storms, spoiled food

Practicing the Skill

Turn to Chapter 13 and read the Animated History called "American Trails West" on pages 424–425. Follow the steps above to create a model of a covered wagon.

3.1 Formulating Historical Questions

Defining the Skill

Formulating historical questions means asking questions about events and trends in history. These questions might ask how or why something happened, why someone acted a certain way, or how different conditions might have changed an event. To decide if a historical question is reasonable, ask yourself (1) whether the answer is important or not, and (2) if enough information exists to answer it.

Applying the Skill

The following passage describes the Boston Tea Party. Use the strategies listed below to help you formulate questions about this historical event.

How to Formulate Questions

Strategy **1** First ask about the basic facts of the event using the questions Who, What, When, Where, Why, and How.

Strategy **2** Think about where the event fits into the sequence of history. What events led up to it? What were its results?

Strategy **3** Formulate a central question about the event. Make sure it is neither too narrow nor too broad and can be answered from the sources available.

> ### THE BOSTON TEA PARTY
>
> In 1773, British Parliament passed the Tea Act. The Tea Act gave the British East India Company control over the American tea trade. Colonists would have to pay a tax on this regulated tea.
>
> Protests against the Tea Act took place all over the colonies. One such protest occurred in Boston. The Sons of Liberty, a secret society that opposed the British, organized what came to be known as the Boston Tea Party.
>
> On the evening of December 16, 1773, a group of men disguised as Native Americans boarded three tea ships docked in Boston Harbor. They destroyed 342 chests of tea. Many colonists rejoiced at the news. They believed that Britain would now see how strongly colonists opposed taxation without representation.
>
> The Boston Tea Party aroused fury in Britain. In 1774, Parliament passed a series of laws to punish the Massachusetts colony. The British reaction fanned the flames of rebellion in the 13 colonies.

Make a Web

Making a web will help you formulate historical questions. In the web shown here, the center oval asks a central question about the event. More narrow questions—ones that help explore the broader question—are noted in the outer ovals.

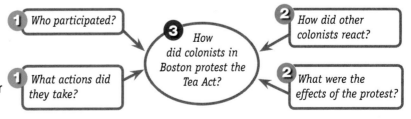

Practicing the Skill

Turn to Chapter 4, Section 1, "New England: Commerce and Religion." Read "Harvesting the Sea" on page 96, and make a web of narrow and broad historical questions about New England's coastal commerce.

3.2 Identifying and Using Primary and Secondary Sources

Defining the Skill

Primary sources are materials written or made by people who lived during historical events and witnessed them. They can be letters, journal entries, speeches, autobiographies, artwork, government documents, census surveys, or financial records. **Secondary sources** are materials written by people who did not participate in an event. History books are secondary sources.

Applying the Skill

The following passage contains both a primary source and a secondary source. Use the strategies listed below to help you read them.

How to Identify and Use Primary and Secondary Sources

Strategy ① Distinguish secondary sources from primary sources. The first paragraph is a secondary source that explains something about the primary source in the next paragraph.

Strategy ② Analyze the primary source and consider why the author produced it. Consider what the document was supposed to achieve and who would read it.

Strategy ③ Identify the author of the primary source and note when and where it was written.

> ① The core idea of the Declaration is based on the philosophy of John Locke that people have unalienable rights that government cannot take away. Jefferson stated this belief in what was to become the Declaration's best-known passage.
>
> ② We hold these truths to be self-evident, that all men are created equal, that they are endowed by their Creator with certain unalienable Rights, that among these are Life, Liberty and the pursuit of Happiness.
>
> ③ —Thomas Jefferson, *The Declaration of Independence*, 1776

Make a Chart

Making a chart will help you summarize information from primary sources and secondary sources. The chart below summarizes the information from the passage you just read.

Author	*Thomas Jefferson*
Document	*The Declaration of Independence*
Notes on Primary Source	*The Declaration says that "all men are created equal" and that people have "unalienable rights." These rights include life, liberty, and the pursuit of happiness.*
Notes on Secondary Source	*Jefferson based his ideas on those of John Locke. Locke had written about rights that governments could not take away from the people.*

Practicing the Skill

Turn to Chapter 6, Section 3, "The Road to Lexington and Concord." Read "British Control Begins to Slip" on page 172, and make a chart like the one above to summarize the information in the primary source and the secondary source.

3.3 Using a Database

Defining the Skill

Using a database allows you to find and retrieve information on a specific topic quickly and easily. By selecting keywords from your topic, you can search a database for related materials and sort them by date, format, or relevance.

Databases for Historical Research

- The Archival Research Catalog (ARC) – a database of many historic documents, photographs, maps, and other artifacts in the collection of the National Archives in Washington, D.C.
- The University of Virginia Library's Historical Census Browser – an easy-to-use online database of population and housing data from 1790 to 1960.

Applying the Skill

The image below shows a screen from a database of materials related to the Battle of Gettysburg. Use the strategies listed below to help you use the database.

How to Use a Database

Strategy ❶ You can broaden or narrow your search of the database. For example, if your search produced too few materials, you can search using more general keywords or a larger date range.

Strategy ❷ The title of the item alone will rarely give you enough information to judge whether or not it will be useful to you. Read all the fields.

Strategy ❸ Many valuable sources of information, including some newspapers and magazines, are not available in digital format. To view some materials, you may have to go to the library.

❶ **Database results for search terms "Civil War" AND "Gettysburg"**

❷ Title	Collection	Date	Available Formats
Battle of Gettysburg	maps	August 11, 1864	• original • digital
Rebel Sharpshooter	photographs	July 5, 1863	• original
Letters	documents	June 1861–1906	• original
Military service records	documents	1890–1912	❸ • original • microfilm
Casualty lists	data files	1861–1865	• original • digital
Union military orders	documents	1861–1865	• original
Diagrams of Confederate positions	engineering drawings	1861–1876	• original

Practicing the Skill

Turn to Chapter 12, Section 2, "Jackson's Policy Toward Native Americans." Read "Trail of Tears" on pages 405–406. Then go to the Archival Research Catalog on the Internet and search the database for "Trail of Tears." Compile the results in a table like the one above.

3.4 Paraphrasing

Defining the Skill

When you **paraphrase**, you restate a sentence, paragraph, or passage in your own words. Unlike a summary, which includes only the most important ideas, a paraphrase includes all information and is about the same length as the original. When paraphrasing, you change the structure of the sentence, as well as individual words.

Applying the Skill

The passage below describes the development of the idea of manifest destiny in the mid-1800s. Use the strategies listed below to help you paraphrase the passage.

How to Paraphrase

Strategy ① Think about the ideas that each sentence is trying to communicate. Then express the same ideas in your own words.

Strategy ② In addition to using different vocabulary, you must use your own sentence structures. Do not copy the grammar of the original.

Strategy ③ Paraphrasing is useful in research papers to avoid cluttering your report with too many quotations. But remember always to cite your source, even for a paraphrase.

> **MANIFEST DESTINY**
>
> Many Americans believed that the United States was destined to stretch across the continent from the Atlantic Ocean to the Pacific Ocean. In 1845, a newspaper editor name John O'Sullivan gave a name to that belief. O'Sullivan wrote, "Our manifest destiny [is] to overspread and possess the whole of the continent which Providence [God] has given us for the development of the great experiment of liberty. . . ." Manifest destiny suggested that expansion was not only good but bound to happen—even if it meant pushing Mexicans and Native Americans out of the way. After James K. Polk's election in 1844, manifest destiny became government policy.
>
> —John Q. Author, in *A History Book*

Write a Paraphrase

Write your paraphrase in the same form as the original. The following paragraph paraphrases the passage above.

The idea that the United States was meant to cover the continent from the east coast to the west coast was a common one among Americans. Newspaper editor John O'Sullivan coined the term "manifest destiny" in 1845. ① O'Sullivan believed that God wanted Americans to spread their system of government all across the continent. According to manifest destiny, the widespread growth of America was both positive and unstoppable. ② The fact that Mexicans and Native Americans were already occupying parts of the continent did not matter. The U.S. government officially pursued manifest destiny after Polk became president in 1844. ③ Source: *A History Book*, by John Q. Author

Practicing the Skill

Turn to Chapter 1, Section 2, "Societies of Africa." Read "One African's Story" on page 11, and paraphrase the section in your own words.

3.5 Outlining

Defining the Skill

An **outline** is a summary of the information you plan to include in a written piece, and how you plan to structure it. A topic outline begins with a shortened version of the thesis statement. Roman numerals identify the major parts of the essay, followed by key ideas and supporting details listed with letters and Arabic numerals. Ways to organize your ideas include chronological order, cause-and-effect, and order of degree.

Applying the Skill

The outline shown here is a plan for a report on the Lewis and Clark expedition. Use the strategies listed below to help you create an outline.

How to Outline

Strategy 1 Write a possible title for the essay, along with your thesis statement, at the top of your outline.

Strategy 2 The body of the essay is where you discuss the points that support your thesis. List each main point after a capital letter.

Strategy 3 List supporting details below each main point with Arabic numerals. In general, there should be at least two details that support each main idea. If you have only one detail for a main idea, you may need more research.

> **1** The Accomplishments of the Lewis and Clark Expedition
>
> **Thesis statement:** The Lewis and Clark expedition made important contributions to the expansion of the U.S. in the 19th century.
>
> I. Introduction
> **2** II. **Body:** Three goals accomplished by the Lewis and Clark expedition
>   A. Increased knowledge of the geography of the American West
>   **3** 1. Learned there was no all-water route across the continent
>   2. Made more accurate maps than had previously existed of areas west of St. Louis
>   B. Established good relations with Native Americans
>   **3** 1. Guidance of Sacagawea and the Shoshone
>   2. Assistance of the Nez Perce
>   C. Discovered natural resources
>   **3** 1. Navigated Missouri, Clearwater, Snake, and Columbia Rivers
>   2. Sketched edible plants and animals
> III. Conclusion

Practicing the Skill

Prepare an outline for an essay called "The Impact of the Emancipation Proclamation on the Civil War." Refer to Chapter 17, Section 1, "The Emancipation Proclamation" on pages 537–540, as a resource for your outline.

3.6 Forming and Supporting Opinions

Defining the Skill

When you **form opinions**, you interpret and judge the importance of events and people in history. You should always **support your opinions** with facts, examples, and quotes.

Applying the Skill

The following passage describes events that followed the gold rush. Use the strategies listed below to form and support your opinions about the events.

How to Form and Support Opinions

Strategy ① Look for important information about the events. Information can include facts, quotations, and examples.

Strategy ② Form an opinion about the event by asking yourself questions about the information. For example, How important was the event? What were its effects?

Strategy ③ Support your opinions with facts, quotations, and examples. If the facts do not support the opinion, then rewrite your opinion so it is supported by the facts.

THE IMPACT OF THE GOLD RUSH

By 1852, the gold rush was over. ① While it lasted, about 250,000 people flooded into California. ① This huge migration caused economic growth that changed California. ① The port city San Francisco grew to become a center of banking, manufacturing, shipping, and trade. ① However, the gold rush ruined many *Californios*. *Californios* are the Hispanic people of California. The newcomers did not respect *Californios*, their customs, or their legal rights. ① In many cases, Americans seized their property.

Native Americans suffered even more. ① Thousands died from diseases brought by the newcomers. ① Miners hunted down and killed thousands more. ① By 1870, California's Native American population had fallen from 150,000 to only about 30,000.

Make a Chart

Making a chart can help you organize your opinions and supporting facts. The following chart summarizes one possible opinion about the impact of the gold rush.

② Opinion	*The effects of the gold rush were more negative than positive.*
③ Facts	*Californios were not respected, and their land was stolen.* *Many Native Americans died from diseases, and others were killed by miners.* *Their population dropped from 150,000 to about 30,000.*

Practicing the Skill

Turn to Chapter 11, Section 3, "Nationalism and Sectionalism." Read "The Monroe Doctrine" on page 385, and form your own opinion about the United States' reaction to European colonialism. Make a chart like the one above to summarize your opinion and the supporting facts and examples.

3.7 Essay

Defining the Skill

An **essay** is a written presentation consisting of (1) a thesis, and (2) an argument supported by details and evidence. A thesis is a statement that answers the question you are exploring in your essay. The argument explains why you believe your thesis is true. An argument is based on accurate evidence (facts, examples, statistics, etc.) from which you draw logical conclusions that help prove your thesis.

Applying the Skill

The page shown here is from an essay on the role of the cotton gin in the growth of slavery. Analyze the writer's use of these strategies in the essay.

How to Write an Essay

Strategy 1 Use the introduction to state your thesis and provide important background information.

Strategy 2 The body of the essay is where you present your argument. Often, you can present each point of your argument in a separate paragraph.

Strategy 3 Fill out each paragraph with details and evidence that support the main point.

Practicing the Skill

Turn to Chapter 11, Section 1, "Early Industry and Inventions." Read "One American's Story" on page 365, "The Lowel Mills Hire Women" on page 367, and "Comparing Perspectives" on page 366. Then, write an essay around a thesis statement about the working conditions for women in the Lowell mills.

THE COTTON GIN AND THE GROWTH OF SLAVERY

1 A warm climate and fertile soil made the southern states ideal for agriculture. In the late 1700s, cash crops such as tobacco, indigo, rice, and sugar cane were grown on plantations using enslaved labor. The demand for that labor grew dramatically after new technology made cotton the dominant cash crop in the South. Eli Whitney's invention of the cotton gin in 1793 led to an increase in the use of slave labor in the United States at the end of the 18th century.

2 Separating seeds and other debris from cotton fibers by hand was slow and very expensive. Whitney's gin made the cleaning process fast and easy. Sold at a lower price, cotton became the most commonly used fiber in textile production. As the demand for cotton grew, so did the demand for labor in the form of slaves.

Many plantations that had grown tobacco, rice, or indigo switched to cotton. From the increased profits on cotton, plantation owners could purchase more slaves. If soiled by storms, cotton was worthless. So many laborers were needed to pick cotton quickly before bad weather could destroy the crop.

Cotton could be grown on smaller plots than sugar cane and still make a profit. As a result, more people began to farm, more land was cultivated, and more labor was needed. **3** In Georgia, for example, from 1790 to 1810 (a period during which the cotton gin was invented), the number of slaves increased 104 percent.

3.8 Constructed Response

Defining the Skill

A **constructed response** requires you to write your own answer to a question, rather than to make a choice among provided answers. A constructed-response item consists of an "exhibit"—a document or artifact, such as a quotation, map, drawing, or photograph—and a series of questions about the exhibit and related history. Often, the answer can be found within the exhibit, but some questions require your own knowledge of the subject.

Applying the Skill

Shown here are three sample constructed-response items along with answers. Use the strategies listed below to help you answer constructed-response questions.

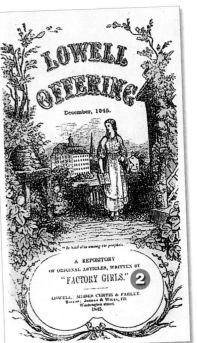

How to Answer Constructed-Response Questions

Strategy ❶ Unless the directions specify otherwise, you do not need to write your answers in complete sentences.

Strategy ❷ Look for clues to answer a question. One clue for the second question is in the exhibit—the date the magazine was published (1845). The second clue is in the question itself, which provides a description of the Industrial Revolution.

Strategy ❸ The third question requires you to synthesize your own knowledge about the Industrial Revolution with information in the exhibit. This response refers to specific details in the exhibit and compares them to the student's own knowledge about factory work in the 1800s.

1. Who wrote the articles published in the *Lowell Offering*?

   ❶ *young women who worked in factories*

2. At the time the *Lowell Offering* was published, ❷ what movement was replacing hand tools with machines, and farming with manufacturing?

   the Industrial Revolution

3. Does the cover illustration accurately reflect the daily lives of young women employed in factories? Why or why not?

   ❸ *No. In the illustration, the girl is standing in a wooded area holding a book, which makes her daily life look peaceful and leisurely, when factory girls actually worked 12-hour days in noisy, crowded mills.*

Practicing the Skill

Turn to Chapter 9, Section 3, "The Federalists in Charge." Read the excerpt of the letter from Benjamin Banneker to Thomas Jefferson on page 327, and formulate a constructed response to the following question: Why do you think Banneker wrote these words to Jefferson?

3.9 Extended Response

Defining the Skill

An **extended response** is a detailed answer to a complex question about an exhibit or topic. It requires more time and thought to answer than a constructed response. Many extended-response questions ask you to write an essay on a given topic, using information from the exhibit and your own knowledge.

Applying the Skill

Shown here is a sample extended-response item along with its answer. Use the strategies listed below to help you answer extended-response questions.

How to Answer Extended-Response Questions

Strategy 1 Carefully read or study the exhibit and the question that follows.

Strategy 2 Take notes or diagram important information on a separate sheet of paper.

Strategy 3 Create a rough outline for your essay on a separate sheet of paper. Then use the outline to write your answer.

Practicing the Skill

Turn to Chapter 17, Section 2, "War Affects Society." Read "Economic and Social Change" on pages 545–547, and formulate an extended response to the following question: What impact did the Civil War have on American society?

Read the passage about religion in some of the colonies. How did these colonies' ideas of religious tolerance help shape attitudes about diversity in the United States today?

RELIGIOUS TOLERATION IN THE COLONIES

William Penn founded Pennsylvania in 1681 when King Charles II gave him a large piece of land in America as repayment for debts to his family. Penn, a Quaker, organized his colony to provide a safe haven for Quakers and other persecuted peoples. Lord Baltimore founded Maryland in 1632 to create a refuge for Roman Catholics fleeing persecution in England. To attract other settlers besides Catholics, Maryland passed the Toleration Act in 1649. Like William Penn and Lord Baltimore, James Oglethorpe also wanted to help people persecuted for their religion, especially Protestants. He founded the Georgia colony, where all religions were welcome.

In response to religious persecution in Europe in the 1600s, the colonies of Pennsylvania, Maryland, and Georgia each offered settlers religious freedom. Whether to provide a safe haven for persecuted people or to attract more settlers, the founders of these colonies believed it important not to exclude anyone from living there based on religion. The ideas of religious tolerance in the Middle and Southern Colonies helped shape attitudes toward religious diversity in the United States today.

Those who had been persecuted for their beliefs in Europe greatly valued the freedom of religion they found in the colonies, where people of many faiths often lived side-by-side. As America developed from individual colonies into a nation, the freedom to worship became an expectation of society. Many states refused to ratify the U.S. Constitution until the founders agreed to add a Bill of Rights, the first of which protected religious freedom.

The toleration that started in the colonies extends today in the United States. . . .

3.10 Creating a Multimedia Presentation

Defining the Skill

Movies, CD-ROMs, television, and computer software are different kinds of media. To **create a multimedia presentation**, you need to collect information in different media and organize them into one presentation.

Applying the Skill

Use the strategies listed below to help you create your own multimedia presentation.

How to Create a Multimedia Presentation

Strategy ① Identify the topic of your presentation and decide which media are best for an effective presentation. For example, you may want to use slides or posters to show visual images of your topic. Or, you may want to use CDs or audiotapes to provide music or spoken words.

Strategy ② Research the topic in a variety of sources. Images, text, props, and background music should reflect the historical period of the event you choose.

Strategy ③ Write the script for the oral portion of the presentation. You could use a narrator and characters' voices to tell the story. Primary sources are an excellent source for script material. Make sure the recording is clear so that the audience will be able to understand the oral part of the presentation.

Strategy ④ Videotape the presentation. Videotaping the presentation will preserve it for future viewing and allow you to show it to different groups of people.

③
```
                    Narrator
Lee's plan on July 3 was to attack the middle of the Union
line along Cemetery Ridge with 15,000 Confederate soldiers.
But General Longstreet disagreed with
Lee's strategy.

                    Longstreet
It is my opinion that no 15,000 men ever arrayed for battle
can take that position.

                    Narrator
Lee refused to change his mind. He wanted to see the
battle—and the war—end that day.

                     Pickett
[to Longstreet] General, shall I advance?

                    Narrator
Longstreet, foreseeing disaster, could not speak. He
only bowed to Pickett in a silent order of "Advance".

                     Pickett
[shouting] Charge the enemy and remember old Virginia!
```

Practicing the Skill

Turn to Chapter 16, "The Civil War Begins" Choose a topic from the chapter, and use the strategies listed above to create a multimedia presentation about it.

4.1 Using a Search Engine

Defining the Skill

A **search engine** is a computer program that looks for, gathers, and reports information available on the Internet. Using a search engine helps you find such information quickly and easily. By entering key words into a search engine, you will generate a list of Web pages and sites that contain those words.

Applying the Skill

Shown here is a list of results from a search for information on Harriet Tubman's work on the Underground Railroad. Use the strategies listed below to get better results when you search the Internet.

How to Use a Search Engine

Strategy ① Be specific when searching to get more relevant information. Use quotation marks around exact phrases that you want the engine to search for as a whole. Narrow your search with plus and minus signs. For example, to include Harriet Tubman in your search but exclude Levi Coffin, you would enter "+Tubman –Coffin" in the search box.

Strategy ② The brief excerpt that appears under the title is actual text from the page. Read it carefully for clues as to whether or not the site contains useful information. The first result, for example, shows a quotation from Tubman, which might indicate that there are more pirmary sources on the Web site.

Strategy ③ Read the title of the Web site. Although a site might meet the search criteria, sometimes you can tell by reading the title that it will not be useful. The third result, for example, is a quiz that probably will not help your research.

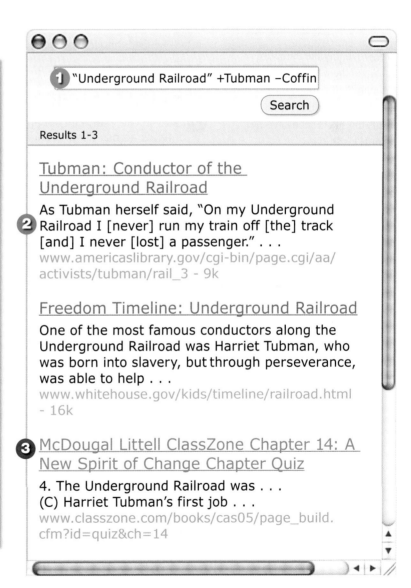

① "Underground Railroad" +Tubman –Coffin

Search

Results 1-3

Tubman: Conductor of the Underground Railroad

② As Tubman herself said, "On my Underground Railroad I [never] run my train off [the] track [and] I never [lost] a passenger." . . .
www.americaslibrary.gov/cgi-bin/page.cgi/aa/activists/tubman/rail_3 - 9k

Freedom Timeline: Underground Railroad

One of the most famous conductors along the Underground Railroad was Harriet Tubman, who was born into slavery, but through perseverance, was able to help . . .
www.whitehouse.gov/kids/timeline/railroad.html - 16k

③ **McDougal Littell ClassZone Chapter 14: A New Spirit of Change Chapter Quiz**

4. The Underground Railroad was . . . (C) Harriet Tubman's first job . . .
www.classzone.com/books/cas05/page_build.cfm?id=quiz&ch=14

Practicing the Skill

Turn to Chapter 3, Section 2, "New England Colonies," and read about Anne Hutchinson on page 70. Then look for Web sites about Hutchinson and her trial using an Internet search engine. Jot down the three sites that you feel provide the best information.

4.2 Evaluating Internet Sources

Defining the Skill

Evaluating Internet sources will help you decide if the information you find online is trustworthy. Reliable Internet sources generally:

- are created by a credible author, with the backing of an educational institution or government agency;
- have content that is well-researched and free from bias with sources cited.

Applying the Skill

Shown here is a Web page about the Lincoln-Douglas debates. Use the strategies listed below to help you evaluate Internet sources.

How to Evaluate Internet Sources

Strategy 1 Identify the author of the material and the organization, if any, that supports the site. In the example here, the URL includes ".edu," which means the site is sponsored by an educational institution.

Strategy 2 Examine the content for accuracy and thoroughness. Are sources cited? Are there signs of bias? How recently was it created or updated?

Strategy 3 Consider how well the page or site is organized. Is it easy to read and navigate? Do images provide useful information?

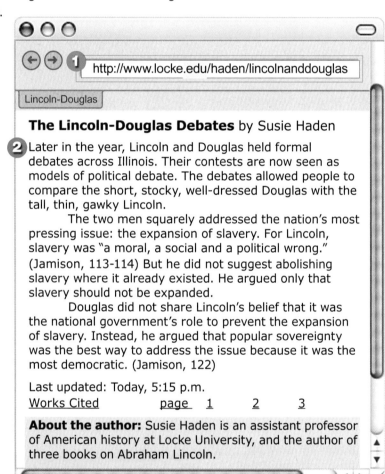

http://www.locke.edu/haden/lincolnanddouglas

Lincoln-Douglas

The Lincoln-Douglas Debates by Susie Haden

Later in the year, Lincoln and Douglas held formal debates across Illinois. Their contests are now seen as models of political debate. The debates allowed people to compare the short, stocky, well-dressed Douglas with the tall, thin, gawky Lincoln.

The two men squarely addressed the nation's most pressing issue: the expansion of slavery. For Lincoln, slavery was "a moral, a social and a political wrong." (Jamison, 113-114) But he did not suggest abolishing slavery where it already existed. He argued only that slavery should not be expanded.

Douglas did not share Lincoln's belief that it was the national government's role to prevent the expansion of slavery. Instead, he argued that popular sovereignty was the best way to address the issue because it was the most democratic. (Jamison, 122)

Last updated: Today, 5:15 p.m.
Works Cited   page 1   2   3

About the author: Susie Haden is an assistant professor of American history at Locke University, and the author of three books on Abraham Lincoln.

Make a Chart

Making a chart can help you evaluate Internet sources. The chart below contains notes on the Web page you just read.

1 Source	Author	University professor, expert on Lincoln
	Sponsor	Locke University (.edu)
2 Content	Accuracy & objectivity	Good, no evidence of bias, sources cited
	Thoroughness	Good
	Up-to-date	Yes
3 Style & Functionality	Organization	Clear
	Legibility	Good, easy to read
	Ease of navigation	Yes, links provided to each page of site

Practicing the Skill

Go to the Library of Congress Web site and find the exhibition on Lewis and Clark. Use the above strategies to evaluate the exhibition's reliability as a historical source about the Corps of Discovery. Create a chart like the one here to organize your evaluation.

4.3 Recognizing Bias

Defining the Skill

Bias is the presentation of only one side of an issue. A biased source is not objective: it exhibits a point of view influenced by its author's emotions or personal preferences. Bias can also appear in the form of advertising to try to persuade you to patronize a product or service. Recognizing bias will help you evaluate whether or not a source is reliable.

Applying the Skill

Shown here is a Web page about Thomas Jefferson's first term as president. Use the strategies listed below to identify words and tone that indicate bias.

How to Recognize Bias

Strategy 1 Read the Web page carefully, looking for evidence of the author's point of view. Note places where the author expresses a personal opinion. Consider word choice.

Strategy 2 Think critically about the text. Decide whether or not it seems balanced. Does it present both sides of an argument?

Strategy 3 Use the evidence you have gathered to judge whether or not the material is biased.

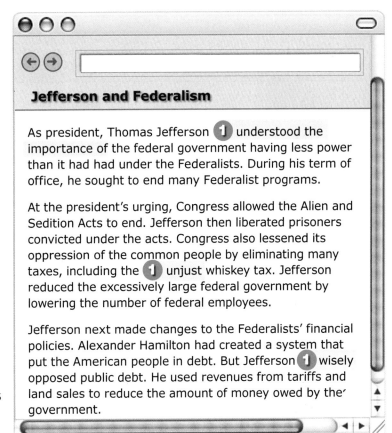

Jefferson and Federalism

As president, Thomas Jefferson 1 understood the importance of the federal government having less power than it had had under the Federalists. During his term of office, he sought to end many Federalist programs.

At the president's urging, Congress allowed the Alien and Sedition Acts to end. Jefferson then liberated prisoners convicted under the acts. Congress also lessened its oppression of the common people by eliminating many taxes, including the 1 unjust whiskey tax. Jefferson reduced the excessively large federal government by lowering the number of federal employees.

Jefferson next made changes to the Federalists' financial policies. Alexander Hamilton had created a system that put the American people in debt. But Jefferson 1 wisely opposed public debt. He used revenues from tariffs and land sales to reduce the amount of money owed by the government.

Make a Chart

Making a chart will help you recognize bias in online materials. The chart below shows how bias appears in the Web site.

1 Evidence of Point of View	Author shows his own belief ("the importance of") that the federal government needed to have less power. Word choice: unjust, wisely
2 Think Critically	Makes all Federalist policies sound bad. Does not tell Hamilton's "side of the story."
3 Bias	Biased in favor of Jefferson and small government. Author's purpose is to persuade reader that Federalism is bad.

Practicing the Skill

Search the Web for an article about an event or figure in American history. Using the above strategies, create a chart to identify any instances of bias in the content of the article. If you notice bias, consider how it could be written more objectively.

Alabama
4,557,808 people
52,218 sq. mi.
Rank in area: 30
Entered Union in 1819

Montgomery

Tallahassee

Florida
17,789,864 people
59,909 sq. mi.
Rank in area: 22
Entered Union in 1845

Baton Rouge

Louisiana
4,523,628 people
49,650 sq. mi.
Rank in area: 31
Entered Union in 1812

Juneau

Alaska
663,661 people
616,240 sq. mi.
Rank in area: 1
Entered Union in 1959

Atlanta

Georgia
9,072,576 people
58,970 sq. mi.
Rank in area: 24
Entered Union in 1788

Augusta

Maine
1,321,505 people
33,738 sq. mi.
Rank in area: 39
Entered Union in 1820

Phoenix

Arizona
5,939,292 people
113,998 sq. mi.
Rank in area: 6
Entered Union in 1912

Honolulu

Hawaii
1,275,194 people
6,641 sq. mi.
Rank in area: 43
Entered Union in 1959

Annapolis

Maryland
5,600,388 people
12,297 sq. mi.
Rank in area: 42
Entered Union in 1788

Little Rock

Arkansas
2,779,154 people
53,178 sq. mi.
Rank in area: 29
Entered Union in 1836

Boise

Idaho
1,429,096 people
83,570 sq. mi.
Rank in area: 14
Entered Union in 1890

Boston

Massachusetts
6,398,743 people
9,240 sq. mi.
Rank in area: 44
Entered Union in 1788

Sacramento

California
36,132,147 people
158,854 sq. mi.
Rank in area: 3
Entered Union in 1850

Springfield

Illinois
12,763,371 people
57,914 sq. mi.
Rank in area: 25
Entered Union in 1818

Lansing

Michigan
10,120,860 people
96,716 sq. mi.
Rank in area: 11
Entered Union in 1837

Denver

Colorado
4,665,177 people
104,093 sq. mi.
Rank in area: 8
Entered Union in 1876

Indianapolis

Indiana
6,271,973 people
36,418 sq. mi.
Rank in area: 38
Entered Union in 1816

St. Paul

Minnesota
5,132,799 people
86,938 sq. mi.
Rank in area: 12
Entered Union in 1858

Hartford

Connecticut
3,510,297 people
5,543 sq. mi.
Rank in area: 48
Entered Union in 1788

Des Moines

Iowa
2,966,334 people
56,271 sq. mi.
Rank in area: 26
Entered Union in 1846

Jackson

Mississippi
2,921,088 people
48,282 sq. mi.
Rank in area: 32
Entered Union in 1817

Dover

Delaware
843,524 people
2,396 sq. mi.
Rank in area: 49
Entered Union in 1787

Topeka

Kansas
2,744,687 people
82,276 sq. mi.
Rank in area: 15
Entered Union in 1861

Jefferson City

Missouri
5,800,310 people
69,704 sq. mi.
Rank in area: 21
Entered Union in 1821

Washington

District of Columbia
550,521 people
68 sq. mi.
Created 1790

Frankfort

Kentucky
4,173,405 people
40,409 sq. mi.
Rank in area: 37
Entered Union in 1792

Helena

Montana
935,670 people
147,042 sq. mi.
Rank in area: 4
Entered Union in 1889

Sources: U.S. Census Bureau, *American Factfinder* online: 2005 Population Estimates. *CIA World Factbook* online. *Encyclopaedia Britannica Almanac* 2006. *Rand McNally Goode's World Atlas,* 20th ed., 2000.

Nebraska
1,758,787 people
77,353 sq. mi.
Rank in area: 16
Entered Union in 1867

Ohio
11,464,042 people
44,825 sq. mi.
Rank in area: 34
Entered Union in 1803

Texas
22,859,968 people
267,256 sq. mi.
Rank in area: 2
Entered Union in 1845

Nevada
2,414,807 people
110,560 sq. mi.
Rank in area: 7
Entered Union in 1864

Oklahoma
3,547,884 people
69,898 sq. mi.
Rank in area: 20
Entered Union in 1907

Utah
2,469,585 people
84,898 sq. mi.
Rank in area: 13
Entered Union in 1896

New Hampshire
1,309,940 people
9,282 sq. mi.
Rank in area: 46
Entered Union in 1788

Oregon
3,641,056 people
97,126 sq. mi.
Rank in area: 9
Entered Union in 1859

Vermont
623,050 people
9,614 sq. mi.
Rank in area: 45
Entered Union in 1791

New Jersey
8,717,925 people
8,214 sq. mi.
Rank in area: 47
Entered Union in 1787

Pennsylvania
12,429,616 people
46,055 sq. mi.
Rank in area: 33
Entered Union in 1787

Virginia
7,567,465 people
42,328 sq. mi.
Rank in area: 35
Entered Union in 1788

New Mexico
1,928,384 people
121,589 sq. mi.
Rank in area: 5
Entered Union in 1912

Rhode Island
1,076,189 people
1,231 sq. mi.
Rank in area: 50
Entered Union in 1790

Washington
6,287,759 people
70,634 sq. mi.
Rank in area: 18
Entered Union in 1889

New York
19,254,630 people
54,077 sq. mi.
Rank in area: 27
Entered Union in 1788

South Carolina
4,255,083 people
31,190 sq. mi.
Rank in area: 40
Entered Union in 1788

West Virginia
1,816,856 people
24,230 sq. mi.
Rank in area: 41
Entered Union in 1863

North Carolina
8,683,242 people
52,670 sq. mi.
Rank in area: 28
Entered Union in 1789

South Dakota
775,933 people
77,116 sq. mi.
Rank in area: 17
Entered Union in 1889

Wisconsin
5,536,201 people
65,498 sq. mi.
Rank in area: 23
Entered Union in 1848

North Dakota
636,677 people
70,699 sq. mi.
Rank in area: 19
Entered Union in 1889

Tennessee
5,962,959 people
42,143 sq. mi.
Rank in area: 36
Entered Union in 1796

Wyoming
509,294 people
97,813 sq. mi.
Rank in area: 10
Entered Union in 1890

United States: *Major Dependencies*

- American Samoa—62,700 people; 90 sq. mi.
- Guam—165,000 people; 217 sq. mi.
- Commonwealth of Puerto Rico—3,898,000 people; 5,324 sq. mi.
- Virgin Islands of the United States—109,000 people; 171 sq. mi.
- Midway Islands—no indigenous inhabitants; 6.2 sq. mi.
- Wake Island—no indigenous inhabitants; 6.5 sq. mi.

Presents of the United States

Here are some little-known facts about the presidents of the United States:

- First president born in the new United States: **Martin Van Buren** (eighth president)
- Only president who was a bachelor: **James Buchanan**
- First left-handed president: **James A. Garfield**
- Largest president: **William H. Taft** (6 feet 2 inches, 332 pounds)
- Youngest president: **Theodore Roosevelt** (42 years old)
- Oldest president: **Ronald Reagan** (77 years old when he left office in 1989)
- First president born west of the Mississippi River: **Herbert Hoover** (born in West Branch, Iowa)
- First president born in the 20th century: **John F. Kennedy** (born May 29, 1917)

1 George Washington
1789–1797
No Political Party
Birthplace: Virginia
Born: February 22, 1732
Died: December 14, 1799

2 John Adams
1797–1801
Federalist
Birthplace: Massachusetts
Born: October 30, 1735
Died: July 4, 1826

3 Thomas Jefferson
1801–1809
Democratic-Republican
Birthplace: Virginia
Born: April 13, 1743
Died: July 4, 1826

4 James Madison
1809–1817
Democratic-Republican
Birthplace: Virginia
Born: March 16, 1751
Died: June 28, 1836

5 James Monroe
1817–1825
Democratic-Republican
Birthplace: Virginia
Born: April 28, 1758
Died: July 4, 1831

6 John Quincy Adams
1825–1829
Democratic-Republican
Birthplace: Massachusetts
Born: July 11, 1767
Died: February 23, 1848

7 Andrew Jackson
1829–1837
Democrat
Birthplace: South Carolina
Born: March 15, 1767
Died: June 8, 1845

8 Martin Van Buren
1837–1841
Democrat
Birthplace: New York
Born: December 5, 1782
Died: July 24, 1862

9 William H. Harrison
1841
Whig
Birthplace: Virginia
Born: February 9, 1773
Died: April 4, 1841

10 John Tyler
1841–1845
Whig
Birthplace: Virginia
Born: March 29, 1790
Died: January 18, 1862

11 James K. Polk
1845–1849
Democrat
Birthplace: North Carolina
Born: November 2, 1795
Died: June 15, 1849

12 Zachary Taylor
1849–1850
Whig
Birthplace: Virginia
Born: November 24, 1784
Died: July 9, 1850

13 Millard Fillmore
1850–1853
Whig
Birthplace: New York
Born: January 7, 1800
Died: March 8, 1874

14 Franklin Pierce
1853–1857
Democrat
Birthplace: New Hampshire
Born: November 23, 1804
Died: October 8, 1869

15 James Buchanan
1857–1861
Democrat
Birthplace: Pennsylvania
Born: April 23, 1791
Died: June 1, 1868

16 Abraham Lincoln
1861–1865
Republican
Birthplace: Kentucky
Born: February 12, 1809
Died: April 15, 1865

17 Andrew Johnson
1865–1869
Democrat
Birthplace: North Carolina
Born: December 29, 1808
Died: July 31, 1875

18 Ulysses S. Grant
1869–1877
Republican
Birthplace: Ohio
Born: April 27, 1822
Died: July 23, 1885

19 Rutherford B. Hayes
1877–1881
Republican
Birthplace: Ohio
Born: October 4, 1822
Died: January 17, 1893

20 James A. Garfield
1881
Republican
Birthplace: Ohio
Born: November 19, 1831
Died: September 19, 1881

21 Chester A. Arthur
1881–1885
Republican
Birthplace: Vermont
Born: October 5, 1829
Died: November 18, 1886

22 24 Grover Cleveland
1885–1889, 1893–1897
Democrat
Birthplace: New Jersey
Born: March 18, 1837
Died: June 24, 1908

23 Benjamin Harrison
1889–1893
Republican
Birthplace: Ohio
Born: August 20, 1833
Died: March 13, 1901

25 William McKinley
1897–1901
Republican
Birthplace: Ohio
Born: January 29, 1843
Died: September 14, 1901

26 Theodore Roosevelt
1901–1909
Republican
Birthplace: New York
Born: October 27, 1858
Died: January 6, 1919

27 William H. Taft
1909–1913
Republican
Birthplace: Ohio
Born: September 15, 1857
Died: March 8, 1930

28 Woodrow Wilson
1913–1921
Democrat
Birthplace: Virginia
Born: December 28, 1856
Died: February 3, 1924

29 Warren G. Harding
1921–1923
Republican
Birthplace: Ohio
Born: November 2, 1865
Died: August 2, 1923

Presidents of the United States

30 Calvin Coolidge
1923–1929
Republican
Birthplace: Vermont
Born: July 4, 1872
Died: January 5, 1933

31 Herbert C. Hoover
1929–1933
Republican
Birthplace: Iowa
Born: August 10, 1874
Died: October 20, 1964

32 Franklin D. Roosevelt
1933–1945
Democrat
Birthplace: New York
Born: January 30, 1882
Died: April 12, 1945

33 Harry S. Truman
1945–1953
Democrat
Birthplace: Missouri
Born: May 8, 1884
Died: December 26, 1972

34 Dwight D. Eisenhower
1953–1961
Republican
Birthplace: Texas
Born: October 14, 1890
Died: March 28, 1969

35 John F. Kennedy
1961–1963
Democrat
Birthplace: Massachusetts
Born: May 29, 1917
Died: November 22, 1963

36 Lyndon B. Johnson
1963–1969
Democrat
Birthplace: Texas
Born: August 27, 1908
Died: January 22, 1973

37 Richard M. Nixon
1969–1974
Republican
Birthplace: California
Born: January 9, 1913
Died: April 22, 1994

38 Gerald R. Ford
1974–1977
Republican
Birthplace: Nebraska
Born: July 14, 1913
Died: December 26, 2006

39 James E. Carter, Jr.
1977–1981
Democrat
Birthplace: Georgia
Born: October 1, 1924

40 Ronald W. Reagan
1981–1989
Republican
Birthplace: Illinois
Born: February 6, 1911
Died: June 5, 2004

41 George H. W. Bush
1989–1993
Republican
Birthplace: Massachusetts
Born: June 12, 1924

42 William J. Clinton
1993–2001
Democrat
Birthplace: Arkansas
Born: August 19, 1946

43 George W. Bush
2001–
Republican
Birthplace: Connecticut
Born: July 6, 1946

Gazetteer

A gazetteer is a dictionary of geographical terms and place names. This Gazetteer identifies important places and geographical features in this book. Entries include a short description, often followed by page numbers. Arabic numbers refer to a text page on which the entry is discussed; numbers in italics refer to a map where the place appears. In addition, some entries include rounded-off geographical coordinates.

Afghanistan nation in Central Asia. Capital: Kabul. *A24–A25*

Africa world's second largest continent.

Alabama 22nd state. Capital: Montgomery. *A34–A35*

Alamo Texas mission in San Antonio captured by Mexico in 1836. (29°N 98°W) *431*

Alaska 49th state. Capital: Juneau. *A34–A35*

Antarctica continent at the South Pole.

Antietam Maryland creek; site of bloodiest day's fighting in the Civil War. (39°N 77°W) *526*

Appalachian Mountains mountain range running from Alabama into Canada. *A36–A37*

Appomattox Court House town near Appomattox, Virginia, where Lee surrendered to Grant on April 9, 1865. (37°N 79°W) *554*

Arizona 48th state. Capital: Phoenix. *A34–A35*

Arkansas 25th state. Capital: Little Rock. *A34–A35*

Asia world's largest continent.

Atlantic Ocean ocean forming east boundary of the United States.

Australia island country between Indian and Pacific ocean; Capital: Canberra. Also the world's smallest continent. *A24–A25*

Austria-Hungary one of the Central Powers in World War I; after the war, divided into smaller countries. *719*

Aztec Empire region of what is now Mexico, once under Aztec control.

Backcountry identification for former undeveloped region beginning in the Appalachian Mountains and extending west. *118*

Baltimore Maryland city on Chesapeake Bay. (39°N 77°W)

Bay of Pigs (Bahía de Cochinos) inlet on south coast of Cuba; site of 1961 ill-fated, U.S.-backed Cuban invasion attempt.

Beringia former land bridge connecting Asia with North America and now under waters of Bering Strait. (66°N 169°W).

Berlin capital of Germany; divided into East and West Berlin, 1948–1989. (53°N 13°E) *847*

Boston capital of Massachusetts; site of early colonial unrest and conflict. (42°N 71°W) *38, 96*

Bull Run stream 30 miles southwest of Washington, D.C.; site of first land battle of Civil War. (39°N 78°W)

Bunker Hill hill now part of Boston; its name misidentifies Revolutionary War battle fought at nearby Breed's Hill. (42°N 71°W) *190*

Cahokia Illinois Mound Builders site; village taken from British by Clark in 1778. (39°N 90°W) *209*

California 31st state. Capital: Sacramento. *A34–A35*

Canada nation sharing northern U.S. border. Capital: Ottawa. *A28*

Caribbean Sea expanse of the Atlantic Ocean between the Gulf of Mexico and South America. *A30–A31*

Central America area of North America between Mexico and South America. *A30–A31*

Charleston as Charles Town, largest Southern colonial city; South Carolina site of first Civil War shots, at offshore Fort Sumter. (33°N 80°W) *80*

Charlestown former town, now part of Boston; site of both Bunker and Breed's hills. (42°N 71°W) *190*

Chesapeake Bay inlet of the Atlantic Ocean, located in Virginia and Maryland. *A36–A37*

Chicago large Illinois city on Lake Michigan. (42°N 88°W)

China large nation in Asia. Capital: Beijing. *A24–A25*

Colorado 38th state. Capital: Denver. *A34–A35*

Concord Massachusetts town and site of second battle of the Revolutionary War. (42°N 71°W)

Confederate States of America nation formed by 11 Southern states during the Civil War. Capital: Richmond, Virginia. *509*

Connecticut 5th state. Capital: Hartford. *A34–A35*

Cuba Caribbean island south of Florida. Capital: Havana. *A24–A25*

Delaware 1st state. Capital: Dover. *A34–A35*

District of Columbia (D.C.) self-governing federal district between Virginia and Maryland, made up entirely of the city of Washington, the U.S. capital. (39°N 77°W)

Dominican Republic nation sharing the island of Hispaniola with Haiti. Capital: Santo Domingo. *A24–A25*

Eastern Hemisphere the half of the world that includes Europe, Africa, and Asia. *A6*

El Salvador Central American nation. Capital: San Salvador. *A24–A25*

England southern part of Great Britain. *A24–A25*

English Channel narrow waterway separating Great Britain from France. *823*

Erie Canal all-water channel dug out to connect the Hudson River with Lake Erie. *363, 381*

Europe second smallest continent, actually a peninsula of the Eurasian landmass.

Florida 27th state. Capital: Tallahassee. *A34–A35*

Fort McHenry fort in Baltimore harbor where 1814 British attack inspired U.S. national anthem. (39°N 77°W) *355*

Fort Sumter fort in Charleston, South Carolina, harbor where 1861 attack by Confederates began the Civil War. (33°N 80°W) *509, 524*

Fort Ticonderoga fort in New York on Lake Champlain; site of battles during French and Indian War and the Revolutionary War. (44°N 73°W) *145, 178, 200*

France nation in western Europe; it aided America in the Revolutionary War. Capital: Paris. *A24–A25*

Gadsden Purchase last territory (from Mexico, 1853) added to continental United States. *A38–A39*

Georgia 4th state. Capital: Atlanta. *A34–A35*

Germany nation in central Europe; once divided into West and East Germany, 1949–1990. Capital: Berlin. *A24–A25, 742, 847*

Gettysburg Pennsylvania town and site of 1863 Civil War victory for the North that is considered the war's turning point. (40°N 77°W) *551*

Ghana first powerful West African trading empire. *14*

Great Britain European island nation across from France; it consists of England, Scotland and Wales. *A24–A25*

Great Lakes five connected lakes—Ontario, Erie, Huron, Michigan, and Superior—on the U.S. border with Canada. *A24–A25*

Great Plains vast grassland region in the central United States. *A36–A37*

Guam Pacific island, possession of United States. *A24–A25, 829*

Gulf of Mexico body of water forming southern U.S. boundary from east Texas to west Florida. *A30–A31*

Haiti nation sharing the island of Hispaniola with Dominican Republic. Capital: Port-au-Prince. *A30–A31*

Harlem neighborhood of New York City, home to large African-American community since 1910s. *764–766*

Harpers Ferry village today in extreme eastern West Virginia where John Brown raided stored U.S. weapons in 1859. (39°N 78°W)

Hawaii 50th state. Capital: Honolulu. *A34–A35*

Hiroshima Japanese city destroyed by U.S. atomic bomb dropped to end World War II. (34°N 132°E) *829*

Hispaniola West Indies island (shared today by Dominican Republic and Haiti) that Columbus mistook for Asia. *A30–A31*

Hudson River large river in eastern New York. *113, 200*

Idaho 43rd state. Capital: Boise. *A34–A35*

Illinois 21st state. Capital: Springfield. *A34–A35*

Indiana 19th state. Capital: Indianapolis. *A34–A35*

Indian Territory area, mainly of present-day Oklahoma, that in the 1800s became land for relocated Native Americans. *405*

Iowa 29th state. Capital: Des Moines. *A34–A35*

Iran Middle East nation. Capital: Tehran. *A24–A25, 947*

Iraq Middle East nation whose 1990 invasion of Kuwait led to the Persian Gulf War. Capital: Baghdad. *A24–A25, 947*

Ireland island country west of England whose mid-1800s famine caused more than one million people to emigrate to America. Capital: Dublin. *A24–A25*

Israel Jewish nation in the Middle East. Capital: Jerusalem. *A24–A25*

Italy nation in southern Europe. Capital: Rome. *A24–A25*

Jamestown community in Virginia that was the first permanent English settlement in North America. *59, 80*

Japan island nation in east Asia. Capital: Tokyo. *A24–A25, 829*

Kansas 34th state. Capital: Topeka. *A34–A35*

Kentucky 15th state. Capital: Frankfort. *A34–A35*

Kosovo province of the Yugoslavian republic of Serbia.

Kuwait tiny, oil-rich Middle East nation. Capital: Kuwait City. *947*

Latin America region made up of Mexico, Caribbean Islands, and Central and South America, where Latin-based languages of Spanish, French, or Portuguese are spoken. *A30–A31*

Lebanon Middle East country on the Mediterranean coast. Capital: Beirut. *A24–A25*

Lexington Massachusetts town and site of first Revolutionary War battle in 1775. (42°N 71°W)

Little Bighorn River Montana site of Sioux and Cheyenne victory over Custer. (46°N 108°W)

Little Rock capital of Arkansas and site of 1957 school-desegregation conflict.

Los Angeles 2nd largest U.S. city, on California's coast.

Louisiana 18th state. Capital: Baton Rouge. *A34–A35*

Louisiana Purchase land west of the Mississippi River purchased from France in 1803. *347, 436*

Lowell Massachusetts city built in early 1800s as planned factory town. (43°N 71°W)

Maine 23rd state. Capital: Augusta. *A34–A35*

Mali early West African trading empire succeeding Ghana empire. *14*

Maryland 7th state. Capital: Annapolis. *A34–A35*

Massachusetts 6th state. Capital: Boston. *A34–A35*

Mexico nation sharing U.S. southern border. Capital: Mexico City. *A30–A31*

Michigan 26th state. Capital: Lansing. *A34–A35*

Middle East eastern Mediterranean region that includes countries such as Iran, Iraq, Syria, Kuwait, Jordan, Saudi Arabia, Israel, and Egypt.

Minnesota 32nd state. Capital: St. Paul. *A34–A35*

Mississippi 20th state. Capital: Jackson. *A34–A35*

Mississippi River second longest U.S. river, south from Minnesota to the Gulf of Mexico.

Missouri 24th state. Capital: Jefferson City. *A34–A35*

Missouri River longest U.S. river, east from the Rockies to the Mississippi River.

Montana 41st state. Capital: Helena. *A34–A35*

Montgomery Alabama capital and site of 1955 African-American bus boycott. (32°N 86°W)

Nagasaki Japanese port city, one-third of which was destroyed by U.S. atomic bomb dropped to end World War II. (33°N 130°E) *829*

Nebraska 37th state. Capital: Lincoln. *A34–A35*

Nevada 36th state. Capital: Carson City. *A34–A35*

New England northeast U.S. region made up of Maine, New Hampshire, Vermont, Massachusetts, Rhode Island, and Connecticut. *72*

New France first permanent French colony in North America. *38*

New Hampshire 9th state. Capital: Concord. *A34–A35*

New Jersey 3rd state. Capital: Trenton. *A34–A35*

New Mexico 47th state. Capital: Santa Fe. *A34–A35*

New Netherland early Dutch colony that became New York in 1664. *38*

New Orleans Louisiana port city at mouth of the Mississippi River. *355*

New Spain former North American province of the Spanish Empire, made up mostly of present-day Mexico and the southwest United States. *42*

New York 11th state. Capital: Albany. *A34–A35*

New York City largest U.S. city, at the mouth of the Hudson River; temporary U.S. capital, 1785–1790.

Nicaragua Central American nation. Capital: Managua. *A24–A25*

Normandy region of northern France where Allied invasion in 1944 turned tide of World War II.

North America continent of Western Hemisphere north of Panama-Colombia border.

North Carolina 12th state. Capital: Raleigh. *A34–A35*

North Dakota 39th state. Capital: Bismarck. *A34–A35*

North Korea Communist country in Asia, bordering eastern China. Capital: Pyongyang. *852*

North Vietnam northern region of Vietnam, established in 1954; reunified with South Vietnam in 1975 after Vietnam War. *911*

Northwest Territory U.S. land north of the Ohio River to the Great Lakes and west to the Mississippi River; acquired in 1783. *240, 320*

Ohio 17th state. Capital: Columbus. *A34–A35*

Ohio River river that flows from western Pennsylvania to the Mississippi River.

Oklahoma 46th state. Capital: Oklahoma City. *A34–A35*

Oregon 33rd state. Capital: Salem. *A34–A35*

Oregon Country former region of northwest North America claimed jointly by Britain and the United States until 1846. *347, 434*

Oregon Trail pioneer wagon route from Missouri to the Oregon Territory in the 1840s and 1850s. *421*

Pacific Ocean world's largest ocean, on the west coast of the United States.

Panama Canal ship passageway cut through Panama in Central America, linking Atlantic and Pacific oceans. (8°N 80°W) *709*

Paris capital city of France. (49°N 2°E)

Pearl Harbor naval base in Hawaii; site of surprise Japanese aerial attack in 1941. (21°N 158°W) *805*

Pennsylvania 2nd state. Capital: Harrisburg. *A34–A35*

Persian Gulf waterway between Saudi Arabia and Iran, leading to Kuwait and Iraq. *947*

Philadelphia large port city in Pennsylvania; U.S. capital, 1790–1800. (40°N 76°W) *113*

Philippine Islands Pacific island country off the southeast coast of China. Capital: Manila. *701*

Plymouth town on Massachusetts coast and site of Pilgrim landing and colony. (42°N 71°W) *69*

Poland central European republic on the Baltic coast. Capital: Warsaw. (52°N 21°E) *A24–A25, 742*

Portugal nation in southwestern Europe; leader in early oceanic explorations. Capital: Lisbon. *A24–A25, 30*

Potomac River river separating Virginia from Maryland and Washington, D.C.

Puerto Rico Caribbean island that has been U.S. territory since 1898. *A30–A31*

Quebec major early Canadian city; also a province of eastern Canada. *38*

Rhode Island 13th state. Capital: Providence. *A34–A35*

Richmond Virginia capital that was also the capital of the Confederacy. (38°N 77°W)

Rio Grande river that forms part of the border between the United States and Mexico. *435*

Roanoke Island island off the coast of North Carolina; 1585 site of the first English colony in the Americas. (36°N 76°W) *59*

Rocky Mountains mountain range in the western United States and Canada. *A36–A37*

Russia large Eurasian country, the major republic of the former Soviet Union (1922–1991). Capital: Moscow. *A24–A25*

St. Augustine oldest permanent European settlement (1565) in the United States, on Florida's northeast coast. (30°N 81°W) *38*

St. Lawrence River Atlantic-to-Great Lakes waterway used by early explorers of mid-North America. *38*

St. Louis Missouri city at the junction of the Missouri and Mississippi rivers. (39°N 90°W) *363*

San Antonio Texas city and site of the Alamo. (29°N 99°W) *431*

San Francisco major port city in northern California. (38°N 123°W)

San Salvador West Indies island near the Bahamas where Columbus first landed in the Americas. (24°N 74°W)

Santa Fe Trail old wagon route from Missouri to Santa Fe in Mexican province of New Mexico. *421*

Scotland northern part of the island of Great Britain. *A24–A25*

Serbia republic, part of the former Yugoslavia. Capital: Belgrade. *A24–A25*

Sierra Nevada mountain range near the Pacific coast.

Songhai early West African trading empire succeeding Mali empire. *12*

South America continent of Western Hemisphere south of Panama-Colombia border.

South Carolina 8th state. Capital: Columbia. *A34–A35*

South Dakota 40th state. Capital: Pierre. *A34–A35*

South Korea East Asian country bordering North Korea. Capital: Seoul. *852*

South Vietnam southern region of Vietnam, established in 1954; reunified with North Vietnam in 1975 after Vietnam War. *911*

Soviet Union (U.S.S.R.) country created in 1922 by joining Russia and other republics; in 1991, broken into independent states. *843*

Spain nation in southwestern Europe; early empire builder in the Americas. Capital: Madrid. *A24–A25, 30*

Tennessee 16th state. Capital: Nashville. *A34–A35*

Tennessee Valley area of Appalachian Mountains drained by the Tennessee River. *791*

Tenochtitlán Aztec Empire capital; now site of Mexico City. *30*

Texas 28th state. Capital: Austin. *A34–A35*

Timbuktu city and trading center of ancient Mali. *14*

Utah 45th state. Capital: Salt Lake City. *A34–A35*

Valley Forge village in southeast Pennsylvania and site of Washington's army camp during winter of 1777–1778. (40°N 75°W) *193, 207, 208*

Vermont 14th state. Capital: Montpelier. *A34–A35*

Vicksburg Mississippi River site of major Union victory (1863) in Civil War. (32°N 91°W) *553, 556*

Vietnam country in Southeast Asia; divided into two regions (1954–1975), North and South, until end of Vietnam War. Capital: Hanoi. *A24–A25, 907, 911*

Virginia 10th state. Capital: Richmond. *A34–A35*

Washington 42nd state. Capital: Olympia. *A34–A35*

Washington, D.C. capital of the United States since 1800; makes up whole of District of Columbia (D.C.). (39°N 77°W) *274*

West Africa region from which most Africans were brought to the Americas.

Western Hemisphere the half of the world that includes the Americas. *A6*

West Indies numerous islands in the Caribbean Sea, between Florida and South America. *A30–A31*

West Virginia 35th state. Capital: Charleston. *A34–A35, 513*

Wisconsin 30th state. Capital: Madison. *A34–A35*

Wounded Knee South Dakota site that was scene of 1890 massacre of Sioux. (43°N 102°W)

Wyoming 44th state. Capital: Cheyenne. *A34–A35*

Yorktown Virginia village and site of American victory that sealed British defeat in Revolutionary War. (37°N 77°W) *216*

English Glossary

54th Massachusetts Volunteers regiment of African-American soldiers that gained fame for its courageous assault on Fort Wagner, South Carolina (p. 536)

abolition the movement to stop slavery (p. 464)

Act of Toleration Maryland law that forbade religious persecution (p. 76)

Alamo, Battle of the battle between Texas and Mexico in 1836 (p. 426)

Albany Plan of Union first formal proposal to unite the colonies (p. 142)

Alien and Sedition Acts series of four laws enacted in 1798 to reduce the political power of recent immigrants (p. 326)

aliens immigrants who are not yet citizens (p. 326)

alliance people or nations involved in a pact or treaty (p. 26)

ally (AL•eye) a country that agrees to help another country achieve a common goal (p. 204)

amendment addition to a document (p. 248)

American Federation of Labor (AFL) a national organization of labor unions founded in 1886 by Samuel Gompers (p. 656)

American System plan introduced in 1815 to make America economically self-sufficient (p. 378)

amnesty official pardon (p. 570)

Anaconda Plan Union strategy to defeat the Confederacy (p. 510)

anarchist person who believes in anarchism or a society that has no government at all (p. 656)

Angel Island San Francisco Bay immigration station for Asian immigrants (p. 640)

Anglo English-speaking settler in the Southwest (p. 600)

annex join or merge territory into an existing political unity such as a country or state (p. 426)

Antietam, Battle of battle in Maryland that ended Lee's first invasion of the North (p. 522)

Antifederalists people who opposed ratification of the Constitution (p. 248)

Anti-Imperialist League group of influential Americans who believed the United States should not deny other people the right to govern themselves (p. 698)

Appalachian Mountains mountain range stretching from eastern Canada south to Alabama (p. 116)

Appomattox Court House town in Virginia where Lee surrendered to Grant (p. 548)

apprentice (a•PREN•tis) one who is learning a trade from an experienced craftsperson (p. 126)

arsenal place where weapons are kept (p. 234)

Articles of Confederation plan for national government ratified in 1781 (p. 234)

artillery cannon and large guns (p. 176)

artisans skilled craftspeople, such as blacksmiths and cabinet makers (p. 110)

assimilate to absorb into a culture (p. 402)

assimilation the process of blending into society (p. 640)

attorney general nation's top legal officer; today also the head of the Department of Justice (p. 312)

Aztec Native American civilization that spread through what is now Mexico (p. 4)

Backcountry the far western edges of the colonies (p. 94)

Bacon's Rebellion 1676 rebellion in Virginia (p. 102)

banish to force someone to leave a place (p. 66)

Bear Flag Revolt rebellion by Americans in 1846 against Mexican rule of California (p. 432)

bickering petty quarreling (p. 480)

Bill of Rights first ten amendments to the U.S. Constitution (p. 248)

black codes laws passed by Southern states that limited the freedom of former slaves (p. 570)

Black Death deadly disease that spread through Europe in the 14th century (p. 16)

boomtown town that experiences sudden growth in population or economic activity (p. 600)

border states slave states that bordered states in which slavery was illegal (p. 510)

Boston Massacre incident in 1770 in which British troops fired on and killed American colonists (p. 160)

Boston Tea Party incident in 1773, when colonists protested British policies by boarding British ships and throwing their cargoes of tea overboard (p. 160)

Boxer Rebellion 1900 nationalist uprising in China (p. 706)

boycott refusal to buy (p. 156)

buffalo soldier name Native Americans gave to African-American soldiers in the West (p. 600)

Bull Moose Party progressive political party in 1912 presidential election (p. 678)

Bull Run, First Battle of first major battle of the Civil War (p. 510)

business cycle the pattern of good and bad economic times (p. 630)

cabinet group of Executive department heads that serve as the President's chief advisers (p. 312)

California Gold Rush migration of thousands of settlers to California in search of gold (p. 438)

Californios settlers of Spanish or Mexican descent who populated California (p. 438)

carpetbagger Northerner who went to the South after the Civil War to help with Reconstruction (p. 570)

cash crops crops raised to be sold for money (p. 102)

Catholics Christian followers of the Roman Catholic Church (p. 16)

cede surrender, or give up (p. 318)

Charles Town, Battle of British siege of Charles Town (Charleston), South Carolina, in May 1780, in which the Americans suffered their worst defeat of the war (p. 212)

charter written contract giving the right to establish a colony (p. 60)

checks and balances the ability of each branch of government to exercise checks, or controls, over the other branches (p. 242)

Chinese Exclusion Act 1882 law which banned Chinese immigration (p. 640)

citizen person owing loyalty to and entitled to protection of a state or nation (p. 234)

civil rights rights granted to all citizens (p. 570)

civilization complex society in which people share key characteristics such as language and religion (p. 4)

clans large groups of families that claim a common ancestor (p. 116)

Clayton Antitrust Act legislation that strengthened the Sherman Antitrust Act's power (p. 678)

coercion (ko•ER•shun) practice of forcing someone to act in a certain way by use of pressure or threats (p. 352)

Columbian Exchange transfer of plants, animals and diseases between the Western and Eastern hemispheres (p. 40)

Commander-In-Chief the President in his role as commander of all armed forces (p. 536)

committee of correspondence organization formed to exchange information about British policies and American resistance (p. 160)

common shared land where public activities took place (p. 94)

compromise settlement of differences in which each side gives up something it wants (p. 582)

Compromise of 1850 series of laws intended to settle the major disagreements between free states and slave states (p. 480)

Compromise of 1877 agreement that decided the 1876 presidential election (p. 582)

Conestoga wagons covered wagons introduced by German immigrants (p. 110)

Confederate States of America confederation formed in 1861 by the Southern states after their secession from the Union (p. 498)

Confederation Congress national legislative body formed by the Articles of Confederation (p. 234)

congregation a group of people who belong to the same church (p. 66)

conquistador (kahn•KEES•tuh•dawr) Spanish soldier that explored the Americas and claimed land for Spain (p. 26)

conscription military draft (p. 542)

conservation controlling resource usage (p. 672)

Constitutional Convention 1787 meeting at which the U.S. Constitution was created (p. 242)

consumer person who buys something (p. 662)

Continental Army America's Patriot army during the Revolutionary War (p. 176)

contractor private supplier (p. 516)

converts people who accept a new religious belief (p. 418)

Copperheads Northern Democrats who favored peace with the South (p. 542)

corporation a business owned by investors who buy part of it through shares of stock (p. 630)

corps (kor) a number of people acting together for a similar purpose (p. 344)

cotton gin machine that made cleaning seeds from cotton faster (p. 372)

Crittenden Compromise compromise introduced in 1861 that might have prevented secession (p. 498)

Daughters of Liberty organization of colonial women formed to protest British policies (p. 160)

Dawes Act 1887 law that distributed reservation land to individual Native American owners (p. 608)

Declaration of Independence document that declared American independence from Britain (p. 176)

denomination distinct religious group (p. 110)

depression a severe economic slump (pp. 408, 582)

desert (duh•ZERT) to leave military duty without permission (p. 204)

direct primary primary in which voters, not party conventions, choose candidates to run for public office (p. 672)

dislodge remove (p. 548)

disputes (dis•PYOOTS) disagreements (p. 222)

dissenter (dih•SEHN•tuhr) a person who disagrees with an official church (p. 66)

diversity variety (p. 76)

doctrine of nullification idea that a state had the right to nullify, or reject, a federal law that it considers unconstitutional (p. 394)

Dred Scott v. *Sandford* 1856 Supreme Court case in which a slave, Dred Scott, sued for his freedom; the court ruled against Scott (p. 490)

duties taxes placed on imported goods (p. 160)

Eighteenth Amendment constitutional amendment enacting Prohibition (p. 682)

electoral votes votes made by members of the Electoral College, which elects the president and vice president (p. 582)

elite highest-ranking social group (p. 76)

Ellis Island New York Harbor immigration station for European immigrants (p. 640)

emancipate to free (p. 536)

Emancipation Proclamation document issued by Lincoln that declared that all slaves in Confederate territory were free (p. 536)

Embargo Act of 1807 law that forbade American ships from sailing to foreign ports and closed American ports to British ships (p. 352)

emigrant person who leaves a country (p. 450)

encomienda grant of Native American slave labor (p. 40)

English Bill of Rights 1689 laws protecting the rights of English subjects and Parliament (p. 136)

Enlightenment philosophical movement stressing human reason (p. 126)

enlist to join the armed forces (p. 516)

Erie Canal waterway that connected New York City with Buffalo, New York (p. 378)

executive branch government department that enforces laws (p. 242)

Exodusters name for African Americans who settled on the Great Plains (p. 616)

export to send abroad for trade or sale (p. 40)

factory system method of production using many workers and machines in one building (p. 364)

fall line the point at which waterfalls prevent large boats from moving farther upriver (p. 116)

Fallen Timbers, Battle of 1794 battle between Native Americans and American forces (p. 318)

famine (FAM•ihn) severe food shortage leading to starvation (p. 450)

Federal Judiciary (joo•DISH•ee•ER•ee) **Act** 1789 law passed by the first Congress that set up lower Federal courts (p. 312)

Federal Reserve Act law that created the modern banking system (p. 678)

federalism system of government in which power is shared between the national (or federal) government and the states (p. 248)

The Federalist **papers** ratification essays published in New York newspapers (p. 248)

Federalists people who supported ratification of the Constitution (p. 248)

Fifteenth Amendment constitutional amendment that stated citizens could not be stopped from voting "on account of race, color, or previous condition of servitude" (p. 582)

fireside chats series of radio talks in which FDR explained his policies in a casual style (p. 784)

First Continental Congress meeting of delegates from most of the colonies, called in reaction to the Intolerable Acts (p. 168)

Ford's Theatre theater in Washington, D.C. where Lincoln was shot (p. 558)

foreign policy relations with the governments of other nations (p. 326)

Fort Sumter a Union fort in the harbor of Charleston, South Carolina (p. 510)

forty-niner person who went to California to find gold in 1849 (p. 438)

Founders people who helped create the U.S. Constitution (p. 242)

Fourteenth Amendment constitutional amendment that made all people born in the U.S. (including former slaves) citizens (p. 570)

Freedman's Bureau federal agency set up to help former enslaved people (p. 570)

freedmen's school school set up to educate newly freed African Americans (p. 576)

Free-Soil Party a political party dedicated to stopping the expansion of slavery (p. 480)

French and Indian War war of 1754–1763 between Britain, France, and their allies for control of North America (p. 142)

French Revolution revolution overthrowing the government in France that began in 1787 and ended in violence and mass executions (p. 318)

frontier parts of the West that were occupied mainly by Native Americans, rather than settlers (p. 596)

Fugitive Slave Act an 1850 law to help slaveholders recapture runaway slaves (p. 480)

Fundamental Orders of Connecticut document that has been called the first written constitution in America (p. 66)

galleon sailing ship (p. 34)

Gettysburg, Battle of battle in 1863 in Pennsylvania when Union forces stopped a Confederate invasion of the North (p. 548)

Ghana West African kingdom that prospered between A.D. 700 and 1000 (p. 10)

Gilded Age late 1800s era of fabulous wealth (p. 630)

Glorious Revolution events of 1688–1689, during which the English Parliament invited William and Mary to replace James II as monarchs (p. 136)

gold standard a policy under which the government backs every dollar with a certain amount of gold (p. 616)

Grange organization formed in 1867 to meet the social needs of farm families (p. 616)

Great Awakening Christian religious movement (p. 126)

Great Compromise agreement to establish a two-house national legislature, with all states having equal representation in one house and each state having representation based on its population in the other house (p. 242)

great famine a widespread food shortage that killed thousands of Europeans (p. 16)

Great Migration (17th Century) the movement of tens of thousands of English settlers to New England during the 1630s (p. 66)

Great Plains the area from the Missouri River to the Rocky Mountains (p. 596)

greenback paper money introduced during the Civil War (p. 542)

Greenville, Treaty of 1795 treaty in which 12 Native American tribes ceded control of much of Ohio and Indiana to the U.S. government. (p. 318)

Guadalupe Hidalgo (gwah•duh•LOOP•ay hih•DAHL•go), **Treaty of** treaty that ended the War with Mexico (p. 432)

guerillas (guh•RIL•uhz) small bands of fighters who weaken the enemy with surprise raids and hit-and-run attacks (p. 194)

hacienda large farm or estate (p. 40)

Harpers Ferry a federal arsenal in Virginia captured in 1859 during an antislavery revolt (p. 490)

Haymarket Affair 1886 union protest (p. 656)

headright land grant given to one who could pay his or her way to the colonies (p. 60)

heritage tradition (p. 136)

Homestead Act 1862 law that offered 160 acres free to anyone who agreed to live on and improve the land for five years (p. 616)

Homestead Strike violent strike at Andrew Carnegie's Homestead, Pennsylvania, steel mills in 1892 (p. 656)

House of Burgesses the Virginia assembly, which was the first representative assembly in the American colonies (p. 60)

Huguenots French Protestants (p. 76)

Hull House settlement house founded by Jane Addams in Chicago (p. 640)

hygiene conditions and practices that promote health (p. 516)

immigrant person who settles in a new country (p. 450)

impeach to formally accuse the president of misconduct in office (p. 570)

imperialism policy by which stronger nations extend their economic, political, or military control over weaker nations (p. 694)

impressment the act of seizing by force; between 1803 and 1812, the British impressed, or kidnapped, about 6,000 American sailors to work on British ships (p. 352)

inaugurate (in•AW•gyuh•rate) to formally swear in or induct into office (p. 312)

Inca Native American civilization that developed in what is now Peru (p. 4)

income tax tax on earnings (p. 542)

indentured servant one who worked for a set time without pay in exchange for a free passage to America (p. 60)

Indian Removal Act 1830 law that called for the government to negotiate treaties requiring Native Americans to relocate west (p. 402)

Indian Territory an area to which Native Americans were moved that covered what is now Oklahoma and parts of Kansas and Nebraska (p. 402)

indigo plant that produces a deep blue dye (p. 102)

Industrial Revolution the economic changes of the late 1700s, when large-scale manufacturing replaced farming as the main form of work (p. 364)

inflation an increase in prices and a decrease in the value of money (p. 408)

Intolerable Acts series of laws, known in Britain as the Coercive Acts, meant to punish Massachusetts and clamp down on resistance in other colonies (p. 168)

investor person who puts money into a project to earn a profit (p. 60)

Islam religion that teaches there is one God, named Allah, and Muhammad is his prophet (p. 10)

Jacksonian democracy the idea of widening political power to more of the people (p. 394)

Jamestown the first permanent English settlement in North America (p. 60)

Jay's Treaty agreement that ended the dispute with Britain over American shipping during the French Revolution (p. 318)

Jim Crow laws enacted in Southern states designed to separate white and black people (p. 650)

joint-stock company company funded by a group of investors (p. 60)

judicial branch government department that interprets laws (p. 242)

judicial review principle that states that the Supreme Court has the final say in interpreting the Constitution (p. 338)

Judiciary Act of 1801 law that let President John Adams fill federal judgeships with Federalists (p. 338)

Kansas-Nebraska Act 1854 law that established the territories of Kansas and Nebraska and gave their residents the right to decide whether to allow slavery (p. 480)

Kentucky and Virginia Resolutions Resolutions passed by Kentucky and Virginia in 1798 giving the states the right to declare acts of Congress null and void (p. 326)

King Philip's War 1675–1676 Native American uprising against the Puritan colonies (p. 94)

Knights of Labor an organization of workers from all trades formed after the Civil War (p. 656)

Know-Nothing Party political party in the United States during the 1850s that was against recent immigrants and Roman Catholics (p. 450)

Kongo Central African kingdom that ruled during the 1400s (p. 10)

Ku Klux Klan secret group that used violence to try to restore Democratic control of the South and keep African-Americans powerless (p. 576)

labor union group of workers who band together to seek better working conditions (p. 456)

Land Ordinance of 1785 law that established a plan for dividing the federally owned lands west of the Appalachian Mountains (p. 234)

land speculators (SPEC•yuh•LAY•tors) people who buy land in the hope that it will increase in value (p. 418)

legislative branch government department that makes laws (p. 242)

leisure freedom from time-consuming duties (p. 662)

levy impose or raise a tax (p. 234)

Lewis and Clark expedition group that explored the Louisiana Territory and lands west; also known as the Corps of Discovery (p. 344)

Lexington and Concord first battles of the Revolutionary War (p. 168)

liberation the act of setting someone free (p. 536)

literacy the ability to read and write (p. 126)

Little Bighorn, Battle of the 1876 battle in which the Sioux and Cheyenne killed an entire force of U.S. troops (p. 608)

lode deposit of mineral buried in rock (p. 600)

Lone Star Republic nickname of the Republic of Texas once free from Mexico (p. 426)

long drive journey that takes cattle by foot to a railway (p. 600)

Louisiana Purchase American purchase of the Louisiana Territory from France in 1803 (p. 344)

Lowell mills textile mills located in the factory town of Lowell, Massachusetts (p. 364)

Loyalists Americans who supported the British (p. 168)

lynch to kill by hanging without due process of law (p. 576)

Magna Carta charter of English political and civil liberties (p. 136)

majority rule system of government in which more than one half of a group holds the power to make decisions binding the entire group (p. 248)

malaria infectious disease spread by mosquitoes (p. 706)

Mali West African kingdom that ruled from about 1200 to 1400 (p. 10)

manifest destiny belief that the U.S. was meant to expand from coast to coast (p. 432)

maroon runaway or fugitive slave (p. 48)

mass culture common culture experienced by a large number of people (p. 662)

Maya ancient Native American civilization of Mesoamerica (p. 4)

Mayflower Compact document that helped establish the practice of self-government (p. 66)

mechanical reaper a device that cuts grain (p. 364)

melting pot a place where cultures blend (p. 640)

mercantilism (MUR•kuhn•tee•LIHZ•uhm) economic system that increased money in a country's treasury by creating a favorable balance of trade (pp. 26, 60)

mercenary (MUR•suh•NAIR•ee) a professional soldier hired to fight for a foreign country (p. 194)

Merrimack Confederate ironclad ship, later renamed the *Virginia* (p. 516)

Mesoamerica region that stretches from modern-day Mexico to Nicaragua (p. 4)

Mexican cession Mexican territory surrendered to the United States at the end of the war with Mexico (p. 432)

Mexicano (may•hi•KAH•noh) Spanish word for a person of Mexican heritage; a Spanish-speaking person in the Southwest whose ancestors had come from Mexico (p. 600)

middle passage middle leg of the triangular trade route that brought captured Africans to the Americas to serve as slaves (p. 48)

migrate to move from one region to another (p. 4)

migration movement of people from one country or locality to another (p. 438)

militia a force of armed civilians pledged to defend their community (p. 168)

Minutemen group of armed civilians, trained to be ready to fight "at a minute's warning" (p. 168)

mission settlement created by the Spanish church in order to convert Native Americans to Christianity (p. 40)

missionary person sent by the Church to convert Native Americans to Christianity (p. 26)

Missouri Compromise laws enacted in 1820 to maintain balance of power between slave and free states (p. 378)

Monitor Union ironclad ship (p. 516)

monopoly business that gains control of an industry by eliminating other competitors (p. 630)

Monroe Doctrine U.S. policy opposing European interference in the Western Hemisphere (p. 378)

Mormon member of a church founded by Joseph Smith in 1830 (p. 418)

mountain men trappers and explorers who opened up the western pioneer trails (p. 418)

muckraker (MUHK•RAYK•er) writer who exposed corruption in American society (p. 672)

Muslim follower of the religion of Islam (p. 10)

NAACP National Association for the Advancement of Colored People (p. 650)

nationalism a feeling of pride, loyalty, and protectiveness towards one's country (p. 378)

nativist native-born American who wanted to eliminate foreign influence (p. 450)

Navigation Acts laws passed by the English government to ensure that England made money from its colonies' trade (p. 94)

Ndongo Central African kingdom that ruled during the 1400s (p. 10)

neutral (NEW•truhl) not favoring any one side (p. 194)

New France first permanent French settlement in North America (p. 34)

New Jersey Plan proposal for a legislature in which each state would have one vote (p. 242)

New Netherland first permanent Dutch colony in North America (pp. 34, 82)

Nineteenth Amendment constitutional amendment that gave women the vote (p. 682)

nomadic characterized by moving from place to place (p. 608)

nondenominational not favoring any particular religion (p. 222)

nonsedentary societies people who move continually in search of food (p. 4)

North Atlantic current clockwise ocean current that flows between Northern Europe and the Caribbean Sea (p. 16)

Northwest Ordinance law that described how the Northwest Territory was to be governed (p. 234)

Northwest Territory lands northwest of the Appalachians, covered by the Land Ordinance of 1785 (p. 234)

nullification idea that a state could cancel a federal law within the state (p. 326)

Open Door Policy U.S. policy proposed in 1899 which stated no single country should have a monopoly on trade with China (p. 706)

Oregon Trail trail that ran westward from Independence, Missouri, to the Oregon Territory (p. 418)

outposts (OWT•posts) military bases, usually located on the frontier (p. 222)

overseers people who watch over and direct the work of slaves (p. 102)

pacifist (PAS•uh•fist) someone who is opposed to all war (p. 194)

pact formal agreement; a bargain (p. 142)

Panama Canal canal through the Isthmus of Panama that connects the Atlantic and Pacific (p. 706)

Panic of 1837 widespread fear about the state of the economy that spread after Van Buren took office (p. 408)

Panic of 1873 financial panic in which banks closed and the stock market crashed (p. 582)

Paris, Treaty of (1763) treaty that ended the war between France and Britain (p. 142)

Paris, Treaty of (1783) the 1783 treaty that ended the Revolutionary War (p. 222)

Parliament England's chief lawmaking body (p. 136)

patents government documents giving an inventor the exclusive right to make and sell an invention for a specific number of years (p. 630)

Patriots Americans who sided with the rebels (p. 168)

patronage (PA•truh•nihj) exchanging government jobs and contracts for political support (p. 672)

patroon person rewarded with a large land grant for bringing 50 settlers to New Netherland (p. 82)

Pearl Harbor Hawaiian port; granted by 1887 treaty to the United States for use as a refueling station for U.S. ships (p. 694)

persecute (PUR•sih•KYOOT) to mistreat (p. 66)

Philadelphia settlement on the Delaware River that became the fastest growing city in the colonies (p. 110)

Pickett's Charge failed assault on Union positions on final day of Battle of Gettysburg (p. 548)

Piedmont the broad plateau that lies at the foot of the Blue Ridge Mountains of the Appalachian range (p. 116)

Pilgrims Separatist group that traveled to America to gain religious freedom (p. 66)

Pinckney's (PINK•neez) **Treaty** 1795 treaty with Spain allowing Americans to use the Mississippi River and to store goods in New Orleans (p. 318)

plantation large farm that raises cash crops (p. 40)

platform statement of beliefs (p. 498)

Platt Amendment agreement stating the United States' right to intervene in Cuban affairs (p. 698)

Plessy* v. *Ferguson 1896 Supreme Court case that upheld the legality of segregation (p. 650)

plunder steal from, ransack (p. 522)

political machine organization that controls a local government (p. 640)

political party group of people that tries to promote its ideas and influence government (p. 326)

Pontiac's Rebellion Native American revolt against the British colonies (p. 142)

Populist Party political party formed in 1890s that wanted a policy that would raise crop prices (p. 616)

populous heavily populated (p. 510)

precedent (PRE•seh•dent) an example that becomes standard practice (p. 312)

prejudice (PREHJ•uh•dihs) a negative opinion that is not based on facts (p. 450)

printing press device that mechanically printed pages by pressing inked forms onto paper, invented in about 1455 (p. 16)

privateer (pry•vuh•TEER) a privately owened ship that has been granted permission by a wartime government to attack an enemy's merchant ships (p. 204)

Proclamation of 1763 British declaration that forbade colonists from settling west of the Appalachians (p. 142)

progressivism (pruh•GREHS•ih•VIHZ•uhm) reform movements that sought to raise living standards and correct wrongs in American society (p. 672)

prohibition (PROH•uh•BIHSH•uhn) legal ban on the production, possession, and sale of alcohol (p. 682)

prolong to lengthen (in time) (p. 536)

prominent important and well known (p. 136)

proprietary colony colony governed by a single owner, or proprietor (p. 76)

protective tariff a tax on imported goods that protects a nation's businesses from foreign competition (p. 378)

Protestants Christian group that broke away from the Catholic Church (p. 16)

Pueblo Native Americans who built great mud-brick cities (p. 4)

"pull" factor a reason or force that causes people to choose to move to a new place (p. 450)

Pullman Strike nationwide railway strike that spread throughout the rail industry in 1894 (p. 656)

Puritans English dissenters who wanted to reform the Church of England (p. 66)

"push" factor a reason or force that causes people to leave their native land (p. 450)

Quakers group of Protestant dissenters (p. 66)

Quartering Act act requiring the colonists to quarter, or house, British soldiers and provide them with supplies (p. 156)

Quebec, Battle of battle that led to the British victory in the French and Indian War (p. 142)

racism belief that some people are inferior because of their race (p. 48)

Radical Republican congressman who favored using federal power to rebuild the South and promote African-American rights (p. 570)

radical person who takes extreme political positions (p. 338)

ragtime music that blended African-American songs and European musical forms (p. 662)

ratification act of official confirmation (p. 234)

ratify approve (p. 558)

Reconstruction period from 1865 to 1877, in which the U.S. government attempted to rebuild the Southern society and governments (p. 570)

redoubt (re•DOWT) a small fort (p. 212)

Reformation movement that divided the church between Catholics and Protestants (p. 16)

region distinct area of land (p. 76)

Renaissance a time of increased interest in art and learning in Europe (p. 16)

rendezvous (RAHN•day•voo) a meeting (p. 194)

republic state, country or nation in which people elect representatives to govern (p. 234)

Republican Party political party formed in 1854 by opponents of slavery (p. 490)

reservation land set aside by the U.S. government for Native American tribes (p. 608)

revenue income (p. 678)

robber baron a business leader who became wealthy through dishonest methods (p. 630)

Roosevelt Corollary United States' claim of right to interfere in the affairs of Latin American countries (p. 706)

Rough Riders members of the First U. S. Volunteer Cavalry, organized by Theodore Roosevelt during the Spanish-American War (p. 698)

royal colony colony ruled by the king's appointed officials (p. 60)

S

Sahara a large desert in Northern Africa (p. 10)

Sand Creek Massacre 1864 attack in which as many as 200 Cheyenne were killed by the Colorado militia (p. 608)

Santa Fe Trail trail that began in Missouri and ended in Santa Fe, New Mexico (p. 418)

Saratoga (sair•uh•TOH•guh), **Battles of** a series of conficts in 1777 near Albany, New York (p. 194)

savanna flat grassland with abundant wildlife, thorny bushes and scattered trees (p. 10)

scalawag white Southerner who supported Radical Reconstruction (p. 570)

Scots-Irish the name give to people from the borderlands of Scotland and England and from the region of northern Ireland (p. 116)

secede (sih•SEED) to withdraw (pp. 394, 498)

Second Battle of the Marne battle that was the turning point of the war (p. 734)

Second Continental Congress America's government during the Revolutionary War (p. 176)

Second Great Awakening renewal of religious faith in the 1790s and early 1800s (p. 456)

Second New Deal 1935-1937 extension of Roosevelt's First New Deal (p. 784)

sectionalism loyalty to the interests of one's own region or section of the country (p. 378)

sedentary societies people who settled in permanent villages or towns (p. 4)

sedition stirring up rebellion against a government (p. 326)

segregation (seh•greh•GA•shun) the separation of races (p. 650)

semisedentary societies people who settled in villages or towns but moved every few years in search of food (p. 4)

Seneca Falls Convention a women's rights convention held in Seneca Falls, New York (p. 464)

settlement house community center providing help to immigrants and the poor (p. 682)

Seven Days' Battles Confederate victory during which Lee stopped the Union campaign against Richmond (p. 522)

Seventeenth Amendment amendment that provided for direct election of U.S. senators (p. 678)

Shaker member of a Christian sect that practiced communal living and did not allow marriage and childbearing (p. 456)

sharecropping system under which landowners gave poor farmers seed, tools, and land to cultivate in exchange for part of their harvest (p. 576)

shareholder an investor who buys part of a company through shares of stock (p. 630)

Shays's Rebellion uprising of Massachusetts farmers who wanted debt relief (p. 234)

Sherman Antitrust Act law that made it illegal for corporations to gain control of industries by forming trusts (p. 672)

Sherman's March to the Sea Union General Sherman's destructive march across Georgia (p. 548)

Shiloh, Battle of bloody battle in Tennessee won by Grant (p. 522)

siege when enemy forces surround a town or city in order to force it to surrender (p. 176)

Siege of Vicksburg the surrounding of the city of Vicksburg, Mississippi, by Union forces (p. 548)

Sixteenth Amendment amendment that gave Congress the power to create income taxes (p. 678)

slash-and-burn process of clearing land by cutting down and burning trees (p. 4)

slave codes law passed to regulate the treatment of slaves (p. 48)

slave someone who is captured for use in forced, unpaid labor (p. 10)

slavery practice of one person being owned by another (p. 48)

slum neighborhood with overcrowded and dangerous housing (p. 640)

smallpox highly infectious and often fatal disease (p. 142)

smuggling importing or exporting goods illegally (p. 94)

social gospel movement reforms based on Christian values (p. 640)

socialism system in which the state controls the economy (p. 656)

society group of people with common interests, customs and way of life (p. 4)

sod the top layer of prairie soil that contains thick, tightly tangled grass roots (p. 616)

sodbusters name for pioneer farmers on the Great Plains (p. 616)

solar time time based on the calculations of the sun's passage across the sky (p. 596)

Sons of Liberty secret society formed to opposed British policies (p. 156)

South Atlantic current counter clockwise current that flows between Africa and South America (p. 16)

Spanish Armada large fleet of ships sent to invade England and restore Catholicism (p. 34)

Spanish-American War 1898 war that began when the United States demanded Cuba's independence from Spain (p. 698)

speculate to buy as an investment (p. 156)

sphere of influence areas where foreign nations claimed special rights and economic privileges (p. 706)

spirituals religious folk songs (p. 372)

spoils system the practice of giving government jobs to political backers (p. 394)

Stamp Act law requiring all legal and commercial documents to carry and official stamp showing that a tax had been paid (p. 156)

standard time the time zones devised by railroad companies (p. 596)

states' rights the idea that the states have certain rights that the federal government cannot overrule (p. 326)

steerage the cheapest deck on a ship (p. 450)

stock market place where shares of ownership in companies are bought and sold (p. 582)

Stono Rebellion 1739 slave rebellion in South Carolina (p. 102)

strategy (STRA•tuh•jee) an overall plan of action (p. 194)

strike to stop work to demand better working conditions (p. 456)

subsistence farming producing just enough food for one's needs (p. 94)

suffrage the right to vote (p. 464)

Sugar Act law placing a tax on sugar, molasses, and other products shipped to the colonies (p. 156)

sweatshop place where workers labored long hours under poor conditions for low wages (p. 640)

Tammany Hall New York City political machine (p. 640)

Tariff of Abominations 1828 law that significantly raised tariffs on raw materials and manufactured goods (p. 394)

tariff tax on imported goods (p. 312)

Tejanos (tay•HAH•nohs) people of Mexican heritage who consider Texas their home (p. 426)

Tejas (tay•HAHS) name the Spanish explorers gave present-day Texas (p. 426)

temperance movement campaign to stop the drinking of alcohol (p. 456)

tenements run-down and overcrowded apartment houses (p. 640)

Thirteenth Amendment Constitutional amendment that ended slavery (p. 558)

Three-Fifths Compromise agreement that three-fifths of a state's slave population would be counted for representation and taxation (p. 242)

threshing machine a device that separates kernels of wheat from their husks (p. 364)

Tidewater flat land along the coast (p. 76)

tolerance acceptance of different opinions (p. 66)

Tordesillas (tawr•day•SEEL•yahs), **Treaty of** 1494 treaty in which Spain and Portugal agreed to divide lands of the Western hemisphere between them and move the Line of Demarcation to the west (p. 26)

Townshend Acts acts passed by Parliament in 1767 to tax imports in the colonies (p. 160)

Trail of Tears forced removal of the Cherokee from their homeland to Indian Territory (p. 402)

transcontinental railroad railroad that spanned the U.S. continent (p. 596)

triangular trade complex system of transatlantic exchange of slaves, rum, sugar, and molasses (p. 94)

tribute (TRIHB•yoot) payment in exchange for protection (p. 352)

trust a legal body created to hold stock in many companies, often within an industry (p. 630)

U.S.S. *Maine* a U.S. warship that exploded off of Havana, Cuba, on February 15, 1898 (p. 698)

Uncle Tom's Cabin novel published by Harriet Beecher Stowe in 1852 that showed slavery as brutal and immoral (p. 480)

Underground Railroad a series of escape routes used by slaves escaping the South (p. 464)

uprising rebellion (p. 510)

urbanization growth of cities resulting from industrialization (p. 640)

Valley Forge site in southeast Pennsylvania where Washington and his army camped in the winter of 1777–1778 (p. 204)

vaquero (vah•KAIR•oh) Spanish term for cowhand (p. 600)

vaudeville live entertainment that featured song, dance and comedy (p. 662)

veto (VEE•to) to prevent from becoming law (p. 570)

vigilante (vij•uh•LAN•tee) person who takes the law into his or her own hands (p. 600)

Virginia Plan proposal for a two-house legislature with representation according to each state's population or wealth (p. 242)

Virginia Statute for Religious Freedom statement of religious liberty, written by Thomas Jefferson (p. 222)

war hawk westerner who supported the War of 1812 (p. 352)

Whig Party political party formed by Henry Clay, Daniel Webster, and other Jackson opponents (p. 408)

Whiskey Rebellion a 1794 protest against the government's tax on whiskey by backcountry farmers (p. 318)

Wilderness Road a trail into Kentucky (p. 204)

Wilmot Proviso 1846 proposal that outlawed slavery in any territory gained from the War with Mexico (p. 480)

Wounded Knee Massacre mass killing by U.S. soldiers of as many as 300 unarmed Sioux at Wounded Knee, South Dakota, in 1890 (p. 608)

writ of habeas corpus law that prevents the government from holding citizens without formal charges (p. 542)

writs of assistance search warrants used to enter homes or businesses to search for smuggled goods (p. 160)

XYZ Affair 1797 incident in which French officials demanded a bribe from U.S. diplomats (p. 326)

yellow journalism style of journalism that exaggerates and sensationalizes the news (p. 698)

Yorktown, Battle of final battle of the war, in which French and American forces led by George Washington defeated British General Cornwallis (p. 212)

Spanish Glossary

54th Massachussets Volunteers [voluntarios del regimiento 54° de Massachussets] *s.* regimiento de soldados afro-americanos que se hicieron famosos por su coraje en el asalto a Fort Wagner, Carolina del Sur (pág. 536)

A

abolition [abolición] *s.* movimiento para acabar con la esclavitud (pág. 464)

Act of Toleration [Acta de Tolerancia] *s.* ley de Maryland que prohibía la persecución religiosa (pág. 76)

Alamo, Battle of the [batalla de El Álamo] *s.* batalla entre Texas y México, 1836 (pág. 426)

Albany Plan of Union [Plan de Unión de Albano] *s.* primera propuesta formal para unir las colonias (pág. 142)

Alien and Sedition Acts [Actas de Extranjeros y de Sedición] *s.* serie de cuatro leyes promulgadas en 1798 para reducir el poder político de los inmigrantes recién llegados (pág. 326)

aliens [extranjeros] *s.* inmigrantes que no son aún ciudadanos (pág. 326)

alliance [alianza] *s.* pacto o tratado en el que hay pueblos o naciones involucradas (pág. 26)

ally [aliado] *s.* un país que accede a ayudar a otro país para lograr un objetivo común (pág. 204)

amendment [enmienda] *s.* adjunto hecho a un documento (pág. 248)

American System [Sistema Americano] *s.* plan introducido en 1815 para convertir a EE.UU. en un país económicamente autosuficiente (pág. 378)

amnesty [amnistía] *s.* perdón oficial (pág. 570)

Anaconda Plan [Plan Anaconda] *s.* estrategia de la Unión para derrotar a la Confederación (pág. 510)

anarchist [anarquista] *s.* persona que cree en una sociedad que no tiene ningún gobierno (pág. 656)

Angel Island [*Angel Island*] *s.* estación de inmigración en la Bahía de San Francisco para los inmigrantes asiáticos (pág. 640)

Anglo [anglo] *s.* colono de habla inglesa asentado en el Suroeste (pág. 600)

annex [anexar] *v.* unir o agregar territorio a una unidad política ya existente, tal como un país o un estado (pág. 426)

Antietam, Battle of [batalla de Antietam] *s.* batalla en Maryland que terminó con la primera invasión de Lee en el Norte (pág. 522)

Antifederalists [antifederalistas] *s.* personas que se oponían a la ratificación de la Constitución (pág. 248)

Anti-Imperialist League [Liga Anti-imperialista] *s.* grupo de estadounidenses influyentes que opinaban que Estados Unidos no debían negar a otros pueblos el derecho a autogobernarse (pág. 698)

Appalachian Mountains [Montes Apalaches] *s.* cadena montañosa que se extiende desde el este de Canadá hasta Alabama (pág. 116)

Appomattox Court House [Appomattox Court House] *s.* ciudad de Virginia donde Lee se rindió a Grant (pág. 548)

apprentice [aprendiz] *s.* alguien que está aprendiendo un oficio con un artesano con experiencia (pág. 126)

arsenal [arsenal] *s.* donde se guardan armas (pág. 234)

Articles of Confederation [Artículos de la Confederación] *s.* plan para el gobierno nacional ratificado en 1781 (pág. 234)

artillery [artillería] *s.* cañones y armas grandes (pág. 176)

artisans [artesanos] *s.* personas especializadas en algún oficio (pág. 110)

assimilate [asimilar] *v.* absorber una cultura (pág. 402)

assimilation [asimilación] *s.* el proceso de integrarse en una sociedad (pág. 640)

attorney general [fiscal general] *s.* el máximo funcionario legal de la nación; hoy en día también el jefe del Departamento de Justicia (pág. 312)

Aztec [azteca] *s.* civilización de indígenas americanos que se propagó en lo que hoy es México (pág. 4)

B

backcountry [*backcountry*] *s.* las partes más lejanas hacia el Oeste de las colonias (pág. 94)

Bacon's Rebellion [Rebelión de Bacon] *s.* rebelión que tuvo lugar en Virginia en 1676 (pág. 102)

banish [desterrar] *v.* obligar a alguien a abandonar un lugar (pág. 66)

Bear Flag Revolt [Revuelta de la Bandera del Oso] *s.* rebelión estadounidense contra el gobierno mexicano de California en 1846 (pág. 432)

bickering [riña] *s.* pelea de poca importancia (pág. 480)

Bill of Rights [Declaración de Derechos] *s.* las primeras diez enmiendas a la Constitución de EE.UU. (pág. 248)

black codes [*black codes*] *s.* leyes aprobadas por los estados del Sur que limitaban la libertad de los antiguos esclavos (pág. 570)

Black Death [muerte negra] *s.* enfermedad mortal que se extendió por Europa en el siglo XIV (pág. 16)

boomtown [ciudad de crecimiento rápido] *s.* pueblo que tiene una explosión repentina de población o de actividad económica (pág. 600)

border state [estados de la frontera] *s.* estados esclavistas que tenían frontera con otros estados en los que la esclavitud era ilegal (pág. 510)

Boston Massacre [masacre de Boston] *s.* incidente en el que las tropas británicas abrieron fuego y mataron a colonos norteamericanos en 1770 (pág. 160)

Boston Tea Party [Motín del té en Boston] *s.* incidente que tuvo lugar en 1773 cuando los colonos protestaron contra la política británica abordando barcos británicos y arrojando sus cargas de té por la borda (pág. 160)

Boxer Rebellion [Rebelión Bóxer] *s.* levantamiento nacionalista en China en 1900 (pág. 706)

boycott [boicot] *v.* negarse a comprar (pág. 156)

buffalo soldier [soldado búfalo] *s.* nombre que los indígenas norteamericanos dieron a los soldados afro-americanos en el Oeste (pág. 600)

Bull Moose Party [Partido del Alce] *s.* partido político progresista de las elecciones presidenciales de 1912 (pág. 678)

Bull Run, First Battle of [primera batalla de Bull Run] *s.* primera gran batalla de la Guerra Civil (pág. 510)

business cycle [ciclo económico] *s.* patrón de buenos y malos tiempos para la economía (pág. 630)

cabinet [gabinete] *s.* grupo de miembros del Ejecutivo que sirven como principales asesores al Presidente (pág. 312)

California Gold Rush [fiebre del oro californiana] *s.* emigración de miles de colonos a California en busca de oro (pág. 438)

Californios *s.* colonos de ascendencia española o mexicana que poblaron California (pág. 438)

carpetbagger [*carpetbagger*] *s.* residentes en el Norte que fueron al Sur después de la Guerra Civil para ayudar con la Reconstrucción (pág. 570)

cash crops [cultivo comercial] *s.* cultivo destinado a ser vendido a cambio de dinero (pág. 102)

Catholics [católicos] *s.* cristianos seguidores de la Iglesia Católica Romana (pág. 16)

cede [ceder] *v.* rendirse o capitular (pág. 318)

Charles Town, Battle of [batalla de Charles Town] *s.* asedio británico a Charles Town (Charleston), Carolina del Sur, en mayo de 1780, en el que los norteamericanos sufrieron su peor derrota en la guerra (pág. 212)

charter [carta] *s.* contrato por escrito que otorga el derecho a establecer una colonia (pág. 60)

checks and balances [sistema de equilibrio de poderes] *s.* capacidad de cada rama del gobierno para ejercer control sobre las otras (pág. 242)

Chinese Exclusion Act [Acta de Exclusión de Chinos] *s.* ley de 1882 que prohibía la inmigración china (pág. 640)

citizen [ciudadano] *s.* persona que debe lealtad a un estado o nación y que tiene derecho a su protección (pág. 234)

civil rights [derechos civiles] *s.* derechos otorgados a todos los ciudadanos (pág. 570)

civilization [civilización] *s.* sociedad compleja en la que el pueblo comparte rasgos clave como el lenguaje y la religión (pág. 4)

clans [clanes] *s.* grupos grandes de familias que dicen tener un ancestro común (pág. 116)

Clayton Antitrust Act [Acta Antitrust Clayton] *s.* ley que reforzó la efectividad del Acta Antitrust de Sherman (pág. 678)

coercion [coerción] *s.* obligar a alguien a actuar de cierta manera mediante el uso de presión o amenazas (pág. 352)

Columbian Exchange [intercambio colombino] *s.* traslado de animales, plantas y enfermedades entre los hemisferios oriental y occidental (pág. 40)

Commander-In-Chief [comandante en jefe] *s.* rol que ejerce el Presidente como comandante de todas las fuerzas armadas (pág. 536)

committee of correspondence [comité de correspondencia] *s.* organización formada para intercambiar información sobre la política británica y la resistencia norteamericana (pág. 160)

common [campo comunal] *s.* tierra compartida donde tenían lugar las actividades públicas (pág. 94)

communism [comunismo] *s.* sistema político en el que el gobierno controla la economía para llevar a cabo la posesión común de toda propiedad (pág. 672)

compromise [concesión] *s.* acuerdo por el que cada lado cede algo de lo que reclama (pág. 582)

Compromise of 1850 [Concesión de 1850] *s.* serie de leyes cuyo objetivo era poner fin a los desacuerdos más graves entre los estados libres y los estados esclavistas (pág. 480)

Compromise of 1877 [Concesión de 1877] *s.* acuerdo por el que se decidieron las elecciones presidenciales de 1876 (pág. 582)

Conestoga wagons [carromatos conestoga] *s.* carromatos cubiertos introducidos por los inmigrantes alemanes (pág. 110)

Confederate States of America [Estados Confederados de América] *s.* confederación formada por los estados del Sur en 1861 después de abandonar la Unión (pág. 498)

Confederation Congress [Congreso de la Confederación] *s.* cuerpo nacional legislativo formado por Artículos de la Confederación (pág. 234)

congregation [congregación] *s.* grupo de personas que pertenecen a la misma iglesia (pág. 66)

Congress of Racial Equality, CORE [Congreso para la Igualdad Racial] *s.* organización que planificaba los *Freedom Rides* (viajes por la libertad) (pág. 884)

conquistador [conquistador] *s.* soldado español que exploró las Américas reclamando tierra para España (pág. 26)

conscription [conscripción] *s.* reclutamiento militar (pág. 542)

conservation [conservación] *s.* control del uso de los recursos (pág. 672)

Constitutional Convention [Convención Constitucional] *s.* reunión de 1787 en la que se creó la Constitución de Estados Unidos (pág. 242)

consumer [consumidor] *s.* persona que compra algo (pág. 662)

Continental Army [Ejército Continental] *s.* ejército patriota norteamericano durante la Guerra de Independencia (pág. 176)

contractor [contratista] *s.* suministrador privado (pág. 516)

converts [conversos] *s.* personas que adoptan una nueva creencia religiosa (pág. 418)

Copperheads [*copperheads*] *s.* demócratas del Norte que estaban a favor de la paz con el Sur (pág. 542)

corporation [corporación] *s.* negocio que es propiedad de inversores que compran su parte en acciones de bolsa (pág. 630)

corps [cuerpo] *s.* un grupo de personas que actúan juntas por una meta común (pág. 344)

cotton gin [despepitadora de algodón] *s.* máquina que limpiaba las semillas de algodón más rápido (pág. 372)

Crittenden Compromise [Concesión de Crittenden] *s.* concesión introducida en 1861 que podría haber evitado la secesión (pág. 498)

Daughters of Liberty** [Hijas de la Libertad] *s.* organización que formaron las mujeres de las colonias para protestar contra la política británica (pág. 160)

Dawes Act [Acta de Dawes] *s.* ley de 1887 que distribuyó las tierras de las reservas entre propietarios indígenas (pág. 608)

Declaration of Independence [Declaración de Independencia] *s.* documento que declaró la independencia estadounidense de Gran Bretaña (pág. 176)

deficit spending [gasto deficitario] *s.* usar dinero prestado para invertir en programas del gobierno (pág. 784)

denomination [denominación] *s.* determinado grupo religioso (pág. 110)

depression [depresión] *s.* un declive económico severo (pág. 408, 582)

desert [desertar] *v.* abandonar el ejército sin permiso (pág. 204)

direct primary [primarias directas] *s.* primarias en las que los votantes, no las convenciones de los partidos, eligen a los candidatos que compiten por puestos públicos (pág. 672)

dislodge [sacar] *v.* quitar (pág. 548)

disputes [disputa] *s.* desacuerdos (pág. 222)

dissenter [disidente] *s.* persona en desacuerdo con una iglesia oficial (pág. 66)

diversity [diversidad] *s.* variedad (pág. 76)

doctrine of nullification [doctrina de la anulación] *s.* idea de que un estado tiene el derecho a anular, o rechazar, una ley federal que considera inconstitucional (pág. 394)

Dred Scott vs. Sandford [Dred Scott contra Sandford] *s.* caso de 1856 en la Corte Suprema en que un esclavo, Dred Scott, fue a juicio para pedir su libertad; la corte falló contra Scott (pág. 490)

duties [impuestos] *s.* arancel que se pone a los productos de importación (pág. 160)

Eighteenth Amendment** [Enmienda Decimoctava] *s.* enmienda constitucional que puso en práctica la Prohibición (pág. 682)

electoral votes [votos electorales] *s.* votos hechos por el Colegio Electoral, quien elige al presidente y vicepresidente (pág. 582)

elite [élite] *s.* grupo social de más alto rango (pág. 76)

Ellis Island [Ellis Island] *s.* estación de inmigración en la Bahía de Nueva York para emigrantes europeos (pág. 640)

emancipate [emancipar] *v.* liberar (pág. 536)

Emancipation Proclamation [Proclama de Emancipación] *s.* documento promulgado por Lincoln en el que declaraba la libertad de todos los esclavos en territorio Confederado (pág. 536)

Embargo Act of 1807 [Acta de Embargo de 1807] *s.* ley que prohibía a los barcos estadounidenses navegar a puertos extranjeros y cerraba los puertos estadounidenses a los barcos británicos (pág. 352)

emigrant [emigrante] *s.* persona que deja un país (pág. 450)

encomienda [encomienda] *s.* concesión del trabajo de los indígenas norteamericanos esclavizados (pág. 40)

English Bill of Rights [Declaración Inglesa de Derechos] *s.* leyes de 1689 que protegían los derechos de los súbditos ingleses y de su Parlamento (pág. 136)

Enlightenment [Ilustración] *s.* movimiento filosófico que subrayaba la razón humana (pág. 126)

enlist [alistarse] *v.* unirse a las fuerzas armadas (pág. 516)

Erie Canal [Canal de Erie] *s.* vía de agua que conectaba la Ciudad de Nueva York con Buffalo (pág. 378)

executive branch [poder ejecutivo] *s.* departamento del gobierno que hace cumplir las leyes (pág. 242)

Exodusters [*Exodusters*] *s.* nombre que se le daba a los afro-americanos que se asentaban en las Grandes Llanuras (pág. 616)

export [exportar] *v.* enviar al extranjero para el comercio o la venta (pág. 40)

Factory system** [*factory system*] *s.* método de producción que utilizaba a trabajadores y máquinas en un mismo edificio (pág. 364)

fall line [línea de descanso] *s.* punto en el que las cataratas impiden a los barcos grandes seguir navegando río arriba (pág. 116)

Fallen Timbers, Battle of [batalla de Fallen Timbers] *s.* lucha entre los indígenas norteamericanos y las fuerzas estadounidenses (pág. 318)

famine [hambruna] *s.* escasez grave de alimentos que resulta en el hambre (pág. 450)

Federal Judiciary Act of 1789 [Acta de la Judicatura Federal] *s.* ley de 1789 aprobada por el primer Congreso que estableció las cortes federales menores (pág. 312)

Federal Reserve Act [Acta de la Reserva Federal] *s.* ley que creaba el sistema bancario moderno (pág. 678)

federalism [federalismo] *s.* sistema de gobierno en el cual el poder es compartido entre el gobierno nacional (o federal) y los estados (pág. 248)

The Federalist **papers** [The Federalist *papers*] *s.* ensayos de ratificación publicados en los periódicos de Nueva York (pág. 248)

Federalists [federalistas] *s.* personas que apoyaban la ratificación de la Constitución (pág. 248)

Fifteenth Amendment [Enmienda Decimoquinta] *s.* enmienda constitucional que establecía que no se podía impedir de votar a los ciudadanos "por motivos de raza, color, o haber sido esclavos" (pág. 582)

First Continental Congress [Primer Congreso Continental] *s.* reunión de delegados de casi todas las colonias convocada como reacción a las Actas Intolerables (pág. 168)

Ford's Theatre [Teatro Ford] *s.* teatro en Washington, D.C., donde Lincoln fue asesinado (pág. 558)

foreign policy [política exterior] *s.* relaciones con los gobiernos de otras naciones (pág. 326)

Fort Sumter [*Fort Sumter*] *s.* fuerte de la Unión en el puerto de Charleston, Carolina del Sur (pág. 510)

forty-niner [minero del 49] *s.* persona que fue a California buscando oro en 1849 (pág. 438)

Founders [padres fundadores] *s.* personas que ayudaron a redactar la Constitución de EE.UU. (pág. 242)

Fourteenth Amendment [Enmienda Decimocuarta] *s.* enmienda constitucional que convirtió en ciudadanos a todas las personas nacidas en EE.UU. (incluidos los antiguos esclavos) (pág. 570)

Freedmen's Bureau [Agencia Federal de Libertos] *s.* agencia federal establecida para ayudar a los antiguos esclavos (pág. 570)

freedmen's school [escuelas para libertos] *s.* escuelas creadas para educar a los afro-americanos recién liberados (pág. 576)

Free-Soil Party [Partido del Suelo Libre] *s.* partido político dedicado a frenar la expansión de la esclavitud (pág. 480)

French and Indian War [Guerra franco-indígena] *s.* guerra entre Bretaña, Francia, y sus aliados de 1754 a 1763 por el control de Norteamérica (pág. 142)

French Revolution [Revolución Francesa] *s.* revolución derrocando el gobierno de Francia que comenzó en 1787 y terminó en violencia y ejecuciones (pág. 318)

frontier [frontera] *s.* partes del Oeste que fueron ocupadas principalmente por indígenas norteamericanos, en vez de colonos (pág. 596)

Fugitive Slave Act [Acta del Esclavo Fugitivo] *s.* ley de 1850 que permitía a los propietarios de esclavos capturar a los esclavos huidos (pág. 480)

Fundamental Orders of Connecticut [Órdenes Fundamentales de Connecticut] *s.* documento que ha sido considerado la primera constitución escrita en Norteamérica (pág. 66)

galleon [galeón] *s.* barco para la navegación (pág. 34)

Gettysburg, Battle of [batalla de Gettysburg] *s.* batalla de 1863 en Pennsylvania donde las fuerzas de la Unión evitaron una invasión Confederada del Norte (pág. 548)

Ghana [Ghana] *s.* reino de África Occidental que prosperó entre 700 y 1000 d. C. (pág. 10)

Gilded Age [Edad Dorada] *s.* época de fabulosa riqueza a finales del siglo XIX (pág. 630)

Glorious Revolution [Revolución Gloriosa] *s.* eventos sucedidos entre 1688 y 1689, por los cuales el Parlamento inglés invitó a William y Mary a reemplazar a James II como monarca (pág. 136)

gold standard [patrón oro] *s.* política bajo la cual el gobierno respalda cada dólar con una cierta cantidad de oro (pág. 616)

Grange [*Grange*] *s.* organización formada en 1867 para satisfacer las necesidades de las familias de agricultores (pág. 616)

Great Awakening [Gran Despertar] *s.* movimiento religioso cristiano (pág. 126)

Great Compromise [Gran Concesión] *s.* acuerdo para establecer una legislatura nacional con dos cámara en la que todos los estados tienen la misma representación en una cámara y en la otra su representación se basa en la población (pág. 242)

great famine [gran hambruna] *s.* generalizada escasez de alimentos que mató a miles de europeos (pág. 16)

Great Migration, 17th Century [Gran Migración, siglo XVII] *s.* movimiento de miles de colonos ingleses a Nueva Inglaterra durante la década de 1630 (pág. 66)

Great Plains [Grandes Llanuras] *s.* área situada entre el río Missouri y las Montañas Rocosas (pág. 596)

greenback [*greenback*] *s.* papel moneda introducido durante la Guerra Civil (pág. 542)

Greenville, Treaty of [Tratado de Greenville] *s.* tratado firmado en 1795 por el que 12 tribus indígenas norteamericanas cedían el control de la mayor parte de Ohio e Indiana al gobierno de EE.UU. (pág. 318)

Guadalupe Hidalgo, Treaty of [Tratado de Guadalupe Hidalgo] *s.* tratado de 1848 que puso fin a la Guerra con México (pág. 432)

guerrillas [guerillas] *s.* pequeñas bandas de combatientes que debilitan al enemigo con rebatos y de golpe y fuga (pág. 194)

hacienda [hacienda] *s.* granja o propiedad grande (pág. 40)

Harpers Ferry [Harpers Ferry] *s.* arsenal federal en Virginia, capturado en 1859 durante una revuelta antiesclavista (pág. 490)

Haymarket Affair [asunto Haymarket] *s.* protesta sindical en 1886 (pág. 656)

headright [*headright*] *s.* tierra entregada a las personas que podían pagar, por sus propios medios, su viaje hacia las colonias (pág. 60)

heritage [herencia] *s.* tradición (pág. 136)

Homestead Act [Acta de Heredades] *s.* ley de 1862 por la que se ofrecían 160 acres de terreno gratis a quien quisiera vivir en él y mejorarlo durante cinco años (pág. 616)

Homestead Strike [huelga de haciendas] *s.* huelga violenta en la hacienda de Andrew Carnegie, en los molinos de acero de Pensilvania, en 1892 (pág. 656)

House of Burgesses [Cámara de los Burgueses] *s.* asamblea de Virginia; la primera asamblea representativa en las colonias norteamericanas (pág. 60)

Huguenots [hugonotes] *s.* protestantes franceses (pág. 76)

Hull House [Casa Hull] *s.* centro comunitario fundado por Jane Addams en Chicago (pág. 640)

hygiene [higiene] *s.* condiciones y prácticas que favorecen la salud (pág. 516)

immigrant [inmigrante] *s.* persona que se asienta en un país nuevo (pág. 450)

impeach [encausar] *v.* acusar formalmente al presidente de mala conducta durante su mandato (pág. 570)

imperialism [imperialismo] *s.* política por la cual naciones más fuertes extienden su control económico, político y militar sobre naciones más débiles (pág. 694)

impressment [leva] *s.* acto de tomar por la fuerza; entre 1803 y 1812, los británicos aprisionaron, o secuestraron, a 6.000 marineros norteamericanos para que sirvieran en la marina británica (pág. 352)

inaugurate [investir] *v.* jurar un cargo formalmente o hacerlo jurar (pág. 312)

Inca [inca] *s.* civilización indígena americana que se desarrolló en lo que hoy en día es Perú (pág. 4)

income tax [impuesto sobre la renta] *s.* impuesto sobre las ganancias (pág. 542)

indentured servant [sirviente por contrato] *s.* persona que trabajaba por un plazo fijado sin cobrar a cambio de un pasaje gratis a América (pág. 60)

Indian Removal Act [Acta de Traslado de Indios] *s.* ley de 1830 que obligaba al gobierno a negociar tratados para forzar a los indígenas norteamericanos a trasladarse al oeste (pág. 402)

Indian Territory [Territorio Indio] *s.* área a la que fueron trasladados los indígenas norteamericanos, que cubría lo que en la actualidad es Oklahoma y partes de Kansas y Nebraska (pág. 402)

indigo [índigo] *s.* planta que produce un tinte azul oscuro (pág. 102)

Industrial Revolution [Revolución Industrial] *s.* cambios económicos a finales del siglo XVIII por los que la fabricación a gran escala reemplazó a la agricultura como forma principal de empleo (pág. 364)

infamy [mala reputación] *s.* mala fama (pág. 806)

inflation [inflación] *s.* aumento de los precios y disminución del valor del dinero (pág. 408)

Intolerable Acts [Actas Intolerables] *s.* serie de leyes, conocidas en Gran Bretaña como Actas Coercitivas, dirigidas a castigar a Massachussets y a contener la resistencia de las otras colonias (pág. 168)

investor [inversor] *s.* persona que pone dinero en un proyecto para obtener beneficios (pág. 60)

Islam [Islam] *s.* religión que enseña que hay un solo Dios, llamado Alá, y Mahoma es su profeta (pág. 10)

Jacksonian democracy [democracia Jacksoniana] *s.* idea de ampliar el poder político a una parte mayor del pueblo (pág. 394)

Jamestown [Jamestown] *s.* primer asentamiento inglés permanente en Norteamérica (pág. 60)

Jay's Treaty [Tratado de Jay] *s.* acuerdo que puso fin a la disputa con Gran Bretaña sobre la navegación de barcos norteamericanos durante la Revolución Francesa (pág. 318)

Jim Crow [*Jim Crow*] *s.* leyes promulgadas en los estados del Sur con el propósito de separar a blancos y negros (pág. 650)

joint-stock company [compañía de acciones compartidas] *s.* compañía fundada por un grupo de inversores (pág. 60)

judicial branch [poder judicial] *s.* departamento del gobierno que interpreta las leyes (pág. 242)

judicial review [control judicial] *s.* principio que afirma que la Corte Suprema tiene la última palabra en la interpretación de la Constitución (pág. 338)

Judiciary Act of 1801 [Acta de la Judicatura de 1801] *s.* ley que permitió al presidente John Adams elegir a los nuevos jueces entre los Federalistas (pág. 338)

Kansas-Nebraska Act [Acta de Kansas-Nebraska] *s.* ley de 1854 que estableció los territorios de Kansas y Nebraska y otorgó a sus residentes el derecho a permitir o no la esclavitud (pág. 480)

Kentucky and Virginia Resolutions [Resoluciones de Kentucky y Virginia] *s.* resoluciones aprobabas por Kentucky y Virginia en 1798 que daban a los estados el derecho a anular actas del Congreso (pág. 326)

King Philip's War [Guerra de rey Philip] *s.* levantamiento indígena norteamericano (1675-1676) contra las colonias Puritanas (pág. 94)

Knights of Labor [Caballeros del Trabajo] *s.* organización de trabajadores de todos los oficios formada tras la Guerra Civil (pág. 656)

Know-Nothing Party [Partido No-Sé-Nada] *s.* partido político formado en Estados Unidos durante la década de 1850 en contra de los nuevos inmigrantes y los católicos romanos (pág. 450)

Kongo [Congo] *s.* reino de África Central que gobernó en el siglo XV (pág. 10)

Ku Klux Klan [Ku Klux Klan] *s.* grupo secreto que utilizaba la violencia para intentar devolver el control a los Demócratas en el Sur y mantener sin poder a los afro-americanos (pág. 576)

labor union [organización sindical] *s.* grupos de trabajadores que se asocian para buscar condiciones mejores de trabajo (pág. 456)

Land Ordinance of 1785 [Ordenanza de la Tierra de 1785] *s.* ley que establecía un plan para dividir los territorios que poseía el gobierno federal al oeste de los Montes Apalaches (pág. 234)

land speculators [especuladores urbanísticos] *s.* personas que compran tierra esperando que aumente de valor (pág. 418)

legislative branch [poder legislativo] *s.* departamento del gobierno que elabora las leyes (pág. 242)

leisure [ocio] *s.* libertad de obligaciones exigentes (pág. 662)

levy [gravar] *v.* imponer o recaudar un impuesto (pág. 234)

Lewis and Clark expedition [expedición de Lewis y Clark] *s.* grupo que exploró el Territorio de Luisiana y las tierras al oeste; también conocido como Cuerpo de Descubrimiento (pág. 344)

Lexington and Concord [Lexington y Concord] *s.* primeras batallas de la Guerra de Independencia (pág. 168)

liberation [liberación] *s.* acto de dar la libertad (pág. 536)

literacy [alfabetización] *s.* saber leer y escribir (pág. 126)

Little Bighorn, Battle of the [batalla de Little Bighorn] *s.* batalla de 1876 en la que los sioux y los cheyenne mataron a una tropa de EE.UU. (pág. 608)

lode [filón] *s.* depósito mineral enterrado en la roca (pág. 600)

Lone Star Republic [República de la Estrella Solitaria] *s.* apodo de Texas tras separarse de México (pág. 426)

long drive [*long drive*] *s.* viaje que lleva al ganado a pie hasta el ferrocarril (pág. 600)

Louisiana Purchase [Compra de Luisiana] *s.* compra estadounidense del Territorio francés de Luisiana en 1803 (pág. 344)

Lowell mills [hilanderías de Lowell] *s.* fábricas de tejidos en la ciudad industrial de Lowell, Massachusetts (pág. 364)

Loyalists [leales] *s.* norteamericanos que apoyaban a los británicos (pág. 168)

lynch [linchar] *v.* condenar a una persona a la horca sin seguir ningún proceso legal (pág. 576)

Magna Carta [Carta Magna] *s.* carta de libertades civiles y políticas de Inglaterra (pág. 136)

majority rule [gobierno de la mayoría] *s.* sistema en el que más de la mitad de un grupo tiene poder para tomar decisiones por todo el grupo (pág. 248)

malaria [malaria] *s.* enfermedad contagiosa que propagan los mosquitos (pág. 706)

Mali [Malí] *s.* reino de África Occidental que predominó entre 1200 y 1400 (pág. 10)

manifest destiny [destino manifiesto] *s.* creencia de que EE.UU. estaban destinados a expandirse de costa a costa (pág. 432, 706)

maroon [cimarrón] *s.* esclavo huido o fugitivo (pág. 48)

mass culture [cultura de masas] *s.* cultura común que comparte un grupo grande de personas (pág. 662)

Maya [maya] *s.* antigua civilización indígena de Mesoamérica (pág. 4)

Mayflower Compact [Convenio del Mayflower] *s.* documento que ayudó a establecer el gobierno autónomo (pág. 66)

mechanical reaper [cosechadora mecánica] *s.* máquina que corta el grano (pág. 364)

melting pot [crisol de culturas] *s.* lugar donde se mezclan las culturas (pág. 640)

mercantilism [mercantilismo] *s.* sistema económico que aumenta las divisas del tesoro de un país al crear una balanza comercial favorable (pág. 26, 60)

mercenary [mercenario] *s.* soldado profesional contratado para servir a un país extranjero (pág. 194)

Merrimack [Merrimack] *s.* acorazado Confederado, rebautizado después como *Virginia* (pág. 516)

Mesoamerica [Mesoamérica] *s.* región que se extiende desde lo que hoy es México hasta Nicaragua (pág. 4)

Mexican cession [cesión mexicana] *s.* territorio mexicano que se entregó a Estados Unidos al final de la guerra con México (pág. 432)

Mexicano [mexicano] *s.* persona de herencia mexicana (pág. 600)

middle passage [paso central] *s.* parte media de la ruta del comercio triangular que llevaba africanos capturados a las Américas para servir (pág. 48)

migrate [migrar] *v.* trasladarse de una región a otra (pág. 4)

migration [migración] *s.* movimiento de personas desde una localidad a otra (pág. 438)

militia [milicia] *s.* fuerza de civiles armados que juran defender su comunidad (pág. 168)

Minutemen [soldados al minuto] *s.* grupo de civiles armados, preparados para luchar un minuto después de ser avisados (pág. 168)

mission [misión] *s.* asentamiento creado por la iglesia española para convertir a los indígenas al cristianismo (pág. 40)

missionary [misionero] *s.* persona enviada por la Iglesia para a los indígenas convertir al cristianismo (pág. 26)

Missouri Compromise [Compromiso de Missouri] *s.* leyes promulgadas en 1820 para mantener el equilibrio de poderes entre los estados esclavistas y los libres (pág. 378)

Monitor [Monitor] *s.* acorazado de la Unión (pág. 516)

monopoly [monopolio] *s.* negocio que toma el control de una industria eliminando a sus competidores (pág. 630)

Monroe Doctrine [doctrina Monroe] *s.* política de EE.UU de oponerse a la injerencia europea en el hemisferio occidental (pág. 378)

Mormon [mormón] *s.* miembro de una iglesia fundada por Joseph Smith en 1830 (pág. 418)

mountain men [hombres de la montaña] *s.* tramperos y exploradores que abrieron senderos de pioneros en el Oeste (pág. 418)

muckracker [escarbador] *s.* escritor que destapaba la corrupción de la sociedad estadounidense (pág. 672)

Muslim [musulmán] *s.* seguidor del Islam (pág. 10)

NAACP [ANPPC] *s.* Asociación Nacional para el Progreso de las Personas de Color (pág. 650)

nationalism [nacionalismo] *s.* sentimiento de orgullo, lealtad y protección hacia el país propio (pág. 672)

nativist [nativista] *s.* persona nacida en EE.UU. que quería eliminar la influencia extranjera (pág. 450)

Navigation Acts [Actas de Navegación] *s.* leyes aprobadas por el gobierno inglés para asegurarse de que Inglaterra obtenía dinero del comercio de sus colonias (pág. 94)

Ndongo [Ndongo] *s.* reino de África Central que predominó en el siglo XVI (pág. 10)

neutral [neutral] *adj.* que no está a favor de ningún bando (pág. 194)

New France [Nueva Francia] *s.* primer asentamiento permanente francés en Norteamérica (pág. 34)

New Jersey Plan [Plan de New Jersey] *s.* propuesta de una legislatura en la que cada estado tendría un voto (pág. 242)

New Netherland [Nueva Holanda] *s.* primera colonia holandesa permanente en Norteamérica (pág. 34, 82)

Nineteenth Amendment [Enmienda Decimonovena] *s.* enmienda constitucional que dio el voto a las mujeres (pág. 682)

nomadic [nómada] *adj.* que se caracteriza por trasladarse de un lugar a otro (pág. 608)

nondenominational [aconfesional] *adj.* que no está a favor de ninguna religión concreta (pág. 222)

nonsedentary societies [sociedades nómadas] *s.* personas que se trasladaban continuamente buscando alimentos (pág. 4)

North Atlantic current [corriente del Atlántico Norte] *s.* corriente oceánico que circula en el sentido de las agujas del reloj entre Europa y el mar Caribe (pág. 16)

Northwest Ordinance [Ordenanza de la Tierra del Noroeste] *s.* ley que describía cómo se gobernaría el Territorio del Noroeste (pág. 234)

Northwest Territory [Territorio del Noroeste] *s.* tierras al noroeste de los Apalaches, cubiertas por la Ordenanza de la Tierra de 1785 (pág. 234)

nullification [anulación] *s.* idea de que un estado puede cancelar una ley federal dentro de ese estado (pág. 326)

Open Door Policy [política de puertas abiertas] *s.* política de EE.UU. propuesta en 1899 por la cual ningún país debería tener el monopolio del comercio con China (pág. 706)

Oregon Trail [Ruta de Oregón] *s.* ruta que iba hacia el oeste desde Independence, Missouri, al Territorio de Oregón (pág. 418)

outposts [puesto fronterizo] *s.* bases militares, situadas generalmente en la frontera (pág. 222)

overseers [capataces] *s.* personas que vigilan y dirigen el trabajo de los esclavos (pág. 102)

pacifist [pacifista] *s.* alguien que se opone a todas las guerras (pág. 194)

pact [pacto] *s.* acuerdo formal; trato (pág. 142)

Panama Canal [Canal de Panamá] *s.* canal que atraviesa el istmo de Panamá y conecta los océanos Atlántico y Pacífico (pág. 706)

Panic of 1837 [pánico de 1837] *s.* temor extendido sobre el estado de la economía tras la toma de posesión de Van Buren (pág. 408)

Panic of 1873 [Pánico de 1873] *s.* pánico financiero que provocó el cierre de los bancos y que la bolsa se desplomara (pág. 582)

Paris, Treaty of, 1763 [Tratado de París, 1763] *s.* tratado que puso fin a la guerra entre Francia e Inglaterra (pág. 142)

Paris, Treaty of, 1783 [Tratado de París, 1783] *s.* tratado que puso fin a la Revolución (pág. 222)

Parliament [Parlamento] *s.* el organismo legislativo más importante de Inglaterra (pág. 136)

patents [patentes] *s.* documentos del gobierno que otorga a un inventor el derecho en exclusiva de fabricar y vender un invento durante un número específico de años (pág. 630)

Patriots [Patriotas] *s.* estadounidenses que se pusieron del lado de los rebeldes (pág. 168)

patronage [patrocinio] *s.* intercambiar puestos en el gobierno y contratos a cambio de apoyo político (pág. 672)

patroon [encomendero holandés] *s.* persona a quien se recompensaba con un gran lote de terreno por llevar 50 colonos a Nueva Amsterdam (pág. 82)

Pearl Harbor *s.* puerto hawaiano; cedido por un tratado en 1887 a Estados Unidos como estación para aprovisionar de combustible sus barcos (pág. 694)

persecute [perseguir] *v.* maltratar (pág. 66)

Philadelphia [Filadelfia] *s.* asentamiento en el río Delaware que se convirtió en la ciudad de mayor crecimiento de las colonias (pág. 110)

Pickett's Charge [carga de Pickett] *s.* asalto fallido a posiciones de la Unión el último día de la batalla de Gettysburg (pág. 548)

Piedmont [Piedmont] *s.* la amplia llanura que queda a los pies de las montañas Blue Ridge en los Apalaches (pág. 116)

Pilgrims [peregrinos] *s.* grupo separatista que viajó a Norteamérica para conseguir libertad religiosa (pág. 66)

Pinckney's Treaty [Tratado de Pinckney] *s.* tratado de 1795 por el que España permitió a los norteamericanos usar el río Mississippi y almacenar mercancías en Nueva Orleáns (pág. 318)

plantation [plantación] *s.* granja de gran tamaño donde hay cultivos comerciales (pág. 40)

platform [plataforma] *s.* declaración de creencias (pág. 498)

Platt Amendment [Enmienda Platt] *s.* acuerdo que afirmaba el derecho de los Estados Unidos de intervenir en los asuntos cubanos (pág. 698)

Plessy* vs. *Ferguson *s.* caso de 1893 en la Corte Suprema que ratificó la legalidad de la segregación (pág. 650)

plunder [saquear] *v.* robar, piratear (pág. 522)

political machine [maquinaria política] *s.* organización que controla un gobierno local (pág. 640)

political party [partido político] *s.* grupo de personas que intentan promover sus ideas e influir en el gobierno (pág. 326)

Pontiac's Rebellion [rebelión de Pontiac] *s.* revuelta indígena norteamericana contra las colonias británicas (pág. 142)

popular sovereignty [soberanía popular] *s.* sistema de gobierno regido por el pueblo (pág. 244)

Populist Party [Partido Populista] *s.* partido político formado en la década de 1890 a favor del aumento del precio en los cultivos (pág. 616)

populous [populoso] *adj.* muy poblado (pág. 510)

precedent [precedente] *s.* ejemplo que se convierte en práctica habitual (pág. 312)

prejudice [prejuicio] *s.* opinión negativa que no se basa en datos (pág. 450)

printing press [imprenta] *s.* máquina que imprimía páginas de forma mecánica y que se inventó alrededor de 1455 (pág. 16)

privateer [corsario] *s.* barco de propiedad privada a cuyo dueño se ha concedido permiso para atacar a barcos mercantes enemigos en tiempo de guerra (pág. 204)

Proclamation of 1763 [Proclamación de 1763] *s.* declaración británica que prohibió a los colonos asentarse al oeste de los Apalaches (pág. 142)

progressivism [progresismo] *s.* movimientos reformistas que buscaban mejorar las condiciones de vida y corregir los males de la sociedad estadounidense (pág. 672)

prohibition [prohibición] *s.* entredicho legal impuesto en la producción, posesión y venta de alcohol (pág. 682)

prolong [prolongar] *v.* alargarse en el tiempo (pág. 536)

prominent [prominente] *adj.* importante y muy conocido (pág. 136)

proprietary colony [colonia propietaria] *s.* colonia gobernada por un solo propietario (pág. 76)

protective tariff [arancel proteccionista] *s.* impuesto sobre productos importados que protege los negocios de una nación frente a la competencia extranjera (pág. 378)

Protestants [protestantes] *s.* grupo cristiano que se separó de la Iglesia Católica (pág. 16)

Pueblo [pueblo] *s.* indígenas norteamericanos que construyeron grandes ciudades de adobe (pág. 4)

"pull" factor [factor de atracción] *s.* razón o fuerza que hace a la gente mudarse a un nuevo lugar (pág. 450)

Pullman Strike [huelga Pullman] *s.* huelga nacional de ferrocarriles que se extendió por la industria del ferrocarril en 1894 (pág. 656)

Puritans [puritanos] *s.* disidentes ingleses que querían reformar la Iglesia de Inglaterra (pág. 66)

"push" factor [factor de repulsión] *s.* razón o fuerza que hace a la gente abandonar su país de origen (pág. 450)

Quakers [cuáqueros] *s.* grupo de disidentes protestantes (pág. 66)

Quartering Act [Acta de Alojamiento] *s.* acta que obligaba a los colonos a alojar a soldados británicos y a proporcionarles suministros (pág. 156)

Quebec, Battle of [batalla de Quebec] *s.* batalla que condujo a la victoria británica en la Guerra Franco-Indígena (pág. 142)

racism [racismo] *s.* creencia de que algunas personas son inferiores debido a su raza (pág. 48)

radical [radical] *s.* persona que toma posiciones políticas extremas (pág. 338)

Radical Republican [republicano radical] *s.* congresista a favor de usar el poder federal para reconstruir el Sur y promover los derechos de los afroamericanos (pág. 570)

ragtime [*ragtime*] *s.* música que mezclaba las canciones afro-americanas y el estilo musical europeo (pág. 662)

ratification [ratificación] *s.* acto de confirmación oficial (pág. 234)

ratify [ratificar] *v.* aprobar (pág. 558)

Reconstruction [Reconstrucción] *s.* período entre 1865 y 1877 en el que el gobierno de EE.UU. intentó reconstruir la sociedad y el gobierno del Sur (pág. 570)

redoubt [reducto] *s.* pequeño fuerte (pág. 212)

Reformation [Reforma] *s.* movimiento que dividió a la iglesia en católicos y protestantes (pág. 16)

region [región] *s.* área de tierra definida (pág. 76)

Renaissance [Renacimiento] *s.* época en la que aumentó el interés por el arte y el conocimiento en Europa (pág. 16)

rendezvous [*rendezvous*] *s.* encuentro (pág. 194)

republic [república] *s.* estado, país o nación en donde la gente elige representantes para el gobierno (pág. 234)

Republican Party [Partido Republicano] *s.* partido político formado en 1854 por opositores a la esclavitud (pág. 490)

reservation [reservación] s. tierra reservada por el gobierno de EE.UU. para las tribus de indígenas norteamericanos (pág. 608)

revenue [renta] s. ingresos (pág. 678)

robber baron [*robber baron*] s. líder económico que se hizo muy rico mediante métodos deshonestos (pág. 630)

Roosevelt Corollary [corolario de Roosevelt] s. reivindicación de EE.UU. para intervenir en los asuntos de los países latinoamericanos (pág. 706)

Rough Riders [*Rough Riders*] s. miembros del Primer Regimiento de Voluntarios de Caballería de EE.UU., organizado por Theodore Roosevelt durante la Guerra Hispanoamericana (pág. 698)

royal colony [colonia real] s. colonia gobernada por funcionarios nombrados por el rey (pág. 60)

Sahara [Sahara] s. gran desierto en el norte de África (pág. 10)

Sand Creek Massacre [masacre de Sand Creek] s. ataque en 1864 en el que unos 200 cheyenne fueron asesinados por la milicia de Colorado (pág. 608)

Santa Fe Trail [Ruta de Santa Fe] s. ruta que comenzaba en Missouri y terminaba en Santa Fe, Nuevo México (pág. 418)

Saratoga, Battles of [batallas de Saratoga] s. serie de conflictos en 1777 cerca de Albany, Nueva York (pág. 194)

savanna [sabana] s. pradera llana con abundante vida animal, arbustos espinosos y árboles dispersos (p. 10)

scalawag [*scalawag*] s. hombre blanco del Sur que apoyó la Reconstrucción de los radicales (pág. 570)

Scots-Irish [escoceses-irlandeses] s. nombre dado a la gente que proviene de las tierras en la frontera de Escocia e Inglaterra o de la región de Irlanda del Norte (pág. 116)

secede [separarse] v. retirarse (pág. 394, 498)

Second Continental Congress [Segundo Congreso Continental] s. gobierno de Norteamérica durante la Guerra de Independencia (pág. 176)

Second Great Awakening [Segundo Gran Despertar] s. renovación de la fe religiosa a finales del siglo XVIII y principios del XIX (pág. 456)

sectionalism [seccionalismo] s. lealtad a los intereses de la propia región o sección del país (pág. 378)

sedentary societies [sociedades sedentarias] s. personas que se asentaban en pueblos o ciudades estables (pág. 4)

sedition [sedición] s. provocar una rebelión contra un gobierno (pág. 326)

segregation [segregación] s. separación racial (pág. 650)

semisedentary societies [sociedades semi-sendentarias] s. personas que se asentaba en pueblos o ciudades pero se trasladaban a los pocos años en busca de alimentos (pág. 4)

Seneca Falls Convention [Convención de Seneca Falls] s. convención a favor de los derechos de las mujeres celebrada en Seneca Falls, Nueva York (pág. 464)

settlement house [casa de asistencia] s. centro comunitario que proporcionaba ayuda a los inmigrantes y a los pobres (pág. 682)

Seven Days' Battles [batallas de los Siete Días] s. victoria Confederada en la que Lee detuvo la campaña de la Unión contra Richmond (pág. 522)

Seventeenth Amendment [Enmienda Decimoséptima] s. enmienda que proveyó la elección directa de los senadores estadounidenses (pág. 678)

Shaker [*Shaker*] s. miembro de una secta cristiana que vivía en comuna y no permitía el matrimonio o tener hijos (pág. 456)

sharecropping [aparcería] s. sistema mediante el cual los propietarios daban a los granjeros pobres semillas, herramientas y tierras para cultivar a cambio de parte de sus cosechas (pág. 576)

shareholder [accionista] s. inversor que compra parte de una compañía en acciones de bolsa (pág. 630)

Shays's Rebellion [rebelión de Shays] s. levantamiento de los granjeros de Massachusetts que querían la cancelación de sus deudas (pág. 234)

Sherman Antitrust Act [Acta Antitrust de Sherman] s. ley que ilegalizó el control de las industrias por parte de las corporaciones mediante la formación de trusts (pág. 672)

Sherman's March to the Sea [marcha al mar de Sherman] s. marcha destructiva del general Sherman a través de Georgia (pág. 548)

Shiloh, Battle of [batalla de Shiloh] s. batalla sangrienta en Tennessee que ganó Grant (pág. 522)

siege [asediar] v. cuando las fuerzas enemigas rodean un pueblo o ciudad para obligarla a rendirse (pág. 176)

Siege of Vicksburg [asedio de Vicksburg] s. rendición de la ciudad de Vicksburg, Mississippi, a las tropas de la Unión (pág. 548)

Sixteenth Amendment [Enmienda Decimosexta] s. enmienda que dio al Congreso poderes para establecer impuestos sobre la renta (pág. 678)

slash-and-burn [tala y quema] s. proceso de limpiar la tierra cortando y quemando árboles (pág. 4)

slave [esclavo] s. alguien que es capturado para usarlo en trabajos forzados sin cobrar (pág. 10)

slave codes [códigos de esclavos] s. ley aprobada para regular el trato a los esclavos (pág. 48)

slavery [esclavitud] s. práctica por la que una persona pertenece a otra (pág. 48)

slum [barriada] s. vecindario superpoblado y con edificios peligrosos (pág. 640)

smallpox [viruela] s. enfermedad altamente contagiosa y a menudo mortal (pág. 142)

smuggling [contrabandear] v. importar o exportar productos de forma ilegal (pág. 94)

social gospel movement [movimiento de evangelización social] s. reformas basadas en los valores cristianos (pág. 640)

socialism [socialismo] *s.* sistema en el que el estado controla la economía (pág. 656)

society [sociedad] *s.* grupo de gente con intereses, costumbres y formas de vida comunes (pág. 4)

sod [terrón] *s.* primera capa del suelo de la pradera que tiene raíces gruesas y enredadas (pág. 616)

sodbusters [*sodbusters*] *s.* nombre de los granjeros pioneros en las Grandes Llanuras (pág. 616)

solar time [hora solar] *s.* hora basada en los cálculos del movimiento del sol por el cielo (pág. 596)

Sons of Liberty [Hijos de la Libertad] *s.* sociedad secreta formada para oponerse a las políticas británicas (pág. 156)

South Atlantic current [corriente del Atlántico Sur] *s.* corriente que circula en sentido contrario a las agujas del reloj entre África y América del Sur (pág. 16)

Spanish Armada [Armada española] *s.* gran flota enviada para invadir Inglaterra y restaurar el catolicismo (pág. 34)

Spanish-American War [Guerra Hispanoamericana] *s.* guerra de 1898 que comenzó cuando EE.UU. exigió a España la independencia de Cuba (pág. 698)

speculate [especular] *v.* comprar como inversión (pág. 156)

sphere of influence [esfera de influencia] *s.* áreas donde las naciones extranjeras demandan derechos especiales y privilegios económicos (pág. 706)

spirituals [espirituales] *s.* canciones religiosas populares (pág. 372)

spoils system [sistema de despojos] *s.* práctica de dar puestos en el gobierno a los partidarios políticos (pág. 394)

Stamp Act [Acta del Timbre] *s.* ley que exigía que todos los documentos legales y comerciales llevaran un sello oficial demostrando que se había pagado un impuesto (pág. 156)

standard time [hora estándar] *s.* zonas horarias ideadas por las compañías de ferrocaril (pág. 596)

states' rights [derechos estatales] *s.* idea de que los estados tienen ciertos derechos que el gobierno federal no puede denegar (pág. 326)

steerage [tercera clase] *s.* la cubierta más barata de un barco (pág. 450)

stock market [bolsa de valores] *s.* lugar donde se compran y venden las acciones de las compañías (pág. 582)

Stono Rebellion [Rebelión de Stono] *s.* rebelión de esclavos en 1739 en Carolina del Sur (pág. 102)

strategy [estrategia] *s.* plan general de acción (pág. 194)

strike [huelga] *s.* dejar de trabajar para exigir mejores condiciones laborales (pág. 456)

subsistence farming [agricultura de subsistencia] *s.* producir sólo alimentos para consumo propio (pág. 94)

suffrage [sufragio] *s.* derecho al voto (pág. 464)

Sugar Act [Acta del Azúcar] *s.* ley que creaba un impuesto sobre el azúcar, la melaza y otros productos enviados por barco a las colonias (pág. 156)

sweatshop [maquiladora] *s.* lugar donde se trabaja muchas horas, en malas condiciones y por poco dinero (pág. 640)

Tammany Hall [Tammany Hall] *s.* maquinaria política en Nueva York (pág. 640)

tariff [arancel] *s.* impuesto sobre productos importados (pág. 312)

Tariff of Abominations [Arancel de las Abominaciones] *s.* ley de 1828 que aumentaba significativamente los aranceles de las materias primas y de los productos manufacturados (pág. 394)

Tejanos [Tejanos] *s.* gente de herencia mexicana que consideran Texas su hogar (pág. 426)

Tejas [Tejas] *s.* nombre designado por los exploradores españoles a la tierra que hoy día es Texas (pág. 426)

temperance movement [movimiento de la moderación] *s.* campaña para evitar el consumo de alcohol (pág. 456)

tenements [casa de vecindario] *s.* apartamentos superpoblados y deteriorados (pág. 640)

Thirteenth Amendment [Enmienda Decimotercera] *s.* enmienda que puso fin a la esclavitud (pág. 558)

Three-Fifths Compromise [Concesión de los Tres Quintos] *s.* acuerdo por el que los tres quintos de la población de un estado esclavista se contarían para la representación y los impuestos (pág. 242)

threshing machine [trilladora] *s.* máquina que separa los granos de trigo de la paja (pág. 364)

Tidewater [agua de marea] *s.* zona de llanuras costeras (pág. 76)

tolerance [tolerancia] *s.* aceptación de distintas opiniones (pág. 66)

Tordesillas, Treaty of [Tratado de Tordesillas] *s.* tratado de 1494 por el cual España y Portugal acordaron repartirse las tierras del hemisferio occidental y trasladaron al oeste la Línea de Demarcación (pág. 26)

Townshend Acts [Actas de Townshend] *s.* actas aprobadas por el Parlamento en 1767 para intensificar el control británico de las colonias (pág. 160)

Trail of Tears [Marcha de las Lágrimas] *s.* el desplazamiento forzado de los cherokee desde su tierra natal hasta el Territorio Indígena (pág. 402)

transcontinental railroad [ferrocarril transcontinental] *s.* ferrocarril que recorría el continente norteamericano (pág. 596)

triangular trade [comercio triangular] *s.* complejo sistema de intercambio transatlántico de esclavos, ron, azúcar y melaza (pág. 94)

tribute [tributo] *s.* pago a cambio de protección (pág. 352)

trust [*trust*] *s.* organismo legal creado para controlar acciones de muchas compañías, a menudo de la misma industria (pág. 630)

U.S.S. *Maine* [*U.S.S.* Maine] *s.* acorazado estadounidense que explotó en La Habana, Cuba, el 15 de febrero de 1898 (pág. 698)

Uncle Tom's Cabin [La cabaña del Tío Tom] *s.* novela publicada por Harrriet Beecher Stowe en 1852 que mostraba la esclavitud como una práctica brutal e inmoral (pág. 480)

Underground Railroad [ferrocarril subterráneo] *s.* serie de rutas de huida utilizadas por los esclavos para escapar del Sur (pág. 464)

uprising [levantamiento] *s.* rebelión (pág. 510)

urbanization [urbanización] *s.* crecimiento de las ciudades como resultado de la industrialización (pág. 640)

Valley Forge [Valley Forge] *s.* lugar al suroeste de Pensilvania donde Washington y su ejército acamparon el invierno de 1777-1778 (pág. 204)

vaquero [vaquero] *s.* término para una persona que trabaja con ganado (pág. 600)

vaudeville [vodevil] *s.* entretenimiento ligero que incluía canciones, bailes y comedia (pág. 662)

veto [veto] *v.* impedir que se convierta en ley (pág. 570)

vigilante [vigilante] *s.* persona que se toma la justicia por su mano (pág. 600)

Virginia Plan [Plan Virginia] *s.* propuesta de una legislatura con dos cámaras con representación en cada una según la población o riqueza de cada estado (pág. 242)

Virginia Statute for Religious Freedom [Estatuto de Virginia para la Libertad de Culto] *s.* declaración a favor de la libertad religiosa, escrito por Thomas Jefferson (pág. 222)

war hawk [halcón de guerra] *s.* persona del Oeste que apoyó la Guerra de 1812 (pág. 352)

Whig Party [Partido *Whig*] *s.* partido político formado por Henry Clay, Daniel Webster, y otros opositores a Jackson (pág. 408)

Whiskey Rebellion [Rebelión del Whiskey] *s.* protesta contra los impuestos del gobierno sobre el whiskey que realizaron los granjeros campesinos (pág. 318)

Wilderness Road [*Wilderness Road*] *s.* sendero que terminaba en Kentucky (pág. 204)

Wilmot Proviso [Provisión de Wilmot] *s.* propuesta de 1846 que ilegalizaba la esclavitud en cualquier territorio ganado en la guerra con México (pág. 480)

Wounded Knee Massacre [Masacre de Wounded Knee] *s.* asesinato en masa de unos 300 sioux desarmados a manos de soldados estadounidenses en Wounded Knee, Dakota del Sur, en 1890 (pág. 608)

writ of habeas corpus [escrito de habeas corpus] *s.* ley que impide al gobierno retener a los ciudadanos sin cargo formal (pág. 542)

writs of assistance [escritos de allanamiento] *s.* orden judicial que se usa para entrar en domicilios o negocios en busca de mercancía de contrabando (pág. 160)

XYZ Affair [Asunto XYZ] *s.* incidente de 1797 en el que oficiales franceses demandaron de los diplomáticos norteamericanos un soborno (pág. 326)

yellow journalism [periodismo amarillo] *s.* estilo de periodismo que exagera las noticias, en busca del sensacionalismo (pág. 698)

Yorktown, Battle of [batalla de Yorktown] *s.* batalla final de la guerra, en la que fuerzas francesas y estadounidenses lideradas por George Washington derrotaron al general británico Cornwallis (pág. 212)

Index

Page references in **boldface** indicate Key Terms & Names and Background Vocabulary that are highlighted in the main text.
Page references in *italics* indicate illustrations, charts, and maps.

Acknowledgments

Text Acknowledgments

Chapter 6, page 175: Excerpt from *Johnny Tremain* by Esther Forbes. Copyright © 1943 by Esther Forbes Hoskins, copyright renewed © 1971 by Linwood M. Erskine, Jr., Executor of the Estate of Esther Forbes Hoskins. Reprinted by permission of Houghton Mifflin Company. All rights reserved.

Chapter 16, page 530: Excerpt from *Across Five Aprils* by Irene Hunt. Copyright © 1964 by Irene Hunt. All rights reserved. Reprinted by permission of Penguin Putnam.

Chapter 20, page 666: Excerpt from *Dragonwings* by Laurence Yep. Copyright © 1975 by Laurence Yep. Used by permission of HarperCollins Publishers.

The editors have made every effort to trace the ownership of all copyrighted material found in this book and to make full acknowledgment for its use. Omissions brought to our attention will be corrected in a subsequent edition.

Art Credits

All maps, with the exception of World Atlas maps, created by GeoNova LLC.

Cover and Title Page *George Washington* The Granger Collection, New York; *Sacajawea* Connie Ricca/Corbis; *Mariano Vallejo* Courtesy of The Bancroft Library University of California, Berkeley, General Vallejo. Houseworth & Co. Photographs. Houseworth's Souvenir Photographs: 5; *Frederick Douglass* J. R. Eyerman/Time Life Pictures/Getty Images; *Abraham Lincoln* Archivo Iconografico, S.A./Corbis; *Jane Addams* Bettmann/Corbis; *eagle* iStockphoto.com; *flag* PhotoDisc/Getty Images; *Yosemite* Jose Fuste Raga/Corbis; *clouds* PhotoDisc.

Section & American Spirit Banner *American flag* PhotoDisc Red/Getty Images; **Historic Decisions of the Supreme Court** *courthouse* Royalty-Free/Corbis; *justice* Royalty-Free/Corbis; **Geography & History Banner** *compass* Harnett/Hanzon/Getty Images; **Interactive Primary Source Banner** *glasses, pen, document* Royalty-Free/Corbis; *quill pen, magnifying glass on letter* Royalty-Free/Corbis; *Constitution with quill pen* Comstock; **Table of Contents Banner** *American flag* Comstock; *Rocky Mountains* Digital Stock; *White House* Comstock; *Constitution* Comstock.

Table of Contents
iii McDougal Littell/Houghton Mifflin Co.; **vii** *bottom right* Detail, *Benjamin Franklin* (ca. 1785), Joseph Siffred Duplessis. Oil on canvas, 72.4 x 59.6 cm. National Portrait Gallery, Smithsonian Institution, Washington, DC. Gift of the Morris and Gwendolyn Cafritz Foundation/Art Resource, New York; **x** *bottom right* Courtesy of the State Preservation Board, Austin, Texas. CHA 1989.96, Photographer Perry Huston, 7/28/95, post conservation; **xii** *bottom right* The Granger Collection, New York; **xiv** *bottom right* Bettmann/Corbis.

Special Features & Reading for Understanding
xxiv *center left* Bizuayehu Tesfaye/AP Images; *bottom center* AP Images; *bottom right* Thinkstock Images/Jupiter Images; *frame* Shutterstock; *stamp* AP Images; **xxv** *top right* National Museum of American History, Smithsonian Institution Negative # 74-2491; *center left* The Granger Collection, New York; *center inset* California Gold Rush Guide, 1849/The Granger Collection, New York; **xxvi** *top* Pixel Images, Inc./McDougal Littell/Houghton Mifflin Co.

Geography Handbook
S30 *top right* Peter Pearson/Getty Images; *bottom left* Bob Torrez/Getty Images; **A1** *top* Onne van der Wal/Corbis; *bottom* Andy Sacks/Getty Images; **A2** *top* Steve Dunwell/Index Stock Imagery; *bottom* Christopher Pfuhl/AP Images; **A3** Brian Snyder/Reuters/Corbis; **A4** *bottom left* Lockheed Martin; **A8** *top* Lester Lefkowitz/Corbis; *bottom* Tom Bean/Corbis; *center* George Steinmetz/Corbis; **A9** *top* Steve Satushek/Getty Images; *bottom* Keith Wood/Getty Images; **A10** *top* Jessica Rinaldi/Reuters/Corbis; **A11** Michael Melford/Getty Images; **A12** Illustration by Ken Goldammer/McDougal Littell/Houghton Mifflin Co.; **A14** *bottom* Atlantide Phototravel; *center right* Bill Pogue/Getty Images; *center left* Walter Rawlings/Getty Images; **A15** *top* Najlah Feanny/Corbis SABA; *bottom* Jeff Greenberg/PhotoEdit; **A16** Brooks Kraft/Corbis; **A17** *left* Gregory Bull, Staff/AP Images; *right* James Leynse/Corbis; **A18** Medioimages/Getty Images.

World Atlas
A20 Image created by Reto Stockli with the help of Alan Nelson, under the leadership of Fritz Hasler/NASA. **A21–A39** All maps © Rand McNally.

Unit 1
1 Corbis; **2** *bottom right* Biblioteca Augusta Perugia/Dagli Orti/The Art Archive; *bottom center* Werner Forman/Corbis; *bottom left* Charles & Josette Lenars/Corbis; **3** *top right* The Granger Collection, New York; *center right* Werner Forman Archive; *center left* Macduff Everton/Corbis; *bottom* Sextant, English (brass), English School, (18th century)/Private Collection/The Bridgeman Art Library International; **5** *top right* Werner Forman/Art Resource, NY; *center right* Palazzo Pitti Florence/Dagli Orti (A)/The Art Archive; **6** *center right* SuperStock; **7** George H. H. Huey/Corbis; **8** *top* The Granger Collection, New York; *inset* Medioimages/Getty Images Royalty-Free; **8–9** Wide Group/Getty Images; **9** *top* George H. H. Huey/Corbis; **10** Illustration by Geoff Kornfeld; *bottom left* Gianna Dagli Orti/Corbis; *top left* Getty Images/Royalty-Free; *center left* Keith Dannemiller/Corbis; **12** *center right* Frans Lemmens/Getty Images; **13** *center right* Erich Lessing/Art Resource, NY; *top right* Sandro Vannini/Corbis; **14** Werner Forman Archive; **16** SSPL/The Image Works; **17** *center right* Stock Montage/Getty Images; *top right* Bibliothèque Universitaire de Mèdecine, Montpellier/Dagli Orti/The Art Archive; **18** The Granger Collection, New York; **19** *center* Sandro Vannini/Corbis; *right* Bibliothèque Universitaire de Mèdecine, Montpellier/Dagli Orti/The Art Archive; *left* Werner Forman/Art Resource, NY; **20** Four pocket compasses (wood & brass) by German School, (15th century) © British Museum, London, UK/© Boltin Picture Library/The Bridgeman Art Library; **21** *top* Werner Forman/Art Resource, NY; *bottom left* Biblioteca Augusta Perugia/Dagli Orti/The Art Archive; **22** North Wind Pictures Archive/Alamy; **23** *The Venetian Ambassador's Interview in an Oriental City or, The Reception of Domenico Trevisani in Cairo in 1512* (oil on panel), Italian School, (16th century)/Louvre, Paris, France, Giraudon/The Bridgeman Art Library International; **24–25** Library of Congress, Washington, DC; **24** *bottom left* Museum of Modern Art Mexico/Dagli Orti/The Art Archive; *bottom right* Inca kero, or wooden beaker, Southern Highlands, Peru, 16th century © British Museum, London, UK/The Bridgeman Art Library; **25** *center* Jeffrey L. Rotman/Corbis; *bottom* The Granger Collection, New York; **26** New-York Historical Society, New York, USA/The Bridgeman Art Library; **27** *top right* Museo de la Torre del Oro Seville/Dagli Orti/The Art Archive; *center* Snark/Art Resource, NY; **28** Monastery of the Rabida, Palos, Spain/Dagli Orti/The Art Archive; **29** Archivo Iconografico, S.A./Corbis; **31** Bildarchiv Preusssischer Kulturbesitz/Art Resource, NY; **32** *right* American Museum of Natural History, New York, USA/The Bridgeman Art Library; *left* Gianni Dagli Orti/Corbis; **34** *The Launching of English Fireships on the Spanish Fleet off Calais with Queen Elizabeth I (1533-1603) on Horseback on Shore*, by Flemish School, (17th century) Private Collection/Rafael Valls Gallery, London, UK/The Bridgeman Art Library; **35** *center* Bettmann/Corbis; *top right* Museo de la Torre del Oro Seville/Dagli Orti/The Art Archive; **37** Elizabeth I, Armada portrait, c.1588 (oil on panel), English School, (16th century)/Private Collection/The Bridgeman Art Library; **40** Tom Bean/Corbis; **41** *center right* The Granger Collection, New York; *top right* Museo de la Torre del Oro Seville/Dagli Orti/The Art Archive; **42** Bettmann/Corbis; **43** Helmet and Shield: Collection of the Oakland Museum of California, Gifts of Herbert Hamlin and Dr. W. Michael Mathes. Body Armor: The DeYoung Museum of San Francisco; **48** *Slaves Below Deck of Albanez* (date unknown), Francis Meynell. Copyright © National Maritime Museum Picture Library, London.; **49** *center* Fotomas Index/Bridgeman Art Library; *top right* Museo de la Torre del Oro Seville/Dagli Orti/The Art Archive; **50** *Portrait of a Negro Man*, c.1780 (oil on canvas), Ramsay, Allan (1713-84) (attr. to)/Royal Albert Memorial Museum, Exeter, Devon, UK/The Bridgeman Art Library International; **51** Corbis; **53** *top* Museo de la Torre del Oro Seville/Dagli Orti/The Art Archive; *bottom right* Museumof Modern Art Mexico/Dagli Orti/The Art Archive; *bottom left* Archivo Iconografico, S.A./Corbis; **54** Museo de la Torre del Oro Seville/Dagli Orti/The Art Archive; **55** Museo de America Madrid Dagli Orti/The Art Archive.

Unit 2
56–57 *Old State House*, Boston, 1801 (oil on panel) by Marston, James Brown (1775-1817) Massachusetts Historical Society, Boston, MA, USA/The Bridgeman Art Library; **58** *bottom left* Getty Images; *bottom center* Tobacco plant (nicotiana tabacum) (1633), woodcut from Thomas Johnson's "Herball"/The Granger Collection, New York; **59** *bottom* British Library/HIP/Art Resource, New York; *center* Penn's Treaty With the Indians (1830 - 1840), Edward Hicks. Oil on canvas. The Bayou Bend Collection, gift of Alice C. Simkins in memory of Alice Nicholson Hanszen/Museum of Fine Arts, Houston (B.77.46) Photograph by Francis G. Mayer/Corbis; **61** *top right* Richard T. Nowitz/Corbis; *center* Carolina Algonquin Indians Fishing (ca. 1585), John White. Watercolor. The Granger Collection, New York; **63** Detail, *Pochahontas, Daughter of Powhatan Chief* (ca 1616), Anonymous, after 1616 engraving by Simon van de Passe. Oil on canvas, 76.8 cm x 64.1 cm. National Portrait Gallery, Smithsonian Institution, Washington, DC/Art Resource, New York; **64** Spencer Platt/Getty Images; **65** New Line/Merie W. Wallace/The Kobal Collection ; **67** *center* John Winthrop (1834), Charles Osgood, after portrait by anonymous artist. Oil on canvas. The Granger Collection, New York; *top right* Richard T. Nowitz/Corbis; **68** Richard T. Nowitz/Corbis;

Acknowledgments **R79**

69 *inset* Tim Wright/Corbis; 70 Culver Pictures/The Art Archive; 71 *The Hanging of Mary Dyer* (1906), Basil King. Lithograph, after Howard Pyle/The Bridgeman Art Library; 73 Toby Talbot/AP Images; 74 Joseph Sohm/The Image Works; 76 Library of Congress Prints and Photographs Division (LC-USZ62-61452); 77 Illustration by Christian Hook; *top right* Richard T. Nowitz/Corbis; 79 The Colonial Williamsburg Foundation; 80 *inset* The Granger Collection, New York; 82 The Granger Collection, New York; 83 *center* Stock Montage/Getty Images; *top right* Richard T. Nowitz/Corbis; 85 Illustrations by Andrew Wheatcroft; *all* The Colonial Williamsburg Foundation; *cap* The Colonial Williamsburg Foundation. Gift of Mrs. Cora Ginsburg; 87 *top right* Richard T. Nowitz/Corbis; *bottom* Mary Evans Picture Library ; *top left* Snark/Art Resorce, New York; 88 Merie W. Wallace/New Line/The Kobal Collection; 89 *top left* Richard T. Nowitz/Corbis; *bottom left* John Winthrop (1834), Charles Osgood, after portrait by anonymous artist. Oil on canvas. The Granger Collection, New York; 91 Public Domain; 92 *bottom left* The Granger Collection, New York; *center left* Howard Pyle/The Granger Collection, New York; 93 *bottom* The Granger Collection, New York; 95 *center Self-Portrait* (ca. 1680),Thomas Smith. Oil on canvas, 24.75 x 23.75 inches. Worcester Art Museum, Worcester, Massachusetts. Museum Purchase (1948.19); *top right* Detail, *Southeast Prospect of the City of Philadelphia* (1720), Peter Cooper. Oil on canvas, 20" x 87". The Library Company of Philadelphia; 97 *right* Mary Evans Picture Library; *left* © 2001, 2006 Stars and Stripes. Used with permission.; 98 *right inset Trade Castles and Forts of West Africa* (Stanford University Press, 1964), A.W. Lawrence. Plate 44; taken from "Tilforladelig Efterretning om Kysten Guinea" ("A reliable account of the coast of Guinea") Ludwig Romer (Copenhagen, 1760)/Stanford University Press; *left inset* The Granger Collection, New York; 99 Hulton Archive/Getty Images; 100 *right John Freake* (ca.1671-1674), Anonymous. Oil on canvas, 42.5 x 36.8 inches. Worcester Art Museum, Worcester, Massachusetts. Sarah C. Garver Fund (1963.135); *left Portrait of Elizabeth Clarke Freake and Baby Mary* (ca. 1671-1674), Anonymous. Oil on canvas, 42.5 x 36.8 inches. Worcester Art Museum, Worcester, Massachusetts. Gift of Mr. and Mrs. Albert W. Rice (1963.134) ; 101 North Wind Picture Archives; 102 *yarn* Dorothy Miller; *indigo plant* The New York Botanical Garden; 103 *center right George Mason of Gunston Hall* (1858), Louis Mathieu Didier Guillaume, after John Hesselius. Oil on canvas, 76.20 x 63.50 cm (30 x 25 inches). (1858.2) Virginia Historical Society; *top right* Detail, *Southeast Prospect of the City of Philadelphia* (1720), Peter Cooper. Oil on canvas, 20" x 87". The Library Company of Philadelphia; 106 Angelo Hornak/Corbis; 108 David Lyons/Alamy; 108–109 Illustration by Sebastian Quigley/Linden Artists Ltd.; 110 The Granger Collection, New York; 111 *center right Penn's Treaty With the Indians* (1830 - 1840), Edward Hicks. Oil on canvas. The Bayou Bend Collection, gift of Alice C. Simkins in memory of Alice Nicholson Hanszen/Museum of Fine Arts, Houston (B.77.46) Photograph by Francis G. Mayer/Corbis; *top right* Detail, *Southeast Prospect of the City of Philadelphia* (1720), Peter Cooper. Oil on canvas, 20" x 87". The Library Company of Philadelphia; 112 Lithograph, 1875/The Granger Collection, New York; 113 Royalty-Free/Corbis; 114 Photograph by John Schilling, Courtesy of Peter Wentz Farmstead, Department of Parks and Heritage Services, Montgomery County PA; 116 Ric Ergenbright; 117 Illustration by Roger Stewart; *top right* Detail, *Southeast Prospect of the City of Philadelphia* (1720), Peter Cooper. Oil on canvas, 20" x 87". The Library Company of Philadelphia; 118 *inset* Michael P. Gadomski/Photo Researchers, Inc.; 121 *top left* Detail, *Southeast Prospect of the City of Philadelphia* (1720), Peter Cooper. Oil on canvas, 20" x 87". The Library Company of Philadelphia; *bottom left* New York Botanical Garden; 124 *both* The Granger Collection, New York; 125 *bottom right* Stuart Dee/Getty Images; *bottom left* The Granger Collection, New York; 126 Colonial Williamsburg Foundation; 127 *center* Illustration from Henry Mouzon, Jr., "Map of the Parish of St. Stephen's in Craven County" (1775), South Carolina Historical Society; *top right* Colonial Williamsburg Foundation; *bottom* Gown, silk textile 1740s, remodeled 1780-1795, silk damask with appliquéd silk. From the collection of Doris Langley Moore. The Colonial Williamsburg Foundation; 129 Colonial Williamsburg Foundation; 130 *top* The Granger Collection, New York; *center, bottom* Library of Congress Prints and Photographs Division; 131 Colonial Williamsburg Foundation; 132 *Benjamin Franklin* (ca. 1785), Joseph Siffred Duplessis. Oil on canvas, 72.4 x 59.6 cm. National Portrait Gallery, Smithsonian Institution, Washington, DC. Gift of the Morris and Gwendolyn Cafritz Foundation/Art Resource, New York; 133 *Franklin's Experiment, June, 1752* (1876), Currier & Ives. Museum of the City of New York/Corbis; 134–135 Illustrations by Luigi Galante; 135 The Colonial Williamsburg Foundation; 136 British Picture Library; 137 *center Increase Mather* (1688), Jan Van Spriett. Oil on canvas. Massachusetts Historical Society/The Granger Collection, New York; *top right* The Colonial Wiliamsburg Foundation; 138 David Frazier/Getty Images; 139 The Granger Collection, New York; 140 Illustrations by Rogue Element; 142 *Death of General Richard Montgomery* (1865), Alonzo Chappel. Oil on canvas. Chicago Historical Museum/The Bridgeman Art Library; 143 *center* The Granger Collection, New York; *top right* The Colonial Wiliamsburg Foundation; 145 *inset* Detail, *Braddock's Defeat* (1903), Edward Deming. State Historical Society of Wisconsin Museum Collection, SHSW #42.488; 147 The Granger Collection, New York; 149 *top*

left The Colonial Wiliamsburg Foundation; *bottom left* Detail, *Benjamin Franklin* (ca. 1785), Joseph Siffred Duplessis. Oil on canvas, 72.4 x 59.6 cm. National Portrait Gallery, Smithsonian Institution, Washington, DC. Gift of the Morris and Gwendolyn Cafritz Foundation/Art Resource, New York; 151 *The Death of General Wolfe* (ca. 1771), Benjamin West. Oil on panel, 43.2 x 61 cm. Private collection/The Bridgeman Art Library.

Unit 3

152–153 Burstein Collection/Corbis; 154 Illustration by Thomas Bayley; *right* Military and Historical Image Bank; *left George III* (ca. 1762), Allfter Allan Ramsay. Oil on canvas. Scottish National Portrait Gallery, Edinburgh, Scotland/The Bridgeman Art Library; 155 *bottom left* Pennsylvania Society of the Sons of the Revolution; *bottom right* Don Troiani/Military and Historical Image Bank; 156 *George III* (1794), David Dodd. Oil on canvas. Private Collection/The Bridgeman Art Library; 157 *center Mrs. Richard Bache* (Sarah Franklin) (1793), John Hoppner. Oil on canvas, 30 1/8 x 24 7/8 inches. (76.5 x 63.2 cm). Catherine Lorillard Wolfe Collection, Wolfe Fund, 1901 (01.20),The Metropolitan Museum of Art, New York; *top right* Colored engraving (1770), Paul Revere. The Granger Collection, New York; 158 *bottom* Emmet Collection, Manuscripts and Archives Division, The New York Public Library; *top* The Granger Collection, New York; 159 The Granger Collection, New York; 161 Illustration by Patrick Faricy; *top right* Colored engraving (1770), Paul Revere. The Granger Collection, New York; 162 *window* Colonial Williamsburg Foundation; *dress* The Granger Collection, New York; *clock* Georgian longcase clock with marquetry case, 18th century/Private Collection/Bonhams, London/The Bridgeman Art Library; *fabric* Floral design with peonies, lilies and roses for Spitalfields silk (1744), Anna Maria Garthwaite/Victoria and Albert Museum/The Bridgeman Art Library; *book The Constitutions of the Freemasons* (1723), Dr James Anderson, London/Bibliotheque Nationale, Paris/Archives Charmet/The Bridgeman Art Library; *telescope* Reflecting Table Telescope (18th century), English. Brass and leather. Private Collection/The Bridgeman Art Library; *glasses* Wine glasses, (18th century), English. Private Collection/The Bridgeman Art Library; 164 Colored engraving (1770), Paul Revere. The Granger Collection, New York; 165 *right John Adams after 1783* (Detail) (ca. 1783), Anonymous, after John Singleton Copley. Oil on canvas, 20 1/4 x 13 5/8 inches (51.43 x 34.61 cm). Seth K. Sweetser Fund (23.180), Museum of Fine Arts, Boston; *left Samuel Adams* (Detail) (ca. 1772), John Singleton Copley. Oil on canvas, 49 1/2 x 39 1/2 inches (125.73 x 100.33 cm). Deposited by the City of Boston (L-R 30.76c), Museum of Fine Arts, Boston; 167 *right A Society of Patriotic Ladies* (1775), Philip Dawe. Mezzotint. British Cartoon Collection, (LC-USZC4-4617) Library of Congress; *left* Library of Congress, Prints and Photographs Division (LC-USZC4-1583); *bottom* The Granger Collection, New York; 168 *Paul Revere* (1768), John Singleton Copley. Oil on canvas, 35 1/8 x 28 1/2 inches (89.22 x 72.39 cm). Gift of Joseph W. Revere, William B. Revere and Edward H. R. Revere (30.781), Museum of Fine Arts, Boston; 169 *center* Art Resource, New York; *top right* Colored engraving (1770), Paul Revere. The Granger Collection, New York; 170 Bettmann/Corbis; 171 The Granger Collection, New York; 172 *Abigail Smith Adams* (ca. 1766), Benjamin Blyth. Pastel on paper, 57.3 x 44.8 cm. Massachusetts Historical Society, Boston MA/Corbis; 173 Illustration, Bibby's Annual (1909), Ernest Crofts. Mary Evans Picture Library; 175 McDougal Littell/Houghton Mifflin Co.; 176 Detail, *Thomas Jefferson* (1786), Mather Brown. Oil on canvas, 90.8 x 72.4 cm. Bequest of Charles Francis Adams, National Portrait Gallery, Smithsonian Institution/Art Resource, New York; 177 *center Mrs. Gage* (1771), John Singleton Copley. Oil on canvas. Private Collection/The Bridgeman Art Library ; *top right* Colored engraving (1770), Paul Revere. The Granger Collection, New York; 179 Lauren McFalls/McDougal Littell/Houghton Mifflin Co.; 180 *both* The Granger Collection, New York; 181 *all* Pennsylvania Society of the Sons of the Revolution; 182 *all* The Granger Collection, New York; 184 The Granger Collection, New York; 189 *top left* Colored engraving (1770), Paul Revere. The Granger Collection, New York; *bottom right* Don Troiani/Military and Historical Image Bank; *bottom left* The Granger Collection, New York; 191 Military and Historical Image Bank; 192 *bottom left* The Granger Collection, New York; 193 *bottom right* National Park Service, Harpers Ferry Center, artist Don Troiani http://www.cr.nps.gov/museum/exhibits/revwar/image_gal/vafoimg//csfront.html; *bottom left* Guilford Courthouse National Military Park; 195 *top right* Bob Krist/Corbis; *center right The Copley Family* (1776/1777), John Singleton Copley. Oil on canvas, 1.841 m x 2.292 m (72 1/2" x 90 1/4"). Andrew W. Mellon Fund, © 1999 Board of Trustees, National Gallery of Art, Washington DC; 196 *both* North Wind Picture Archives; 197 Réunion des Musées Nationaux/Art Resource, NY; 199 The Granger Collection, New York; 200 Photo courtesy of the Historical and Military Image Bank www.historicalimagebank.com; 202 *center left* Albert Konschak; *bottom left* Richard T. Nowitz/Corbis; *top left* Albert Konschak; 202–203 Illustration by Sebastian Quigley/Linden Artists Ltd.; 203 *top right* Kelly Culpepper/Transparencies, Inc.; 204 Photograph courtesy Peabody Essex Museum, Joseph Howard, Watercolor 19 3/4 x 27 3/4 in. Built 1799, Salem, MA, 850 tons. ; 205 *center right* www.davidrwagner.com; *top right* Bob Krist/Corbis; 206 British Cartoon Collection, Library of Congress, (LC-USZ62-45442); 207 *Marquis de Lafayette* (1757-1834), c.1781-85 (oil on canvas) by Francesco Giuseppe Casanova (c.1732-1803), New-York Historical

Society, New York, USA/Bridgeman Art Library; **208** *top left* Courtesy National Park Service, Museum Management Program and Guilford Courthouse, National Military Park, GUCO 1603 http://www.cr.nps.gov/museum/exhibits/revwar/image_gal/gucoimg/guco1603amputation.html; **208** *top right* Valley Forge National Historical Park ; *bottom left* National Park Service, Harpers Ferry Center, artist Don Troiani, http://www.cr.nps.gov/museum/exhibits/revwar/image_gal/gucoimg/medicalcare.html; *right* North Wind Picture Archives; **209** *George Rogers Clark* (1976), Rosemary Brown Beck. Oil on canvas. From the Collection of the Indiana State Museum and Historic Sites; **210** Historical Society of Pennsylvania (HSP), James Forten, n.d., Leon Gardiner Collection; **211** *top right* The Granger Collection, New York; **212** Robert K. Ander; **213** *center right* Andy Thomas; *top right* Bob Krist/Corbis; **214** *left* The Granger Collection, New York; *right* Heribert Proepper/AP Images; **217** The Granger Collection, New York; **218** Illustrations by Rogue Element; **220** *both* The Granger Collection, New York; **221** *center right* William L. Clements Library, University of Michigan; *center left* National Portrait Gallery, Smithsonian Institution/Art Resource, NY; *top right* The Granger Collection, New York; **222** The Granger Collection, New York; **223** *center right* United States Postal Service. All rights reserved. Used with permisssion/The Granger Collection, New York; *top right* Bob Krist/Corbis; **224** Illustrations by Rogue Element; **226** The Granger Collection, New York; **227** *inset* The Granger Collection, New York; *frame* PhotoDisc/Getty Images; **229** *top* Bob Krist/Corbis; *bottom* The Granger Collection, New York; **230** *Marquis de Lafayette* (1757-1834), c.1781-85 (oil on canvas) by Francesco Giuseppe Casanova (c.1732-1803), New-York Historical Society, New York, USA/Bridgeman Art Library; **231** The Granger Collection, New York; **232** *bottom left* The Granger Collection, New York; *bottom right* American flag, c.1781 (wool & cotton), American School, (18th century)/© Collection of the New-York Historical Society, USA,/The Bridgeman Art Library International; **233** *bottom right* Peggy & Ronald Barnett/Corbis; *bottom left* The Granger Collection, New York; **235** *center right* The Granger Collection, New York; *top right* Bettmann/Corbis; **238** *View of New Orleans from the Plantation of Marigny, 1803* (oil on canvas), Woiseri, J. L. Bouquet de (fl.1797-1815)/© Chicago Historical Museum, USA,/The Bridgeman Art Library International; **240** *center left* The Granger Collection, New York; *bottom right* Ohio Historical Society; **241** Illustration by Roger Stewart; *survey tool* Copyright © John E. Fletcher & Arlan R. Wiler/National Geographic Image Collection; **243** *center inset* The Granger Collection, New York; *center right* Dennis Degnan/Corbis; *top right* Bettmann/Corbis; **244** Corbis; **249** *center right* The Granger Collection, New York; *top* Bettmann/Corbis; **250** *right John Jay* (1745-1829) 1786 (oil on canvas), Wright of Derby, Joseph (1734-97)/© Collection of the New-York Historical Society, USA,/The Bridgeman Art Library International; *left* Bettmann/Corbis; **251** Bettmann/Corbis; **252** AP Images; **253** Bettmann/Corbis; **256** *bottom left* Corbis; **257** *top left* Bettmann/Corbis; **259** *The Constitutional Convention, 1787*, by Allen Cox, Negative # 70681. Architect of the Capitol; **260** *center left* The Granger Collection, New York; *bottom right* Bettman/Corbis; **261** *top left* Norm Dettlaff/AP Images; *center right* Karen Kasmauski/Corbis; *bottom left* Mike Lane; **262** J. L. Atlan/Corbis Sygma; **263** Steve Warmowski/Jacksonville Journal-Courier/The Image Works; **264** Illustrations by Rogue Element; **265** *top right* Terry Ashe/Time Life Pictures/Getty Images; *center right* David Bacon/The Image Works; **266** *top* National Archives; *bottom left* Richard T. Nowitz/Corbis; **267** The Granger Collection, New York; **268** Peter Lennihan/AP Images; **269** Bettman/Corbis; **270–271** Illustrations by Rogue Element; **271** Jay Penni/McDougal Littell/Houghton Mifflin Co.; **272** *bottom left* Ahn Young-Joon/AP Images; *bottom center* U.S. Navy/Handout/CNP/Corbis; *bottom right* George Hall/Corbis; **273** *bottom left* Brownie Harris/Corbis; **273** *bottom right* Reuters/Corbis; **274** Royalty-Free/Corbis; **276** Illustrations by Rogue Element; **277** Bettmann/Corbis; **278** *top right* Library of Congress, Washington, DC (cwpb 01131); *center left* The Granger Collection, New York; *top left* Eric Draper/White House/Handout/CNP/Corbis; *center right* Wally McNamee/Corbis; *bottom* Bettmann/Corbis; **280** Mark Wilson, Staff/Getty Images; **283** Jack Kurtz/The Image Works; **284** Mike Theiler/Reuters/Corbis; **286** *top left* The Granger Collection, New York; **286–287** Tom Dodge/AP Images; **287** *bottom right* Spencer Grant/PhotoEdit; **288** Alan Klehr/Getty Images; **289** The Granger Collection, New York; **290** Getty Images; **291** 1976 Matt Herron/Take Stock; **292** The Granger Collection, New York; **293** Bettmann/Corbis; **294** Bettmann/Corbis; **295** Francis Miller/Getty Images; **296** *bottom center* Wedgwood Slave Emancipation Society medallion, c.1787-90 (jasperware) by William Hackwood (c.1757-1829), © Private Collection/The Bridgeman Art Library; *bottom left* The Granger Collection, New York; *top right* Associated Press, AP Images; **297** *bottom center* The Art Archive/Museum of the City of New York/47.225.12; *bottom right* Franklin D. Roosevelt Library; **299** Bob Lang; **301** Bettmann/Corbis; Seth Wenig/Reuters/Corbis; **303** *bottom* Will & Deni McIntyre/Corbis; *center right* Royalty-Free/Corbis; **304** NewsCom/PR Newswire; **305** Mary Kate Denny/PhotoEdit; **306** Michael Newman/PhotoEdit.

Unit 4

308–309 Yale University New Haven/The Art Archive; **310** *bottom left* Library of Congress, Washington, DC (cph 3b52213); *bottom center* SSPL/The Image Works; **311** *bottom left Birthplaces of John Adams and John Quincy Adams*, G. Frankenstein (1849). Courtesy of the National Park Service, Adams National Historical Park; *bottom center* Chateau de Blerancourt/Dagli Orti/The Art Archive; **312** Larry Downing/Reuters/Corbis; **313** *top right* The Granger Collection, New York; *center right* New York Times; **314** The Granger Collection, New York; **315** North Wind Picture Archives; **316** Illustrations by Rogue Element; **319** *center right* North Wind Picture Archives; *top right* The Granger Collection, New York; **320** Ohio Historical Society; **322** *The Women of Les Halles Marching to Versailles, 5th October 1789* (watercolor on paper) Jean-Francois Janinet (1752-1814) © Bibliotheque Nationale, Paris, France/Archives Charmet/The Bridgeman Art Library; **324** *bottom right* The Philadelphia Museum of Art/Art Resource, NY; *top* Library of Congress, Washington, DC (LC-USZ62-88324); *bottom left* American Numismatic Society; **325** *center left* Joseph Sohm/Visions of America/Corbis; *bottom left* Andre Jenny/Alamy; *top right* British Museum/HIP/Art Resource, New York; *center, bottom center* Dagli Orti/The Art Archive; *center right* John Hicks/Corbis; **327** *both* The Granger Collection, New York; **328** Fenimore Art Museum, Cooperstown, NY; **329** Illustration by Andrew Wheatcroft; **330** The Granger Collection, New York; **331** Photos courtesy of the Military & Historical Image Bank www.historicalimagebank.com; **333** *top left* The Granger Collection, New York; **333** *bottom left* Chateau de Blerancourt/Dagli Orti/The Art Archive; **334** *bottom A Thames Wharf*, c1750 Samuel Scott, oil on canvas, Victoria & Albert Museum, London, UK/The Bridgeman Art Library ; **336** *bottom left* Smithsonian American Art Musuem, Washington, DC/Art Resource, NY; *bottom right* The Granger Collection, New York; **336–337** Library of Congress, Prints and Photographs Division (g3300-ct000584); **337** *center left* From the Archives of the Ernst Mayr Library of the Museum of Comparative Zoology, Harvard University; *bottom left* © 2006 Harvard University, Peabody Museum, 99-12-10/53110.2 T3042.1.1; *bottom right* Bettmann/Corbis; **339** *center right* Smithsonian Institution; *top right* Monticello/Thomas Jefferson Foundation, Inc.; **340** *top right* Thomas Jefferson Polygraph, Special Collections, University of Virginia Library (image provided by Monticello/Thomas Jefferson Foundation, Inc.); *all others* Monticello/Thomas Jefferson Foundation, Inc.; **342** *Chief Justice John Marshall* (date unknown). Rembrandt Peale. Oil on canvas. Collection of the Supreme Court of the United States; **344** *both* Independence National History Park; **345** *top right* Monticello/Thomas Jefferson Foundation, Inc.; *center right* The Granger Collection, New York; **347** *top* Sam Abell/National Geographic Image Collection; *center right* Historical Picture Archive/Corbis; *all others* Smithsonian American Art Museum, Washington, DC/(Detail) Art Resource, New York; **348** *right* Library of Congress, Washington, DC; *left* The Granger Collection, New York; **350** *bottom* Navaswan/Taxi/Getty Images; *top* David Muench Photography; **351** *top left* David Muench/Corbis; *top right* Connie Ricca/Corbis; *center left* Annie Griffiths Belt/Corbis; *bottom right* Olivier Cirendini/Lonely Planet Images; **352** The Granger Collection, New York; **353** *center right* The Granger Collection, New York; *top right* Monticello/Thomas Jefferson Foundation, Inc.; **354** *both* The Granger Collection, New York; **356** Bettmann/Corbis; **357** Brooklyn Museum/Corbis; **359** *top left* Monticello/Thomas Jefferson Foundation, Inc.; *bottom right* Smithsonian American Art Musuem, Washington, DC/Art Resource, NY; *bottom left* The Granger Collection, New York; **360** *both* The Granger Collection, New York; **361** The Granger Collection, New York; **362** *bottom right Portrait of Euphemia Toussaint*, c.1825 (miniature on ivory) by Meucci, Anthony (fl.1825) © Collection of the New-York Historical Society, USA/The Bridgeman Art Library; *bottom left* Hulton Archive/Getty Images; **363** *bottom center* Collection of The New-York Historical Society, negative number X.48; *bottom right* National Museum of American History, Smithsonian Institution. Negative # 74-2491; **364** Hulton Archive/Getty Images; **365** *both* American Textile History Museum; **366** *background* The Granger Collection, New York; *inset* David H. Wells/Corbis; **367** The Granger Collection, New York; **368** *center* Thomas Kraft/TRANSTOCK INC.; *bottom* Michael Freeman/Corbis; *center left* Photo By Stock Montage/Getty Images; *top* The Granger Collection, New York; **370** *top left, center left* Bettmann/Corbis; *bottom left* Corbis; **370–371** Illustration by Michael Mundy; **372** National Museum of American History, Smithsonian Institution; **373** *center right* Library of Congress, Prints and Photographs Division; *top right* American Textile History Museum; **375** *right* Tim Rand/Getty Images; *left* The Granger Collection, New York; **376** *Nat Turner (1800-31) with fellow insurgent slaves during the Slave Rebellion of 1831* (coloured engraving) by American School, (19th century) © Private Collection/Peter Newark American Pictures/The Bridgeman Art Library; **377** *inset* The Granger Collection, New York; *top right* Art Media/Heritage-Images/The Image Works; **378** Joseph Sohm; ChromoSohm Inc./Corbis; **379** *center right Portrait of Henry Clay* (1777-1852) (oil on canvas) by Jarvis, John Wesley (1780-1840) Private Collection/© Christie's Images/The Bridgeman Art Library ; *top right* American Textile History Museum; **381** SSPL/The Image Works; **383** Hulton Archive/Getty Images; **385** Bettmann/Corbis; **387** *top* American Textile History Museum; *bottom left* National Museum of American History, Smithsonian Institution; *bottom right* Bettmann/Corbis; **388** *right* Bettmann/Corbis; *left* Stock Montage/Getty Images.

Unit 5

390–391 *Three American Indian Chiefs, c.1900* (photogravure) (b&w photo) by Curtis, Edward Sheriff (1868-1952) Private Collection/The Bridgeman Art Library; 392 *left* The Granger Collection, New York; 392 *right* Bettmann/Corbis; 393 *left* North Wind Picture Archives/Alamy; *right* The Granger Collection, New York; 394 Chateau de Blerancourt/Dagli Orti/The Art Archive; 395 *center right Margaret Bayard Smith*, Charles Bird King. Oil on canvas. Redwood Library and Athenaem, Newport, Rhode Island, www.redwoodlibrary.com; *top right* Sonda Dawes/The Image Works; 396 Topham/The Image Works; 397 Michael Dwyer/AP Images; 399 Illustration by Vilma Ortiz-Dillon; 400 *top* Corbis; *bottom* The Art Archive/Culver Pictures; 401 *Henry Clay* (1777-1852) (b/w photo) by American Photographer, (19th century) Private Collection/Peter Newark American Pictures/The Bridgeman Art Library ; *frame* PhotoDisc/Getty Images; 402 The Granger Collection, New York; 403 *center right* Library of Congress, Washington, DC (LC-USZC4-2566); *top right* Sonda Dawes/ The Image Works; 404 *Sash, c.1820s* (wool and beads) American School (19th century), © Peabody Essex Museum, Salem, Massachusetts, USA/ The Bridgeman Art Library ; 406 Billy E. Barnes/PhotoEdit; 407 *Portrait of Osceola* (1804-38) (oil on canvas), George Catlin (1794-1872)/Private Collection/The Bridgeman Art Library; 408 Bettmann/Corbis; 409 *center right* The Art Archive/National Archives Washington, DC; *top right* Sonda Dawes/The Image Works; 410 Panoramic Images/Getty Images; 411 The Granger Collection, New York; 412 The Granger Collection, New York; 413 *bottom left* Bettmann/Corbis; *top left* Sonda Dawes/The Image Works; 414 The Granger Collection, New York; 415 The Granger Collection, New York; 416 *bottom right* Courtesy of the Oakland Museum of California; *bottom left* Smithsonian American Art Museum, Washington, DC/(Detail)Art Resource, New York; 416–417 Ric Ergenbright; 417 *bottom left* Courtesy of the Oakland Museum of California; *bottom center* Photos courtesy of the Military & Historical Image Bank www. historicalimagebank.com; *center right* Gift of Ruth Koerner Oliver/Buffalo Bill Historical Center, Cody, Wyoming/The Art Archive; 419 *inset* The Granger Collection, New York; *center right* William Manning/Corbis; *top right* Robert Y. Ono/Corbis; 420 The Granger Collection, New York; 421 *inset* Museum of the American West/Autry National Center; 422 *bottom left* James L. Amos/Corbis; *top right* Royalty-Free/Getty Images; *center right* Museum of the American West/Autry National Center; *bottom right* James L. Amos/Corbis; 424 *top left* North Wind/Nancy Carter/North Wind Picture Archives; *center left* David Muench/Corbis; *bottom left* The Granger Collection, New York; 424–425 Illustration by Steve Weston/ Linden Artists Ltd.; 426 Richard Cummins/Corbis; 427 *center right* Prints and Photographs Collection, Mary Austin Holley File, The Center for American History, The University of Texas at Austin; CN00165; *top right* Robert Y. Ono/Corbis; 428 *both* The Granger Collection, New York; 429 The Granger Collection, New York; 430 Courtesy of the State Preservation Board, Austin, Texas (CHA 1989.96). Photograph by Perry Huston; 432 *right* Library of Congress Prints and Photographs Division (LC-USZC2-3798); *left* Courtesy of the California History Room, California State Library, Sacramento, California; 433 *center right* The Granger Collection, New York; *top right* Robert Y. Ono/Corbis; 437 Christie's Images/Corbis; 438 *center right* Courtesy of the Oakland Museum of California; 439 *center right* Courtesy of the California History Room, California State Library, Sacramento, California ; *top right* Robert Y. Ono/Corbis; 440 *inset* Courtesy of The Bancroft Library University of California, Berkeley, General Vallejo. Houseworth & Co. Photographs. Houseworth's Souvenir Photographs: 5; *top left* Courtesy of The Bancroft Library University of California, Berkeley, Shaw, S. W., artist Kuchel & Dresel (active ca. 1853-ca. 1865), lithographer Britton & Rey (active 1851-1902), printer [18--] lithograph, color 53.9 x 68.8 cm. ; 441 Sherwin Crasto/Reuters/Corbis; 442 Courtesy of the Oakland Museum of California; 444 *bottom left* The Granger Collection, New York; *center right* Collection of the Oakland Museum of California, Gift of Anonymous Donor. Photography by Isaac W. Baker; *top right* The Granger Collection, New York; 445 *top left* Robert Y. Ono/Corbis; *bottom right* Courtesy of the State Preservation Board, Austin, Texas. CHA 1989.96, Photographer Perry Huston, 7/28/95, post conservation.; *bottom left* The Granger Collection, New York; 446 The Granger Collection, New York; 448 *bottom right* Stuart Ramson/AP Images; *bottom left* View of St. Paul's Chapel and the Broadway Stages, New York (color litho), American School, (19th century) /, © Collection of the New-York Historical Society, USA /The Bridgeman Art Library International; 449 Emigrant illustrations by Rogue Element; *others* The Granger Collection, New York; 450 Courtesy of the Milwaukee County Historical Society, Milwaukee, Wisconsin; 451 *both* Museum of the City of New York/Corbis; 454 Brown Brothers 455 Library of Congress, Washington, DC; 457 *center right* The Granger Collection, New York; *top right* Museum of the City of New York/Corbis; 458 Archive Photos/ Getty Images; 459 Brown Brothers; 460 Lauren McFalls/McDougal Littell/ Houghton Mifflin Co.; 461 *top right* NBAE/Getty Images; *inset* Will & Deni McIntyre/Getty Images; 462 *left* Bettmann/Corbis; 464 *center right* The Granger Collection, New York; 465 *center right* General Research & Reference Division, Schomburg Center for Research and Black Culture, The New York Public Library, Astor, Lenox and Tilden Foundations; *top right* Museum of the City of New York/Corbis 466 Detail, *Frederick Douglass* (1844), Elisha Hammond. Oil on canvas, 69.9 cm x 71.1 cm. National Portrait Gallery, Smithsonian Institution/Art Resource, New York; 467 Hulton Archive/Getty Images; 468 *left* Mike Simons/Getty Images; *right* Library of Congress Prints and Photographs Division (LC-USZC4-4659); 469 *top right* Corbis; 470 *bottom right* Stuart Ramson/AP Images; 472 McDougal Littell/Houghton Mifflin Co.; 473 *top* Museum of the City of New York/Corbis; *bottom right* The Granger Collection, New York; *bottom left* Detail, *Frederick Douglass* (1844), Elisha Hammond. Oil on canvas, 69.9 cm x 71.1 cm. National Portrait Gallery, Smithsonian Institution/Art Resource, New York; 474 *bottom* Copyright © Collection of The New York Historical Society/The Bridgeman Art Library; *center* Bettmann/Corbis; 475 The Granger Collection, New York.

Unit 6

476–477 Carolyn Kaster/AP Images; Don Burk/AP Images; 478 *cards* (ca. 1850), American. Color lithograph. Dallas Historical Society, Texas/The Bridgeman Art Library; *bottom right* Schomburg Center/Art Resource, NY; 479 *both* The Granger Collection, New York; 481 *both* The Granger Collection, New York; 482 Illustrations by Rogue Element; 483 David J. and Janice Frent Collection; 484 *top right* Bettmann/Corbis; *center inset* Lithograph, Robertson, Seibert & Shearman, New York, ca.1859. Library of Congress Prints and Photographs Division (LC-USZC4-2356); 485 Stock Montage/Getty Images; 486 The Granger Collection, New York; 488 *bottom inset Bird's-Eye View of New Orleans and Suburbs* (1873), American School. Color lithograph. Collection of the New-York Historical Society/The Bridgeman Art Library; 488–489 Robert Holmes/Corbis; 489 *top left Loading the Steamboat with Cotton Bales from a Plantation* (ca1860), American School. Color engraving. Private Collection. Peter Newark American Pictures/The Bridgeman Art Library; 489 *center right Slave Quarters, Evan-Hall Plantation* (ca. 1860), George Francois Mugnier. Albumen photograph. Louisiana State Museum; 490 Getty Images; 491 *center right FugitiveSlave Law Convention, Cazenovia, New York, August 22, 1850*, Ezra Greenleaf Weld. (Accession Number 84.XT.1582.5). Daguerreotype, 1/6 Plate. Image: 6.7 x 5.4 cm (2 5/8 x 2 1/8 in.) ; Mat: 8.1 x 7 cm (3 3/16 x 2 3/4 in.). The J. Paul Getty Museum, Los Angeles; *top right* The Granger Collection, New York; 492 Illustration by Rogue Element; 493 *Frank Leslie's Illustrated Newpaper*, June 27, 1857. Wood engraving after photograph by Fitzgibbon. Library of Congress Prints and Photographs Division (LC-USZ62-79305); 494 The Granger Collection, New York; 495 Rick Wilking/AP Images; 496 Richmond Times-Dispatch/AP Images; 497 *John Brown Going to His Hanging* (1942), Horace Pippin. Oil on canvas, 24 1/8" x 301/4" (61.3 x 76.8 cm). John Lambert Fund (1943.11), Pennsylvania Academy of the Fine Arts, Philadelphia; 498 Brady-Handy Photograph Collection, Library of Congress, Prints and Photographs Division (LC-BH82-2417); 499 *top right, center right* The Granger Collection, New York; *frame* PhotoDisc; 501 Courtesy of the Lloyd Ostendorf Collection; 502 South Carolina Historical Society; 503 The Granger Collection, New York; 505 *top left* The Granger Collection, New York; *bottom left* Bettmann/Corbis; 506 *bottom* The Granger Collection, New York; *top Frank Leslie's Illustrated Newpaper*, June 27, 1857. Wood engraving after photograph by Fitzgibbon. Library of Congress Prints and Photographs Division (LC-USZ62-79305); 508 *bottom left* Library of Congress, Prints and Photographs Division (LC-USZC2-2804); *center left, center right* The Chicago Historical Society; *bottom center* Museum of the City of New York/Corbis; 509 *center* Military and Historical Image Bank; *right* Military and Historical Image Bank ; 510 *Bombardment of Fort Sumter, Charleston Harbour, 12th & 13th April 1861* (ca. 1865), Currier & Ives. Color lithograph. Library of Congress/The Bridgeman Art Library; 511 *center right* Public Domain; *top right* Carolyn Kaster/ AP Images; *frame* Jupiter Images; 512 Library of Congress Prints and Photographs Division (LC-USZ62-11897); 514 *left* Library of Congress Prints and Photographs Division (LC-DIG-ppmsca-08386); *right* Library of Congress Prints and Photographs Division (LC-DIG-cwpbh-03116); *left & right insets* Photograph by Hugh Talman/Smithsonian Images; 515 Museum of the City of New York/Corbis; 516 *The 'Monitor' and the 'Merrimac', the First Fight between Ironclads in 1862* (1886), after Julian Oliver Davidson. Lithograph. Published by Louis Prang & Co. Private Collection/The Bridgeman Art Library; 517 *center right* Bureau of Archives and History, New Jersey State Library; *top right* Carolyn Kaster/AP Images; *frame* Jupiter Images; 518 *top* Hulton Archive/Getty Images; *jacket & cap* Military and Historical Image Bank ; 519 *bottom* Bettmann/Corbis; *bottom inset* Hugh Talman/Smithsonian Institute; *top* Military and Historical Image Bank; 520 *top right* Corbis; *top left* Andrew J. Russell/Corbis; *rifle* Photograph by Dave King/Confederate Memorial Hall, New Orleans/Dorling Kindersley ; *bottom right* Time Life Pictures/Getty Images; *grenade* Armed Forces History, Division of History of Technology, National Museum of American History; 522 Bettmann/ Corbis; *frame* Jupiter Images; 523 *top right* Carolyn Kaster/AP Images; 524 Library of Congress Prints and Photographs Division (LC-USZC4-1910); 525 *bottom right* Brad C. Bower/AP Images; 527 *Home, Sweet Home* (ca. 1863), Winslow Homer. Oil on canvas, 21 1/2" x 16 1/2", (54.6 x 41.9 cm). Patrons' Permanent Fund (1997.72.1), National Gallery of Art/Christie's Images/The Bridgeman Art Library ; 528 Military & Historical Image Bank; 529 *top left* Library of Congress Prints and Photographs Division

(LC-DIG-cwpb-00238); *top right* George Eastman House; *photograph in viewer Confederate Soldiers as They Fell, Near the Burnside Bridge at the Battle of Antietam, September 1862*, Alexander Gardner. Glass negative, wet collodion process. Library of Congress Prints and Photographs Division (LC-B811- 555); **530** McDougal Littell/Houghton Mifflin Co.; **531** *top left* Carolyn Kaster/AP Images; *bottom left* Library of Congress Prints and Photographs Division (LC-DIG-ppmsca-08386); **534** *bottom left The Freedman* (1863), John Quincy Adams Ward. Bronze, 19 1/2" x 14 3/4" x 9 3/4" (49.5 x 37.5 x 24.8 cm). Gift of Charles Anthony Lamb and Barea Lamb Seeley, in memory of their grandfather, Charles Rollinson Lamb, 1979 (1979.394), Metropolitan Museum of Art, New York; *bottom right Siege of Vicksburg–13, 15, & 17 Corps, Commanded by Gen. U.S. Grant, Assisted by the Navy under Admiral Porter–Surrender, July 4, 1863* (1888), Kurz and Allison, Art Publishers, Chicago. Lithograph. Library of Congress Prints and Photographs Division (LC-USZC4-1754); **535** *bottom Lee Surrendering at Appomattox*, Thomas Lovell, National Geographic Image Collection; **536** Lee Snider Photo Images/Corbis; **537** *center right* Time Life Pictures/Getty Images; *top right The Fall of Richmond, Virginia* (1865), Currier and Ives. Lithograph. Private Collection/The Bridgeman Art Library; **538** *The Hour of Emancipation* (1863), William Tolman Carlton. Oil on canvas. Private Collection/© Christie's Images/The Bridgeman Art Library; **539** *Freedom to the Slave* (1863). Lithograph, Philadelphia. National Museum of American History, Smithsonian Institution; **540** Kean Collection/Getty Images; **541** Jonathan Wiggs/Boston Globe; **542** *both* Courtesy of the Federal Reserve Bank of Atlanta Monetary Museum; **543** *center* The Museum of the Confederacy; **543** *top right The Fall of Richmond, Virginia* (1865), Currier and Ives. Lithograph. Private Collection/The Bridgeman Art Library; **544** The Granger Collection, New York; **546** Corbis; **547** Abraham Lincoln Presidential Library, Springfield, Illinois; **548** Eric Mencher/Getty Images; **549** *center right* Adams County Historical Society, Gettysburg, Pennsylvania; *top right The Fall of Richmond, Virginia* (1865), Currier and Ives. Lithograph. Private Collection/The Bridgeman Art Library; **550–551** Brad C. Bower/AP Images; **552** *right* Time Life Pictures/Getty Images; *left* Detail, *Ulysses S. Grant* (1864), Mathew Brady. Albumen silver print. National Portrait Gallery, Smithsonian Institution/Art Resource, New York; **554** *The Fall of Richmond*, Virginia (1865), Currier and Ives. Lithograph. Private Collection/The Bridgeman Art Library; **556–557** Illustration by Brian Berley; **558** Time Life Pictures/Getty Images; **559** *center right Portrait of Walt Whitman* (ca. 1853), Gabriel Harrison. Quarter plate daguerreotype, 4 1/4" x 3 1/4" (10.8 x 8.3 cm). Humanities and Social Sciences Library/ Rare Books Division, New York Public Library; *top right The Fall of Richmond, Virginia* (1865), Currier and Ives. Lithograph. Private Collection/The Bridgeman Art Library; **560** *top right Incidents of the War: Harvest of Death* (Gettysburg,1863), Timothy H. O'Sullivan. Published by Alexander Gardner in "Gardner's Photographic Sketch Book of the War," Vol I, 1866. (LC-B8184-7964-A) Library of Congress Prints and Photographs Division; *top left* The Granger Collection, New York; *frame* PhotoDisc; **561** AP Images; **563** Alexander Gardner (1863)/AP Images; **565** *top left The Fall of Richmond, Virginia* (1865), Currier and Ives. Lithograph. Private Collection/The Bridgeman Art Library; *bottom left* Time Life Pictures/ Getty Images; **567** *A Ride for Liberty, or The Fugitive Slaves* (ca. 1862), Johnson, J. Eastman. Oil on paper board, 21 15/16" x 26 1/8" (55.8 x 66.4 cm). Brooklyn Museum of Art, New York (40.59a-b), Gift of Gwendolyn O. L. Conkling/The Bridgeman Art Library ; **568** *bottom center* The Granger Collection, New York; *bottom left* Corbis; **569** Farmland illustrations by Rogue Element; *bottom left* Dorling Kindersley; *bottom right* Carolyn Kaster/AP Images; **571** *center right* The Granger Collection, New York; *top right* Hisham Ibrahim/Getty Images; **572** The Granger Collection, New York; **573** The Granger Collection, New York; **574** Michael Siluk/The Image Works; **575** The Granger Collection, New York; **576** The Granger Collection, New York; **577** *center right* Corbis; *center* Hisham Ibrahim/Getty Images; **578** *right* Medford Historical Society Collection/ Corbis; *background* Richard T. Nowitz/Corbis; *background inset* Buddy Mays/Corbis; **579** The Granger Collection, New York; **580** Illustrations by Rogue Element; **581** *top inset* The Chicago Historical Society; *top* The Granger Collection, New York; **582** Bettmann/Corbis; **583** *bottom The Shackle Broken–by the Genius of Freedom*. Color lithograph. Published by E. Sachs & Co., Baltimore, 1874. The Chicago Historical Society; *center* Library of Congress, Washington, DC; *top right* Hisham Ibrahim/Getty Images; **584** *both* Bettmann/Corbis; **585** The Granger Collection, New York; **586** The Granger Collection, New York; **587** Illustration by Rogue Element; **588** Jeff Greenberg/Index Stock Imagery; **589** *top left* Hisham Ibrahim/Getty Images; *bottom right, bottom left* The Granger Collection, New York; **590** © 2006 The Children's Museum of Indianapolis, Inc. Photograph by Wendy Kaveney.

Unit 7

592–593 Library of Congress, Washington, DC (cph 3g04637); **594** *left* Library of Congress, Prints and Photographs Division Washington, DC (LC-USZC2-4891); *right* Craig J. Brown/Index Stock Imagery; **595** *bottom left* Werner Forman/Art Resource, NY; *center left* Bill Manns/The Art Archive; **596** Annie Griffiths Belt/Corbis; **597** *center right* Pajaro Valley Historical Association; *top right* The Granger Collection, New York; **598** *center left* Iris & B. Gerald Cantor Center for Visual Arts at Stanford University; **599** National Museum of American History/The Smithsonian Institution; **600** Smithsonian Institution; **601** *center right* Bill Manns/The Art Archive ; *top right* The Granger Collection, New York; **602** Courtesy of the Oakland Museum of California; **603** *cowboy* Bill Manns/The Art Archive; *cowgirl* Courtesy of Colorado Historical Society, (ID Number F40608, 10027838). All Rights Reserved; *boots* Dorling Kindersley; *hat* Kansas State Historical Society; *spurs* Museum of the American West/Autry National Center; **604** Royalty-Free/Corbis; **605** Bill Manns/The Art Archive ; *frame* PhotoDisc; **606** The Granger Collection, New York; **607** Courtesy of Colorado Historical Society, (William H. Jackson Collection, ID number 20101514. All Rights Reserved; **608** Smithsonian Institution; **609** *center right* State Historical Society of North Dakota; *top right* The Granger Collection, New York; **610** *all* National Archives Washington DC/The Art Archive ; **611** Southwest Museum Pasadena/Laurie Platt Winfrey/The Art Archive; **612** Burton Historical Collection, Detroit Public Library; **613** Buffalo Bill Historical Center, Cody, Wyoming; Chandler-Pohrt Collection, Gift of Mary J. and James R. Jundt; NA.204.4; **614** *bag,* Buffalo Bill Historical Center, Cody, Wyoming; Gift of Mrs. Henry H.R. Coe; NA. 106.128A *calumet,* Buffalo Bill Historical Center, Cody, Wyoming; Gift of Mrs. Richard A. Pohrt; NA. 502.195.2 *basket* Buffalo Bill Historical Center, Cody, Wyoming; Simplot Collection, Gift of J.R. Simplot; NA. 506.69"; *moccasins* Southwest Museum of the American Indian/Autry National Center; *bottom* National Archives, Washington, D.C./The Art Archive; ; **615** *top* Bill Manns/The Art Archive; **617** *center right* Solomon D. Butcher Collection, Nebraska State Historical Society; *top right* The Granger Collection, New York; **618** Solomon D. Butcher Collection, Nebraska State Historical Society; **619** Bill Stormont/Corbis; **620** Illustrations by Rogue Element; **621** Bettmann/Corbis; **622** *right* National Archives and Records Administration; *left* Craig J. Brown/Index Stock Imagery; *center left* Royalty-Free/Corbis; *center right* National Archives, Washington, D.C./The Art Archive; **623** Library of Congress Prints and Photographs Division; **624** *top right* Corbis; *bottom right, center left* Bettmann/Corbis; *bottom center* Museum of the American West/Autry National Center; **625** *top* The Granger Collection/New York; *bottom left* Tom Bean/Corbis; **626** Library of Congress, Washington, DC; **627** *Indians Attacking a Pioneer Wagon Train* (oil on canvas), Remington, Frederic (1861-1909)/Private Collection, Peter Newark American Pictures/The Bridgeman Art Library; **628** *bottom left* Library of Congress, Washington, DC; *bottom right* Dinodia Images/ Alamy; *bottom center* Bettmann/Corbis; **629** *bottom center* SSPL/The Image Works; *Rockefeller* The Granger Collection, New York; *Carnegie* Hulton Archive/Getty Images; *bottom right* Eric Risberg/AP Images; **631** *center right* The Queens Borough Public Library, Long Island Division, Latimer Family Papers Collection; *top right* Lake County Museum/Corbis; **632** Lake County Museum/Corbis; **633** *Edison & Bell* Stock Montage/Getty Images; *phone & lightbulb* SSPL/The Image Works; *background* Mansell/ Time & Life Pictures/Getty Images; **634** Corbis; **635** *both* The Granger Collection, New York; **636** *left* Bettmann/Corbis; *right* Jacob A Riis/ Museum of the City of New York/Getty Images; **637** Dagli Orti/The Art Archive; **638** *center left* Lake County Museum/Corbis; *bottom left* Dave King/Dorling Kindersley; *bottom right* Courtesy of Phil Baggley/ Workington Iron and Steel; **639** *bottom* Bettmann/Corbis; *center right* Matther Warc/Dorling Kindersley; **641** *center right* The Granger Collection, New York; *top right* Lake County Museum/Corbis; **642** Bancroft Library/University of California at Berkeley; **643** The Granger Collection, New York; **644** Mario Tama/Getty Images; **645** *top* Jacob A. Riis/Getty Images; *center right* Bettmann/Corbis; **646** The Granger Collection, New York; **647** The Granger Collection, New York; **648** *both* The Granger Collection, New York; **648–649** Illustration by Nick Rotundo/ Bizzy Productions, Inc.; **651** *center right* Marianne Barcellona/Time Life Pictures/Getty Images; *top right* Lake County Museum/Corbis; **652** *left* The Granger Collection, New York; *right* Library of Congress, Washington, DC; **653** *top right* The Granger Collection, New York; **654** *left* Time Life Pictures/Library of Congress/Getty Images; *right* C.M. Battey/Getty Images; **655** Mary Ann Chastain/AP Images; **656** Bettmann/ Corbis; **657** *center right* Library of Congress, Washington, DC (LC- DIG-ggbain-18170); *top right* Lake County Museum/Corbis; **658** The Granger Collection, New York; **659** The Granger Collection, New York; **660** Bettmann/Corbis; **661** The Granger Collection, New York; **662** Bettmann/ Corbis; **663** *center right* The Granger Collection, New York; **663** *top right* Lake County Museum/Corbis; **664** *bottom* Library of Congress, Washington, DC (LC-USZ62-21467A); *center right* The Granger Collection, New York; **665** Museum of the City of New York/The Art Archive; **666** McDougal Littell/Houghton Mifflin Co.; **667** *top left* Lake County Museum/Corbis; *bottom right, bottom left* The Granger Collection, New York; **668** Royalty-Free/Getty Images; **669** The Granger Collection, New York; **670** *left* Jeff Vanuga/Corbis; *center* Bettmann/Corbis; **671** *bottom left* Culver Pictures/The Art Archive; *bottom right* The Granger Collection, New York; **673** *center right* Corbis; *top right* Bettmann/Corbis; **674** Roswell Daily Record/AP Images; **675** Corbis; **676** Ric Ergenbright; **677** David J. & Janice L. Frent Collection/Corbis; **678** David J. & Janice L. Frent Collection/Corbis; **679** *center right* David J. & Janice L. Frent Collection/ Corbis; *top right* Bettmann/Corbis; **682** The Granger Collection, New York; **683** *both* Bettmann/Corbis; **684** *bottom* Corbis; *left Abigail Smith Adams* (ca. 1766), Benjamin Blyth. Pastel on paper, 57.3 x 44.8 cm. Massachusetts Historical Society, Boston, MA/Corbis; **684** *center* The Granger Collection, New York; **685** *top left* Bettmann/Corbis; *bottom left* AP Images; *top right* David J. & Janice L. Frent Collection/Corbis; *bottom right* The Herald-Dispatch/AP Images; **686** Bettmann/Corbis; **687** *bottom* Culver Pictures/The Art Archive/Picture Desk; *top* Bettmann/Corbis; **689** *top left* Bettmann/Corbis; *bottom left, bottom right* Corbis; **690** The Granger Collection, New York; **691** Underwood & Underwood/Corbis; **692** *bottom left* Richard Cummins/SuperStock; *bottom right* Royalty-Free/Corbis; **692–693** Bettmann/Corbis; **693** *bottom left* Rout of Foreign Troops by Boxers at Beicang near Diantsin. Qing Dynasty (ca. 1900). Woodcut. Donated by E.B. Howell (1948,0710,0.6), The British Museum; *bottom right* Julie Plansencia/AP Images; **694** The Granger Collection, New York; **695** *center* MPI/Hulton Archive/Getty Images; *right* The Granger Collection, New York; **697** *inset* Frank and Frances Carpenter Collection/Library of Congress, Prints and Photographs Division (LC-USZ62-108293); *top* Charles O'Rear/Corbis; **698** The Chicago Historical Society; **699** *center* Richard Drew/AP Images; *top right* The Granger Collection, New York; **700** *top* The Yellow Kid (June 5, 1897), Richard Felton Outcoult. Magazine cover illustration. Library of Congress Prints and Photographs Division (AP2. Y5 1897); *bottom* Jeremy Horner/Corbis; **705** American insurance company advertisement, 1909/The Granger Collection, New York; **706** Corbis; **707** *center* Matthew Calbraith Perry (ca.1854), Anonymous. Color wood-block print. Published in Miki Kosai's Ikoku Ochiba Kage, Tokyo, ca. 1854. National Portrait Gallery, Smithsonian Institution/Art Resource, New York; *top right* The Granger Collection, New York; **709** Illustration by Nick Rotundo/Bizzy Productions, Inc.; **710** The Granger Collection, New York; **713** *top left* The Granger Collection, New York; *bottom left* Royalty-Free/Corbis; *bottom right* Detail, Matthew Calbraith Perry (ca.1854), Anonymous. Color wood-block print. Published in Miki Kosai's Ikoku Ochiba Kage, Tokyo, ca. 1854. National Portrait Gallery, Smithsonian Institution/Art Resource, New York; **715** Culver Pictures.

Epilogue
716 *left* Library of Congress, Prints & Photographs Division, [LC-USZ62-123456]; *right* Bettmann/Corbis; **717** *top right* Florida Division of Library and Information; *top right inset* Library of Congress, Prints & Photographs Division; *center left* The Granger Collection, New York; *bottom right* Bettmann/Corbis; **718** *right* Dorothea Lange/Library of Congress, Prints & Photograhs Division, FSA/OWI Collection, [LC-USF34-9058-C]; *left* Bettmann/Corbis; **719** *top right* Mary Evans Picture Library; *tank* Corbis; *center left* Joe Raedle/Getty Images; *bottom right* Getty Images; **720** *right* Bettmann/Corbis; *left* Time Life Pictures/Getty Images; **721** *top right* Getty Images; *left* Bettmann/Corbis; *bottom right* Smithsonian Institution National Museum of American History, Division of Politics and Reform, Negative Number 2000-6287; **722** *right* Wally McNamee; *left* Corbis; **723** *top right* Wolfgang Rattay/Reuters; *center left* Royalty-Free/Corbis; *bottom right* Sara K. Schwittek/Reuters. *Flag* PhotoDisc/Getty Images

Skillbuilder Handbook
R18 Library of Congress, Wahington, DC; **R24** Courtesy of the Lloyd Ostendorf Collection; **R25** McDougal Littell/Houghton Mifflin; **R26** McDougal Littell/Houghton Mifflin; **R34** The Granger Collection, New York; **R36** Christopher Barth/AP Images.

Presidents of the United States
Illustrations by Patrick Faricy.

All other illustrations by
McDougal Littell/Houghton Mifflin Co.

MICHIGAN

Michigan Grade Level Social Studies Content Expectations: Eighth Grade—United States History

MICHIGAN GRADE LEVEL CONTENT EXPECTATIONS

GRADE 8

Foundations In United States History and Geography ERAs 1–3

These foundational expectations are included to help students draw upon their previous study of American history and connect 8th grade United States history with the history studied in 5th grade. To set the stage for the study of U.S. history that begins with the creation of the U.S. Constitution, students should be able to draw upon an understanding of these politics and intellectual understandings.

F1   Political and Intellectual Transformations

F1.1   Describe the ideas, experiences, and interactions that influenced the colonists' decisions to declare independence by analyzing

   1. *colonial ideas about government (e.g., limited government, republicanism, protecting individual rights and promoting the common good, representative government, natural rights) (C2)*

   2. *experiences with self-government (e.g., House of Burgesses and town meetings) (C2)*

   3. *changing interactions with the royal government of Great Britain after the French and Indian War (C2)*

F1.2   Using the Declaration of Independence, including the grievances at the end of the document, describe the role this document played in expressing

   1. *colonists' views of government*

   2. *their reasons for separating from Great Britain. (C2)*

F1.3   Describe the consequences of the American Revolution by analyzing the

   1. *birth of an independent republican government (C2)*

   2. *creation of Articles of Confederation (C2)*

   3. *changing views on freedom and equality (C2)*

   4. *and concerns over distribution of power within governments, between government and the governed, and among people (C2)*

Integrated United States History

U3   USHG ERA 3 – Revolution and the New Nation

U3.3 Creating New Government(s) and a New Constitution

Explain the challenges faced by the new nation and analyze the development of the Constitution as a new plan for governing. [Foundations for Civics HSCE Standard 2.2.]

Note: Expectations U3.3.1–U3.3.5 address content that was introduced in Grade 5, but ask for explanation and analysis at a higher level than expected in Grade 5. They are included here to support in-depth discussion of the historical and philosophical origins of constitutional government in the United States. (U3.3.6)

8 – U3.3.1   Explain the reasons for the adoption and subsequent failure of the Articles of Confederation (e.g., why its drafters created a weak central government, challenges the nation faced under the Articles, Shays' Rebellion, disputes over western lands). (C2)

8 – U3.3.2   Identify economic and political questions facing the nation during the period of the Articles of Confederation and the opening of the Constitutional Convention. (E1.4)

8 – U3.3.3   Describe the major issues debated at the Constitutional Convention including the distribution of political power, conduct of foreign affairs, rights of individuals, rights of states, election of the executive, and slavery as a regional and federal issue.

8 – U3.3.4   Explain how the new constitution resolved (or compromised) the major issues including sharing, separating, and checking of power among federal government institutions, dual sovereignty (state-federal power), rights of individuals, the Electoral College, the Three-Fifths Compromise, and the Great Compromise.

8 – U3.3.5   Analyze the debates over the ratification of the Constitution from the perspectives of Federalists and Anti-Federalists and describe how the states ratified the Constitution. (C2) (*National Geography Standard 3, p. 148*)

8 – U3.3.6   Explain how the Bill of Rights reflected the concept of limited government, protections of basic freedoms, and the fear of many Americans of a strong central government. (C3)

8 – U3.3.7   Using important documents (e.g., Mayflower Compact, Iroquois Confederacy, Common Sense, Declaration of Independence, Northwest Ordinance, Federalist Papers), describe the historical and philosophical origins of constitutional government in the United States using the ideas of social compact, limited government, natural rights, right of revolution, separation of powers, bicameralism, republicanism, and popular participation in government. (C2)

U4   USHG ERA 4 – Expansion and Reform (1792–1861)

U4.1 Challenges to an Emerging Nation

Analyze the challenges the new government faced and the role of political and social leaders in meeting these challenges.

8 – U4.1.1   **Washington's Farewell** – Use Washington's Farewell Address to analyze the most significant challenges the new nation faced and the extent to which subsequent Presidents heeded Washington's advice. (C4)

8 – U4.1.2   **Establishing America's Place in the World** – Explain the changes in America's relationships with other nations by analyzing treaties with American Indian nations, Jay's Treaty (1795), French Revolution, Pinckney's Treaty (1795), Louisiana Purchase, War of 1812, Transcontinental Treaty (1819), and the Monroe Doctrine. (C4) *(National Geography Standard 13, p. 161)*

8 – U4.1.3   **Challenge of Political Conflict** – Explain how political parties emerged out of the competing ideas, experiences, and fears of Thomas Jefferson and Alexander Hamilton (and their followers), despite the worries the Founders had concerning the dangers of political division, by analyzing disagreements over

    1.   relative power of the national government (e.g., Whiskey Rebellion, Alien and Sedition Acts) (C3) *(National Geography Standard 13, p. 169)*

    2.   foreign relations (e.g., French Revolution, relations with Great Britain) (C3) *(National Geography Standard 13, p. 169)*

    3.   economic policy (e.g., the creation of a national bank, assumption of revolutionary debt) (C3, E2.2)

8 – U4.1.4   **Establishing a National Judiciary and Its Power** – Explain the development of the power of the Supreme Court through the doctrine of judicial review as manifested in *Marbury v. Madison* (1803) and the role of Chief Justice John Marshall and the Supreme Court in interpreting the power of the national government (e.g., *McCullouch v. Maryland, Dartmouth College* v. *Woodward, Gibbons* v. *Ogden*). (C3, E1.4, 2.2)

U4.2 Regional and Economic Growth

Describe and analyze the nature and impact of the territorial, demographic, and economic growth in the first three decades of the new nation using maps, charts, and other evidence.

8 – U4.2.1   **Comparing Northeast and the South** – Compare and contrast the social and economic systems of the Northeast and the South with respect to geography and climate and the development of

    1.   agriculture, including changes in productivity, technology, supply and demand, and price (E1.3,1.4) *(National Geography Standard 14, p. 171)*

    2.   industry, including entrepreneurial development of new industries, such as textiles (E1.1)

    3.   the labor force including labor incentives and changes in labor forces (E1.2)

    4.   transportation including changes in transportation (steamboats and canal barges) and impact on economic markets and prices (E1.2,1.3) *(National Geography Standard 3, p. 148)*

    5.   immigration and the growth of nativism *(National Geography Standard 9, p. 160)*

    6.   race relations

    7.   class relations

8 – U4.2.2   **The Institution of Slavery** – Explain the ideology of the institution of slavery, its policies, and consequences.

8 – U4.2.3   **Westward Expansion** – Explain the expansion, conquest, and settlement of the West through the Louisiana Purchase, the removal of American Indians (Trail of Tears) from their native lands, the growth of a system of commercial agriculture, and the idea of Manifest Destiny. (E2.1) (*National Geography Standard 6, p. 154*)

8 – U4.2.4   **Consequences of Expansion** – Develop an argument based on evidence about the positive and negative consequences of territorial and economic expansion on American Indians, the institution of slavery, and the relations between free and slaveholding states. (C2) (*National Geography Standard 13, p. 169*)

U4.3 Reform Movements

Analyze the growth of antebellum American reform movements.

8 – U4.3.1   Explain the origins of the American education system and Horace Mann's campaign for free compulsory public education. (C2)

8 – U4.3.2   Describe the formation and development of the abolitionist movement by considering the roles of key abolitionist leaders (e.g., John Brown and the armed resistance, Harriet Tubman and the Underground Railroad, Sojourner Truth, William Lloyd Garrison, and Frederick Douglass), and the response of southerners and northerners to the abolitionist movement. (C2) (*National Geography Standard 6, p. 154*)

8 – U4.3.3   Analyze the antebellum women's rights (and suffrage) movement by discussing the goals of its leaders (e.g., Susan B. Anthony and Elizabeth Cady Stanton) and comparing the Seneca Falls Resolution with the Declaration of Independence. (C2)

8 – U4.3.4   Analyze the goals and effects of the antebellum temperance movement. (C2)

8 – U4.3.5   Evaluate the role of religion in shaping antebellum reform movements. (C2)

U5   USHG ERA 5 – Civil War and Reconstruction (1850–1877)

U5.1 The Coming of the Civil War

Analyze and evaluate the early attempts to abolish or contain slavery and to realize the ideals of the Declaration of Independence.

8 – U5.1.1   Explain the differences in the lives of free blacks (including those who escaped from slavery) with the lives of free whites and enslaved peoples. (C2)

8 – U5.1.2   Describe the role of the Northwest Ordinance and its effect on the banning of slavery (e.g., the establishment of Michigan as a free state). (*National Geography Standard 12, p. 167*)

8 – U5.1.3   Describe the competing views of Calhoun, Webster, and Clay on the nature of the union among the states (e.g., sectionalism, nationalism, federalism, state rights). (C3)

8 – U5.1.4   Describe how the following increased sectional tensions

1.   the Missouri Compromise (1820)

2.   the Wilmot Proviso (1846)

3.   the Compromise of 1850 including the Fugitive Slave Act

4.   the Kansas-Nebraska Act (1854) and subsequent conflict in Kansas

5.   the Dred Scott v. Sandford decision (1857)

6.   changes in the party system (e.g., the death of the Whig party, rise of the Republican party and division of the Democratic party)

(C2; C3) (*National Geography Standard 13, p. 169*)

8 – U5.1.5   Describe the resistance of enslaved people (e.g., Nat Turner, Harriet Tubman and the Underground Railroad, John Brown, Michigan's role in the Underground Railroad) and effects of their actions before and during the Civil War. (C2)

8 – U5.1.6   Describe how major issues debated at the Constitutional Convention such as disagreements over the distribution of political power, rights of individuals (liberty and property), rights of states, election of the executive, and slavery help explain the Civil War (C2). (*National Geography Standard 13, p. 169*)

U5.2 Civil War

Evaluate the multiple causes, key events, and complex consequences of the Civil War.

8 – U5.2.1   Explain the reasons (political, economic, and social) why Southern states seceded and explain the differences in the timing of secession in the Upper and Lower South. (C3, E1.2) (*National Geography Standard 6, p. 154*)

8 – U5.2.2   Make an argument to explain the reasons why the North won the Civil War by considering the

1.   critical events and battles in the war

2.   the political and military leadership of the North and South

3.   the respective advantages and disadvantages, including geographic, demographic, economic and technological (E1.4) (*National Geography Standard 15, p. 173*)

8 – U5.2.3   Examine Abraham Lincoln's presidency with respect to

1.   his military and political leadership

2.   the evolution of his emancipation policy (including the Emancipation Proclamation)

3.   and the role of his significant writings and speeches, including the Gettysburg Address and its relationship to the Declaration of Independence (C2)

8 – U5.2.4   Describe the role of African Americans in the war, including black soldiers and regiments, and the increased resistance of enslaved peoples.

8 – U5.2.5 Construct generalizations about how the war affected combatants, civilians (including the role of women), the physical environment, and the future of warfare, including technological developments. (*National Geography Standard 14, p. 171*)

U5.3 Reconstruction

Using evidence, develop an argument regarding the character and consequences of Reconstruction.

8 – U5.3.1 Describe the different positions concerning the reconstruction of Southern society and the nation, including the positions of President Abraham Lincoln, President Andrew Johnson, Republicans, and African Americans.

8 – U5.3.2 Describe the early responses to the end of the Civil War by describing the
1. policies of the Freedmen's Bureau (E2.2)
2. restrictions placed on the rights and opportunities of freedmen, including racial segregation and Black Codes (C2, C5)

8 – U5.3.3 Describe the new role of African Americans in local, state and federal government in the years after the Civil War and the resistance of Southern whites to this change, including the Ku Klux Klan. (C2, C5) (*National Geography Standard 10, p. 162*)

8 – U5.3.4 Analyze the intent and the effect of the Thirteenth, Fourteenth, and Fifteenth Amendments to the Constitution.

8 – U5.3.5 Explain the decision to remove Union troops in 1877 and describe its impact on Americans.

U6   USHG ERA 6 – THE DEVELOPMENT OF AN INDUSTRIAL, URBAN, AND GLOBAL UNITED STATES (1870–1930)

Grade 8 begins to address trends and patterns in the last half of the 19th century, through 1898.

U6.1 America in the Last Half of the 19th Century

Analyze the major changes in communication, transportation, demography, and urban centers, including the location and growth of cities linked by industry and trade, in last half of the 19th century. The purpose of this section is to introduce some of the major changes in American society and the economy in the last part of the 19th Century. This era will be addressed in-depth and with greater intellectual sophistication in the high school United History and Geography content expectations.

8 – U6.1.1 **America at Century's End** – Compare and contrast the United States in 1800 with the United States in 1898 focusing on similarities and differences in
1. territory, including the size of the United States and land use (*National Geography Standards 1 and 16, pp. 144 and 196*)
2. population, including immigration, reactions to immigrants, and the changing demographic structure of rural and urban America (E3.2) (*National Geography Standards 9 and 12, pp. 160 and 167*)
3. systems of transportation (canals and railroads, including the Transcontinental Railroad), and their impact on the economy and society (E1.4, 3.2) (*National Geography Standard 11, p. 164*)

4. governmental policies promoting economic development (e.g., tariffs, banking, land grants and mineral rights, the Homestead Act) (E.2.2) *(National Geography Standard 16, p. 176)*

5. economic change, including industrialization, increased global competition, and their impact on conditions of farmers and industrial workers (E1.4, 2.1, 3.2) *(National Geography Standard 11, p. 164)*

6. the treatment of African Americans, including the rise of segregation in the South as endorsed by the Supreme Court's decision in *Plessy v. Ferguson*, and the response of African Americans

7. the policies toward American Indians, including removal, reservations, the Dawes Act of 1887, and the response of American Indians *(National Geography Standard 13, p. 169)*

U6.2 Investigation Topics and Issue Analysis (P2)

Use the historical perspective to investigate a significant historical topic from United States History Eras 3-6 that also has significance as an issue or topic in the United States today.

8 – U6.2.1   United States History Investigation Topic and Issue Analysis, Past and Present –

Use historical perspectives to analyze issues in the United States from the past and the present; conduct research on a historical issue or topic, identify a connection to a contemporary issue, and present findings (e.g., oral, visual, video, or electronic presentation, persuasive essay, or research paper); include causes and consequences of the historical action and predict possible consequences of the contemporary action. *(National Geography Standard 9 and 10, pp. 160 and 162)*

Examples of Investigation Topics and Questions (and examples from United States History)

Balance of Power – How has the nation addressed tensions between state and federal governmental power? (e.g., Articles of Confederation, U.S. Constitution, states' rights issues, secession, others)

Liberty vs. Security – How has the nation balanced liberty interests with security interests? (e.g., Alien and Sedition Acts, suspension of habeas corpus during the Civil War)

The Government and Social Change – How have governmental policies, the actions of reformers, and economic and demographic changes affected social change? (e.g., abolitionist movement, women's movement, Reconstruction policies)

Movement of People – How has the nation addressed the movement of people into and within the United States? (e.g., American Indians, immigrants)

Public Discourse, Decision Making, and Citizen Involvement (P3, P4)

P3.1 Identifying and Analyzing Issues, Decision Making, Persuasive Communication About a Public Issue, and Citizen Involvement

8 – P3.1.1   Identify, research, analyze, discuss, and defend a position on a national public policy issue.

1. Identify a national public policy issue.

2. Clearly state the issue as a question of public policy orally or in written form.

3. Use inquiry methods to trace the origins of the issue and to acquire data about the issue.

4. Generate and evaluate alternative resolutions to the public issue and analyze various perspectives (causes, consequences, positive and negative impact) on the issue.

5. Identify and apply core democratic values or constitutional principles.

6.   Share and discuss findings of research and issue analysis in group discussions and debates.

7.   Compose a persuasive essay justifying the position with a reasoned argument.

8.   Develop an action plan to address or inform others about the issue

P4.2 Citizen Involvement

8 – P4.2.1   Demonstrate knowledge of how, when, and where individuals would plan and conduct activities intended to advance views in matters of public policy, report the results, and evaluate effectiveness.

8 – P4.2.2   Engage in, activities intended to contribute to solving a national or international problem studied.

8 – P4.2.3   Participate in projects to help or inform others (e.g., service learning projects).

211-09-t